Lecture Notes in Computer Science

Edited by G. Goos and J. Hartmanis

483

Grzegorz Rozenberg (Ed.)

Advances in Petri Nets 1990

Springer-Verlag

Berlin Heidelberg New York London Paris
Tokyo Hong Kong Barcelona Budapest

Volume Editor

Grzegorz Rozenberg
Department of Computer Science, Leiden University
P. O. Box 9512, 2300 RA Leiden, The Netherlands

CR Subject Classification (1991): F.1–3, C.1–2, D.4, I.6

ISBN 3-540-53863-1 Springer-Verlag Berlin Heidelberg New York
ISBN 0-387-53863-1 Springer-Verlag New York Berlin Heidelberg

© Springer-Verlag Berlin Heidelberg 1991
Printed in Germany

Printing and binding: Druckhaus Beltz, Hemsbach/Bergstr.
2145/3140-543210 – Printed on acid-free paper

Preface

The idea behind the series of volumes "Advances in Petri Nets" is to present to the general computer science community recent results which are the most representative and significant for the development of the area.

The main source of papers for "Advances" is the annual "International Conference on Applications and Theory of Petri Nets". The "best" papers from the latest conferences are considered for the series (however, they go through an independent refereeing process and, if accepted, they often appear in "Advances" in a quite revised and extended form). Independently of the conference papers, "Advances" present also papers submitted directly for publication in "Advances" - potential authors are encouraged to submit papers directly to the editor of "Advances".

The main aims of "Advances" are:

(1) to present to the "outside" scientific community a fair picture of recent advances in the area of Petri nets, and

(2) to encourage those interested in applications and the theory of concurrent systems to take a closer look at Petri nets and then join the group of researchers working in this fascinating and challenging area.

To facilitate (2) above, "Advances" also contain surveys and tutorials on various topics from Petri nets. The current volume contains a tutorial on refinements of Petri nets by W. Brauer, R. Gold, and W. Vogler, and a tutorial on analysis and synthesis of free choice systems by J. Esparza and M. Silva. The tutorials have been prepared in the framework of the ESPRIT BRA Project DEMON.

"Advances in Petri Nets 1990" covers the 10th "International Conference on Applications and Theory of Petri Nets" held in Bonn, Germany in June 1989. I would like to thank the members of the program committee and especially the chairman G. De Michelis for the help in selecting papers from the workshop to be submitted for "Advances".

Special thanks go to the referees of the papers in this volume who very often are responsible for considerable improvements of papers presented here. The referees were: P. Azema, R. Bhatia, W. Brauer, F. De Cindio, J.M. Colom, J. Desel, R. Devillers, J. Esparza, U. Goltz, R. Hopkins, J. Jeffrey, K. Jensen, P. Juanole, A. Kiehn, M. Koutny, M. Lindqvist, J.C. Lloret, Marinescu, J. Martinez, G. Memmi, T. Murata, M. Nielsen, G. Nutt, A. Pagnoni, L. Pomello, W. Reisig, C. Simone, V. Sliva, E. Smith, P.S. Thiagarajan, S. Tu, R. Valette, W. Vogler, K. Voss.

Leiden, November 1990
G. Rozenberg
Editor

Table of Contents

A Survey of Behaviour and Equivalence Preserving Refinements of Petri Nets

Wilfried Brauer*)
Robert Gold*)
Walter Vogler*)

Institut für Informatik, Technische Universität München
Arcisstr. 21, D-8000 München 2

ABSTRACT   Results on refinements of places and transitions in Petri nets are surveyed. Such refinements may either transform a net to a refined net with the same behaviour, where behaviour often means safeness or liveness. Or they may transform semantically equivalent nets to refined nets which are semantically equivalent again. Here the semantics of a net is a description of the possible runs incorporating information on choices to a varying degree.

Keywords: Concurrent system, top-down design, Petri net, place/transition net, refinement, liveness, safeness, deadlocking, failures semantics, partial order semantics, interval order, history preserving bisimulation

CONTENTS

*) This work was partially supported by the ESPRIT Basic Resarch Action No. 3148 DEMON (Design Methods Based on Nets)

0. Introduction

In a top-down design of a concurrent system one starts with a coarse model of the system and refines it stepwise by replacing parts of the model by more detailed models. This way one always has to deal with relatively small subproblems, which also can be distributed between several designers. More importantly, this approach supports a modular verification and analysis of the design: one can verify some properties of the coarse model, which is relatively easy since the model is small; then one can deduce some properties of the final design provided the refinement process follows some rules. Such rules and the help they provide in the system analysis is the topic of this paper.

In a Petri net, refinement means replacing a transition or a place by some net. In the literature mostly refinement of transitions is studied, and an example of transition refinements may look like illustrated in the following example.

The life of a philosopher – as computer scientists see it – can roughly be modelled as shown in Figure 0.1, see [Dij71].

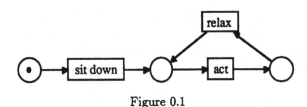

Figure 0.1

The philosopher sits down at a table and there he (or she) does something repeatedly. If we have a closer look at what he does, we see that he may either eat or think (Figure 0.2); thus refinement may introduce some choice.

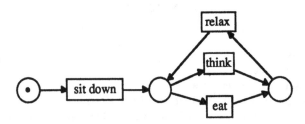

Figure 0.2

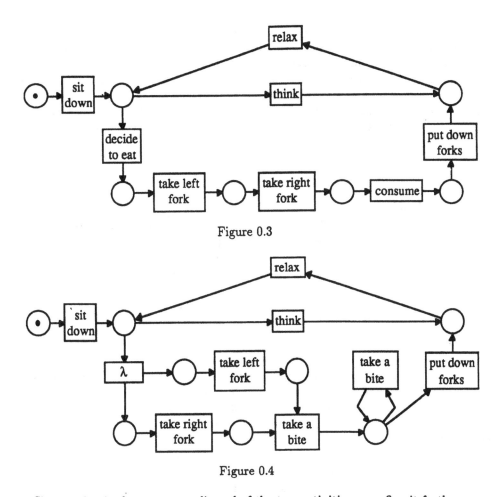

Figure 0.3

Figure 0.4

Since eating is the more complicated of the two activities we refine it further, e.g. as in Figure 0.3. Here we see that refinement may replace an action by a sequence of actions.

Alternatively, we can refine *eat* as shown in Figure 0.4. Here we can see several things: In this refinement the decision to eat is seen as an invisible action, and instead of leaving the corresponding box empty we have labelled it with the empty word λ. Secondly, in this case the forks that are needed for the meal are taken independently, i.e. refinement can introduce concurrency. Thirdly, this philosopher may have an arbitrary number of bites before he puts down the forks again, thus the inserted net may allow repetitions, i.e. have cycles. Finally we see that transitions are labelled with actions and several transitions may represent the same visible action.

All these refinements seem to be quite sensible. For example, the original net was safe and live in the sense that always some transition was enabled. These properties are preserved by the presented refinements. On the other hand, some properties have changed, too: The refined nets are capable of actions that were not present in the coarse first model. Thus if we consider the behaviour of a net as being defined by the possible actions, we will not expect that refinement is behaviour preserving. Instead two nets with the same behaviour should always be refined to nets that have the same behaviour again, if we refine both in the same way. In this case we can determine the behaviour of the refined net from the behaviour of the unrefined one.

Consequently, this survey consists of two main parts: Section 3 deals with a number of results regarding behaviour preserving refinements (where we regard property preservation as a special case of behaviour preservation). Section 4 gives results on refinements that preserve behaviour equivalence.

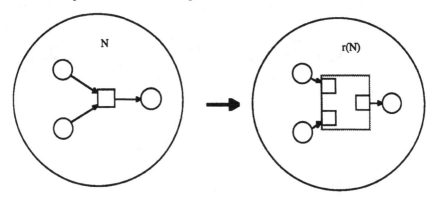

Figure 0.5

Schematically, the refinements of the above example look like it is shown in Figure 0.5. A transition is replaced by some net which is in some way connected to the places adjacent to the original transition. Various techniques for embedding the new net and various classes of nets that may replace a transition (or a place) have been suggested and accordingly the results on the preservation of behaviour and behaviour equivalence vary.

After defining some basic notions on Petri nets and their behaviour in Sections 1 and 2 we introduce in Section 3.1 a basic embedding technique, which is often used: The refinement net D that is going to replace the transition t has some initial transitions representing the begin of t and some final transitions representing the end of t. The net D is embedded in such a way that the preset of t is in the preset of the initial transitions and the postset of t is in the postset of the final transitions.

Section 3.2 surveys [Val79], [SM83] and [Mül85] where this technique (with only one initial and one final transition) is used. Different classes of refinement nets are defined and corresponding results on behaviour preservation are given. In Section 3.3 a different technique is introduced which embeds by merging places [Vog87]. There modules are defined as those refinement nets that always allow a behaviour preserving refinement; then it is characterized which refinement nets are modules.

In Section 3.4 we deal with the refinement of places, [Vog90b]. Such a refinement is put into the context of a general synchronization operator on nets which composes nets by merging transitions.

Section 4 deals with the preservation of behaviour equivalence. Refinements of this type have also been studied in a setting of process algebras like CCS [AH88], [NEL89], [Ace90], and in a setting of event structures in the sense of [NPW81] and transition systems, which can both be seen as special Petri nets [GG89], [GW89], [Gla90], [GG90], [Vog90c]. We concentrate here on the papers [BDKP89], [GG90] and [Vog90a], which deal with nets. After some introductory remarks in Section 4.1 we discuss in Section 4.2 which refinement nets can be used in this context.

Behaviour in Section 4 is concerned with the actions a net can perform. In the behaviour description we can also incorporate information on branching, i.e. at which stages of a run which choices are made. Section 4.3 deals with linear time and failures semantics which incorporate no or only some information on branching. Results in this subsection, [Vog90a], show that partial order semantics is useful in this setting (this has independently been done in [GG89] for event structures), but they also show to what degree it is necessary. The full interplay of branching and partial order semantics is modelled by history preserving bisimulation, discussed in Section 4.4. Refinement preserves this equivalence as shown in [BDKP89] (see also [GG89] for event structures), but only under some restrictions: Especially the self-concurrent firing of transitions is discussed.

We conclude this introduction by mentioning some related approaches that we will not discuss in detail: If we view Figure 0.5 as a transformation from right to left, we get a coarsening, an application of a net morphism in the sense of [GSW80]. These net morphisms are graph-theoretic in spirit. They give a framework for our considerations, but are themselves of limited interest here, since they are not closely related to the behaviour of nets. Some ideas of restricting them to more behaviour-oriented morphisms can be found in [DM88], [DM89].

Another sort of net morphisms is defined in [Win87] and subsequently in [MM88], [DMM89], [NRT90], and these morphisms are very much behaviour oriented. Here the framework is category theory; quite likely there are close relations to the graph-theoretic frame we work in, but for the moment they remain to be evaluated. Similar remarks hold for [PS89], [PS90a], where morphisms are defined which are much more concerned with places.

A very different idea of refinement is elaborated in [Kie89], [Kie90]: Whereas in this paper refinement is always an embedding of a refinement net into some host net, in [Kie89], [Kie90] a transition may be something like a procedure call: Firing it creates an incarnation of a corresponding subnet. Such calls may also be recursive.

This idea is certainly very natural, but these net systems lead to a larger class of behaviours, i.e. they do not stay within the framework of Petri nets. Therefore we have felt that this paper is beyond the scope of our survey. It should be mentioned that within the framework of net systems we get a compositional semantics. Especially the semantics of a refined net system can easily be computed from the semantics of the unrefined net system by substitution. We encourage the reader to consult [Kie89] and [Kie90] where he/she can find results that address net systems from a formal language theoretic point of view as well as results on compositional verification for these net systems.

1 Basic definitions

We will deal with *labelled place/transition-nets* $N = (S_N, T_N, W_N, M_N, l_N)$, where
- S_N, T_N are disjoint sets of *places* and *transitions*,
- $M_N : S_N \to I\!N_0$ is the *initial marking*,
- $W_N : S_N \times T_N \cup T_N \times S_N \to I\!N_0$ gives the *arc weights*,
- $l_N : T_N \to \Sigma \cup \{\lambda\}$ is a *labelling* of the transitions with labels from a fixed infinite alphabet Σ or with the empty string $\lambda \notin \Sigma$. The elements of Σ are *actions*, which may be represented by several different transitions; transitions with label λ stand for *internal* actions; these transitions perform *silent moves*.

For all refinement techniques that we present in this paper places are supposed to have infinite capacities (with the exception of [Mül85]). Therefore we have no capacity function. The sets S_N and T_N need not be finite. If some authors require this, we will note this later on. We call a net N *finite* if S_N and T_N are finite. From W_N we deduce the set of arcs $F_N = \{(x, y) \mid W_N(x, y) \neq 0\}$. In some papers unlabelled nets are considered. In these cases the labelling l_N can be assumed to be the identity; often we will simply omit the labelling. We will use the following definitions:

- $^\bullet x := \{y \in S_N \cup T_N \mid (y, x) \in F_N\}$, $x^\bullet := \{y \in S_N \cup T_N \mid (x, y) \in F_N\}$ for $x \in S_N \cup T_N$ are called the *pre-*, *postset* resp. of x; for subsets X of $S \cup T$ we put $^\bullet X = \cup_{x \in X} {}^\bullet x$ and $X^\bullet = \cup_{x \in X} x^\bullet$;

- N is called *T-restricted* if $\forall t \in T_N : {}^\bullet t \neq \emptyset, t^\bullet \neq \emptyset$;

- $M : S_N \to I\!N_0$ is called a *marking*;

- $t \in T_N$ is *enabled* under a marking M if $\forall s \in S_N : W_N(s, t) \leq M(s)$; this is denoted by $M[t\rangle$;

- the firing of a transition t that is enabled under M yields the follower marking M' where $\forall s \in S_N : M'(s) := M(s) - W_N(s, t) + W_N(t, s)$; this is denoted by $M[t\rangle M'$;

- this definition is extended to transition sequences: $w \in T_N^*$ is enabled under a marking M yielding the follower marking M', denoted by $M[w\rangle$ and $M[w\rangle M'$, if $w = \lambda$ and $M = M'$ or if $w = w't$, $w' \in T_N^*$, $t \in T_N$ such that $M[w'\rangle M_1$ and $M_1[t\rangle M'$; M' is denoted by $M(w)$;

- a transition sequence that is enabled under the initial marking is called a *firing sequence*; the set of all firing sequences of N is denoted by $FS(N)$;

- the labelling l_N is extended in the usual way to sequences $w \in T^*$ by $l_N(\lambda) = \lambda$, $l_N(wt) = l_N(w)l_N(t)$;

- $a \in \Sigma \cup \lambda$ is *image enabled* under a marking M if $\exists w \in T_N^* : l_N(w) = a \wedge M[w\rangle$; this is denoted by $M[a\rangle\rangle$; if w yields the follower marking M' we write $M[a\rangle\rangle M'$; observe that w is a sequence of transitions which are labelled by λ with one exception (if $a \neq \lambda$), which is labelled a.

- $l_N(FS(N))$ is called the *language* of N;

- $[M\rangle := \{M' : S_N \to I\!N_0 \mid \exists w \in T_N^* : M[w\rangle M'\}$ is called the set of *markings reachable* from the marking M;

- $[M_N\rangle$ is called the set of *reachable markings*;

- $t \in T_N$ is *live* if $\forall M \in [M_N)\ \exists M' \in [M) : M'[t\rangle$;
- N is *live* if all $t \in T_N$ are live;
- $s \in S_N$ is *m-bounded* if $\forall M \in [M_N) : M(s) \leq m$;
- $s \in S_N$ is *bounded* if there exists $m \in \mathbb{N}_0$ such that s is m-bounded;
- $s \in S_N$ is *safe* if s is 1-bounded;
- N is *(m-)bounded* if all $s \in S_N$ are $(m\text{-})$bounded;
- N is *safe* if N is 1-bounded;
- $t \in T_N$ is *dead* if $\forall M \in [M_N) : \neg M[t\rangle$.

Sometimes we will need the *restriction* of a relation. Let $r \subseteq X \times Y$ be a relation and $X' \subseteq X, Y' \subseteq Y$. The relation $r \cap (X' \times Y') \subseteq X \times Y$ is denoted by $r|_{X' \times Y'}$. If r is a function, then the function $r \cap (X' \times Y)$ is denoted by $r|_{X'}$. For a sequence $w \in A^*$ over some set A and an element a of A we denote the *number of occurrences* of a in w by $\#(w, a)$. For the *disjoint union* of two sets we use the symbol $\dot\cup$, i.e. $X = Y \dot\cup Z$ iff $X = Y \cup Z$ and $Y \cap Z = \emptyset$.

A function $X \to \mathbb{N}_0$ is called a *multiset* over X where X is a set. The firing rule defined above can be extended to multisets of transitions. Let N be a net, let $s \in S_N, t \in T_N$ and u a multiset over T_N.

- $u^-(s) := \sum_{t \in T_N} u(t) W_N(s, t), \quad u^+(s) := \sum_{t \in T_N} u(t) W_N(t, s)$,
  $\Delta u(s) := u^+(s) - u^-(s)$;
- u is *enabled* under a marking M if $\forall s \in S_N: u^-(s) \leq M(s)$; this is denoted by $M[u\rangle$; u is called a *step*;
- the multiset $t + t$ has value 2 at t and 0 everywhere else; for $t_1 \neq t_2$ the multiset $t_1 + t_2$ has value 1 at t_1 and t_2 and 0 everywhere else;
- two transitions t_1, t_2 are *in conflict* if $\exists M \in [M_N) : M[t_1\rangle, M[t_2\rangle, \neg M[t_1 + t_2\rangle$;
- N is called *conflict-free* if $\forall t_1, t_2 \in T_N : t_1 \neq t_2 \Rightarrow t_1, t_2$ are not in conflict;
- N is called *sequential* if $\forall M \in [M_N)\ \forall t_1, t_2 \in T_N : \neg M[t_1 + t_2\rangle$;
- a transition t is *self-concurrent* if $\exists M \in [M_N) : M[t + t\rangle$;
- an action a is *auto-concurrent* if $\exists M \in [M_N) : \exists t_1, t_2 \in T_N : l_N(t_1) = l_N(t_2) = a \wedge M[t_1 + t_2\rangle$; note that $l_N(t)$ is auto-concurrent if t is self-concurrent, but not the other way round.

In general we do not distinguish between isomorphic nets, partial orders (see below) etc.

2 Behaviour of Petri nets

For the study of refinement techniques we need some notions of behaviour. In the previous section we have already introduced liveness, boundedness and safeness. These are very basic notions of behaviour, where two nets have the same behaviour if either both are live or both are not live etc.

Very often the behaviour of a net is described by its language. There are two aspects in which this semantics can be seen as unsatisfactory:

- It is an interleaving semantics, i.e. it does not distinguish between the concurrent execution of actions and their execution in arbitrary order. Instead one could take a partial order semantics like the set of (images of) partial words or of (event structures of) processes.
- It is a linear time semantics (like processes and partial words), i.e. it contains no information at which stage of an execution which choices have been made. Instead one could work with failures semantics which contains some information on the choices – this semantics has been developed for TCSP [BHR84], [BR84]. Or one could model the branching behaviour completely by taking a class of bisimilar transition systems as semantics; this has most often been studied for CCS [Mil83], [Par81]. Both are interleaving semantics.

In the following we define the above mentioned behaviour notions and the related equivalences. These are those equivalences of nets we will need in this paper. For a more detailed discussion of equivalences of Petri nets see [PS90b].

Definition 2.1

Two nets N_1, N_2 are called *language-equivalent* if $l_{N_1}(FS(N_1)) = l_{N_2}(FS(N_2))$.

Another well-known notion of behaviour are processes; they are intended to model the causality of a system run.

Definition 2.2

A *causal net* is a triple $N = (B, E, F)$, where
- B, E are finite, disjoint sets of *conditions* and *events*,
- $F \subseteq B \times E \cup E \times B$ is the *flow relation* (by F^+ we denote the transitive closure of F, by ${}^\bullet x$ and $x^\bullet$ we denote the pre-, postset resp. of $x \in B \cup E$, i.e. ${}^\bullet x := \{y \in B \cup E \mid (y, x) \in F\}$, $x^\bullet := \{y \in B \cup E \mid (x, y) \in F\}$),
- $\forall x, y \in B \cup E : (x, y) \in F^+ \Rightarrow (y, x) \notin F^+$ (acyclicity),
- $\forall b \in B : |{}^\bullet b| \leq 1, |b^\bullet| \leq 1$ (no branching of places).

A *process* $\pi = (B, E, F, p)$ of a net $N = (S_N, T_N, W_N, M_N, l_N)$ *enabled* under a marking M consists of a causal net (B, E, F) and a labelling $p : B \cup E \to S_N \cup T_N$ such that
- $p(B) \subseteq S_N$, $p(E) \subseteq T_N$,
- $\forall s \in S_N : M(s) = |p^{-1}(s) \cap \{b \in B \mid {}^\bullet b = \emptyset\}|$ (minimal conditions correspond to the marking M),
- $\forall e \in E \, \forall s \in S_N : W_N(s, p(e)) = |p^{-1}(s) \cap {}^\bullet e|$, $W_N(p(e), s) = |p^{-1}(s) \cap e^\bullet|$ (transition environments are respected).

We write $M[\pi\rangle$ in this situation. The marking M' reached after the firing of π is defined by $\forall s \in S_N : M'(s) = |p^{-1}(s) \cap \{b \in B \mid b^\bullet = \emptyset\}|$ (denoted by $M[\pi\rangle M'$). A process of a net N enabled under the initial marking is simply called *process of N*. The *initial process* of a net N, denoted by $\pi_0(N)$, is the unique process of N with an empty set of events.

For the following we need some definitions about partial orders.

Definition 2.3

Let $(A, <)$ be a finite strict partial order, i.e. let $<$ be a transitive, irreflexive relation on a finite set A, and let $\beta : A \to X$ be a function into some set X, called a labelling. Then $(A, <, \beta)$ is called a *strict partial order labelled over X*.

For a strict partial order $(A, <)$, for $k, l \in A$ and $B \subseteq A$ we define, as usual, $l \leq k :\Leftrightarrow l < k \vee l = k$ and $\downarrow B := \{l \in A | \exists k \in B : l \leq k\}$. We call B *downward-closed*, if $B = \downarrow B$.

Let $(A_i, <_i, \beta_i)$, $i = 1, 2$, be strict partial orders labelled over X. They are said to be *isomorphic*, if there exists a bijection $\alpha : A_1 \to A_2$ that is *label* and *order preserving*, i.e. $\beta_1(k) = \beta_2(\alpha(k))$ and $k <_1 l \Leftrightarrow \alpha(k) <_2 \alpha(l)$ for all $k, l \in A_1$. α is called an *isomorphism*. $(A_1, <_1, \beta_1)$ is called *prefix* of $(A_2, <_2, \beta_2)$ if $A_1 \subseteq A_2$, $A_1 = \downarrow_2 A_1$, $<_1 = <_2|_{A_1 \times A_1}$, $\beta_1 = \beta_2|_{A_1}$.

A process $\pi = (B, E, F, p)$ of a net N enabled under some marking M defines a strict partial order labelled over $S_N \cup T_N$, namely $(B \cup E, F^+, p)$.

Definition 2.4

Let N be a net and $\pi_i = (B_i, E_i, F_i, p_i)$, $i = 1, 2$, be processes of N enabled under some marking M. Then π_1 is a *prefix* of π_2 if $(B_1 \cup E_1, F_1^+, p_1)$ is a prefix of $(B_2 \cup E_2, F_2^+, p_2)$. We also call π_2 an *extension* of π_1.

From a process we derive a strict partial order labelled over Σ
 - by supressing all conditions and those events labelled by λ-transitions and
 - by changing the labels of the remaining events from transitions of N to their labels.

Definition 2.5

Let $\pi = (B, E, F, p)$ be a process of a net N enabled under some marking M. The *event structure* of π is the strict partial order $ev(\pi) := (A, <, \beta)$ labelled over Σ, where $A := \{e \in E | l_N(p(e)) \neq \lambda\}$, $< := F^+|_{A \times A}$, $\beta := l_N \circ p|_A$.

We say that $ev(\pi)$ is *enabled* under M yielding the follower marking M', denoted by $M[ev(\pi)\rangle\rangle$, and $M[ev(\pi)\rangle\rangle M'$, if π is a process in N that is enabled under M yielding the follower marking M'. Two nets N_1, N_2 are called *process-equivalent* if $\{ev(\pi) | \pi$ is a process of $N_1\} = \{ev(\pi) | \pi$ is a process of $N_2\}$.

A third notion of behaviour, which is a less well-known partial order semantics of nets, is based on so-called partial words [Gra81]. Intuitively a partial word can be seen as the causal ordering of the events in a system run together with a partial observation of this run; consequently also causally independent events can be ordered.

Definition 2.6

Let N be a net, let $p = (A, <, \beta)$ be a strict partial order labelled over T_N, $C \subseteq A$, M be a marking of N. The multiset βC over T_N is defined by $\beta C(t) := |\beta^{-1}(t) \cap C|$. p

is said to be *enabled* (under M_N) if $\forall B, C \subseteq A, B \cap C = \emptyset$: If all elements of C are pairwise unordered, and B and $B \cup C$ are downward-closed, then

$$\forall s \in S_N : (\beta C)^-(s) \leq M_N(s) + \sum_{l \in B} \Delta\beta(l)(s).$$

Then p is called a *partial word* of N. The *image* of p, $(A', <', \beta')$, is the strict partial order labelled over Σ defined by $A' := \{a \in A \mid l_N(\beta(a)) \neq \lambda\}$, $<' := < \mid_{A' \times A'}$, $\beta' := l_N \circ \beta \mid_{A'}$.

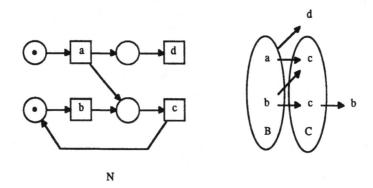

Figure 2.1

Figure 2.1 shows a net N and a partial word enabled in N, where some sets B and C are indicated. The unordered elements of C can be fired independently, if we respect the given precedences, i.e. fire the elements of B first.

The following translation of failures semantics to nets can be found in [Pom86]. In [Vog89] it has been shown to be just the right semantics for the modular construction of nets, if one uses a certain well-known synchronization operator and is interested in nets that cannot deadlock. There is also a variant that takes divergence into account. Divergence or internal looping is an infinite firing sequence of silent moves that might occur at some reachable marking.

Definition 2.7

The *(interleaving) failures semantics* of a net N is $\mathcal{F}(N) = \{(v, X) \mid v \in \Sigma^*, X \subseteq \Sigma, \exists w \in FS(N) : l_N(w) = v \wedge \forall a \in X : \neg M(w)[a\rangle)\}$. Two nets N_1, N_2 are $\mathcal{F}$-*equivalent* if $\mathcal{F}(N_1) = \mathcal{F}(N_2)$.

Figure 2.2 shows two nets which are not failures equivalent: Only the second net can perform a such that no b is possible, it can refuse b after a. Formally, we have $(a, \{b\}) \in \mathcal{F}(N_2) - \mathcal{F}(N_1)$.

On the other hand, the nets of Figure 2.3 are not distinguished by failures semantics, since only the second net can perform a such that bc is not possible. This is because of the fact that failures semantics only has a 'look-ahead' of 1. These nets are distinguished by bisimilarity.

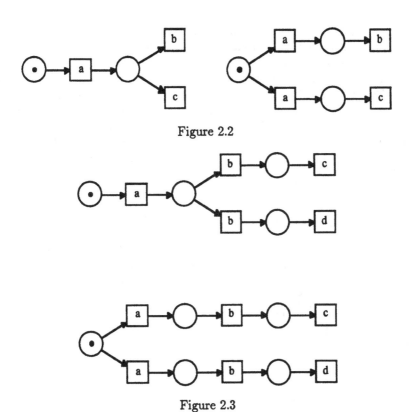

Figure 2.2

Figure 2.3

Definition 2.8

Two nets N_1, N_2 are *(interleaving) bisimilar* if there is a *bisimulation*, i.e. a relation $\rho \in [M_{N_1}\rangle \times [M_{N_2}\rangle$ with

- $(M_{N_1}, M_{N_2}) \in \rho$,
- for all $M_1 \in [M_{N_1}\rangle$ and all $M_2 \in [M_{N_2}\rangle$ such that $(M_1, M_2) \in \rho$ we have:
  if there is $a \in \Sigma \cup \{\lambda\}$ and $M_1' \in [M_{N_1}\rangle$ such that $M_1[a\rangle\rangle M_1'$ then for some M_2' we have $M_2[a\rangle\rangle M_2'$ and $(M_1', M_2') \in \rho$,
  if there is $a \in \Sigma \cup \{\lambda\}$ and $M_2' \in [M_{N_2}\rangle$ such that $M_2[a\rangle\rangle M_2'$ then for some M_1' we have $M_1[a\rangle\rangle M_1'$ and $(M_1', M_2') \in \rho$.

3 Behaviour preserving refinements

3.1 A basic technique for the refinement of transitions

In this chapter we define a refinement technique, which is widely used in the literature. We give the definition of the refinement nets, i.e. the nets that substitute transitions, and a description, how this substitution is done.

A *refinement net* D is a net, which contains a special place, called the *idle place*, denoted by $idle_D$. We assume that the arcs from and to the idle place have weight 1. The set of places of D is $S_D \dot\cup \{idle_D\}$. This is a slight abuse of notation, since here S_D

is not the set of all places of D; the additional place represents the interface to a *host* net, i.e. the net into which D is inserted and 'really' belongs to the host. The idle place is removed, when D is inserted into a host. The transitions in the postset of the idle place are called *initial transitions*, those in the preset of the idle place are called *final transitions* (Figure 3.1.1). (It is also possible that a transition is initial and final at the same time, also that there are no initial or no final transitions.)

The *refined net* is constructed by removing a transition t from the host and inserting the refinement net (without the idle place). To the preset of each initial transition the preset of t is added and to the postset of each final transition the postset of t is added (Figure 3.1.2).

initial transitions   final transitions

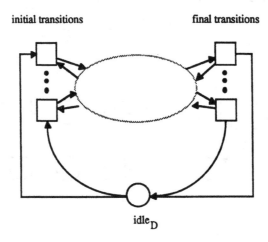

idle$_D$

Figure 3.1.1 A refinement net D

Definition 3.1.1

Let N be a net, $t \in T_N$ and D a refinement net. We assume that $S_N \cup T_N$ and $S_D \cup T_D$ are disjoint. Refining t by D yields the refined net, denoted by $N[t/D]$, which is defined by:

$$S_{N[t/D]} = S_N \dot\cup S_D$$

$$T_{N[t/D]} = (T_N - \{t\}) \dot\cup T_D$$

$$W_{N[t/D]}(x,y) = \begin{cases} W_N(x,y), & \text{if } x,y \in S_N \cup (T_N - \{t\}) \\ W_D(x,y), & \text{if } x,y \in S_D \cup T_D \\ W_N(x,t), & \text{if } x \in S_N \text{ and } y \text{ is an initial transition} \\ W_N(t,y), & \text{if } y \in S_N \text{ and } x \text{ is a final transition} \\ 0, & \text{otherwise} \end{cases}$$

$$M_{N[t/D]}(s) = \begin{cases} M_N(s), & \text{if } s \in S_N \\ M_D(s), & \text{if } s \in S_D \end{cases}$$

$$l_{N[t/D]}(x) = \begin{cases} l_N(x), & \text{if } x \in T_N - \{t\} \\ l_D(x), & \text{if } x \in T_D \end{cases}$$

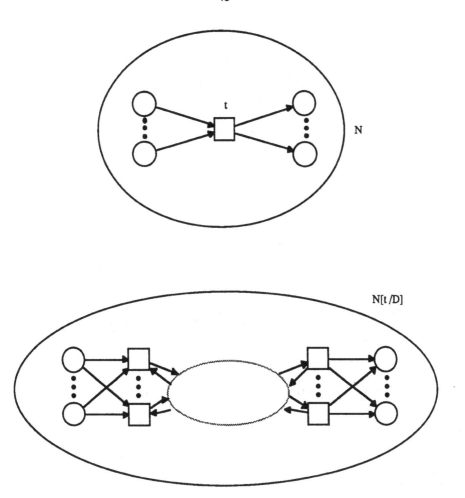

Figure 3.1.2

The marking of the idle place is not relevant for the refinement technique. But it will be relevant, when we study the behaviour of the refinement net in order to determine the behaviour of the refined net. This refinement technique obviously also applies to unlabelled nets.

The first and the second refinement step in the introduction are performed with the refinement nets shown in Figure 3.1.3.

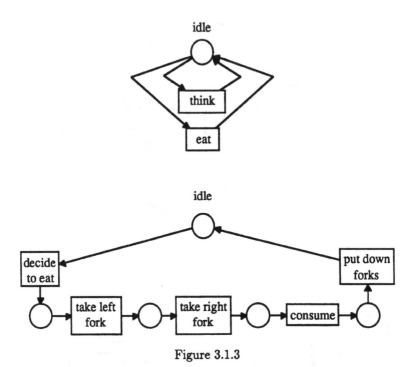

Figure 3.1.3

3.2 Refinement nets with one initial and one final transition

The first attempts on behaviour preserving refinement of transitions are based on the idea that the firing of a transition has a 'beginning' and an 'end'. Therefore transitions can be split in one initial transition, which models the 'beginning', an inner part and one final transition, which models the 'end'. In this approach, the refinement net does not have an initial conflict, i.e. we can not refine *act* to a choice between *eat* and *think* as shown in the introduction. But of course we could embed this choice between an internal initial and an internal final transition.

In [Val79] a refinement net[†] with one initial transition ($t_{initial}$) and one final transition (t_{final}) with $t_{initial} \neq t_{final}$ is called *block*. In order to study the behaviour of a block the idle place is initially marked with one token (Figure 3.2.1).

For the refinement by an arbitrary block we cannot expect behaviour preservation. Therefore we only use well-formed blocks.

Definition 3.2.1

A block D is called *well-formed*, if
- D is live
- $\forall M \in [M_D\rangle : (M(idle_D) > 0 \Rightarrow M = M_D)$
- $\forall t \in T_D : (M_D[t\rangle \Rightarrow t = t_{initial})$.

[†] Throughout the chapters 3.2 and 3.3 all nets are supposed to be unlabelled and finite.

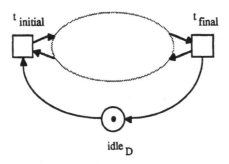

Figure 3.2.1

Well-formed blocks can simulate a transition: The only transition that can activate D is the initial transition. Thus a simulation can only start, if the environment — which is represented by the idle place — allows this. If D is activated, always a transition sequence can fire that enables the final transition, since D is live. Hence every simulation can be finished. The firing of the final transition marks the idle place, i.e. produces the output for the environment. Now we have reached the initial marking again, i.e. a well-formed block does not have a 'memory', just like a procedure call does not depend on earlier calls. During the simulation of a transition t by D the idle place is empty. Therefore it is not possible to start a second simulation of t before the first is finished. Only when the simulation has come to an end, a new simulation can be initiated by the initial transition. The environment of t in a host net N has to ensure this property, therefore the transition that is refined must not be 2-enabled by any reachable marking of N. A transition $t \in T_N$ is k-enabled ($k \in I\!N_0$) by a marking M, if

$$\forall s \in S_N : k \cdot W_N(s, t) \leq M(s).$$

Then the following results concerning behaviour preservation are obtained.

Theorem 3.2.2 ([Val79])

Let N be a net, $t \in T_N$ a transition that is not 2-enabled by any reachable marking and D a well-formed block. Then we have for $N[t/D]$ as defined in 3.1.1:

(i) N bounded $\Leftrightarrow$ $N[t/D]$ bounded
(ii) N and D safe $\Leftrightarrow$ $N[t/D]$ safe
(iii) N live $\Leftrightarrow$ $N[t/D]$ live.

In [SM83] this refinement technique is generalized such that it is possible to refine a transition that is not $(k + 1)$-enabled by any reachable marking even if $k + 1 > 2$. To achieve this, well-formedness must be strenghtened (to k-well-behavedness). 1-well-behavedness is a slightly relaxed version of well-formedness, but is sufficient for behaviour preservation, if the transition is not 2-enabled by any reachable marking.

Definition 3.2.3

Let D be a block as defined above but with k tokens on the idle place ($k \in I\!N_0$). Such a block D is k-well-behaved, if

- $t_{initial}$ is live in D
- $\forall w \in FS(D) : \#(w, t_{initial}) \geq \#(w, t_{final})$
- $\forall w_1 \in FS(D) : (\#(w_1, t_{initial}) > \#(w_1, t_{final})$
  $\Rightarrow \exists w_2 \in (T_D - \{t_{initial}\})^+ : w_1 w_2 \in FS(D) \wedge \#(w_1, t_{initial}) = \#(w_1 w_2, t_{final}))$

Let us examine, how a k-well-behaved block D simulates a transition t. Since we have k tokens on the idle place, at most k simulations can be started simultanously. Liveness of the initial transition ensures that at least one simulation is possible. Because of the third condition every run of D can be finished (by the firing of the final transition). The second condition says that the idle place is k-bounded, since every firing of the final transition corresponds to a firing of the initial transition. When all simulations are finished, there are k tokens on the idle place, but the reached marking may differ from the initial marking on the inner places: D may have a 'memory'.

The first block depicted in Figure 3.2.2 is well-formed and therefore 1-well-behaved, but it is not 2-well-behaved. The second block is not well-formed, since t is not live, but 1-well-behaved. If we put two tokens on the idle place it is possible that t gets activated and fires. Then there are unfinished runs of D. Thus the second block is not 2-well-behaved.

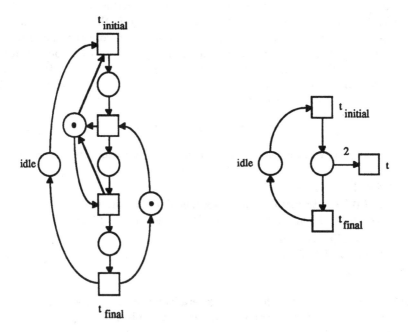

Figure 3.2.2

The following result is analogous to Theorem 3.2.2.

Theorem 3.2.4 ([SM83])

Let N be a net, $t \in T_N$ a transition that is not $(k+1)$-enabled by any reachable marking and D a k-well-behaved block. Then we have for $N[t/D]$ as defined in 3.1.1 the following results:

   (i) N m-bounded, D m'-bounded $\Rightarrow$ $N[t/D]$ $(\max(m, m'))$-bounded
   (i') $N[t/D]$ m-bounded $\Rightarrow$ N m-bounded
   (ii) N and D safe $\Rightarrow$ $N[t/D]$ safe
   (ii') $N[t/D]$ safe $\Rightarrow$ N safe
   (iii) N and D live, condition $(*)$ holds $\Rightarrow$ $N[t/D]$ live
   (iii') $N[t/D]$ live $\Rightarrow$ N live

where
$$\forall M \in [M_N) \; \exists M' \in [M] : t \; k\text{-enabled by } M' \qquad (*)$$

Note that we have to require that D is m'-bounded in (i) and that D is live in (iii), since k-well-behavedness does not ensure boundedness of D and only ensures liveness of $t_{initial}$. On the contrary, in the definition of well-formedness liveness of D is explicitly stated, boundedness follows from liveness of t_{final} and the fact that the firing of t_{final} reproduces the initial marking. If we compare well-formedness and 1-well-behavedness, we have — besides the difference we have just stated — that the condition 'no memory' in well-formedness is not demanded for 1-well-behavedness. Hence this condition is not necessary for behaviour preservation. Furthermore it is also not necessary that only the initial transition is enabled initially.

Example: If we look at Figure 3.2.3 we see that the conditions of Theorem 3.2.4 are satisfied with $k = 2$; the nets N and D are live, but $(*)$ does not hold since t is never 2-enabled and the refined net $N[t/D]$ (which is identical to D but with only one token on $idle_D$) is not live. Liveness of N and D is not sufficient for liveness of $N[t/D]$, since liveness of D is tested with two tokens on the idle place, but if inserted into N there is only one token supplied by N. Therefore liveness of a transition in D does not carry over to $N[t/D]$.

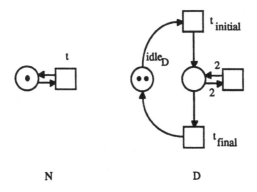

N   D

Figure 3.2.3

For practical reasons we are interested in deciding, whether a refinement is behaviour preserving, i.e. whether the conditions of Theorem 3.2.4 hold. Note that here only finite nets are considered.

Theorem 3.2.5 ([SM83])
  (i) It is decidable, whether for a given net N and a transition $t \in T_N$ there exists $M \in [M_N\rangle$ such that t is $(k+1)$-enabled by M for a given $k \in \mathbb{N}_0$.
 (ii) It is decidable, whether a given block is k-well-behaved for a given $k \in \mathbb{N}_0$.
(iii) It is decidable, whether a given net satisfies condition $(*)$ for a given $k \in \mathbb{N}_0$.

In [SM83] it is suggested to use the same refinement technique also for the refinement of places. The place s that should be refined is split as shown in Figure 3.2.4. Then the transition t is refined. The results gained for the refinement of transitions can be transfered to this case.

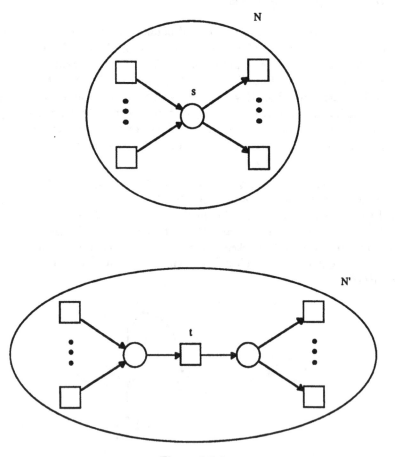

Figure 3.2.4

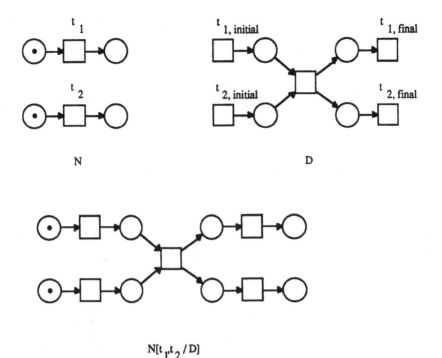

Figure 3.2.5

In [Mül85] a technique for the refinement of several transitions by one net is proposed. An example is shown in Figure 3.2.5: t_1, t_2 are refined by D.

This is a very interesting generalization, and it allows especially to compose several nets by a medium net: We can choose one transition from every net and refine them by a common net. But this generalization does not really fit into our framework of refinement of places and transitions, but rather concerns the exchange of general subnets; therefore we will not deal with it in this paper in full generality. For a more detailed discussion of this technique see [BC90].

However, if we restrict this technique of [Mül85] to the refinement of only one transition, then the nets used for refinement are similar to the blocks defined above, except that the idle place is split into two places, called the input place and the output place $(input_D, output_D)$. Furthermore we demand that $^\bullet t_{initial} = \{input_D\}$ and $t^\bullet_{final} = \{output_D\}$ (see Figure 3.2.6).

Figure 3.2.6

The refined net is constructed by removing a transition t and inserting the refinement net (without the input and the output place) as presented in 3.1.

The requirements on refinement nets are strengthened in the definition below such that it is possible to refine an arbitrary transition without any enabledness condition. Therefore an arbitrary number of tokens on the input place are considered. But note that this is also a restriction, since there exist well-behaved blocks that are not refinement nets in the sense of [Mül85] and thus are excluded there.

Definition 3.2.6 ([Mül85])

Let D be a refinement net in the sense of [Mül85] (see above). D is called *completely m-permeable* ($m \in I\!N_0$) if

$$\forall M \in [M_{D_m}) \; \exists w \in T_D^* : M[w)M' \land M'(input_D) = 0 \land M'(output_D) = m$$

where D_m is constructed from D by placing m tokens on the input place, i.e. $D_m = (S_D \cup \{input_D, output_D\}, T_D, W_D, M_{D_m})$ with $M_{D_m}(input_D) = m$, $M_{D_m}(output_D) = 0$, $M_{D_m}(s) = M_D(s)$, for all $s \in S_D$.

D is called *completely permeable* if D is completely m-permeable for all $m \in I\!N_0$.

In the above definition the environment is represented by the m tokens we put on the input place. If D is a completely m-permeable refinement net, every 'run' of D_m can be prolonged such that all tokens on the input place are transmitted to the output place. Thus m simultaneous firings of a transition are simulated.

For the following result concerning preservation of liveness we need the definition of lively completely permeable refinement nets.

Definition 3.2.7 ([Mül85])

Let D be a completely permeable refinement net. D is *lively completely m-permeable* ($m \in I\!N_0$), if

$$\forall t \in T_D \; \forall M \in [M_{D_m}) : M(input_D) + M(output_D) = m \Rightarrow \exists M'' \in [M') : M''[t),$$

where M' is the marking with $M'(input_D) = M(input_D) + 1$ and $M'(s) = M(s)$ for $s \in S_D \cup \{output_D\}$. D is *lively completely permeable*, if D is lively completely m-permeable for all $m \in I\!N_0$ (for D_m see Definition 3.2.6).

The above definition is very close to liveness of D_m. But for the examination of liveness of a transition t we restrict ourselves to reachable markings M in D_m, where some of the m tokens that we put initially on the input place stay on the input place and the rest of those tokens are already transmitted to the output place. This means that in such a state there is no unfinished run of D_m. If the environment puts an additional token on the input place in such a marking M (let the resulting marking be M'), then there has to be a marking M'' reachable from M' such that t can be fired under M''.

Theorem 3.2.8 ([Mül85])

Let N be a net, $t \in T_N$ and D a completely permeable refinement net. If N is live and D is lively completely permeable, then $N[t/D]$ is live.

A similar result is obtained for the refinement of several transitions by one refinement net. Note that in [Mül85] nets with capacities are used, but for Theorem 3.2.8 it is required that the places in the postset of the transition t have infinite capacities. This is necessary as the example in Figure 3.2.7 shows. No decidability results are shown in [Mül85].

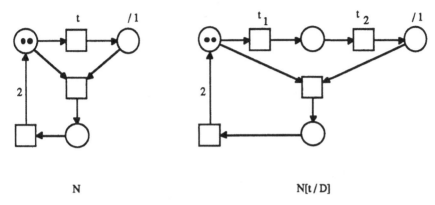

Figure 3.2.7 N is live, $N[t/D]$ is not live.

3.3 An alternative technique for the refinement of transitions

Let us discuss the basic refinement technique defined in 3.1. Let N be a net and t a transition in N that is refined by some refinement net D. In the refined net every place s in the preset of t is connected with every initial transition of D with the weight of the arc between s and t. Symmetrically final transitions and places in the postset of t are connected. Thus the firing of an initial transition absorbs the same number of tokens from each place in the preset of t as the firing of t. These tokens cannot be distributed between two initial transitions or between an initial transition and a transition not belonging to D. Symmetrically the firing of a final transition produces the same number of tokens on each place in the postset of t as the firing of t. Especially, it is not possible that some output is produced and used by the environment before the rest is produced. We say that *distributed input* and *distributed output* is not allowed.

In [Vog87] a refinement technique is proposed, where distributed input and distributed output is possible (Figure 3.3.1). A transition t is removed and a daughter-net D is inserted by identifying all places in the preset of t with some special places of D, called the input places, and all places in the postset of t with some other places of D, called the output places. Thus several initial transitions (the postset of the input places) and several final transitions (the preset of the output places) are allowed.

Hence the set of places of a *daughter-net* D should be the disjoint union of a non-empty set I_D of input places, a set S_D of inner places, and a non-empty set O_D of output places. Furthermore we assume that $^\bullet I_D = \emptyset = O_D^\bullet$ and that input and output

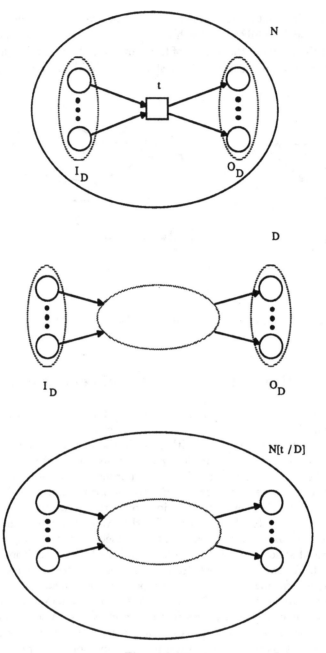

Figure 3.3.1

places are not marked under the initial marking. For simplicity we assume that the weights on arcs to or from the transition t that is refined are 1.

Since distributed input and output is possible, this refinement technique is more general than the basic refinement technique. But it can only be applied to a transition

t, if ${}^\bullet t = I_D$ and $t^\bullet = O_D$. Otherwise the refinement is not possible. (If ${}^\bullet t \cap t^\bullet = \emptyset$, $|{}^\bullet t| = |I_D|$ and $|t^\bullet| = |O_D|$, then we can rename the places in I_D and O_D such that ${}^\bullet t = I_D$ and $t^\bullet = O_D$ and apply the refinement technique; observe that the result of the refinement might be different for different renamings.)

Definition 3.3.1

Let N be a net, $t \in T_N$ such that $\forall s \in S_N : W_N(s,t) \leq 1, W_N(t,s) \leq 1$ and let D be a daughter-net as defined above such that ${}^\bullet t = I_D, t^\bullet = O_D$. We assume that $S_N \cup T_N$ and $S_D \cup T_D$ are disjoint. Refining t by D yields the refined net, denoted by $N[t/D]$, which is defined by:

$$S_{N[t/D]} = S_N \dot\cup S_D$$

$$T_{N[t/D]} = (T_N - \{t\}) \dot\cup T_D$$

$$W_{N[t/D]}(x,y) = \begin{cases} W_N(x,y), & \text{if } x,y \in S_N \cup (T_N - \{t\}) \\ W_D(x,y), & \text{if } x,y \in S_D \cup I_D \cup O_D \cup T_D \\ 0, & \text{otherwise} \end{cases}$$

$$M_{N[t/D]}(s) = \begin{cases} M_N(s), & \text{if } s \in S_N \\ M_D(s), & \text{if } s \in S_D \end{cases}$$

In the previous chapter, blocks were designed such that they simulate a transition. As a result we got behaviour preservation. Now we look at things the other way round. We give the desired property, namely N and $N[t/D]$ should have equivalent behaviour, and try to determine, which daughter-nets ensure this. These daughter-nets are called modules.

The main problem is to define an appropriate notion of behaviour. The following definition requires a close correspondence of the reachable markings in N and $N[t/D]$. This seems reasonable, since properties like liveness or boundedness depend on the reachable markings.

Definition 3.3.2 ([Vog87])

Let D be a daughter-net. D is called a *module* if, for all nets N and all $t \in T_N$ with $\forall s \in S_N : W_N(s,t) \leq 1, W_N(t,s) \leq 1$ and ${}^\bullet t = I_D, t^\bullet = O_D$, the nets N and $N[t/D]$ have the same behaviour, i.e.

$$\forall M \in [M_{N[t/D]}\rangle \; \exists M' \in [M_N\rangle, \; w \in T_D^* :$$
$$M[w\rangle M'' \wedge M''|_{S_N} = M' \wedge$$
$$(M'[t\rangle \Rightarrow \exists w'' \in T_D^* : M''[w''\rangle \wedge M''(w'')|_{S_N} = M'(t))$$

This behaviour notion means the following. Each reachable marking M in the refined net corresponds to a reachable marking M' in N after normalization of M by a firing sequence of D, and if t is enabled under the corresponding marking M', then the firing of t can be simulated by a transition sequence w'' in D, i.e. the marking reached after the firing of t corresponds to the marking reached after the firing of w''.

The next theorem follows from Definition 3.3.2 and [Vog87, Theorem 1 (iv), Corollary 1, Definition 3, Proposition 1].

Theorem 3.3.3

Let N be a net, $t \in T_N$ such that $\forall s \in S_N : W_N(s,t) \leq 1, W_N(t,s) \leq 1$ and let D be a module such that $^\bullet t = I_D, t^\bullet = O_D$.

- If s is a m-bounded place of N, then s is m-bounded in $N[t/D]$.
- A transition $t' \neq t$ of N is live in N if and only if it is live in $N[t/D]$.
- Let N and D' be bounded, where D' is constructed from D by removing the input and output places, i.e.

$$D' = (S_D, T_D, W_D|_{S_D \times T_D \cup T_D \times S_D}, M_D|_{S_D}).$$

Then $N[t/D]$ is bounded.

Like refinement nets in the sense of [Mül85] a module D can be used for the refinement of an arbitrary transition t (if $^\bullet t = I_D$ and $t^\bullet = O_D$) without any enabledness condition.

The main result in [Vog87] is a characterization of modules that does not involve the (test-) nets N but only the daughter-net that is in question.

Theorem 3.3.4 ([Vog87])

A daughter-net D is a module if and only if

(i) $\forall t \in T_D : ((\exists s_1, s_2 \in I_D : W_D(s_1, t) \neq W_D(s_2, t)) \Rightarrow t$ is dead in $D')$
where D' is constructed from D by removing the input places, i.e.

$$D' = (S_D \cup O_D, T_D, W_D|_{(S_D \cup O_D) \times T_D \cup T_D \times (S_D \cup O_D)}, M_D|_{S_D \cup O_D})$$

(ii) $\forall m \in \mathbb{N}_0 \ \forall M \in [M_{D_m}) \exists w \in T_D^* : M[w)M' \wedge \forall s \in O_D : M'(s) = m$
where D_m is constructed from D by placing m tokens on each input place, i.e.
$D_m = (S_D \cup I_D \cup O_D, T_D, W_D, M_{D_m})$ with $M_{D_m}(s) = m$, for all $s \in I_D$, $M_{D_m}(s) = M_D(s)$, for all $s \in S_D$, $M_{D_m}(s) = 0$, for all $s \in O_D$.

Condition (i) means that distributed input is not allowed for modules. Figure 3.3.2 shows an example, where D does not satisfy this condition. The transition t in N needs the two tokens on the places in its preset for firing. In the refined net it is possible to start a simulation of the firing of t by firing t_1. Thereby only one token is removed from the preset of t. The other token remains there and can be used for firing t_2, a transition not belonging to D. The tokens are distributed between the initial transitions of D and transitions in the environment of t. As a consequence the marking in $N[t/D]$ reached after the firing of $t_1 t_2$ does not correspond to a reachable marking in N. Thus in this setting one can prove that distributed input must be forbidden, while distributed output is possible — which generalizes the refinements of the previous subsection. Note that condition (i) includes the possibility that some transition takes e.g. twice as many tokens from $^\bullet t$ as t, thus starts two (or more) simulations of t simultaneously.

Condition (ii) is a generalization of the condition in Definition 3.2.6 to sets of input and output places. There is an obvious similarity between modules and completely permeable refinement nets as defined by [Mül85]. Modules generalize these refinement nets, since they allow several initial and final transitions and distributed output, but

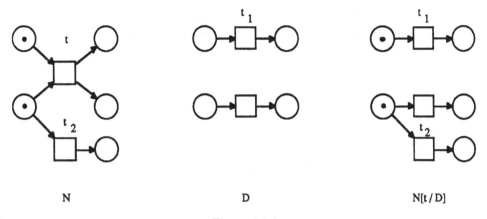

N   D   N[t / D]

Figure 3.3.2

they are also slightly restricted, since they can only be used to refine a transition with a given number of input and a given number of output places.

We have the following decidability result (whose proof is by reduction to the liveness problem).

Theorem 3.3.5 ([Vog87])
It is decidable, whether a given daughter-net is a module.

3.4 A technique for the refinement of places

Another desirable operation on nets besides refinement is the composition of nets. Both operations should be combined in order to support the modular and hierarchical net design. There are two main techniques used in the literature: composition by merging of places or by merging of transitions. The first corresponds to asynchronous communication between the two nets, the second means synchronization of actions of the nets.

So far refinement was defined as a separate operator on nets. Now we consider refinement only as a special case of net composition. Then both operations can be treated by the same formalism and results gained for net composition can be transfered. Since this is not a paper about net composition, we will just very informally survey one paper that studies specifically the connection between net composition and refinement, namely [Vog90b].

In this chapter nets are supposed to be labelled with actions from a set Σ or with the empty string λ. Nets are possibly infinite.

An operator $\|_A$ for the parallel composition with synchronization is defined e.g. in [Vog90b]: two nets N_1 and N_2 are composed to a net $N_1 \|_A N_2$ by merging equally labelled transitions with labels in a synchronization set $A \subseteq \Sigma$. For this all a-labelled transitions are split up (if $a \in A$) such that each a-labelled transition from one net can be combined with every a-labelled transition from the other net. This operator corresponds to the parallel composition with synchronization of TCSP; it means that the nets are put in parallel such that actions from A are synchronized.

For the modular construction of nets we consider two nets N_1 and N_2 as equivalent, if exchanging them in any context preserves the behaviour. A simple notion of behaviour is the existence or non-existence of deadlocks: a net N can *deadlock* if there is $M \in [M_N\rangle$ such that $\forall a \in \Sigma : \neg M[a\rangle$ (i.e. no action is image enabled under M). But there may be λ-transitions enabled under M. Now nets N_1, N_2 are *deadlock-equivalent* if for all nets N and $A \subseteq \Sigma : N \parallel_A N_1$ cannot deadlock if and only if $N \parallel_A N_2$ cannot deadlock.

Deadlock-equivalence is an external equivalence (see [Bau88]), since the nets must be tested in all environments N. But deadlock-equivalence can be characterized by an internal equivalence that involves only the nets N_1, N_2 and no other nets.

Theorem 3.4.1 ([Vog89], [Vog90b])
Let N_1, N_2 be nets such that $\Sigma - (l_{N_1}(T_{N_1}) \cup l_{N_2}(T_{N_2})) \neq \emptyset$. Then N_1 is deadlock-equivalent to N_2 if and only if N_1 is $\mathcal{F}$-equivalent to N_2.

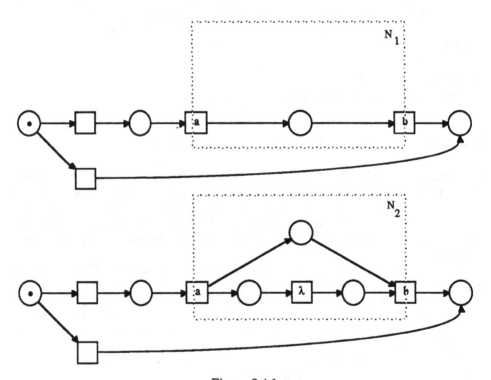

Figure 3.4.1

Now we transfer the definitions and results from net composition to refinement. In order to describe the refinement of places via parallel composition we fix an atomic net N_p, i.e. a net with only one place p, with transition set T_p and the identity as labelling. We call a net N an N_p-*host*, if it contains N_p as an induced subnet - except for the transition lablelling, which might be different in N. Now we can consider an N_p-host N as being constructed from some net N_1 and N_p by parallel composition $\|_{T_p}$ and a relabelling of the transitions adjacent to p; combining the net N_1 and some net D in the same way, we obtain the refined net $N[p/D]$.

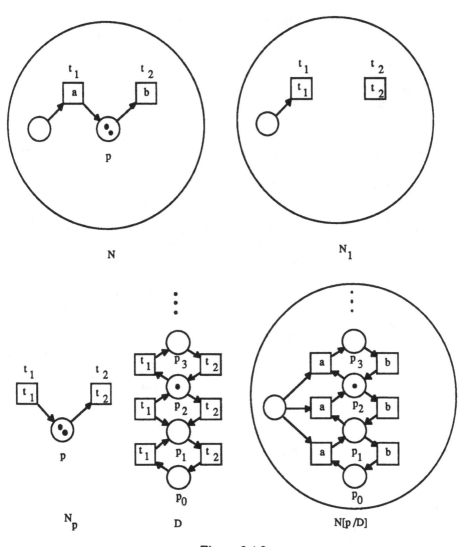

Figure 3.4.2

Such a place refinement may look like in Figure 3.4.1. Since the parallel composition operator possibly involves the splitting of transitions, a place refinement can also look like it is shown in Figure 3.4.2; here the net D is infinite, and the place p is replaced by an infinite sequence $p_0, p_1, p_2, \ldots$ such that one token on p_i corresponds to i tokens on p.

A net D is called N_p-*deadlock-module* if for all N_p-hosts N: N cannot deadlock $\Leftrightarrow N[p/D]$ cannot deadlock. In contrast to the definition of deadlock-equivalence we use as test nets only those nets N that contain the place p and a special surrounding of p.

N_p-deadlock-modules are defined in the same style as modules in [Vog87]. The desired property, behaviour preservation, is demanded for every host net N.

Theorem 3.4.2 ([Vog90b])

A net D is an N_p-deadlock-module if and only if N_p and D are $\mathcal{F}$-equivalent. Moreover we have in this case that $\mathcal{F}(N) = \mathcal{F}(N[p/D])$ and that N and $N[p/D]$ are even bisimilar.

The last part of this theorem is due to the fact that an N_p-deadlock-module is in some sense deterministic, and studying these deterministic nets is the specific adaption of the general approach of net composition to the special case of place refinement. Thus for place refinement we have only required a very simple sort of behaviour preservation, but automatically gained behaviour preservation in a very strong sense. Since D must be deterministic, it is possible to decide, whether for a given finite D the nets N_p and D are $\mathcal{F}$-equivalent. Hence with Theorem 3.4.2 it is decidable, whether D is an N_p-deadlock-module. In contrast to this result it is in general undecidable, whether two nets are $\mathcal{F}$-equivalent, even if the nets are finite.

Let us remark that in [Vog90b] for the refinement of transitions the dual approach is taken. For this a composition operator for nets by merging of places is defined. Then we have the same technique that was used in [Vog87] but now in the framework of modular construction of nets. Therefore failures semantics is used, and the conditions for modules are formulated in terms of this semantics. Next it is studied in which sense modules for transition refinement may be considered as deterministic.

For both approaches also a variation is considered that takes divergence into account, and similar results for both net composition techniques are obtained.

4. Congruences with respect to action refinement

4.1 Motivation

The topic of this part is action refinement: In this section all transitions are labelled by actions, and when we refine a net we replace every transition with some given label by a copy of the same refinement net. E.g. we want to be able to replace every action *exchange_x_y* by a sequence *move_x_to_h*; *move_y_to_x*; *move_h_to_y*. Furthermore, our interest is semantic equivalence of nets, and we require that equivalent nets must have at least the same language.

In this situation we cannot expect that action refinement is e.g. language preserving: If we replace *exchange_x_y* by the sequence *move_x_to_h*; *move_y_to_x*; *move_h_to_y*, then the refined net can perform totally different actions than the unrefined net. Hence these two nets cannot possibly have the same language. Thus we have quite a different starting point compared with the last section where the refined and the unrefined net were expected to be equivalent, i.e. to have the same relevant properties or to have the same behaviour in some other sense.

Instead we are interested in the preservation of semantic equivalence: Refining equivalent nets in the same way should give equivalent refined nets. In other words, we look for semantic equivalences that are congruences with respect to refinement.

Recently research into this field has attracted much interest. Some first attempts to add a refinement operator to process algebras like CCS can be found in [Hen87], [AH88], [NEL89], [Ace90]; refinements of event structures in the sense of [NPW81] and transition systems (which can both be seen as special Petri nets) are studied in [GG89], [GW89], [Gla90], [GG90], [Vog90c]; a split operator for Petri nets that splits every action into a sequence of two actions was introduced in [GV87], while general action refinements for Petri nets are studied in [Dev88], [BDKP89], [GG90], [Vog90a].

What makes the issue of action refinement so interesting (especially to the Petri net community) is its connection to partial order semantics. In [Pra86] and [CDP87] it is suggested that partial order semantics is useful when considering action refinement, see also [Lam86]. In [CDP87] the following example is discussed:

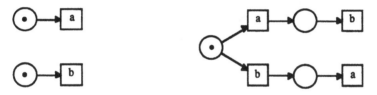

Figure 4.1.1

The nets of Figure 4.1.1 are interleaving bisimilar, but if we refine a to a sequence $a_1 a_2$ the first net can perform $a_1 b a_2$ while the second cannot, i.e. the refined nets do not even have the same language.

Hence the two nets should be distinguished, which can be done by using some partial order semantics. It is argued in [CDP87] that partial order semantics gives a congruence for refinement, indeed. We will present precise results below.

4.2 Refinement technique and refinement nets

Before we can look for a congruence w.r.t. refinement we have to decide what refinement technique and what refinement nets we want to use.

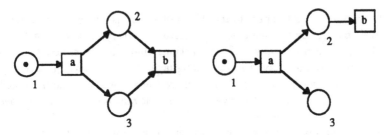

Figure 4.2.1

In the two papers [BDKP89], [Vog90a], which we will mainly refer to, distributed input or output are forbidden. This can be explained by the following examples, see [Vog90a].

Figure 4.2.1 shows two nets which are sequential and conflict-free. Since they have the same language they also have the same event structures of processes and are (interleaving) bisimilar, too, and they certainly should be semantically equivalent. Figure 4.2.2 shows a net that in view of the results in Section 3.3 one might consider as a suitable refinement net with distributed output.

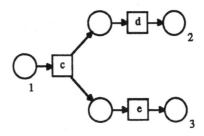

Figure 4.2.2

Refining the a-labelled transitions with this net transforms the nets of Figure 4.2.1 to the nets in Figure 4.2.3. The second of these refined nets can perform *cdbe* while the first one cannot, hence there cannot be an acceptable semantic equivalence that is a congruence w.r.t. this sort of refinement.

One might feel that in the context of this section we should use refinements that preserve behaviour w.r.t. the markings, e.g. in the sense of Definition 3.3.2. Then we can also use the results of the previous section regarding behaviour preservation. This would especially forbid distributed input. But we can also give an argument against distributed input that is valid in our context alone. In fact, it is symmetrical to the above example.

The nets of Figure 4.2.4 should certainly be semantically equivalent. But if we refine the b-labelled transitions with the net shown in Figure 4.2.5 we get the nets of Figure 4.2.6; the second can perform *cad*, while the first cannot.

As a consequence of these observations we use the basic refinement technique of Section 3.1 in order to define action refinement:

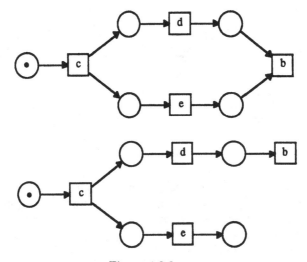

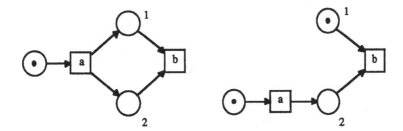

Figure 4.2.3

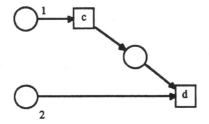

Figure 4.2.4

Figure 4.2.5

Definition 4.2.1

An *action refinement* r is a pair (a, D) where $a \in \Sigma$ and D is a refinement net as in Section 3.1. For a net N the refined net $r(N)$ is obtained by replacing every a-labelled transition by a copy of D as explained in Definition 3.1.1.

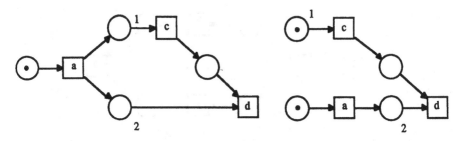

Figure 4.2.6

In [GG90] a different technique for action refinement is presented, which allows initial and final concurrency while avoiding distributed input or output. We will explain this technique by way of the above example. If we refine the second net of Figure 4.2.1 by (a, D) with D as in Figure 4.2.2, then the postset of the a-labelled transition is replaced by the cartesian product of this postset and the set $\{2, 3\}$ of output places of D, and analogously for the preset. The transitions of N and D are connected to these new places in the natural way as shown in Figure 4.2.7.

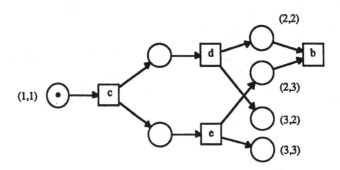

Figure 4.2.7

We see that this net cannot perform the undesirable sequence $cdbe$; here we do not have a distributed output in the sense that part of the output can be used by the environment while some other part has not been produced, yet. But this technique allows final (and initial) concurrency since the refinement net D finishes its simulation by firing concurrently d and e.

This technique seems to be very promising, but not much has been proven so far – except a result of [GG90] that compares the refinements of a special class of acyclic safe nets with the refinements of event structures in the sense of [NPW81].

There is another property that is – rather surprisingly – necessary for an action refinement net. In the approach of [Val79] refinement nets do not have a memory, compare Section 3.1. This restriction is not necessary for the results of [Val79], but it turns out to be necessary in the context of action refinement. The nets shown in Figure 4.2.8 should be semantically equivalent by the same reasoning as above. Figure 4.2.9 shows a refinement net D describing the alternation of actions a_1 and a_2, i.e. D 'remembers' the parity of the number of simulations it has performed. Refining a by D yields the nets of Figure 4.2.10, where the first can only perform $a_1 b a_2$ while the second can only perform $a_1 b a_1$. Again we conclude that we cannot allow such a refinement net.

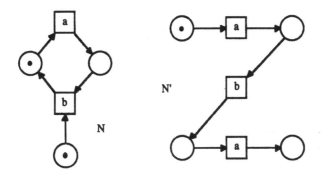

Figure 4.2.8

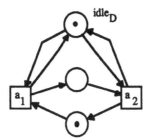

Figure 4.2.9

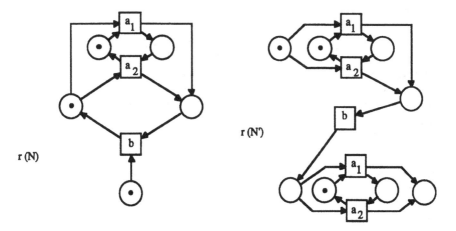

Figure 4.2.10

Also we cannot allow that a non-initial transition is initially enabled. Consider the refinement net of Figure 4.2.11. If we refine the nets of Figure 4.2.8 with this refinement net, then the first can only perform one d while the second can perform d twice.

Figure 4.2.11

Consequently, the refinement nets in this section will have a considerable similarity with the well-formed blocks of [Val79].

4.3 Interval word semantics

In this section we will mainly report the results of [Vog90a], and the nets in this subsection may also be infinite. We will present two linear time and a failures semantics for safe nets which induce congruences w.r.t. action refinement. Especially, partial order semantics is shown to be useful and, to a certain degree, even necessary for this purpose.

Definition 4.3.1

A *V-refinement net* D is a safe refinement net with the following properties:
  i) $M_D(idle_D) = 1$
 ii) For all reachable markings M of D there is some $M' \in [M\rangle$ with $M'(idle_D) = 1$
iii) For all reachable markings M of D $M(idle_D) = 1$ implies $M = M_D$.
 iv) Only initial transitions of D are enabled under M_D, and some initial transition is enabled under M_D.
  v) No final transition is λ-labelled.

Comparison with [GG90] suggests that condition ii) and the second part of iv) might be unnecessary to obtain the results below. Condition v) is a rather technical condition necessary for the result on failures semantics.

The first result of [Vog90a] shows that linear time partial order semantics induces a congruence w.r.t. action refinement. A similar result for event structures can be found in [GG89].

Theorem 4.3.2

For safe nets process equivalence is a congruence w.r.t. action refinement with V-refinement nets.

The main aim of [Vog90a] is to determine the coarsest congruence w.r.t. refinement contained in failures equivalence. Crucial for this purpose is the notion interval order.

Definition 4.3.3

A partial order $(A, <)$ is an *interval order* if there are closed intervals $I(x) \subseteq \mathbb{R}$, $x \in A$, such that $x < y$ if and only if for all $z \in I(x)$, $z' \in I(y)$ we have $z < z'$.

An *interval partial word* (*ipw*) $p = (A, <, l)$ of a safe net N is a partial word of N such that $(A, <)$ is an interval order. An *interval partial word with termination set* (*ipwt*) $p = (A, <, l, ter)$ consists of an *ipw* $(A, <, l)$ and a set $ter \subseteq A$ containing at least all non-maximal elements of A.

The marking reached after an *ipwt* p is

$$M_N + \sum_{x \in ter} W_N(l(x), .) - \sum_{x \in A} W_N(., l(x)).$$

The *image* of p is $(A', <', l', ter')$, where $A' = \{x \in A \mid l_N \circ l(x) \neq \lambda\}$, $ter' = ter \cap A'$, and $<'$ and l' are the restrictions of $<$ and $l_N \circ l$ to A'.

The idea of an *ipwt* is the following: The elements of A are occurrences of transitions of N. In an interval observation of a system run we observe in which order such occurrences begin and end. Thus each occurrence corresponds to a time interval. If two such intervals overlap, then we can directly observe that the corresponding transition occurrences are concurrent. If one interval is as a whole earlier than the other, then the corresponding transition occurrence preceeds the other. This way the partial order of an *ipwt* can be observed. Figure 4.3.1 shows two examples of intervals and the corresponding interval orders (more precisely the images of some *ipwt*'s are shown).

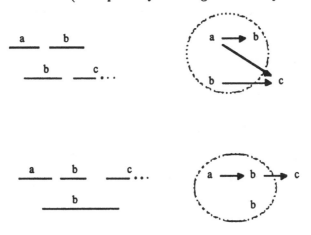

Figure 4.3.1

We can add a termination set to an interval partial word to indicate that the corresponding transition occurrences have already terminated. Such a set is indicated in Figure 4.3.1 by a dotted line; thus the two observations have stopped in the middle of the time interval belonging to c. Naturally, if $x \in A$ is not maximal, then something has begun after the occurrence of $l(x)$, hence x must belong to the termination set.

In an interval observation we observe the beginning and ending of transition occurrences. One might wonder whether we can describe such an observation in the following way without using partial order semantics: We split every action into a sequence of two and take a usual sequential observation of the resulting system, i.e. an element of its language. (This approach is taken in [Hen87] and [AH88]). But both the above interval observations correspond to the sequence $a_1 b_1 a_2 b_1 b_2 c_1 b_2$ in the splitted system. Hence with an interval observation we observe not only that action b occurs concurrently to itself, we also observe which of these occurrences ends first.

Interval orders can be characterized by the forbidden substructure depicted in Figure 4.3.2 as shown by the following result of [Fis70]:

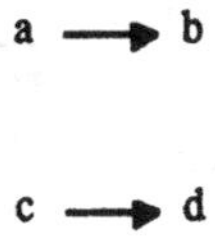

$$a \longrightarrow b$$

$$c \longrightarrow d$$

Fig. 4.3.2

Theorem 4.3.4

A partial order $(A, <)$ (on a finite or countably infinite set A) is an interval order if and only if for all $a, b, c, d \in A$ we have: $a < b$ and $c < d$ implies $a \leq d$ or $c \leq b$.

We can define a linear time semantical equivalence based on interval partial words and a sort of failures semantics based on interval partial words with termination set.

Definition 4.3.5

Safe nets are *interval word equivalent* if they have the same set of images of interval partial words.

For a safe net N we define

$$ref\,\mathcal{F}(N) = \{(p, X) \mid p \text{ is the image of an } ipwt\ q \text{ of } N,$$
$$\text{and for the marking } M \text{ reached after } q \text{ and every } a \in X : \neg M[a\rangle)\}.$$

Two safe nets N_1, N_2 are *ref $\mathcal{F}$-equivalent* if $ref\,\mathcal{F}(N_1) = ref\,\mathcal{F}(N_2)$.

In [Vog90a] the following results are shown:

Theorem 4.3.6

For safe nets interval word equivalence is a congruence w.r.t. action refinement with V-refinement nets.

Theorem 4.3.7

For safe nets *ref $\mathcal{F}$-equivalence* is the coarsest congruence w.r.t. action refinement with V-refinement nets contained in failures equivalence.

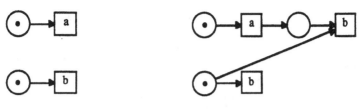

Fig. 4.3.3

In fact, the proofs and results of [Vog90a] also show that interval word equivalence is the coarsest congruence w.r.t. action refinement contained in language equivalence. Hence here we have results that show that some partial order semantics is not only useful for action refinement, but in fact the power of partial order semantics is necessary, too.

Let us consider some examples to see that interval word semantics is less discriminating than process semantics. Figure 4.3.3 shows two nets which are interval word equivalent, but not process equivalent: Only the second net can perform a and then some b that is necessarily after a, but this cannot be observed by an interval observation.

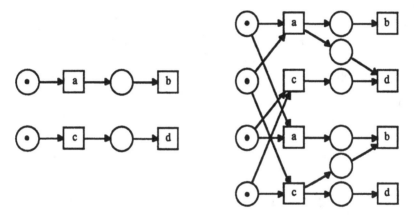

Fig. 4.3.4

Also Figure 4.3.4 shows two nets which are interval word, but not process equivalent. The image partial word of Figure 4.3.2 is the event structure of a process of the first, but not of the second net. Such an image partial word cannot be observed by an interval observation, compare Figure 4.3.1 and Figure 4.3.2.

An equivalence which is based on a duration of transition occurrences can already be found in [GV87]; we will give the definition of this ST-bisimilarity in the next subsection. In the meantime, it has been shown in [Gla90] for event structures without silent moves that ST-bisimilarity is a congruence for action refinement. In the same paper also ST-traces are introduced, and it is shown that we can base a congruence on these, too. It should be remarked that ST-traces are a (more or less) sequential representation of $ipwt$'s. Interval orders are also studied in the context of action refinement for a process algebra in [NEL89].

Two final remarks: The proof of the congruence result of Theorem 4.3.7 does not depend too much on the specific properties of interval orders; therefore it seems likely that also some failures semantics based on the event structures of processes can be shown to induce a congruence w.r.t. action refinement. Note that such a failures semantics will have to distinguish again between transitions that have terminated and those that have not. E.g. in [PS90b] a failures semantics TCF based on the event structures of processes, but without such a distinction, is defined; Figure 3.3.5 of this paper shows an example of two nets that are TCF-equivalent, but are not TCF-equivalent after refinement.

Furthermore, it is announced in [Vog90a] that a variation of Theorem 4.3.7 for a failures semantics with divergence can be shown. This has been worked out, but here the proof depends crucially on the properties of interval orders.

4.4 History preserving bisimulation

We have seen in the last subsection that partial order semantics can be very useful when looking for a congruence w.r.t. action refinement. Thus when looking for a bisimulation type congruence it is natural to consider a combination of partial order semantics and bisimulation. The most straightforward combination is pomset bisimulation [BC87], where one changes Definition 2.8 by considering $M[ev(\pi))\rangle M'$, π a process, instead of $M[a)\rangle M'$. Somewhat surprisingly, pomset bisimilarity is not a congruence, see [Dev88], [GG89]: The two nets of Figure 4.4.1 (see [Dev88]) are pomset bisimilar, but if we refine a to $a_1 a_2$ then only the first net can perform a_1 in such a way that no b is possible afterwards.

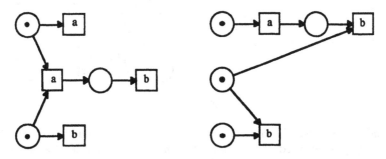

Fig. 4.4.1

Therefore a more intricate combination of partial order semantics and bisimulation seems to be necessary. Such a combination has been developed in [RT88] under the name of BS-bisimulation, and has also been studied in [DDM89] for a semantics for CCS; in [GG89] it is given the name history preserving bisimulation – a name we will stick to – and shown to induce a congruence w.r.t. action refinement for event structures without silent moves. If we translate this notion to Petri nets we get the fully concurrent bisimulation of [BDKP89], and we will report now the results of this paper. (All nets in [BDKP89] are finite and T-restricted.)

In pomset bisimulation, system states are described by markings as usual., In order to transform one state to another, a partial order of actions is performed, which is generated from a process. For the bisimulation it is required that such a state transformation in one system is matched by a transformation in the other system involving an isomorphic partial order of actions.

In history preserving bisimulation, a system state is described by the process that leads to this state. When a bisimulation relates two states the processes that lead to these states must have isomorphic event structures. Naturally, a state transformation is an extension of one process π to another π'. For the bisimulation we do not only require that the part we have added to π can be matched in the second system: We require that the isomorphism from the event structure of π can be extended to the event structure of π'; without this requirement the results would fail as shown in [BDKP89].

Definition 4.4.1

Nets N_1 and N_2 are *history preserving bisimilar*, denoted $N_1 \approx_h N_2$, if there exists a *history preserving bisimulation*, i.e. a set

$$\mathcal{B} \subseteq \{(\pi_1, \pi_2, f) \mid \pi_1 \text{ is a process of } N_1, \pi_2 \text{ a process of } N_2,$$
$$f : ev(\pi_1) \to ev(\pi_2) \text{ is an isomorphism}\}$$

such that:
  i) $(\pi_0(N_1), \pi_0(N_2), \emptyset) \in \mathcal{B}$ (i.e. the initial processes are related.)
  ii) For all $(\pi_1, \pi_2, f) \in \mathcal{B}$:
    a) If the process π_1' of N_1 is an extension of π_1, then there exists an extension π_2' of π_2 and an extension f' of f such that $(\pi_1', \pi_2', f') \in \mathcal{B}$
    b) vice versa

As observed in [BDKP89] it is — in this definition — sufficient to consider the case that π_1' has one event more than π_1. In [BDKP89] two sorts of refinement nets are studied:

Definition 4.4.2

A refinement net D is a *simple refinement net* if
  i) $M_D(idle_D) = 1$ and for all $s \in S_D - \{idle_D\} : M_D(s) = 0$
  ii) For all reachable markings M of D $M(idle_D) > 0$ implies $M = M_D$.
  iii) No transition of T_D is dead.

If we compare this definition with Definition 4.3.1 we note that i) is a rather severe restriction. It seems that this severeness is not necessary for the results below, but motivated by the proof technique. Condition iii) looks like a counterpart to 4.3.1 ii), thus it is also probably not necessary.

As we will see below, an even simpler sort of refinement net is needed, which is based on state machine nets. Such a refinement net introduces no concurrency.

Definition 4.4.3

A simple refinement net D is an *SM-refinement net*, if for all $t \in T_D$ we have $|^\bullet t| = 1 = |t^\bullet|$ and $W_D(^\bullet t, t) = 1 = W_D(t, t^\bullet)$.

The first congruence result of [BDKP89] applies to nets where the refined transitions are not self-concurrent and where there are no internal (λ-labelled) transitions immediately after them.

Theorem 4.4.4

Let $r = (a, D)$ be an action refinement with a simple refinement net D. Let N_1, N_2 be two nets such that for every a-labelled transition t of N_1 or N_2 we have
 - t is not self-concurrent
 - $t' \in t^{\bullet\bullet}$ implies that t' is not λ-labelled.
Then $N_1 \approx_h N_2$ implies $r(N_1) \approx_h r(N_2)$.

Let us exhibit two examples that show the necessity of the two restrictions on the nets N_1 and N_2. The two nets of Figure 4.4.2 are obviously history preserving bisimilar, but the second net has a self-concurrent a-transition.

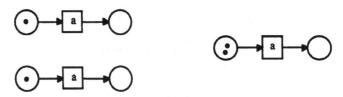

Fig. 4.4.2

If we refine the a-actions by the net of Figure 4.4.3 the results are not even process equivalent: Figure 4.4.3 also shows the event structure of a process that only the second refined net can exhibit.

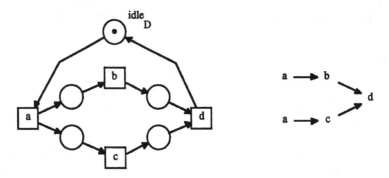

Fig. 4.4.3

The second example is taken from [BDKP89] and is also given in [GW89]: The nets of Figure 4.4.4 are history preserving bisimilar, where the additional a-transition of the second net is matched by the a- and the λ-transition of the first net together.

If we refine all a-actions by the sequence cd, then the second net can perform c such that no b is possible, while the first cannot.

As a consequence of the first example one might restrict attention to safe nets, as it is done in [Vog90a] and also advocated in [GG90]. One can also restrict the refinement nets: The following is again a result of [BDKP89].

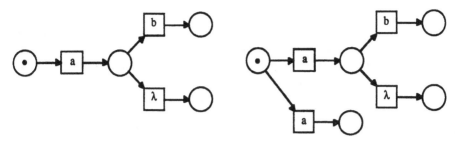

Fig. 4.4.4

Theorem 4.4.5

Let $r = (a, D)$ be an action refinement with an SM-refinement net D. Let N_1, N_2 be two nets such that for every a-labelled transition t of N_1 or N_2 we have

$- t' \in t^{\bullet\bullet}$ implies that t' is not λ-labelled.

Then $N_1 \approx_h N_2$ implies $r(N_1) \approx_h r(N_2)$.

The second example above indicates that history preserving bisimulation might not be the right notion for the refinement of nets with silent moves, see below. One might also wonder whether history preserving bisimulation is necessary to obtain a congruence w.r.t. action refinement which respects bisimilarity. This is probably not the case:

The following type of bisimulation is defined in [GV87]. As already mentioned in the last subsection, this interleaving ST-bisimulation is based on the idea that the occurrence of a transition has a duration. Consequently, we will deal with the begin and the end of such an occurrence, and the states of the net also involve information on the transitions that have started but not finished yet. The bisimulation has to match these still active transitions, and it is important that this matching is kept fixed:

Definition 4.4.6

Safe nets N_1, N_2 without silent moves are *interleaving ST-bisimilar* if there exists an *interleaving ST-bisimulation*, i.e. a set

$$\mathcal{B} \subseteq \{((M_1, A_1), (M_2, A_2), f) \mid M_1 \subseteq S_{N_1}, A_1 \subseteq T_{N_1}, M_2 \subseteq S_{N_2}, A_2 \subseteq S_{N_2},$$
$$f : A_1 \to A_2 \text{ is a label-preserving bijection}\}$$

such that

i) $((M_{N_1}, \emptyset), (M_{N_2}, \emptyset), \emptyset) \in \mathcal{B}$

ii) $((M_1, A_1), (M_2, A_2), f) \in \mathcal{B}$ and $M_1[t_1\rangle$ implies that there is some $t_2 \in T_{N_2}$ and some f' such that
   - $M_2[t_2\rangle$ and $l_{N_1}(t_1) = l_{N_2}(t_2)$
   - $f'(t_1) = t_2$ and $f'(t) = f(t)$ for all $t \in A_1$
   - $((M_1 - {}^\bullet t_1, A_1 \cup \{t_1\}), (M_2 - {}^\bullet t_2, A_2 \cup \{t_2\}), f') \in \mathcal{B}$

iii) vice versa

iv) $((M_1, A_1), (M_2, A_2), f) \in \mathcal{B}$ and $t_1 \in A_1$ implies $((M_1 \cup t_1^\bullet, A_1 - \{t_1\}), (M_2 \cup t_2^\bullet, A_2 - \{t_2\}), f|_{A_1 - \{t_1\}}) \in \mathcal{B}$, where $t_2 = f(t_1)$

v) vice versa

Very recently some interesting results regarding this equivalence have been obtained. In [Gla90] it is shown that interleaving ST-bisimilarity is a congruence w.r.t. action refinement for event structures without silent moves, which can easily be extended to include silent moves [Vog90c]. One can expect that this result can be generalized to nets (if we keep care of self-concurrency).

In [Vog90c] even more is shown: The general idea of ST-bisimulation can also be applied to pomset and history preserving bisimulation. Thus we have for event structures with silent moves that interleaving (or pomset or history preserving) ST-bisimilarity is the coarsest congruence w.r.t. action refinement which respects interleaving (or pomset or history preserving) bisimilarity. History preserving ST-bisimulation has independently been developed in [Dev90] under the name maximality preserving bisimulation. Similar results as Theorems 4.4.4 and 4.4.5 above have been obtained by [Dev90], only that a special treatment of silent moves is not necessary anymore.

We conclude by mentioning a problem about history preserving bisimulation: Since system states are given by processes, even a finite safe net may generate infinitely many states; therefore it is not obvious how one can decide whether finite safe nets are history preserving bisimilar. In [Vog90c] an alternative formulation for history preserving bisimulation of safe nets without silent moves is given: This so-called OM-bisimulation is based on ordered markings; an ordered marking is a set of tokens together with a pre-order which describes in which causal order the tokens are generated. OM-bisimilarity can be decided by exhaustive search.

Acknowledgement

We thank Lucia Pomello and the three anonymous referees for their valuable comments.

References

[Ace90]   L. Aceto: Full abstractions for series-parallel pomsets. Technical Report 1/90, Dept. Comp. Sci. Univ. of Sussex, Brigthon, 1990.

[AH88]   L. Aceto and M. Hennesy: Towards action-refinement in process algebras. Technical Report 3/88, Dept. Comp. Sci. Univ. of Sussex, Brigthon, 1988.

[Bau88]   B. Baumgarten: On internal and external characterizations of PT-net building block behaviour. In: G. Rozenberg, editor, Advances in Petri Nets 1988, Lect. Notes Comp. Sci. 340 (1988) 44–61.

[BC87]   G. Boudol and I. Castellani: On the semantics of concurrency: Partial orders and transition systems. In: H. Ehrig et al., editors, TAPSOFT 87, Vol. I, Lect. Notes Comp. Sci. 249 (1987) 123–137.

[BC90]   L. Bernardinello, F. de Cindio: A survey of basic net models and modular net classes. submitted to Advances in Petri Nets.

[BDKP89] E. Best, R. Devillers, A. Kiehn, and L. Pomello: Fully concurrent bisim-
          ulation. Technical Report LIT-202, Univ. Bruxelles, 1989; to appear in
          Acta Informatica.

[BHR84]   S.D. Brookes, C.A.R. Hoare, and A.W. Roscoe: A theory of communicating
          sequential processes. J. ACM 31 (1984) 560–599.

[BR84]   S.D. Brookes and A.W. Roscoe: An improved failures model for communi-
          cating processes. In: S.D. Brookes, A.W. Roscoe, and G. Winskel, editors,
          Seminar on Concurrency, Lect. Notes Comp. Sci. 197 (1984) 281–305.

[CDP87]   L. Castellano, G. De Michelis, and L. Pomello: Concurrency vs. interleav-
          ing: An instructive example. Bull. EATCS 31 (1987) 12–15.

[DDM89]   P. Degano, R. De Nicola, and U. Montanari: Partial orderings descrip-
          tions and observations of nondeterministic concurrent processes. In: J.W.
          de Bakker et al., editors, Proc. REX School / Workshop Linear Time,
          Branching Time and Partial Order in Logic and Models of Concurrency.
          Noordwijkerhout, 1988, Lect. Notes Comp. Sci. 354 (1989) 438–466

[Dev88]   R. Devillers: On the definition of a bisimulation notion based on partial
          words. Petri Net Newsletter 29 (1988) 16–19.

[Dev90]   R. Devillers: Maximality preserving bisimulation. Technical Report LIT-
          214, Univ. Bruxelles, 1990.

[Dij71]   E.W. Dijkstra: Hierarchical ordering of sequential processes. Acta Infor-
          matica 1 (1971) 115–138.

[DM88]   J. Desel and A. Merceron: P/T-systems as abstractions of C/E-systems.
          In: G. Rozenberg, editor, Advances in Petri Nets 1989, Lect. Notes Comp.
          Sci. 424 (1990) 105–127.

[DM89]   J. Desel and A. Merceron: Vicinity respecting morphisms. In: Proc. 10th
          Int. Conf. Applications and Theory of Petri Nets, Bonn, 1989, 115–138;
          to appear in Advances in Petri Nets 1990.

[DMM89]   P. Degano, J. Meseguer, and U. Montanari: Axiomatizing net computations
          and processes. In Proc. 4th Ann. Symp. Logic in Comp. Sci. LICS 89,
          Asilomar, USA, 1989, 175–185.

[Fis70]   P.C. Fishburn: Intransitive indifference with unequal indifference intervals.
          J. Math. Psych. 7 (1970) 144–149.

[GG89]   R.J. v. Glabbeek and U. Goltz: Equivalence notions for concurrent systems
           and refinement of actions. In: A. Kreczmar and G. Mirkowska, editors,
           MFCS 89, Lect. Notes Comp. Sci. 379 (1989) 237–248.

[GG90]   R.J. v. Glabbeek and U. Goltz: Refinement of actions in causality based
           models. Technical report, Arbeitspapiere der GMD 428, 1990.

[Gla90]   R.J. v. Glabbeek: The refinement theorem for ST-bisimulation semantics.
           In: M. Broy and C.B. Jones, editors, Proc. IFIP Working Conference
           on Programming Concepts and Methods, Sea of Galilee, Israel, 1990, to
           appear.

[Gra81]   J. Grabowski: On partial languages. Fundamenta Informaticae IV.2 (1981)
           428–498.

[GSW80]   H.J. Genrich and E. Stankiewicz-Wiechno: A dictionary of some basic
           notions of net theory. In: W. Brauer, editor, Net Theory and Applications,
           Lect. Notes Comp. Sci. 84 (1980) 519–531.

[GV87]   R.J. v. Glabbeek and F. Vaandrager: Petri net models for algebraic theories
           of concurrency. In: J.W. de Bakker et al., editors, PARLE Vol. II, Lect.
           Notes Comp. Sci. 259 (1987) 224-242.

[GW89]   R.J. v. Glabbeek and W.P. Weijland: Refinement in branching time se-
           mantics. Technical Report CS-R8922, CWI, Amsterdam, 1989.

[Hen87]   M. Hennessy: Axiomatising finite concurrent processes. Technical Report
           4/87, Dept. Comp. Sci. Univ. of Sussex, Brigthon, 1987.

[Kie89]   A. Kiehn: A Structuring Mechanism for Petri Nets. PhD thesis, Technical
           Report TUM-I8902, Inst. Informatik, Techn. Univ. München, 1989.

[Kie90]   A. Kiehn: Petri net systems and their closure properties. In: G. Rozenberg,
           editor, Advances in Petri Nets 1989, Lect. Notes Comp. Sci. 424 (1990)
           306-328.

[Lam86]   L. Lamport: On interprocess communication I. Distributed Comp. 1 (1986)
           77–85.

[Maz84]   A. Mazurkiewicz: Traces, histories, graphs: Instances of a process monoid.
           In: M.P. Chytil et al., editors, Proceeding of the 11th Symposium on Math-
           ematical Foundations of Computer Science (MFCS), Lect. Notes Comp.
           Sci. 176 (1984) 115–133.

[Mil83]   R. Milner: Calculi for synchrony and asynchrony. Theor. Comput. Sci. 25 (1983) 267–310.

[MM88]   J. Meseguer and U. Montanari: Petri nets are monoids: A new algebraic foundation for net theory. In: Proc. 3rd Ann. Symp. Logic in Comp. Sci. LICS 88, Edinburgh. IEEE Computer Soc. Press, Washington (1988) 155–164.

[Mül85]   K. Müller: Constructable Petri nets. Elektr. Inf. Kybern. 21 (1985) 171–199.

[NEL89]   M. Nielsen, U. Engberg, and K. Larsen: Partial order semantics for concurrency. In: J.W. de Bakker et al., editors, Proc. REX School / Workshop Linear Time, Branching Time and Partial Order in Logic and Models of Concurrency. Noordwijkerhout, 1988, Lect. Notes Comp. Sci. 354 (1989) 523-548.

[NPW81]   M. Nielsen, G.D. Plotkin, and G. Winskel: Petri nets, event structures and domains I. Theor. Comput. Sci. 13 (1981) 85–108.

[NRT90]   M. Nielsen, G. Rozenberg, and P.S. Thiagarajan: Elementary transition systems. Techn. Rep. 90-13, Univ. Leiden, 1990.

[Par81]   D. Park: Concurrency and automata on infinite sequences. In: P. Deussen, editor, Proc. 5th GI Conf. on Theoretical Comp. Sci., Lect. Notes Comp. Sci 104 (1981) 167–183.

[Pom86]   L. Pomello: Some equivalence notions for concurrent systems - an overview. In: G. Rozenberg, editor, Advances in Petri Nets 85, Lect. Notes Comp. Sci. 222 (1986) 381–400.

[Pra86]   V. Pratt: Modelling concurrency with partial orders. Int. J. Parallel Prog. 15 (1986) 33–71.

[PS89]   L. Pomello and C. Simone: A state transformation preorder over a class of EN-systems. In: Proc. 10th Int. Conf. Applications and Theory of Petri Nets, Bonn, 1989.

[PS90a]   L. Pomello and C. Simone: Preorders of concurrent systems. Internal report, DSI, Milano, 1990.

[PS90b]   L. Pomello and C. Simone: A survey of equivalence notions for net based systems. submitted to Advances in Petri Nets.

[RT88]   A. Rabinovich and B.A. Trakhtenbrot: Behaviour structures and nets. Fundamenta Informaticae 11 (1988) 357–404.

[SM83]   I. Suzuki and T. Murata: A method for stepwise refinement and abstraction of Petri nets. J. Comp. Sys. Sci. 27 (1983) 51–76.

[Val79]   R. Valette: Analysis of Petri nets by stepwise refinement. J. Comp. Sys. Sci. 18 (1979) 35–46.

[Vog87]   W. Vogler: Behaviour preserving refinements of Petri nets. In: G. Tinhofer and G. Schmidt, editors, Graph-Theoretic Concepts in Computer Science, Proc. WG 86, Bernried, Lect. Notes Comp. Sci. 246 (1987) 82–93.

[Vog89]   W. Vogler: Failures semantics and deadlocking of modular Petri nets. Acta Informatica 26 (1989) 333–348.

[Vog90a]   W. Vogler: Failures semantics based on interval semiwords is a congruence for refinement. In: C. Choffrut and T. Lengauer, editors, STACS 90, Lect. Notes Comp. Sci. 415 (1990) 285–297; to appear in Distributed Computing

[Vog90b]   W. Vogler: Failures semantics of Petri nets and the refinement of places and transitions. Technical Report TUM-I9003, Inst. Informatik, Techn. Univ. München, 1990.

[Vog90c]   W. Vogler: Bisimulation and action refinement. Technical Report SFB-Bericht Nr. 342/10/90A, Inst. Informatik, Techn. Univ. München, 1990.

[Win87]   G. Winskel: Petri nets, algebras, morphisms, and compositionality. Inform. and Computation 72 (1987) 197–238.

A Distributed Simulator for High Order Petri Nets

B.Bütler, R.Esser, R.Mattmann

Corporate Research and Development
Landis & Gyr Betriebs AG
CH-6300 Zug Switzerland

Abstract

This paper describes a distributed simulator of high order Petri nets for a parallel computer. It shows how the inherent parallelism of a Petri net can be used to obtain a fast simulator. The design decisions made in implementing a distributed simulator in hardware and software are discussed and a detailed description of both is given.

The simulator is a component of a suite of tools which allow the construction of specifications of embedded systems. A special form of Predicate/Transition net is used as a model of a specification. This allows the real time simulation of a sufficiently refined specification, which can then be used as a system prototype or implementation.

Keywords:
Embedded Systems, Executable Specification, Petri nets, Distributed Simulator, CSP, Interconnection Architecture, Transputer, Occam.

1. Introduction

High order Petri nets are used to specify the behaviour of embedded systems. The principles of using Petri nets as a design method are discussed in [Reisig 86] and [Winkler 86]. The software tool SPECS offers a graphics based editor with integrated sequential simulator [Dähler 87] and an object oriented net library facility for the reusing of nets [Oswald 90]. The animated simulator aids in the construction of a specification which correctly models the behaviour of a system. This animation facility allows easy detection of errors in specifications. [Pulli 88] shows that such a net simulator is also suitable for giving formal semantics to informal specification methods such as RTSA/SD [Ward 85], enabling them to be simulated with SPECS.

The testing of a specification of an embedded system in its real environment requires a simulator that is able to execute a net in real time. Sequential simulators are usually too slow, therefore a multiprocessor system has been built *(the Simulation Engine)* enabling Petri nets to be executed much faster using a distributed simulation algorithm. The *Simulation Engine*, allows via extensive IO capabilities, a simulation of a system to be embedded in its actual environment. This functioning prototype of the specified system can be used to conduct field tests.

Nets specifying an embedded system contain a high degree of parallelism which can be used to obtain an efficient system simulation. This characteristic is reflected in the choice of hardware and software used to implement the simulator.

2. The Specification of Embedded Systems with Nets

The specification of embedded systems can be divided into two phases. In the first phase the system is modeled together with a representation of its environment with a high order Petri net (i.e. Predicate/Transition net (PrT-net) [Genrich 87]) (Fig. 2a). During the simulation the token flow is animated graphically on the screen where the user can study the behaviour of the system with its environment. Interactive stepwise refinement of the net is then carried out to eliminate ambiguities.

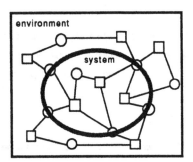
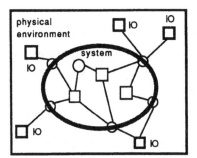

Fig. 2a Petri net of a system and
its environment

Fig. 2b Petri net system coupled with
its physical environment

In the second phase the part of the net which models the system is transformed and simulated on a special hardware *(Simulation Engine)*. It interacts through dedicated IO interfaces with its real physical environment which replaces the modelled one (Fig. 2.b). A prototype is thus generated whose behaviour matches the specified system in its own real time environment and snapshots of the system's states can be captured and displayed in SPECS as a token distribution. An error found in the system's real time behaviour can be corrected and tested by repeating phases one and two which therefore also updates the specification because the same net is used as a system specification and as a system implementation on the *Simulation Engine*.

The result of the second phase is a tested prototype, which can be used directly or whose specification can be used to implement the final product.

3. Design Considerations for the Real Time Simulator

Sequential simulators of high order Petri nets on a conventional von Neumann computer have proven to be inadequate for real time simulations. A system architecture which closely matches the semantics of Petri nets was found. This consists of a suitable net class, programming model and computer architecture.

The net class defines the expressiveness of a specification tool and must allow embedded systems to be modelled. The programming model defines how easily a net class can be implemented and should be chosen so that the characteristics of nets can be naturally expressed. The computer architecture forms the last element in the triad and must be able to support the programming model as closely as possible. A decision was made not to use a general purpose computer and attempt to fit the problem to it, but to define a computer architecture for the problem of simulating embedded systems with nets.

3.1 Net Class

An informal description of the currently defined *FunPrE-net* class (predicate/event net with functions) follows:
- A net consists of *S-elements*, *T-elements*, *arcs*, *tokens* and *inscriptions*.
- The T-elements can be inscribed with a side effect free *firing function* which consists of a *condition* and an *action*.
- The inscriptions on arcs either define formal identifiers for tokens flowing along them or specify a constant value a token must have to be able to traverse the arc.
- The tokens are either undefined black tokens or carry a list of attributes with them. An attribute has either an integer, real, boolean, symbolic type or an array of a type.
- The S-elements contain either zero or one token.
- The firing rule is influenced by a firing condition and a firing action in the following way: the firing condition computes a relationship based on the attributes of input tokens, while the firing action computes the attributes of output tokens. The formulation of firing conditions and firing actions is made with side effect free functions which contain attributes of the input tokens as arguments.

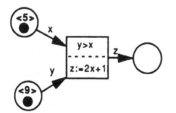

Fig 3.1 Predicate/event net with
activated T-element

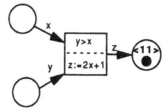

Fig 3.1b Net after firing

These nets can be regarded as predicate/event nets (PrE-nets) with the added capability of containing functional program fragments. In them T-elements can not be regarded as transformation schemes [Genrich 87] as the maximum capacity of S-elements is only one, thus T-elements can only be activated once by any distribution of tokens at any one time. This net class is sufficiently powerful in describing embedded systems. As FunPrE-nets are not far removed from PrT-nets the theoretical tools for PrT-nets can be used to analyse FunPrE-nets. These tools will be integrated into the system at a later date.

3.2 The Programming Model

The characteristics of Petri nets, especially the inherent parallelism which affect the choice of a programming model, are described below.

a) Parallelism:

T-elements that do not share either input or output S-elements fire independently of each other (concurrently).

b) Locality:

Whether a T-element can fire or not is only dependent on its immediate input and output S-elements.

c) Decentralised conflict adjudication:

Conflicts where more than one T-element requires the same input token or place for an output token can be solved without the aid of a global arbiter.

d) Nondeterminism:

Nondeterminism in the firing rules of Petri nets occurs in three places: (1) It is not determined when more than one fireable T-element will in fact fire. (2) In a conflict situation it is not determined which T-element will fire. (3) The choice of which combination of possible valid tokens that will be used when a T-element fires can not be previously determined.

A programming model which can express in a natural way these characteristics is required. Parallelism, dataflow, functional, object and process oriented approaches are supported by various programming models. Hoare's *Communicating Sequential Processes* (CSP) [Hoare 85] is an appropriate process based model for expressing the semantics of Petri nets.

In CSP a Petri net can be considered to be made up of active T-element processes and reactive S-element processes. When firing, the T-element processes transform tokens which are regarded as resources managed by S-element processes.

3.2.1 Communicating Sequential Processes

CSP is founded on a sound mathematical theory that can be expressed as a list of algebraic rules. The model defines *process, parallelism, nondeterminism* and *communication* and how they can be used in a specification. This specification can be used to develop, implement and verify embedded systems (Hoare: "Computer systems which continuously act and interact with their environment").

- *Processes* in CSP are a mathematical abstraction of the interaction between a system and its environment and run dependently or independently of each other.
- CSP allows systems to be naturally divided into subsystems which run in parallel with one another and with the system's environment.

- The introduction of nondeterminism is a method of abstraction where the exact knowledge of a system's behaviour can be ignored until a later date.

- Two processes can communicate with each other when one process sends a message at the exact moment the other process receives the message.

3.3 Computer Architecture

It is desirable to have a computer architecture that reflects the programming model as closely as possible. In multiprocessing architectures a choice must be made between common memory bus based systems or 'message passing interconnection architectures' having no common memory.

Petri nets and CSP are both networks without global states, therefore a computer architecture need not have global memory. This solution has the advantage that the speed at which a simulation can be carried out can increase linearly with the increase in processing and communication power if the network contains enough inherent parallelism.

Common memory systems contain an inherent bottle neck that prevents a linear speed up being achieved and a multiprocessor system without common memory is better suited to support the large number of simple processes needed to implement a simulator.

At the moment the only commercial integrated circuit (IC) which directly supports an interconnection architecture is the INMOS Transputer™ [INMOS 87]. This IC provides a powerful integer and floating point processor in addition to four very fast communication links that, via an asynchronous DMA driven protocol, provide communication with neighbouring processors. The Transputer was developed to support the efficient execution of programs written in the Occam™ language [May 87], which is a language that supports parallel programming using Hoare's CSP paradigm. An Occam program consists of processes that are composed of other processes. Occam processes communicate with one another through unidirectional unbuffered communication channels.

These channels also provide synchronisation between processes, as the sender and receiver process 'rendezvous' when communicating.

The addition of configuration statements allows an Occam program to be distributed on a network of interconnected Transputers. Processes are placed on processors and communication channels are mapped onto hardware links. A near linear speed up can be obtained for certain classes of problems.

To enable the efficient simulation of any Petri net it is advantageous to keep the interconnection of processors flexible. An ideal hardware configuration for any simulated net can then be obtained. Subnets, which run in parallel, can be placed on physically separated processors.

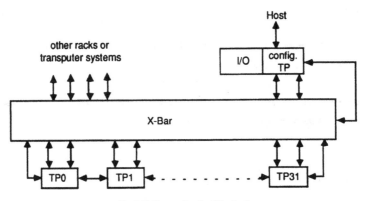

Fig 3.3 Computer Architecture

A fully configurable hardware network is only feasible for small numbers of processing elements as the complexity of the crossbar switch required to establish every link increases quadratically with the number of processing elements. By restricting the topology to always include a Hamiltonian path we simplify the hardware at the cost of being unable to directly mimic trees or other structures without Hamiltonian paths. This restriction does not affect the simulation of real nets. A Hamiltonian path connects all processors in a linear array which can be hard wired, and the additional two links are brought out to be switched via a programmable crossbar switch. Through the hard wired path the program code for each processor can be downloaded and at runtime be used for interprocessor communication. The remaining two links can be used to connect a processor to any two other processors. An additional Transputer oversees the programming of the crossbar switch and also serves as an IO processor enabling data to be input and output. A complete system consists of a rack containing 32 processors while larger systems can be configured by connecting racks and/or other specialised Transputer based systems (i.e. for graphics) together.

4. Simulator Algorithm

The aim of a distributed simulator is to fire independent T-elements in parallel. The simulator should run efficiently on any number of processors, thus care should be taken to prevent overheads in the simulation from increasing with the number of processors used.

One simulation strategy would divide a net up into subnets and simulate them sequentially on each processor however, in such a non-homogeneous simulator communication between subnets would be awkward to implement. Occam makes no distinction between processes running within a single processor and processes distributed among many processors, thus alleviating the need for such a non-homogeneous simulator.

As the Occam implementation on the Transputer is intended to handle large numbers of parallel processes efficiently [INMOS 87 pp. 6-7], we can map each S- and T-element onto an individual Occam process. A token is represented as a local variable of a S-element process which manages it as a resource. A T-element will attempt to fire and if successful causes tokens to be moved from one S-element to another. The decision whether a T-element can fire or not occurs without any global knowledge or global clock.

A conflict between two or more T-elements should be solved locally. A decentralised adjudication scheme aids in maintaining the maximum amount of parallelism in a simulation, preventing possible bottlenecks from occurring. T-elements reserve their S-elements using a reservation protocol enabling conflicts to be solved locally and at the same time preventing S- and T- processes from becoming deadlocked or livelocked.

The firing of a T-element is dependent on three conditions: All input tokens must be present, the attributes of these tokens must fullfil the firing condition and all output S-elements must be able to accept the output tokens. Inherent in the algorithm is the ability to abort a firing attempt if one of the three conditions is not fulfilled and a new attempt is then only made when conditions have changed sufficiently to allow the T-element a possible chance of firing. This guarantees that no processor time is wasted in fruitless polling.

4.1 Functional Description

The implementation of the distributed simulator for the FunPrE-net class is based upon the following constraints: tokens have multiple attributes, firing rules are extended with firing conditions and actions and S-elements have a maximum capacity of one. This functional description is taken from the viewpoint of a single T-element however, in the distributed simulator every T-element attempts to fire in parallel using the following steps:

1) A T-element attempts to reserve all of its input S-elements in a predefined order by sending a message to each one. A S-element will then be reserved if it has a token and is not already reserved and will send the T-element either a 'go' message, which includes the values of the current token, or a 'nogo' message. Whether a T-element was sent a 'go' or 'nogo' message is remembered by the S-element.

2) If all of the input S-elements have been successfully reserved, the T-element will then calculate its firing condition and if appropriate calculate the attributes of the generated output tokens. Then in an analogous fashion the T-element attempts to reserve all of its output S-elements.

3) If successful the T-element can fire by removing all of its input tokens and placing the generated output tokens on its output S-elements and also releasing the reservation by the T-element. If a T-element is unsuccessful during a reservation phase it will free all S-elements previously reserved. It will then wait until it receives a message from every S-element that could not be previously reserved. A free S-element will send such a message to all input T-elements when there is space for a token or to all output T-elements when a token becomes available.

4) A T-element which cannot fire due to its firing condition not being met will wait until at least one of its input S-elements has received a new token. This is accomplished by having each waiting T-element being remembered in a second list by the S-elements concerned. When a S-element receives a new token it will then inform all waiting T-elements in this list.

The reservation strategy used in step 1 (reserving S-elements in a fixed order) is a well-known strategy for preventing deadlocks in distributed systems, [Taubner 88] discusses this approach when used for simulating Petri nets. Analysis of nets has shown that a considerable number of S-elements are not involved in conflicts. As a result in non conflict situations simplified S-elements can be used. These S-elements do not need to be reserved and to be freed by their neighbouring T-elements. This substantially decreases the number of messages exchanged for a T-element to fire.

As the token capacity is limited, the output S-elements must also be reserved (step 2) to ascertain whether tokens can be placed upon them. Conflicts between T-elements competing to place tokens on common S-elements must also be solved.

If token attributes do not need to be tested to decide whether a S-element can accept them, then it would be possible to calculate these token attributes only after a successful reservation of all output S-elements has been made. This would be true if the maximum capacity of S-elements is one, as in FunPrE-net class, or if the number of tokens (up to the S-element capacity) carrying the same attributes is allowed. This would prevent unnecessary calculations of output token attributes.

4.2 Nondeterminism

A net contains nondeterminism when two or more T-elements are in conflict with each other. Which one fires cannot be determined in advance. The nondeterministic behaviour that such a net is modelling is expressed by the nondeterminism of CSP, the programming model. In Occam, which is an implementation of CSP, the alternative statement ALT is the construct used to express nondeterminism. It allows a process to wait for communication on more than one channel simultaneously.

In the distributed simulator a conflict is solved with the aid of such an ALT statement. The implementation of the ALT-statement by the current Occam compiler is deterministic, therefore conflicts in nets are solved deterministically. However it is straightforward to implement a fair, random or prioritised construct which would replace the ALT statement, thus changing the manner in which conflicts are solved.

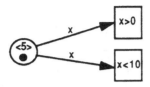

Fig 4.2 Conflict

5. Automated Generation of a Distributed Simulation Program

To distribute the constituent simulator processes efficiently on a number of processors a measure of the interprocess communication and process load needs to be made. The clustering of processes onto processors must aim to minimise cluster to cluster communication while providing a balanced load distribution.

Process load and communication rely not only on the net topology but also on the external environment of a net (inputs and outputs) and the complexity of the fire conditions and actions. Experience has shown that by assigning default process loads and by optimising communication between clusters, obtained by statically analysing the net, a reasonable initial distribution can be obtained. Work has also been carried out using a monitor program which enables exact statistics on process load and communication to be returned. These results can then be used in a further process distribution.

5.1 Distribution

The simulator performance depends on how well individual processes are distributed on processors. It is very important to balance the total computational load, memory requirements and communication bandwidth on every processor. This problem is known as the mapping problem and belongs to the class of NP-complete problems. It is the object of various works in which graph theory has been applied to implement heuristic and evolutionary solutions [Kropf 87] [Schütte 88].

Most nets can not be directly mapped onto a network of processors. This requires that processes be clustered together and placed on individual processors and the concentrating of software communication channels onto hardware communication links, with perhaps some channels being routed via other processors. To accomplish this additional processes must be added (multiplexer, demultiplexer and router processes) but as these processes also buffer messages the synchronisation between processes is lost and an asynchronous message passing paradigm must be used.

After some experience with an existing configuration tool [Kropf 87] which analyses an Occam program and generates a distribution for a specific hardware topology, a net specific configuration tool was designed that also generates a hardware topology for a configurable hardware. This approach, in addition to generating a software topology, generates an optimal hardware configuration for a particular net.

The configuration uses a simulated annealing algorithm to cluster processes. Simulated annealing attempts to model the physical annealing process found in metallurgy where a body is cooled at a specific rate to induce structural properties like hardness. In the configurer the energy function used to simulate annealing is dependent upon the cumulated process load differences and communication requirements between clusters and time. The configurer attempts to minimise this energy function ignoring hardware constraints however, when automatically placing the partitions on processors, multiplexers and routers may be inserted.

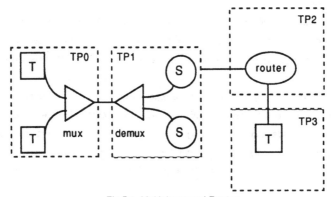

Fig 5.1 Multiplexer and Router

An Occam program containing all processes assigned to a cluster is then automatically generated for every processor. Every T-process has an associated fire function process with which it communicates during the reservation cycle, this fire function process is unique and can not be called from a library unlike S-, T-, multiplexer and router processes. All processes making up cluster are called, and therefore executed, in parallel.

Figure 5.2 shows the configuration file automatically generated by the SPECS tool. In the configuration file clusters (SC mainXX) are assigned to processors and communication channels to hardware links. Processor 32 is an I/O processor which provides physical interfaces between the simulated net and its environment. Processors 4 and 31 route messages to the I/O processor.

```
... SC main0
... SC main1
... SC main2
... SC main3
... SC main4
... SC main31
... SC graphic

[34] CHAN OF ANY c:

PLACED PAR

 PROCESSOR 0 T8
 ... link assignments
 main0(c[0] , c[1] , c[2] , c[3] , c[16] , c[17] , c[23] , c[22])

 PROCESSOR 1 T8
 ... link assignments
 main1(c[3] , c[2] , c[4] , c[5] , c[18] , c[19] , c[21] , c[20])

 PROCESSOR 2 T8
 ... link assignments
 main2(c[5] , c[4] , c[6] , c[7] , c[20] , c[21] , c[17] , c[16])

 PROCESSOR 3 T8
 ... link assignments
 main3(c[7] , c[6] , c[8] , c[9] , c[22] , c[23] , c[19] , c[18])

 PROCESSOR 4 T8
 ... link assignments
 main4(c[9] , c[8] , c[10] , c[11] , c[24] , c[25] , c[28] , c[29])

 PROCESSOR 31 T8
 ... link assignments
 main31(c[12] , c[13] , c[14] , c[15] , c[26] , c[27] , c[25] , c[24])

 PROCESSOR 32 T8
 ... link assignments
 graphic(c[15], c[14], c[30], c[31])
```

Fig 5.2 Configured Occam Program

Figure 5.3 shows the automatically generated program for one processor. The "#USE" statements include the element libraries which include all ordinary net elements. Fire functions are unique for every T-element and are generated by parsing connector and T-element inscriptions. CHAN declarations define channels which connect elements together. This interconnection of elements is defined by the net topology. All elements are called in parallel (PAR statement) in which individual elements communicate with their neighbours over communication channels. Keyboard.handler and time.handler are special T-elements which introduce I/O into the net. Multiplexers have been automatically inserted to concentrate software channels onto the available hardware links.

```
PROC main1 (CHAN OF ANY in0, out0, in1, out1,
                    in2, out2, in3, out3)
  ... VALs
  #USE "netprot.tsr"
  #USE "netel.tsr"
  ...  PROC fire.func3
  ...  PROC fire.func5
  ...  PROC fire.func6
  ...  PROC fire.func7
  ...  PROC fire.func11

  [39][2] CHAN OF ANY chan.pair:
  [7] CHAN OF fire.data.protocol from.fire:
  [7] CHAN OF fire.data.protocol to.fire:

  PAR
    keyboard.handler(0, 15,
     "keyboard",
     [97, 100, 104, 109, 115],    -- valid keys
     chan.pair [1], -- output
     chan.pair[28], -- daisy.in
     chan.pair[29]) -- daisy.out

    transition(3, 22,
     [chan.pair FROM 2 FOR 2], -- inputs
     [chan.pair FROM 4 FOR 1], -- outputs
     from.fire[1], to.fire[1],
     chan.pair[29], -- daisy.in
     chan.pair[30]) -- daisy.out
    fire.func3(from.fire[1], to.fire[1])

    transition(5, 24,
     [chan.pair FROM 5 FOR 2], -- inputs
     [chan.pair FROM 7 FOR 1], -- outputs
     from.fire[2], to.fire[2],
     chan.pair[30], -- daisy.in
     chan.pair[31]) -- daisy.out
    fire.func5(from.fire[2], to.fire[2])

    transition(6, 25,
     [chan.pair FROM 8 FOR 2], -- inputs
     [chan.pair FROM 10 FOR 1], -- outputs
     from.fire[3], to.fire[3],
     chan.pair[31], -- daisy.in
     chan.pair[32]) -- daisy.out
    fire.func6(from.fire[3], to.fire[3])

    transition(7, 26,
     [chan.pair FROM 11 FOR 2], -- inputs
     [chan.pair FROM 13 FOR 1], -- outputs
     from.fire[4], to.fire[4],
     chan.pair[32], -- daisy.in
     chan.pair[33]) -- daisy.out
    fire.func7(from.fire[4], to.fire[4])

    transition(11, 30,
     [chan.pair FROM 14 FOR 3], -- inputs
     [chan.pair FROM 17 FOR 3], -- outputs
```

```
     from.fire[5], to.fire[5],
     chan.pair[33], -- daisy.in
     chan.pair[34]) -- daisy.out
    fire.func11(from.fire[5], to.fire[5])

    time.handler(12, 31,
     "Stop Watch Timer",
     10,  -- delay in ms
     -2147483645,   -- token.symbol
     chan.pair [21], -- output
     chan.pair[34], -- daisy.in
     chan.pair[35]) -- daisy.out

    predicate(0, 0,
     chan.pair,
     [1], -- inputs
     [2,5,22,23,8,11], -- outputs
     35, -- daisy.in
     36, -- daisy.out
     "") -- initial tokens

    predicate(3, 3,
     chan.pair,
     [24,10,13,7], -- inputs
     [25,3,12,6], -- outputs
     36, -- daisy.in
     37, -- daisy.out
     "") -- initial tokens

    predicate(8, 8,
     chan.pair,
     [21], -- inputs
     [26,27,14], -- outputs
     37, -- daisy.in
     38, -- daisy.out
     "") -- initial tokens

    mdx4(in1,out1,
     chan.pair[18][1], chan.pair[18][0],
     chan.pair[15][1], chan.pair[15][0],
     chan.pair[26][0], chan.pair[26][1],
     chan.pair[19][1], chan.pair[19][0])
    mdx3(in3,out3,
     chan.pair[16][1], chan.pair[16][0],
     chan.pair[27][0], chan.pair[27][1],
     chan.pair[38][1], chan.pair[38][0])
    mdx6(in2,out2,
     chan.pair[25][0], chan.pair[25][1],
     chan.pair[24][0], chan.pair[24][1],
     chan.pair[22][0], chan.pair[22][1],
     chan.pair[23][0], chan.pair[23][1],
     chan.pair[4][1], chan.pair[4][0],
     chan.pair[9][1], chan.pair[9][0])
    mdx2(in0,out0,
     chan.pair[28][0], chan.pair[28][1],
     chan.pair[17][1], chan.pair[17][0])
                    :
```

Fig. 5.3 Generated Occam program for 1 processor

5.2 Remote Control

The problem of detecting the (abnormal) termination of processes is present in all distributed systems. It is also usually a requirement that the system be controlled and/or monitored from a central computer.

The workstation based SPECS tool with its graphics based user interface serves as the central control and monitoring system for the simulator in such a way that the whole environment appears homogeneous. Requirements are the ability to start, stop, step a simulation, the reading and writing of the token distribution and the ability to send various statistics back to the central computer.

All S- and T-element processes are connected in a daisy chain together with a process on the central computer allowing the control of every net element. Control messages in every element are handled in parallel with little disturbance to the main simulation process. This daisy chain is also used by special I/O T-elements to forward and receive messages with the I/O processor where the physical interfaces are situated.

6. Results

A simulator has been developed by careful weighing of all the design and implementation considerations. The reservation of an input S-element by a T-element requires a message and an acknowledgement message to be sent, with a complete firing cycle requiring between three and five communication steps to be carried out. In nets with hundreds or even thousands of elements the majority of S- and T-elements are inactive and consume no processor time.

As an example we have distributed the Railway net defined in [Genrich 87] for 64 sections, for various number of trains and processors.

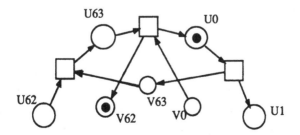

Fig 6.1 Part of the railway system with 64 sections

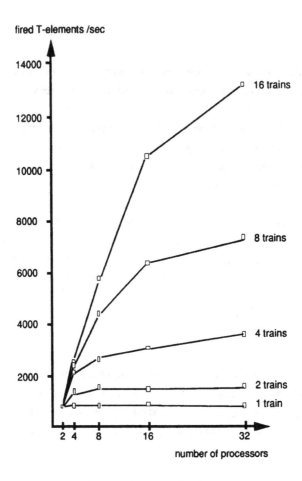

Fig. 6.2 Simulator performance for the railway system

The simulator firing rate is dependent on the number of trains (parallelism) and the number of processors used. If there is enough parallelism in the net (number of concurrent fireable T-elements) then the firing rate increases near linear with the number of processors used. If the number of processors used exceeds the parallelism in the net no remarkable slow down results through the distribution overhead.

7. Conclusion

FunPrE-nets have been shown to be suitable for specifying embedded systems. Predicate/Transition nets because of their compact description, would be better as a specification method, unfortunately this would bury parallelism that could be used to obtain an efficient simulator. Current work shows how nets which allow multiple tokens to occupy the same S-element can be efficiently simulated. When a certain token distribution multiply enables a T-element to fire then the firings can be carried out in parallel. This can be done by automatically transforming a PrT-net into a PrE-net or by dynamically creating T-element processes during a simulation.

At present the side effect free firing conditions and actions are written in a Pascal-like language. Side effects would, of course, introduce some degree of global knowledge and would affect how a net could be distributed on a processor array. It would be useful to consider a functional language (i.e. Lisp) for defining firing functions.

Should a net containing a conflict be simulated then any solution which solves the conflict is in principle correct. In practice however it may be desirable to solve conflicts fairly so that all paths in a net may eventually be tested. A distributed and fair conflict solving approach is described in [Chandy 84]. However it is open to question whether a user would be prepared to accept reduced simulator performance.

Using CSP as a foundation a real time distributed simulator has been written. A parallel computer which supports the CSP paradigm has also been built expressly to support the simulator. This foundation has proven useful in understanding the concepts of process, nondeterminism and distributed systems.

The simulator can execute high order Petri nets in real time and can be regarded as a prototype of the specified system. It is therefore possible to test specifications of embedded systems in their environment. Languages and methods of programming highly parallel computer systems are still in their infancy but it has been shown that Petri nets can be used in this area to good effect.

8. Related Work

A comparison and classification of strategies for distributed simulators is given in [Taubner 88]. He looks at three aspects of distributed simulations: the control distribution (how tokens are managed), reservation strategies and the solving of conflicts. The classification of the reservation strategy used for the FunPrE-net class can be described as follows: it is based on a control distribution centered on S-elements, reservation is made of a token and conflicts are solved by reserving S-elements in a fixed order. It is interesting that Taubner uses Occam to describe various simulation strategies.

Two papers have appeared describing parallel simulators [Hartung 88], [Heinrich 88]. Both recommend a parallel computer with common memory and have a concept of global states. It will be interesting to see which concept (common memory or message passing) proves in the future more attractive for high speed simulation of large nets. We are convinced that any sort of common memory system will be a bottleneck to system performance and that message passing is for Petri nets a more natural concept whose advantages lie in the ease at which the size of nets or size of parallel computer can be scaled up.

Acknowledgements

We would like to thank Dr. H. Genrich of the GMD Bonn for his interest and detailed comments of our work and the unknown referee of this paper for his helpful suggestions. Our introduction into the Transputer world was made less painful by the help of P. Kropf and J. Boillat from the University of Bern with whom configuration tools are being developed.

Bibliography

[Chandy 84]: K.M. Chandy, J. Misra
"*The Drinking Philosophers Problem*" ACM Transactions on Programming Languages and Systems, Vol. 6. No. 4. October 1984; pp. 632-646

[Dähler...87]: J. Dähler, P. Gerber, H.-P. Gisiger, A. Kündig
"*A Graphical Tool for the Design and Prototyping of Distribute Systems.*" ACM Software Engineering Notes. Vol. 12. No. 3. July 1987

[Genrich 88]: H. Genrich
"*Equivalence Transformations of PrT-nets.*" In: Proc. 9th European Workshop on Applications and Theory of Petri nets 1988; pp. 229-248

[Genrich 87] H. Genrich
"*Predicate/Transition Nets.*" In: Lecture Notes in Computer Science 254, Petri Nets: Central Models and Their Properties, Springer Verlag 1987; Eds.: W. Brauer, W. Reisig and R. Rozenberg; pp. 207-247

[Hoare 85]: C.A.R. Hoare
"*Communicating Sequential Processes.*" Prentice-Hall International Series in Computer Science 1985

[Hartung 88]: G. Hartung
"*Programming a closely coupled multiprocessor system with high level Petri nets.*" In: Proc. 8th Petri Net Workshop, Zaragoza Spain, 489-508 (1987)

[Heinrich...88]: A. Heinrich, W. Ameling
"*Multiprocessor System Architecture for the Execution of Higher Petri Nets.*"In: Proc. 9th European Workshop on Application and Theory of Petri Nets.

[Kropf 87]: P. Kropf
"*An Analysis and Reconfiguration Tool for Mapping Parallel Programs onto Transputer Networks*" Interner Bericht am Institut für Informatik Universität Bern

[May 87]: D. May
"*Occam 2 language definition*" INMOS Limited March 1987

[INMOS 87]:

"*IMS T800 Transputer data sheet*" INMOS Limited April 1987

[Oswald 90]: H. Oswald, R. Esser, R. Mattmann

"*An Environment for Specifying and Executing Hierachical Petri Nets*" In: Proc. 12th International Conference on Software Engineering, Nice, France, March 1990

[Pulli... 88]: P. Pulli, J. Dähler, H.-P. Gisiger, A. Kündig

"*Execution of Ward's Transformation Schema on the Graphic Specification and Prototyping Tool SPECS.*" CompEuro 88, Brussels, 11.-14.4.1988

[Reisig 86] W. Reisig

"*Embedded System Description using Petri Nets.*" In: Lecture Notes in Computer Science 284, Embedded Systems, Eds.: A. Kündig, R.E. Bührer, J. Dähler; pp. 18-62

[Schütte...88]: A. Schütte, F. Opfer, Ch. Asp

"*Automatische Prozesskonfiguration in Occam2*" Informationstechnik it 30 (1988) 4, R. Oldenbourg Verlag

[Taubner 88]: D. Taubner

"*On the Implementation of Petri Nets.*" In: Lecture Notes in Computer Science 340, Advances in Petri Nets 1988, Eds.: G.Rozenberg, pp. 418-439

[Ward...85]: P.T. Ward, S.J. Mellor

"*Structural Development for Real-Time Systems*", Vol.1-3. Yourdon Press. New York. 1985

[Winkler 86]: P. Winkler

"*Anforderungsbeschreibung mit Netzmodellen.*" Automatisierungstechnische Praxis atp, Vol. 28 No.1 (1986), pp. 32-39

Petri nets with uncertain markings

Janette Cardoso

LAAS-CNRS and UFSC, Florianópolis-Brazil, e-mail lcmi@brufsc.bitnet

Robert Valette

LAAS-CNRS 7, avenue du Colonel Roche F-31077 Toulouse, e-mail robert@laas.laas.fr

Didier Dubois

LSI-UPS 118, Route de Narbonne F-31062 Toulouse, e-mail dubois@irit.fr

ABSTRACT After having described the importance and the complexity of monitoring Flexible Manufacturing Systems, this paper shows the interest of introducing uncertainty and imprecision within Petri net based models. These two concepts are then introduced through a modification of the marking of a Petri net with Objects, and of its interpretation (external conditions associated with the transitions). It is shown how, in some cases, uncertainty is propagated and how, sometimes, it is possible to go back to certainty. Finally, an illustrative example is described.

Keywords possibility logic, Petri Nets, fuzzy dates, F.M.S., imprecise, uncertain.

Contents

1 Introduction

1.1 The hierarchical control architecture

Due to its complexity, Flexible Manufacturing System (FMS) Control is commonly decomposed into a hierarchy of the following abstraction levels: planning, scheduling, global coordination and real-time monitoring, sub-systems coordination and local control.

Each level operates on a certain model of the manufacturing system. The upper level models are more aggregated but also more global. The decisions made at each level have to be a refinement of the decisions made at the upper levels.

At the same time, each level supervises the behavior of the level just below. This is done by checking that the current state of a given level is consistent with the update messages sent by lower level.

Let us consider these levels in detail.

Planning: operates with manufacturing ratios, i.e. number of parts to be manufactured per week or per month. At this level, a pre-allocation of the machines is done in order to reduce the combinatorial explosion of the scheduling level.

Scheduling: is the level where the manufacturing plan is elaborated. A sequence for the execution of each operation on each machine (the *schedule*) is built. It checks that the quantity of planned products is feasible. When flexibility is required, the operations are not totally ordered, a set of feasible schedules or a manufacturing policy is produced.

Global coordination: its function is to update the state representation of the workshop in real-time. It has to check that no abnormal update message is received in order to guarantee a certain consistency between the actual state of the workshop and the technical data base (fault detection). We call this *supervising the shop floor*. It has also to compare the set of the operations which are possible (because the required resources are free in the shop) with the set of the operations which have to be done in order to respect the manufacturing schedule (or policy) and consequently to make the right decisions in real-time. We call this *real-time decision*.

Sub-system coordination: realizes the coordination of subsystems such as the transportation system, the manufacturing cells or workstations, the storage units etc. No more global optimization is required. The decisions taken at this level derive directly from the decisions taken at the global coordination level. The manufacturing plan is normally not explicitly involved.

Local control: implements the real-time control of the machines, the devices etc. No decision is made at this level.

1.2 Real-time decision within a schedule

In the sequel, we focus on the global coordination level. The representation of a Flexible Manufacturing System by means of Petri nets, in order to model conveniently resource allocations, implies the use of a kind of high level net. As rule-based approach, specifically for scheduling and real-time decisions are already commonly used for FMS management [ea86] [EE86], it seems natural to employ Predicate/Transition nets [Gen87] where each transition is considered as a rule with variables and each place as a set of entities verifying some predicate.

The concept of object class, defined as a set of properties or attributes in the same way as in object-oriented sense, is also very convenient because the modeling of a shop floor is frequently based on the actual objects (parts, machines, tools, etc...) circulating in it. A way of integrating object-oriented approach and Predicate/Transition nets has been already developed with the Petri Nets with Objects

(PNO) [SB85]. The variables attached to the arcs in the PNO are substituted by objects rather than by constants as in Predicate/Transition nets. It is why we have chosen this model, but this does not mean that the concepts of rule and object class could not be integrated in an approach based on colored nets.

As the Petri net depicts resource allocation mechanisms, firing a transition with available tokens corresponds to making a decision compatible with the shop floor state and with the manufacturing policy. A token that remains in a place associated with the input queue of a machine (containing the parts waiting for an operation) after the scheduled date means a violation of this policy [Ata87].

1.3   Supervising the shop floor

The supervising function is responsible for detecting any abnormal behavior of the physical part of the shop floor. Its requirements are twofold and contradictory: it has to be strict in order to avoid any fault propagation but it has also to be tolerant of human interventions in order to avoid floods of alarms in such situations.

A Petri net description of a shop floor allows a systematic strict supervision: each event corresponding to a normal behavior has to be associated with a transition. Two situations may occur in case of an error: either the transition is enabled and is never fired, or the event occurs and the transition is not enabled. The first case corresponds to checking that a scheduled event occurs before some deadline (watchdog). In Petri nets with Objects, such situations are easily modeled by a token attribute containing the duration of normal operation. A token remaining in a place (that represents for instance a machining operation) more than this duration means that either the machine failed or that the foreseen operation duration was incorrect. The second case corresponds to the occurrence of an event attached to a transition that cannot be fired for the current marking i.e. in the current state. In this situation, when the event is known to be the consequence of a human intervention, instead of activating an alarm, it is better to try to update the shop floor state correctly.

The problem is consequently to be tolerant in specific cases and so to decompose the events in three classes:

- those corresponding to normal operation,

- the forbidden ones,

- the acceptable ones.

For example, let us consider an automatic guided vehicle stopped between two contacts (the contacts are the only positions where the controller can detect and send commands to the vehicles) in a transport system. After a human intervention supposed to solve the trouble either by restarting the vehicle or by dragging it to the maintenance station, the normal event is the arrival at the next contact, the forbidden ones are the arrival at any other contact, but an acceptable event is the arrival at the maintenance station. This example will be used later and it will be explained in more detail in the sequel.

In order to make the expression of the notion of *acceptable* events possible, it is required to use a logic including the notion of imprecision or uncertainty.

In the case of Petri nets, we should express the fact that the existence of an object modeled by a token is known but that its location is imprecise (the token may be contained in more than a place).

The aim of this paper is to apply Petri Net theory and possibilistic logic to treat the shop floor supervising problem.

Some concepts are general, they deal with imprecise marking and transition firing. On the contrary the way it is decided that imprecision is increased or decreased is application dependent (specifically sections 3.4 and 6).

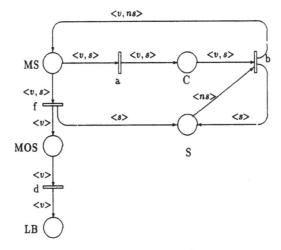

Figure 1: Transport system

2 The possibilistic logic

According to several authors [BZ88] [KF88] [DP88a], one way of simplifying the description of a very complex system is to allow some degree of uncertainty in this description. Statements obtained from this simplified system are *less precise but their relevance to the original system is fully maintained*.

We shall deal with two categories of uncertainty expressed by the terms vagueness and imprecision. In general [KF88], vagueness is associated with the difficulty of making sharp or precise distinctions in the world; that is, some domain of interest is vague if it cannot be delimited by sharp boundaries. Imprecision, on the other hand, is associated with one-to-many relations, that is, situations in which the choice between two or more alternatives is left unspecified.

The problems that we find when we deal with the FMS are well represented by these two categories at the different levels of abstraction.

When we deal with the scheduling level, the execution time may be known with some imprecision or, due to the complexity of a plan, we want to preserve some flexibility. In this case, the set of admissible schedules will not have a sharp boundary and we use the concept of vagueness. So, the interval between the earliest date and the due date is a fuzzy interval. The concept of fuzzy set provides a basic mathematical framework for dealing with vagueness [KF88].

At the global coordination level, we have to supervise the possible abnormal situations. The FMS may find itself in a situation which may have one among several possible causes. This situation is captured quite well by the term imprecision, the basic mathematical framework of which is provided by the concept of possibility distribution and possibility measure. Indeed, a possibility measure evaluates the *possibility* that an arbitrary element of the universal set X - also named the reference set - belongs to the individual crisp subsets A_i of X.

Let us consider the example of the automatic guided vehicles again. These vehicles follow automatically some circuits, their locations are only known at some points that are called *contacts*. They can only receive a command (stop, go, itinerary change) when they are on such a contact. In order to avoid collision, the circuits are decomposed into sections and the vehicles have to be controlled in such a manner that at a given time each section can only contains one vehicle.

The Petri net in figure 1 describes the coordination of such a transport system: transitions a, b and the places MS (*vehicle moving along a section*), C (*vehicle on a contact*) and S (*section free*) represents

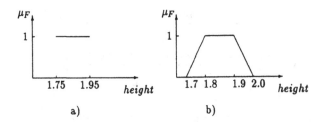

Figure 2: The knowledge about John's height is: a) imprecise, b) fuzzy

the normal system operation. The variable v represents a vehicle, s is some section, and ns is the next section. The transition b indicates that vehicle $< v >$ goes from section $< s >$ to the next section $< ns >$.

The place MS contains the tuples $< v, s >$ such that $< v >$ moves along $< s >$. The place C contains the vehicles $< v >$ on a contact. The place S contains the free sections $< s >$.

The transitions f and d depict an abnormal behavior: vehicle $< v >$ battery failed and $< v >$ has been manually removed from section $< s >$ and driven to the load battery station LB. The place MOS represent the movement of $< v >$ out of the sections.

In this example, the universal set X is the set of such vehicles that are in the transport system. Each vehicle has a location in the shop, and so, belongs to a specific subset. For instance, we can be interested in the following ones:

- A_1, the vehicles which are on a contact, represented by place C (predicate C in the Predicate-Transition net),

- A_2, the vehicles which are moving along a section, represented by place MS,

- $A_3 = A_1 \cup A_2$, the vehicles which are in a section, represented by places C and MS.

Each subset is well defined, but at a given moment we may ignore in what subset the vehicle is. We will present in the next section the basic definitions about the possibilistic measures.

2.1 Basic definitions

Let π_f be the possibility distribution that delimits the fuzzy set F of the more or less possible values of f. If μ_F is the membership function of F, we have by definition

$$\forall x \in X, \quad \pi_f(x) = \mu_F(x) \tag{1}$$

Assume for example that the information we have about *John's height* is the fuzzy set F in figure 2.b. The membership function μ_F can be interpreted as a possibility distribution π_f, because the values of the support ($\mu_F \neq 0$) are mutually exclusive candidates for John's height [DP88a]. The possibility for John being $1.50m$ (or $2.20m$) tall is zero, that for $1.85m$ tall is one.

A particular case of fuzzy information is imprecision, where the membership function μ_F values are restricted to 0 or 1 such as in figure 2.a.

With a given statement concerning an information, a possibility measure Π can be associated. Let us assume that we ask the following question: what is the possibility Π for John's height be an element of a subset A of X (A is supposed be a crisp set i.e. A is not fuzzy). In this case, the universal set X is the set of heights. For example, we can intuitively say that the possibility measure Π for John being greater than $1.60m$ is 1 with the information given by figure 2.b.

When the set X is finite, the possibility measure Π can be defined in terms of its values on the subsets of single elements (singletons) of X:

$$\forall A \subseteq X, \quad \Pi(A) = \max_{x \in A} \pi(x),$$

where $\pi(x) = \Pi(\{x\})$.

The necessity measures N are related to the possibility measures Π by the equation

$$N(A) = 1 - \Pi(\bar{A}) \tag{2}$$

where $\bar{A}$ is the complement of A, $\bar{A} = X - A$. This equation is a numerical expression of a duality relationship between the modalities of the possible and the necessary (in modal logic), which postulates that an event is necessary when its contrary is impossible.

In the sequel we shall consider mainly the case where X is finite (it is the set of the places in a Petri net), and the information imprecise.

3 Uncertainty in markings

3.1 Petri nets with Objects

As it has been mentioned in section 1.2, Petri nets with objects are used to describe the coordination mechanisms of the FMS control. It is not the purpose of this paper to give the formal definition of this class of Predicate/Transition net. Its chief feature is that a token is a tuple of unique instances of some classes (or sub-classes). A class denotes a set of similar but unique objects [Boo86]. For instance we have the classes *vehicle* and *section* in the net in figure 1. A token in place MS (tuple $< v_1, s_1 >$) represents a particular vehicle v_1 in a specific section s_1. A tuple describes a dynamic relation involving two or more object instances.

As the variable attached to the arcs are substituted by object instances, they are also typed by the corresponding object class. In the Petri net in figure 1, variable $< v >$ is of class *vehicle* and variable $< s >$ of class *section*. Each class is defined by a list of attributes.

Ubiquity appears when a given object belongs to more than one place, when a given place contains a given object with an arity greater than one or when an object appears in two different tuples contained in two different places [SB85]. *As a given physical object cannot be in two different states, the Petri Net with Objects describing the shop floor has to be without ubiquity.* For instance, a vehicle v_1 cannot be, at the same time, moving in a section (v_1 is in place MS) and stopped at a contact (v_1 is in place C). In fact, the non ubiquity notion is a natural consequence of the object-oriented approach. Another way of defining non ubiquity is to say that a given object instance is available in a unique exemplary and is visible at a unique place (in a unique state).

In the next section, we shall show that ubiquity will be interpreted as imprecision about the object instance location.

3.2 Imprecise marking

Traditionally, the marking of a Petri net is defined as the mapping M of the set of places P to the set $\mathcal{N}$ of natural numbers.

$$M : P \longrightarrow \mathcal{N}$$

So, if O is the set of objects and O^* the set of tuples of objects, the marking M of a PNO is defined by:

$$M : O^* \text{x} P \longrightarrow \mathcal{N}$$

When the net is without ubiquity the marking can be defined as

$$M : O^* \longrightarrow P$$

In order to have an image for any element of O^* we introduce a virtual place ϕ containing all the defined tuples of objects which are not in a place of the net and we define P_ϕ as $P \cup \{\phi\}$.

The marking can also be represented by:

$$M : O^* \longrightarrow \{P_\phi \longrightarrow \{0,1\}\} \tag{3}$$

or

$$M : O^* \times P_\phi \longrightarrow \{0,1\}.$$

If $M(o^*,p) = 1$, the tuple of object instances o^* is in the place p.

This way of representing the marking allows us to treat nets with ubiquity as well as without ubiquity. We can represent an ubiquity situation where a tuple of object instance is in two places p_1 and p_2:

$$M(o^*,p_1) = M(o^*,p_2) = 1$$

PNO without ubiquity

During the normal operation, we work with the PNO without ubiquity. As a matter of fact, within the shop floor, a part is always in one and only one site.

PNO with ubiquity

When an abnormal event occurs, no part, tool or automated guided vehicle can suddenly disappear from the manufacturing workshop but it may happen that we are not sure of its location. As it has been mentioned in section 2, this will be expressed by uncertainty attached to the occupancy of a token at a place.

We are certain of the existence of an object while its location is imprecise i.e. the object occupies more than one place, leading to ubiquity.

It is obvious that any decision involving a command of a machine or a resource allocation requires a certain knowledge i.e. the absence of imprecision. In order to represent this imprecision, we might introduce a possibility distribution π_{o^*} [DP88b] assigned to each tuple $o^* \in O^*$ and defined on the set P_ϕ. The set of all these functions describe the marking in a way which resembles (3). π_{o^*} is the possibility distribution that delimits the possibles locations of tuple o^*, i.e. the possible places the object instances belong to. In fact, we note π_{o^*} as a short-way for $\pi_{l(o^*)}$, where $l(o^*)$ is the location of o^*. The value of $\pi_{o^*}(p)$ is the possibility the location of o^* be p. From an initial value given by the initial marking, new values are computed after each event by transition firings as it will be explained in the sequel.

Clearly, the possibility distribution assigned to an element of a tuple is the same as that of the tuple. If a given element appears in more than one tuple for a place, then its possibility will be the maximum value over the corresponding tuples.

As far as no transition firing is concerned, we shall work directly with the possibility distributions of the object instances (tuples are split):

$$o \in O \quad \pi_o : P_\phi \longrightarrow \{0,1\} \tag{4}$$

and consider it as a partial representation of the marking (regardless of the notion of tuple).

Moreover, it must be pointed out that we will restrict our study to the case where π_o is either zero or one (the fuzzy case will not be considered).

We can then make the following statements:

- $\pi_o(p) = 1$ represents the fact that p is a *possible* location of o,

- $\pi_o(p) = 0$ expresses the *certainty* that o is not present in place p.

- It can happen that $\pi_o(p) = 1$ and $\pi_o(p') = 1$ for $p \neq p'$ at a given time, i.e. object o may be in place p or place p'.

Indeed, saying that it is completely possible (possibility equal to 1) that *the location of o is p* is much weaker than saying that it is completely certain *that the location of o is p*. In fact, the first statement does not forbid another location p' to be also completely possible for o [DP88b], i.e. does not forbid that the location of o is uncertain.

As it has been mentioned in section 2, the reference set (in our case P_ϕ) is partitioned into subsets that are singletons i.e. $A_i = \{p_i\}$. Let us assume that the following expression holds:

$$\forall p_i \neq p, \ \pi_o(p_i) = 0$$
$$\pi_o(p) = 1 \tag{5}$$

Then, the possibility that the location of o be p, $l(o) = p$, is equal to possibility that the location of o belongs to set A, $l(o) \in A$. In other words,

$$\pi_o(p) = \Pi(\{p\}) = \Pi(A) = 1$$

Now let us assume that

$$\Pi(\bar{A}) = \max_{p \in \bar{A}} \pi_o(p) = 0$$

where $\bar{A} = P_\phi - A$ Using equation 2, we obtain

$$N(A) = N(\{p\}) = 1$$

that is we are certain that the object o belongs to the place p. In other words there is no ubiquity concerning the token o.

Finally, it must be pointed out that the possibility distributions are defined at a given time. As a matter of fact, they can be considered either as functions defined on O in P_ϕ for a given t or as a function of t for an object o and a given place p.

Remark: Let us consider once again the example in figure 1. When it is certain that v_1 is on a contact we have:

$$\Pi_{v1}(\{C\}) = N_{v1}(\{C\}) = 1 \ \text{ and } \ \Pi_{v1}(\{MS, S, MOS, LB\}) = 0$$

If we know that v_2 is in normal operation we have

$$\Pi_{v2}(\{MS, C\}) = 1 \ \text{ and } \ \Pi_{v2}(\{S, MOS, LB\}) = 0$$

Consequently the knowledge derived from the place invariants can be easily translated into the form of a necessity measure. As an example let us consider the place invariant $M(MS, s_1) + M(C, s_1) + M(S, s_1) = 1$ meaning that a section s_1 is always free, or occupied by a vehicle which is either moving or at a contact. It can be written $N_{s1}(\{MS, C, S\}) = 1$ which implies $\Pi_{s1}(\{MS, C, S\}) = 1$ and $\Pi_{s1}(\{MOS, LB\}) = 0$.

3.3 Firing a transition

In a Petri net with an imprecise marking, transitions can be fired in two different ways: certain or pseudo-firing (uncertain firing).

The first case corresponds to the classical firing of a transition and therefore necessitates that the locations of all the involved tokens are certain (no ubiquity for them). The action associated with the transition is executed.

In the second case, the firing does not correspond to an evolution of the system modeled by the Petri net which is known with certainty. It rather means that we are making some *inference* about its state. The actions associated with the transition are not executed because actual commands can only be performed when the knowledge is certain. We call it *pseudo-firing*.

Pseudo-firing is performed by computing new possibility distributions for some object instances (those which would have moved for a classical firing). Uncertainty about the location of these objects will be increased. In other words, the sets of the places where their possibility distributions are equal to one will be larger. Uncertainty will increase until the occurrence of an event allowing to deduce the location of the objects with certainty.

In doing so, we avoid the occurrence of contradiction in case of abnormal behavior of the system. As soon as an incident occurs, we operate with uncertain knowledge in order to be able to take into account a larger set of possible events (update messages received from the shop floor). The occurrence of one of these events allows us to go back to a certain knowledge.

3.4 Imprecision introduced by the interpretation

3.4.1 Interpreted Petri net

A practical utilization of Petri nets implies an interpretation of the net i.e. the association of labels to the transitions in order to describe a condition and an action together. The condition is an extra firing condition involving either data (for example token attributes in a Petri net with Objects) or the occurrence of external events. Consequently, in an interpreted net, a transition can only be fired when the marking is sufficient and when this extra condition is true. The action depicts data modifications or commands sent to the environment.

By means of the interpretation it is possible to differentiate the situations for which a transition a is enabled into three cases:

- a is not fired (in order to synchronize its firing with a specific event which will occur eventually),

- a is pseudo-fired because from a piece of information just received we infer that some abnormal behavior is possible,

- a is fired immediately.

Consequently, we define the interpretation $\mathcal{I}$ of a Petri net by attaching to each transition another authorization function $\eta_{x_1...x_n}$ that plays the part of the extra firing condition:

$$\eta_{x_1...x_n} : T \longrightarrow \{false, uncertain, true\} \tag{6}$$

where $x_1...x_n$ are the variables associated to the incoming arcs of a.

Let us assume that $o_1...o_n$ is a possible substitution to $x_1...x_n$ for firing a. If $\eta_{o_1...o_n}(a)$ is

- **false**, transition a cannot be fired.

- **uncertain**, a will be fired, and the imprecision will be increased; it is a **pseudo-firing** depicted in detail in section 3.5.

- **true** and if the location of $o_1...o_n$ is precise, a will be fired.

- **true** and the location of $o_1...o_n$ is imprecise, then a new computation of the possibility distribution of these tokens will be done in order to go back to certainty. This will be explained in part 4.

Let us consider figure 3. Transition a can be fired with various instantiations of the variables $< x >$ and $< y >$ by object instances contained in the places 1 and 2 respectively. Let us assume that the objects contained in place 1 have an attribute *date*, the authorization functions η_{xy} can be given:

$$\eta_{xy}(a) = \forall y \begin{cases} uncertain & if & (t < x.date) \wedge (signal(x)) \\ true & if & (t \geq x.date) \wedge (signal(x)) \\ false & otherwise \end{cases} \tag{7}$$

In the case of figure 3 two substitutions are possible: $\eta_{o_1 o_3}(a)$ and $\eta_{o_2 o_3}(a)$ will be obtained by substituting $< x >$ by o_1 or by o_2 and $< y >$ by o_3.

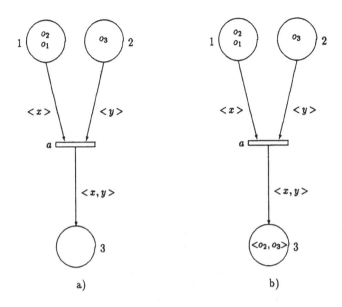

Figure 3: Example of a transition and an imprecise marking

This function has the following semantics. Before time *date*, the arrival of a message from the shop floor signaling that object $< x >$ was involved in the event a, is *possible* but does not correspond to a normal behavior. Either the message is erroneous, or the representation of the shop floor state within the controller (the Petri net marking) is not consistent with the actual state. The imprecision about object $< x >$ will increase and the transition associated with event a will be pseudo-fired.

On the other hand, receiving the message after time *date* corresponds to the normal behavior. So the firing of a should be a normal firing and the update of the shop floor state should be done with certainty.

Let us assume that:

$$o_1.date = 20 \quad \text{and} \quad o_2.date = 40$$

and that the current time is $t = 30$. If the message $signal(o_1)$ is received from equation 7 we have $\eta_{o_1\,o_3}(a) = true$. Transition a is then fired normally. On the contrary, if message $signal(o_2)$ is received, we have $\eta_{o_2\,o_3}(a) = uncertain$ and the firing of a should be a $pseudo-firing$, increasing so the imprecision.

3.4.2 Time Petri net

The example given above shows that timing considerations are important pieces of information when deciding to pseudo-fire a transition. Instead of introducing time in the token attributes, it is possible to handle it explicitly.

In [CD89] a specific use of time Petri net is shown. Actually the interval $[\tau_1, \tau_2]$ associated with a transition a in a time Petri net can be seen as an imprecise enabling duration. After an enabling duration of τ_1 (time units), the transition a is pseudo-fired. Then, a normal firing of a is performed either when the occurrence of the event associated with it is reported or when the enabling duration reaches the value τ_2. In fact, in this work, instead of the interval $[\tau_1, \tau_2]$ we have used a fuzzy interval $[\tau_1', \tau_1, \tau_2, \tau_2']$ meaning that the normal value for the duration is an element of $[\tau_1, \tau_2]$, while an element of $[\tau_1', \tau_1] or [\tau_2, \tau_2']$ is not excluded.

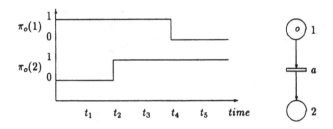

Figure 4: Pseudo-firing of a transition

3.5 Detailed pseudo-firing mechanism

Let us consider the pseudo-firing of a transition a in the context of an interpreted Petri net. This is done when $\eta(a)$ takes the value *uncertain*, the object location being certain or uncertain.

In this paper, we restrict ourselves to the case where the possibility distributions of the objects used for the firing of a are equal to zero in the output places of a. In fact, if this restriction is not made, restoring certainty could turn out to be impossible because more than one firing sequence would lead from the last certain marking to the new one. When this restriction is violated, a message has to be sent to the human operator in order to inform him that automatic restoration of a consistent state representation of the shop is no longer possible.

Pseudo-firing is performed in the following way: possibility distributions $\pi_o(p)$ are set to one for all the objects o concerned with all the input places of transition a (substituted to variables) and in all the output places of a in which the objects would have been put for a normal firing. It must be pointed out that the possibility distributions of these objects are not set to zero in the input places of a. Indeed, this mechanism corresponds to an augmentation of the imprecision.

The imprecision concerning the marking is a way of considering a set of situations (the normal one and acceptable ones) globally. Instead of considering only one marking for the Petri net, we consider a set of markings *abbreviated* in the form of an imprecise marking. Pseudo-firing a transition a consists in adding to all the preceding markings all the new ones obtained after firing a. In other words, to the situations such that the event *firing a* may occur eventually, we add the situations such that the event *firing a* may have occurred in the past.

Let us consider the example concerning the shop floor supervision. Imprecision will increase until the occurrence of one of the two following events:

- a message arrives from the shop floor which will be used to update our knowledge of the shop;

- or a message is sent to the human operator signaling that automatic knowledge restoration is no longer possible (either the possibility of the objects in the output places is equal to *one*, or too much time has passed with no message arriving from the shop floor.

Let us consider figure 4. It represents the possibility distributions $\pi_o(1)$ and $\pi_o(2)$ for the object o and the places 1 and 2 as a function of time.

The semantics are the following:

- at time $t1$, the fact that place 1 contains the object o means that the occurrence of event a for o will be possible in the future,

- at time $t2$, suppose $\eta_o(a) = uncertain$: the pseudo-firing of a for o occurs and uncertainty increases,

- at time $t3$ the marking is imprecise, the occurrence of a for o may have happened in the past but it is possible that it will happen only in the future,

- at time $t4$, an event that is certain allows the deduction of a precise location for o, in other words pseudo-firing of a for o terminates, which is equivalent to a normal firing of a from the marking as it was at time $t1$,

- at time $t5$ it is known with certainty that transition a fired for o in the past, a cannot be fired in the future for o without a shop floor state modification i.e. the execution of a cycle by o.

Let us go back to figure 3. If $signal(o_2)$ occurs at time 30, the marking described in b) would be obtained by the pseudo-firing of a by the tuple $< o_2, o_3 >$. When an object o is drawn in a place p it means that the possibility distribution $\pi_o(p) = 1$ otherwise $\pi_o(p) = 0$.

4 Certainty recovery

4.1 Principles

At this point, we have explained how, in case of an abnormal operation, the imprecision of the shop floor state representation can be modeled. It must be pointed out that the imprecision concerns only some objects and that the locations of the others is known with certainty. This means that the part of the manufacturing shop which is not altered by the abnormal operation operates normally.

The restoration of certainty occurs when for a transition a, $\eta(a)$ is *true* for a tuple containing objects with an uncertain location.

As previously stated in section 3.3, normal firing implies certainty, and as it has been explained in section 3.2, certainty derives from the fact that the possibility distribution π_o is equal to one for only one place. Consequently, it is necessary to have a procedure for the new computation of the possibility distribution that achieves this goal, taking into account the new information received i.e. the fact that $\eta(a)$ is *true*.

4.2 Algorithm

As it has been mentioned formerly, discussing figure 4, *pseudo-firing* a transition a can be considered as the beginning of a normal firing. In fact, we put the tokens in the output places but we do not remove them from the input places. This is because we are not certain if the transition a has to be fired or not. When we compute again the possibility distributions of the objects, we have to decide for every transition which has been pseudo fired if it has been actually fired or not. In the first case, we say that we decide a *pseudo-firing achievement* (a has to be fired), in the second case we decide a *pseudo-firing cancellation* (a has not to be fired).

In other words:

pseudo-firing achievement: we have concluded that the transition has to be fired because the corresponding event in the shop floor actually occurred. The possibility distributions of the objects involved in the firing are reset to zero for the input places of the transition.

pseudo-firing cancellation: we have concluded that the transition has not to be fired because the corresponding event in the shop floor did not occur. The possibility distribution of the objects involved in the firing are reset to zero for the output places of the transition.

Let us emphasize the restriction which we have made: no pseudo-firing is performed when the possibility distribution of the objects is equal to one in the output places already. We will also assume that no transition is, at a given time, in the process of pseudo-firing for more than one tuple of objects. This restriction corresponds to the classical hypothesis of simple breakdown in the diagnostic systems.

We assume that we are in the case where a message has just arrived and is such that $\eta(a) = $ true. The procedure for the computation of the possibility distribution is thus the following one:

1 If the transition a is in process of pseudo-firing (we had previously $\eta(a) =$ uncertain), *cancel* this firing (firing cancellation), go to 2,

2 put into list LP the input and output places of a, go to 3,

3 if LP is empty, go to 6 else let p be first element of LP, remove p of LP, go to 4,

4 if there is an input transition t of p different from a in process of pseudo-firing, *achieve* this firing, put the input and output places of t which are different from p into LP, then go to 4; else go to 5,

5 if there is an output transition t of p different from a in process of pseudo-firing, *cancel* this firing, put the input and output places which are different from p into LP, then go to 5; else go to 3,

6 the normal firing of transition a can be performed because the location of the objects are certain. There is only one place p' where o_i belongs to: $\pi_{o_i}(p') = 1$ and $\pi_{o_i}(p_k) = 0$, $p_k \neq p'$ (see section 3.2).

This procedure terminates because the number of places and transitions is finite and by assumption (no pseudo-firing is performed when the possibility distribution of the objects is equal to one in the output places already) no cycle of possible places for an object can exist.

As stated above an imprecise marking is an abbreviated way of taking into account a set of acceptable markings. This algorithm is a way of eliminating of this set all the markings which are not such that transition a is enabled before firing it. This is possible because the places p for which $\pi_o(p) \neq 0$ represents alternative locations for o and thus alternative markings. The assumption that when a pseudo-firing is performed, no object o is introduced in p if $\pi_o(p) \neq 0$ is essential also.

Imprecise marking is an abbreviation that allows to recognize a sequence of events even when it is only *partially observed*. Some transitions of the firing sequence are not signaled but the fact that they correspond to events which have occurred is inferred by means of imprecise markings and certainty restoration.

5 Analysis

Imprecision is a way of describing a set of alternatives for a given situation, leaving the choice of one of these alternatives open.

In the case of a Petri net with imprecise markings, the set of the alternatives for a given object o is the set of places p such that $\pi_o(p) = 1$, i.e. the set of the possible locations of o. The sets of transitions that are being pseudo-fired (before pseudo-firing achievement or cancellation) describe possible paths for the objects. The paths are legal but only one can be true.

Let us consider a Petri net PN, an initial marking M_0, and the corresponding set of the reachable markings $\mathcal{A}(PN, M_0)$. An imprecise marking $\mathcal{M}$ is simply a connected subset of $\mathcal{A}(PN, M_0)$. Certainty restoration consists of choosing correctly an alternative, i.e. a marking which belongs to $\mathcal{M}$ and thus necessarily which is an element of $\mathcal{A}(PN, M_0)$.

Consequently no specific analysis of Petri nets with imprecise markings is required. All the analysis that was done on the net before the introduction of uncertainty remain valid.

Let us now consider the place invariants. As stated above they can be translated into the form of necessity measures concerning some object instances for some subset of places. As imprecision is only increased or decreased by means of transition firings (pseudo-firing, pseudo-firing achievement, pseudo-firing cancellation), these necessity measures are always verified and they give no new information about the marking of the net. It is why they are not used in the algorithm for restoring certainty (in the same way place invariant are not used in token players). Actually, the differences between our work and other works about imprecision in discrete event systems is the computations of the possibility distributions performed by us are more efficient because they take into account the control structure of the discrete event system (i.e. the Petri net directly).

6 Example

Let us now consider the illustrative example concerning the transportation system again. The fact that s and ns are not independent is expressed by the authorization function $\eta_{s\,ns}(b)$ attached to transition b. The transition a represents the arrival of the vehicle $< v >$ at a contact. Its authorization function is the following one:

$$\eta_v(a) = \begin{cases} true & \text{if} & signal(v) \\ uncertain & \text{if} & t > (v.dis + tmax_2) \\ false & \text{otherwise} \end{cases}$$

where $signal(v)$ is the message sent by a contact when $< v >$ arrives.

It is assumed that vehicles $< v >$ have an attribute dis which contains the date when $< v >$ entered section $< s >$. This attribute is used as a watch dog in order to detect when a vehicle remains for too long when moving along the section. Sometimes the vehicle stops because it has detected something in front of it, for example a human operator crossing the shop floor. It can be put in to operation again by manual reset and will finally reach the next contact. Sometimes it is the battery that is discharged and the vehicle has to be driven manually to the maintenance station. The transport system coordination has to tolerate the two situations and to release the concerned section when it is certain that the vehicle has been driven away. As the movement out of the section to the maintenance station (from place MS to place MOS) is not controlled by the transport system coordinator, no signal is given informing that in the actual system transition f is fired. However it is this firing which releases the section.

The following authorization function is therefore attached to f:

$$\eta_v(f) = uncertain \ \text{if} \ t > (v.dis + tmax), \ \text{else} \ false$$

where t is the current time and $tmax$ the maximum duration for crossing a section. The authorization function $\eta_v(d)$ is identical to $\eta_v(a)$.

Consequently, when a vehicle $< v >= v_i$ remains for too long time on a section $< s >= s_j$, a pseudo-firing of transition f is done. The possibility distribution π_{vi} is equal to one for the places MS and MOS and π_{sj} is equal to one for MS and S. It must be pointed out that section s_j cannot be allocated to another vehicle although its name appears in place S because its location is not certain.

As the marking is uncertain, transition a as well as transition d are enabled for the tuple $< v_i, s_j >$. Let us suppose that, after a delay, transition a also is pseudo-fired. Now, transitions a and d, as well as transition b if section s_{j+1} is free, are enabled. One of them will be fired after the receiving of a message and a recomputation of the possibility distributions of v_i and s_j as stated in the algorithm in the preceding section.

Let us consider the cases when transition d has to be fired. Pseudo-firing of transition f is achieved, and that of transition a is canceled. The location of the token $< v_i >$ in place MOS is certain and transition d is fired. As a side-effect of the algorithm, the location of token $< s_j >$ becomes certain into place S and this means that this section will be allocated eventually to a vehicle leaving section s_{j-1} (certain firing of transition b).

7 Conclusion

This paper is a first attempt to introduce uncertainty in the marking of a Petri net in order to take into account abnormal events as well as normal operation. The advantage of doing so is that the combinatorial explosion of the complexity of the Petri net is avoided because a larger set of transitions can be considered as enabled by a given marking, however with uncertainty.

Further work is now underway in order to be able to consider fuzzy markings. This means that the possibility distributions will be defined on the interval $[0,1]$ rather than on the set $\{0,1\}$. This will allow the utilization of fuzzy intervals for operation durations as well as for the intervals defined by the earliest starting time and the due date. In doing so it will be possible to monitor the plan execution as well as to supervise the shop floor by means of the same representation of the shop floor state.

Acknowledgement:
This work has been partially supported by G.I.P. PROMIP (midi pyrénées research group in production systems). The first author would like to acknowledge the financial support of CAPES/Brazil.
We thank the three referees for their comments.

References

[Ata87] H. Atabakhche. *Utilisation conjointe de l'intelligence artificielle et des réseaux de Petri: Application au contrôle d'exécution d'un plan de fabrication.* PhD thesis, Université Paul Sabatier, Toulouse, december 1987.

[Boo86] Grady Booch. Object-oriented development. *IEEE Trans. on Software Engineering,* SE-12:211–221, 1986.

[BZ88] R. E. Bellman and L. A. Zadeh. Decision-making in a fuzzy environment. In R. R. Yager, editor, *Fuzzy sets and applications.* John Wiley and Sons, 1988.

[CD89] R. Valette J. Cardoso and D. Dubois. Monitoring manufacturing systems by means of petri nets with imprecise markings. In *IEEE International Symposium on Intelligent Control 1989,* pages 233–238, Albany, New York, september 1989.

[DP88a] D. Dubois and H. Prade. An introduction to possibilistic and fuzzy logics. In P. Smets, editor, *Non-Standard logics for automated reasoning.* Academic Press, 1988.

[DP88b] D. Dubois and H. Prade. *Possibility Theory: an approach to computerized processing of uncertainty.* Plenum Press, 1988. Translation of Théorie de possibilités published by Masson in 1985.

[ea86] E. Bensana et all. An expert system approach to industrial job-shop scheduling. In *IEEE International Conference on Robotics and automation,* San Francisco, april 1986.

[EE86] J. Erschler and P. Esquirol. Decision-aid in job-shop scheduling: a knowledge based approach. In *IEEE International Conference on Robotics and automation,* San Francisco, april 1986.

[Gen87] H.J. Genrich. Predicate/transition nets. Technical report, Institut fur methodische Grundlagen, may 1987.

[KF88] G.J. Klir and T.A. Folger. *Fuzzy sets uncertainty and information.* Prentice-Hall, 1988.

[SB85] C. Sibertin-Blànc. High-level petri nets with data structures. In *Workshop on Applications and Theory of Petri nets,* Finland, june 1985.

CONVEX GEOMETRY AND SEMIFLOWS IN P/T NETS.
A COMPARATIVE STUDY OF ALGORITHMS FOR
COMPUTATION OF MINIMAL P-SEMIFLOWS

J.M. Colom and M. Silva

Dpto. Ingeniería Eléctrica e Informática - Universidad de Zaragoza
María de Luna, 3 (Actur) 50015 ZARAGOZA (Spain)

ABSTRACT. P-semiflows are non-negative left anullers of a net's flow matrix. The importance of these vectors lies in their usefulness for analyzing net properties. The concept of minimal p-semiflow is known in the context of Mathematical Programming under the name "extremal direction of a cone". This connection highlights a parallelism between properties found in the domains of P/T nets and Mathematical Programming. The algorithms known in the domain of P/T nets for computing elementary semi-flows are basically a new rediscovery, with technical improvements with respect to type of problems involved, of the basic Fourier-Motzkin method. One of the fundamental problems of these algorithms is their complexity. Various methods and rules for mitigating this problem are examined. As a result, this paper presents two improved algorithms which are more efficient and robust when handling "real-life" Nets.

Keywords: Structural analysis of P/T nets, Minimal semiflows, Convex Geometry, Extremal direction of a cone, Algorithms to compute all minimal semiflows, Tests of minimality.

CONTENTS

1. INTRODUCTION

Various techniques have been developed for analyzing P/T nets [APN 87], [SILV 85]. These include those based on linear invariant relations drawn from the structure of the net (they belong to the so-called structural analysis techniques). Their computation is based on the left or right anullers of a matrix representing the structure of the net (*flows*).

This paper is divided into two parts. The first presents the close relationship between *non-negative flows* (semiflows), a concept used in net theory, and the *direction of a cone*, which belongs to the domain of Convex Geometry (and the related field of Mathematical Programming). This coincidence provides properties and algorithms developed independently in the two fields. [KRUC 87] and [TREV 86] are surveys on properties and algorithms related to semiflows from the perspective of P/T nets (in [MART 84] and

[TREV 86] can be found a performance evaluation of several of these algorithms). In Mathematical Programming [MATH 80] and [WILL 86] are also surveys in the topic.

The second part is devoted to a *review* and *improvement* of the algorithms existing for calculating semiflows. In these algorithms, the well-known Fourier-Motzkin method (the first reference dates back to 1826 [FOUR 1826]) is used to eliminate variables from systems of linear inequalities. However, the basic algorithms for calculating the extremal directions of a cone using this method were presented as original methods when they appeared in very diverse fields. This rediscovery phenomenon is a strongly recurring theme with these algorithms. The following references, classified by fields, have described them as innovations:

-Linear systems of equations: [FARK 02],[MOTZ 36],[CHER 64],[KOHL 67].
-Parametric programming: [DUFF 74].
-Mathematical logic: [LANG 27].
-Integer Linear Programming: [WILL 76].
-P/T Nets: [MART 81] (the first publication on the subject), [TOUD 81],[ALAI 82], [KRUC 87].

The number of extremal directions of a cone can be exponential [MART 81], [WILL 86]. Therefore, one of the fundamental problems in calculating them is the complexity. Various algorithms, with a plethora of minor variants containing different heuristics, have been developed for the·purpose. Their common aim is to reduce the computational cost (execution time and memory occupation) as much as possible.

Following [MATH 80], this paper classifies the known algorithms and introduces new variants which give excellent performance in handling "real" models of concurrent systems described with nets.

The basic terminology of Convex Geometry used in this work follows [CHVA 83]. Fundamental concepts of P/T nets are denoted following [SILV 87]. Section 2 presents the concepts of invariant and linear flow in a net and their relation with concepts in the field of Mathematical Programming.

The rest of the paper is organized as follows. Section 3 presents two basic approaches for calculating a generator of semiflows, and gives different solutions for improving the efficiency of these algorithms. Section 4 establishes the general implementation characteristics of the algorithms, and the examples which will be used a basis for comparison. Sections 5 and 6 examine implementations of variants of each of the approaches given the performance figures. The experimental phase in which the real performance of the algorithms were tested for several examples takes near two months of CPU time for a VAX 11/750. The presentation of variants in §5 (and §6) is not done reflecting the experimental plans but in an (didactical) incremental way. Data concerning several "significative" examples are reflected in different tables in such a way that the reader can appreciate by him/her self the performance improvement each variant implies. Finally, §7 compares the most efficient and robust implementations of each approach.

2. LINEAR FLOWS AND SEMIFLOWS IN P/T NETS

2.1. Some basic concepts and results

A *p-flow* is a vector $Y:P \to \mathbb{Q}$ such that $Y^T \cdot C = 0$, where C is the flow matrix of the net. The p-flows of a P/T net characterize the structural linear p-invariants of form: $\forall M_0$, $\forall M \in R(N,M_0)$, $Y^T \cdot M = Y^T \cdot M_0$, where $R(N,M_0)$ is the set of reachable markings of P/T net N from the initial marking M_0.

Proposition 2.1. Let N be a net. Given an arbitrary M_0, the invariant $Y^T \cdot M = Y^T \cdot M_0$ holds $\forall M \in R(N,M_0)$ iff $Y^T \cdot C = 0$. ◆

The set of p-flows is a vector space (orthogonal to the space of rows in C). Therefore, the p-flows can be generated from a *basis* of the space. Non-negative p-flows are called *conservative components* or *p-semiflows* (vectors $Y: P \to \mathbb{N}$ such that $Y^T \cdot C = 0$). The following terminology is used with p-semiflows [MEMM 78]: The *support* of a p-semiflow, Y: $\|Y\| = \{p \mid Y(p) > 0\}$. A p-semiflow, Y, is *canonical* iff the g.c.d. of its non-null elements is one. A P/T net is *conservative* iff there exists a p-semiflow such that $\|Y\| = P$.

The set of a net's canonical p-semiflows can be infinite, since the weighted sum of any two p-semiflows is a p-semiflow. A *generator set* of p-semiflows, $\Psi = \{Y_1, Y_2,...,Y_q\}$, is made up of the least number of them which will generate any p-semiflow as follows:

$$Y = \sum_{Y_j \in \Psi} k_j \cdot Y_j, \, k_j \in \mathbb{Q} \text{ and } Y_j \in \Psi.$$

The p-semiflows $Y_j \in \Psi$ are said to be *minimal*.

Proposition 2.2 [SIFA 79], [SILV 85]. A p-semiflow is minimal iff it is canonical and its support does not contain strictly the support of any other p-semiflow. ◆

Corollary 2.3 [SILV 85].The p-semiflow generator of a net is finite and unique. ◆

The number of minimal p-semiflows is less than or equal to the number of incomparable vectors of dimension n (n=|P|) [SILV 85]: n° of minimal semiflows$\leq \binom{n}{\lceil n/2 \rceil}$. Where $\binom{*}{*}$ denotes a combinatory number and $\lceil * \rceil$ denotes rounding up to an integer. In practice this number is still too gross a bound for the number of p-semiflows.

2.2.   P-semiflows and Mathematical Programming

The concepts related to p-semiflows are known in other fields such as Mathematical Programming, Convex Geometry, etc. However, the mutual ignorance of these fields is apparent from the fact that each has its own terminology (table 1). The calculation of generators of p-flows and p-semiflows is the problem considered in this work. In the case of p-flows, the problem is solved using the classic calculation of a basis of a space orthogonal to a given one (see, for example, [KANN 79]). On the other hand, the case of p-semiflows has given rise to various works proposing original algorithms for calculating minimal p-semiflows [MART 81], [TOUD 81], [ALAI 82], [KRUC 87].

P/T nets [BRAM 83]	Convex Geometry [CHVA 83]
p-semiflow	Direction of a positive cone
Set of p-semiflows	Positive Convex Cone
Minimal p-semiflow	Extremal Direction of a positive cone
Generator of p-semiflows	Set of Extremal Directions of a positive cone
Supports Inclusion	Dominance [DUFF 74]

Table 1.   Correspondence of terms in Petri Nets and Convex Geometry.

Once the relationships between Convex Geometry and semiflow related concepts has been established, the algorithms existing in the first domain for calculating the extremal directions of a cone are classified below (following [MATH 80]). The goal is to place those developed for nets in the same context (given the equivalence between a minimal p-semiflow and the extremal direction of a cone).

a)   *Algorithms based on pivoting operations* [BALI 61], [DYER 77], [MANA 68], [MATH 73], [MURT 68].
      These are inspired by the operations performed by the simplex algorithm to solve Linear Programming Problems(LPP) [DANT 63]. The idea is based on the fact that

the solutions of the LPP dealt with by simplex are the extremal points of a polyhedron which describes the constraints of the LPP. To compute the extremal directions of a cone $A \cdot X = 0$, $X \geq 0$ a normalization constraint is added ($\mathbb{1}^T \cdot X \leq 1$) which transforms the original cone into a polytope in which each extremal point is associated with an extremal direction of the original cone. Starting from one of these solutions, these algorithms go through all the extremal points of the polytope using the same method as simplex uses to go from one solution to another (*pivoting*). The variants on this algorithm are based on different strategies to avoid repeating extremal points.

As Matheiss mentions in [MATH 80], these algorithms are very sensitive to the existence of *degenerate* solutions of the system of constraints (solutions with basic variables of value zero), and it is necessary to add special techniques to handle degeneracy (lexicographic or perturbation methods, see chapter 6 of [HADL 62]) which drastically reduce the algorithms' efficiency. Probably *this is the reason why this type of algorithm has no counterpart in the P/T net computation of semiflows: nets' problems are usually strongly degenerate.*

b) ***Algorithms not based on pivoting.***
These can be viewed as variants of the Fourier-Motzkin elimination method for solving systems of linear inequalities [FOUR 1826], [FARK 02], [MOTZ 36],[CHER 64], [KOHL 67], [WILL 86].

The basic idea is to eliminate variables from the system by adding to them *all* the inequalities resulting from positive linear combinations of pairs of inequalities. The method proceeds by eliminating all the variables and memorizing, for each final inequality, the coefficients of the positive linear combination of rows which generated it. These coefficients are the extremal directions of the cone (semiflows).

The computational difficulty of the method lies in the large number of inequalities added in the process of eliminating variables. Many of them are *redundant* and can be discarded. The different variants published [MOTZ 36], [KOHL 67], etc, seek the common goal of braking the growth of the new inequalities by eliminating the redundant ones. All the variants known so far for calculating the set of minimal p-semiflows of a P/T net fall into this group.

The rest of this article is devoted to presenting two improved algorithms for calculating p-semiflows in P/T nets. They are based on the above Fourier-Motzkin method. The proposed algorithms are found to give an improvement of between one and two orders of magnitude over the algorithms studied and programmed for P/T nets [MART 84], [TREV 86].

3. COMPUTATION OF MINIMAL P-SEMIFLOWS

There are two approaches, each one containing many variants, for calculating the minimal p-semiflows. Nevertheless, it is very important to remark from the very beginning that both approaches are based on a unique method: the Fourier-Motzkin Method (§2.2b). These approaches are: (1) Algorithms which start from the net flow matrix, and (2) Algorithms which start from a basis of p-flows.

One of the problems with this sort of algorithm is the high memory occupation due to the addition of new rows (that can be redundants) in the Fourier-Motzkin method and because of the combinatory nature of the problem. To alleviate this situation, mechanisms are added to the basic algorithms in order to detect and eliminate redundancies, together with a series of heuristic rules which will help to control this combinatory explosion. Section 3.1 presents the algorithms corresponding to the two basic approaches examined here and emphasizes that, though they start from different approaches, they are essentially the same method. Section 3.2 presents mechanisms used with P/T nets for eliminating redundancies and their parallelism with methods in Mathematical Programming.

3.1. Basic Algorithms for computation of minimal p-semiflows

The basic algorithms corresponding to the two approaches for computing the minimal p-semiflows are:

ALGORITHM 1. Calculation of the minimal p-semiflows, Y, from the flow matrix C of the net: $Y^T \cdot C = 0$, $Y \geq 0$ (the algorithm given in [MART 81], and the first algorithm given in [ALAI 82] or [TOUD 81] belong to this class).

ALGORITHM 1. OBTAINING THE MINIMAL P-SEMIFLOWS FROM THE FLOW MATRIX, C
(1) $A := C$, $Y := I_n$ { I_n is an identity matrix of dimension n }
(2) **For** i:=1 **to** m **do**   { m is the number of transitions in the net }
    2.1   Add to the matrix $[Y \mid A]$ all the rows which are linear combinations of pairs of rows of $[Y \mid A]$ and which annul the i-th column of A.
    2.2   Eliminate from $[Y \mid A]$ the rows in which the i-th column of A is non-null.
(3) The rows of matrix Y are p-semiflows of the net. Among them are all the minimal p-semiflows (after a transformation of the rows of Y into canonical p-semiflows).

Each row of matrix Y memorizes the coefficients of the positive linear combination of rows of matrix C which generated the row of A with the same index. In step (3) of the algorithm, the rows of A are null and therefore each row Y_i is a p-semiflow.

Proposition 3.1 [MART 81]. Algorithm 1 generates all the minimal p-semiflows of the net N. They are a subset of the rows of Y obtained after execution. ◆

Column k is said to be *actively annulled* if it is not null (so that operations must be performed to annul it). The following can be easily proven.

Proposition 3.2 [COLO 89]. Algorithm 1 actively annuls r=rank(C) linearly independent columns of matrix C. ◆

ALGORITHM 2. Computation of the minimal p-semiflows from a basis of p-flows (the next algorithm to that which start from the flow matrix C in [ALAI 82] or [TOUD 81] and the algorithm given in [KRUC 87] belong to this group). This algorithm is based on the fact that every p-semiflow belongs to the p-flow vector space, that is:

$$Y \text{ is a semiflow} \iff \exists\, \lambda \text{ such that } B\cdot\lambda = Y \geq 0 \qquad [1]$$

where the columns of matrix B are a basis of p-flows. This basis is arbitrary; nevertheless, one basis can always be found such that every p-semiflow is a positive linear combination of the basis [e.g. $B^T = [E \mid D]$ where D is a positive diagonal submatrix of dimension n-r and r=rank(C)]. Basis of this type will be used in the sequel. Using [1], the calculation of p-semiflows consists merely of operating with the following system of inequalities:

$$Y^T = \lambda^T \cdot B^T \geq 0,\ \lambda \geq 0 \text{ and } B^T = [E \mid D] \qquad [2]$$

ALGORITHM 2. OBTAINING THE MINIMAL P-SEMIFLOWS FROM A BASIS B OF P-FLOWS
(1) $A := B^T$ {B has dimension nx(n-r), where r is the rank of C}
(2) **For** i:=1 **to** r **do**   {r is the number of actively annulled columns of B^T}
    2.1 Add to matrix A all the rows resulting from positive linear combinations of pairs of rows of A which annul the i-th column of A.
    2.2 Eliminate from A all the rows in which the i-th column is negative.
(3) The rows of matrix A are p-semiflows of the net. Among them are the minimal p-semiflows (after a transformation of the rows of A into canonical p-semiflows).

Essentially, the above algorithm is an alternative implementation of algorithm 1 with a different starting matrix based on a basis of p-flows, B. In fact, introducing *slack variables*, h, into [2] leads to the following homogeneous system:

$$[\lambda^T \; h^T].\begin{bmatrix} B^T \\ -I_n \end{bmatrix} = 0, \quad \lambda \geq 0, h \geq 0 \qquad\qquad [3]$$

Therefore, algorithm 2 solves the same type of problem as algorithm 1. The difference between Algorithms 1 and 2 lies in the following simplifications at the conceptual implementation level: (a) The vector λ do not need to be memorized (unlike the vectors Y in algorithm 1) since the important aspect of this algorithm are the combinations (p-semiflows): $\lambda^T.B^T = h^T = Y^T \geq 0$; (b) The submatrix $-I_n$ [3] is not included. For this reason, step 2.2 only eliminates those rows whose i-th column in A is negative, unlike algorithm 1 which also eliminates those whose i-th column is positive.

3.2. Conditions for removing non-minimal p-semiflows

The algorithms presented in §3.1 can also generate non-minimal p-semiflows. Two alternative characterizations of non-minimal p-semiflows are given in this section in view to eliminating them. One is based on their supports (proposition 2.2) and the other on the rank of certain submatrices of the original matrix which are associated with each p-semiflow. From these characterizations we get necessary and sufficient conditions for eliminating superfluous rows.

A) Characterization of non-minimal p-semiflows by their supports.

A p-semiflow is non-minimal iff its support contains strictly that of another or it is not canonical (proposition 2.2). In Mathematical Programming this is called *dominance* in [DUFF 74] and *inclusion of sets of indices* in [KOHL 67]. First we look at the implementation in algorithm 1. The implementation in algorithm 2 is analogous, although adapted to the initial problem it solves and fitted to the simplifications which 2 contains compared to 1. For this reason it is presented later.

A first implementation is got by applying proposition 2.2 in the moment the new row is generated. Proposition 3.3 establishes the necessary and sufficient conditions under which a new row generated while annulling column k should not be added to matrix [A | Y]. Let N^k be the net obtained from N by removing transitions k+1, ..., m.

Proposition 3.3. [COLO 89] Let [A | Y] be the matrix of algorithm 1 after annulling k-1 columns, where Y only contains the minimal p-semiflows of N^{k-1}. Let $[a_u \mid y_u]$ be a row obtained (not necessarily the first row) while annulling column k as a combination of $[a_i \mid y_i]$ and $[a_j \mid y_j]$. y_u is a non-minimal p-semiflow of N^k *iff* there exists a row y_e, in Y, such that $y_i \neq y_e \neq y_j$, $\|y_e\| \subseteq \|y_u\|$. ◆

According to proposition 3.3, a new row cannot eliminate any previous one (except in the case of *equality* of supports and then the new one is eliminated). Therefore, we only need to check whether the support of the new p-semiflow contains that of an existing one (the supports do not decrease: *monotony* property). The important remark here is that the comparison of supports *is performed in one direction* (i.e. it is a unidirectional test). By including comparison of supports in algorithm 1 as described, only the minimal p-semiflows of the net N are obtained. This is because initially $\mathbf{Y}$ contains only the minimal p-semiflows of N^0 and therefore, in any subsequent step k, $\mathbf{Y}$ will only contain the minimal p-semiflows of N^k (proposition 3.3).

A second implementation of support comparison is obtained if it is applied after annulling a column or set of columns in algorithm 1 (i.e. after step 2.2). Corollary 3.4 shows the condition to include in this case.

Corollary 3.4. Let $[A \mid \mathbf{Y}]$ be the matrix in algorithm 1 after annulling column k and eliminating all the rows in which the k-th column of submatrix A is non-null. Let $[a_u \mid \mathbf{y}_u]$ be a row of this matrix. $\mathbf{y}_u$ is a non-minimal p-semiflow of N^k iff row $[a_u \mid \mathbf{y}_u]$ was generated while annulling column k and it contains the support of a row $\mathbf{y}_v$ already present in the submatrix $\mathbf{Y}$. ♦

From the above corollary, support comparison should be performed: (1) between the rows generated in step k, to determine whether their support is contained in, or contains that of, any other (bidirectional test) and; (2) between a new row and those generated in the steps before k (unidirectional test).

If support comparison is implemented at the end of the algorithm, it is necessary to compare each p-semiflow with all the others, since they are all new. [MART 81] presents an algorithm in which support comparison is performed after annulling a column or set of columns but, unlike corollary 3.4, each p-semiflow is compared with all the others.

In the published algorithms based on the approach of algorithm 2 [ALAI 82], [TOUD 81] support comparison to eliminate non-minimal p-semiflows is always performed at the end of the algorithm. A possible explanation for the fact that other alternatives have not been developed is that in the intermediate steps of this algorithm, we do not have the minimal p-semiflows of any subnet N^k, in contrast with algorithm 1. This means that a priori it appears that similar conditions to proposition 3.3 or corollary 3.4 cannot be applied.

Below we show how to include support comparison in algorithm 2 analogously to the methods presented for algorithm 1, since the two algorithms are essentially the same. Consider the problem solved by algorithm 2 in the form given in [3]. Applying algorithm 1 to [3] we can calculate its extremal directions $[\lambda^T \; h^T]$. Taking into account that a p-semiflow, Y, is given by $Y^T=h^T=\lambda^T \cdot B^T \geq 0$, proposition 3.5 relates the minimality of the support of Y to the extremal directions $[\lambda^T \; h^T]$ of [3].

Proposition 3.5. [COLO 89] A p-semiflow $Y^T=h^T=\lambda^T \cdot B^T \geq 0$, $\lambda \geq 0$ is non-minimal iff $[\lambda^T \; h^T]$ is a non-extremal direction of the cone defined by [3]. ♦

According to proposition 3.5, the elimination of redundant rows is performed by calculating the extremal directions $[\lambda^T \; h^T]$ of the cone defined by [3], and therefore in the same way as in algorithm 1. The implementation of support comparison in algorithm 2 requires that a diagonal Boolean matrix, I_{n-r}, be adjoined to B^T. This memorizes the support of vector λ of [3]. Thus, the initial matrix is of the form [A | **Y**] and initially $A=B^T$ and $\mathbf{Y}=I_{n-r}$. The combination of rows is performed on the complete matrix [A | **Y**] so that in A the operations are arithmetic, and in **Y** they are logic unions of Boolean vectors. The support of vectors h of [3] is the support of the corresponding rows of A restricted to the set of non-negative columns of A.

On the basis of the above, proposition 3.6 gives the necessary and sufficient conditions under which a p-semiflow is non-minimal in algorithm 2. These correspond to locating the test at the point when new rows are generated. Let $(a_k \mid \mathbf{y}_k)$ be the k-th row of matrix [A | **Y**] and let ($\|a_k\|$/non_negative_columns) be the support of row a_k restricted to the non-negative columns of A.

Proposition 3.6. A row, $[a_j \mid \mathbf{y}_j]$, generated as a combination of two rows of [A | **Y**] is non-extremal (i.e. it will not be added to [A | **Y**]) iff there exists another row, $[a_k \mid \mathbf{y}_k]$, different from the two which generate the j-th row, such that ($\|a_k\|$/non_negative_columns) $\cup \|\mathbf{y}_k\| \subseteq$ ($\|a_j\|$/non_negative_columns)$\cup\|\mathbf{y}_j\|$. ♦

The condition of proposition 3.6 can be found in the field of Mathematical Programming in [CHER 64]. However, here it is presented a slightly different form, and the arguments for the proof are quite different. [KRUC 87] presents an algorithm similar to [CHER 64] and contains the same support comparison.

B) Characterization of the non-minimal p-semiflows based on the rank of certain incidence submatrices of the net.

This characterization was first presented in the field of nets in [MART 81]. An analogous characterization in the field of LP can be found in [MURT 71].

Proposition 3.7 [MART 81]. A p-semiflow Y is minimal iff the cardinal of its support is one unit higher than the rank of the submatrix made up of the rows l_i of C such that Y[i] is not zero. ♦

With this characterization we can decide whether one p-semiflow is minimal without considering the rest. It is a property which can be computed directly on the p-semiflow. However, its direct application is limited by the computational cost of calculating the rank of a submatrix for each p-semiflow.

Proposition 3.7 applies to algorithm 1. Applying it to algorithm 2 simply requires to replace the matrix in the statement ($\begin{bmatrix} B^T \\ -I_n \end{bmatrix}$ instead of C) and replace the p-semiflows Y with the extremal directions $[\lambda^T \ h^T]$ of the cone defined by [3]. Section 5.2 gives a rule which, while taking advantage of this characterization, gives a sufficient condition for non-minimality based on an easily calculated upper bound of the rank of the submatrix.

4. SOME PRELIMINARY QUESTIONS ON IMPLEMENTATION AND PERFORMANCE EVALUATION.

Sections 5 and 6 evaluate the implementations of different variants of the basic algorithms for calculating p-semiflows presented in §3.1. These variants are obtained by adding different algorithmic peculiarities which, a priori, can be expected to improve performance.

In the presentation and subsequent discussion of the implementation of each of the solutions, we start from a basic algorithm to which we gradually add those solutions which have proven to be effective. Thus, in the presentation the algorithm is improved step by step as the discussion advances (incremental improvement). Section 4.1 presents the examples which will be used to evaluate and compare the different variants. Section 4.2 gives the technical characteristics common to all variants, the data structures and the execution environment.

4.1. Examples used to evaluate performance

Each variant will be used to calculate the minimal semiflows of a series of nets, in order to evaluate its effect on the algorithm's performance. The criteria used to select the set of nets are: (1) Nets which model *sufficiently large real systems* for the execution time and memory occupation to be significant; (2) Nets with various *execution problems*: nets which do or do not generate redundant rows, nets with a very small or very large number of semi-flows, etc.; (3) *Parametrable* nets (i.e. while keeping their basic structure, they can be made arbitrarily large by changing a series of parameters such as number of users, resources, ...).

Example	Places	Transit.	Rank(C)	p-semiflows	t-semiflows
MU_0504	20	4	4	1024	1
F1_085	255	170	85	170	85
PC1_4040	242	240	161	81	1600
PC2_3030	242	240	181	62	900
BD_03	34	18	15	133	3
BD_04	61	32	28	1023	4
FE_1515	240	225	210	99	15
TE_02	32	46	20	130	30
TE_03	57	96	39	947	75
B5_03	31	18	15	73	3
B5_04	57	32	28	495	4
B6_04	49	32	28	117	4
B6_05	81	50	45	1104	5

Table 2. Some characteristics of the examples used to evaluate performance

The nets used in this paper are the following (table 2):

MU_0504. The number of minimal p-semiflows is u^m. In the example: u=4, m=5.

F1_085. Models a protocol for the use of shared resources, based on the "dining philosophers" problem ([JENS 87] page 285). It is parametrized by the number of philosophers (users). The example has 85 philosophers.

PC1_4040. Models the interaction of 40 producer processes with 40 consumer processes via a limited capacity store ([MART 84] page 118).

PC2_3030. Models 30 producers and 30 consumers accessing a limited capacity store in mutual exclusion ([TREV 86] page 193).

BD_03, BD_04. Models a data base management system with n managers ([JENS 87] page 268). In the examples n=3 and n=4, respectively.

FE_1515. Models a system of control for a circular railway with u trains and v stretches of line, ([GENR 87] page 208). In the example u=v=15.

TE_02, TE_03. Models a telephone system. The parameter is the number of subscribers. In the examples it is 2 and 3 respectively, ([JENS 87] page 272).

B5_03, B5_04. These are PNs BD_03 and BD_04 respectively from which the implicit place "inactive" has been eliminated (figure 10 in [JENS 87], page 268).

B6_04, B6_05. PNs BD_04, BD_05 respectively without the implicit places "inactive", "waiting" and "performing" ([JENS 87], page. 268, figure 10).

Tables concerning the algorithm performances only contain those examples that are relevants for the considered variant. An extensive analysis can be found in [COLO 89].

4.2. Preliminary comments on the implementations

The basic algorithms and their variants are implement in PASCAL on a VAX 11/750 with operating system VMS v.4.4. Times were measured by equipping the programs with standard operating system routines to capture the CPU process time to a precision of hundredth of a second (times are given in seconds in the tables). During the previous experiments to take measures of time a problem on quality of figures obtained has been observed. The consumption of CPU time of programs to compute minimal p-semiflows is strongly dependent on load of machine, number of memory pages associated to the process and available physical memory. For this, all measures has been obtained in an *ideal environment* whose characteristics are: only one user process in execution simultaneously (i.e. the process to compute the minimal p-semiflows), 4098 pages of memory for the process, 8 Mbytes of central memory. The data structures used were:

a) Matrices A^k and B^k (algorithms 1, 2 of figures 2, 3) were represented by a list of rows, and each row by a list of non-null elements. The reasons for this are: (1) More compact memory, since A^k, B^k are very sparse matrices; (2) The list structure makes it easier to eliminate and add rows;

b) The vector supports were represented by *PASCAL set* structures, with each element accessed by its index. This is due to the efficiency of operations with sets, and to memory compactness.

Numbers and arithmetic operations were in integers, with steps being taken to avoid operations such as multiplication by one or zero.

5. EFFICIENT IMPLEMENTATION OF THE ALGORITHM FOR CALCULATING THE MINIMAL P-SEMIFLOWS STARTING FROM THE FLOW MATRIX

This section analyzes variants of algorithm 1, presented in §3.1. Before, going into detail, it should be pointed out that (as far as we know) there is no "absolute best" version. The following exposition is constructive and explanatory in that variants are progressively introduced to the previous "best" version in order to improve its performance. Reference will be made to [TREV 86] for performance comparison, since it is a recent study of characteristics similar to this paper. However, many of the variants proposed here have no counterpart in [TREV 86]. In the next subsections, several questions will be discussed in order to obtain the "best" algorithm of this type.

5.1. Location of support comparison

The problem addressed here is *where to locate* the elimination of non-minimal semiflows based on support comparison. The basic alternatives are: (1) when a new row is generated, (2) after annulling a column or set of columns, and (3) at the end of the algorithm. Algorithms A1, A2 and A3, described below, implement these variants. In them, to improve their efficiency, the support of each row of Y is memorized as a set of indices. So the support of a new row of Y is the union of the supports of the rows of Y which generate it. Therefore, support comparison can be performed without additional calculations (Note: In these algorithms, the column to annul is selected using the heuristics which proved most efficient, see §5.2).

Algorithm A1: *Location before generating the linear combination of a new row (proposition 3.3)*. Before getting a new row of A ,the support of the new row of Y is calculated. If it contains the support of an existing row (*unidirectional* test), then the combination is not made (a computational saving). The a priori advantage of A1 is that it eliminates redundant rows as they are generated, thus avoiding unnecessary accumulations. However, there are cases in which only minimal semiflows are generated. In these cases, A1 has worse performance than the variants below.

Algorithm A2: *Location after eliminating a column (corollary 3.4)*. The procedure is applied after annulling a column, k, and eliminating all the rows of [A | Y] whose column k in submatrix A is non-null. This algorithm "accumulates" a higher number of rows in [A | Y] than does A1.

Algorithm A3: *Location at the end of the algorithm*. Support comparison is performed between each semi-flow and all the rest (bidirectional test). The disadvantage of this variant is the large number of non-minimal semi-flows which can accumulate. It is included here so as to compare its performance.

[TREV 86] only discusses the variant A2. Table 3 gives the execution times and memory occupations of variants A1, A2 and A3. From the table we can draw the following conclusions:

1) *Examples F1_085, PC1_4040, PC2_3030, B6_05*. Only minimal p-semiflows are generated, and the times for the three variants are comparable (the time difference between A1 and A3 varies between +18.94% for PC2_3030 and -10.32% for B6_05, A2 falls between A1 and A3). In the first three examples, A3 is more efficient since the number of rows throughout the execution is of the order of the initial number, and fewer support comparisons are performed. A1 is the least efficient (even with the unidirectional test!). In B6_05 the terms are inverted due to the explosion of

p-semiflows (from 81 initial rows we get 1104 minimal p-semiflows). Therefore, although A3 performs fewer comparisons, any saving is offset by the bidirectional test. A2 is close to the least favorable situation in each case: in the first three examples, because it performs more tests than A3, and in B6_05, because the test it performs is bidirectional.

Example	Alg.	Max. R.	Elimin.	Comp. T.	%Comp.T.	Total T.
F1_085	A1			3,49	24,14%	14,46
	A2	254	0	3,49	25,40%	13,74
	A3			1,76	14,15%	12,44
PC1_4040	A1			2,83	14,43%	19,60
	A2	241	0	2,83	15,07%	18,78
	A3			0,61	3,57%	17,10
PC2_3030	A1			4,08	16,41%	24,87
	A2	242	0	3,95	16,67%	23,69
	A3			0,50	2,39%	20,91
B6-05	A1			48,49	68,19%	71,11
	A2	1104	0	60,62	75,03%	80,79
	A3			59,02	74,43%	79,30
BD_04	A1	1023	6483	51,15	65,75%	77,80
	A2	6847	6483	12822,43	99,31%	12911,08
	A3	—	—	—	—	—
FE_1515	A1	240	7941	50,99	36,65%	139,12
	A2	529	7941	153,08	31,78%	481,54
	A3	—	—	—	—	—
TE_03	A1	949	117212	472,50	62,08%	761,15
	A2	—	—	—	—	—
	A3	—	—	—	—	—
B5_04	A1	495	2663	14,77	55,09%	26,81
	A2	2863	2663	400,37	92,01%	435,14
	A3	—	—	—	—	—

Max. R.: Max. number of rows of [A I D] which are present at any one time.
Elim.: Total number of redundant rows eliminated by support comparison.
Comp. T.: Total time used in support comparison.
%Comp.T.: Support comparison time as percentage of total execution time.
Total T.: Total algorithm execution time.
— : No measurements possible due to overflow in dynamic data storage.

Table 3. Time performance (in seconds) of variants A1, A2 and A3.

2) *Examples BD_04, FE_1515, TE_03, B5_04.* In this case, the decreasing order of efficiency is always A1, A2, A3. These examples generate a large number of non-minimal p-semiflows. A1 is the most efficient since it eliminates them as they are generated. A3 is the most permissive variant (it filters least), and gives the worst results. So bad in fact that it overflows the assigned memory and the system aborts before concluding! A2's filter is more permissive than A1 but more restrictive than A3. Therefore, computation concludes in several cases. However, performance is quite

poor since the cost of support comparison using corollary 3.4 is quadratic in the number of rows generated.

According to the above results, there is no absolute optimum variant. *A1 is adopted for inclusion in the final solution since it is the most robust* . That is, in the unfavorable cases, the time difference from the others is not excessive, and in cases where a large number of p-semiflows, particularly non-minimal ones, are generated, it has a significant advantage over A2 and A3 (i.e. it performs the calculation in a significantly shorter period, and successfully finishes in cases where the others abort).

5.2. Heuristics for selecting the columns to annul

This section presents *heuristics* whose aim is to limit the number of rows added in each iteration, by selecting the column whose elimination will generate the fewest new rows (the algorithm is valid for any order of column annulment). Let π_k and v_k be the number of positive and negative elements, respectively, of the column k of A which we wish to annul. The number of new rows to add, by combining pairs of rows, is $\pi_k \cdot v_k$. The $\pi_k + v_k$ rows used to annul column k are eliminated at the end of the iteration. The *expansion factor* is the net number of new rows added in annulling column k: $F(k) := \pi_k \cdot v_k - (\pi_k + v_k)$.

Therefore, a priori it might appear "a good policy" to select for annulment the column with lowest expansion factor. However, minimality in the number of rows added *in each iteration* does not guarantee that this choice will be optimum for the algorithm *as a whole* (it is a heuristic). Variant A1 presented in §5.1 contains one of these heuristics. A4, A5, A6 implement additional rules to emphasize the importance of having a good rule of this type (table 4).

Algorithm A1. [MART 84] Select the first column with a negative expansion factor, or if there is none, that with lowest value of $\pi_k.v_k$. Choosing the first one to appear reduces the time of sequential searches through the lists implementing the matrix.

Algorithm A4. The columns are selected in the order they appear in the incidence matrix. This rule can lead to very bad results. This is because it is possible to initially select columns with large expansion factors, thus generating a large number of rows (in table 4 the examples with no numerical data for A4 require more than 1 day of CPU).

Algorithm A5. First select the columns with highest expansion factor. This rule is the extreme case, and leads to very long execution times. As in A4, the reason lies in the number of non-minimal rows generated (note the increase in the number of rows eliminated in comparison with A6 and A1).

Algorithm A6. Select the column with the lowest expansion factor.

Example	Alg.	Max Nº R	Elim. C.	Select T.	Total T.
F1_085	A1			2,87	14,46
	A5	254	0	3,63	15,65
	A6			3,62	15,80
	A4			2,86	14,86
PC1_4040	A1		0	6,03	19,60
	A5	241	80	9,22	35,19
	A6		0	8,04	21,84
	A4		80	6,88	28,31
PC2_3030	A1		0	7,30	24,87
	A5	242	30	9,59	31,14
	A6		0	9,24	26,95
	A4		30	7,63	27,89
BD_03	A1	133	100	0,15	2,95
	A5	238	5511	0,41	45,39
	A6	133	100	0,15	2,97
	A4	541	33744	0,72	254,28
BD_04	A1	1023	6483	0,42	77,80
	A5	—	—	—	
	A6	1023	6483	0,42	78,82
	A4	—	—	—	
FE_1515	A1	240	7941	18,60	139,12
	A5	293	52620	27,68	704,45
	A6	240	7941	18,26	138,61
	A4	240	7656	18,32	174,15
TE_02	A1	130	392	0,27	6,10
	A5	451	73242	3,59	476,12
	A6	130	392	0,29	6,02
	A4	144	1948	0,78	27,84
TE_03	A1	949	117212	2,11	761,15
	A5	—	—	—	—
	A6	949	117212	1,92	768,39
	A4	—	—	—	—
B5_03	A1	73	53	0,11	1,56
	A5	216	4122	0,33	33,08
	A6	73	53	0,10	1,57
	A4	321	15738	0,56	120,17
B6_03	A1	24	0	0,08	0,46
	A5	94	460	0,19	6,11
	A6	24	0	0,06	0,52
	A4	94	460	0,27	8,68
B6_04	A1	117	0	0,26	3,63
	A5	6681	3021480	37,79	58558,6
	A6	117	0	0,30	2,84
	A4	—	—	—	

Max Nº R: Maximum number of rows of [A I D] which are present at any one time.
Elim. C: Total number of p-semiflows eliminated by support comparison.
T. comp.: Total time used in support comparison.
% T.comp.: Support comparison time as percentage of total execution time.
T. total: Total algorithm execution time.
T. select: Total time used to calculate the column to annul
— : Not shown as execution times are higher than 24 hours.

Table 4. Comparison of the different policies for selecting the column to annul.

In table 4, for FE_1515, TE_03, B5_03 and B6_03 the column selection times for A1 are slightly higher than those for A6, which is unexpected. This is due to errors in the measuring system (note that the errors are at the limits of precision, 1 hundredth of a second). A simple statistical study shows that the performance of A1 is normally slightly better than A6. The compromise lies in the fact that column selection is usually faster in A1 (the first column with negative factor), while A6 calculates the expansion factors of all the columns in order to select the column with the lowest. A1 is the solution retained.

5.3. Prior elimination of a maximal set of linearly dependent columns of the incidence matrix C

The number of actively eliminated columns is equal to the rank of C, r (proposition 3.2). The rest of the columns, m-r, are annulled during the annulment of the others. Therefore, one possible improvement could be to initially eliminate m-r linearly dependent columns, since memory occupation is reduced, in polynomial time, to r columns. The row combination time can also be expected to fall. The following variants are considered for implementing this potential improvement:

Algorithm 1. Operate directly on matrix C. (Retained for comparison)

Algorithm 7. Triangularization of C by columns. We get a matrix with r linearly independent columns to which we apply A1.

Algorithm 8. Select r linearly independent columns of C. The chosen columns are with "low" expansion factor. The selection procedure applied is: First choose the column with the lowest factor. Add to the set a column which is linearly independent of those already included and which has the lowest expansion factor of those remaining, until r columns have been chosen.

The triangularized matrix normally has a filling factor (non-null elements over total elements) greater than the case of selecting r linearly independent columns. This is due to operations performed between columns. In the results of A7 (Table 5) we observe the following:

(a) Because of the above, the expected reduction in row combination time, due to the shorter rows, is offset in some cases by the higher number of operations performed;

(b) In some examples, more non-minimal p-semiflows are generated than in A1 (142 compared with 100 in BD_03). This is due to the higher filling factor, which leads to more combinations. This can drastically increase execution time (in BD_04 and TE_03 is more than 24 hours of CPU).

In all cases, the time for selecting the column to annul is significantly lower than A1, due to the shorter rows in the matrix (between 50 and 60% for the examples studied). The balance of the above phenomena, together with the triangularization time, leads to longer times than in A1 for most of the examples (the highest increase is 13.52% for PC1_4040). However, in B6_04 and FE_1515 the times are shorter (20% and 1.62%, respectively). Nevertheless, the existence of examples for which execution time mushrooms (BD_04, TE_03) leads us to rule out solution A7 because it is not robust. In general, we can say that the structure of the incidence matrix should not be altered, as it conditions the evolution of the algorithm. From the time results of A8 (Table 5) we observe the following: (a) Row combination time is lower than for A1. In this case, unlike A7, the reduction is clear, since the columns have not been altered; (b) Support comparison time is lower than for A1 (this reduction is 9.24% for TE_03). This is because non-minimal p-semiflows are eliminated by the first one in the matrix, and support comparison is not extended to all rows (i.e. selecting r linearly independent columns generates the p-semiflows in a different order from A1, in the examples studied here). This new order is advantageous for support comparison.

Example	Alg.	Max.R.	Elim.C.	Reduc.T	Comb.T.	Total T.	Total T.A1
F1_085	A7	254	0	2,14	8,16	14,58	14,46
	A8	254	0	5,66	7,86	18,71	
PC1_4040	A7	241	0	5,07	11,16	22,25	19,60
	A8	241	0	15,30	10,37	33,20	
PC2_3030	A7	242	0	4,84	12,97	26,33	24,87
	A8	242	0	15,55	13,19	39,89	
B6_04	A7	117	0	0,36	1,67	2,95	3,63
	A8	117	0	0,44	1,75	3,08	
BD_03	A7	133	142	0,34	2,39	4,38	2,95
	A8	133	100	0,24	1,60	2,94	
BD_04	A7	—	—	—	—	—	77,80
	A8	1023	6483	0,66	25,90	76,32	
FE_1515	A7	240	7941	5,30	68,00	136,90	139,02
	A8	240	7941	16,64	66,71	149,03	
TE_03	A7	—	—	—	—	—	761,15
	A8	949	117212	1,72	287,45	718,76	

Max. R.: Maximum number of rows of [A I D] which are present at any time.
Elim. C: Total number of p-semiflows eliminated by support comparison.
Total T.: Total algorithm execution time.
Reduc T.: Total time for eliminating linearly dependent columns of C
Comb. T.: Total time for linear combination of rows.
Total T. A1: Total time of algorithm A1.

Table 5. Evaluation of variants for eliminating linearly dependent columns

Column selection time is lower than for A1 and in the same proportion as A7. Therefore, variant A8 has no clear advantages. In most cases, the time difference (positive or negative) is of the order of the time taken to select r linearly independent columns. Only in TE_03 is the difference significative, and this improvement is not due to a reduction in the size of the matrix but to a reduction in the support comparison time thanks to the different order in which the p-semiflows are generated. For these reasons, this variant will not be retained (i.e. at this moment A1 is the retained variant).

5.4. Classification of the matrix rows

The rows of $U=[A \mid \Psi]$ can be classified into matrices $U_{(0)}$, $U_{(+)}$ and $U_{(-)}$ containing the rows of U in which column k of A is null, positive and negative, respectively. To annul column k of A, each row of $U_{(+)}$ is combined with each row of $U_{(-)}$. The new rows are added to matrix $U_{(0)}$. Once column k is annulled, $U_{(0)}$ is the initial matrix U for annulling column k+1. But first, matrices $U_{(+)}$ and $U_{(-)}$ are removed. This solution reduces the number of tests needed to select two rows whose values in column k of A are non-null and of opposite sign. Thus, to annul a column of A needs [nrows·(nrows-1)/2] tests to detect the pair of rows to combine, where nrows is the number of rows before beginning the annulment of the column. In this variant, only [nrows] tests are required to initially separate the rows. This ordering of the calculations also reduces the number of iterations of step 2.1 of algorithm 1 and therefore reduces the index update time, loops test time, etc. Table 6 gives the results for A9. The proposed solution is quite efficient since it gives an improvement over A1 of between 50% (F1_085, PC1_4040, PC2_3030) and 9% (B5_04,TE_03). Therefore, A9 is the retained variant at this moment.

Example	Max. Nº R.	Elim. C	Total T. A9	Total T.A1
F1_085	254	0	6,35	14,46
PC1_4040	241	0	9,85	19,60
PC2_3030	242	0	13,77	24,87
B6_05	1104	0	57,85	71,11
BD_04	1023	6483	67,50	77,80
FE_1515	240	7941	109,48	139,12
TE_03	949	117212	699,63	761,15
B5_04	495	2663	24,42	26,81

Max. Nº R: Max. number of rows of matrix [A I D] present at any one time
Elim. C: Total number of p-semiflows eliminated by support comparison.
Total T. A9: Total time for algorithm A9.
Total T. A1: Total time for algorithm A1

Table 6. Performance of algorithm A9 which classifies the rows of matrix C

5.5. Prior elimination of transitions with only one input and one output place: Elimination of sequences (A10).

Transitions such that $|{}^\bullet t| = |t^\bullet| = 1$ represent pure sequences. Initial elimination of these transitions has the following advantages: (a) The matrix is reduced by one row for each of these transitions, since: $F(k):=(\pi_k \cdot v_k)-(\pi_k+v_k)= -1$; (b) After annulling the column, support comparison is not necessary. In effect, we have generated an intermediate p-semiflow whose support is the only one containing ${}^\bullet t$ and $t^\bullet$ (i.e. if one place in a sequence belongs to a p-semiflow, then so do all the places in the sequence).

Table 7a gives the performance of algorithm A10 which contains this. It is not a significant improvement on A9 (in F1_085 and B5_04 the times appears to be worse, but the difference is within the precision limits of the measuring system). This is because these columns are the first to be selected in A9 because of the column selection rule. Therefore, the time reduction is achieved by inhibiting support comparison. However, these columns are eliminated early in the algorithm, and the number of rows is small, so the saving in time is small. This variant is very effective for calculating t-semiflows, since eliminating sequences annuls all the columns of the matrix (case of examples MU_0504, F1_085, B6_05, BD_03, BD_04, FE_1515 and B5_04).This improvement will be incorporated into later variants.

5.6. Fast test of minimality

By characterizing the non-minimal p-semiflows using the rank of certain submatrices of C, we can reduce the determination of minimality to the p-semiflow itself (§3.2). Therefore, applying this characterization may be of interest. To avoid the cost of computing the rank of these submatrices, we resort to *upper bounds of the rank*, which give only sufficient conditions for minimality.

Corollary 5.1. A p-semiflow Y is non-minimal if card($\|Y\|$)>rank_upperbound+1. ♦

In the sequel we will call this the *fast test of minimality*. It is an initial filter for eliminating non-minimal p-semiflows (sufficient condition), faced to support comparison (necessary and sufficient condition). The goodness of the filter depends on the upper bound of the rank used.

In [MART 81] the upper bound is the *number of non-null columns* of the submatrix composed of the rows of C corresponding to the places belonging to the support of the p-semiflow. Applying it in intermediate stages of the algorithm we use the matrix made up of the actively annulled columns, instead of C. In the context of Mathematical Programming, the upper bound proposed in [KOHL 67] is equal to the number of actively annulled columns. This upper bound is greater or equal than that of [MART 81] since the null columns of the submatrix of C are counted in calculating the upper bound (i.e. it is a poorer filter). This disadvantage is magnified in P/T nets, since the flow matrix is usually sparse, and there are often null columns in the submatrices where the upper bound of the rank is calculated. To implement the rule given in [KOHL 67] we only need to know the cardinal of the support of the p-semiflow and the number of actively annulled columns. Thus, the test simply involves comparing two integers. **Algorithm A12** implements this rule. There are two solutions for implementing the [MART 81] rule:

Algorithm A11a. For each row, *memorize* the union of the supports of the rows of C indexed by the support of the p-semiflow. For a new row it is obtained from the union of the memorized supports for the two rows which generate it.

Algorithm A11b. For each row, *calculate* the union of the supports of all the rows of C indexed by the support of the new p-semiflow.

Then, in both cases, calculate the cardinal of the set obtained, restricted to the columns which have been actively annulled up to that point. This value is the upper bound of the rank. These algorithms bring out the classic tradeoff between execution time and memory occupation. We will not use the solution in algorithm A11b , since A11a gives better time performance at the expense of a small increase in memory occupation (because of the efficient representation of the supports of the p-semiflows by sets). In the examples which only generate minimal p-semiflows, the times for the two algorithms are practically equal. However, in those which generate a large number of non-minimal p-semiflows, the execution time of algorithm A11b can be double that of A11a (for FE_1515 7.941 non-minimal p-semiflows are generated, and the execution time of A11a is 50.10% that of A11b; for TE_03 117.212 non-minimal p-semiflows are generated, and the execution time of A11a is 72.20% that of A11b).

Table 7 gives the results for A10, A11a and A12. The times for calculating the upper bounds are included in the times for annulling a column (column T.L.C. in table 7). We can draw the following conclusions from the table:

1) The fast test of minimality improves performance in those cases where a large number of non-minimal p-semiflows are generated, since the test eliminates many of them, thus avoiding the need for support comparison. In B5_04, 100% of the non-minimal p-semiflows are eliminated by this test, with a time reduction of 22.07% compared to A10 (without test). For TE_03 the test eliminates 75% of the non-minimal p-semiflows, and the time reduction is 30.19% with respect to A10.

a) Algorithm A10.

Example	C.A	M.R.		E.C.	TES	T.L.C.	T.S.	T.S.C.	T.E±	T.T.
MU_0504	4	1103		0	0,00	6,33	0,01	20,32	0,04	26,70
F1_085	85	257		0	0,06	3,06	0,28	2,89	0,26	6,55
PC1_4040	161	241		0	4,07	3,85	0,17	1,22	0,54	9,85
PC2_3030	181	242		0	2,97	6,36	0,61	2,25	0,86	13,05
B6_05	45	1367		0	0,56	16,15	0,02	39,59	0,20	56,52
BD_03	15	159		100	0,01	1,45	0,07	1,04	0,06	2,63
BD_04	28	1188		6483	0,01	23,51	0,09	42,17	0,22	66,00
FE_1515	210	243		7941	0,09	59,01	3,64	43,37	3,55	109,66
TE_03	39	1477		117212	0,13	242,20	0,22	448,18	1,45	692,19
B5_04	28	604		2663	0,02	11,10	0,14	13,10	0,15	24,51

b) Algorithm A11 (fast test of minimality from [MART 81]) [SOLUTION A11a]

Example	C.A	M.R.	E.T	E.C.	TES	T.L.C.	T.S.	T.S.C.	T.E±	T.T.
MU_0504	4	1103	0	0	0,01	8,09	0,00	21,79	0,05	29,93
F1_085	85	257	0	0	0,07	3,21	0,31	3,04	0,30	6,93
PC1_4040	161	241	0	0	4,00	3,77	0,29	1,18	0,52	9,76
PC2_3030	181	242	0	0	2,92	6,73	0,74	2,34	0,88	13,61
B6_05	45	1367	0	0	0,59	17,74	0,02	40,40	0,19	58,94
BD_03	15	158	56	44	0,01	1,73	0,00	0,84	0,08	2,66
BD_04	28	1187	2839	3644	0,02	29,56	0,08	37,49	0,21	67,36
FE_1515	210	243	1392	6549	0,09	68,60	3,60	40,86	3,66	116,81
TE_03	39	1477	88062	29150	0,13	270,72	0,19	210,61	1,54	483,19
B5_04	28	603	2663	0	0,02	10,97	0,07	7,89	0,15	19,10

c) Algorithm A12 (fast test of minimality from [KOHL 67])

Example	C.A	M R.	E.T.	E.C.	TES	T.L.C.	T.S.	T.S.C.	T.E±	T.T.
MU_0504	4	1103	0	0	0,01	7,64	0,00	21,40	0,07	29,12
F1_085	85	257	0	0	0,07	3,32	0,31	2,82	0,25	6,77
PC1_4040	161	241	0	0	4,19	3,84	0,26	1,08	0,51	9,88
PC2_3030	181	242	0	0	3,04	6,76	0,70	2,24	0,86	13,60
B6_05	45	1367	0	0	0,61	17,84	0,02	39,42	0,20	58,09
BD_03	15	159	1	99	0,02	1,69	0,02	1,05	0,09	2,87
BD_04	28	1188	1	6482	0,02	32,31	0,10	43,15	0,24	75,82
FE_1515	210	243	745	7196	0,09	68,29	3,58	42,35	3,69	118,00
TE_03	39	1477	71326	45886	0,13	279,71	0,19	261,45	1,50	542,98
B5_04	28	604	1	2662	0,02	14,28	0,07	13,15	0,23	27,75

C.A.	:	Number of actively annulled columns (rank of C)
M.R.	:	Peak number of rows present at any one time during the algorithm
E.T.	:	Number of rows eliminated using the fast test of minimality
E.C.	:	Number of rows eliminated using support comparison
TES	:	Time for eliminating place-transition-place sequences
T.L.C.	:	Time for linear combinations of pairs of rows
T.S.	:	Time for selecting the column to annul
T.S.C.	:	Time for support comparison
T.E ±	:	Time for elimination of matrices $U^k_{(+)}$ and $U^k_{(-)}$
T.T.	:	Total Time for the algorithm

Table 7. Performance of the algorithm which starts from the incidence matrix C, with algorithms A11 and A12, which use the fast test of minimality.

2) In the examples which only generate minimal p-semiflows, the perturbation introduced by the test never exceeds 7% of the execution time with respect to A10 (the maximum perturbation arises for FE_1515 with 6.5%).

3) The upper bound of the rank proposed in [MART 81] is more efficient than that of [KOHL 67] in all the cases which generate non-minimal p-semiflows, both in terms of the number of rows eliminated, and of total execution time. In some cases which do not generate non-minimal p-semiflows, the [KOHL 67] rule perturbs the algorithm least, as expected, due to its lower calculation requirements (the comparison only involves two integers).

Therefore, the solution in algorithm A11 will be added into the final algorithm.

5.7. Conclusions

From the variants on algorithm 1 evaluated in previous sections, the following improvements will be used to obtain the "best" algorithm of this type:

1) Support comparison (§5.1) before generating a new row as a linear combination of two other rows. The test is unidirectional (i.e. it checks if the support of the new p-semiflow contains that of any existing one).
2) Select the column to annul using the rule (§5.2): First column with a negative expansion factor or, if there is none, that with the lowest value of $\pi_k \cdot \upsilon_k$.
3) Classification of the rows of the matrix (§5.4), before annulling column k, into 3 matrices which group the rows whose column k is zero, negative or positive, respectively.
4) Prior elimination of sequences ($\{t \mid |\bullet t|=1 \wedge |t\bullet|=1\}$).(§5.5).
5) Fast test of minimality (§5.6) using the upper bound proposed in [MART 81].

Algorithm 1 presented in figure 1 incorporates these characteristics. To summarise, this algorithm is considered to be the "best" because:

1) It *calculates* the minimal p-semiflows for a broad range of nets, even though there are many redundant rows (*robustness*). This is due to the early elimination of non-minimal p-semiflows (economy of memory).
2) Although other variants are more efficient for some nets, the time difference with respect to this algorithm is not significant. However, these variants are not capable of completing the algorithm with some examples for which algorithm 1 (figure 1) gives reasonable performance.

ALGORITHM 1 Computation of p-semiflows
0. Annul all columns k of U^0 in which $\pi_k=v_k=1$
1. Select the first non-null column k of U^0 such that $\pi_k \cdot v_k- (\pi_k+v_k)<0$ or a column k which minimizes $\pi_k \cdot v_k$.
2. **While k≠null do**
3.   Move the rows j of U^{k-1} such that $A^{k-1}[j,k]=0$ to U^k
4.   Move the rows j of U^{k-1} such that $A^{k-1}[j,k]<0$ to $U_{(-)}$
5.   Move the rows j of U^{k-1} such that $A^{k-1}[j,k]>0$ to $U_{(+)}$
6.   row 1:= index_first_row $(U_{(-)})$
7.   **While** row 1 ≠ null **do**
8.   row 2:=index_first_row $(U_{(+)})$
9.   **While** row 2 ≠ null **do**
10. $\|Y\| := \|\Psi_{(-)}[\text{row } 1,-]\| \cup \|\Psi_{(+)}[\text{row } 2,-]\|$ {Compute support of the new p-semiflow Y}
11.   **If** cardinal $(\|Y\|)\leq$ rank_upperbound + 1 **Then**
12.   **If** $\|Y\|$ does not contain the support of another p-semiflow of Ψ^k or $\Psi_{(+)}$ or $\Psi_{(-)}$
13.   **Then** Add $\alpha \cdot U_{(-)}[\text{row } 1,-]+\beta \cdot U_{(+)}[\text{row } 2,-]$ to U^k where $\alpha=|A_{(+)}[\text{row } 2,k]|$ and $\beta=|A_{(-)}[\text{row } 1,k]|$
14.   Divide the new row by the h.c.d. of the non-null elements
15.   Memorize $\|Y\|$
                    EndIf
                  EndIf
16.   row 2:=index_next (row 2)
            EndWhile
17.   row 1:=index_next (row 1)
        EndWhile
18.   Eliminate all rows of $U_{(+)}$ and $U_{(-)}$
19.   Select the first non-null column of U^k such that $\pi_k \cdot v_k - (\pi_k+v_k)<0$ or a column k which minimizes $\pi_k \cdot v_k$
    EndWhile

Notation
C   the PN incidence matrix (dimensions nxm and rank r)
I   identity matrix nxn
U^k matrix $[A^k | \Psi^k]$ where
        for k=0 A^k=C and Ψ^k=I
        for k>0 A^k is the matrix resulting from annulling k columns of C
                  Ψ^k is the matrix which memorizes the coefficients of linear combinations of rows of C
$U_{(-)}$ the matrix which contains the rows of U^{k-1} whose k-th column is negative
$U_{(+)}$ the matrix which contains the rows of U^{k-1} whose k-th column is positive
π_k,v_k the number of positives and negatives in column k of A^k

Figure 1. Algorithm for calculating the minimal p-semiflows starting from the incidence matrix C, incorporating the improvements from section 5.

3) The performance of algorithm 1 (Figure 1) is significantly better than the algorithms given in [TREV 86] (these were implemented on C in a VAX 11/750 with operating system UNIX Berkeley 4.2, while the algorithms presented here were implemented in PASCAL on the same machine with operating system VMS 4.4). For the purposes of comparison, for example BD_03 the time in [TREV 86] is 31.48 sec; here it is 2.66 sec. For the example PC2_2020 in [TREV 86] 102.80 seconds, while here it is 7.13 seconds. In both cases the improvement is more than one order of magnitude.

It is interesting to note that the prior elimination of sequences is extraordinarily effective for calculating minimal t-semiflows, since in the examples F1_085, B6_05, BD_03, BD_04, FE_1515, B5_04, it is not then necessary to apply the full algorithm. Furthermore, in no example are non-minimal t-semiflows generated, which must be due to the different logic underlying t-semiflows in "models of real systems".

6. EFFICIENT IMPLEMENTATION OF THE ALGORITHM FOR CALCULATING THE MINIMAL P-SEMIFLOWS, STARTING FROM A BASIS OF P-FLOWS

6.1. Potential improvements to introduce into the algorithm

This section analyzes the variants of algorithm 2 (§3.1) in the same way as section 5 did for algorithm 1. The aim is to introduce a series of potential improvements. Some of these are taken directly from section §5 since they have the same effect on algorithm 2, due to its similarity to algorithm 1. These are:

1) Rule for selecting the column to annul. Select the first column k for which $\pi_k \cdot v_k - v_k < 0$ (the difference between this expansion factor and that in algorithm 1 is that here it only eliminates rows whose column k is negative) or which minimizes $\pi_k \cdot v_k$. The comments made in §5.2 are applicable here.
2) Classification of the rows of the matrix into three matrices in which the column to be annulled is zero, positive and negative, respectively. Unlike §5.4, at the end of the iteration, only the matrix in which the column is negative is eliminated.
3) Elimination of non-minimal p-semiflows. We use the conditions presented in proposition 3.6. Support comparison is located before generating the linear combination to get the new row. The reasons for this are analogous to those given in §5.1, and are based on analogous computational results.
4) Application of the fast test of minimality, using the upper bound of the rank from [MART 81]. This corresponds to the number of non-null columns in the submatrix $\begin{bmatrix} B^T \\ -I_n \end{bmatrix}$

which is associated with the direction $[\lambda^T h^T]$ of the cone in equation [3] of §3.2. To calculate it we simply determine the cardinal of the set resulting from the union of the following sets of column indices, restricted to columns annulled in the current iteration: (a) Union of the supports of the rows of B^T whose index belongs to the support of λ; (b) Support of the new row to add (which coincides with the union of the supports of I_n whose index belongs to the support of h).

6.2. Choosing the initial basis of p-flows

One particularly delicate point in implementing this algorithm is choosing the initial basis of p-flows. Considerations here are analogous to that presented in §5.3. In §3.1 the only condition imposed on it was that it should have the form B=[E | D] where D is a positive diagonal matrix with dimensions (n-r) x (n-r) (r is the rank of the flow matrix C). [ALAI 82] and [TOUD 81] give algorithms for calculating these basis in the context of calculating p-semiflows from a basis of p-flows. However, the basis obtained by these algorithms later lead to extraordinarily large execution times and memory occupations during the calculation of p-semiflows!. This is because these algorithms make no effort to get basis in which the matrix E is as sparse as possible. As a result, the columns of this matrix normally have high expansion factors, and are very likely to generate numerous non-minimal p-semiflows. In other words, as in §5.3, the efficiency of these algorithms for calculating p-semiflows in P/T nets depends on the initial matrices being quasi-empty. Therefore, any operation which tends to fill the initial matrices will normally give rise to a disproportionate increase in the number of rows generated, and will give poor performance in practice. Below is an heuristic algorithm for calculating a basis, whose aim is to get a basis B=[E | D] in which the matrix E is "as sparse as possible".

Algorithm. Computation of Basis B=[E | D] with "a small" filling factor for E.
1. A:=C, F:=I_n
2. Select a column k of A for which $\pi_k = v_k = 1$. If none exists, select a column k for which $\pi_k \cdot v_k$ is minimum.
3. **While k≠null do**
   3.1. Select the first row of [A | F] whose column k in A is non-null. Let j be the index of this row.
   3.2 Add to the matrix [A | F] all the rows resulting from linear combination of row j with rows of [A | F] whose k-th column of A is non-null and the result of which annuls the k-th column of A. Note: If both rows have the same sign in column k, the one which changes sign to annul column k is j.
   3.3 Eliminate from [A | F] all rows in which the column k of A is non-null.
   3.4 Select a column k of A for which $\pi_k = v_k = 1$. If none exists, select a column k for which $\pi_k \cdot v_k$ is minimum.
4. The rows of matrix F are a basis of p-flows of the PN of the form F=[E | D] where D is positive diagonal.

The above algorithm triangularizes the incidence matrix C by treating only r (the rank of C) columns. Each of the triangularization stages pivots on a different row, which is eliminated, since no further operations are performed on it. At the end, r different rows of matrix C have been pivoted on, leaving n-r rows with null value, which have not been pivoted on. Therefore, n-r columns of F make up a positive diagonal submatrix of the basis. Steps 2 and 3.4 of the algorithm seek to perform as few operations as possible on the rows in order to keep the resulting basis as empty as possible. For this purpose, the algorithm selects those columns which require fewest combinations for their elimination: $\pi_k = v_k = 1$ or minimum $(\pi_k \cdot v_k)$.

6.3. Algorithm performance

Table 8 shows the execution time and memory occupation for algorithm 2, with the improvements presented here for calculating minimal p-semiflows. We observe the following:

(1) In general, the time taken to calculate the basis is small compared with the total time (0.88% for TE_03). However, for PC1_4040 and PC2_3030 it is 80% of the total. This is because the minimal p-semiflows form a basis of the p-flow space. Therefore, most of the time is used in calculating a basis, and the algorithm for calculating p-semiflows merely transforms it to get a non-negative basis;

Example	C.A.	M R.	E.T.	E.C.	T.B.	T.L.C.	T.S.	T.S.C.	T.T.
MU_0504	4	1026	0	0	0.10	8.29	0.02	19.54	27.95
F1_085	85	171	0	0	3.45	2.95	1.27	1.34	9.01
PC1_4040	40	81	0	0	13.28	1.89	0.53	0.23	15.93
PC2_3030	60	62	0	0	18.94	3.20	0.88	0.28	23.30
B6_05	5	1362	0	0	0.91	20.19	0.05	40.32	61.47
BD_03	9	143	82	18	0.28	1.64	0.06	0.61	2.59
BD_04	16	1116	5664	819	0.69	30.71	0.06	28.80	60.26
FE_1515	210	151	1297	6359	25.94	150.98	3.47	28.12	208.51
TE_03	14	1060	32541	1547	1.29	113.29	0.08	31.92	146.58
B5_04	16	534	2330	333	0.56	13.04	0.11	6.98	20.69

C.A.	:	Number of actively annulled columns
M R.	:	Maximum number of rows present at any one time during algorithm
E.T.	:	Number of rows eliminated by the fast test of minimality
E.C.	:	Number of rows eliminated by support comparison
T.B.	:	Time for calculating a base of p-flows
T.L.C.	:	Time for linear combinations of pairs of rows
T.S.	:	Total time used to calculate the column to annul
T.S.C.	:	Time for support comparison
T.T.	:	Total Time for algorithm

Table 8. Performance of the algorithm which starts from a basis of p-flows.

ALGORITHM 2   Computation of minimal p-semiflows
0.   Select the first non-null column k of B^o such that $\pi_k v_k - v_k < 0$ or, if none exists, the first for which $\pi_k \cdot v_k$ is minimum.
1.   **While** k≠null **do**
2.   Move the rows j of U^{k-1} such that $B^{k-1}[j,k]=0$ to U^k
3.   Move the rows j of U^{k-1} such that $B^{k-1}[j,k]<0$ to $U_{(-)}$
4.   Move the rows k of U^{k-1} such that $B^{k-1}[j,k]>0$ to $U_{(+)}$
5.   row 1:=index_first_row $(U_{(-)})$
6.   **While** row 1 ≠ null **do**
7.   row 2:=index_first_row $(U_{(+)})$
8.   **While** row 2≠null **do**
9. $\|Y\|=\{\|U_{(-)}[row1,-]\| \cup \|U_{(+)}[row2,-]\|\} \cap \{non\text{-}negative\ columns\}$
10.   **If** cardinal$(\|Y\|) \leq$ rank_supremant + 1
                     Then
11.   **If** the support of the new p-semiflow does not contain that of any of U^k, $U_{(-)}$ or $U_{(+)}$ {prop.3.6}
12.   **Then** Add $\alpha \cdot B_{(-)}[row\ 1,-] + \beta \cdot B_{(+)}[row\ 2,-]$ to B^k where $\alpha=|B_{(+)}[row\ 2,k)]|$ and $\beta=|B_{(-)}[row\ 1,k]|$
13.   Divide the new row by the g.c.d. of the non-null elements
14.   Add $(\|\lambda\|_{(-)}[row\ 1] \cup \|\lambda\|_{(+)}[row\ 2])$ to $\|\lambda\|^k$
                     EndIf
                     EndIf
15.   row 2:=next_index (row 2)
                EndWhile
16.   row 1:=next_index (row 1)
           EndWhile
17.   Eliminate all rows of $U_{(-)}$
18.   Add to U^k all the rows of $U_{(+)}$
19.   Select the first non-null column of B^k s. t. $\pi_k v_k - v_k < 0$ or, if none exists, the first for which $\pi_k v_k$ is minimum.
     EndWhile

Notation
B^T a basis of p-flows [dimensions (n-r)xn where r is the rank of C]. $B^T = [E \mid D]$ where D is a positive diagonal matrix.
U^k matrix $[B^k \mid \|\lambda\|^k]$ where   for k=0, $B^k = B^T$ and $\|\lambda\|^k_i = \{i\}$ $\forall i=1,..,$ n-r
                              for k>0, B^k is the matrix resulting from annulling k columns of B^T .
$\|\lambda\|^k$ is a vector of sets, each of which memorizes the rows of B^T which generated the corresponding row of B^k
$U_{(-)}$ matrix containing the rows of U^{k-1} in which the k-th column of B^{k-1} is negative
$U_{(+)}$ matrix containing the rows of U^{k-1} in which the k-th column of B^{k-1} is positive
π_k,v_k the number of positives and negatives in column k of B^k

Figure 2. Algorithm for computing the minimal p-semiflows, from a basis of p-flows.

(2)   In some examples, the number of actively annulled columns is very small in relation to the number of places (in B7_04, 3 actively annulled columns compared with 37 places; the rank of C is 28). This effect can be explained by the column selection rule used in calculating the basis. Selecting columns k of C for which $\pi_k = v_k = 1$ generates

p-flows in which the two places belong to the sequence (transition t_k) characterizing that column have positive coefficients . If the places ${}^\bullet t_k$ and $t_k{}^\bullet$ satisfy $|({}^\bullet t_k){}^\bullet| = |{}^\bullet(t_k{}^\bullet)|=1$ then this is the only p-flow which will contain them, and the column will be non-negative.

(3) The fast test of minimality is as efficient as in algorithm 1, and filters a large number of non-minimal p-semiflows before support comparison is performed.

In the case of calculating t-semiflows, in many cases a basis of t-flows is itself the generator set for minimal t-semiflows. Figure 2 gives the final algorithm for this approach, including the improvements discussed here. The algorithm starts from a basis of p-flows calculated using the algorithm given above.

7. PERFORMANCE COMPARISON OF THE "BEST" ALGORITHMS

A comparative analysis, using the time and memory occupation data from tables 7 (A11) and 8, of the algorithm adopted as the "best" in each of the two approaches, we draw the following conclusions:

(a) *Neither algorithm can be considered better than the other.* Algorithm 1 in figure 1 is significantly better than algorithm 2 (figure 2) for FE_1515; the opposite is true for TE_03;

(b) *The execution times are of the same order of magnitude* the difference between them varying between +43.97% and -69.66% for the examples here. Unfortunately, we have no way of knowing, a priori, which of the algorithms will be more efficient for a given net. In fact, the theoretical models of complexity we can built actually give so big figures that almost no practical information is obtained.

8. CONCLUSIONS

By identifying the concept of minimal p-semiflows in P/T nets with that of the extremal direction of a cone in Mathematical Programming we bridge the gap between these rather separate disciplines. The domain of PNs contributes the interpretation and use of these concepts in modeling and analysis of complex concurrent systems. The mutual ignorance of these disciplines has led to each developing its own algorithms for calculating minimal p-semiflows. This is not the only instance of this rediscovery phenomenon. The basic Fourier (or Fourier-Motzkin) algorithm has been reinvented a surprising number of times. Probably, it is the algorithm which has most often been renamed!. This has occurred not only in Mathematical Programming, but also in such distant fields as Mathematical Logic [LANG 27]. The algorithms for calculating minimal p-semiflows are of identical nature to those in the field of Mathematical Programming. However, they have some characteristics peculiar to type of problems handled in the domain of nets.

In this work has been shown that there exists two basic approaches, that leads to many different algorithms, to compute minimal p-semiflows in P/T nets. But essentially only one common basic scheme is underlying to both approaches: The Fourier-Motzkin Method. The first uses the flow matrix as its starting point [MART 81] and the other uses a base of p-flows [ALAI 82], [TOUD 81]. The performance analysis sought to find the most *efficient* and *robust* algorithm for each approach. This analysis was presented on incrementally studying the different alternatives given for non-minimal p-semiflow elimination, heuristics, etc., (§5 and §6).

This paper makes several contributions to the problem of calculating minimal p-semiflows:

(1) It gives two original implementations of these algorithms, one starting from the incidence matrix, C, and the other from a base of p-flows, B;

(2) The algorithms' performance has been found to exceed that of the algorithms given in recent studies such as [TREV 86]; even in more than one order of magnitude!

(3) The two algorithms are conceptually very close. The basic differences are in some simplifications introduced to handle the particular problems dealt with in each case. In general, they are found to be comparable in terms of performance, although one may be better than the other for a particular case.

At the time this paper has been written we have no way of knowing, a priori, which algorithm will perform better on a particular problem.

ACKNOWLEDGEMENTS

The authors are indebted to four anonymous referees whose comments and suggestions helped us in improving the final version of the paper. This work was supported in part by the DEMON Esprit Basic Research Action 3248, and the Plan Nacional de Investigación Grant TIC-0358/89

REFERENCES

[ALAI 82] ALAIWAN H.,MEMMI G.: Algorithmes de Recherche des Solutions Entieres Positives d'un Systeme Lineaire d'Equations Homogenes. *Revue Technique-CSF,vol.14, nº 1*, Mars, pp. 125-135.

[APN 87] *Petri Nets: Central Models and their Properties. Advances in Petri Nets 1986, Proceedings of an Advanced Course*, Bad Honnef, September 1986. LNCS 254, Springer Verlag, Berlin.

[BALI 61] BALINSKI, M.L.: An Algorithm for Finding all Vertices of Convex Polyhedral Sets. *SIAM IX*, pp. 72-78.

[BRAM 83] BRAMS G.W.: *Réseaux de Petri. Theorie et pratique* , Masson, Paris.

[CHER 64] CHERNIKOVA N.V.: Algorithm for Finding a General Formula for the Nonnegative Solutions of a System of Linear Equations, *U.S.S.R. Computational Mathematics and Mathematical Physics IV*, pp. 151-156.

[CHVA 83] CHVATAL V.: *Linear Programming*, W.H. Freeman and Company, New York, 1983.

[COLO 89] COLOM J.M.: *Métodos de análisis estructural de Redes de Petri basados en Programación Lineal y Geometría Convexa*. Tesis Doctoral. Universidad de Zaragoza. June 1989.

[DANT 63] DANTZIG G.B.: *Linear Programming and Extensions*. Princeton University Press.

[DINE 27] DINES L.L.: On Positive Solutions of a System of Linear Equations, *Annals of Mathematics 28*, pp. 386-392.

[DUFF 74] DUFFIN R.J.: On Fourier's Analysis of Linear Inequality Systems, *Mathematical Programming Study 1*, American Elsevier Publishing Company, New York, pp. 71-95.

[DYER 77] DYER M.E., PROLL L.G.: An Algorithm for Determining All Extreme Points of a Convex Polytope. *Math. Programming XII*, pp. 81-96.

[FARK 02] FARKAS J.: Theorie der einfachen Ungleichungen. In: *Journal für die reine und andgewandte Mathematik*, 124, pp. 1-27.

[FOUR 1826] FOURIER J.B.J.: Solution d'une Question Particuliere du Calcul des Inegalités. In *Oeuvres II*, pp. 317-328, Gauthier-Villars, Paris.

[GENR 87] GENRICH H.J.: Predicate/Transition Nets. In [APN 87], pp. 207-247.

[HADL 62] HADLEY G.: *Linear Programming*. Addison Wesley, Reading, Massachusetts.

[JENS 87] JENSEN K.: Coloured Petri Nets. In [APN 87], pp. 248-299.

[KANN 79] KANNAN, R., BACHEM A.: Polynomial Algorithms for Computing the Smith and Hermite Normal Forms of an Integer Matrix. *SIAM J. Comp.*, vol. 8, pp. 499-507.

[KOHL 67] KOHLER D.A.: Projections of Convex Polyhedral Sets. *Report ORC 67-29, Operations Research Center*, University of California at Berkeley.

[KRUC 87] KRUCKEBERG F., JAXY M.: Mathematical Methods for Calculating Invariants in Petri Nets, *Advances in Petri Nets 1987 (Ed. Grzegorz Rozenberg) LNCS 266*, Springer Verlag.

[LANG 27] LANGFORD C.H: Some Theorems on deducibility.*Annals of Mathematics* I,28, pp.16-40.

[MANA 68] MANAS M., NEDOMA J.: Finding All Vertices of a Convex Polyhedron. *Numer. Math. XII*, pp.226-229.

[MART 81] MARTINEZ J., SILVA M.: A Simple and Fast Algorithm to Obtain all Invariants of a Generalized Petri Net. *Second European Workshop on Application and Theory of Petri Nets*, Bad Honnef, September, pp. 411-422.

[MART 84] MARTINEZ J.: *Contribución al Análisis y Modelado de Sistemas Concurrentes mediante Redes de Petri*. Tesis Doctoral . Universidad de Zaragoza, Octubre 1984.

[MATH 73] MATTHEISS T.H.: An Algorithm for Determining Irrelevant Constraints an All Vertices in Systems of Linear Inequalities. *Operations Res. 21*, pp. 247-260.

[MATH 80] MATHEISS T.H.,RUBIN D.S.: A Survey and Comparison of Methods for Finding all Vertices of Convex Polyhedral Sets *Mathematics of Ops. Res.*, Vol.5, No.2, May, pp.167-185.

[MEMM 78] MEMMI G: *Fuites et semiflots dans les réseaux de Petri*. Thése de Docteur Ingenieur. Univ. Pierre et Marie Curie, Paris VI, Paris, Decembre.

[MOTZ 36] MOTZKIN T.S.: *Beitrage zur Theorie der Linearen Ungleichungen*, Doctoral Thesis, University of Zurich.

[MURT 68] MURTY K.G.: Solving the Fixed Charge Problem by Ranking the Extreme Points. *Operations Res. XVI*, pp. 268-279.

[MURT 71] MURTY K.G.: Adjacency on Convex Polyhedra, *SIAM. Rev. XIII*, pp. 377-386.

[SILV 85] SILVA M.: *Las Redes de Petri en la Automática y la Informática*. Editorial AC, Madrid.

[SILV 87] SILVA M., COLOM J.M.: On the Computation of Structural Synchronic Invariants in P/T nets, *Advances in Petri Nets 1988 (g. Rozenberg, ed.), LNCS 340*, Springer Verlag, Berlin, pp 386-417.

[TOUD 81] TOUDIC J.M.: *Algorithmes d'analyse structurelle de réseaux de Petri*. These 3éme Cycle, Université Pierre et Marie Curie, Paris VI, Octobre.

[TREV 86] TREVES N.: *Le Calcul d'Invariants dans le Réseaux de Petri a Predicats Transitions Unaires*. Thése de Docteur de 3éme cycle, Univ. de Paris-Sud, Centre d'Orsay, Novembre, Paris.

[WILL 76] WILLIAMS H.P.: Fourier-Motzkin Elimination Extension to Integer Programming Problems. *Journal of Combinatorial theory (A) 21*, pp. 118-123.

[WILL 86] WILLIAMS H.P.: Fourier's Method of Linear Programming and its Dual, *American Mathematical Monthly*, Nov. 1986, pp. 681-695.

IMPROVING THE LINEARLY BASED CHARACTERIZATION OF P/T NETS

J.M. Colom and M. Silva

Dpto. Ingeniería Eléctrica e Informática - Universidad de Zaragoza
María de Luna, 3 (Actur) 50015 ZARAGOZA (Spain)

ABSTRACT. The state equation is a linear description of the reachable markings and firing count vectors of a P/T net. It has the disadvantage that its solution space, in general, includes additional integer unreachable or/and unfirable vectors. As a result, the analysis of properties using this linear characterization, usually leads to necessary or sufficient conditions for satisfying it, but not both. The appearance of these spurious solutions is due to the fact that the state equation does not take into account the order in which transitions fire.

The existence of methods which *a priori* eliminate spurious solutions of the direct state equation would bring structural verification methods closer to behavioural methods. Two elimination methods are presented here. Both are based on adding to the state equation linear restrictions which (partially) check the transition firing rule.

The first consists of checking that every marking which is a solution of the state equation has a sequence of predecessor markings, and that the transition firing rule holds in that sequence. The second is based on the addition of implicit places to the net [SILV 85] which are linearly non-redundant in the state equation. Some of these places are associated to initially marked traps, and the elimination of unreachable markings they perform is based on a well-known fact: initially marked traps remain always marked. The reasoning on structural deadlocks leads to the complementary fact: initially unmarked deadlocks remains always unmarked. In this case the linear restrictions are based on the annullation of marking variables belonging to places in the deadlock. Last but not least, another important point is the characterization by means of one single Linear Programming Problem (LPP) of those implicit places which are structurally implicit. The interesting fact here is that the theoretical complexity to solve a LPP is polynomial and the practical complexity is linear [SAKA 84].

Keywords: Linear descriptions of P/T nets, Structural analysis of P/T nets, Linear state equation, Spurious solutions, Implicit place, Structurally implicit place, Cutting implicit place, Deadlocks and Traps, Linear Programming.

CONTENTS

1. INTRODUCTION

One of the main problems in a linearly based analysis of properties of a P/T net (i.e. analysis from linear invariants or from the net state equation) is that, in general, one can get either necessary or sufficient conditions, but not both (semidecision algorithm). This is because the set of integer marking vectors that satisfies the linear invariants is greater than the set of reachable markings of the P/T net. To illustrate this we consider the net of figure 1.a. The set of reachable markings (obtained by playing the token game from the initial marking) is presented in figure 1.b by means of white boxes. The integer marking vectors that satisfy the marking invariants [there is only one linear invariant: $2 \cdot m(p_1) + m(p_2) + m(p_3) + m(p_4) + m(p_5) = 2$] are the reachable ones and some non-reachable integer marking vectors represented by shaded boxes. These last vectors will be called *spurious solutions*.

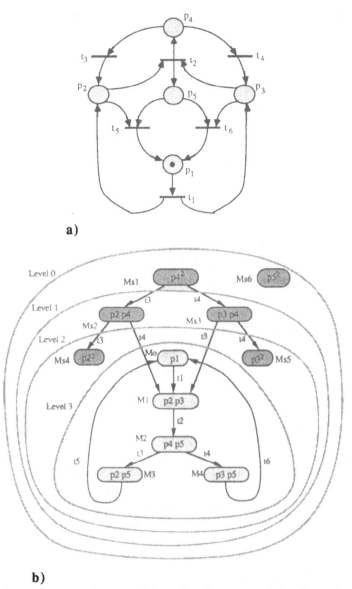

b)

Figure 1. a) Binary, live net. b) Potential reachability graph of the figure 1.a net [Notes: (1) The meaning of lines named "Level i" will be given in §3; (2) The shaded nodes correspond to unreachable integer marking solutions].

The elimination of spurious integer solutions is clearly of great interest: a linearly based analysis can fail because of these solutions. That is, after removing spurious solutions it is possible to conclude in some cases in which previously it was not possible. In the example of figure 1.a, if we try to verify that the initial marking is a home state, by means of the linearly based procedure presented in [JOHN 87], we do not conclude because of the spurious solutions M_{s4}, M_{s5} and M_{s6} (they are total deadlocks, figure 1.b). Later, it is proved that the initial marking is a home state by removing previously all the spurious solutions.

The purpose of this work is to eliminate spurious solutions of the net state equation by adding linear restrictions designed to incorporate necessary conditions derived from the transition firing rule. Evidently, the firing rule cannot be considered in its entirety, since this, in the general case, is equivalent to building the graph of the net's reachable markings. This would undermine one of the basic advantages of using the state equation for analysis: the fact that it is a compact, linear description.

Two methods, based on different principles, are developed in order to remove some but in general not all spurious solutions. The first (§3) consists in proving the existence of a sequence of predecessor markings, of a given length, for each marking vector which is a solution of the state equation. The method checks the transition firing rule in this sequence. One of the disadvantages of this method is the rapid increase in the dimension of the resulting system of equations as a function of the length of the studied sequence.

The second method (§5) is based on the addition to the net of some structurally implicit places [SILV 80]. Their initial marking is computed to be the minimum that make them implicit. If the corresponding marking variables are not redundant in the convex set theory sense [LUEN 72], they will eliminate spurious solutions from the direct state equation. In other words, the new state equation (obtained by adding implicit places to the direct state equation) improves the characterization of the P/T net behaviour: spurious firing count vectors and, eventually, spurious marking vectors are eliminated. The explanation, in net terms, of why some of these implicit places eliminate unreachable markings is based on the existence of a set of places associated with each implicit place which is an initially marked trap. Since an initially marked trap cannot be unmarked, the state equation solutions which are eliminated are those marking vectors in which the traps have markings smaller than a residual minimum value.

Each method involves a different approach to introducing the firing rule into the state equation, and both do so partially. In spite of this only partial introduction, in practice they lead to very good linear representations of the net, in the sense that in many cases the integer solutions of the new system of equations are almost exclusively the reachable markings and characteristic vectors of the firing sequences of the net.

This paper is organized as follows. Section 2 presents the concepts and notations to be used in the paper, together with different linear descriptions of a net and relations between them. Special emphasis is put on the limitations of the state equation to describe the behaviour of a net. Section 3 develops the first method for eliminating spurious solutions. It leads to a classification of the state equation integer solution space. In the case of structurally bounded nets, the maximum length of the sequence which must be considered to attain the maximum improvement is finite. Section 4 introduces the concept of implicit and structurally implicit places. A structurally implicit place (SIP) is characterized by means of a single Linear Programming Problem (LPP). This LPP will be the basis for the discussion in §5. Section 5 develops the method based on the addition of implicit places. The first task it to characterize the implicit places which allow solutions of the state equation (not necessarily integer) to be eliminated. By interpreting the reasons why some of these places eliminate unreachable markings, it is deduced that at least one of their sets of implying places is a marked trap.

2. BASIC CONCEPTS AND NOTATIONS

2.1 Generalities

The general objective of this preliminary section is to introduce the main notation regarding P/T nets that is used in the sequel (following [BEST 85] and [SILV 85]).

A *place/transition net*, N, is a fourtuple, $N=<P,T,Pre,Post>$, where $P=\{p_1,p_2,...,p_n\}$ is the set of places, $T=\{t_1,t_2,...,t_m\}$ is the set of transitions ($P \cap T = \emptyset$), and *Pre* (*Post*) is the pre (post) incidence function representing the input (output) arcs Pre: $PxT \rightarrow \mathbb{N}$(Post : $PxT \rightarrow \mathbb{N}$), and $\mathbb{N} = \{0,1,2,3,...\}$.

A function $M: P \rightarrow \mathbb{N}$ is called a *marking*. A *marked P/T net*, $<N,M_0>$, is a P/T net, N, with an initial marking M_0. A transition $t \in T$ is *enabled at* M iff for all $p \in P: M(p) \geq Pre(p,t)$. If $t \in T$ is enabled at a marking M, then t may be *fired* yielding a new marking M' given by the equation: $M'(p)=M(p)-Pre(p,t)+Post(p,t)$ for all $p \in P$ (this definition is also called the transition firing rule). $M[t>M'$ denotes that M' is reached from M by firing t.

A finite sequence of transitions, $\sigma=t_1t_2 ...t_u$, is a *finite firing sequence* of $<N,M_0>$ iff there exists a sequence $M_0t_1M_1t_2M_2... t_uM_u$ such that for all i, $1 \leq i \leq u: M_{i-1}[t_i> M_i$. Marking M_u is said to be *reachable* from M_0 by firing σ: $M_0[\sigma>M_u$. An infinite sequence of transitions, $\sigma=t_1t_2t_3...$, is an *infinite firing sequence* of $<N,M_0>$ iff there exists a sequence $M_0t_1M_1t_2....$ such that for all i, $1 \leq i: M_{i-1}[t_i>M_i$.

Let $R(N,M_0)$ be the set of all markings reachable from M_0. Let $L(N,M_0)$ be the set of all firing sequences and their suffixes in $<N,M_0>$: $L(N,M_0)=\{\sigma \mid M[\sigma>$ and $M \in R(N,M_0)\}$.

Let: * $\bar{\sigma}:T\to\mathbb{N}$ be σ's *characteristic vector* (i.e. the Parikh mapping of σ) whose i-th component, $\bar{\sigma}(t_i)$, is the number of occurrences of transition t_i in σ.

* PRE=$[a_{ij}]$ ($1\leq i\leq n$, $1\leq j\leq m$), where a_{ij}= Pre(p_i,t_j), be the pre-incidence matrix of the net. PRE(p) (PRE(t)) will denote the row (column) of the pre-incidence matrix corresponding to place p (transition t).

* POST=$[b_{ij}]$ ($1\leq i\leq n$, $1\leq j\leq m$), where b_{ij}=Post(p_i,t_j), be the post-incidence matrix of the net. POST(p) [POST(t)] will denote the row [column] of the post-incidence matrix corresponding to place p [transition t].

* C=$[c_{ij}]$ ($1\leq i\leq n$, $1\leq j\leq m$), where c_{ij}=Post(p_i,t_j) - Pre(p_i,t_j), be the incidence matrix of the net. C(p) [C(t)] will denote the row [column] of the incidence matrix corresponding to place p [transition t].

* $\bullet p$ [$p\bullet$] be the *Pre-set [Post-set] of p:* $\bullet p$={t I Post(p,t)$\neq$0} [$p\bullet$={t I Pre(p,t)$\neq$0}].

* $\bullet t$ [$t\bullet$] be the *Pre-set [Post-set] of t:* $\bullet t$={p I Pre(p,t)$\neq$0} [$t\bullet$={p I Post(p,t)$\neq$0}].

A marked net <N,M_0> is said to be *(marking) bounded* iff there exists a finite $k\in\mathbb{N}$ such that for all place p_i and for all reachable marking M, M $\in$ R(N,M_0), M(p_i) $\leq$ k (if k=1 the marked net is called *binary*). A net is *structurally bounded* if it is bounded for each initial marking, M_0. A transition t$\in$ T is *live* in <N,M_0> iff for all M $\in$ R(N,M_0), there exists M' $\in$ R(N,M) such that M' enables t. The marked net <N,M_0> is *live* iff all t$\in$ T are live (i.e. liveness in nets guarantees the possibility of infinite activity of all the transitions in the net). N is *structurally live* iff there exists M_0 such that <N,M_0> is live.

An *R-component* (Repetitive component) is a function (vector) X:T$\to\mathbb{N}$ such that X$\neq$0 and C·X$\geq$0. A *T-flow* is a function (vector) X:T$\to\mathbb{Z}$ such that X$\neq$0 and C·X=0. Non negative T-flows are called *consistent components* or *T-semiflows*. A *P-flow* is a function (vector) Y:P$\to\mathbb{Z}$ such that Y$\neq$0 and Y^T·C=0. Non negative P-flows are called *conservative components* or *P-semiflows*. ||X|| [||Y||] is called the *support of* X [Y] iff ||X||={t$\in$ T I X(t)$\neq$0} [||Y||={p$\in$ P I Y(p)$\neq$0}]. An (R-component, P-flow) T-flow, I, of N is called *minimal* iff there exists no (R-component, P-flow) T-flow I' of N with ||I'|| $\subset$ ||I||. A net is *repetitive* iff there exists an R-component, X, such that X$\geq$1. A net is *consistent* iff there exists a T-flow, X, such that X$\geq$1. A net is *conservative* iff there exists a P-flow, Y, such that Y$\geq$1. A *pure net* is a P/T net such that for all p $\in$ P: $\bullet$p $\cap$ p$\bullet$ = $\emptyset$. A *Marked Graph* (MG) is a P/T net such that for all p$\in$ P I$\bullet$pI=Ip$\bullet$I=1. A *State Graph* (SG) is a P/T net such that for all t$\in$ T I$\bullet$t I=It$\bullet$I=1.

2.2 On linearly based descriptions of P/T nets

Let C be the incidence matrix of a pure marked net <N,M_0>. From the definition of C and the transition firing rule the following equivalence holds: M[t_i>M' *iff* M'=M+C.e_i

(this relation is called *state equation* of the P/T net) where M, $M' \in R(N, M_0)$, and $e_i: \{1,...,m\} \to \{0,1\}$ such that $e_i[j] = 0$ for all $j \neq i$ and $e_i[i]=1$. Let M_f be a reachable marking from M_0 through a firing sequence $\sigma = t_1 t_2 \ldots t_f$. Writing the state equation for $i=1, 2, \ldots, f$ and summing them up, we obtain: $M_f = M_0 + C \cdot \sum_{k=1}^{f} e_k$, which can be rewritten as $M_f = M_0 + C.\bar{\sigma}$, where $\bar{\sigma} = \sum_{k=1}^{f} e_k$ is the characteristic vector of σ. Therefore, the existence of a nonnegative integer vector $\bar{\sigma}$ satisfying the last expression is a necessary condition for M_f to be reachable from M_0. In other words, if we consider the system of equations presented below where M and $\bar{\sigma}$ are vectors of variables, every reachable marking of the net $<N, M_0>$ is a solution of it.

$$[S^0] \qquad \boxed{\begin{array}{l} M = M_0 + C \cdot \bar{\sigma} \\ M \geq 0, \ \bar{\sigma} \geq 0 \end{array}}$$

This linear system is usually but inappropiately called the *state equation* associated with the marked P/T net $<N, M_0>$. A marking M' is called *potentially reachable* iff M' is an integer solution of the state equation (i.e. $\exists \ \bar{\sigma} \in \mathbb{N}^m$ such that $M' = M_0 + C \cdot \bar{\sigma} \geq 0$). The set of potentially reachable markings can be represented by means of a graph, where the nodes are the integer marking solutions of the state equation. Two nodes M and M' are connected by a directed arc iff there exists a transition $t \in T$ such that $M[t > M'$. This graph is called *Potential Reachability Graph* (PRG). The following two remarks show limits of the state equation as description of the net behaviour:

1) There can be potentially reachable markings which are unreachable markings of the net.

2) The vector $\bar{\sigma}$ does not uniquely define a sequence σ, with the result that information on the order of transition firing has been lost, and this information is fundamental for studying certain net properties, like liveness.

Example 2.1. Limitations of the state equation for describing a net.

The integer solutions of the state equation of the net in figure 1.a are the vectors shown in figure 1.b. If $M_0 = (10000)$, the markings M_{si} ($i=1..6$) are not reachable since there is no σ firable from M_0 which leads to these markings. Therefore, every $\bar{\sigma}$ which satisfies the state equation for M_{si} ($i=1..6$) represents firing sequences which at some point violate the transition firing rule. For example, the vector $\bar{\sigma}_{s1} = (320011)$ satisfies the state equation for M_{s1}. However, none of the sequences characterized by $\bar{\sigma}_{s1}$ are applicable: From M_0 transitions t_1, $t_2 \in \|\bar{\sigma}_{s1}\|$ can fire. After firing t_1, t_2 only t_3 or t_4 is firable, but since they do no appear in $\|\bar{\sigma}_{s1}\|$ any subsequent firing of transitions of $\|\bar{\sigma}_{s1}\|$ will violate the firing rule. ♦

The state equation gives a linear representation of the P/T net. Alternative linear representations of the reachable markings have been used in the literature by means of marking invariants of the net. They are obtained by premultiplying the state equation by vectors Y which are left anullers of C (i.e. $Y^T \cdot C = 0 \Rightarrow Y^T \cdot M = Y^T \cdot M_0$). The following are three different linear representations of the reachable markings:

a) Potentially Reachable markings defined by the net State equation, $PR^S(N,M_0) = \{M \mid M = M_0 + C \cdot \bar{\sigma}, M \geq 0, \bar{\sigma} \geq 0\}$.

b) Potentially Reachable markings defined by a Basis of linear invariants, $PR^B(N,M_0) = \{M \mid B^T \cdot M = B^T \cdot M_0, M \geq 0,$ the columns of matrix B are a basis of p-flows$\}$.

c) Potentially Reachable markings defined by the set of minimal non negative invariants, $PR^{\Psi}(N,M_0) = \{M \mid \Psi^T \cdot M = \Psi^T \cdot M_0, M \geq 0,$ the columns of matrix Ψ are the minimal p-semiflows$\}$.

Proposition 2.1 [COLO 89]. Let $<N,M_0>$ be a marked P/T net.

1) $R(N,M_0) \subseteq PR^S(N,M_0) \subseteq PR^B(N,M_0) \subseteq PR^{\Psi}(N,M_0)$.

2) If N is consistent, $PR^S(N,M_0) = PR^B(N,M_0)$.

3) If N is conservative, $PR^B(N,M_0) = PR^{\Psi}(N,M_0)$.

4) If N is structurally bounded and structurally live, $PR^S(N,M_0) = PR^B(N,M_0) = PR^{\Psi}(N,M_0)$.

5) If N is a marked graph (MG), $PR^S(N,M_0) = PR^B(N,M_0)$. If the MG is strongly connected, $PR^B(N,M_0) = PR^{\Psi}(N,M_0)$ and if it contains at least a token in each circuit, $R(N,M_0) = PR^S(N,M_0)$.

6) If N is a state graph (SG), $PR^B(N,M_0) = PR^{\Psi}(N,M_0)$. If the SG is strongly connected, $PR^S(N,M_0) = PR^B(N,M_0)$ and if it contains at least one token, $R(N,M_0) = PR^S(N,M_0)$. ◆

Proposition 2.1 establishes that a description of the reachable markings based on $PR^S(N,M_0)$, $PR^B(N,M_0)$ or $PR^{\Psi}(N,M_0)$ in general implies the existence of elements in these sets which are unreachable markings. Because of these unreachable markings, it may not be possible to ascertain whether a property holds for a given net, even though it may in fact hold. That is, one can get either necessary or sufficient conditions, but not both (semidecision algorithm). Two examples of this are given below.

Example 2.2. Determination of the bound of place p4 in figure 1.a.

The bound of place p4 in figure 1.a can be calculated from the following LPP [SILV 87],

$$\begin{array}{ll} \max & e_{p4}^T \cdot M \\ \text{s.t.} & M = M_0 + C \cdot \bar{\sigma} \\ & M \geq 0, \bar{\sigma} \geq 0 \end{array}$$

where e_{p4}: $P \rightarrow \{0,1\}$ such that $e_{p4}[p]=0$ for all $p \neq p_4$ and $e_{p4}[p_4]=1$. An optimum solution of this LPP is: $M_{op}^T=(00020)$ and $\bar{\sigma}_{op}^T= (320011)$. Therefore, we conclude that the bound of p_4 is 2. However, M_{op} is an unreachable marking, as shown in example 2.1, and the real bound is one (see figure 1.b). ◆

The above example considered a quantitative property, and gave a non reachable upper bound of the real value of the place marking. In the case of qualitative properties, the existence of spurious solutions may prevent one concluding a property holds, even though the net may verify it (example 2.3).

Example 2.3. Study of the deadlock-freeness in the P/T net in figure 1.a.

The net in figure 1.a will be deadlock-free **if** the three systems shown below have no solution. Each one of these systems represents a different marking pattern for which no transitions can be fired in an ordinary P/T net (i.e. a net where the arcs have a weight equal to one) [MART 84]. For example, in system [1] the additional restrictions to the state equation mean that the following transitions cannot be fired: t_1 since $M[p_1]=0$; t_2 and t_5 since $M[p_2]=0$; t_2 and t_6 since $M[p_3]=0$; and, t_3 and t_4 since $M[p_4]=0$ (i.e. all transitions are unfirable).

$\exists$ M s.t. $M=M_0+C\cdot\bar{\sigma}$		$\exists$ M s.t. $M=M_0+C\cdot\bar{\sigma}$		$\exists$ M s.t. $M=M_0+C\cdot\bar{\sigma}$
	$M{\geq}0, \bar{\sigma}{\geq}0$		$M{\geq}0, \bar{\sigma}{\geq}0$	$M{\geq}0, \bar{\sigma}{\geq}0$
[1]	$M[p_1]=0, M[p_2]=0$	**[2]**	$M[p_1]=0, M[p_2]=0$	**[3]** $M[p_1]=0, M[p_3]=0$
	$M[p_3]=0, M[p_4]=0$		$M[p_4]=0, M[p_5]=0$	$M[p_4]=0, M[p_5]=0$

The above systems have the following marking solutions, [1]: $M^T=(00002)$, [2]: $M^T=(00200)$, [3]: $M^T=(02000)$. That is, one cannot conclude regarding the absence of deadlocks. However, the above solutions are unreachable markings (see figure 1.b). Later, it will be shown how a more precise linearly based description of that net allows to conclude that it is deadlock free using the same method. ◆

3. REMOVING POTENTIALLY REACHABLE MARKINGS WITHOUT PREDECESSORS

3.1. Basic Principle

The method developed in this section to remove spurious solutions is based on a necessary condition for a marking M to be reachable from M_0, via a sequence σ with characteristic vector $\bar{\sigma}$. It consists in verifying the existence of a potentially reachable marking M'≥0 which allows M to be reached by firing a transition t ∈ ||σ̄||, M'[t >M. That is, the last transition of sequence σ is t, σ=σ₀t, and therefore σ̄=σ̄₀+e_t, where e_t is the characteristic firing vector of t. According with this, the outlined reachability condition follows the scheme: M₀+C.σ̄₀=M'[t >M (i.e. M'∈ PR^S(N,M₀) and firing t keeps the transition firing rule). This is a necessary condition, since σ̄₀ is a characteristic vector for which there may be no admissible firing sequence. The markings M which satisfy the above criterion are characterized by the following system of equations:

$$
[S^1_0] \quad
\begin{array}{lll}
[1] & M'=M_0+C\cdot(\bar{\sigma}-e) & \{\text{Reachability of M' from } M_0\} \\
[2] & M=M'+C\cdot e & \{\text{Reachability of M from M'}\} \\
[3] & 1^T\cdot e = 1 & \{\text{M is reached from M' by firing one transition} \in ||e||\} \\
[4] & M'\geq PRE\cdot e & \{\text{Verification of the firing rule for } ||e||\} \\
[5] & \bar{\sigma}-e\geq 0 & \{\text{Condition for non-negativity of } \bar{\sigma}_0\} \\
[6] & M',M\geq 0,\ \bar{\sigma},e\geq 0 & \{\text{Conditions of non-negativity}\}
\end{array}
$$

where e is the characteristic firing vector of one single transition t∈||σ̄||. Evidently, σ̄₀= σ̄-e. If n is the number of places and m is the number of transitions the system [S^1₀] has 3n+m+1 equations and 2n+2m variables. The introduction of some trivial algebraic modifications into [S^1₀] leads to the system [S^1], which is more compact since it does not contain the vector M'. It has 2n+m+1 equations and n+2m variables:

$$
[S^1] \quad
\begin{array}{lll}
[1+2] & M=M_0+C\cdot\bar{\sigma} & \\
[2+4] & M-POST\cdot e\geq 0 & [2+4=4-1] \\
[3] & 1^T\cdot e=1 & \\
[5] & \bar{\sigma}-e\geq 0 & \\
[6] & M\geq 0,\ \bar{\sigma}\geq 0,\ e\geq 0 &
\end{array}
$$

[S^1] shows that, in order to satisfy the transition firing rule, restrictions must be added to the state equation. These new equations permit some spurious solutions of the state equation to be removed (solutions M of the net state equation without predecessor markings). This elimination is only partial, since the existence of sequences with characteristic vector σ̄₀ (example 3.1) is not verified.

Example 3.1. Elimination of solutions of the state equation using [S^1].
Vectors M_{s1} and M_{s6} (Fig. 1b) are not solutions of the system [S^1]. This is due to the fact that no solution of the original state equation allows them to be reached by firing a transition. By computing the bound of place p_4 taking [S^1] into account, we conclude that the marking bound of p_4 is one (see example 2.2). Solutions M_{s2}, M_{s3}, M_{s4} and M_{s5} are not eliminated since the vector M_{s1} is a solution of the original state equation which allows

these markings to be reached. This shows that the transition firing rule is only partially considered. ◆

Nevertheless, it should be pointed out that for non reversible nets (in particular, for non consistent nets) $[S^1]$ can exclude the initial marking [see Fig. 1.a with $M_0=(00020)^T$]. Moreover, the following is trivially true: $R(N,M_0) \subseteq PR^{(1)}(N,M_0) \cup \{M_0\} \subseteq PR^S(N,M_0)$, where $PR^{(1)}(N,M_0)$ is the set of solutions M of $[S^1]$.

The scheme outlined in $[S^1]$ could have been obtained by decomposing $\bar{\sigma}$ into two non-negative vectors, $\bar{\sigma}=\bar{\sigma}_0+\bar{\sigma}_1$. This would lead to a system similar to $[S^1{}_0]$ of the form:

$$[S'] \quad \boxed{\begin{array}{l} M'=M_0+C\cdot(\bar{\sigma}-\bar{\sigma}_1) \\ M=M'+C\cdot\bar{\sigma}_1 \\ 1^T\cdot\bar{\sigma}_1 > 0, \quad \bar{\sigma}-\bar{\sigma}_1 \not\geq 0 \\ M\geq 0, \ M'\geq 0 \\ \bar{\sigma}\geq 0, \ \bar{\sigma}_1 \geq 0 \end{array}}$$

The system $[S']$ is less restrictive than $[S^1]$. In fact, $[S']$ only eliminates vectors $M=M_0+C\cdot\bar{\sigma}$ for which every σ with characteristic vector $\bar{\sigma}$ leads to intermediate markings with a negative component. Thus, for example, M_{s1} is a potentially reachable marking in figure 1.b, it is not a solution of $[S^1]$ but it is a solution of $[S']$ with $\bar{\sigma} = (320011)$, $\bar{\sigma}_1 = (210011)$, $M'=M_0+C\cdot(\bar{\sigma}-\bar{\sigma}_1)=(00011)^T$ and $M_{s1}=M'+C\cdot\bar{\sigma}_1$. If the net is consistent, it can be proven that no spurious solution is eliminated by $[S']$.

3.2. Generalizing the scheme

In the preceding section the existence of *one* predecessor marking for every potentially reachable marking was considered. This scheme can be generalized to the existence of *a sequence* of k predecessor markings. That is, a marking M is reachable if it satisfies the state equation for a $\bar{\sigma}\geq 0$ such that $\bar{\sigma} = \bar{\sigma}_0 + e_k + ... + e_1$ (where e_i, i=1..k, is the characteristic vector of one single transition) and in the intermediate steps the transition firing rule is kept. Therefore, a necessary condition for M to be reachable is to verify that there exist $M_1, M_2, ..., M_k \geq 0$ such that: $M_0 + C\cdot\bar{\sigma}_0 = M_1[t_1>M_2[t_2> .... M_{k-1}[t_{k-1}>M_k[t_k>M$ (i.e. $t_i \in \|e_i\|$, i = 1..k). The algebraic expression of this condition leads to the system $[S^k]$ presented below. Denoting $PR^{(k)}(N,M_0)$ as the set of solutions M of $[S^k]$, for all P/T net $<N,M_0>$ the following holds: $R(N,M_0) \subseteq PR^{(k)}(N,M_0) \cup \{M_0\} \cup \{M_0[t_i>\} \cup...\cup \{M_0[t_1...t_k>\} \subseteq ... \subseteq PR^{(1)}(N,M_0) \cup \{M_0\} \subseteq PR^S(N,M_0)$.

$$[S^k]$$

$$M = M_0 + C \cdot \overline{\sigma}$$
$$M - POST \cdot e_1 \geq 0$$
$$M - C \cdot e_1 - POST \cdot e_2 \geq 0$$
$$\bullet \bullet \bullet \bullet \bullet \bullet$$
$$M - C \cdot \left(\sum_{i=1}^{k-1} e_i \right) - POST \cdot e_k \geq 0$$
$$1^T \cdot e_i = 1 \ , \ \forall \, i = 1 \dots k$$
$$\overline{\sigma} - \sum_{i=1}^{k} e_i \geq 0$$
$$M \geq 0, \overline{\sigma} \geq 0, e_i \geq 0, \ \forall \, i = 1 \dots k$$

$[S^k]$ represents an iterative scheme for which, depending on the desired degree of confidence in the conclusions of the structural verification of a property, the number of steps, k, to be considered in the system $[S^k]$ can be chosen. The disadvantage of this technic is the rapid increase of the dimensions of this system on increasing the length of the predecessor marking sequence: For a sequence of length k, $(k+1) \cdot n + m + k$ equations and $n + (k+1) \cdot m$ variables are involved. This method can be extremely effective for some nets (e.g. for some nets for which the only integer solutions of $[S^k]$ are the reachable markings and the characteristic vectors of the firing sequences, see examples 3.2 & 3.3).

Example 3.2. Net in which the integer marking solutions of $[S^2]$ are the reachable markings.

The PRG of the net in figure 2.a is shown in figure 2.b. Let $M_0^T = (01100100)$. The markings M_{s1}, M_{s2} and M_{s3} are unreachable. To eliminate these solutions, sequences of length 2 should be considered in $[S^k]$ (i.e. the only integer solutions of $[S^2]$ are the reachable markings). Unfortunately, the dimension of $[S^2]$ is 32 equations and 26 variables, while that of the state equation is 8 equations and 14 variables. An interesting aspect of this example comes to light when we calculate the bound of the place p_2. Using the state equation, this is found to be 2 (due to M_{s1} and M_{s2}). In the system $[S^2]$, M_{s1} and M_{s2} have been eliminated and therefore, the bound on this place is one. However, the maximum marking of p_2 in the convex set which defines the solution space of $[S^2]$ in $\mathbb{R}^+$ is: $M_s^T = (1/2 \ 3/2 \ 1/2 \ 0 \ 0 \ 1 \ 0 \ 0)$, $\overline{\sigma}_s^T = (0 \ 1 \ 1 \ 1/2 \ 1/2 \ 1/2)$; which maintains that p_2 is binary since the markings are integers (i.e. using real arithmetic, we reach the same conclusions as in integer arithmetic, with a lower computational cost). ♦

Example 3.3. In fig. 1.b we can see that for the net in figure 1.a, we need to consider $k = 3$ in $[S^k]$. ♦

The method presented induces a binary relation, $\Re$, on the set of potentially reachable markings defined as: Two potentially reachable markings M_i and M_j are related, $M_i \, \Re \, M_j$, iff they have the same maximum sequence length of predecessor marking vectors. Because this relation is based on the equality of integers, it leads to an equivalence relation (i.e. reflexive, symmetric and transitive properties are trivially verified). Therefore, according to relation $\mathfrak{R}$, the set of integer solutions of the state equation is classified into a set of classes or levels. Each level is formed of solutions with the same maximum sequence length of predecessor marking vectors. In the examples given here, the graphs of integer solutions show this classification by means of a series of concentric closed lines. The vectors between two consecutive lines make up a class or level. If the lines are numbered inwards starting from zero, these numbers represent the length of the longest sequence of predecessor markings for the vectors enclosed between one line and the next, with the exception of the innermost line (e.g. see figure 1.b).

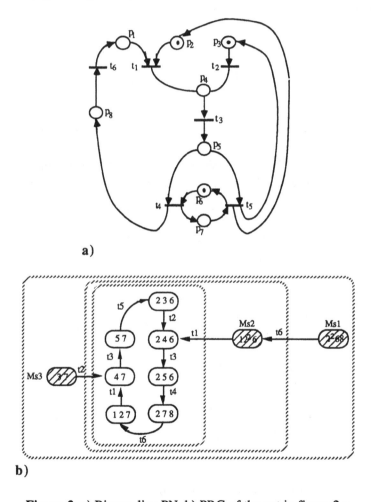

Figure 2. a) Binary, live PN. b) PRG of the net in figure 2.a.

One of the limitations of the proposed method is the existence of nets in which the state equation has unreachable markings but where $[S^k]$ does not eliminate, whatever is k, the sequence length considered. These cannot be eliminated since they have an infinite sequence of predecessor markings. The boundedness in the number of levels of the potential reachability graph is an interesting question. A trivial answer to this problem is the following result: If N is structurally bounded, the number of levels in the PRG is bounded (in fact it is bounded by the number of integer solutions of the state equation). For some unbounded P/T nets, the number of levels can be infinite since the set of integer solutions is infinite. Unfortunately, it has not been possible to find a method which, a priori, allows to calculate the length of the predecessor marking sequence to consider in equation $[S^k]$ (in fact, such a method may not exist in general). In [COLO 89] a property is presented that establishes the point beyond which no further increase in the sequence length allows any more integer solutions of the state equation to be eliminated (saturation).

4. STRUCTURALLY IMPLICIT PLACES

An implicit place is one which never restricts the firing of its output transitions. Let N be any net and N_p be the net resulting from adding a place p to N. If M_o is an initial marking of N, $M_o \cup m_o(p)$ denotes the initial marking of N_p. The incidence matrix of N is C and l_p is the incidence vector of place p. The state equation of the net N_p is:

$$[S] \quad \boxed{\begin{array}{l} M - C \cdot \bar{\sigma} = M_o \\ m(p) - l_p \cdot \bar{\sigma} = m_o(p) \\ M \geq 0, \ m(p) \geq 0, \ \bar{\sigma} \geq 0 \end{array}}$$

Definition 4.1. (Implicit place [SILV 85]). Given a net $<N_p, M_o \cup m_o(p)>$, the place p is implicit (IP) iff $L(N_p, M_o \cup m_o(p)) = L(N, M_o)$ [i.e. it preserves the firing sequences]: $\forall M \in R(N, M_o)$, **if** $M \geq PRE[t_k]$ **then** $m(p) \geq pre(p, t_k)$. ♦

A place is an IP depending on the initial marking, M_o. Places which can be implicit for any M_o are said to be structurally implicit.

Definition 4.2. (Structurally implicit places). Given a net N_p, the place p is structurally implicit (SIP) iff for all M_o of N, there exists an $m_o(p)$ such that p is an IP in $<N_p, M_o \cup m_o(p)>$. ♦

Example 4.1. Differences between IP and SIP.
The place p is an IP in both nets in figure 3, which are live and bounded. In figure 3.b the place p is a SIP since for all M_o p is an IP if $m_o(p) \geq m_o(p2) + m_o(p3)$ (removing it does not alter the net's firing sequences). However, the place p in figure 3.a is not a SIP since if

$M_0 = (1\,0\,0\,1\,1\,0\,0\,0\,1)$, for p to be an IP requires that $m_0(p)=\infty$. Thus, the sequence $t_2t_4t_6$ can fire an infinite number of times in the net without the place p. ♦

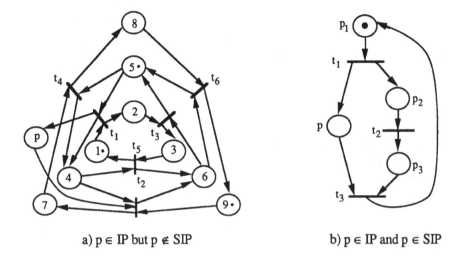

a) $p \in IP$ but $p \notin SIP$ b) $p \in IP$ and $p \in SIP$

Figure 3. Difference between an implicit place and a structurally implicit place.

The literature contains two approaches to SIPs: (a) [BERT 87] in which only a direct instrumentalization of the concept of non-extremal variable from Convexity Theory [LUEN 72] is used (see [COLO 89] where this is discussed). Sufficient conditions for a place to be an SIP are given; (b) [SILV 85] uses the preservation of firing sequences to obtain a necessary and sufficient condition for a place to be a SIP.

This paper follows the approach presented in [SILV 85] together with a contribution from Linear Programming Theory (LP). Firstly, necessary and sufficient conditions for a place to be a SIP are given. Then the conditions for which these places are IPs for a given M_0 are presented. The use of Linear Programming allows alternative proofs and, what is more important, a polynomial time computation algorithm to decide if a place is SIP and to compute an upper bound of the minimum initial marking that makes it implicit.

Theorem 4.1. A place p is a SIP in N_p iff there exists $Y \geq 0$ such that $Y^T \cdot C \leq l_p$. ♦

Proof
⇒) Let p be a SIP and $\nexists$ $Y \geq 0$, $Y^T \cdot C \leq l_p$. Therefore, $\exists X \geq 0$ such that $C \cdot X \geq 0$ and $l_p \cdot X < 0$ (Alternatives Theorem [SAKA 84]). Let there be an M_0 which allows a sequence σ to fire in N such that $\bar{\sigma} = X$ (e.g. $M_0 = PRE \cdot X$). Then, σ can fire an infinite number of times (since $C \cdot X \geq 0$). Adding p to N, $\bar{\sigma} = X$ can fire an infinite number of times, only if $m_0(p) = \infty$ [since $m(p) = m_0(p) + l_p \cdot \bar{\sigma} = m_0(p) + l_p \cdot X < m_0(p)$]. That is, p is not an IP for at least one M_0 and therefore is not a SIP.

$\Leftarrow$) Let p be a place such that $\exists Y \geq 0$ and $Y^T \cdot C \leq l_p$. Premultiplying [S] by $[Y^T \mid -1]$ the following equation is obtained: $m(p) = Y^T \cdot M + (l_p - Y^T \cdot C) \cdot \bar{\sigma} + [m_o(p) - Y^T \cdot M_o]$. For any M_o of N, if t_k is a transition such that: $t_k \in p\bullet$, $M \in R(N, M_o)$ and $M[t_k > M'$, choose $m_o(p)$ satisfying $m_o(p) \geq Y^T \cdot M_o + \max\{pre(p, t_i), \forall t_i \in p\bullet\}$. This implies using the previous equation that $m(p) \geq pre(p, t_k)$ [since $Y^T \cdot M \geq 0$, $(l_p - Y^T \cdot C) \geq 0$] and therefore p has enough tokens to fire t_k in N_p. Thus, for all M_o there exists an $m_o(p)$ for which p is an IP (i.e. it is a SIP). ◆

The $m_o(p)$ considered in the above proof is in many cases larger than strictly necessary (e.g. the place p9 defined as $l_{p9} = (1\ 0\ 0\ 0\ -1\ 0)$ in the net in figure 2.a is a SIP; the initial marking required in the proof of theorem 4.1 is 2, and the required minimum initial marking is zero). This can have different consequences, depending on whether we wish to: (1) Eliminate an IP, since some (e.g. the place p9 above) will not be eliminated; (2) Add an IP, since it may contain a larger $m_o(p)$ than necessary (frozen tokens).

Theorem 4.2. Let p be a SIP. An upper bound of the minimum initial marking, $m_o(p)$, for which p is an IP is $m_o(p) = \max\{0, v\}$, where

$$
\begin{aligned}
v = \min \quad & Y^T \cdot M_o + \mu \\
\text{s.t.} \quad & Y^T \cdot C \leq l_p,\ Y \geq 0 \\
& Y^T \cdot PRE[t_k] + \mu \geq pre(p, t_k)\ \forall t_k \in p\bullet
\end{aligned}
$$

◆

Proof

For a given M_o, a sufficient condition for a SIP p to be an IP is (it is only sufficient because the solutions of the state equation can be unreachable markings):

$$
\left|
\begin{aligned}
& \forall M = M_o + C \cdot \bar{\sigma} \text{ with } M \geq 0,\ \bar{\sigma} \geq 0 \\
& M \geq PRE[p\bullet] \cdot \bar{\sigma}_{p\bullet} \\
& 1^T \cdot \bar{\sigma}_{p\bullet} = 1,\ \bar{\sigma}_{p\bullet} \geq 0
\end{aligned}
\right.
\qquad
\begin{aligned}
\Rightarrow\ & m(p) = m_o(p) + l_p \cdot \bar{\sigma} \geq pre(p, p\bullet) \cdot \bar{\sigma}_{p\bullet} \\
& (\text{or } m_o(p) \geq -l_p \cdot \bar{\sigma} + pre(p, p\bullet) \cdot \bar{\sigma}_{p\bullet})
\end{aligned}
$$

where $\bar{\sigma}_{p\bullet}$ is a characteristic vector restricted to the subset of transitions $p\bullet$. The minimum $m_o(p)$ which makes p an IP is bounded by the maximum of the above function $-l_p \cdot \bar{\sigma} + pre(p, p\bullet) \cdot \bar{\sigma}_{p\bullet}$ (because $m_o(p) \geq -l_p \cdot \bar{\sigma} + pre(p, p\bullet) \cdot \bar{\sigma}_{p\bullet} \Rightarrow m_o(p) \geq \max[-l_p \cdot \bar{\sigma} + pre(p, p\bullet) \cdot \bar{\sigma}_{p\bullet}]$). This maximum is computed by the following dual linear programing problems (LPPs):

$v = \max \quad -l_p \cdot \bar{\sigma} + pre(p, p\bullet) \cdot \bar{\sigma}_{p\bullet}$ $\quad\quad \text{s.t.} \quad M - C \cdot \bar{\sigma} = M_o$ [P1] $\quad\quad\quad M \geq PRE[p\bullet] \cdot \bar{\sigma}_{p\bullet}$ $\quad\quad\quad\quad 1^T \cdot \bar{\sigma}_{p\bullet} = 1$ $\quad\quad\quad\quad M \geq 0,\ \bar{\sigma} \geq 0,\ \bar{\sigma}_{p\bullet} \geq 0$	$v = \min\ Y^T \cdot M_o + \mu$ $\quad\quad \text{s.t.} \quad Y^T \cdot C \leq l_p$ [D1] $\quad\quad Y^T \cdot PRE[t_k] + \mu \geq pre(p, t_k),\ \forall t_k \in p\bullet$ $\quad\quad\quad\quad Y \geq 0$

Since p is a SIP, problem [D1] always has a solution. If $v \geq 0$, $m_o(p) = Y^T \cdot M_o + \mu$ where Y, μ is an optimum solution of [D1]. If v is negative, $m_o(p)=0$ is taken. ◆

An important point derived from theorem 4.2 is that: given a marked net $<N, M_o>$, by means of one single Linear Programming Problem (LPP) as those in theorem 4.2, a SIP which is an IP can be detected (and so eliminated) in polynomial time. The place p is a SIP iff the LPP in theorem 4.2 for p has a feasible solution (theorem 4.1). Moreover, if the initial marking of p in the marked net is greater or equal to that computed by theorem 4.2 place p is an IP (i.e. the net can be reduced removing p, see example 4.2). It is said that this computation is polynomial in time because the theoretical complexity to solve a Linear Programming Problem is polynomial [SAKA 84] and the practical complexity is linear since the simplex algorithm, though of exponential complexity, behaves linearly in practice.

Example 4.2. Detection of an IP which is a SIP.
Let p_9 be a place defined in the net in figure 2.a as $l_{p9}=(1\ 0\ 0\ 0\ -1\ 0)$ and let $m_o(p_9)=0$ be its initial marking. Place p is a SIP since there exists $Y^T = (001110100) \geq 0$ such that $Y^T \cdot C \leq l_{p9}$ [i.e. $l(p_3)+ l(p_4)+ l(p_5)+ l(p_7) = l(p_9)$]. This vector Y and $\mu = -1$ is an optimum solution of the LPP in theorem 4.2. Therefore, $m_o(p_9) \geq Y^T \cdot M_o + \mu = 0$. Thus, the net in figure 2.a with place p_9 can be reduced removing this place. ◆

Some questions related with IPs are discussed below, permitting the vectors Y of theorem 4.1 to be interpreted in terms of nets, and to be classified.

Definition 4.3. (Implying places). Let p be an IP for M_o and let $Y \geq 0$ be such that $Y^T \cdot C \leq l_p$ (i.e. structural condition for p to be SIP, Theorem 4.1). The support of Y, $\|Y\|$, is said to be a *set of implying places of p* iff Y is an optimal solution of the LPP in theorem 4.2. ◆

In general, the set of implying places *is not unique* [see figure 4]. The set of implying places *can also be empty* (if $Y=0$).

The variable m(p) of a SIP can be written in terms of the other variables of the state equation (i.e. M and $\bar{\sigma}$). In terms of nets, this means that the marking of an IP can be calculated as a function of the marking of other places and/or the number of transition firings. Therefore, two categories of IP can be defined depending on the solutions Y and on the equation $Y^T \cdot C \leq l_p$. Premultiplying the state equation of N_p by $(Y^T \mid -1)$ gives: $m(p) = -Y^T \cdot M_o + m_o(p) + Y^T \cdot M + (l_p - Y^T \cdot C) \cdot \bar{\sigma}$. Two cases arise from this expression:

a) *Marking structurally implicit place (MSIP).* There is a set of implying places $\|Y\|$ such that $l_p - Y^T \cdot C = 0$. Therefore, their marking is a linear function of the marking of a set of implying places (except for a constant): $m(p) = -Y^T \cdot M_o + m_o(p) + Y^T \cdot M$. That is, the MSIP preserve the firing sequences and their marking is a redundant state variable.

b) *Firing structurally implicit place (FSIP).* There is no a set of implying places $\|Y\|$ such that $l_p - Y^T \cdot C = 0$ (i.e. for all Y, $l_p - Y^T \cdot C = ay \not\geq 0$). The marking depends also on the number of firings of certain transitions: $m(p) = -Y^T \cdot M_0 + m_0(p) + Y^T \cdot M + ay \cdot \bar\sigma$.

If the PN is live, firing structurally implicit places are unbounded. Figures 4.a and 4.b give an example of each type of SIP.

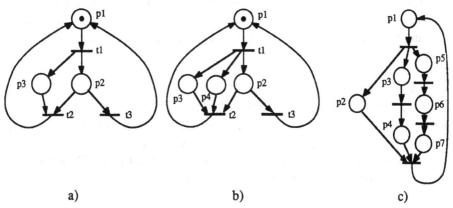

a)   b)   c)

Figure 4. a) p_3 is a FSIP, $m(p_3)=m(p_2)+\bar\sigma(t_3)$. **b)** p_3 is a MSIP, $m(p_3)=m(p_4)$; and $\{p_2\}$ or $\{p_4\}$ are sets of implying places. **c)** Sets of implying places of p_2 are $\{p_3, p_4\}$ if $M_0=$ (1000100) and $\{p_5, p_6, p_7\}$ if $M_0 = $ (1010000).

5. SPURIOUS SOLUTIONS AND IMPLICIT PLACES

The contents of this section is based on the following remark: *certain SIP can be IP for a given M_0, while they are not non-extremal variables in the convexity theory sense* [LUEN 72]. The addition of this kind of places (constraints) allows to reduce the number of spurious solutions of the state equation (firability vectors and, possibly, marking vectors). Two examples of eliminating solutions are given below. The first eliminates potentially reachable markings (so unfirable characteristic vectors), while the second only eliminates unfirable characteristic vectors.

Example 5.1. Elimination of marking vectors from the state equation.
Consider the net in figure 1.a and the SIP defined as $l_{\bar{p4}} = $ (0 -1 1 1 0 0). Its initial marking is (Theorem 4.2) $m_0(\bar{p4}) = Y^T \cdot M_0 + \mu = 1$ with $Y^T = $ (21101), $\mu = -1$ and $Y^T \cdot C = l_{\bar{p4}}$, and for every optimum solution $\mu < 0$. Adding this place eliminates the vectors M in

which $m(p_4) \geq 2$ since then $m(\bar{p}_4) < 0$ (this conclusion is also drawn from the p-invariant which induces $\bar{p}_4$: $m(p_4) + m(\bar{p}_4) = 1$). ♦

Example 5.2. Elimination of characteristic vectors only.

Let us define a place p for the net in figure 1.a as $l_p = (0\ \text{-}1\ 2\ 1\ 0\ 0)$. For every optimum solution of the theorem 4.2 LPP, $\mu < 0$. One of these solutions is, $Y^T = (21101)$, $\mu = -1$, $Y^T \cdot C = (0\ \text{-}1\ 1\ 1\ 0\ 0) \nleq l_p$ and $m_o(p) = 1$ [**Note:** another optimum solution is $Y_1^T = (32102)$, $\mu_1 = -2$, $Y_1^T \cdot C = (0\ \text{-}1\ 2\ 1\ \text{-}1\ 0) \nleq l_p$ and $m_o(p) = 1$]. This place eliminates the solution $M^T = (00020)$, $\bar{\sigma}_1^T = (320011)$. However, it does not eliminate marking M since there exists a $\bar{\sigma}_2^T = (431021)$ for which this marking is a solution of the state equation (Vector $\bar{\sigma}_2$ is obtained from vector $\bar{\sigma}_1$ by adding the t-semiflow $X^T = (111010)$. ♦

In other words, the addition of such IPs allows to cut the convex closure defined by the net state equation. For any added IP, we will assume in the sequel they are pure (i.e. self-loop free) and therefore characterised by their row in the incidence matrix. The following are some a few interesting questions, considered in the next paragraphs:

a) Which SIPs that are IPs for a given M_0 cut spurious solutions?
b) Which solutions do they cut?
c) Why is the cut produced? (net interpretation)
d) How can be a given spurious firability or marking vector removed?
e) Determine a set of SIPs that produce the maximum cut in the original convex closure. That is, how to compute "one of the best" linearly based descriptions of a given net?

5.1 Characterising the implicit places that produce a cut of spurious solutions and the cut performed.

The basic principle lies in the fact that not every SIP which is an IP in a net is a non-extremal variable (i.e. a redundancy in the state equation whose elimination will not alter the solution space). However, the addition or elimination of an IP does not alter the reachable markings of a P/T net $<N, M_0>$ (since it preserves the net's firing sequences). Therefore, the addition of IPs which are not non-extremal variables permits the elimination of spurious solutions of the state equation. These places are found by introducing information about the firing preconditions of the SIP's output transitions which is not directly contained in the state equation (Theorem 4.2). This allows to obtain an initial marking for these places which may be smaller (when $\mu < 0$) than the minimum required for the marking variable to be non-extremal. The next theorem establishes necessary and sufficient conditions which an IP must meet so that its addition to a net eliminates spurious solutions [these IPs will be called *Cutting Implicit Places* (CIP)].

Theorem 5.1. Cutting Implicit Places (CIP)

Let $<N,M_0>$ be a marked net and p be a pure SIP which is an IP with an initial marking given by Theorem 4.2. Adding p to $<N,M_0>$ eliminates at least one solution of its state equation iff $\mu_i<0$ for every feasible solution Y_i, μ_i of the LPP in theorem 4.2 such that $Y_i^T.M_0 + \mu_i = m_0(p)$. ♦

Proof

Adding p to $<N,M_0>$ eliminates a solution of its state equation iff $m(p)$ is not a non-extremal variable in the state equation of $<N_p, M_0 \cup m_0(p)>$ [LUEN 72]. $m(p)$ is not a non-extremal variable iff the LPP [P] and its dual, [D], have optimum negative values (Non Extremal Variable Theorem [LUEN 72]).

$$[P] \quad \begin{array}{ll} \min & m(p) \\ \text{s.t.} & M = M_0 + C \cdot \bar{\sigma} \\ & m(p) = m_0(p) + l_p \cdot \bar{\sigma} \\ & M \geq 0, \bar{\sigma} \geq 0 \end{array} \qquad [D] \quad \begin{array}{ll} \max & -Y^T \cdot M_0 + m_0(p) \\ \text{s.t.} & Y^T \cdot C \leq l_p \\ & Y \geq 0 \end{array}$$

That is, $0 > \min[m(p)] = \max[-Y^T \cdot M_0 + m_0(p)] \geq -Y^T \cdot M_0 + m_0(p)$, for all $Y \geq 0$ such that $Y^T \cdot C \leq l_p$. Therefore, adding p to $<N,M_0>$ eliminates at least one solution of its state equation iff

$$Y^T \cdot M_0 > m_0(p), \text{ for all } Y \geq 0 \text{ such that } Y^T \cdot C \leq l_p \quad [*]$$

Every vector Y which is a solution of the LPP [D] is also a solution of the LPP in theorem 4.2 if μ is selected in accordance with equation $Y^T \cdot PRE[p\bullet] + \mu \cdot 1^T \geq pre(p,p\bullet)$. In addition, if p is pure then for all $Y \geq 0$ such that $Y^T \cdot C \leq l_p$ implies that: $Y^T \cdot PRE[p\bullet] \geq pre(p,p\bullet)$; that is, there are solutions with $\mu \leq 0$. Also, $m_0(p) = \max\{0, v\}$ where v is the optimum value of the LPP in theorem 4.2 for the place p.

In view of the above points, and following the inequality [*], two cases arise:

Case 1. $m_0(p) = v \geq 0$. The only solutions of the theorem 4.2 LPP which satisfy $Y^T.M_0 + \mu = m_0(p)$ are the optimum solutions of that LPP since $m_0(p)$ is its optimum value. If equation [*] holds for all $Y \geq 0$ such that $Y^T \cdot C \leq l_p$, it also holds for $Y = Y_{op}$, where Y_{op} is an optimum solution. Therefore, $Y^T.M_0 > m_0(p) = Y_{op}^T \cdot M_0 + \mu_{op}$ implies that $\mu_{op} < 0$. Also, if $\mu_{op} < 0$ for every optimum solution Y_{op}, μ_{op} then $Y^T.M_0 > Y_{op}^T \cdot M_0 + \mu_{op} = m_0(p)$ for all $Y \geq 0$ such that $Y^T \cdot C \leq l_p$ since any of these vectors Y with $\mu = 0$ (p is pure) is a feasible solution of the LPP in theorem 4.2.

Case 2. $m_0(p) = 0$ and $v < 0$. Trivially, inequality [*] holds iff $\mu < 0$ for every feasible solution Y, μ of the theorem 4.2 LPP such that $Y^T.M_0 + \mu = m_0(p) = 0$. ♦

Theorem 5.1 guarantees the elimination of a solution of the state equation by adding CIPs. The following theorem characterises the cut performed by one of these places.

Theorem 5.2. Characterisation of the cut produced by one CIP

The following system characterises the set of spurious solutions of the state equation (i.e. vectors $M \geq 0, \bar{\sigma} \geq 0$) which are eliminated by a CIP p,

$$
\boxed{
\begin{array}{l}
M = M_o + C \cdot \bar{\sigma} \\
Y^T.M + \mu + [l_p - Y^T.C].\bar{\sigma} < 0 \\
M \geq 0, \bar{\sigma} \geq 0
\end{array}
}
$$

where $Y \geq 0, \mu < 0$ is any feasible solution of the theorem 4.2 LPP for p such that $m_o(p) = Y^T.M_o + \mu$ (theorem 5.1). ◆

Proof

If p is a CIP, m(p) is not a non-extremal variable (theorem 5.1): Thus, there exist solutions $M \geq 0, \bar{\sigma} \geq 0$ of the original state equation for which the variable m(p) is negative (Non-Extremal Variables Theorem [LUEN 72]). The solutions eliminated are those for which $m(p) < 0$.

$$
[S_1] \quad
\boxed{
\begin{array}{l}
M = M_o + C \cdot \bar{\sigma} \\
m(p) = m_o(p) + l_p \cdot \bar{\sigma} \\
M \geq 0, m(p) \geq 0, \bar{\sigma} \geq 0
\end{array}
}
\qquad
[S_2] \quad
\boxed{
\begin{array}{l}
M = M_o + C \cdot \bar{\sigma} \\
Y^T.M + \mu + [l_p - Y^T.C].\bar{\sigma} \geq 0 \\
M \geq 0, \bar{\sigma} \geq 0
\end{array}
}
$$

The new description of net behavior will be given by the system $[S_1]$, where according to the above the cutting inequation is $m(p) \geq 0$. Eliminating m(p) in system $[S_1]$ (taking into account that $m(p) \geq 0$) the system $[S_2]$ can be obtained. In this case, the cutting inequation is $Y^T.M + \mu + [l_p - Y^T.C].\bar{\sigma} \geq 0$, where Y and μ are a feasible solution of the theorem 4.2 LPP for the CIP such that $Y^T.M_o + \mu = m_o(p)$. This inequation in $[S_2]$ is the complementary inequation to that which expresses the cut in theorem 5.2. ◆

Obviously, from the above theorem the set of spurious solutions eliminated by a set of CIPs are the solutions of all systems as described in theorem 5.2 which are associated with each CIP of the set. The following corollary gives conditions under which a CIP eliminates a potentially reachable marking.

Corollary 5.1. Let $<N, M_o>$ be a net and p a CIP. Place p eliminates a potentially reachable marking, M_s, if for all $\bar{\sigma} \geq 0$ such that $M_s = M_o + C \cdot \bar{\sigma}$, $(M_s, \bar{\sigma})$ is a solution of the system in theorem 5.2 ◆

A particular case of corollary 5.1. If the theorem 4.2 LPP for the CIP p admits a solution $Y \geq 0$, $\mu < 0$ such that $Y^T.M_0 + \mu = m_0(p)$ and $Y^T.C = l_p$ then p eliminates at least one vector M. This is trivially deduced from theorem 5.2 since $Y^T.C = l_p$ imply that the term dependent on $\bar{\sigma}$ disappears and the expression is valid for all $\bar{\sigma}$ which satisfies the state equation for at least one marking. In this case, the set of vectors M eliminated by p are the integer solutions of the following linear system:

$$[S_3] \qquad \boxed{\begin{array}{l} M = M_0 + C \cdot \bar{\sigma} \\ Y^T.M < -\mu \\ M \geq 0, \bar{\sigma} \geq 0 \end{array}}$$

The CIP of the example 5.2 produces a cut that is characterized by means of the linear system of theorem 5.2, and the cut produced by the CIP of example 5.1 is characterized by a linear system as $[S_3]$ because in this case $Y^T.C = l_p$.

5.2. Interpreting the elimination of spurious marking vector solutions

This section interprets, in terms of nets, the elimination of unreachable markings by adding CIPs. The idea is to find out what information these places give about the net possible behavior which is not directly contained in the state equation (the conditions in theorem 5.1 are structural except where M_0 is concerned). It is shown that a necessary condition for a CIP to eliminate unreachable markings from the state equation is that it should have an associated set of places which make up a marked trap. The eliminated markings are precisely those in which the trap is unmarked or contains a number of tokens lower than a residual minimum related to the value of the variable μ. First, some details of notation and terminology are discussed.

A *trap* is a subset of places $\theta \subseteq P$ in a net N, such that $\theta^\bullet \subseteq {}^\bullet\theta$. A well-known property [HACK 72], [SILV 85] of these structural elements is recalled below.

Lemma 5.1. Let $<N,M_0>$ be a P/T net and $\theta \subseteq P$ a trap. If θ is initially marked, then θ is marked throughout the net's evolution. ♦

The structural concept of a trap lets us interpret in net terms the reason why certain CIPs in theorem 5.1 eliminate unreachable markings. A first step (theorem 5.3) interprets the possible solutions, Y, of the theorem 4.2 LPP for which $\mu < 0$ and $Y^T.C=l_p$.

Theorem 5.3. Let p be a CIP in $<N_p, M_0 \cup m_0(p)>$. For every solution $Y \geq 0$, $\mu < 0$ of the theorem 4.2 LPP such that $Y^T.M_0 + \mu = m_0(p)$ and $Y^T.C = l_p$, $\|Y\|$ is a marked trap. ♦

Proof

Let p be a CIP such that the theorem 4.2 LPP has a solution $Y \geq 0$, $\mu < 0$, $Y^T.M_0 + \mu = m_0(p)$ and $Y^T.C = l_p$. Decomposing this last equation we get:

$$Y^T \cdot POST\ [p\bullet] - Y^T \cdot PRE\ [p\bullet] = -pre[p,p\bullet] < 0 \qquad [1]$$

$$Y^T \cdot POST\ [\bullet p] - Y^T \cdot PRE\ [\bullet p] = post[p,\bullet p] > 0 \qquad [2]$$

$$Y^T \cdot POST\ [T-(p\bullet \cup \bullet p)] - Y^T \cdot PRE\ [T- (p\bullet \cup \bullet p)] = 0 \qquad [3]$$

Substituting the second equation of the theorem 4.2 LPP, $Y^T \cdot PRE[p\bullet] - \mu \cdot \mathbf{1}^T \geq pre[p,p\bullet]$, into [1] gives: $Y^T \cdot POST[p\bullet] = Y^T \cdot PRE[p\bullet] - pre[p,p\bullet] \geq -\mu \cdot \mathbf{1}^T > 0$. This inequality, and equations [2] and [3] give: for all t_k such that $t_k \in \|Y\|\bullet$ (i.e. $Y^T \cdot PRE[t_k] \neq 0$) implies that $t_k \in \bullet\|Y\|$ (i.e. $Y^T \cdot POST[t_k] \neq 0$). That is: $\|Y\|\bullet \subseteq \bullet\|Y\|$ (i.e. $\|Y\|$ is a trap in N). The trap $\|Y\|$ is marked since $\mu < 0$ and $m_0(p)=Y^T \cdot M_0+\mu \geq 0$. Therefore, $Y^T \cdot M_0 > 0$. ◆

From the special solutions Y of the theorem 4.2 LPP for p, considered in the above theorem, the following trivial result is deduced: $p\bullet \subseteq \|Y\|\bullet \cap \bullet\|Y\|$. That is, $\|Y\| \cup \{p\}$ is a marked trap.

According to theorem 5.3, the existence of CIPs which eliminate markings implies the existence of a set of places which is a marked trap. Since an initially marked trap remains marked (Lemma 5.1), the existence of this residual marking is the key to interpreting the value of μ in theorem 5.1, and the reason for the elimination of unreachable markings when these places are added.

Theorem 5.4. Let p be a CIP and let $Y \geq 0$, $\mu < 0$ be a solution of the theorem 4.2 LPP for p such that $Y^T.M_0 + \mu = m_0(p)$ and $Y^T.C = l_p$. The minimum of the sum, weighted by vector Y, of the marking of places in trap $\|Y\|$ is $-\mu$. ◆

Proof. This interpretation can be easily obtained from the above system [S3]. ◆

In the above corollary, if vector $Y \in \{0,1\}^n$ then $-\mu$ is the minimum number of tokens which the trap defined by places $\|Y\|$ can contain.

5.3 A heuristic procedure for computing implicit places that eliminate a/some given unreachable markings

The heuristic procedure below aims to eliminate a marking vector, M, which is an integer solution of the state equation, but is suspected *a priori* to be non reachable (i.e. it is a spurious solution). For this purpose, a CIP (if one exists) with an associated initially marked trap that is unmarked at the marking M (Lemma 5.1) is computed.

Procedure. Elimination of one spurious marking by means of a CIP.
1) Obtain a net N' removing the marked places of N at M together with their input and output arcs: p ∈ P such that M[p] > 0. The resulting subnet is fully unmarked at M.
2) Compute an initially marked (i.e. for M_0) trap θ in N'. If there exists one of these traps, there is an initially marked trap that is empty at M, what violates Lemma 5.1. Therefore M is unreachable.
3) Add to <N,M_0> a SIP p such that $Y_\theta^T \cdot C = l_p$, $\|Y_\theta\| = \theta$ and $m_0(p)$ computed using theorem 4.2. ◆

An example illustrating the use of this procedure is given bellow.

Example 5.3. Application of the procedure to the PN in figure 1.a.
The purpose is to refine the conclusions obtained from the binarity analysis of place p_4, that was carried out in example 2.2. The place p_4 could not be decided to be binary because $M_{s1}=(00020)^T$ was a solution of the state equation. We are looking for a CIP that eliminates this marking which is supposed unreachable.

Computing a CIP which will eliminate marking M_{s1}

Step 1. In the net in figure 1.a place p_4 must be eliminated since it have tokens.
Step 2. The resulting subnet has a trap $\theta_a=\{p_1, p_2, p_3, p_5\}$.
Step 3. Taking vector $Y_a^T=(1\ 1\ 1\ 0\ 1)$ with $\|Y_a\| = \theta_a$ we get the IP p_a of the form: $l_{pa} = Y_a^T \cdot C = (1\ -1\ 1\ 1\ -1\ -1)$. Theorem 4.2 gives the initial marking of p_a, $m_0(p_a)=0$. The optimum solution of the LPP in that theorem is the vector Y_a and $\mu_a = -1$.

The place p_a eliminates the potentially reachable marking M_{s1}. However, it is not the only possible solution. A different choice of the weighting vector, $Y_b^T=(2\ 1\ 1\ 0\ 1)$ leads to the IP p_b: $l_{pb} = Y_b^T \cdot C = (0\ -1\ 1\ 1\ 0\ 0)$; $\mu_b = -1$ and $m_0(p_b) = 1$ [see example 5.1]. p_b also eliminates solution M_{s1}.

Considering the state equation of the original net plus the above computed CIP p_a (or p_b), if the marking bound of p_4 is computed again as in example 2.2, value 1 is obtained (i.e. the real marking bound). Observe that place p_a induces the p-invariant $m(p_1) + m(p_4) + m(p_a) = 1$ (place p_b induces the p-invariant $m(p_4) + m(p_b) = 1$) which allows to conclude on the binarity of p_4. ◆

The stated procedure is polynomial in time because: (a) The computation of N' is linear in the number of places; (b) The computation of an initially marked trap in the net N' can be done by one single LPP as in [ESPA 89], considering the additional restriction

$Y^T \cdot M_0 \geq 1$ (i.e. $\|Y\|$ is an initially marked trap). Therefore, it is polynomial; (c) The computation of the CIP is polynomial in time since it can be done by the LPP of theorem 4.2.

The procedure can be generalised to try to eliminate several markings simultaneously by means of a single CIP. This generalisation modifies the step 1 of the procedure: Obtain a net N' removing all the marked places of N under at least one of the markings to be eliminated together with their input and output arcs. Example 5.4 illustrate this case.

Example 5.4. Elimination of several markings by one single CIP (Figure 1.a).
Let us try to eliminate marking vectors $M_{s4} = (02000)^T$ and $M_{s1} = (00020)^T$.

Computing a CIP which will eliminate marking M_{s4} and M_{s1}

Step 1. In the net in figure 1.a places p_2 and p_4 must be eliminated because they have tokens in M_{s4} or M_{s1}.

Step 2. The resulting subnet contains an initially marked trap $\theta_c = \{p_1, p_3, p_5\}$.

Step 3. Taking vector $Y_c^T = (1\ 0\ 1\ 0\ 1)$ with $\|Y_c\| = \theta_c$ we get the IP p_c of the form: $l_{pc} = Y_c^T \cdot C = (0\ 0\ 0\ 1\ 0\ -1)$. Theorem 4.2 gives for the initial marking of p_c, $m_0(p_c) = 0$. The optimum solution of the LPP in that theorem is the vector Y_c and $\mu_c = -1$.

If place p_c is added to the original net, markings M_{s4} and M_{s1} are eliminated from the solution space of state equation. This can be proven by the new p-invariant induced by p_c: $m(p_1) + m(p_2) + m(p_4) + m(p_c) = 1$.

Even more, according with the new p-invariant $M = (01010)$ is also eliminated. Let N_c be the net in figure 1.a, resulting from the addition of place p_c computed above. The study of the deadlock-freeness in N_c requires the three systems of example 2.3 (the state equations that appears in the systems refer now to net N_c), plus the following additional system,

$$
\begin{array}{ll}
\exists\ M\ \text{s. t.} & M = M_0 + C \cdot \bar{\sigma} \\
& M \geq 0, \bar{\sigma} \geq 0 \\
[4] & M[p_1] = 0,\ M[p_2] = 0 \\
& M[p_4] = 0,\ M[p_a] = 0
\end{array}
$$

The system above and system [3] in example 2.3 have no solution. Unfortunately, systems [1] and [2] do have solutions and therefore we cannot conclude on the deadlock-freeness of the net. We will try to eliminate their integer solutions in the following example by means of one single CIP. ♦

Example 5.5. Let us try to eliminate marking vectors $M_{s6}=(00002)^T$ and $M_{s5}=(00200)^T$, integer solutions of systems [1] and [2] of example 2.3. These solutions prevent us to conclude on the deadlock-freeness of the net.

Step 1. Places p_3 and p_5 of the net in figure 1.a are eliminated.

Step 2. There is not an initially marked trap in the resulting subnet after step 1. Therefore, there is not one single CIP which eliminate markings M_{s6} and M_{s5}. ◆

We proceed now according to the procedure. That is, we will try to eliminate each marking by means of one CIP. The example below shows it.

Example 5.6. Removing markings $M_{s6}=(00002)^T$ and $M_{s5}=(00200)^T$.

Removing marking M_{s6} by means of one single CIP.

Step 1. The place p_5 must be removed from the net in figure 1.a because it is marked at M_{s6}.

Step 2. The subnet resulting from step 1 contains an initially marked trap $\theta_d = \{p_1, p_2, p_3, p_4\}$.

Step 3. Taking vector $Y_d^T = (11110)$ with $\|Y_d\| = \theta_d$ we get the IP p_d: $l_{pd} = Y_d^T \cdot C = (1-10000)$; $\mu_d = -1$ and $m_0(p_d)=0$. It can be proven that this place eliminates marking M_{s6} because it induces the p-invariant: $m(p_1) + m(p_5) + m(p_d) = 1$.

Removing marking M_{s5} by means of one single CIP.

Step 1. The place p_3 is removed from the net in figure 1.a.

Step 2. In resulting subnet there exists an initially marked trap $\theta_e = \{p_1, p_2, p_5\}$.

Step 3. Taking vector $Y_e^T = (11001)$ with $\|Y_e\| = \theta_e$ we get the IP p_e: $l_{pe} = Y_e^T \cdot C = (0010-10)$; $\mu_e = -1$ and $m_0(p_e) = 0$. It can be proven that this place eliminates marking M_{s5} because it induces the p-invariant: $m(p_1) + m(p_3) + m(p_4) + m(p_e)=1$. ◆

Adding the CIPs p_c, p_d and p_e obtained above to the net in figure 1.a, and performing a similar computation to the one of example 2.3 (but on the new P/T net) we can prove that the net is deadlock-free. Moreover, the addition of these three CIPs allows to conclude that M_0 is a home state (using the algorithms presented in [JOHN 87]), what was not possible in the original net (of course, if M_0 is a home state then the net is reversible for this initial marking).

5.4. Maximum elimination of unreachable markings by means of CIPs.

This section presents a procedure which together with the interpretation of the section 5.2 lead to a set of CIPs to add to the net which eliminates the maximum number of unreachable markings. To present and illustrate the procedure an example is given below based again on the net in figure 1.a.

Example 5.7. Elimination of potentially reachable markings by CIPs.
Consider the net in figure 1.a. Below are introduced with the example the steps to calculate the CIPs which eliminate the unreachable markings.

Step 1. *Computing the minimal initially marked traps.* This net has three minimal traps (figure 5): $\theta_1 = \{p_1, p_2, p_5\}$, $\theta_2 = \{p_1, p_2, p_3, p_4\}$ and $\theta_3 = \{p_1, p_3, p_5\}$. These traps are initially marked since they contain p_1.

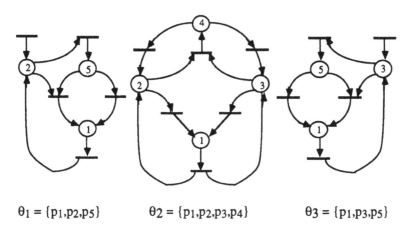

$$\theta_1 = \{p_1, p_2, p_5\} \qquad \theta_2 = \{p_1, p_2, p_3, p_4\} \qquad \theta_3 = \{p_1, p_3, p_5\}$$

Figure 5. Minimal traps (marked) of P/T net in figure 1.a.

Step 2. *Determination of the IPs* For each of the above traps, calculate a SIP by selecting the vectors $Y_{\theta i} \in \{0,1\}^n$ and $\|Y_{\theta i}\| = \theta_i$. These places are (figure 6.a): $l_{p\theta 1} = Y_{\theta 1}^T \cdot C = (0\ 0\ 1\ 0\ -1\ 0)$; $l_{p\theta 2} = Y_{\theta 2}^T \cdot C = (1\ -1\ 0\ 0\ 0\ 0)$; $l_{p\theta 3} = Y_{\theta 3}^T \cdot C = (0\ 0\ 0\ 1\ 0\ -1)$

Step 3. *Initial markings of the IPs calculated in step 2.* The initial marking of the $p_{\theta i}$ is calculated from theorem 4.2, giving:

$p_{\theta 1})$ Optimum solution: $Y_{\theta 1} = (1\ 1\ 0\ 0\ 1)$, $\mu_{\theta 1} = -1$
       Initial marking: $m_0(p_{\theta 1}) = Y_{\theta 1}^T \cdot M_0 + \mu_{\theta 1} = 0$

$p_{\theta 2})$ Optimum solution: $Y_{\theta 2} = (1\ 1\ 1\ 1\ 0)$, $\mu_{\theta 2} = -1$
       Initial marking: $m_0(p_{\theta 2}) = Y_{\theta 2}^T \cdot M_0 + \mu_{\theta 2} = 0$

$p_{\theta 3})$ Optimum solution: $Y_{\theta 3} = (1\ 0\ 1\ 0\ 1)$, $\mu_{\theta 3} = -1$
       Initial marking: $m_0(p_{\theta 3}) = Y_{\theta 3}^T \cdot M_0 + \mu_{\theta 3} = 0$

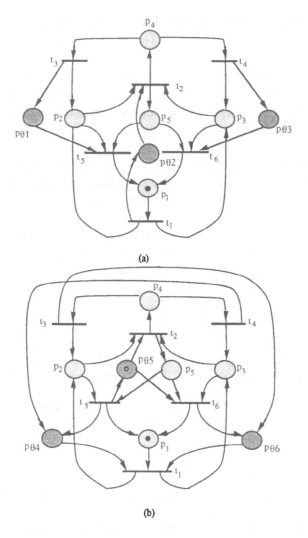

(a)

(b)

Figure 6. P/T net of figure 1 with two different sets of IP.

VERIFICATION.

Adding the above IPs to the net eliminates all the spurious integer solutions from the state equation of net $<N,M_0>$. The $p_{\theta i}$ introduce the following invariant relations:

$p_{\theta 1}$) $M(p_1) + M(p_2) + M(p_5) \geq 1$, $\forall M \in R(N,M_0)$ {i.e. θ_1 contains at least 1 token}

$p_{\theta 2}$) $M(p_1) + M(p_2) + M(p_3) + M(p_4) \geq 1$, $\forall M \in R(N,M_0)$ {i.e. θ_2 contains at least 1 token)

$p_{\theta 3}$) $M(p_1) + M(p_3) + M(p_5) \geq 1$, $\forall M \in R(N,M_0)$ {i.e. θ_3 contains at least 1 token}

Table 1 shows the unreachable markings which are removed by the above invariant relations. They are induced by adding the calculated implicit places.

Unreachable markings		•	•	•	•		•		•		
	$M(p_1)$	1	0	0	0	0	0	0	0	0	0	0
$2 \cdot M(p_1)+M(p_2)+M(p_3)+M(p_4)+M(p_5)=2$	$M(p_2)$	0	2	0	0	0	1	1	1	0	0	0
(the only minimal p-invariant)	$M(p_3)$	0	0	2	0	0	1	0	0	1	1	0
	$M(p_4)$	0	0	0	2	0	0	1	0	1	0	1
	$M(p_5)$	0	0	0	0	2	0	0	1	0	1	1
$\theta_1 \Rightarrow M(p_1) + M(p_2) + M(p_5) \geq 1$				x	x					x		
$\theta_2 \Rightarrow M(p_1) + M(p_2) + M(p_3) + M(p_4) \geq 1$						x						
$\theta_3 \Rightarrow M(p_1) + M(p_3) + M(p_5) \geq 1$			x		x			x				

Table 1. Integer solutions of the state equation eliminated by CIPs (figure 1.b).

The elimination of these spurious solutions can be checked in a different way if the minimal p-semiflows of $<N,M_o>$ are calculated with the three added CIPs. These p-semiflows induce the following marking invariants:

$$2 \cdot M(p_1) + M(p_2) + M(p_3) + M(p_4) + M(p_5) = 2$$
$$M(p_1) + M(p_5) + M(p_{\theta 2}) = 1$$
$$M(p_1) + M(p_2) + M(p_4) + M(p_{\theta 3}) = 1$$
$$M(p_1) + M(p_3) + M(p_4) + M(p_{\theta 1}) = 1$$
$$M(p_1) + M(p_4) + M(p_{\theta 1}) + M(p_{\theta 2}) + M(p_{\theta 3}) = 1$$

These invariants prove that none of the vectors M_{si} in figure 1.b are solutions of the new state equation.   ◆

The set of computed CIPs is not, in general, the only one since it depends on the weighting vectors (see figure 6.b where an alternative set of CIPs to that in example 5.7 is shown). The technique of adding CIPs does not guarantee that the addition of the equations corresponding to the implicit places will eliminate all the integer spurious solutions from the original net (i.e. the technique is not complete). This is shown in the next example.

Example 5.8. The net in figure 7 is non-live, and the only reachable marking is the initial one (p_4 and p_5 with one token each). Proceeding as in example 5.4 we get:

Step 1. Minimal marked traps $\theta_1=\{p_1, p_3, p_5, p_7\}$; $\theta_2=\{p_2, p_4, p_6, p_7\}$
Step 2. Determining the SIPs $lp_{\theta 1}=Y_{\theta 1}^T \cdot C=(0000000)$; $lp_{\theta 2}=Y_{\theta 2}^T \cdot C=(0000000)$
   [These are non-pure places which are input and output places of the trap transitions (i.e. $\theta^{\bullet}_2={}^{\bullet}\theta_2$ and $\theta^{\bullet}_1={}^{\bullet}\theta_1$ respectively) with arcs of weight one.]

Step 3. Computing the initial marking

$p\theta 1)$ Optimum solution: $Y_{\theta 1}^T = (0000000)$, $\mu_1=1$ or $Y_{\theta 1}^T =(1010101)$, $\mu_1=0$

      Initial marking: $m_0(p\theta 1) = 1$

$p\theta 2)$ Optimum solution: $Y_{\theta 2}^T =(0101011)$, $\mu_2=0$ or $Y_{\theta 2}^T =(0000000)$, $\mu_2=1$

      Initial marking: $m_0(p\theta 2) = 1$

Therefore, add the equations: $m(p\theta 1)=m_0(p\theta 1)=1$ and $m(p\theta 2)=m_0(p\theta 2)=1$ to the state equation. These do not eliminate any unreachable solution from figure 7.b. They simply express that each trap always contains at least one token (note that the same conclusion is drawn from the minimal invariants of the net). In addition, no weighting $Y'_{\theta 1}\geq 0$, $Y'_{\theta 2}\geq 0$, $\|Y'_{\theta 1}\|=\theta_1$, $\|Y'_{\theta 2}\|=\theta_2$ is found which will lead to an IP which eliminates the spurious solutions.   ◆

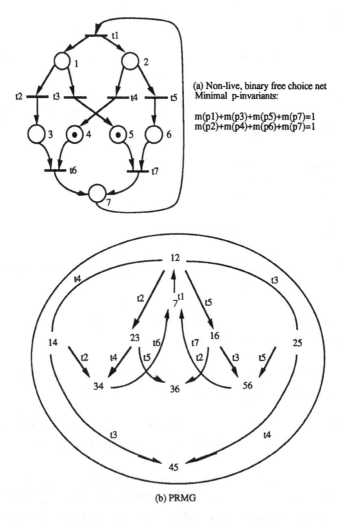

(a) Non-live, binary free choice net
Minimal p-invariants:

$$m(p1)+m(p3)+m(p5)+m(p7)=1$$
$$m(p2)+m(p4)+m(p6)+m(p7)=1$$

(b) PRMG

Figure 7.   PN with unreachable markings.

For some subclasses of nets, the situation described in example 5.8 hold for every minimal trap in the net. Therefore, the rule developed in this section does not eliminate any marking solution of the state equation. This is the case with live bounded Marked Graphs, and fits the well-known property that the set of reachable markings coincides with the set of integer solutions M of its state equation.

Nevertheless, in the above example it can also be applied another reasoning, complementary to that developed with traps, to remove spurious solutions. It is based on the fact that an initially unmarked deadlock remains unmarked. In this example $\{p_1, p_2, p_3, p_6\}$ is an initially unmarked deadlock and all integer spurious solutions can be removed by adding to the state equation the set of linear equations: $m(p_1)=0$, $m(p_2)=0$, $m(p_3)=0$ and $m(p_6)=0$. Observe that in this case the new state equation has the initial marking M_0 as the only integer solution (i.e. the PN is deadlocked).

6. CONCLUSIONS

Structural analysis of P/T nets using linear algebra techniques has the advantage of the efficiency of the algorithms used for this purpose. However, one disadvantage is that usually one can only obtain necessary or sufficient conditions, but not both (semidecision algorithms). This is a result of the fact that the net state equation characterises not only the reachable marking vectors, and the characteristic vectors of the firing sequences, but also spurious solutions. These spurious solutions arise because the state equation does not check that every characteristic vector which is a solution of the state equation leads to at least one valid firing sequence.

An attractive goal for bringing structural analysis closer to behavioural analysis is the elimination of spurious solutions while maintaining the representation's linearity.

This paper has presented two methods for eliminating spurious solutions of the state equation. They are based on adding to the net a series of linear restrictions which partially verify the transition firing rule. The two methods do this differently, by incorporating information not directly contained in the state equation. Though of different efficiency, in many cases they can eliminate all the spurious integer solutions.

The first method consists of checking that for every potentially reachable marking there is a predecessor marking (or sequence of markings) from which it can be reached by firing one or several transitions. This gives a necessary condition for every characteristic vector which solves the new equation to have at least one valid firing sequence. This method is conceptually simple, but has the disadvantages that the system dimensions grow rapidly with the length of the sequence considered, and that markings reachable from M_0 with sequences of equal or shorter length may be eliminated. Unfortunately, no practical method has been found to calculate the maximum sequence length to be studied. The theoretical bound can be derived for structurally bounded nets gives an upper bound to big for practical purposes.

The second method is based on adding to the net certain implicit places (which are also structurally implicit) whose marking variable is not redundant in the state equation (i.e. it is not a non-extremal variable [LUEN 72] of the state equation, thus it can be eliminated along with its equation). An implicit place preserves the net firing sequences; i.e. adding an implicit place does not eliminate any reachable marking. Therefore, the implicit places which are not non-extremal variables restrict the state equation solution space (theorem 5.1). The elimination performed by these places has its origin in the initial marking calculated for them to be implicit (theorem 4.2). This calculation takes into account the firing preconditions of the implicit place's output transitions, giving an initial marking smaller than required for its marking variable to be redundant in the state equation. This type of implicit place is not discussed in [BERT 87] because its definition of an implicit place (redundant place) imposes *a priori* that the variable μ be non-negative.

Another important point is the characterisation by means of a single Linear Programming Problem of implicit places which are structurally implicit. Therefore, the theoretical complexity of this calculation is polynomial [SAKA 84] and the practical complexity is linear; this is because the simplex algorithm , though of exponential complexity, behaves linearly in practice.

The interpretation in net terms of why cutting implicit places eliminate potentially reachable markings is based on the existence of a set of places associated with each of these places which is an initially marked trap. Since a marked trap cannot be completely unmarked, the solutions eliminated are those marking vectors in which the trap has a marking smaller than a residual minimum. This interpretation of the elimination of solutions by adding implicit places permits a procedure regarding the implicit places to add in order to achieve maximum elimination, namely one implicit place per minimal initially marked trap. The method can be extended by considering also initially unmarked deadlocks.

ACKNOWLEDGEMENTS

The authors are indebted to five anonymous referees whose comments and suggestions helped us in improving the final version of the paper. This work was supported in part by the DEMON Esprit Basic Research Action 3248, and the Plan Nacional de Investigación Grant TIC-0358/89

REFERENCES

[BERT 87] BERTHELOT G.: Transformations and Decompositions of Nets. *Petri Nets: Central Models and their Properties. Advances in Petri Nets 1986, Proceedings of an Advanced Course*, Bad Honnef, September 1986. LNCS 254, Springer Verlag, Berlin, pp.359-376.

[BEST 85] BEST E., FERNANDEZ C.: Notations and Terminology on Petri Net Theory. *Newsletter 20*, May 1985, pp. 1-15.

[COLO 89] COLOM J.M.: *Análisis estructural de Redes de Petri, Programación Lineal y Geometría Convexa*. Ph. D. Thesis, Depto. Ingeniería Eléctrica e Informática, Universidad de Zaragoza, June.

[ESPA 89] ESPARZA J., SILVA M.: A Polynomial-time Algorithm to Decide Liveness of Bounded Free Choice Nets, *Internal Report*, Dept. de Ingeniería Eléctrica e Informática, Universidad de Zaragoza.

[HACK 72] HACK M.H.T.: *Analysis of Production Schemata by Petri Nets*. M.S. thesis, TR-94, Project MAC, MIT, Cambridge, Mass.

[JOHN 87] JOHNEN C.: `SUJET: Analyse Algorithmique des Reseaux de Petri: Verification d'Espace d'Accueil, Systemes de Reecriture*. These Doctoral, Université de Paris-Sud, Decembre 1987.

[LUEN 72] LUENBERGER D.G.: *Introduction to Linear and Non Linear Programming*. Addison-Wesley Publishing Company, Reading, Massachssets.

[MART 84] MARTINEZ J.: *Contribución al Análisis y Modelado de Sistemas Concurrentes mediante Redes de Petri*. Tesis Doctoral. Universidad de Zaragoza, Octubre 1984.

[SAKA 84] SAKAROVITCH M.: *Optimisation Combinatoire. Méthodes Mathématiques et Algorithmiques*. Hermann, Paris.

[SILV 80] SILVA M.: Simplification des Reseaux de Petri par Elimination des Places Implicites. *Digital Processes 6*, pp. 245-256.

[SILV 85] SILVA M.: *Las Redes de Petri en la Automática y la Informática*. Editorial AC, Madrid.

[SILV 87] SILVA M., COLOM J.M.: On the Computation of Structural Synchronic Invariants in P/T nets, *Procs. of the Eighth European Workshop on Application and Theory of Petri Nets*, Zaragoza, June 1987, pp. 237-258. Also in *Advances in Petri Nets 88*, LNCS 340, Springer Verlag, 1989, pp. 387-417.

LINEAR INVARIANTS IN COMMUTATIVE HIGH LEVEL NETS

Jean Michel Couvreur
Université Paris VI - C.N.R.S. MASI - C3
4 Place Jussieu, 75252 Paris Cedex 05, France

Javier Martínez
Universidad de Zaragoza - Dpto. de Ingeniería Eléctrica e Informática
María de Luna 3, 50015 Zaragoza, Spain

ABSTRACT. Commutative nets are a subclass of colored nets whose color functions belong to a ring of commutative diagonalizable endomorphisms. Although their ability to describe models is smaller than that of colored nets, they can handle a broad range of concurrent systems. Commutative nets include net subclasses such as regular homogeneous nets and ordered nets, whose practical importance has already been shown.

Mathematical properties of the color functions of commutative nets allow a symbolic computation of a family of generators of flows. The method proposed decreases the number of non-null elements in a given color function matrix, without adding new columns. By iteration, the entire matrix is annulled and a generative family of flows is obtained. The interpretation of the invariants associated with each flow is straightforward.

Keywords. Linear invariants, flow computation, structural analysis methods, subclasses of Petri nets, colored nets

CONTENTS

1. INTRODUCTION

Petri nets are a family of tools with which concurrent systems can be modeled. One of their main advantages is that the constructed models can be analyzed. The best-known of these nets are the place/transition nets. In them, the tokens contained in any place are identical, and the arcs are labeled by natural numbers.

Colored nets can be considered as high level nets in relation to place/transition nets. They permit the construction of more concise and abstract models. Their tokens are distinguished by a differentiating attribute denoted color. In a colored net, a place can contain a non-negative number of colored tokens, or colors. A transition admits various firing modes, parametrized by colors. An arc from a transition to a place (or from a place to a transition) is labeled by a linear function (color function) which determines the colors to be added to (or to be removed from) the place upon firing the transition.

Many results on place/transition net analysis have been elucidated (see, for example (Brams 83), (Silva 85) or (Reisig 85)). Little has been done to generalize these results to high level nets. This paper concentrates on the problem of calculating linear invariants in colored nets. These invariants are the bases for the structural analysis of a net (Jensen 81) (Genrich,Lautenbach 83). The linear invariants can be directly deduced from the left annihilators or flows of the net's incidence matrix.

(Silva et al. 85) presents a method for calculating flows in colored nets, based on a generalization of the Gauss elimination method applied to the net's incidence matrix. In the general case, the process is controlled by heuristic rules which do not guarantee that a generative family of flows will be obtained.

Other works have studies the problem of calculating flows in subclasses of colored nets. Thus there are papers on unary nets (Vautherin,Memmi 85); factorizable nets with commutative functions (Alla et al. 85); regular nets (Haddad 87); associative nets and ordered nets (Haddad, Couvreur 88); etc.

This paper presents commutative nets (§2), a subclass of colored nets which contains regular homogeneous nets, ordered nets, and projection nets (which are defined in §2.3), among others. The fact that we consider a subclass of nets limits the capacity for modeling. However, commutative nets can describe a broad range of practical problems (communication protocols; queue, ring and counter management systems; filters; etc..).

One compensation is that the possibilities of analyzing the models are greatly enhanced.

The color functions of a commutative net belong to a ring of commutative diagonalizable endomorphisms. Section §3 studies these properties and their effect on calculating the flows of a net.

Section §4 deals with the problem of calculating a generative family of flows for a commutative net. The key result is the algorithm presented in §4.3 which, when applied to a color function matrix, decreases the number of non-null functions in a given column. By iteration, the entire color function matrix is annulled, giving a generative family of flows.

Finally, §5 gives some examples of modeling with commutative nets in order to illustrate the ideas presented before. In each case, a generative family of flows is computed, and the corresponding linear invariants are obtained and interpreted.

2. COMMUTATIVE HIGH LEVEL NETS

2.1 Definition of a colored net

Definition 2.1.1: A *colored net* is a 6-tuple $CPN=<P,T,C,W^+,W^-,M_0>$ where:
- P is a non-empty set of places
- T is a non-empty set of transitions
- $C: P \cup T \rightarrow \Omega$, where Ω is a set of finite non-empty sets
- W^+ (W^-) is the pre-(post-) incidence matrix of $P \times T$, where $W^+(p,t)$ ($W^-(p,t)$) is a function of $C(p) \times C(t)$ in N (the set of natural numbers).
- M_0, the initial marking, is a vector indexed by the elements of P, where $M_0(p)$ is a function of $C(p)$ in N.

Notes:
- The color functions $W^+(p,t)$ and $W^-(p,t)$ are matrices $C(p) \times C(t)$ with coefficients in N which, consequently, define respective linear applications of $Bags(C(t))$ in $Bags(C(p))$. ($Bags(A)$ is the set of multisets over A).
- The initial marking $M_0(p)$ of place p takes its values in $Bags(C(p))$.

Definition 2.1.2: The *transition firing rule* is given by:
- A transition t is firable under a marking M with respect to a color c_t of $C(t)$ if and only if: $\forall p \in P$, $\forall c \in C(p)$, $M(p)(c) \geq W^+(p,t)(c,c_t)$
- Firing a transition t with respect to the color c_t of $C(t)$ leads to a new marking M' defined by:

$$\forall p \in P, \ \forall c \in C(p), \ M'(p)(c) = M(p)(c) + W^+(p,t)(c,c_t) - W^-(p,t)(c,c_t)$$

Definition 2.1.3: The *incidence matrix* of a colored net is defined by:$W=W^+-W^-$, where $W(p,t)$ is a linear mapping whose associated matrix $C(p) \times C(t)$ takes values in Z. When a transition t is fired with respect to a color $c_t \in C(t)$ then, for every color

$c_p \in C(p)$, $W(c_p, c_t)$ gives the number of colors c_p to be added to (if the number is positive) or to be removed from (if it is negative) place p.

2.2 Definition of a commutative net

Definition 2.2.1: A *homogeneous net* is a colored net in which the domains of all its places and transitions are identical.

Notes:
- In a homogeneous net, the color functions are endomorphisms of Bags(C), where C is the common domain of the colors of places and transitions.
- We denote **E** as the vector space Bags(C) over the field **Q** (rational numbers) and End(E) as the ring of endomorphisms on **E**.

Definition 2.2.2:Two endomorphisms f and g are *commutative*   iff   f.g = g.f

Definition 2.2.3:Let f be an endomorphism of End(E). The function f is said to be *diagonalizable* on the field of complex numbers if there exists an invertible matrix H such that $H.f.H^{-1}$is a complex diagonal matrix.

Proposition 2.2.1 (Chambalad 72) (Blyth,Robertson 86): *Characterization of diagonalizable functions.* Let f be an endomorphism of End(E). Then the following two statements are equivalent:

(i) There exists a polynomial, P(x), without multiple complex roots, which annuls the function f:
    P(f)=0
    P(x) has no multiple factors

(ii) The function f is diagonalizable on the field of complex numbers.

Definition 2.2.4: Let $\{u_1,...,u_p\}$ be a finite family of endomorphisms of End(E),we denote $Q[u_1,...,u_p]$ as the subring of polynomials generated by the family.

Definition 2.2.5: A *commutative net*   is a homogeneous net such that the color functions are generated by a finite family of diagonalizable endomorphisms $\{u_1,...,u_p\}$ which commute: $\forall u_i, u_k \in \{u_1,...,u_p\}$ $u_i.u_k = u_k.u_i$

2.3 Subclasses of commutative colored nets

Previous definition allows to define subclasses of commutative nets. In effect, every finite family of commutative and diagonalizable endomorphisms $\{u_1,...,u_p\}$ defines a subclass. Functions $u_1,...,u_p$ will be named elementary functions of the subclass.

Below are the basic characteristics of three subclasses of colored nets which are particular cases of commutative nets.

Regular homogeneous nets (Haddad 87)

Color domain: $C=C_1 \times ... \times C_k$, where $C_1, ... , C_k$ are color sets.
Family of elementary functions: $\{1, S_1, ... , S_k\}$ where 1 is the identity function and S_i is the **diffusion** function on C_i:

$$S_i(X_1, ... , X_k) = \sum_{y_i \in C_i} <X_1, ... , X_{i-1}, y_i , X_{i+1}, ... , X_k>$$, where X_j $(1 \leq j \leq k)$ is a variable taking values in $Bag(C_j)$.

There exist polynomials $P_i(x)$, without multiple roots, which annul the functions S_i :

$$P_i(X) = X^2 - n_i.X = 0 ; \quad P_i(S_i) = S_i^2 - n_i.S_i = 0, \quad \text{with} \quad n_i = Card(C_i)$$

The diffusion functions commute :

$$S_i.S_j(X_1, ... , X_k) = S_j.S_i(X_1, ... , X_k) = \sum_{y_i \in C_i, y_j \in C_j} <X_1, ... ,y_i , ...,y_j , ... , X_k>$$

Ordered nets (Haddad,Couvreur 88)

Color domain: $C=C_1 \times ... \times C_k$, where $C_1, ... , C_k$ are ordered color sets:

$$C_i = \{c_{i,0}, c_{i,1}, ... , c_{i,n_i-1}\} \quad (1 \leq i \leq k) .$$

Family of elementary functions: $\{1, s_1, ... , s_k\}$ where 1 is the identity function and s_i is the **successor** function on color set C_i:

$$s_i(X_1, ... , X_k) = <X_1, ... , X_{i-1}, X_i \oplus 1, X_{i+1}, ... , X_k>$$, where X_j $(1 \leq j \leq k)$ is a variable taking values in $Bag(C_j)$ and $\oplus 1$ is the unary operator **successor** defined for each color set C_j ($c_{j,0} \oplus 1 = c_{j,1}$; $c_{j,1} \oplus 1 = c_{j,2}$; ... ; $c_{j,n_j-1} \oplus 1 = c_{j,0}$)

There exist polynomials $P_i(x)$, without multiple roots, which annul the functions s_i:

$$P_i(X) = X^{n_i} - 1 ; \quad P_i(s_i) = s_i^{n_i} - 1 = 0, \quad \text{where} \quad n_i = Card(C_i)$$

The successor functions commute :

$$s_i.s_j(X_1, ... , X_k) = s_j.s_i(X_1, ... , X_k) = <X_1, ... ,X_i \oplus 1 , ...,X_j \oplus 1, ... , X_k>$$

Net in figure 6 belongs to ordered net subclass.

Projection nets

Color domain: A
Family of elementary functions: $\{1, \Pi_{A1} , ... , \Pi_{Ak}\}$, where 1 is the identity function and the function Π_{Ai} is the **projection** of A on the subset A_i defined as follows:

if $c \in A_i$ then $\Pi_{Ai}(c) = c$ else $\Pi_{Ai}(c) = 0$

There exist polynomials $P_i(x)$, without multiple roots, which annul the functions Π_{Ai}:

$P_i(X) = X^2 - X; \quad P_i(\Pi_{Ai}) = \Pi_{Ai}^2 - \Pi_{Ai} = 0$

The projection functions commute :

$\Pi_{Ai}.\Pi_{Aj} = \Pi_{Aj}.\Pi_{Ai} = \Pi_{Ai \cap Aj}$

Nets in figures 1, 2, 3, 4 and 5 belong to projection net subclass.

Projection net shown in figure 1 is a color filter. Let E be the domain of colors of places, P and Q, and of transition t. Let A and B be two subsets of E. Functions Π_A and Π_B are defined as follows.

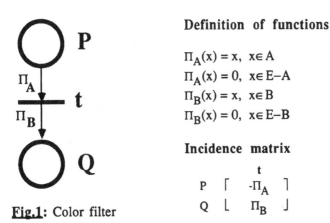

Fig.1: Color filter

Definition of functions

$\Pi_A(x) = x, \quad x \in A$

$\Pi_A(x) = 0, \quad x \in E-A$

$\Pi_B(x) = x, \quad x \in B$

$\Pi_B(x) = 0, \quad x \in E-B$

Incidence matrix

$$\begin{array}{c} \\ P \\ Q \end{array} \begin{array}{c} t \\ \left[\begin{array}{c} -\Pi_A \\ \Pi_B \end{array} \right] \end{array}$$

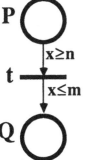

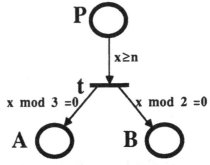

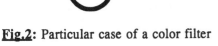

Fig.2: Particular case of a color filter

Fig.3: Selective filter of colors greater than or equal to a threshold n which are multiples of 2 (in B) and of 3 (in A).

Figures 2, 3 and 4 give specific examples of projection nets. In them the color functions labeling arcs appear as predicates, pred(x), instead of using a notation of type Π_A. The correspondence between the two is straightforward:

$x \in A \iff \text{pred}(x)$

Note, finally, that the net in figure 4 can be rewritten in figure 5 by associating predicates with transitions. The transformation rule applied has been introduced in (Genrich 88). This allows us to use predicates, under certain conditions, in the process of computing the flows of a net.

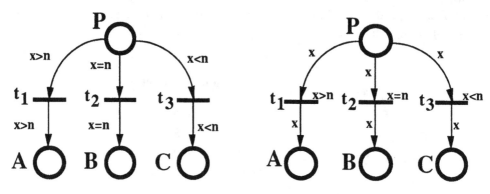

Fig.4: Color selector   **Fig.5**: Alternative form of the net in figure 4

3. PROPERTIES OF THE FUNCTIONS OF A COMMUTATIVE NET

3.1 Stability theorem

Proposition 3.1.1: (Chambalad 72) (Blyth,Robertson 86): *Simultaneous diagonalization.* Let $\{u_1, \dots, u_p\}$ be a finite family of endomorphisms of End(E). Then the following two statements are equivalent:

(i) The family $\{u_1, \dots, u_p\}$ is composed of commutative diagonalizable endomorphisms.

(ii) There exists a matrix H such that the matrix $H.u_i.H^{-1}$ is diagonal for the endomorphisms of $\{u_1, \dots, u_p\}$.

Proposition 3.1.2: *Diagonalizable color function.* Every color function of a commutative net is a diagonalizable function.

Proof:

Let $\{u_1, \dots, u_p\}$ be a family of elementary functions of a commutative net.
Every color function f can be expressed as a polynomial of elementary functions:
$$f = P(u_1, \dots, u_p)$$
The family $\{u_1, \dots, u_p\}$ is composed of diagonalizable endomorphisms which commute. According to propositions 2.2.1 and 3.1.1, there exists a matrix H such that

the matrix $H.u_i.H^{-1}$ is diagonal for the endomorphisms of $\{u_1, \dots, u_p\}$.

Then we have:

$$H.f.H^{-1} = H.P(u_1, \dots, u_p).H^{-1} = P(H.u_1.H^{-1}, \dots, H.u_p.H^{-1})$$

Since the sum and product of diagonal matrices are diagonal matrices, then $H.f.H^{-1}$ is a diagonal matrix. Therefore, the function f is diagonalizable. ◆

3.2 Properties of diagonalizable functions

The aim of this section is to characterise the solutions h of the equation **h.f=0**, where f is a diagonalizable function.

Definition 3.2.1: *Annihilator of a function.* Let f be an endomorphism of End(E). The set of solutions h of h.f=0 is a left ideal. This ideal is called a left annuller and is denoted by Ann(f).

Proposition 3.2.1: *Annihilator of a diagonalizable function.* Given a diagonalizable function f, there exists a polynomial $R(x)$ such that $R(f)$ is a generator of Ann(f).

Proof:

Let f be a diagonalizable function and $P(x)$ a polynomial annihilator of f without multiple roots: P(f)=0.

If $P(0)\neq0$, Let us put $R(x)=P(x)$. Otherwise $(P(0)=0)$ the polynomial $P(x)$ is divisible by x and we put $R(x)=P(x)/x$.

We immediately find that $R(f)$ is an element of Ann(f): $R(f).f=0$

Let us prove that $R(f)$ is a generator of Ann(f):

Since $P(x)$ has not got multiple roots, $R(x)$ and x are relatively prime. Applying Bezout's theorem (Bourbaki 81), there are two polynomials $a(x)$ and $b(x)$ such that:

$$a(x).x + b(x).R(x) = 1$$

Putting x=f we get the following function equation:

$$a(f).f + b(f).R(f) = 1$$

Let h be an element of Ann(f). From the above equation we get:

$$h.a(f).f + h.b(f).R(f) = h.b(f).R(f) = h$$

Therefore, f was generated by the function $R(f)$. ◆

Proposition 3.2.2: *Annihilator of the annihilator of a diagonalizable function.* Given a diagonalizable function f and a polynomial $S(x)$ which is a generator of Ann(f), then the left annihilator of S(f), Ann(S(f)), can be generated by f.

Proof:

1) f is an element of Ann(S(f)) since f . S(f) = 0

2) Let h be an element of Ann(S(f)), i.e. h.S(f)=0. We will prove that h can be expressed as h=g.f, where g belongs to End(E).

We consider two possible cases: $S(0) \neq 0$ and $S(0) = 0$

<u>Case $S(0) \neq 0$</u>: x and S(x) are necessarily relatively prime. Applying Bezout's theorem (Bourbaki 81), there exist two polynomials a(x) and b(x) such that:
$$a(x).x + b(x).S(x) = 1$$
Putting x=f we get the function equation:
$$a(f).f + b(f).S(f) = 1$$
Let h be an element of Ann(S(f)). From the above equation we get:
$$h.a(f).f + h.b(f).S(f) = h.a(f).f = h$$
Therefore, h is of the form g.f with g=h.a(f)

<u>Case $S(0) = 0$</u>: Let us prove that necessarily S(f)=0. This implies that Ann(f)= {0} and, therefore, that f is invertible and that Ann(S(f))=End(E) since f is a generator of Ann(S(f)).

Let P(x) be a non-null polynomial without multiple roots which satisfies P(f)=0 and let R(x) be a polynomial defined by:
If $P(0) \neq 0$ then R(x)=P(x)
else R(x)=P(x)/x   (P(0)=0 means that P(x) is divisible by x)

Since P(x) has no multiple roots, then $R(0) \neq 0$. let us prove that R(x) is a generator of Ann(f). Let c(x) be the highest common denominator of R(x) and S(x).

$c(0) \neq 0$ since c(x) divides R(x) and $R(0) \neq 0$

Since c(x) divides S(x) and $c(0) \neq 0$, there exists a polynomial d(x) which satisfies:
$$S(x) = x.d(x).c(x)$$

Applying Bezout's theorem, there exist two polynomials a(x) and b(x) such that:
$$a(x).S(x) + b(x).R(x) = c(x)$$

Putting x=f we get the function equation:
$$a(f).S(f) + b(f).R(f) = c(f)$$

Multiplying both sides of the equation by f, and taking into account that R(f)=0 and that f.S(f)=0 then we get: f.c(f) = 0.

Therefore: S(f)= f.d(f).c(f) = 0   ♦

Proposition 3.2.3: *Annihilator of the product of two functions.* Given two endomorphism of End(E), f and g, which are diagonalizable and commute with each other, the following holds
$$Ann(f.g) = Ann(f) + Ann(g)$$

Proof:

Let $R(x)$ and $S(x)$ be two polynomials which satisfy:
- $R(f)$ is a generator of Ann(f) and $S(g)$ is a generator of Ann(g)
- $R(0) \neq 0$ and $S(0) \neq 0$

We will prove that every annihilator h of $f.g$ has the form $h1.R(f) + h2.S(g)$, where $h1$ and $h2$ are endomorphisms of End(E).

Applying Bezout's theorem, there are four polynomials $a(x)$, $b(x)$, $c(x)$ and $d(x)$ which satisfy:

$$a(x).x + b(x).R(x) = 1$$
$$c(x).x + d(x).S(x) = 1$$

Putting $x=f$ in the first equation and $x=g$ in the second we get the following equations:

$$a(f).f + b(f).R(f) = 1$$
$$c(g).g + d(g).S(g) = 1$$

Multiplying the two equations element by element and recalling that f and g commute with each other, we get:

$$a(f).c(g).f.g + a(f).d(g).f.S(g) + b(f).c(g).g.R(f) + b(f).d(g).R(f).S(g) = 1$$

Multiplying both elements by function h and taking into account that $h.g.f = h.f.g = 0$ we get:

$$(h.a(f).d(g).f).S(g) + (h.b(f).c(g).g + h.b(f).d(g).S(g)).R(f) = h$$

Therefore, h has the form $h1.R(f) + h2.S(g)$ with:

$$h1 = h.b(f).c(g).g + h.b(f).d(g).S(g) \quad \text{and}$$
$$h2 = h.a(f).d(g).f \qquad \qquad \blacklozenge$$

Corollary 3.2.1: *Annihilator of the product of k-functions.* Given k endomorphisms of End(E), $\{f_1, ..., f_k\}$, which are diagonalizable and commutative, the following holds:

$$\text{Ann}(f_1.f_2. \; .... \; .f_k) = \text{Ann}(f_1) + \text{Ann}(f_2) + \cdots + \text{Ann}(f_k)$$

4. FLOWS OF A COMMUTATIVE NET

4.1 Symbolic flows of a homogeneous net

Definition 4.1.1: A *symbolic flow* of a homogeneous net is a vector F on $(\text{End}(E))^{\text{card}(P)}$ which satisifies the equation: $F . W = 0$

Note: The problem of computing the symbolic flows of a homogeneous commutative net is transformed into that of solving a system of linear equations on the ring End(E).

4.2 Elementary operations

Three types of elementary operations on the commutative net's incidence matrix allow us to get a generative family of flows:
- Adding a new column to the matrix, which is the result of multiplying one of its columns by a given color function.
- Adding to a row of the matrix the result of the multiplication of another row by a given color function.
- Substituting in the matrix the solutions associated with the annullment of a column.

Proposition 4.2.1: Let W be the incidence matrix of a commutative net, h a color function and W' the matrix obtained by adding to W the column resulting from the multiplication of one of its columns by the color function h. Then the flows associated with matrices W and W' are identical.

Proposition 4.2.2: Let W be the incidence matrix of a commutative net, h a color function and W' the matrix obtained by adding to row (b) of W the result of multiplying another of its rows, row (a), by the color function h.
Then $F = (f_1, \ldots, f_a, \ldots, f_b, \ldots, f_k)$ is a flow of W'
iff $F = (f_1, \ldots, f_a + f_b.h, \ldots, f_b, \ldots, f_k)$ is a flow of W.

Proposition 4.2.3: Let W be the incidence matrix of a commutative net, (t) a column of W and $\{G_1, \ldots, G_r\}$ a family which generates the flow associated with column (t). Let us define the matrix G composed of the linear vectors G_i and the matrix W'= G.W . The flows of matrices W and W' are related by the following properties:

(1) F' is a flow of W' $\Leftrightarrow$ F'.G is a flow of W

(2) F is a flow of W $\Leftrightarrow$ there exist F' of W' such that F=F'.G

Proof:

(1) F' is a flow of W' $\Leftrightarrow$ F'.G.W = 0 $\Leftrightarrow$ F'.G is a flow of W

(2) If there exist flows F' of W' such that F=F'.G, according to property (1) F is a flow of W.

If F is a flow of W, F is also a flow of column (t) and can, therefore, be expressed as a linear combination of the family $\{G_1, \ldots, G_r\}$ of the form F'.G. According to property (1) F' is a flow of W'. $\blacklozenge$

4.3 Solution algorithm

With the sequence of elementary operations which will be presented here, we can decrease the number of non-null functions in a given column of the color function matrix without increasing the number of columns. Thus, by iterating this sequence we get a generative family of flows.

Let W be an incidence matrix of the form:

$$
\begin{array}{c}
\\
A_1 \\
\cdots \\
A_r \\
A_{r+1} \\
A_{r+2} \\
\cdots \\
A_p
\end{array}
\left[
\begin{array}{c|c|c}
\mathbf{t} & & \\
f_1 & & \\
\cdots & & \\
f_r & & \\
f_{r+1} & \mathbf{W1} & \\
0 & & \\
\cdots & & \\
0 & &
\end{array}
\right]
$$

Step 1: Add a column

Let $K_i(f_i)$ be a polynomial in f_i which generates $Ann(f_i)$ for $i \in [1,r]$. Let us add to matrix W the column $K_1(f_1). \ \cdots \ . K_r(f_r).t$

$$
\begin{array}{c}
\\
A_1 \\
\cdots \\
A_r \\
A_{r+1} \\
A_{r+2} \\
\cdots \\
A_p
\end{array}
\left[
\begin{array}{c|c|c}
\mathbf{t} & \mathbf{K_1(f_1). \ \cdots \ . K_r(f_r).t} & \\
f_1 & 0 & \\
\cdots & \cdots & \\
f_r & 0 & \\
f_{r+1} & K_1(f_1). \cdots . K_r(f_r).f_{r+1} & \mathbf{W1} \\
0 & 0 & \\
\cdots & \cdots & \\
0 & 0 &
\end{array}
\right]
$$

Step 2: Substitute the flows of the added column

According to the properties of color functions $\{f_1, \ldots , f_r, K_{r+1}(f_{r+1}) \}$ is a family which generates the annihilators of the added column $K_1(f_1). \ \cdots \ . K_r(f_r).t$. Substituting we get:

$$
\begin{array}{c}
\\
A_1 \\
\cdots \\
A_r \\
f_1.A_{r+1} \\
\cdots \\
f_r.A_{r+1} \\
K_{r+1}(f_{r+1}).A_{r+1} \\
A_{r+2} \\
\cdots \\
A_p
\end{array}
\left[
\begin{array}{c|c|c}
\mathbf{t} & \mathbf{K_1(f_1). \ \cdots \ .K_r(f_r).t} & \\
f_1 & 0 & \\
\cdots & \cdots & \\
f_r & 0 & \\
f_1.f_{r+1} & 0 & \\
\cdots & \cdots & \mathbf{W3} \\
f_r.f_{r+1} & 0 & \\
0 & 0 & \\
0 & 0 & \\
\cdots & \cdots & \\
0 & 0 &
\end{array}
\right]
$$

Step 3: Subtract from each row $f_i.A_{r+1}$ the row A_i premultiplied by f_{r+1}

With this we eliminate from column (t) all the added non-null functions. In addition, we can eliminate the added column, since it has been completely annulled.

$$
\begin{array}{c}
A_1 \\
\cdots \\
A_r \\
f_1.A_{r+1}\text{-}f_{r+1}.A_1 \\
\cdots \\
f_r.A_{r+1}\text{-}f_{r+1}.A_r \\
K_{r+1}(f_{r+1}).A_{r+1} \\
A_{r+2} \\
\cdots \\
A_p
\end{array}
\left[
\begin{array}{c|c|c}
t & & \\
f_1 & | & \\
\cdots & | & \\
f_r & | & \\
0 & | & \\
\cdots & | & \mathbf{W4} \\
0 & | & \\
0 & | & \\
0 & | & \\
\cdots & | & \\
0 & |
\end{array}
\right]
$$

5. APPLICATION OF THE COMPUTATION ALGORITHM

5.1 Filter models

We will study the computation of a generative family of flows of the projection net shown in figure 1, which is a color filter.

Incidence matrix

$$
\begin{array}{c}
P \\
Q
\end{array}
\left[
\begin{array}{c}
t \\
-\Pi_A \\
\Pi_B
\end{array}
\right]
$$

Step 1: Add a column

The annihilator of Π_A is $(1-\Pi_A)$.

$$
\begin{array}{c}
P \\
Q
\end{array}
\left[
\begin{array}{c|c}
t & (1-\Pi_A).t \\
-\Pi_A & | & 0 \\
\Pi_B & | & \Pi_B.(1-\Pi_A)
\end{array}
\right]
$$

Step 2: Sustitute the flows of the added column

$$
\begin{array}{c}
P \\
\Pi_A.Q \\
(1-\Pi_B).Q
\end{array}
\left[
\begin{array}{c|c}
t & (1-\Pi_A).t \\
-\Pi_A & | & 0 \\
\Pi_A.\Pi_B & | & 0 \\
0 & | & 0
\end{array}
\right]
$$

Step 3: Add to the row $\Pi_A.Q$ the row P premultiplied by Π_B

$$
\begin{array}{c}
P \\
\Pi_A.Q+\Pi_B.P \\
(1-\Pi_B).Q
\end{array}
\left[
\begin{array}{c}
t \\
-\Pi_A \\
0 \\
0
\end{array}
\right]
$$

Row P can be eliminated by premultiplying by the function $(1 - \Pi_A)$. The computed generative family of flows is:

		P	Q	
(F1)	[	$(1 - \Pi_A)$	0	]
(F2)	[	0	$(1 - \Pi_B)$	]
(F3)	[	Π_B	Π_A	]

Interpreting the invariants associated with the flows:

We denote $P(x)$ the number of colors x in the marking of place P and $P_0(x)$ the number of colors x in the initial marking of place P.

Given that $\Pi_C(x) = x$ if $x \in C$ and $\Pi_C(x) = 0$ if $x \notin C$, we can deduce the following invariant relations:

(F1) $\quad \forall\, x \notin A \qquad (1-\Pi_A)(x) = x - 0 = x \;\Rightarrow\; P(x) = P_0(x) = \text{const}$
Color x belonging to E-A cannot leave place P. $P(x)$ is an invariant.

(F2) $\quad \forall\, x \notin B \qquad (1-\Pi_B)(x) = x - 0 = x \;\Rightarrow\; Q(x) = Q_0(x) = \text{const}$
Color x belonging to E-B cannot reach place Q. $Q(x)$ is an invariant

(F3) $\quad \forall\, x \in A \cap B \quad \Pi_A(x) = \Pi_B(x) = x \;\Rightarrow\; P(x)+Q(x) = P_0(x)+Q_0(x) = \text{const}$
Number of colors $x \in A \cap B$ in places P and Q is invariant.

In a similar way we can compute flows for nets in figures 2, 3 and 4:

Incidence matrix of net in figure 2:

$$
\begin{array}{c}
P \\
Q
\end{array}
\left[
\begin{array}{c}
t1 \\
-[\,x \geq n\,] \\
[\,x \leq m\,]
\end{array}
\right]
$$

Generative family of flows:

		P	Q	
(F1)	[	$[\,x < n\,]$	0	]
(F2)	[	0	$[\,x > m\,]$	]
(F3)	[	$[\,x \leq m\,]$	$[\,x \geq n\,]$	]

Incidence matrix of net in figure 3:

$$
\begin{array}{c}
\quad\quad\quad \textbf{t1} \\
\begin{array}{c}
\text{P} \\
\text{A} \\
\text{B}
\end{array}
\left[
\begin{array}{c}
-[\,x \geq n\,] \\
[\,x \bmod 3 = 0\,] \\
[\,x \bmod 2 = 0\,]
\end{array}
\right]
\end{array}
$$

Generative family of flows:

	P	A	B	
(F1)	[[x < n]	0	0	]
(F2)	[0	[x mod 3 <> 0]	0	]
(F3)	[0	0	[x mod 2 <> 0]]
(F4)	[[x mod 3 = 0]	[x ≥ n]	0	]
(F5)	[[x mod 2 = 0]	0	[x ≥ n]	]
(F6)	[0	[x mod 2 = 0]	[x mod 3 = 0]]

Incidence matrix of net in figure 4:

$$
\begin{array}{c}
\quad\quad\quad\quad \textbf{t1} \quad\quad\quad\quad\quad \textbf{t2} \quad\quad\quad\quad\quad \textbf{t3} \\
\begin{array}{c}
\text{P} \\
\text{A} \\
\text{B} \\
\text{C}
\end{array}
\left[
\begin{array}{ccc}
-[\,x > n\,] & -[\,x = n\,] & -[\,x < n\,] \\
[\,x > n\,] & 0 & 0 \\
0 & [\,x = n\,] & 0 \\
0 & 0 & [\,x < n\,]
\end{array}
\right]
\end{array}
$$

Generative family of flows:

	P	A	B	C	
(F1)	[0	[x ≤ n]	0	0	]
(F2)	[0	0	[x <> n]	0	]
(F3)	[0	0	0	[x ≥ n]]
(F4)	[1	1	1	1	]

5.2 Synchronized clocks arranged on a virtual ring

Figure 6 shows a commutative net which models the synchronization of the local clocks of M stations connected to a virtual ring. The clock of each station, H, has an associated value X. The values or dates of the clocks are synchronized by sending messages along the net. Each station, H, sends a message to the next one, H⊕1 (firing transition t2). When a station H has sent its synchronization message to the next station (the color <H,X> marks place B) and has received the corresponding message from the previous station (the color <H,X> marks place C) it can proceed to update its local clock with the value (date) X⊕1 (firing transition t1).

The domain of the colors of the places and transitions in the net is C1 × C2, where:

C1 = { Stations } = {0 , ··· , M-1}
C2 = { Dates of the local clocks } = {0 , ··· , N-1}
M and N are parameters

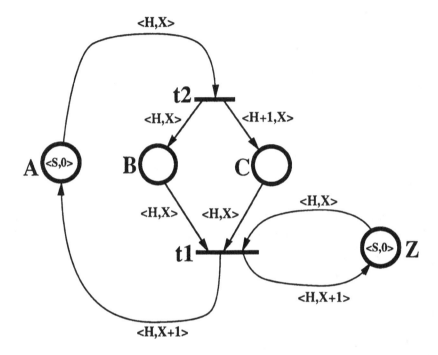

Fig.6: Commutative net which models a protocol for synchronizing the local clocks of stations on a virtual ring. (Note: <S,0> = <0,0> + <1,0> + ... + <M-1,0>)

Incidence matrix

	t1	t2
Z	<H,X⊕1> - <H,X>	0
A	<H,X⊕1>	-<H,X>
B	-<H,X>	<H,X>
C	-<H,X>	<H⊕1,X>

Writing the incidence matrix in terms of functions

To make easier the notation, we have associated names (identifiers) with the color functions of the model:

1   for the "identity" function   { i.e.: **1**(<H,X>) = <H,X> }

λ for the "next_value_of_clock" function

$$\{ \text{ i.e.: } \lambda(<H,X>) = <H,X\oplus 1> \}$$

μ for the "next_station" function $\{ \text{ i.e.: } \mu(<H,X>) = <H\oplus 1,X> \}$

The incidence matrix of the commutative net can be rewritten as:

$$
\begin{array}{c}
 \\
Z \\
A \\
B \\
C
\end{array}
\begin{array}{c}
\mathbf{t1} \\
\left[\begin{array}{c} \lambda - 1 \\ \lambda \\ -1 \\ -1 \end{array}\right.
\end{array}
\begin{array}{c}
\mathbf{t2} \\
\left.\begin{array}{c} 0 \\ -1 \\ 1 \\ \mu \end{array}\right]
\end{array}
$$

By elementary transformations of the incidence matrix we get:

$$
\begin{array}{c}
 \\
Z \\
Z - A - B \\
B \\
C - \mu.B
\end{array}
\begin{array}{c}
\mathbf{t1} \\
\left[\begin{array}{c} \lambda - 1 \\ 0 \\ -1 \\ \mu - 1 \end{array}\right.
\end{array}
\begin{array}{c}
\mathbf{t2} \\
\left.\begin{array}{c} 0 \\ 0 \\ 1 \\ 0 \end{array}\right]
\end{array}
$$

Let us first consider column t2. Only one element remains to be eliminated: function 1 whose polynomial annihilator is polynomial 0: Ann(1)=0. Therefore, row B can be eliminated.

$$
\begin{array}{c}
 \\
Z \\
Z - A - B \\
C - \mu.B
\end{array}
\begin{array}{c}
\mathbf{t1} \\
\left[\begin{array}{c} \lambda - 1 \\ 0 \\ \mu - 1 \end{array}\right.
\end{array}
\begin{array}{c}
\mathbf{t2} \\
\left.\begin{array}{c} 0 \\ 0 \\ 0 \end{array}\right]
\end{array}
$$

Applying the elimination algorithm given in §4.3 to column (t1) we immediately get a generative family of flows:

	Z	Z-A-B	C - μ . B	
(F1)	[S_λ	0	0	]
(F2)	[0	0	S_μ	]
(F3)	[0	1	0	]
(F4)	[$-(\mu - 1)$	0	$(\lambda - 1)$	]

Where: $S_\lambda = 1 + \lambda + ... + \lambda^{N-1}$ is a generator of Ann(λ - 1) and

         $S_\mu = 1 + \mu + ... + \mu^{M-1}$ is a generator of Ann(μ - 1)

Interpreting the invariants associated with the flows:

(F1) $Z(H,0) + \cdots + Z(H,N-1) = 1$

      For each station clock, H, there is only one token (H,X) marking place Z. Then X is the current date of clock H.

(F2) $C(0,X) + \cdots + C(M-1,X) = B(0,X) + \cdots + B(M-1,X)$

      For each date, X, the number of messages (-,X) waiting for updating stations clocks (colors (-,X) marking place C) is equal to the number the station with current date X waiting for an update message (colors (-,X) marking place B).

(F3) $Z(H,X) = A(H,X) + B(H,X)$
A station H, independently of its state (place A or B marked), could send or receive only its clock date, X.

(F4) $C(H,X) - C(H,X\ominus1) = Z(H,X) - Z(H\ominus1,X) + B(H\ominus1,X) - B(H\ominus1,X\ominus1) =$
$= Z(H,X) - A(H\ominus1,X) - B(H\ominus1,X\ominus1)$
The difference between the number of consecutive update messages sent by a station H and not yet received only depends on the state of the stations $H\ominus1$ and H (markings $Z(H,X)$, $A(H\ominus1,X)$ and $B(H\ominus1,X\ominus1)$).

6. CONCLUSION

Commutative nets, a particular case of colored nets, have been introduced. Commutative nets include, as subclasses, regular homogenous nets, ordered nets and projection nets, among others. These nets can model a broad range of concurrent systems of practical importance, such as communication protocols; queue, ring and counter management systems; filters; etc.. Furthermore, other subclasses of nets can be transformed into commutative nets by applying homogenization and decomposition rules.

The color functions which appear both in the model (incidence matrix) and in the process of computing flows belong to a ring of commutative functions which are diagonalizable with respect to a single base. This enables us to compute flows symbolically.

We have proposed an algorithm for computing a flow generator family. The algorithm is based on an elimination method which, in each step, decreases the number of non-null functions in a given column of the color function matrix.

These results are a generalization of those already known for computing flows in regular nets (Haddad 87) and ordered nets (Haddad, Couvreur 88). Furthermore, they complement the method of computation by elimination proposed by (Silva et al. 85) since they give partial solutions to the problem of controlling the elimination algorithm.

ACKNOWLEDGEMENTS

The authors are indebted to the referees for their helpful comments. This work was partially supported by the DEMON Esprit Research Action 3148 and the Plan Nacional de Investigación, Grant TIC-0358/89.

REFERENCES

(Alla et al. 85) H.Alla, P.Ladet, J. Martínez, M. Silva. Modelling and validation of complex systems by coloured Petri nets. *Advances in Petri nets 1984. L.N.C.S. 188,* Springer-Verlag, pp.15-31

(Blyth,Robertson 86) T.S.Blyth, E.F.Robertson. *Linear Algebra (Vol. 4).* Chapman and Hall. London.

(Bourbaki 81) N.Bourbaki . *Algèbre (Chapitres 4 à 7).* Masson. Paris.

(Brams 83) G.W.Brams. *Réseaux de Petri:théorie et pratique.* Masson. Paris

(Chambalad 72) L.Chambalad. *Algèbre multilinaire.* Dunod. Paris

(Genrich 88) H.J.Genrich.Equivalence transformations of PrT-Nets. *9th European Workshop on Application and Theory of Petri Nets. Vol. II.* Venice (Italy). June. pp. 229-248

(Genrich,Lautenbach 83) H.J.Genrich, K.Lautenbach.S-invariance in predicate transition nets.*Informatik Fachberichte 66: Application and Theory of Petri Nets.* A.Pagnoni,G.Rozenberg (eds.). Springer-Verlag. pp. 98-111

(Jensen 81) K.Jensen. Coloured Petri nets and the invariant method. *Theoretical Computer Science 14.* North Holland Publ. Co. pp.317-336

(Haddad 87) S.Haddad. *Une catégorie régulière de réseau de Petri de haut niveau: définition, propietés et reductions. Application à la validation des systèmes distribués.* Ph.D. University Paris VI. June.

(Haddad, Couvreur 88) S.Haddad, J.M.Couvreur. Towards a general and powerful computation of flows for parametrized coloured nets. *9th European Workshop on Application and Theory of Petri Nets. Vol. II.* Venice (Italy). June.

(Reisig 85) W.Reisig. *Petri nets.* EATCS Monographs on Theoretical Computer Science, Vol. 4. Springer Publ. Co.

(Silva 85) M.Silva. *Las redes de Petri en la automática y la informática.* Ed. AC. Madrid.

(Silva et al. 85) M.Silva, J.Martínez, P.Ladet, H.Alla. Generalized inverses and the calculation of invariants for coloured Petri nets. *Technique et science informatique.* Vol.4 n⁰1, pp. 113-126

(Vautherin,Memmi 85) J.Vautherin, G.Memmi. Computation of flows for unary predicates transition nets. *Advances in Petri nets 1984. L.N.C.S. 188,* Springer-Verlag. pp.455-467

Vicinity Respecting Net Morphisms

Jörg Desel

Institut für Informatik
Technische Universität München
Arcisstraße 21
D-8000 München 2

Agathe Merceron

Institut für methodische Grundlagen
Gesellschaft für Mathematik und Datenverarbeitung
Postfach 1240
D-5205 St.Augustin 1

ABSTRACT. Vicinity respecting net morphisms are a restricted class of net morphisms. The restriction requires that pre- and post-sets of elements are respected by the morphisms. However, vicinity respecting net morphisms allow to map S-elements to T-elements and vice versa and can hence formalize contractions of nets.

Amongst some general properties of net morphisms and in particular of vicinity respecting net morphisms it is shown how this concept can be used for net transformations such as abstractions and compositions which preserve global properties. In particular, sufficient conditions for the preservation of coverings by S-components and T-components are given.

Keywords. Net morphisms, synthesis and structure of nets, coarsening and composition of nets.

CONTENTS

0   Introduction

During the design of a (non-sequential) system several aspects of the system are formalized by different models. Some of these models might represent subparts of the system. Their composition leads to a representation of the entire system. On the other hand models may represent the same (part of the) system at different abstraction levels.

It is desirable to have an homogeneous formalism to represent models of different layers. Using such a formalism, properties of models and in particular relations between models can be expressed in a uniform way. Properties of models can be deduced from properties of respective related models.

Examples of such relations between models are abstractions from details. Of course, an abstraction should preserve relevant properties. Another example is the composition of subcomponents. Certain properties of the subcomponents can be deduced from respective properties of the entire system or, conversely, common properties of the subparts carry over to the composed system.

This paper tackles these problems taking Petri Nets to design non-sequential systems and net morphisms to formalize relations between different models, i.e., between different Petri Nets. Petri Nets allow to specify causality, choice (or conflicts) and concurrency (or parallelism) explicitly. We are interested in relations between nets which allow to transfer properties concerning choice and concurrency from some nets to other nets. In particular, we are going to present a class of morphisms which respect coverings by S-components. By the duality between S- and T-components we shall obtain a similar result for T-component coverings.

At a first glance, a Petri Net appears to be a bipartite graph. However, exchanging the two sorts of nodes leads to a completely different interpretation. S-elements and T-elements are dual to each other as choice and concurrency are dual concepts (see [8]).

Branched S-elements allow to specify choice in a structural way. An S-component is a subnet where only the S-elements are branched. It can be seen as a specification of a main stream of conflicts and causal interrelations between these conflicts. S-components can be interpreted as main streams of alternatives allowed by the system at the abstraction level represented by the net. Hence, being covered by S-components is an important property of a net since it allows to know, for any element, to which main alternatives it belongs.

Branched T-elements allow to specify concurrency in a a structural way. All what has been said for S-components can be dually said for T-components. In particular, a T-component covering of a net shows for any element the main streams of concurrency it belongs to.

Given a net, the computation of all its S-components (T-components, respectively) or at least of a covering by S-components is a highly complex task. On the other hand, a well-designed system can be modeled as a composition of simple subparts. If these subparts are (covered by) S-components it remains to prove that the composition of these subparts preserves that property. Other aspects of models can be derived by means of transformations of nets which preserve certain properties – in our case S-component coverings. So there is a need for transformation mechanisms which preserve S-component coverings to avoid the high effort of analysing the respective nets.

The main question addressed in this paper is:

Given a net N which is covered by S-components, how can we derive a higher level of abstraction and/or compose unconnected parts of N such that we get a net N' which is covered by S-components as well?

The method of relating such nets N and N' is given by net morphisms. Roughly speaking, a net morphism is a mapping from elements of a source net to elements of a target net which respects the bipartition and the flow relation of the source net ([5], [6], [4]). Net morphisms and some of their properties are presented in section two.

The question above can be reformulated as:

How can we identify elements of N by means of a surjective morphism such that the property of being covered by S-components carries over to the target net N'?

To answer this question we introduce in the third section vicinity respecting net morphisms. The idea of vicinity respecting morphisms is roughly the following: if two elements are similar enough to be mapped to the same element, then their effect on the environment should be similar as well. Their effect on the environment is given by their adjacent elements (adjacent in the sense of graph theory), which we call their vicinity. Consequently their vicinity should be mapped onto the same set: the vicinity of their common image.

Using morphisms with the local property of respecting the vicinity of elements we present our main result, concerning the global property of S-component coverings, in section four. If a net morphism relates two nets then a sufficient condition for the preservation of S-component coverings by the morphism is: the morphism respects the vicinity of S-elements and, if restricted to any S-component of a given covering, respects the vicinity of T-elements. A dual result holds for T-component coverings. The result is illustrated by means of an example of composition and coarsening of nets with vicinity respecting morphisms.

Section five concludes with discussions and related works.

Throughout this paper we won't give any interpretation of nets such as marking classes or occurrence rules but concentrate on the structure of nets. However, structure and semantics are not independent. The sum of tokens of an S-component remains invariant with respect to transition occurrences. Hence a net covered by S-components is bounded, independently of the marking class considered. In other words, for no S-element the token count can increase infinitely. This kind of structural boundedness is preserved by the morphisms we are going to present.

T-components are related to infinite and cyclic behaviour of nets. For special classes of nets (e.g. for extended-free-choice-nets) it is known that live and bounded nets are covered by S- and T-components [2]. Hence, at least for these nets, to be covered by T-components is a necessary condition for liveness. We shall present a class of morphisms which preserve the property of being covered by T-components.

1 Basic Definitions

Most of the definitions presented in this section closely follow [1].

Definition 1.1

(1) A triple $N = (S, T; F)$ is called a *net* if:

1. $S \cap T = \emptyset$;
2. $F \subseteq (S \times T) \cup (T \times S)$.

(2) The set $X = S \cup T$ is the set of *elements* of the net.

We weaken the definition given in [1] (a net, as defined here, is called *pre-net* in [1]). This allows to consider nets with isolated elements.

Graphically *S-elements* are represented by circles, *T-elements* are represented by squares and the *flow relation* F is represented by arrows between the elements.

We use the following convention:
The indices and primes used to denote a net N are carried over to all parts of N. For example, speaking of a net N'_i, we implicitly understand $N'_i = (S'_i, T'_i; F'_i)$ and $X'_i = S'_i \cup T'_i$.

Notation 1.2

Let x be an element of a net N.
The set $\{y \in X \mid (y, x) \in F\}$ is called *pre-set* of x and is denoted by $^\bullet x$.
The set $\{y \in X \mid (x, y) \in F\}$ is called *post-set* of x and is denoted by $x^\bullet$.

This notion is generalized to sets $A \subseteq X$ of elements: $^\bullet A = \bigcup_{x \in A} {}^\bullet x$, $A^\bullet = \bigcup_{x \in A} x^\bullet$.

Since an element together with its pre-set or post-set will be often used, we introduce the following notion: $^\odot x = {}^\bullet x \cup \{x\}$, $x^\odot = x^\bullet \cup \{x\}$.

In Net Theory, and in this paper in particular, the flow relation F plays a major rôle. While looking how two elements are connected, we will never neglect the direction of the arrows. Hence a path in our sense is a directed path. In strongly connected nets every two elements of a net are connected by means of a directed path.

Definition 1.3

Let N be a net and let $x_1, \ldots, x_n \in X$, $n \geq 1$.
A string $x_1 \ldots x_n$ is called *path* of N if $\forall i \in \{1, \ldots, n-1\}$: $(x_i, x_{i+1}) \in F$.
A net N is *strongly connected* if $X \times X = F^*$.

S-components and *T*-components are particular cases of *subnets*. A subnet is generated by its elements and preserves the flow relation between its elements (see [8]). *S-subnets* are subnets which include for each *S*-element the vicinity of this element as well. *S*-components are strongly connected *S*-subnets without branched *T*-elements.

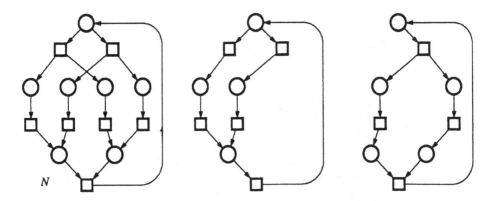

Figure 1: *A net N with one of its two S-components and one of its two T-components. There is one family of S-components and one family of T-components which cover N.*

Definition 1.4

Let N be a net. $X_1 \subseteq X$ generates the *subnet* $N_1 = (S \cap X_1, T \cap X_1, F \cap (X_1 \times X_1))$.

A subnet N_1 is called *S-subnet* if $X_1 = S_1 \cup {}^\bullet S_1 \cup S_1^\bullet$.

A strongly connected S-subnet N_1 of a net N is called *S-component* of N if $\forall t \in T_1$: $|{}^\bullet t \cap S_1| = 1 \wedge |t^\bullet \cap S_1| = 1$ (pre-sets and post-sets are taken with respect to N).

A net N is said to be *covered by S-components* if there exists a family of S-components (N_i), $i \in I$, such that $\forall x \in X \, \exists i \in I: x \in X_i$.

All definitions concerning S-elements or S-components can be dually formulated for T-elements and T-components.

Notation 1.5

If $N = (S, T; F)$ is a net then $N_1 = (S_1, T_1; F_1)$ is a *T-subnet* of N if $(T_1, S_1; F_1)$ is an S-subnet of the net $(T, S; F)$. Similarly, $N_1 = (S_1, T_1; F_1)$ is a *T-component* of N if $(T_1, S_1; F_1)$ is an S-component of $(T, S; F)$ and N is *covered by T-components* if $(T, S; F)$ is covered by S-components.

The net shown in figure 1 is covered by S- and by T-components.

2 Net Morphisms

Viewing one system from different sides, concentrating on different parts, or considering different levels of abstraction, leads to more than one model for one system. These models are of course in some way related to each other.

In General Net Theory the relations between models – here nets – are expressed in terms of relations between the elements of the nets. Special kinds of such relations are given by mappings of nets which consequently are mappings from elements of a source net to

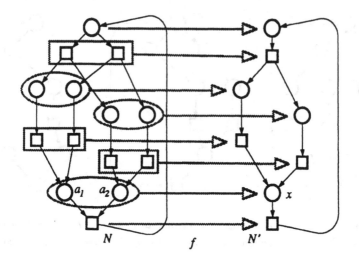

Figure 2: *A net morphism* $f: N \to N'$. *N' is neither covered by T-components nor by S-components.*

elements of a target net. As long as arbitrary mappings are considered there are nearly no interrelations or implications between properties of the nets considered. So additional restrictions on the mappings are required which pay regard to the structure of the nets.

In this section we will define *net morphisms* which have been introduced first in [7]. Net morphisms respect the bipartition of the nodes and the flow relation of the source net as shown in [4]. Using a net morphism, two elements a, b with $(a, b) \in F$ can be mapped to one element – then they are not distinguished in the target net. If this is not the case then their images are in the flow relation of the target net (respecting the flow relation) and additionally the types of the elements are respected (respecting the bipartition). This implies that the image of the S-element of $\{a, b\}$ is an S-element and consequently the image of the T-element of $\{a, b\}$ is a T-element of the target net.

We use the definition given in [6] and [5]. Therefore we first introduce the relation P. An S-element s and a T-element t are in the relation P if t is a T-element adjacent to s.

Definition 2.1

$P = (F \cup F^{-1}) \cap (S \times T)$ is called the *adjacency* relation of a net N.

Definition 2.2

Let N, N' be nets. A mapping $f: X \to X'$ is called *net morphism* (or simply *morphism*), denoted by $f: N \to N'$, if $\forall a, b \in X$:

1. $(a, b) \in P \implies (f(a), f(b)) \in P' \cup \mathrm{id}_{X'}$ and

2. $(a, b) \in F \implies (f(a), f(b)) \in F' \cup \mathrm{id}_{X'}$

where $\mathrm{id}_{X'} = \{(x, x) \mid x \in X'\}$.

Several equivalent definitions of net morphisms can be found in the literature. We use the above version since 2.2.1 and 2.2.2 have separate consequences for the target net.

With 2.2.1 morphisms respect the *bipartition* of the source net. A T-element is allowed to be mapped to an S-element only if all elements of its vicinity (pre-set and post-set) are mapped to the same S-element, and vice versa.

Proposition 2.3

Let $f: N \rightarrow N'$ be a net morphism. Then:

1. $\forall t \in T \; \forall s \in S': f(t) = s \implies f(^\bullet t \cup \{t\} \cup t^\bullet) = \{s\};$
2. $\forall s \in S \; \forall t \in T': f(s) = t \implies f(^\bullet s \cup \{s\} \cup s^\bullet) = \{t\}.$

We deduce immediately the following corollary:

Corollary 2.4

Let $f: N \rightarrow N'$ be a net morphism and let $(a, b) \in F$, $f(a) \neq f(b)$.
Then for $x \in \{a, b\}$ we get $f(x) \in S' \Leftrightarrow x \in S$ and $f(x) \in T' \Leftrightarrow x \in T$.

With 2.2.2 morphisms respect the *flow relation* of the source net. This imposes restrictions on the images of pre-sets and post-sets in the following way:

Proposition 2.5

If $f: N \rightarrow N'$ is a morphism then $\forall a \in X: f(^\odot a) \subseteq {}^\odot f(a)$ and $f(a^\odot) \subseteq f(a)^\odot$.

As single arcs are respected, sequences of arcs which form paths are respected in a certain sense too. Since consecutive elements of a path can be mapped to one element the sequence of images of path elements is not necessarily a path of the target net. Hence we introduce another notion of the image of a path.

Notation 2.6

Given two nets N, N', a mapping $f: X \rightarrow X'$ and a path $a_1 \ldots a_m$ of N, we denote the image $f(a_1 \ldots a_m)$ of the path $a_1 \ldots a_m$ as follows:
The image of a path a is the image of the element a.
Let $m > 1$ and suppose that $f(a_1 \ldots a_{m-1}) = x_1 \ldots x_n$. Then
$f(a_1 \ldots a_m) = x_1 \ldots x_n$ if $f(a_m) = f(a_{m-1}) = x_n$,
$f(a_1 \ldots a_m) = x_1 \ldots x_n f(a_m)$ otherwise.

Corollary 2.7

If $f: N \rightarrow N'$ is a net morphism and $a_1 \ldots a_m$ is a path of N then $f(a_1 \ldots a_m)$ is a path of N'.

In this paper we will be interested to map a net N to a net N', viewing N as a more detailed model of a system than N' (or N' as a coarser model than N). Therefore we are especially interested in surjective mappings.

Note that composing nets is a special case of identifying elements. It can hence be seen as a coarsening and is formally treated by a surjective mapping as well.

Using corollary 2.7, we get:

Corollary 2.8

Let $f: N \to N'$ be a surjective net morphism.
If N is strongly connected, then N' is strongly connected.

Up to now we have considered two given nets and a mapping between them. Another aspect of net mappings is the possibility of *transformation* or *generation* of nets. In these cases only the source net and some information about the mapping is given while the target net is given only implicitly. For generating the elements of the target net the mapping obviously has to be surjective. To have a relation between the structure of the two nets we will consider surjective net morphisms. We call a target net 'generated by the morphism' if not only any element of the target net is generated by some element of the source net but also any arc is generated by some arc of the source net. It turns out that, given the partition of the elements which is generated by the equivalence relation 'is mapped to the same element', the generated target net is unique up to isomorphism. For this reason these morphisms are called *quotients* (in [9] a similar but restricted class of morphisms is called quotients).

Definition 2.9

A surjective net morphism $f: N \to N'$ is called *quotient* if
$\forall (x, y) \in F' \ \exists (a, b) \in F$ with $f(a) = x$ and $f(b) = y$.

The net morphism presented in figure 2 is a quotient.

Notation 2.10

Mappings $f: X \to X'$ are extended to pairs:
$f: X \times X \to X' \times X'$ by $f((a, b)) = (f(a), f(b))$.

With this notion a morphism $f: N \to N'$ is a quotient if and only if $X' = f(X)$ and $F' \subseteq f(F)$.

Dealing with morphisms and subnets we shall need the induced images of subnets and the restricted mappings.

Definition 2.11

Let $f: N \to N'$ be a net morphism and let N_1 be a subnet of N.

$(f(X_1) \cap S', f(X_1) \cap T'; f(F_1) \setminus \mathrm{id}_{X'})$ is called the *net image of N_1 by f* and is denoted by $f(N_1)$.

By $f_{N_1}: X_1 \to f(X_1)$ we denote the restriction of f to X_1, with the range of f restricted to $f(X_1)$. (f_{N_1} is surjective by definition!)

Note that $f(N_1)$ is not necessarily a subnet of N'. Figure 3 gives an example.

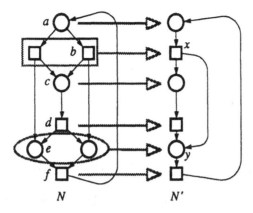

Figure 3: *The image of the subnet generated by $\{a, b, c, d, e, f\}$ is not a subnet of N' because of the arc (x, y).*

With definition 2.11 we get immediately the following proposition and corollary:

Proposition 2.12

If $f: N \rightarrow N'$ is a net morphism and N_1 is a subnet of N then $f_{N_1}: N_1 \rightarrow f(N_1)$ is a quotient.

Corollary 2.13

A morphism $f: N \rightarrow N'$ is a quotient if and only if $N' = f(N)$ and in this case $f = f_N$.

Unfortunately only few properties are transfered from a source net to a target net by a morphism and even by a quotient. Therefore we will define stronger tools in the next section.

We end this section giving a technical lemma that we will use several times in the rest of this paper and which holds for arbitrary surjective mappings.

Lemma 2.14

Let N, N' be nets, N strongly connected, and $|X'| > 1$.
If $f: X \rightarrow X'$ is a surjective mapping then $\forall x \in X'$:

1. $\exists (a, b) \in F$ with $f(a) = x$ and $f(b) \neq x$;
2. $\exists (a, b) \in F$ with $f(b) = x$ and $f(a) \neq x$.

Proof: We show only the first part, the second one being similar.

$|X'| > 1$; let x, y be two distinct elements of X'.

f is surjective; let $c, d \in X$ with $f(c) = x$ and $f(d) = y$.

Since N is strongly connected, there exists a path $a_1 \ldots a_m$ of N with $a_1 = c$ and $a_m = d$.

Let i be the least index such that $f(a_i) = x$ and $f(a_{i+1}) \neq x$.

With $(a, b) = (a_i, a_{i+1})$ we are finished. ∎

3 Vicinity Respecting Net Morphisms

In the example given in figure 2, a_1 is mapped to x but the vicinity of a_1, more precisely its pre-set, is not surjectively mapped to the pre-set of x. A local property of the morphism, namely not respecting the vicinity of a_1, has consequences concerning the global topology of the target net: two paths meet at x and the target net is neither covered by S-components nor by T-components.

A first approach for defining vicinity respecting morphisms could be the following restriction: the pre-set of each element is mapped surjectively to the pre-set of its image and the post-set of each element is mapped surjectively to the post-set of its image, i.e. $f(^\bullet a) = {}^\bullet f(a)$ and $f(a^\bullet) = (f(a))^\bullet$ for each element a (compare the definition of morphism given in [10]).

It can be seen easily that, essentially, with this restriction S-elements have to be mapped to S-elements while T-elements have to be mapped to T-elements. 'Line-reducing' morphisms like those depicted in figure 4 do not respect vicinities in this sense. We want to keep the possibility of mapping an element together with (a part of) its pre-set and (a part of) its post-set to one element of the target net.

Hence for an element a and a vicinity respecting morphism f we have two alternatives concerning the image of the pre-set of a:

$^\bullet f(a)$ is included in $f(^\bullet a)$ or $^\bullet a$ is mapped to $f(a)$. Using the $\odot$-notion, this can be formulated easier as: $f(^\odot a) = {}^\odot f(a)$ or $f(^\odot a) = f(a)$. A similar constraint holds for the post-sets of the elements.

We will first deal with morphisms which respect the vicinity of S-elements. Properties of morphisms which respect the vicinity of T-elements will be deduced by duality.

Definition 3.1

A net morphism $f: N \to N'$ is said to be *S-vicinity respecting* if $\forall a \in S$:

1. $f(^\odot a) = \{f(a)\} \ \lor \ f(^\odot a) = {}^\odot f(a)$ and
2. $f(a^\odot) = \{f(a)\} \ \lor \ f(a^\odot) = f(a)^\odot$.

The morphisms depicted in figure 4 are S-vicinity respecting.

Concentrating on different elements which are mapped to the same image instead of comparing source net and target net leads to another aspect of vicinity respecting morphisms

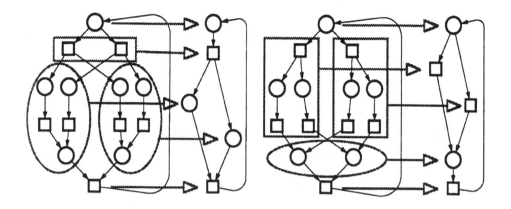

Figure 4: *S-vicinity respecting quotients*

in the case of quotients. In the example of figure 2, one can notice that the S-elements a_1 and a_2 are mapped to the same element x. Their post-sets are also mapped to the same set but this does not hold for their pre-sets. Thus the effect of the element x on its environment can not be seen as an abstraction neither of the effect of a_1 nor of the effect of a_2.

Let f be a vicinity respecting quotient and a and b elements which are similar enough, for a certain view of the model, to be mapped to the same element, i.e. $f(a) = f(b)$. Then what causes these elements to appear i.e. their 'extended pre-sets' should be similar and, consequently, mapped onto the same set, i.e. $f(^{\odot}a) = f(^{\odot}b)$. The same holds for the effect of these elements i.e. their 'extended post-sets': $f(a^{\odot}) = f(b^{\odot})$.

The proposition below shows that these two interpretations of vicinity respecting quotients are equivalent.

Proposition 3.2

Let $f: N \to N'$ be a quotient. f is S-vicinity respecting if and only if $\forall a, b \in S$ such that $f(a) = f(b)$:

1. $f(^{\odot}a) = \{f(a)\} \ \lor \ f(^{\odot}b) = \{f(b)\} \ \lor \ f(^{\odot}a) = f(^{\odot}b);$
2. $f(a^{\odot}) = \{f(a)\} \ \lor \ f(b^{\odot}) = \{f(b)\} \ \lor \ f(a^{\odot}) = f(b^{\odot}).$

Proof: It is immediate that definition 3.1.1 implies *1.* and definition 3.1.2 implies *2.*

We show only that *1.* implies definition 3.1.1, the second part is similar.
Let $a \in S$ such that $f(^{\odot}a) \neq \{f(a)\}$ and let $x \in {}^{\bullet}f(a)$.
Using proposition 2.5 we show only that we can find a $b \in {}^{\bullet}a$ with $f(b) = x$.
Since f is a quotient there is an arc $(c, d) \in F$ with $f(c) = x$ and $f(d) = f(a)$.
Because of proposition 2.3, d is an S-element.
With: $f(^{\odot}a) \neq \{f(a)\}$, $f(^{\odot}d) \neq \{f(d)\}$, $f(d) = f(a)$ and *1.* we have:
$f(^{\odot}a) = f(^{\odot}d)$ i.e. $\exists b \in {}^{\bullet}a$ such that $f(b) = f(c) = x$ which was to prove. ∎

In the proof of proposition 3.2, we show that for any element $x \in {}^{\bullet}f(a)$ there exists an element $b \in {}^{\bullet}a$ with $f(b) = x$. From this fact, we deduce immediately the following corollary:

Corollary 3.3

   Let $f: N \rightarrow N'$ be an S-vicinity respecting quotient. Then $\forall a \in S$:

   1. $f(^{\circ}a) \neq \{f(a)\} \ \Rightarrow \ |{}^{\bullet}f(a)| \leq |{}^{\bullet}a|$;
   2. $f(a^{\circ}) \neq \{f(a)\} \ \Rightarrow \ |f(a)^{\bullet}| \leq |a^{\bullet}|$.

The vicinity respecting concept can be seen as a means to impose restrictions on the flow relation of the target net. Indeed, we have the following relation with quotients:

Proposition 3.4

   Let N be a strongly connected net and $f: N \rightarrow N'$ be a surjective and S-vicinity respecting morphism. Then f is a quotient.

Proof: If $|X'| \leq 1$, then $F' = \emptyset$ and we are finished. So assume $|X'| > 1$.
Let $(x, y) \in F'$. We have to show: $\exists (a, b) \in F$ with $f((a, b)) = (x, y)$.
Either $x \in S'$ or $y \in S'$. W.l.o.g. assume $x \in S'$.
By lemma 2.14, we can find an $a \in X$ with $f(a) = x$ such that $\exists c \in a^{\bullet}$ with $f(c) \neq x$.
Because of proposition 2.3, $a \in S$.
Since f is S-vicinity respecting and $f(a^{\circ}) \neq \{f(a)\}$ we get $f(a^{\circ}) = f(a)^{\circ}$.
$y \in f(a)^{\circ}$, hence there must exist an element $b \in a^{\bullet}$ with $f(b) = y$. ∎

S-vicinity respecting morphisms do not preserve subnets in general. However stronlgy connected S-subnets are respected if they do not collapse to one element.

Proposition 3.5

   Let $f: N \rightarrow N'$ be an S-vicinity respecting morphism and let N_1 be a strongly connected S-subnet of N. Define $N_1' = f(N_1)$. Then:

   1. N_1' is a subnet of N';
   2. If $|X_1'| > 1$ then N_1' is an S-subnet;
   3. $f_{N_1}: N_1 \rightarrow N_1'$ is S-vicinity respecting.

Proof: Assume $|X_1'| > 1$ (otherwise the proposition trivially holds).
1. Obviously $S_1' \subseteq S'$, $T_1' \subseteq T'$ and $F_1' \subseteq F' \cap ((S_1' \times T_1') \cup (T_1' \times S_1'))$.
Let $x, y \in X_1'$ such that $(x, y) \in F'$. We show that $(x, y) \in F_1'$.
Assume w.l.o.g. that x is an S-element.
$f_{N_1}: N_1 \rightarrow N_1'$ is a surjective morphism.
By lemma 2.14 we can find an arc $(a, c) \in F_1$ such that $f_{N_1}(a) = x$ and $f_{N_1}(c) \neq x$.
By corollary 2.4, $a \in S_1$. Since f is S-vicinity respecting and $f(a^{\circ}) \neq \{f(a)\}$

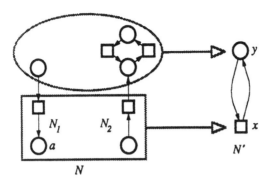

Figure 5: *The image of the subnet N_1 by the S-vicinity respecting quotient is not a subnet because of the arc (x, y).*

($\odot$-notation w.r.t. F) there exists a $b \in a^\bullet$ such that $f(b) = y$.
$b \in T_1$ since N_1 is an S-subnet. Hence $(a, b) \in F_1$ and $f((a, b)) = (x, y) \in F_1'$.

2. We show that $T_1' = {}^\bullet S_1' \cup S_1'{}^\bullet$.
It is clear that $T_1' \subseteq {}^\bullet S_1' \cup S_1'{}^\bullet$ since N_1' is strongly connected (corollary 2.8) and since $|X_1'| > 1$ (N_1' has no isolated elements).
We only show $S_1'{}^\bullet \subseteq T_1'$, ${}^\bullet S_1' \subseteq T_1'$ being similar.
Let $x \in S_1'$, $y \in T'$ such that $(x, y) \in F'$.
Arguing like above, we can find an $a \in S_1$ with $f_{N_1}(a) = x$ and a $b \in a^\bullet$ with $f(b) = y$.
Since $T_1 = {}^\bullet S_1 \cup S_1^\bullet$, $b \in T_1$. Hence $y \in T_1'$, which was to prove.

3. is a consequence of 1. and 2. ∎

The example in figure 5 shows that being strongly connected is in fact a necessary prerequisite for proposition 3.5. In figure 3 we gave an example of a strongly connected subnet which is not an S-subnet. Its image by the S-vicinity respecting quotient is not a subnet of the target net.

An S-component is more than a strongly connected S-subnet. To respect coverings by S-components stronger hypotheses on S-vicinity respecting quotients have to be assumed. This will be the subject of the next section.

By duality we define T-vicinity respecting morphisms and obtain dual results.

Definition 3.6

A morphism $f: N \to N'$ is said to be *T-vicinity respecting* if $\forall a \in T$:

1. $f({}^\odot a) = \{f(a)\} \lor f({}^\odot a) = {}^\odot f(a)$ and
2. $f(a^\odot) = \{f(a)\} \lor f(a^\odot) = f(a)^\odot$.

Corollary 3.7

Let $f: N \to N'$ be a T-vicinity respecting morphism and let N_1 be a strongly connected T-subnet of N. Define $N_1' = f(N_1)$. Then:

1. N_1' is a subnet of N';
2. If $|X_1'| > 1$ then N_1' is a T-subnet;
3. $f_{N_1}: N_1 \to N_1'$ is T-vicinity respecting.

Notation 3.8

A morphism which is S-vicinity respecting and T-vicinity respecting will be called simply *vicinity respecting*.

We end this section showing that proposition 2.7 has a weak converse: any path in N' has a path as pre-image in N, provided that N is strongly connected and that f is vicinity respecting.

Proposition 3.9

Let N be a strongly connected net and let $f: N \to N'$ be a surjective and vicinity respecting morphism. Let $x_1 \ldots x_n$, $n \geq 1$, be a path of N', $a, b \in X$ such that $f(a) = x_1$ and $f(b) = x_n$. Then:

1. There is a path $a_1 \ldots a_m$ of N with $a = a_1$, $m \geq n$, such that $f(a_1 \ldots a_m) = x_1 \ldots x_n$;
2. There is a path $a_1 \ldots a_m$ of N with $b = a_m$, $m \geq n$, such that $f(a_1 \ldots a_m) = x_1 \ldots x_n$.

Proof: We show only the first part of the proposition, the second one being similar.
We proceed by induction on n, the length of the path of N'.
If $n = 1$, there is nothing to show.
Let $x_1 \ldots x_n$, $n > 1$, be a path of N' and suppose there exists a path $a_1 \ldots a_{m-1}$ of N with $m \geq n$, $a_1 = a$ and $f(a_1 \ldots a_{m-1}) = x_1 \ldots x_{n-1}$.
Then $f(a_{m-1}) = x_{n-1}$.
Since f is surjective, there exists a $c \in X$ with $f(c) = x_n$.
Since N is strongly connected, we find a path $a_{m-1} a_m \ldots a_{m+k} c$ from a_{m-1} to c.
Let l be such that a_{m+l} is the first element in the path satisfying $f(a_{m+l}^\odot) \neq \{f(a_{m+l})\}$.
Since f is vicinity respecting, $f(a_{m+l}^\odot) = x_{n-1}^\odot$ i.e. $\exists d \in a_{m+l}$ with $f(d) = x_n$ and we are done. ∎

The example in figure 5 shows the necessity for N to be strongly connected: $f(a) = x$ but there is no path $a_1 \ldots a_m$ with $a_1 = a$ and $f(a_1 \ldots a_m) = xy$.

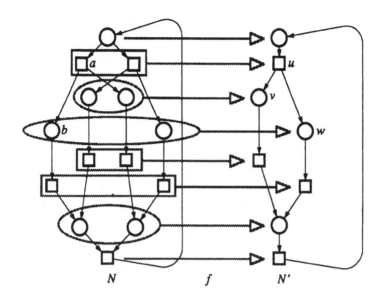

Figure 6: *An S-vicinity respecting quotient which is not T-vicinity respecting if restricted to an S-component*

4 Transformation of S- and T-components

Let us begin this section considering the S-vicinity respecting quotient of figure 6.

The net N is covered by S-components. f is an S-vicinity respecting quotient. However, N' is not anymore covered by S-components. The restriction of f to any S-component is not T-vicinity respecting:

Consider the S-component N_1 containing b. The image of N_1 is the entire net N'.
$f_{N_1}(\{a,b\}) \neq \{f_{N_1}(a)\} = \{u\}$ but $f_{N_1}(\{a,b\}) = \{u,w\} \neq (f_{N_1}(a))^\odot = \{u,v,w\}$. The net image of N_1 is not an S-component of N'.

In figure 4, the quotients restricted to any S-component are T-vicinity respecting.

Proposition 4.1

> Let $f: N \to N'$ be an S-vicinity respecting net morphism and let N_1 be an S-component of N. Define $N'_1 = f(N_1)$ and suppose that $f_{N_1}: N_1 \to N'_1$ is T-vicinity respecting. Then:
>
> If $|X'_1| > 1$ then N'_1 is an S-component of N'.

Proof: Assume $|X'_1| > 1$.
Since N_1 is an S-component, it is an S-subnet. Hence, by proposition 3.5, N'_1 is an S-subnet of N'. Thus $T'_1 = {}^\bullet S'_1 \cup S'^\bullet_1$.

It remains to prove: $\forall y \in T'_1: |{}^\bullet y \cap S'_1| = 1 \wedge |y^\bullet \cap S'_1| = 1$.
Let $y \in T'_1$. We show only: $|{}^\bullet y \cap S'_1| = 1$ ($|y^\bullet \cap S'_1| = 1$ is similar).

Since f_{N_1} is surjective we can find an arc $(b, a) \in F_1$ with $f(b) \neq y$ and $f(a) = y$ by lemma 2.14. Since f_{N_1} is a T-vicinity respecting quotient, with the dual of corollary 3.3 we get $|S_1' \cap {}^{\bullet}y| \leq |S_1 \cap {}^{\bullet}a|$ and $|S_1 \cap {}^{\bullet}a| = 1$ since N_1 is an S-component.

Since N_1 is strongly connected, N_1' is strongly connected by corollary 2.8. Hence with $|X_1'| > 1$ we get $|{}^{\bullet}y \cap S_1'| = 1$. ∎

From proposition 4.1 we deduce:

Theorem 4.2

> Let N be a net which is covered by a family $(N_i), i \in I$ of S-components.
> Let N' be a net without isolated T-elements, i.e. $\forall t \in T' : {}^{\bullet}t \cup t^{\bullet} \neq \emptyset$.
> Let $f: N \rightarrow N'$ be an S-vicinity respecting quotient such that $f_{N_i}: N_i \rightarrow f(N_i)$ is T-vicinity respecting for all $i \in I$. Then N' is covered by S-components.

Proof: In proposition 4.1 we have shown that, given the assumptions above, every S-component of N is either mapped to an S-component of N' or to an element of N'.

Let $x \in X'$. If x is an isolated element then it is an isolated S-element by the assumption and hence, trivially, an S-component. So assume that x is not isolated. Then we can find a $y \in X'$ such that $(x, y) \in F'$ or $(y, x) \in F'$.

Since f is a quotient, there are $a \in S, b \in T$ with $f(\{a, b\}) = \{x, y\}$ and $(a, b) \in P$. N is covered by S-components and hence we can find an $i \in I$ such that $a \in S_i$ and $b \in T_i$. $|X_i'| > 1$ since x and y are distinct elements of $f(N_i)$. Thus $f(N_i)$ is an S-component of N'. ∎

Remark: By proposition 3.5.3 'f is S-vicinity respecting' implies for all $i \in I$: 'f_{N_i} is S-vicinity respecting'. So all the f_{N_i} have to be both S- and T-vicinity respecting. However, this alone does not imply that f is S-vicinity respecting and is not sufficient for N' to be covered by S-components as is shown in figure 2. For both S-components N_i of the net N of figure 2 f_{N_i} is S- and T-vicinity respecting. However, f is not S-vicinity respecting and N' is not covered by S-components.

From theorem 4.2 we deduce that, given a family of S-components which cover the source net, a respective covering of the target net is obtained by the images of the S-components which are not mapped to single non-isolated elements.

The choice of a covering family of S-components is decisive. In the example of figure 7, the quotient is vicinity respecting. Its restriction to either the S-components N_1 which contains a_1, a_2 or to the S-component N_2 which contains a_1', a_2' is T-vicinity respecting. Taking the S-components N_3 and N_4 as a cover of N, with a_1, a_2' belonging to N_3 and a_1', a_2 belonging to N_4, then the restriction of f to any of these S-components is not anymore T-vicinity respecting.

The example points out that the choice of an abstracting and the choice of an S-component covering are not independent. Performing an abstraction one usually wants to preserve certain aspects while other aspects might get lost. A 'good choice' of an S-component

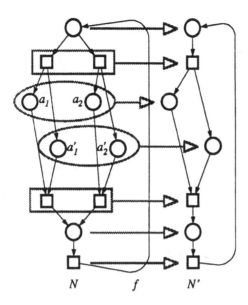

$$N \qquad f \qquad N'$$

Figure 7: *This net has two coverings by S-components. The S-vicinity respecting quotient is such that its restriction to the S-components of one covering is T-vicinity respecting while this does not hold for the other covering.*

covering of the source net is a collection of those S-components which one does not want to loose by the transformation.

The dual version of theorem 4.2 reads as follows:

Theorem 4.3

Let N be a net which is covered by a family $(N_i), i \in I$ of T-components.
Let N' be a net without isolated S-elements, i.e. $\forall s \in S' : {}^\bullet s \cup s^\bullet \neq \emptyset$.
Let $f: N \to N'$ be a T-vicinity respecting quotient such that $f_{N_i}: N_i \to f(N_i)$ is S-vicinity respecting for all $i \in I$. Then N' is covered by T-components.

The net morphisms depicted in figure 4 are vicinity respecting. Their restrictions to each S-component or T-component are also vicinity respecting. Hence their net images are covered by S- and T-components.

A particular case of theorem 4.2 is the composition of S-components. In this case the source net N is the disjoint union of a family of S-components and the mapping, restricted to each of these S-components, is injective (and hence a fortiori T-vicinity respecting). SMD-nets as defined in [1] are a particular case of this construction. For this class the composition of S-components is done only via T-elements. However, this restriction is not necessary for our considerations.

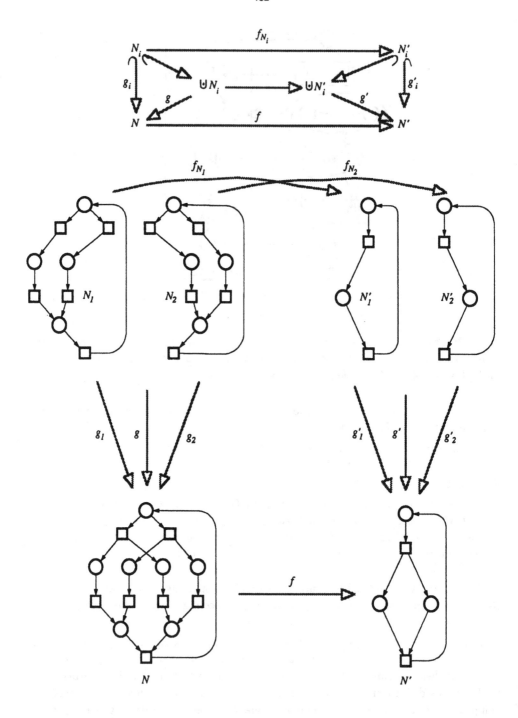

Figure 8: *An example of the commutativity of composition and coarsening of nets*

Conversely, each net which is covered by S-components can be constructed by composing these S-components. So we can reformulate our result as a property of morphisms as follows:

Let N be a net. For each S-element a of an S-component N_1 of N the entire vicinity belongs to the S-component as well by definition. Hence the natural injection $g_1: N_1 \to N$ is S-vicinity respecting but not necessarily surjective.

A covering by S-components N_i $(i \in I)$ can be expressed by a set of morphisms g_i $(i \in I)$ such that each element of N is in $g_i(N_i)$ for at least one i. Using the disjoint union of the S-components $(\bigcup N_i)$, the morphisms g_i induce a quotient g from $\bigcup N_i$ to N.

Now theorem 4.2 reads as follows:

Given

- a family $(N_i), i \in I$ of strongly connected nets with $|^\bullet t| = |t^\bullet| = 1$ for all T-elements (S-components),

- S-vicinity respecting injective morphisms $g_i: N_i \to N (i \in I)$ such that the induced mapping g is a quotient (i.e., N is covered by the N_i),

- an S-vicinity respecting quotient $f: N \to N'$ such that f_{N_i} is T-vicinity respecting for all $i \in I$,

we can find injective S-vicinity respecting mappings $g_i': f(N_i) \to N'$ such that the induced mapping $g': \bigcup f(N_i) \to N'$ is surjective (i.e., N' is covered by the $f(N_i)$).

These interrelations and an example are shown in figure 8.

Again, by duality we can use the same formalism to capture the composition of T-components.

5 Conclusion

After giving some results about morphisms in section two, this paper introduced vicinity respecting morphisms in section three. The vicinity respecting concept expresses a local property of a morphism: roughly speaking, the vicinity of an element is mapped either to the image of the element itself or surjectively to the vicinity of the image. However, vicinity respecting morphisms allow to respect global properties of nets: they allow to transport covering by S-components and covering by T-components from a source net to a target net as it is proved in section four.

Morphisms (in our sense) are used in several places in Net Theory. Examples include the definition of processes of C/E-systems and P/T-systems [5] and the relation between C/E-systems to higher level systems [9]. In these applications morphisms are restricted to map S-elements to S-elements and T-elements to T-elements. We do not have such a restriction and, therefore, our morphisms can shorten nets in their 'length'. The vicinity respecting idea is already present in the morphisms used to define processes since these are T-vicinity respecting, even T-vicinity preserving, i.e. the vicinity of a T-element is mapped injectively onto the vicinity of its image.

In [3], a formalism for abstractions of marked nets is presented. More precisely, P/T-systems are seen as abstractions of C/E-systems. This abstraction is formalized by means of surjective net mappings. For a particular class of P/T-systems (all arc weights are one) this abstraction is vicinity respecting.

The examples given in the paper are more or less simple and symmetric. The main reason for that is our attempt to find simple examples which already show up the phenomena we want to stress. However, the formalism is not restricted to such simple examples since the requirements of vicinity respecting morphisms are purely local. In particular, parts of a source net which are not reflected in the target net, i.e., mapped to one element, may be arbitrary complex.

Another reason is, that we only concentrated on such S-components of target nets which are images of S-components of the respective source nets. Consider the example depicted in figure 8 again. N_1 and N_2 are covered by T-components and so is N. However, the T-components of N are not images of T-components of N_1 or N_2. So the composition of N_1 and N_2 creates new T-components.

More generally, a quotient which preserves the property of being covered by T-components does not necessarily preserve any T-component covering. We are presently working on a characterization of those compositions of S-components which lead to nets covered by T-components.

Other future developments include the preservation of more structural properties of nets. Deadlocks and traps, which are used to characterize live extended-free-choice-nets [2] are candidates for such considerations. Results in this direction might help to develop a modular and compositional calculus for certain classes of nets.

Acknowledgement:
We would like to thank Eike Best, Wolfgang Reisig and Einar Smith for helpful discussions. We also would like to thank several anonymous referees.

References

[1] Best, E.; Fernández C., C.: Notations and Terminology on Petri Net Theory. Arbeitspapiere der GMD Nr.195, GMD St.Augustin, FRG (1986).

[2] Best, E.; Desel, J.: Partial Order Behaviour and Structure of Petri Nets. Formal Aspects of Computing Vol.2 pp.123-138 (1990).

[3] Desel, J.; Merceron A.: P/T-systems as Abstractions of C/E-systems. In: Advances in Petri Nets 1989, Lecture Notes in Computer Science Vol.424 pp.105-127, Springer-Verlag (1990). Extended Version as: Arbeitspapiere der GMD Nr.331, GMD St.Augustin, FRG (1988).

[4] Fernández C., C.: Net Topology I. Interner Bericht der GMD ISF-75-9 GMD St.Augustin, FRG (1975). Net Topology II. Interner Bericht der GMD ISF-76-2, GMD St.Augustin, FRG (1976).

[5] Genrich, H.J; Lautenbach, K.; Thiagarajan, P.S.: Elements of General Net Theory. In: Net theory and Applications; Brauer W. (Ed.), Lecture Notes in Computer Science Vol.84 pp.21-163, Springer-Verlag (1980).

[6] Genrich, H.J; Stankiewicz-Wiechno, E.: A Dictionary of Some Basic Notions of Net Theory. In: Net Theory and Applications; Brauer W. (Ed.), Lecture Notes in Computer Science Vol.84 pp.519-535, Springer-Verlag (1980).

[7] Petri, C.A.: Concepts of Net Theory. Mathematical Foundations of Computer Science: Proceedings of Symposium and Summer School, High Tatras, Sep. 3-8, 1973. Mathematical Institute of the Slovak Academy of Sciences, pp.137-146 (1973).

[8] Petri, C.A.: "Forgotten Topics" of Net Theory. Petri Nets: Applications and Relationships to Other Models of Concurrency. Brauer, W.; Reisig, W.; Rozenberg, G. (Eds.). Lecture Notes in Computer Science Vol.255 pp.500-514, Springer-Verlag (1987).

[9] Smith, E.; Reisig, W.: The Semantics of a Net is a Net – An Exercise in General Net Theory. Voss, K.; Genrich, H.J.; Rozenberg, G. (Eds.): Concurrency and Nets, pp.461-479, Springer-Verlag (1987).

[10] Winskel, G.: A New Definition of Morphism on Petri Nets. STACS 84, Lecture Notes in Computer Science Vol.166 pp.140-150, Springer-Verlag (1984).

REGULAR STOCHASTIC PETRI NETS

C. Dutheillet   S. Haddad

Laboratoire MASI - CNRS UA 818
Université Pierre & Marie Curie
4 place Jussieu
75252 Paris Cedex 05

ABSTRACT : An extension of regular nets, a class of colored nets, to a stochastic model is proposed. We show that the symmetries in this class of nets make it possible to develop a performance evaluation by constructing only a graph of symbolic markings, which vertices are classes of states, instead of the whole reachability graph. Using algebraic techniques, we prove that all the states in a class have the same probability, and that the coefficients of the linear system describing the lumped Markov process can be calculated directly from the graph of symbolic markings.

Keywords : Higher-level net models, stochastic nets.

CONTENTS

0. INTRODUCTION

As they are a function of the number and the complexity of the processes to be represented, Petri net models of distributed computer systems must quickly face problems due to the huge size of the reachability graph.

The use of higher level models (e.g., colored nets, Pr/T nets) can make the task of the modeler easier. However, the existing analysis methods often make it necessary to go back to an equivalent ordinary net, so that there is no improvement in the complexity.

In order to face the exponential increase in the number of states, Jensen [Jen 81a] has introduced in colored Petri nets some equivalence relations that take into account the symmetries of the model. He showed that those relations were directly depending on the type of the color functions. He also defined analysis methods associated with the use of simple functions [Jen 81a, Hub 84].

Research has been done to extend the symmetries in colored nets to the stochastic domain [Zen 85, Lin 87, Chi 88]. Some attempts to reuse the symmetry properties have been proposed. One approach [Zen 85] has been to extend the reduced graph developed by Jensen to a stochastic model. However, when using this technique, the partition of states in classes can lead to a non Markovian process. In [Lin 87], the reduced process is actually Markovian, but no method is provided to build it automatically. The approach in [Chi 88] was to build the reachability graph, to group the states in classes according to some symmetry relation, and then to partition these classes in subclasses until the resulting process is Markovian. In fact, as soon as the color functions are general, no existing method avoids the development of the whole reachability graph. Indeed the simplification due to the symmetries can be used only once the reachability graph has been constructed, even sometimes requiring an expensive preliminary analysis.

This paper aims at showing that in the case of colored nets that do not use general functions, the results obtained during the structural analysis can be extended to the performance evaluation. In order to optimize the analysis, our study is based on a particular class of colored nets, the regular nets [Had 87]. In a regular net, the objects in a class have similar behaviors. The color domains of places and transitions are Cartesian products of object classes. The color functions are Cartesian products and linear combinations of two basic functions, one selecting a unique object in a class, the other synchronizing all the objects of the class. For this class of nets, a condensed representation of the reachability graph, the symbolic reachability graph, can be defined. The symmetry properties of this graph are used to simplify the quantitative analysis of the model.

The paper is organized as follows. In the next section, we give the definition and an example of regular net. Section 3 will presents the construction of the graph of symbolic markings. The stochastic model derived from a regular net will be presented in Section 4. In Section 5, we propose an algorithm for computing the state probabilities from the graph of symbolic markings. Our algorithm maps the symbolic reachability graph on a lumped Markov chain and uses the labels of the symbolic arcs to compute the transition rates. In the last section we prove the correctness of the algorithm. The proof organizes into three steps. First we prove that the developed Markov chain always has a solution such that all the ordinary markings within a symbolic marking have the same probability. Then we show that the lumping condition is verified by the Markov chain, and as a consequence, that the linear system to solve can be reduced. Finally we prove that this reduced system is the one obtained with our algorithm. Moreover, as the number of ordinary markings within a symbolic marking is computed by the algorithm, the ordinary probabilities can be derived without additional operations.

1. REGULAR NETS

Even if they do not have the same expression power as general colored nets, regular nets allow one to model a large class of systems. They have been the starting point for developing important theoretical results, such as reductions and computation of linear place-invariants. They have also allowed to formalize the parametrization which leads to a validation of the system that does not depend on the values of some parameters such as the number of sites, or the number of processes.

1.1 Definition :

A regular net $RN = <P, T, C, I^-, I^+>$ is defined by :

      P the set of places,
      T the set of transitions,
      C the set of object classes : $C = \{C_1, ..., C_n\}$, with $C_i \cap C_j = \emptyset$,
      I^+ and I^- the input and output matrices defined on P x T, which elements I^+, $I^-(p, t)$ are standard color functions of p (defined below).

The color domains $C(p)$ for a place, and $C(t)$ for a transition, are defined as follows : a color domain is made either of the neutral color, or of a Cartesian product of object classes such that all the elements in the product are distinct.

Definition 1.1 : A normalized RN is an RN in which all places and transitions have the same color domain $C = C_1 \times ... \times C_n$.

As every RN can be transformed in a normalized RN without modifying its structural behavior, we will limit our study to that specific class of regular nets. However, the case of non-normalized regular nets and the transformation rule are presented in [Dut 89].

Definition 1.2 : Marking of an object.
A marking is a function $m : P \times C \rightarrow \mathbb{N}$, such that $m(p, c)$ is the number of marks of color c in p. The marking of an object c_i can be defined by the function below :

      $m : C_i \rightarrow [P \times C_1 \times ... \times C_{i-1} \times C_{i+1} \times ... \times C_n \rightarrow \mathbb{N}]$
      $m(c_i)(p, c_1, ..., c_{i-1}, c_{i+1}, ..., c_n) = m(p, c)$ where $c = (c_1, ..., c_n)$.

<u>Definition 1.3</u> : Marking of a color.

The marking of a color c can be defined by the function below :

$$m : C \rightarrow [P \rightarrow \mathbb{N}]$$

$$m(c)(p) = m(p, c)$$

As the three definitions are equivalent, we use the same letter for all the marking functions.

The standard color functions of a regular net are defined from two basic functions :

$$\mathbf{X_i} : C_i \times C \rightarrow \mathbb{N} \quad \text{such that } X_i(c_i', (c_1, ..., c_n)) \quad = Id(c_i, c_i')$$
$$= (\text{If } c_i = c_i' \text{ then } 1 \text{ else } 0).$$

An arc labeled X_i distinguishes exactly one object in the class C_i. The behavior of this object will be independent of the behavior of the other objects of the class when firing the transition.

$$\mathbf{S_i} : C_i \times C \rightarrow \mathbb{N} \quad \text{such that } S_i(c_i', (c_1, ..., c_n)) \quad = 1.$$

An arc labeled S_i means that all the objects in the class C_i play a similar part. It corresponds to a synchronization of all the objects of the class if it labels an input arc. It represents a diffusion to all the objects of the class if it labels an output arc.

Those two basic functions can be combined by :

$$\mathbf{a_i. S_i + b_i. X_i} : C_i \times C \rightarrow \mathbb{N} \quad \text{such that } a_i. S_i + b_i. X_i(c_i', (c_1, ..., c_n))$$
$$= (\text{If } c_i = c_i' \text{ then } (a_i + b_i) \text{ else } a_i).$$

As a consequence, we have $a_i \geq 0$ and $(a_i + b_i) \geq 0$.

<u>Definition 1.4</u> : A standard color function $< a_1. S_1 + b_1. X_1, ... , a_n. S_n + b_n. X_n >$ of a regular net, also denoted by $\prod_{i=1}^{n} <a_i.S_i + b_i.X_i>$, is defined by :

$$\prod_{i=1}^{n} <a_i.S_i + b_i.X_i> : C \times C \rightarrow \mathbb{N},$$

$$\prod_{i=1}^{n} <a_i.S_i + b_i.X_i> ((c'_1, ..., c'_n), (c_1, ..., c_n)) = \prod_{i=1}^{n} <a_i.S_i + b_i.X_i> (c'_i, (c_1, ..., c_n))$$

The initial marking of a regular net, denoted by m_0, must be symmetric, i.e., it must verify the following property :

$$\forall p \in P, \forall c, c' \in C(p), m_0(p, c) = m_0(p, c').$$

1.2 Example :

We consider the net in Figure 1, which models the behavior of a distributed database. This model is derived from a model presented in [Jen 81b], and has also been studied in [Had 87]. A site is made of an active and a passive part.The active part of a site can modify a file, whereas the passive part only takes into account the modifications performed by the other sites. When a site modifies a file, its active part sends a message to all the other sites so that they can take the modification into account, whereas it waits for the acknowledgements (transition T1). The passive part of a site that receives a message modifies its copy of the file (transition T3). If there are several messages for a site, the modifications are done one at a time. Once its copy is modified, a site sends back a message to the one that originated the modification (transition T4). Once all the sites have acknowledged the modification, the waiting site resumes its activity and another site can in turn work on the modified file (transition T2).

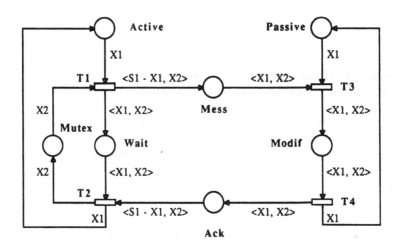

Figure 1 : Regular net model of a database

We consider a distributed database with three sites and two files. There are two color classes in the net: the site class SIT = {s1, s2, s3}, and the file class FIL = {f1, f2}. The initial marking of the net is the following : Active = Passive = SIT, and Mutex = FIL.

In the next section, we show that it is possible to develop a reduced reachability graph for regular nets, the symbolic reachbility graph.

2. SYMBOLIC REACHABILITY GRAPH

In this section, we first present some properties of regular nets that are used in the construction of the symbolic reachability graph (SRG). Unlike Jensen's reachability tree [Hub 84] that develops only once equivalent subtrees, the SRG is obtained by grouping states a priori, thus avoiding to develop any reachable state of the unfolded net. The method for constructing the SRG is then developed. We define the representation of a symbolic marking, and we present a symbolic firing rule that can be used directly on the symbolic markings.

2.1 Definitions and properties :

The properties given here result from the definition of the color domains. Also due to the specificity of the color functions, a basic symmetry property of the model is presented.

Definition 2.1 : let s_i a permutation of C_i. A permutation $s = <s_1, ..., s_n>$ of $(C_1 \times ... \times C_n)$ is defined by

$$s(<c_1, ..., c_n>) = <s_1(c_1), ..., s_n(c_n)>.$$

The group of the permutation of the type $<s_1, ..., s_n>$ will be denoted by S.

Definition 2.2 : let m a marking, $s \in S$ a permutation. Then s.m is a marking defined by :
$$\forall p \in P, \quad s.m(p, c) = m(p, s(c)).$$

Proposition 2.1 : s.m defines an operation of the group S on the marking set MS, i.e.,
$$\forall s, s' \in S, \forall m \in MS, (s \circ s').m = s.(s'.m)$$
$$id.m = m.$$

Definition 2.3 : the orbit of m, reg(m), is defined by $reg(m) = \{s.m, s \in S\}$.

The three following corollaries are standard properties of the operation of a group on a set [Lan 77].

Corollary 2.1 : the orbits reg(m) define a partition of MS that induces an equivalence relation R :
$$m R m' \Leftrightarrow reg(m) = reg(m').$$

The equivalence classes of the relation R are called symbolic markings, denoted by M.

Corollary 2.2 : Let s a permutation, and M a symbolic marking. Let $f_s : M \rightarrow M$, defined by
$$\forall m \in M, \quad f_s(m) = s.m.$$
Then f_s is a bijection.

Corollary 2.3 : Let m, m' $\in$ M. $|\{s \in S, s.m = m'\}| = |S| / |M|$.

We finally give the basic theorem [Had 87], which is a consequence of the type of the color functions :

Theorem 2.1 : $\forall m, m' \in M, \forall t \in T, \forall c \in (C_1 \times ... \times C_n), \forall s \in S,$
$$m[t(c)>m' \Leftrightarrow s.m[t(s(c))>s.m'.$$

2.2 Construction of the SRG :

The construction of the SRG requires that we define the representation of a symbolic marking, and the firing rule that can be applied directly on these symbolic markings. We also present some properties of the SRG. These properties are used to prove that the SRG is relevant for performance evaluation.

2.2.1 Optimal representation of a symbolic marking :

The basic principle for representing a symbolic marking consists in grouping in a subclass all the objects of a class that have the same marking. Therefore, permuting two objects within a subclass will not modify the marking. The identity of the objects in a subclass is then forgotten and only the number of objects is taken into account for each subclass. In this goal, each object class C_i is partitioned in a number of subclasses, $C_i = \{C_{i,1}, ..., C_{i,si}\}$, such that all the objects in a subclass have the same marking. The cardinalities of each subclass, which values are in $\mathbb{N}^+$, verify $\sum_{j=1,si} |C_{i,j}| = |C_i|$. The marking of each place is then similar to an ordinary marking where the subclasses are considered as objects. Thus we can define the marking of a subclass, the marking of a product of subclasses and the permutation on subclasses in the same way as they are defined for objects in Definitions 1.2, 1.3 and 2.1.

Moreover, the grouping must be maximal, i.e., two different subclasses must have different markings. The representation of symbolic markings as defined above is unique within a permutation $<s_1, ..., s_n>$ of the set of subclasses. However, it is possible to define and to calculate a canonical representation for each symbolic marking by an adequate ordering based on the marking of the products of subclasses [Had 87].

Notice that the decomposition in subclasses is local to a symbolic marking. Thus, the subclass $C_{i,j}$ appearing in a symbolic marking M and the same subclass $C_{i,j}$ appearing in a symbolic marking M' may not have related meanings.

2.2.2 Example :

Figure 2 represents one reachable ordinary marking of the net in Figure 1, in which the site s2 has sent a message to the two other sites s1 and s3. The net in Figure 3 gives the symbolic representation of the marking in Figure 2. In this representation, the subclasses have the following cardinalities :

$$|SIT1| = 2 \qquad |FIL1| = 1$$
$$|SIT2| = 1 \qquad |FIL2| = 1$$

But note that ther is not a one to one correspondence between the markings in Figure 2 and Figure 3. In fact, the symbolic marking in Figure 3 represents any ordinary reachable marking in which one site has sent a message to both others.

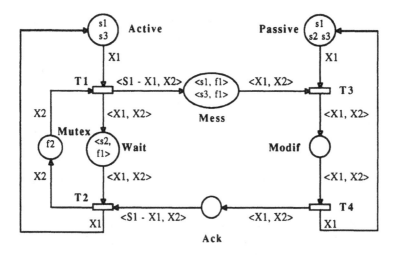

Figure 2 : A reachable ordinary marking of the database model.

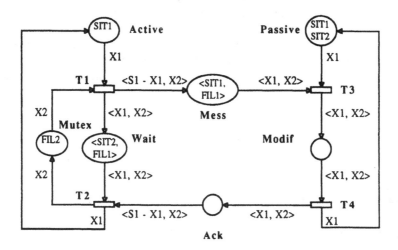

Figure 3 : Symbolic representation of the marking in Figure 2.

2.2.3 Symbolic firing rule :

In order to build the SRG, we first define a symbolic firing rule on the symbolic markings which must be sound i.e., an ordinary marking enables a colored transition if and only if its symbolic marking enables an equivalent symbolic firing and the ordinary marking obtained by the firing belongs to the symbolic marking obtained by the symbolic firing.

The first effect of the symbolic firing will be to split each instantiated subclass in two subclasses, one with the object instantiated in the underlying firing and the other with the remaining objects of the subclass. Thus we formally define this splitting.

Notation : In M, we will denote the partition of the class C_i in $\{C_{i,1}, ..., C_{i,si}\}$ by $C_i = \{C_{i,1}, ..., C_{i,si}\}$. If confusion may arise, $|C_{i,j}|_M$ will denote the cardinality of $C_{i,j}$ in M.

Definition 2.4 : Let M a symbolic marking. Then $M[C_{1,u1}, ..., C_{n,un}]$ is a symbolic marking defined by :
-    If $|C_{i,ui}| > 1$ then
$$C_i = \{C_{i,1}, ..., C_{i,si}, C_{i,si+1}\} \text{ with}$$
$$|C_{i,si+1}| = |C_{i,ui}|_M - 1, \ |C_{i,ui}| = 1, \ |C_{i,j}| = |C_{i,j}|_M \text{ for any } j \neq u_i \text{ and } j \neq s_i+1$$
Else the partition of C_i is unchanged.

-    The marking of the old subclasses is unchanged and the marking of the new subclass $C_{i,si+1}$ is the same as the one of $C_{i,ui}$.

Notice that in $M[C_{1,u1}, ..., C_{n,un}]$ the grouping is not always maximal and that even if the grouping is maximal the representation may not be canonical. But it does not matter since this symbolic marking is just an intermediate marking and it will not appear in the SRG.

The instantiation of a transition in a symbolic firing will be made by choosing a subclass per class instead of an object per class in an ordinary firing. Thus we must define the value of the colored functions for subclasses. This definition is the same as the one for the objects. In the case where an instantiated subclass contains more than one object, the symbolic firing should be enabled for the object instantiated in the underlying firing and for the other objects of the subclass which are not instantiated. Thus the definition should be different but since we apply our definitions on split markings, this case never appears.

Definition 2.5 : Let M a symbolic marking. Then :
$<a_i.S_i + b_i.X_i>$ is a function from $C_i \times \Pi_{j=1,n} C_j \to N$ and
$<a_i.S_i + b_i.X_i> (C_{i,vi}, (C_{1,u1}, ..., C_{n,un})) = $ If $u_i \neq v_i$ then a_i else (a_i+b_i)

Definition 2.6 : Let M a symbolic marking. Then :
$\Pi_{j=1,n} <a_i.S_i + b_iX_i>$ is a function from $\Pi_{i=1,n} C_i \times \Pi_{i=1,n} C_i \dashrightarrow N$ and
$\Pi_{j=1,n} <a_i.S_i + b_iX_i> ((C_{1,v1}, ..., C_{n,vn}), (C_{1,u1}, ..., C_{n,un})) = $
$\Pi_{j=1,n} (<a_i.S_i + b_iX_i> (C_{i,vi}, (C_{1,u1}, ..., C_{n,un})))$

Let M_j a symbolic marking, t a transition, and $(C_{1,u1}, ..., C_{n,un})$ a tuple of subclasses such that $C_{i,ui} \in C_i$. $C_{i,ui}$ is the distinguished subclass of C_i for the firing of t.

Definition 2.7 : t is enabled from M for $(C_{1,u1}, ..., C_{n,un})$ iff :
$\forall p \in P,$
$M[C_{1,u1}, ..., C_{n,un}] (p, C_{1,v1}, ..., C_{n,vn}) \geq I \cdot (p, t) ((C_{1,v1}, ..., C_{n,vn}), (C_{1,u1}, ..., C_{n,un}))$

The symbolic marking M' obtained by firing $t(C_{1,u1}, ..., C_{n,un})$ is calculated with the three following steps :

Step 1 : We apply the incidence functions on $M[C_{1,u1}, ..., C_{n,un}]$ giving a new symbolic marking M_1

$\forall\ p \in P$ (we denote $I = I^+ - I^-$),

$$M_1(p, C_{1,v1}, ..., C_{n,vn}) = M[C_{1,u1}, ..., C_{n,un}] (p, C_{1,v1}, ..., C_{n,vn})$$
$$+ I(p, t) ((C_{1,v1}, ..., C_{n,vn}), (C_{1,u1}, ..., C_{n,un}))$$

Step 2 : as the grouping of states may not be maximal in M_1, it consists in grouping all the subclasses that have same markings giving a new marking M_2. In fact, only the splitted subclasses may be equivalent to previously existing ones.

Step 3 : calculation for M_2 of the canonical representative marking M'.

2.2.4 Example :

We apply the technique to our example. From the initial marking, we show the possible transition firings in the reachability graph (RG), and we represent the same step in the SRG. We will consider the marking of the different places in the following order :

(Active) (Passive) (Mess) (Mutex) (Wait) (Modif) (Ack).

The possible transition firings in the RG are represented in Figure 4 :

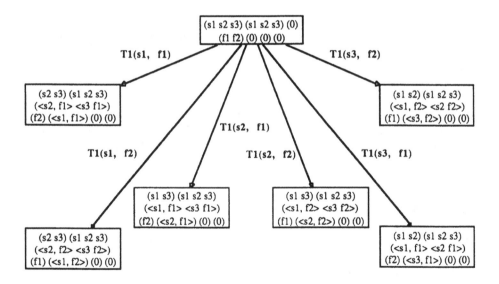

Figure 4 : A set of ordinary firings in the database model.

The SRG corresponding to the same step is the following one : At the beginning, places Active and Passive are marked with a subclass SIT1 of SIT, which is equal to SIT, and Mutex is marked with FIL1 which is a subclass of FIL, FIL1 = FIL. The firing of transition T1 for any couple of objects in SIT1 x FIL1 leads to a unique symbolic marking. This marking is obtained by splitting SIT1 in two subclasses SIT1 and SIT2, and FIL1 in two subclasses FIL1 and

FIL2. The splitting is necessary because the couple of objects for which T1 has been fired now have a marking different from that of the other objects of their former subclasses. This SRG is represented in Figure 5 :

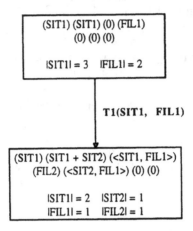

Figure 5 : The SRG associated with Figure 4.

The structure of the complete SRG in case of two sites and two filesis represented in Figure 6. Each node of the graph can be interpreted without knowing the identity of the file or the site that marks any place.

2.2.5 Construction :

The algorithm for constructing the SRG is different from the construction of the ordinary RG only by the firing rule and the labels of the arcs that are made of the transitions and the tuples of firing subclasses, whereas in the RG we have the transition and the tuple of firing objects. Notice that the initial symbolic marking only contains the initial ordinary marking because of the symmetry of the initial marking.

2.2.6 Some properties of the SRG :

Many properties have been proved on the SRG, such as quasi-liveness, and the possibility of finding a home state. However, we will only present some properties that are useful for the derivation of a stochastic model. All the proofs of the propositions given here are in [Had 87].

Proposition 2.2 : The reachability property is equivalent for the ordinary and the symbolic markings :
$$m \in RG \iff reg(m) \in SRG.$$

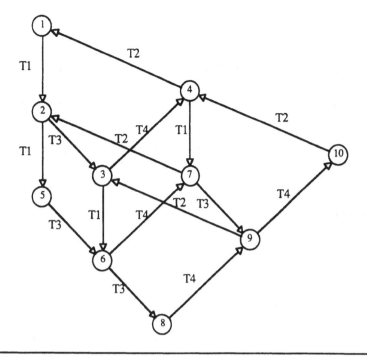

| 1 : no file being modified |
| 2 : 1 file being modified, a message has been sent |
| 3 : 1 file being modified, the second site is performing the modification |
| 4 : 1 file being modified, the second site has sent an acknowledgement |
| 5 : 2 files being modified, 2 messages have been sent |
| 6 : 2 files being modified, one site is performing the modification |
| 7 : 2 files being modified, one site has sent an acknowledgement |
| 8 : 2 files being modified, both sites are performing a modification |
| 9 : 2 files being modified, one site has sent an acknowledgement, the other is performing a modification |
| 10 : 2 files being modified, 2 acknowledgements have been sent |

Figure 6 : The complete SRG of the database model.

<u>Proposition 2.3</u> : There is an exact relation between the arcs of the RG and the SRG.
Let $M = \text{reg}(m)$ and M' two symbolic markings of the SRG. Let $\mathcal{A}_{m,M'}$ the set of arcs going out
of m to any $m' \in M'$, $\mathcal{A}_{M,M'}$ the set of symbolic arcs leading from M to M'. Then there is an
application mapping $\mathcal{A}_{m,M'}$ on $\mathcal{A}_{M,M'}$ such that the reciprocal image of a symbolic arc labelled by
$t(C_{1,u1}, \ldots, C_{n,un})$ is a set of arcs labelled by some $t(c_1, \ldots, c_n)$. The cardinality of this set is
$\Pi_{j=1}^{n} |C_{j,uj}|$.

3. REGULAR STOCHASTIC PETRI NETS

Stochastic Petri nets (SPN's) [Mol 81, Flo 85] are a tool well adapted to the modeling and the performance evaluation of distributed computer systems. In an SPN, a firing delay is associated with each transition. Firing delays are instances of random variables that have a negative exponential probability distribution. The probability that two timed transitions sample exactly the same delay time is zero, so that priority zero transitions are assumed to fire one at a time. The selection of the transition instance to fire among the set of the enabled ones follows a "race" policy [Ajm 85] (the transition that has drawn the least delay is the one that fires). Under these assumptions, the reachability graph is isomorphic to a Markov chain [Mol 81].

Regular Stochastic Petri Nets :

The association of a timing semantics to colored nets, and the extension of some notions such as conflict or confusion, have been clearly defined in [Chi 88]. However, it has also been shown that it was almost impossible to avoid the construction of the reachability graph of the unfolded net when trying to analyze the model. This is the reason why we decided to build our stochastic model only on a subclass of colored nets

As regular nets are a class of colored nets, the rules defined in [Chi 88] apply to Regular Stochastic Petri Nets (RSPN's). A RSPN is then defined as a couple (RN, λ), where RN defines a Regular Net, and λ is a weight function $\lambda : T \times C \rightarrow \mathbb{R}^+$ associating a positive real number with each transition. The value of $\lambda_{t(c)}$ is the mean delay between the moment when (t, c) is enabled and the moment when it actually fires.

Restrictions on the model :

We will neither consider the case of immediate transitions, nor marking-dependent weights, but these extensions have been developed in [Dut 89]. We will further impose that all the color instances of a transition have the same firing rate, so that λ can be redefined as a function $T \rightarrow \mathbb{R}^+$. As all the objects in a class behave the same way, it is not a heavy restriction to believe that they have the same timing constraints.

4. COMPUTATION OF THE STATE PROBABILITIES

All the performance measures of a specific system can be obtained from the computation of the steady-state probabilities. However, complex systems can generate large reachability graphs, thus making the probability computation impossible. In this section, we present an algorithm for computing the steady state probabilities without developping the whole reachability graph. This algorithm is based on a stochastic aggregation of states that is directly derived from the symbolic reachability graph. We first recall the algorithm used in a general case, then we present an algorithm that can be used in the case of regular nets.

4. 1 Usual algorithm

The probability vector P, where p(i) is the steady probability of state i, is usually obtained from the following algorithm :

(1) Unfolding of the net.

(2) Construction of the reachability graph of the unfolded net (the unicity of P is ensured iff there is only one absorbing strongly connected component in the graph), and valuation of the arcs with the rate of the associated transition.

(3) Computation of the square matrix A defined by :
         the dimension of A is the number N of reachable markings,

$$\text{if } i \neq j, \quad a_{i,j} = \sum_{\substack{t(c), \text{ the firing of } t(c) \text{ leads from } i \text{ to } j}} \lambda_{t(c)} ,$$

$$a_{i,i} = - \sum_{j \neq i} a_{i,j}$$

(4) Resolution of the system

$$\begin{cases} P. A = 0 \\ \| P \| = \sum_{i = 1}^{N} p(i) = 1 \end{cases}$$

This algorithm is very general and does not use the particular structure of the Markov chain derived from a regular net. We now present an algorithm which is valid only in the case of regular nets.

4.2 Improved algorithm

The algorithm presented in this section uses some properties of regular nets in order to reduce the complexity of the resolution. In the sequel, a symbolic marking of the SRG will be denoted $M_I, I = 1, \dots, N$.

(1) Construction of the SRG.
     The number of ordinary markings within a symbolic marking is computed during this step with the following formula :

$$|M| = \frac{1}{K} \cdot \prod_{i=1}^{n} \frac{|C_i|!}{|D_{i_1}|! \times \dots \times |D_{i_n}|!}$$

where n_i is the number of subclasses of C_i in the symbolic marking M, and K is the cardinality of the set of the permutations that leave M unchanged when applied to the subclasses of object classes :

$$K = | \{<s_1, ..., s_n> \in S, <s_1, ..., s_n>.M = M\} |.$$

(2) Computation of the square matrix A^* defined by :

the dimension of A^* is the number N' of reachable symbolic markings,

$$\text{if } I \neq J, \quad a^*_{I,J} = \sum_{t(D_1, ..., D_n) \in \mathcal{A}_{M_I,M_J}} \lambda_t .| D_1 |. ... .| D_n |$$

$$a^*_{I,I} = - \sum_{J \neq I} a^*_{I,J}$$

(3) Resolution of the system

$$\begin{cases} Q^* . A^* = 0 \\ \| Q^* \| = \sum_{I=1}^{N'} q^*(M_I) = 1 \end{cases}$$

(4) Computation of the state probability vector Q defined by $q(i) = q^*(M_I) / | M_I |$ for any marking i belonging to the symbolic marking M_I.

The fourth step is optional and depends on the will of the user to get either the probabilities of the classes of states, or the probabilities of the individual states.

N' is generally much less than N, and as the whole reachability graph is never built, the algorithm provides a real improvement in the place necessary for storing the data. Moreover, the improvement is still greater when looking at the complexity of the computation, as the exact resolution of the matricial system has a complexity $O(n^3)$. As for approximate methods, the complexity depends both on the number of states and the number of arcs, our algorithm is still an improvement. It is therefore possible to obtain exact results for large reachability graphs. The results obtained are also often more significant for the user, because the symbolic markings can be easily interpreted. In the next section, we will prove the correctness of the improved algorithm by showing that vectors P and Q are equal.

5. PROOF OF THE ALGORITHM

In this section, we detail the different steps that make the transformation of the algorithm correct. The process associated with the unfolded net is supposed to be ergodic. We first give a sketch of the method we will use to prove the correctness of our improved algorithm. The proof organizes into three steps.

(1) All the markings within a symbolic marking have the same probability.

(2)   We prove that the Markovian lumping condition is fulfilled, and the linear system corresponding to the ordinary matricial equation can be reduced to a system with fewer variables, but which is no longer probabilistic (the solution is not a probability vector). However, the reduced system can be transformed into a probabilistic system by a simple change of variables.

(3)   This probabilistic system is exactly the one computed by our algorithm.

Notation : According to the context, the index of a symbolic marking will be denoted with a capital or a lower case letter. An ordinary marking of the RG will be denoted (i, j) where M_I is the associated symbolic marking, and j is an order number within the symbolic marking. Let $s \in S$ a permutation. Then $s.(i, j)$ will be denoted $(i, s.j)$, where $s.j$ is the order number of $s.(i, j)$ within M_I.

5.1   Equiprobability of the markings :

In this section, we show that as the linear system associated to the Markov chain has a unique solution, the solution is a probability vector such that all the markings in a symbolic marking have the same probability.

We will denote by $Eq(i, k)$ the equation of the system Eq defined by $P.A = 0$, corresponding to the ordinary marking number k of the symbolic marking number i:

$$Eq\,(i, k) : \sum_{J=1}^{N} \sum_{(j,\, q) \in M_J} P_{(j,q)} \cdot a_{(j,\, q)(i,\, k)} = 0.$$

Proposition 5.1 : The transition rate between a state (j, q) and a state (i, k) is the same as the transition rate between $(j, s.q)$ and $(i, s.k)$.

$$\forall\, (j, q),\ \forall\, (i, k),\ \forall\, s \in S,\qquad a_{(j,\, q)(i,\, k)} = a_{(j,\, s.q)(i,\, s.k)}.$$

Proof : Two cases must be considered.
case 1 : $(j, q) \neq (i, k)$: this is a straightforward consequence of the basic Theorem 2.1.
case 2 : $(j, q) = (i, k)$: $a_{(i,\, s.k)(i,\, s.k)}$ is written as

$$a_{(i,\, s.k)(i,\, s.k)} = - \left[\sum_{\substack{J=1 \\ J \neq I}}^{N} \sum_{(j,\, q) \in M_J} a_{(i,\, s.k)(j,\, q)} + \sum_{\substack{(i,\, q) \in M_I \\ q \neq s.k}} a_{(i,\, s.k)(i,\, q)} \right]$$

From Corollary 2.2, we know that a permutation s defines a bijection on a symbolic marking M_I. Therefore, it is equivalent to sum on (i, q) or $(i, s.q)$.

$$a_{(i,\, s.k)(i,\, s.k)} = - \left[\sum_{\substack{J=1 \\ J \neq I}}^{N} \sum_{(j,\, q) \in M_J} a_{(i,\, s.k)(j,\, s.q)} + \sum_{\substack{(i,\, q) \in M_I \\ q \neq k}} a_{(i,\, s.k)(i,\, s.q)} \right]$$

Applying case 1, we obtain :

$$a_{(i, s.k)(i, s.k)} = - \left[\sum_{\substack{J=1 \\ J\neq I}}^{N} \sum_{(j, q)\in M_J} a_{(i, k)(j, q)} + \sum_{\substack{(i, q)\in M_I \\ q \neq k}} a_{(i, k)(i, q)} \right] = a_{(i, k)(i, k)} \qquad \Delta\Delta\Delta$$

Proposition 5.2 : $\{(p_{(i, s.k)})_{(i, k)}\}$ is a solution of the same equation as $\{(p_{(i, q)})_{(i, k)}\}$.

$$\forall (i, k), \quad \sum_{J=1}^{N} \sum_{(j, q)\in M_J} p_{(j, s.q)} \cdot a_{(j, q)(i, k)} = 0.$$

Proof : we write Eq(i, s.k) :

$$\sum_{J=1}^{N} \sum_{(j, q)\in M_J} p_{(j, q)} \cdot a_{(j, q)(i, s.k)} = 0.$$

and applying Corollary 2.2, we change the index (j, q) by (j, s.q)

$$\sum_{J=1}^{N} \sum_{(j, q)\in M_J} p_{(j, s.q)} \cdot a_{(j, s.q)(i, s.k)} = 0.$$

Applying Proposition 5.1, we get

$$\sum_{J=1}^{N} \sum_{(j, q)\in M_J} p_{(j,s.q)} \cdot a_{(j, q)(i, k)} = 0. \qquad \Delta\Delta\Delta$$

As we assume that the system is ergodic, the solution is unique. So $p_{(i, k)} = p_{(i, s.k)}$, and all the markings in a symbolic marking have the same probability.
However, we are going to show that in case the system has multiple solutions, there is always one such that all the markings in a symbolic marking have the same probability, and this solution is computed by our algorithm. If the reader is only interested in ergodic systems, he can jump to Section 5.2.

Proposition 5.3 : $\left\{\left(\dfrac{1}{|M_I|}\cdot\displaystyle\sum_{(i,\,k')\in M_I} p_{(i,\,k')}\right)_{(i,\,k)}\right\}$ is a solution of Eq, i.e.,

$$\sum_{J=1}^{N}\ \sum_{(j,\,q)\in M_J}\left(\frac{1}{|M_J|}\cdot\sum_{(j,\,q')\in M_J}p_{(j,\,q')}\right)\cdot a_{(j,\,q)(i,\,k)}=0.$$

Proof : we apply Proposition 5.2, and we sum on all the possible permutations.

$$\sum_{s\in S}\ \sum_{J=1}^{N}\ \sum_{(j,\,q)\in M_J} p_{(j,s.q)}\cdot a_{(j,\,q)(i,\,k)}=0.$$

$$\sum_{J=1}^{N}\ \sum_{(j,\,q)\in M_J}\left(\sum_{s\in S}p_{(j,\,s.q)}\right)\cdot a_{(j,\,q)(i,\,k)}=0.$$

The application of Corollary 2.3 gives :

$$\sum_{J=1}^{N}\ \sum_{(j,\,q)\in M_J}\left(\frac{|S|}{|M_J|}\cdot\sum_{(j,\,q')\in M_J}p_{(j,\,q')}\right)\cdot a_{(j,\,q)(i,\,k)}=0.$$

Dividing by $|S|$, we get $\displaystyle\sum_{J=1}^{N}\ \sum_{(j,\,q)\in M_J}\left(\frac{1}{|M_J|}\cdot\sum_{(j,\,q')\in M_J}p_{(j,\,q')}\right)\cdot a_{(j,\,q)(i,\,k)}=0.$ △△△

5.2 Reduction of the linear system :

We prove here that the steady-state probability of being in a symbolic marking can be calculated from a system with a reduced number of variables.

Proposition 5.4 : The transition rate out of a symbolic marking M_J to an ordinary marking in M_I has the same value for every marking in M_I. Conversely, the transition rate out of an ordinary marking in M_I to a symbolic marking M_J has the same value for every marking in M_I.
$\forall\ J,\ \forall\ (i,\,k),\ \forall\ s,$

$$\sum_{(j,\,q)\in M_J} a_{(j,\,q)(i,\,k)}=\sum_{(j,\,q)\in M_J} a_{(j,\,q)(i,\,s.k)}$$

$$\sum_{(j,\,q)\in M_J} a_{(i,\,k)(j,\,q)}=\sum_{(j,\,q)\in M_J} a_{(i,\,s.k)(j,\,q)}$$

Note that the second equation of Proposition 2 is equivalent to the strong Markovian lumping condition [Kem 60], which ensures that the aggregation of states will preserve the Markovian property of the process.

Proof : The result is obtained by changing the indexes of the sums and applying Proposition 6.1. ▵▵▵

Let $\bar{p}_I = \dfrac{1}{|M_I|} \cdot \displaystyle\sum_{(i,\,k)\in M_I} p_{(i,\,k)}$ the probability of any marking in M_I for the equiprobable solution,

and $\hat{p}_I = |M_I| \cdot \bar{p}_I$ the probability of being in the symbolic marking M_I.

Let $\overline{Eq}(i, k)$ the following equation : $\displaystyle\sum_{J=1}^{N} \sum_{(j,\,q)\in M_J} \bar{p}_J \cdot a_{(j,\,q)(i,\,k)} = 0.$

Proposition 6.5 : The system $\overline{Eq}$ is such that the equations associated with all the markings in a symbolic marking are the same, i.e.,

$$\forall\ (i, k),\quad \overline{Eq}(i, k) = \overline{Eq}(i, s.k)$$

Proof : $\overline{Eq}(i, k)$: $\displaystyle\sum_{J=1}^{N} \sum_{(j,\,q)\in M_J} \bar{p}_J \cdot a_{(j,\,q)(i,\,k)} = 0.$

$$\sum_{J=1}^{N} \bar{p}_J \cdot \sum_{(j,\,q)\in M_J} a_{(j,\,q)(i,\,k)} = 0.$$

Applying Proposition 5.4, $\displaystyle\sum_{J=1}^{N} \bar{p}_J \cdot \sum_{(j,\,q)\in M_J} a_{(j,\,q)(i,\,s.k)} = 0.$ ▵▵▵

As a consequence, we can consider only one equation by symbolic marking. The system we have to solve is then :

$$\begin{cases} \displaystyle\sum_{J=1}^{N} \bar{p}_J \cdot \sum_{(j,\,q)\in M_J} a_{(j,\,q)(i,\,k)} = 0 \\[2em] \displaystyle\sum_{I=1}^{N} |M_I| \cdot \bar{p}_I = 1. \end{cases}$$

Let $\bar{a}_{I,\,J} = |M_J| \cdot \displaystyle\sum_{(i,\,k)\in M_I} a_{(i,\,k)(j,\,q)}$

Proposition 5.6 : $\displaystyle\sum_{J=1}^{N} \bar{a}_{I,\,J} = 0.$

<u>Proof</u> : $\displaystyle\sum_{J=1}^{N} \bar{a}_{I, J} = \sum_{j=1}^{N} |M_J| \cdot \sum_{(i, k) \in M_I} a_{(i, k)(j, q)}$

Applying Proposition 6.4,

$$= \sum_{J=1}^{N} \sum_{(j, q) \in M_J} \sum_{(i, k) \in M_I} a_{(i, k)(j, q)}$$

$$= \sum_{(i, k) \in M_I} \left(\sum_{J=1}^{N} \sum_{(j, q) \in M_J} a_{(i, k)(j, q)} \right) = 0. \quad \Delta\Delta\Delta$$

Multiplying the first equation by $|M_I|$, we can transform our system in

$$\begin{cases} \displaystyle\sum_{J=1}^{N} \bar{p}_J \cdot \bar{a}_{J, I} = 0 \\[2em] \displaystyle\sum_{I=1}^{N} |M_I| \cdot \bar{p}_I = 1. \end{cases}$$

Introducing the new notation $\hat{a}_{I, J} = \dfrac{\bar{a}_{I, J}}{|M_I|}$, we obtain the final system :

$$\begin{cases} \displaystyle\sum_{J=1}^{N} \hat{p}_J \cdot \hat{a}_{J, I} = 0 \\[2em] \displaystyle\sum_{I=1}^{N} \hat{p}_I = 1. \end{cases}$$

where $\hat{a}_{I, J} = \dfrac{1}{|M_I|} \cdot \displaystyle\sum_{(i, k) \in M_I} \sum_{(j, q) \in M_J} a_{(i, k)(j, q)} \left(= \displaystyle\sum_{(j, q) \in M_J} a_{(i, k)(j, q)} \right)$ with $\displaystyle\sum_{J=1}^{N} \hat{a}_{I, J} = 0.$

The system we have to solve is a stochastic system, and the usual techniques for calculating the steady state probabilities can then be used. The same system would have been obtained using Markovian lumping techniques. And in that case too, it would have been necessary to develop an additional demonstration to prove that all the markings within a symbolic marking have the same probability.

Applied to our example, the above technique allows us to transform a system with 487 variables for the ordinary markings in a system with 46 variables for the symbolic markings.

The gain considerably increases with the cardinalities of the object classes. Moreover, the probabilities of the symbolic markings are often more significant for the modeler than the probabilities of the ordinary markings, making it all the more useful to compute directly the values for the lumped states.

In the next part, we will show that the coefficients $\hat{a}_{I,J}$ can be derived directly from the SRG, and that it is possible to calculate the number of ordinary markings in a symbolic marking, thus allowing us to derive the ordinary probabilities from the probabilities of the symbolic markings.

5.3   Computation of the coefficients of the reduced linear system :

The properties we are going to use to compute the coefficients of the linear system are directly linked to Proposition 2.3.

Let φ the function mapping $\mathcal{A}_{m,M'}$, the set of arcs leading from an ordinary marking m to any marking in the symbolic marking M', on $\mathcal{A}_{M,M'}$, the set of symbolic arcs leading from M, with $m \in M$, to M'. Then we have the following properties :

(1) φ is surjective,

(2)   the same transition labels an arc and its image by φ :
$$\varphi[t'(c_1, ..., c_n)] = t(D_1, ...,D_n) \Rightarrow t' = t,$$

(3) $| \varphi^{-1} [t(D_1, ...,D_n)] | = \prod_{i=1}^{n} |D_i|$

We denote λ_t the rate associated with a transition t, t(A) the transition labeling the symbolic arc A, and D_i^A the subclass of C_i instantiating t(A). So, if t(a) is the transition labeling an ordinary arc a, then t(a) = t(A) for any $a \in \varphi^{-1}(A)$.

Then the coefficients of the reduced linear system can be directly computed with the following formula :

<u>Proposition 6.7</u> : $\hat{a}_{I,J} = \sum_{A \in \mathcal{A}_{M_I,M_J}} \lambda_{t(A)} . | D_1^A | . .... . | D_n^A |$

<u>Proof</u> : From the definition of $\hat{a}_{I,J}$, we have for any $(i, k) \in M_I$:

$$\hat{a}_{I,J} = \sum_{(j, q) \in M_J} a_{(i, k)(j, q)} = \sum_{\substack{a \text{ leading from } (i, k) \text{ to } (j, q) \in M_J}} \lambda_{t(a)}$$

The set of arcs leading from (i, k) to $(j, q) \in M_J$ can be partitioned according to their image by φ. Thus we get :

$$\hat{a}_{I,J} = \sum_{A \in \mathcal{A}_{M_I,M_J}} \sum_{a \in \varphi^{-1}(A)} \lambda_{t(a)}$$

As φ preserves the transition names, this can be also written

$$\hat{a}_{I,J} = \sum_{A \in \mathcal{A}_{M_I,M_J}} \sum_{a \in \varphi^{-1}(A)} \lambda_{t(A)}$$

which is equal to

$$\hat{a}_{I,J} = \sum_{A \in \mathcal{A}_{M_I,M_J}} |\varphi^{-1}(A)| . \lambda_{t(A)}$$

Applying Proposition 2.3, we obtain

$$\hat{a}_{I,J} = \sum_{A \in \mathcal{A}_{M_I,M_J}} \prod_{i=1}^{n} |D_i^A| . \lambda_{t(A)} \qquad \Delta\Delta\Delta.$$

Those values can therefore be calculated directly from the SRG, by giving to an arc a weight depending on the cardinalities of the subclasses of its label. The values of the coefficients for $I = J$ are derived of the nullity of the sum.

6. CONCLUSION

The symmetry properties of regular nets have been used to prove many structural results. In this paper, we have shown that the symmetries can be used also in the case of a quantitative analysis.

We have proved that all the states in a symbolic marking have the same probability, and therefore, that the probabilities of all the ordinary markings can be derived from the resolution of a system which size depends only on the number of symbolic markings. We have given an algorithm for calculating the coefficients of the reduced system directly from the graph of symbolic markings.

The advantages of our method are twofold . On the one hand, the user can choose if he wants the probabilities of the ordinary markings, or if he is only interested in the probabilities of the symbolic markings which are often more significant. On the other hand, the reduction of the system will bring a dramatic improvement in the memory space and the CPU time required to solve large models, and will increase the class of models that can be analytically solved.

Our research directions will be to develop a software tool that will automatically construct the graph of symbolic markings. This tool could be later interfaced with powerful softwares for stochastic Petri nets, such as GreatSPN [Chi 87], or RDPS [Flo 86]. The introduction of immediate transitions and marking-dependent weights has been presented in [Dut 89]. We now intend to analyze less restricted classes of nets that still have symmetry properties. These extended nets include successor functions [Had 88], a non-symmetric initial marking, or color domains with several occurrences of the same object class.

Acknowledgements :

We gratefully acknowledge the three anonymous referees whose pertinent remarks allowed us to improve the quality of this paper.

References

[Ajm 85] M. Ajmone Marsan, G. Balbo, A. Bobbio, G. Chiola, G. Conte, and A. Cumani,
"On Petri Nets with Stochastic Timing", in proc. International Workshop on Timed Petri Nets, pp 80-87, IEEE-CS Press, Torino, Italy (July 1985).

[Ajm 87] M. Ajmone Marsan, G. Balbo, G. Chiola, and G. Conte,
"Generalized Stochastic Petri Nets Revisited : Random Switches and Priorities", in proc. International Workshop on Petri Nets and Performance Models, pp 44-53, IEEE-CS Press, Madison, WI, USA (August 1987).

[Chi 87] G. Chiola,
"A Graphical Petri Net Tool for Performance Analysis", 3rd International Workshop on Modeling Techniques and Performance Evaluation, AFCET, Paris (March 1987).

[Chi 88] G. Chiola, G. Bruno, and T. Demaria,
"Introducing a Color Formalism into Generalized Stochastic Petri Nets", in proc. 9th European Workshop on Application and Theory of Petri Nets, pp 202-215, Venezia, Italy (June 1988).

[Dut 89] C. Dutheillet, S. Haddad,
"Aggregation of States in Colored Stochastic Petri Nets. Application to a Multiprocessor Architecture", in proc. PNPM 89, pp 40-49, IEEE-CS Press, Kyoto, Japan (December 1989).

[Flo 85] G. Florin, S. Natkin,
"Les Réseaux de Petri Stochastiques", AFCET TSI, vol. 4, no. 1, pp 143-160 (January 1985).

[Flo 86] G. Florin,
"RDPS, a Software Package for the Validation and the Evaluation of Dependable Computer Systems", 3rd Proc. IFAC SAFECOMP Workshop, Sarlat, France (October 1986).

[Had 87] S. Haddad,
"Une Catégorie Régulière de Réseaux de Petri de Haut Niveau : Définition, Propriétés et Réductions", Thèse de Doctorat, RR87/197, Laboratoire MASI, Université Paris VI, Paris, France (October 1987).

[Had 88] S. Haddad and J.M. Couvreur,
"Towards a General and Powerful Computation of Flows for Parametrized Coloured Nets", in proc. 9th European Workshop on Application and Theory of Petri Nets, pp 202-215, Venezia, Italy (June 1988).

[Hub 84] P. Huber, A.M. Jensen, L.O. Jepsen, and K. Jensen,
"Towards Reachability Trees for High Level Petri Nets", 5th European Workshop on Application and Theory of Petri Nets, Aarhus, Denmark (1984).

[Jen 81a] K. Jensen,
"Coloured Petri Nets and the Invariant Method", Theoretical Computer Science 14, pp 317-336 (1981).

[Jen 81b] K. Jensen,
"How to Find Invariants for Coloured Petri Nets", Mathematical Foundations of Computer Science, LNCS 118, Springer - Verlag (1981).

[Kem 60] J. G. Kemeny and J. L. Snell,
"Finite Markov Chains", Van Nostrand, Princeton, NJ (1960).

[Lan 77] S. Lang,
"Algebra", Addison - Wesley (1977).

[Lin 87] Chuang Lin and D. Marinescu,
"On Stochastic High Level Petri Nets", in proc. International Workshop on Petri Nets and Performance Models, pp 44-53, IEEE-CS Press, Madison, WI, USA (August 1987).

[Mol 81] M. K. Molloy,
"On the Integration of Delay and Throughput Measures in Distributed in Distributed Processing Models", Ph.D. Dissertation, University of California, Los Angeles, CA, USA (September 1981).

[Zen 85] A. Zenie,
"Colored Stochastic Petri Nets", in proc. International Workshop on Timed Petri Nets, pp 262-271, IEEE-CS Press, Torino, Italy (July 1985).

CIRCUITS, HANDLES, BRIDGES AND NETS

Javier Esparza[*]

Institut für Informatik, Universität Hildesheim

Manuel Silva

Dpto. Ingeniería Eléctrica e Informática, Universidad de Zaragoza

ABSTRACT. This paper introduces two new structural objects for the study of nets: handles and bridges. They are shown to provide sufficient, although not necessary, conditions of good behaviour for general ordinary nets, as well as a new characterisation of structural liveness and structural boundedness for the subclass of Free Choice nets. This characterisation is used to approach a modular synthesis theory of Free Choice nets through the synchronisation of State Machines. The task is fully performed for the restricted subclass of Strict Free Choice nets introduced here.

Keywords: Free Choice nets, Structure Theory, Synthesis.

1. INTRODUCTION

Net structure theory investigates the relationship between the behaviour of a net and its structure (we understand as "structure" the topology of the bipartite graph, plus the possible weights of the arcs and capacities of the places). The purpose of characterising "well behaved" nets using structural properties is twofold:

- *To analyse systems more easily (the analysis problem).* The computational cost of the analysis of structural properties grows usually much more slowly with the net's size than the cost of building the marking graph (or coverability graph).

---

[*] This work was performed while this author was a member of the Dpto. Ingeniería Eléctrica e Informática, Universidad de Zaragoza.

- To design systems granting good behaviour (the synthesis problem). This is achieved giving a design methodology which ensures that the net enjoys the desirable structural properties correlated with good behaviour.

There are very few results of structure theory valid for general ordinary nets. Net subclasses have to be considered to obtain powerful results. In these subclasses, topological objects significant for the behaviour are identified (circuits for Marked Graphs [COMM 71] [GENR 73] [MURA 77], deadlocks and traps for Free Choice nets [HACK 72], small rings for Deterministic Sequential Processes [REIS 83] [SOUI 88]). Then it is proved that behavioural properties are bound to the relationships between these objects, and between these objects and the marking.

In this paper we deal with the synthesis problem for Free Choice nets. There are two main methodologies for the synthesis of systems that find their counterpart in net theory:

-Top-down synthesis. The system is first viewed from a very high-level of abstraction and is stepwise refined until the desired level of detail is reached. In the context of Petri nets, this is equivalent to the refinement of subnets through expansion-reduction rules (this problem is solved for Bipolar Schemes [GENR 84], a subset of Free Choice nets).

- Modular synthesis. The system is divided into modules that can be easily modelled. The problem now is how to compose the modules to yield a well-behaved system. The module usually considered (for instance in the CSP model [HOAR 85]) is the sequential process or automaton. In the field of Petri nets it translates into a safe State Machine.

We are concerned in this paper with the second methodology, which leads us to consider State Machine Decomposable nets (SMD nets for short) [HACK 72] [JANT 81].

While the structure theory of Free Choice nets is very satisfactory with regards to the analysis problem [HACK 72] [THIA 84] [BEST 84], it still lacks results for synthesis. We feel that one of the reasons for this is that the structural objects that support a good part of the theory, namely deadlocks and traps, are inadequate for the synthesis problem. Deadlocks and traps have been proved to be very useful for the analysis of Free Choice nets (they can also be elegantly calculated by means of P-semiflows [LAUT 87]), but do not appear to be meaningful when considering the synthesis problem. We will show in this paper how they can be complemented with other objects, handles and bridges, that lead to results having a clear intuitive meaning. The paper is structured as follows. In section 2 basic definitions and results are given. Section 3 introduces handles and bridges, some elementary properties and relates handles to behavioural properties of ordinary nets. The subclass of Free Choice nets is considered in section 4; structural liveness and structural boundedness (SL&SB for short) is characterised in terms of handles and bridges. This finishes the first part of the paper. In the second part SMD nets are considered. Section 5 gives some definitions and elementary results and introduces the new subclass of Strict Free Choice nets. In section 6 the (modular) synthesis problem of Strict Free Choice nets is solved.

2. BASIC DEFINITIONS AND RESULTS

We use throughout this work a number of known concepts of graph theory and structural net theory. They are defined below, grouped by topics. From the second definition on we focus on ordinary nets.

N denotes the set $N=\{0, 1, 2, 3, ...\}$. $N^+=N-\{0\}$

Definition 2.1 [generalities]

A *place/transition net* (or *P/T net*) is a fourtuple $N= (P, T; F,W)$ where

- P is the set of places
- T is the set of transitions $(P\cap T= \emptyset)$
- $F\subseteq (P \times T) \cup (T \times P)$ is the flow relation
- $W: F\to N^+$ is the weight function.

The elements of $P\cup T$ are called *nodes*. N is *ordinary* iff $\forall (x, y)\in F$: $W((x, y))=1$. Ordinary nets are described by the triple $(P, T; F)$.

N is *pure* iff $\forall x, y\in P\cup T$ such that $(x, y)\in F$: $(y, x)\notin F$.

The *Pre-set* of $x\in P\cup T$ is $^\bullet x= \{y\in P\cup T \mid (y, x)\in F\}$.

The *Post-set* of $x\in P\cup T$ is $x^\bullet= \{y\in P\cup T \mid (x, y)\in F\}$.

A matrix $C = \|c_{ij}\|$ $(1\le i \le n, 1\le j \le m)$ is the *incidence matrix* of $N=(P, T; F)$, where $P=\{p_1, ..., p_n\}$ and $T= \{t_1, ...,t_m\}$ iff $c_{ij}=W(t_j, p_i) - W(p_i, t_j)$.

A function $M: P \to N$ is called a *marking*. A *marked P/T net* $<N,M_0>$, is a P/T net N with an initial marking M_0.

A transition $t\in T$ is *enabled at M* iff $\forall p\in {}^\bullet t$: $M(p)\ge W(p, t)$. If $t_i\in T$ is enabled at a marking M, then t_i may be *fired* yielding a new marking M' given by $M'= M + C \cdot e_{t_i}$, where all the components of vector e_{t_i} are 0 but the ith, whose value is 1.

$M[t>M'$ denotes that M' is reached from M by firing t.

A sequence of transitions, $\sigma=t_1t_2...t_r$, is a *firing sequence* of $<N, M_0>$ iff there exists a sequence $M_0t_1M_1t_2M_2...t_rM_r$ such that $\forall i, 1\le i\le r$: $M_{i-1}[t_i>M_i$. The marking M_r is said to be *reachable* from M_0 by firing σ: $M_0[\sigma>M_r$. $R(N, M)$ is the set of all markings reachable from M. $L(N, M)$ is the set of all firing sequences applicable from M: $L(N, M)=\{\sigma \mid M[\sigma>M'\}$. ♦

Definition 2.2 [subclasses of ordinary nets]

A net N is a *P-graph* or *State Machine* iff each transition has exactly one input place and one output place $(\forall t\in T: |^\bullet t|=|t^\bullet|=1)$.

A net N is a *T-graph* or *Marked Graph* iff each place has exactly one input transition and one output transition ($\forall\ p \in P$: $|{}^\bullet p| = |p^\bullet| = 1$).

A net N is *Free Choice* iff $\forall\ p \in P$ such that $|p^\bullet| \triangleright 1$: ${}^\bullet(p^\bullet) = \{p\}$.

A net N is *Simple* iff $\forall\ t \in T$: ${}^\bullet t$ contains at most one place p such that $|p^\bullet| \triangleright 1$. ◆

Definition 2.3 [subnets]

Let $N=(P, T; F)$ and $N'=(P', T'; F')$ be two nets.

N' is a *subnet* of N and is denoted $N' \subseteq N$ iff $P' \subseteq P$, $T' \subseteq T$ and $F' = F \cap ((P' \times T') \cup (T' \times P'))$.

N' is a *partial subnet* of N and is denoted $N' \leq N$ iff $P' \subseteq P$, $T' \subseteq T$ and $F' \subseteq F \cap ((P' \times T') \cup (T' \times P'))$.

$N' \subseteq N$ is the *input subnet* or *I-subnet* of N (*output subnet* or *O-subnet*) induced by P' iff $T' = {}^\bullet P'$ ($T = P'^\bullet$ for O-subnet).

$N' \subseteq N$ is a *P-component* (*T-component*) of N iff N' is a strongly connected P-graph (T-graph) and $T' = {}^\bullet P' \cup P'^\bullet$ ($P' = {}^\bullet T' \cup T'^\bullet$). ◆

Definition 2.4 [State Machine Decomposable nets]

A net $N = (P, T; F)$ is *State Machine Decomposable* iff there exists a collection $N_i = (P_i, T_i; F_i)$, $1 \leq i \leq a$, $a \in N^+$, of P-components of N such that $P = \cup P_i$, $T = \cup T_i$, $F = \cup F_i$. $\{N_1,..., N_a\}$ is called a *cover* of N, and it is said that N is *covered* by $\{N_1,..., N_a\}$ ◆

Definition 2.5 [paths and circuits]

A *path* of N is an alternating sequence $(x_1, f_1, x_2 ... f_{r-1}, x_r)$ of elements of $X = P \cup T$ and F such that $\forall i\ 1 \leq i \leq r-1$: $f_i = (x_i, x_{i+1})$. If it is allowed that $f_i \in F \cup F^{-1}$ the sequence is an *undirected* path. The *length* of Π is the number r of nodes of the sequence. Π is *elementary* iff all x_i are distinct, except possibly x_1 and x_r. Π' is a subpath of Π iff it is a subsequence of Π that is itself a path.

Let $\Pi_1 = (x_1, ..., x_q)$ and $\Pi_2 = (y_1, ..., y_r)$ be paths such that $x_q = y_1$. The path $\Pi = (x_1, ..., x_q = y_1, ..., y_r)$ is called the *concatenation* of Π_1 and Π_2.

A *general circuit* of N is a path $\Gamma = (x_1, ..., x_r)$ such that $x_1 = x_r$. A general circuit is *elementary* (or just a *circuit*, for short) iff it is elementary as a path. ◆

Note: Paths in ordinary nets will be denoted omitting the arcs of the sequence, $\Pi = (x_1, x_2, ..., x_r)$. It is easy to see that this completely characterizes them. Sometimes, risking confusion, paths will be identified with the set of their nodes.

Definition 2.6 [deadlocks and traps]

$P' \subseteq P$ is a *deadlock* (*trap*) of N iff $P' \neq \emptyset$ and ${}^\bullet P' \subseteq P'^\bullet$ $(P'^\bullet \subseteq {}^\bullet P')$.

A deadlock $D \subseteq P$ (trap $\Theta \subseteq P$) is *minimal* iff there is no deadlock D' such that $D' \subsetneq D$ (trap Θ' such that $\Theta' \subsetneq \Theta$). A deadlock $D \subseteq P$ (trap $\Theta \subseteq P$) is *strongly connected* iff the I–subnet (O–subnet) generated by D (Θ) is strongly connected.

A deadlock (trap) is *marked* iff at least one of its places is marked. ♦

We state an interesting well-known result concerning the concepts of the previous definition.

Proposition 2.1 [HACK 72]

Minimal deadlocks (traps) are strongly connected. ♦

Definition 2.7 [duality and reverse transformations]

Let N=(P, T; F) be an ordinary Petri net.

The net $N^d = (T, P; F)$ is the *dual net* of N. The net $N^{-1} = (P, T; F^{-1})$ is the *reverse net* of N. The net $N^{-d} = (T, P; F^{-1})$ is the *reverse-dual net* of N. ♦

Remark 2.1

Note that, though not the reverse nor the dual of a Free Choice net are necessarily Free Choice, the reverse-dual always is. This will be used later on. ♦

Definition 2.8 [behavioural properties]

A marked net $<N,M_0>$ is said to be *(marking) bounded* iff $\exists$ k∈ N such that $\forall p \in P$ $\forall M \in R(N,M_0)$: $M(p) \leq k$. A net N is *structurally bounded* iff $\forall M_0$: $<N,M_0>$ is bounded.

A transition t∈ T is *live* in $<N, M_0>$ iff $\forall M \in R(N, M_0)$ $\exists$ M'∈ R(N, M) such that M' enables t. The marked net $<N, M_0>$ is live iff all t∈ T are live (i.e. liveness in nets guarantees the possibility of infinite activity of all the transitions in the net). N is *structurally live* iff $\exists$ M_0:$<N,M_0>$ is live.

Let **1** be the vector whose components are all 1. A net N is *conservative* iff there exists a vector Y>**1** such that $Y^T \cdot C = 0$. A net N is *repetitive* (*consistent*) iff there exists a vector X>**1** such that $C \cdot X \geq 0$ ($C \cdot X = 0$). ♦

Notice that structural boundedness is defined using an universal quantifier, while structural liveness requires an existential one.

The property corresponding to the existence of Y>**1** such that $Y^T \cdot C \leq 0$ is namely structural boundedness, as the following proposition shows.

Proposition 2.2 [MEMM 80]

A net N is structurally bounded iff there exists a vector Y>1such that $Y^T \cdot C \leq 0$. ♦

We will make use of Commoner's theorem for Free Choice nets.

Theorem 2.1 [HACK 72] [Commoner's Theorem]

Let <N, M_0> be a marked Free Choice net. <N, M_0> is live iff every deadlock of N contains a marked trap. ♦

3. HANDLES, BRIDGES AND ORDINARY NETS

In the first part of this section handles and bridges, the structures we introduce to complement deadlocks and traps, are defined and some elementary properties stated. The second part provides a sufficient condition for SL&SB of general ordinary nets in terms of handles. This parallels what happens in deadlocks and traps theory, where a sufficient condition for deadlock-freeness (Commoner's property [HACK 72]) is obtained.

3.1 Handles, bridges and elementary properties.

Definition 3.1

Let $N=(P, T; F)$ and N_1 a partial subnet of N. An elementary path $\Pi=(x_1, ..., x_r)$, $r \geq 2$, of N is a *handle* of N_1 iff $\Pi \cap (P_1 \cup T_1)= \{x_1, x_r\}$ (assuming that if $x_1=x_n$ then $\{x_1, x_r\}=\{x_1\}$). It will also be said that N_1 *has* a handle Π. ♦

Figure 1a shows a handle of a circuit. The name was chosen for two reasons. First, its graphical appeal, clear in figure 1. Second, the fact that handles in net theory play a similar role to topological handles in topology. In the same way that every closed surface is topologically equivalent to a sphere with handles, every strongly connected net can be built adding handles to an initial node.

These handles should not be confused with the ones considered in [GENR83] in the field of graph grammars.

Although the concept of handle is the main one on which this paper is based, we make wide use, particularly in proofs, of another structural object, namely bridges.

Definition 3.2

Let $N=(P, T; F)$ and N_1, N_2 partial subnets of N. An elementary path $\Pi=(x_1, ..., x_r)$, $r \geq 2$, is a *bridge* from N_1 to N_2 iff $\Pi \cap (P_1 \cup T_1)=\{x_1\}$ and $\Pi \cap (P_2 \cup T_2)=\{x_r\}$. ♦

Figure 1.b shows a bridge between two paths. Note that N_1 and N_2 need not be disjoint (an example of the disjoint case is a bridge between two islands, one of the non-disjoint case a bridge on a pond).

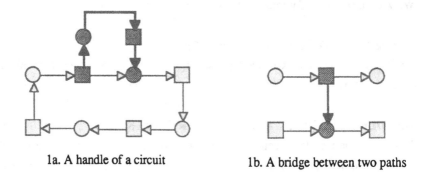

1a. A handle of a circuit   1b. A bridge between two paths

Figure 1. A handle and a bridge

One of the main uses we will make of bridges will be the following: in order to prove the existence of a certain handle of a partial subnet N, we will consider a partial subnet consisting of one single node x such that $N \cap \{x\} = \emptyset$, and will prove that a bridge exists from N to x and another one from x to N. A handle of N can then be then obtained from the concatenation of the two bridges. Nevertheless, the handle may not be just that concatenation, because the resulting path might not be elementary. To avoid this nuisance the following definition is introduced.

Definition 3.3

Let N be a net and $\Pi_1=(x_1, ..., x_q)$, $\Pi_2=(y_1, ..., y_r)$ two elementary paths of N such that $x_q=y_1$. Let x_i be the first node of Π_1 such that $x_i \in \Pi_2$. Consider the two subpaths $\Pi_1'=(x_1, ..., x_i)$ and $\Pi_2'=(x_i, ..., y_r)$ of Π_1 and Π_2 respectively. The path $\Pi=\Pi_1';\Pi_2'$ is called the *elementary concatenation* of Π_1 and Π_2 and is denoted by $\Pi=\Pi_1;;\Pi_2$. ◆

It is clear from the definition that the elementary concatenation of two elementary paths is elementary as well. The following proposition is a trivial consequence of the definitions.

Proposition 3.1

Let $N=(P, T; F)$, $N' \leq N$ and $x \in P \cup T$ such that $N' \cap \{x\} = \emptyset$. Let Π_1 be a bridge from N' to x and Π_2 a bridge from x to N'. Then $\Pi = \Pi_1;;\Pi_2$ is a handle of N'. ◆

In a bipartite graph as a Petri net one of the main features of handles and bridges is the nature of their first and last nodes. We classify them according to this criterion into four subclasses: *PP-, PT-, TP- and TT-handles or bridges* (see Figure 2). The meaning is obvious.It is intuitively clear that both PP- and TT-handles are "nice" for liveness and boundedness while PT- and TP-handles "create problems" that have to be solved. The next proposition shows that "nice" as well as "bad" handles are invariant under the dual and reverse transformations.

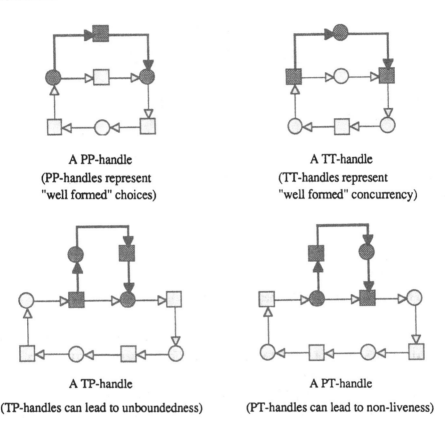

A PP-handle
(PP-handles represent
"well formed" choices)

A TT-handle
(TT-handles represent
"well formed" concurrency)

A TP-handle

A PT-handle

(TP-handles can lead to unboundedness)

(PT-handles can lead to non-liveness)

Figure 2. The four classes of handles

Proposition 3.2

Let $N=(P, T; F)$, $N' \leq N$ and H a XY-handle of N', where both X and Y can be P or T. Let F(N) stand for the reverse, dual or reverse-dual of the primal net N.Then F(H) is a handle of F(N'). Table 3.1 shows the subclass of handles to which F(H) belongs depending on the nature of F. ♦

In this paper we will be mainly concerned with handles of elementary circuits, P-graphs and T-graphs embedded in nets. We prove now that "bad" handles of strongly connected P- and

T-graphs are related to "bad" handles of circuits. In the proof we make use of bridges for the first time.

XY	Reverse	Dual	Reverse-dual
PP	PP	TT	TT
PT	TP	TP	PT
TP	PT	PT	TP
TT	TT	PP	PP

Table 3.1. Transformations of handles in the dual and reverse nets. The sets {PP- and TT-handles} and {PT-and TP-handles} remain invariant under all the tranformations.

In this paper we will be mainly concerned with handles of elementary circuits, P-graphs and T-graphs embedded in nets. We prove now that "bad" handles of strongly connected P- and T-graphs are related to "bad" handles of circuits. In the proof we make use of bridges for the first time.

Proposition 3.3

Let $N=(P, T; F)$ be a net and N_1 a strongly connected P-graph or a strongly connected T-graph of N. If N_1 has a PT- or a TP-handle H, there exists a circuit of N_1 that also has a handle H' of the same class.

Proof. We will exploit proposition 3.2. The invariance of "bad" handles under duality yields without need of proof that if the property is true for a P-graph is also true for a T-graph. We take a P-graph and consider two cases:

i) H is a PT-handle. Let $p \in P$ and $t \in T$ be the first and last nodes of H respectively. If there exists a circuit of N_1 that contains both p and t, we are done (i. e. H'=H). If there is no such circuit, there must exist a circuit Γ of N_1 that contains t but not p. But, as N_1 is a strongly connected P-graph, there must also exist a PP-bridge B from Γ to p. Then H'= B;;H is a PT-handle of Γ.

ii) H is a TP-handle. Use proposition 3.2 again, taking into account that the reverse of a P-graph is a P-graph and the reverse of a PT-handle is a TP-handle. ♦

3.2 Handles and the behaviour of ordinary nets.

We prove in this section how the absence in an ordinary net of "bad" handles, or at least of one of the two subclasses into which they are divided, is a sufficient condition for the net to enjoy some properties of nice behaviour.

Theorem 3.1

Let $N = (P, T; F)$ be a strongly connected net

a) If no circuit of N has a TP-handle, N is structurally bounded.

b) If no circuit of N has a PT-handle, N is repetitive.

Proof.

a) Take $p \in P$. Consider a strongly connected P-graph $N_1 = (P_1, T_1; F_1)$, $N_1 \leq N$ such that $p \in P_1$ and there is no strongly connected P-graph $N_2 \neq N_1$ satisfying $N_1 \leq N_2 \leq N$.

N_1 always exists because N is strongly connected. This implies that there is at least one circuit containing p, and circuits are strongly connected P-graphs.

We claim that if $p' \in P_1$ then all arcs of the form $(t, p') \in F$ satisfy $(t, p') \in F_1$. It is clear that, if this is true, the token count of N_1 can not properly increase, and therefore the number of tokens of p remains bounded for any initial marking. Hence, if this statement is proved we are done.

Assume the claim is not true. Two cases have to be considered:

a.1) $t \notin T_1$. As N is strongly connected, there is a bridge B from N_1 to t. If the first node of B is a place, ii) is contradicted, because $N_1 \cup \Pi$, where $\Pi = B; (t, p')$, would be a strongly connected P-graph bigger than N_1. If it is a transition, then $H = B; (t, p')$ is a TP-handle of N_1. By proposition 3.3, there is also a circuit of N with a TP-handle.

a.2) $t \in T_1$ but $(t, p') \notin F_1$. In this case, $H = (t, p')$ is clearly a TP-handle of N_1.

b) It can be proved that a net N is structurally bounded iff the dual of N, N^d, is repetitive [BRAM 83]. Use then that the dual of a TP-handle is a PT-handle. ♦

Let us see now that nets whose circuits have neither TP nor PT-handles enjoy more behavioural properties than just the ones derived from the "addition" of parts a) and b) of theorem 3.1: the nets of this particular subclass are structurally live. Moreover, the subclass enjoys very nice properties of decomposability and duality, while still being able to model both concurrency and non-determinism.

Theorem 3.2

Let $N = (P, T; F)$ be a strongly connected net such that no circuit of N has a PT- nor a TP-handle. Then :

(a)   N is structurally live.

(b)   N can be covered by P-components (therefore it is conservative).

(c)   N can be covered by T-components (therefore it is consistent).

(d)   The previous properties are also true for the reverse, dual and reverse-dual of N.

Proof. See Annex 1. ♦

4. A NEW CHARACTERISATION OF SL&SB FOR FREE CHOICE NETS

Loosely speaking, the results of the previous section indicate that, in order to be live and bounded, a net has to "solve" the problems raised by the presence of PT- and/or TP-handles of circuits. As ordinary nets can find very different solutions to them, we now consider a restricted subclass, namely Free Choice nets. We show in this section that SL&SB can be characterised for them in terms of handles and bridges. Although the main purpose of this result is to pave the way for the sections to come, concerning synthesis by means of the superposition of automata, we will find as a subproduct a new and nice view of the classical duality results of Free Choice nets. This section is divided in three parts. The first one includes two properties of Live and Bounded Free Choice nets. In the second part we state the main theorem of the section, showing that these properties are also *sufficient* for a Free Choice net to be SL&SB. It is then seen how this result sheds new light on the duality results. Finally, we extend part of the main theorem to Simple nets.

4.1 Two properties of Live and Bounded Free Choice nets.

Let us start our way towards a characterisation of SL&SB with a proposition, conjectured by E. Best and P. Thiagarajan and proved by J. Desel in [DESE 86] in other terms, that was the primary inspiration of this work. In our language, it states that a Free Choice net has no solution for the problems raised by TP-handles.

Proposition 4.1

Let N=(P, T; F) be a Live and Bounded Free Choice net. No circuit of N has TP-handles. ♦

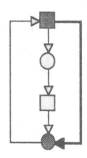 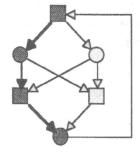 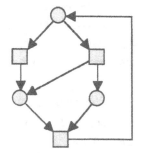

3a. There is a circuit with a TP-handle. The net is SL but unbounded.

3b. A SL&SB Extended Free Choice net containing a circuit with a TP-handle.

3c. No circuit has a TP-hand but the net is not live for any marking.

Figure 3. Illustration of proposition 4.1

Figure 3.a illustrates this proposition. Two remarks should be stated. First, the property is not true for Extended Free Choice nets, as Figure 3.b shows. Second, this is a necessary but not sufficient condition (see Figure 3.c for an example). This naturally raises two questions: Is it possible to add conditions such that together characterize SL&SB? Is there a subset of Free Choice nets for which absence of TP-handles is also sufficient? We will answer the first in this section, and the second in section 6.

When we faced the first question, we thought of a sort of dual condition of proposition 4.1 concerning PT-handles of circuits. But the net of Figure 4 shows that circuits can have PT-handles, as was already pointed out in [DESE 86]. Nevertheless, as the decision taken in place p is free, it was intuitively reasonable that a "signal" had to be sent to the non-selected branch in order to allow transition t to be fired. This signal should travel along a path beginning in a transition of the selected branch and ending in a place of the other one, as happens in the net of Figure 4.

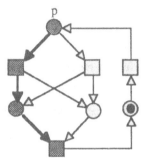

Figure 4. An LSFC net that contains a circuit with a PT-handle.

Proposition 4.2

Let $N=(P, T; F)$ be a Live and Bounded Free Choice net. If a circuit Γ of N has a PT-handle $H=(p_1, t_1, ..., p_r, t_r)$, H is bridged to Γ through a TP-bridge B (see Figure 5).

Proof. Notice first that $p_1 \neq p_r$, because otherwise the net would not be Free Choice. We use a property proven in [THIA 84]: every circuit of N is contained in a P-component. Let N' be a P-component containing Γ. It follows that t_1 also belongs to N', and p_r not (see Figure 5).

Let t be the last transition of H contained in N'. Call H_t the subpath of H such that $H_t=(p_1, ..., t)$ and Π_H to the subpath of Γ whose first and last nodes are p_1 and t_r respectively. As N' is strongly connected, there will exist a bridge $B \subseteq N'$ from t to $\Gamma \cup H_t$. The last node of B must be a place p because N' is a P-graph. If $p \in H_t$, B is a TP-handle of the circuit formed by $(\Gamma \backslash \Pi_H) \cup H$. Therefore $p \in \Gamma$, and B is the bridge we were looking for. ♦

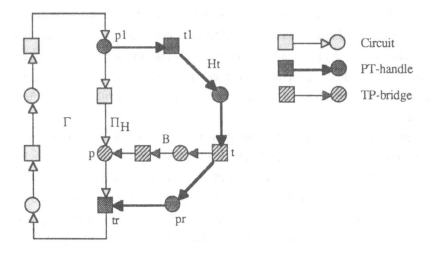

Figure 5. Illustration of proposition 4.2

Remarks 4.1

Proposition 4.1 imposes further restrictions on B. It is easy to see that p∈ Π_H in Γ. Otherwise, a TP-handle of (Γ\Π_H) ∪ H appears.

Moreover, the handle H and the path Π_H can interchange their roles. This implies the existence of another TP-bridge B'=(t', ..., p'), this time from Π_H to H. Proposition 4.1 and 4.2 impose (we will not prove it here):

- B ∩ B' = ∅
- p' is posterior to t in H and p is posterior to t' in Π_H.

Notice as well that the proof of the property of [THIA84] was based in that paper on the fact that a LBFC can be covered by T-components. In [ESPA 90] another proof of proposition 4.2 is given that does not require this. The interest of an independent proof is that later on we will make use of this property to *deduce* the existence of a covering by T-components. ♦

4.2 Characterisation of SL&SB and duality corollaries.

The step to be given now is show that the properties of propositions 4.1 and 4.2 together with the property of strong connectedness are also sufficient for SL&SB of Free Choice nets. We obtain first, using a lemma of [ESPA 89], a slightly improved version of Hack's theorem, which characterises SL&SB in Free Choice nets. Then we show (the proof can be found in Annex 1) that this characterisation is equivalent to the new one based on the properties of handles.

Lemma 4.1 [ESPA 89]

Every strongly connected deadlock of a Free Choice net is union of minimal deadlocks.

♦

As the whole set of places of a strongly connected net forms a strongly connected deadlock, every place of a strongly connected Free Choice net belongs to a minimal deadlock of N.

Theorem 4.1 [HACK 72]

A Free Choice net N is SL&SB iff:

- N is covered by P-components.
- Every minimal deadlock of N generates a P-component. ♦

Notice that theorem 4.1 implies that every SL&SB Free Choice net is a State Machine Decomposable net. It should be remarked also that Hack's theorem is somewhat stronger. It ensures that the net is live and bounded iff, besides the conditions above, minimal deadlocks are marked. The new version of theorem 4.1 is as follows.

Theorem 4.1bis

A Free Choice net N is SL&SB iff :

- N is strongly connected.
- Every minimal deadlock of N generates a P-component.

Proof

⇒) Obvious from theorem 4.1.

⇐) If N is strongly connected, it is covered by minimal deadlocks which generate P–components. ♦

Theorem 4.2

Let N=(P, T; F) be a Free Choice net. N is SL&SB iff:

(a)   N is strongly connected

(b)   No circuit of N has TP-handles

(c)   Every PT-handle of a circuit is bridged to it through a TP-bridge.

Proof See Annex 1. ♦

Corollary 4.2 (Hack's duality theorem)

Let N be a Free Choice net and N^{-d} its reverse-dual. N is SL&SB iff N^{-d} is.

Proof. As the three conditions (a), (b) and (c) of theorem 4.2 are self-reverse-dual, N satisfies the conditions iff N^{-d} does. ♦

Corollary 4.3 (Hack's decomposition theorem)

Let N be a SL&SB Free Choice net. Then N can be covered by T-components.

Proof. N^{-d} is SL&SB by the previous corollary, and by theorem 4.1 can be covered by P-components. As the reverse-dual of a P-component is a T-component, N can be covered by T-components. ♦

The "if" part of theorem 4.2 is also true for Simple nets (in [HOLT 74] this is proven for theorem 4.1, and the conditions of theorem 4.1 and 4.2 are equivalent), but not the "only if" part. Figure 6 shows a SL&SB Simple net that satisfies neither (b) nor (c).

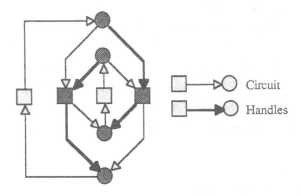

Figure 6. An SL&SB net containing a circuit with TP- and PT- handles.

As was pointed out in the introduction, we are concerned with modular synthesis of Live Free Choice nets through synchronisation of State Machines (structural boundedness is always ensured, as will be recalled in a proposition below). Therefore, we will deal in the second part of the paper with State Machine Decomposable nets (SMD nets). This second part is divided into three sections. We introduce first some concepts and properties of SMD nets. Then a subclass of Free Choice SMD nets is defined. The final section is dedicated to the application of handles and bridges properties to the analysis and synthesis of this subclass.

5. STATE MACHINE DECOMPOSABLE NETS.

5.1 Basic concepts and properties

We start with the well-known result of the structural boundedness of SMD nets. It is based on the fact that the number of tokens of a P-component remains constant for any reachable marking. The proof is omitted.

Proposition 5.1
Let N be a SMD net. Then N is structurally bounded. ♦

Let us consider now the net that remains after "removing" a P-component. The concepts of "remainder" and "removal" are precised in the following definition.

Definition 5.1
Let $N = (P, T; F)$ be a SMD net, $\Re = \{N_1,..., N_a\}$ a cover of N and $N_i \in \Re$. The net $N_i' = (P_i', T_i'; F_i')$ where

$P_i' = \{p \in N_j \mid j \neq i, N_j \in \Re\}$
$T_i' = \{t \in N_j \mid j \neq i, N_j \in \Re\}$
$F_i' = F \cap (P_i' \times T_i') \cup (T_i' \times P_i')$

is called the *neighbourhood* or *environment* of N_i. A *neighbour* of N_i is a connected component of N_i'. ♦

Proposition 5.2
The neighbours of a P-component N_i are strongly connected.
Proof. It follows from definition 5.1 that N_i' is also a SMD net. If N_i' is composed by several isolated subnets (i.e. not connected to each other), each of them must be also SMD and therefore strongly connected. Each of these isolated subnets is a neighbour of N_i. ♦

The relationship between a P-component and its neighbours is established through a subset of transitions. We call them *synchronisations*.

Definition 5.3
Let $N = (P, T; F)$ be a SMD net. A transition $t \in T$ is a *synchronisation* iff $|{}^\bullet t| > 1$ or $|t^\bullet| > 1$. ♦

Proposition 5.3
Let $N = (P, T; F)$ be a SMD net. Every synchronisation $t \in T$ belongs to at least two different P-components of any cover of N. ♦

5.2 A classification of SMD nets

Are Free Choice SMD nets a "natural" subclass of SMD nets, or, on the contrary, are they spread among different "natural" subclasses ? To have an answer we need a criterion upon which a "natural" taxonomy of SMD nets could be founded. We propose the following one: *classify SMD nets attending to how much freedom State Machines are allowed for taking decisions.* It is analogous to the usual criterion of classifying nets by the complexity of their interplay between concurrency and non-determinism, but not equal. The proof is precisely the fact that our criterion splits the class of Free Choice SMD nets in two.

Consider the nets of Figure 4 and Figure 7. Both are Live and Safe Free Choice SMD, and can be seen as the synchronisation of two Strongly Connected State Machines. In the net of Figure 7 the State Machines can take their decisions with *full freedom*, that is, without having to ask for permission to the other one. On the contrary, both State Machines of the net of Figure 4 must agree about the decision (what could be exhibited adding an implicit place that would transform the net into Extended Free Choice). It should be clear that these two are the only posibilities Free Choice SMD nets offer for the synchronisation of Strongly Connected State Machines. Free Choice nets mix these two different situations, that we would like to separate. This is the reason of the next definition.

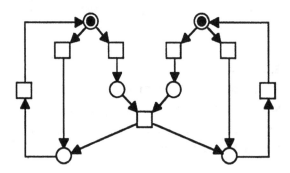

Figure 7. An LSFC net (and therefore SMD). The two State Machines take their decisions freely.

Definition 5.4

Let N= (P, T; F) be an SMD net, and OS={p∈ P such that |p$^•$|>1} (OS stands for output-shared). We will also call p∈ OS a *choice*. N is *Strict Free Choice (SFC)* iff it is Free Choice and there exists a set $\Re$ of P-components of N such that

- N is covered by $\Re$
- $\forall$ N$_i$, N$_j$ ∈ $\Re$, either N$_i$=N$_j$ or N$_i$ ∩ N$_j$ ∩ OS = Ø

In other words, N can be covered by P-components whose choices are pairwise disjoint, or each choice belongs to one and only one State Machine.

The set $\Re$ of P-components is called a *strict decomposition* of N. ♦

Notice in the previous definition that $\Re$ is not unique. It should also be noted that, according to this definition, whenever we speak of Strict Free Choice nets we are assuming that they are State Machine Decomposable.

Our classification of SMD nets is then as follows: Strongly connected MGs and State Machines $\subsetneq$ Strict Free Choice $\subsetneq$ Free Choice SMD $\subsetneq$ Simple SMD $\subsetneq$ General SMD nets

It could be objected that "strictness" is a too strong notion. Consider the two nets of figure 8.

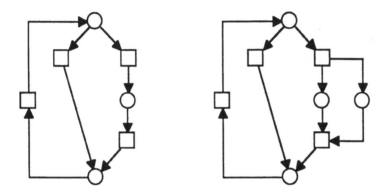

Figure 8. An SFC net (left) and a non-SFC net (right).

The one on the left is obviously SFC. Nevertheless, the addition of an identity place, which is clearly harmless, spoils strictness (the net on the right is not SFC). The answer to this objection is that we are dealing with the synthesis problem. Therefore we should ask whether SFC nets are a natural class from the *synthesis* point of view, that is, whether they are the nets that can be obtained through the synchronisation of State Machines by imposing to the composition *natural* and *meaningful* constraints. The answer to this question is yes: SFC nets are exactly the models of systems of synchronised sequential automata that are not allowed to influence in any way the decisions taken by the others. Solving the synthesis problem of SFC nets answers the question of what can be done with these systems.

6. ANALYSIS AND SYNTHESIS OF STRICT FREE CHOICE NETS

We will prove in this section that Strict Free Choice nets are really simple to analyse and synthesise. In the first part of the section it will be shown that, for this subclass, the conditions of theorem 4.2 can be reduced to only one. This liveness conditions that could be called "low-level", as it will refer to topological concepts not very intuitive, will be given several "high-level" interpretations in the second part. We will show how the interpretations allow a meaningful stepwise construction of *all* structurally live nets of this subclass.

6.1 A characterisation of SL&SB for Strict Free Choice nets.

The key concept of this first part is contained in the next definition.

Definition 6.1

Let $N=(P, T; F)$ be a Free Choice SMD net and $p \in P$ such that $|p^\bullet|>1$ (this places are called *choices*). The choice p is a *killing choice* iff the two following conditions are satisfied:

(a) There exists a decomposition $\Re$ of N such that p belongs to one and only one of the P-components of $\Re$. Call it $N'=(P', T'; F')$.

(b) There exist two synchronizations $t_1, t_2 \in T'$ which belong to the same neighbour NE of N', and two paths $\Pi_1=(p, ..., t_1)$ and $\Pi_2=(p, ..., t_2)$ of N' such that $\Pi_1 \cap \Pi_2 = \{p\}$ (see Figure 9). $\blacklozenge$

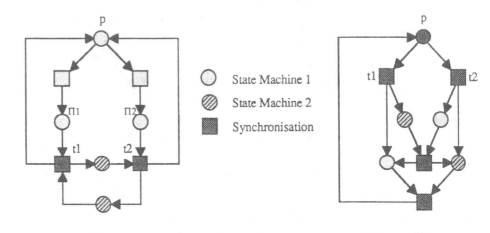

◯	State Machine 1
◍	State Machine 2
◼	Synchronisation

Figure 9. A net containing a
killing choice p.

Figure 10. Net containing no killing
choices that is not live
for any marking.

The name "killing choice" has to be justified. It will be achieved by proving that its existence is a sufficient and necessary condition for structural non-liveness of Strict Free Choice nets (it is also a sufficient one for Free Choice SMD nets, although this result is not contained in this work; the definition was given for Free Choice SMD nets because of this). These results are rather intuitive because of the Free Choice Property. The P-component can direct tokens freely at the killing choice towards synchronizations t_1 or t_2, ignoring where the tokens of the neighbour will be waiting for them. If the P-component chooses wrongly, the tokens of the P-component will reach synchronisation t_1, for instance, while the tokens of the environment are waiting for them in t_2. This leads to a sort of "deadly embrace" between the P-component and its neighbour.

In the particular case of Strict Free Choice nets, killing choices can be given a nicer characterisation. First of all, condition (a) is redundant for this subclass, as every choice of the net satisfies it. But besides that, the following property holds.

Proposition 6.1

Let $N=(P, T; F)$ be a Strict Free Choice net and $N'= (P', T'; F')$ a P-component of a strict decomposition of N. N' contains a killing choice p' iff there exist two synchronizations t_1, $t_2 \in T$ with the same neighbour and a circuit $\Gamma \subseteq N'$ that contains one and only one of them.

Proof.

$\Rightarrow$) Obvious from the definition.

$\Leftarrow$) Suppose Γ contains t_1 but not t_2. As N' is strongly connected, there exists a PT-bridge from Γ to t_2. The first node of this bridge p belongs only to N' because the net is Strict. Therefore p is a killing choice. ◆

This is not true for general Free Choice SMD nets. Figure 10 shows a counterexample: t_1 and t_2 are synchronisations, and there exists a circuit of the white P-component containing t_2, but not t_1. Nevertheless, the net contains no killing choices. The characterisation of structural liveness we present now relates killing choices to "bad" handles of circuits, so that theorem 4.2 can be applied.

Theorem 6.1

Let $N=(P, T; F)$ be a Strict Free Choice net. Then:

a) N contains a killing choice iff it contains a circuit with a TP-handle .

b) If N contains a circuit with a PT-handle, then it also contains a circuit with a TP-handle.

Proof. See Annex 1. ◆

6.2 "High and low level" characterisations of structural liveness.

The fruits of theorem 6.1 are several different characterisations of structural liveness for SFC nets. The one contained in theorem 6.2 corresponds to the "low level" interpretation announced in the introduction. The rest are "high level" interpretations, condensed into theorem 6.3.

Theorem 6.2 ["low level" characterisation of structural liveness]

Let N be a Strict Free Choice net. N is structurally live iff no circuit of N has TP- or PT-handles.

Proof.

⇒) By theorem 6.1, part b), in both cases N has a circuit with a TP-handle. By theorem 4.2, N is not SL&SB. As N is structurally bounded, because it is an SMD net, it follows that N is not structurally live.

⇐) See theorem 3.2. ♦

We have thus proved that Structurally Live Strict Free Choice nets belong to the class of nets of theorem 3.2, and therefore enjoy all the properties of nice behaviour of this class. All but one were already known. The new one is *the preservation of structural liveness under both the reverse and dual transformations, and not only under their composition.* (Note: Take into account that the reverse or the dual of a Strict Free Choice net can be non-Strict or even non-Free Choice; the net of Figure 7 is an example. Nevertheless, though we are leaving the subclass, structural liveness is preserved!). This is a nice confirmation of the interest of defining Strict Free Choice nets as a separate class.

Let us consider now the high level interpretations. One of them requires some concepts of Synchrony Theory, although the use we make of it here will be very light.

Synchrony Theory is a branch of Net Theory devoted to the study of transition firing dependences (the first ideas date back to Petri [PETR67]). These dependences are studied by means of several synchronic concepts, of which multiple slightly different definitions can be found in the literature. Here we only introduce the ones we need. The terminology is taken from [SILV 87]:

Definition 6.2

Let $<N, M_0>$ be a marked net and t_i, t_j transitions of N. $\overline{\sigma}(t_i)$ is the number of times that t_i is fired in σ.

(1) The *firing deviation bound* (*deviation bound*, for short) of t_i with respect to t_j in $<N, M_0>$ is:

$$DB(t_i, t_j) = \sup \{\overline{\sigma}(t_j) \mid \sigma \in L(N, M), M \in R(N, M_0) \text{ and } \overline{\sigma}(t_j) = 0\}$$

(Loosely speaking, the deviation bound is the maximun number of times that t_i can be fired without firing t_j, that can be unbounded).

(2) t_i is in *bounded deviation relation* with respect to t_j in $<N, M_0>$, or $(t_i, t_j) \in BD$, iff $\exists k \in N$ such that $DB(t_i, t_j) \leq k$.

(3) t_i is in *structural bounded deviation relation* with respect to t_j in N, or $(t_i, t_j) \in$ SBD, iff they are in bounded deviation relation for any initial marking M_0. ♦

We employ (3) here. The unique result of Synchrony Theorem we need is very simple and requires no proof.

Proposition 6.3

Let N=(P, T; F) be a strongly connected State Machine and t_i, $t_j \in$ T. $(t_i, t_j) \in$ SBD iff every circuit of N containing t_i contains also t_j. ♦

Now we are ready to state our results.

Theorem 6.3 ["high level" characterizations of structural liveness]

Let N be a Strict Free Choice net and $\Re$ a strict decomposition of N. Let N' stand for a P-component of $\Re$, NE for a neighbour of N' and SY(N', NE) for the set of synchronizations of N' with NE. The following four statements are equivalent:

(a)   N is structurally live.

(b)   N contains no killing choices.

(c) $\forall$ N'$\in \Re$, $\forall$ t_1, $t_2 \in$ SY(N', NE), $(t_1, t_2) \in$ SBD$_{N'}$.

(d) $\forall$ N'$\in \Re$, $\forall$ circuit $\Gamma \subseteq$ N' either SY(N', NE)$\subseteq \Gamma$ or SY(N', NE)$\cap \Gamma = \emptyset$.

Proof

(a) $\Leftrightarrow$ (b). Apply theorems 6.1 and 6.2 .

(b) $\Rightarrow$ (c) Apply propositions 6.1 and 6.3 .

(c) $\Rightarrow$ (d). Use proposition 6.3 .

(d) $\Rightarrow$ (b). Obvious from the definition of killing choice and the fact that N' is strongly connected. ♦

Statements (b), (c) and (d) in the theorem above are different characterisations of structural liveness. Statement (b) is the more suitable to be generalised (remember that it was defined for the general case of Free Choice SMD nets). We consider (c) interesting because one of the common approaches to systems specification is the use of synchronic constraints (see examples for CSP specifications in [HOAR 85] [OLDE 85]). Finally, (d) is a topological version of (c) that is probably the most interesting of the three characterizations for practical purposes. Theorem 6.3 is the base of an algorithm for the modular synthesis of Structurally Live Strict Free Choice nets:

Algorithm 6.1

Step 1. Take a State Machine. Call it N

Step 2. Synchronize N with a new State Machine N' making sure that:

- the resulting net is Strict Free Choice

- one of the conditions (b), (c) or (d) of theorem 6.3 holds.

Repeat Step 2 at will. ♦

We claim that this is a good synthesis algorithm for this subclass. Our first reason is that it allows to generate *all* Structurally Live SFC nets.This derives from the following property of monotonicity that was announced in section 4. We call it *structure monotonicity* for liveness.

Proposition 6.4 [structure monotonicity for liveness]

Let N be a structurally live Strict Free Choice net. Every Strict Free Choice subnet N'⊆ N is structurally live.

Proof. If N' is not structurally live, it contains a circuit Γ with a TP-handle H. Both Γ and H will be also contained in N. ♦

This property is false for Simple nets. If we take out the lower regulation circuit of the structurally live net of Figure 11, the remaining net is dead for any marking.

Now let N be a Structurally Live SFC net. If we take out of N a State Machine, the remaining net will be structurally live by proposition 6.4. We can take another State Machine and go on this way until the remaining net is empty. Reversing the procedure, we can synthesise N by means of the algorithm above.

Our second reason is that of *locality*. At each step of the algorithm, it is necessary to examine only the P-components directly involved in the new synchronisations.

Finally, we think that the concept of killing choice or its synchronic version have more *meaning* for the designer than, say, that of deadlock containing no trap. When a net is not structurally live, they provide a clear image of where the problems are, and can suggest solutions to those problems.

7. CONCLUSIONS

In this work we have introduced new structural objects for the study of nets: *handles* and *bridges*. We have shown how "bad" handles (of circuits) convey unpleasant interplays of concurrency and nondeterminism. Their absence is a sufficient condition for properties of nice behaviour (such as structural boundedness, repetitivity or structural liveness) of ordinary nets. In particular, nets whose circuits have only "nice" handles have proved to be extremely well behaved. Stronger results for the subclass of Free Choice have been obtained, namely a characterisation of structural liveness & structural boundedness that sheds new light on the duality properties of the subclass.

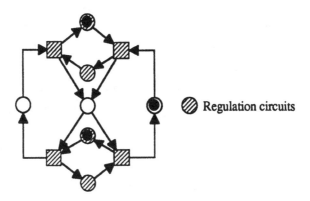

Figure 11.   A Simple net that does not satisfy the SFC properties of structure and marking monotonicity.

This characterisation has proved to be more fruitful than the previous one (in terms of deadlocks and traps) when facing the problem of synthesising Structurally Live Free Choice nets through the synchronisation of State Machines. We have shown that Free Choice SMD nets contain a subclass that had not been previously identified: *Strict Free Choice nets*. The handles and bridges approach has allowed us to give a set of characterisations of structural liveness of this subclass. One of them, of graph-theoretical form, has been used to show that structural liveness of this subclass is "invariant" under two basic transformations on nets (reversal and duality) *separately*. Other ones, that we call "high level", have been proved to provide rules for the *synthesis* of *all* and *only* Structurally Live Strict Free Choice nets by means of the synchronisation of Strongly Connected State Machines. The synthesis algorithm has two interesting properties: *structure monotonicity* for liveness (the system needs to be structurally live after each step of the construction, and therefore possible errors can be detected very early), and *locality* (at each step only a part of the net has to be considered). Moreover, the rules can be expressed in terms of *synchronic relations* on the transitions that synchronize each Strongly Connected State Machine with its neighbourhood. This is important, as synchronic relations have been often employed to specify systems. Alternatively, they can also be expressed in terms of *killing choices*.

ACKNOWLEDGMENTS
The authors wish to thank J.M Colom for helpful discussions, as well as one anonymous referee whose comments improved the paper.

REFERENCES

[BEST 84]   BEST, E.; VOSS, K.: Free Choice Systems have Home States, *Acta Informatica*,vol. 21, pp. 89-100 (1984).

[BEST 87]   BEST, E.: Structure Theory of Petri Nets: The Free Choice Hiatus, *Advanced Course on Petri Nets, Bad Honnef*, Lecture Notes on Computer Science 254-255, Springer Verlag, (1987).

[BETH 87]   BEST, E.; THIAGARAJAN, P.S.: Some classes of live and safe Petri Nets, In: *Concurrency and nets*, Voss, Genrich, Rozenberg eds., Springer Verlag, (1987).

[BRAM 83]   BRAMS, G.W.: *Réseaux de Petri. Theorie et Practique*, (2 tomos), Masson, Paris (1983).

[COMM 71]   COMMONER, F.; HOLT, A.W.; EVEN, S; PNUELI, A.: Marked Directed Graphs, *Journal of Computing and Systems Sciences*, vol. 5, pp. 511-523 (1971).

[DESE 86]   DESEL, J.: A structural property of Free-choice systems, *Petri Net Newsletter* 25, (December 1986).

[ESPA 89]   ESPARZA, J.; BEST, E.; SILVA, M: Minimal deadlocks in Free Choice nets, *Hildesheimer Informatik Fachberichte*, 1/89 (1989).

[ESPA 90]   ESPARZA, J: Structure theory of Free Choice nets, Ph. D. Thesis. To appear in 1990.

[GENR 73]   GENRICH, H.J.; LAUTENBACH, K.: Synchronisationsgraphen, *Acta Informatica*, vol. 2, pp. 143-161 (1973).

[GENR 83]   GENRICH, H.J.; JANSSENS, D.; ROZENBERG, G.; THIAGARAJAN, P.S.: Petri Nets and Their Relation to Graph Grammars, *2nd International Workshop on Graph Grammars and Their Application to Computer Science*, LNCS 153, pp. 115-129 (1983).

[GENR 84]   GENRICH, H.J.; THIAGARAJAN, P.S.: A theory of bipolar synchronisation schemes, *Theoretical Computer Science*, 30, pp. 241-318 (1984).

[HACK 72]   HACK, M.H.T.: *Analysis of production schemata by Petri Nets*. TR-94. MIT. Boston (1972). Corrected June 1974.

[HOAR 85]   HOARE, C.A.R.: *Communicating Sequential Processes*, Prentice/Hall, London (1985).

[HOLT 74]   HOLT, A.W.: Final Report for the Project '*Development of the Theoretical Foundations for Description and Analysis of Discrete Information Systems*', Wakefield , Mass., Applied Data Research, Report CADD-7405-2011 (1974).

[JANT 81]   JANTZEN, M.; VALK, R.: *Formal Properties of Place/Transition-Nets*, LNCS 84, pp. 165-212 (1981).

[LAUT 87]   LAUTENBACH, K.: Linear Algebraic Calculation of deadlocks and traps. In: *Concurrency and Nets*, Voss, Genrich, Rozenberg eds., Springer Verlag (1987).

[MEMM 80]   MEMMI, G.; ROUCAIROL, G.: Linear Algebra in Net Theory. In: *Net Theory and Applications*, Proc. of the first Advanced Course on General Net Theory of Systems and Processes, Brauer ed., LNCS 84, Springer (1980).

[MEMM 83]   MEMMI, G.: *Methode d'analyse de reseaux de Petri. Reseaux a files et applications aux systemes temps reel*, These d'etat (1983)

[MURA 77]   MURATA, T.: Circuit Theoretic Analysis and Synthesis of Marked Graphs, *IEEE Transactions on Circuits and Systems*, vol.cas-24, n² 7, (July 1977).

[OLDE 85]   OLDEROG, E.R.: Semantics, specification and verification. In: *Current Trends in Concurrency*, de Bakker, de Roever, Rozenberg eds., LNCS 224 (1985).

[PETR 67]   PETRI, C.A.: Gründsatzliches zur Beschreibung diskreter Prozesse, *3. Colloquium über Automatentheorie*, Basel, Birkhaüser Verlag (1967).

[REIS 83]   REISIG, W.; MEMMI, G.; BERTHELOT, G.: A control structure for sequential processes synchronized by buffers, *Proc. of the 4th European Workshop on Application and Theory of Petri nets*, Toulouse (1983).

[SILV 85]   SILVA, M.: *Las Redes de Petri en la Automática y la Informática*, Editorial AC, Madrid (1985).

[SILV 87]   SILVA, M.: Towards a Synchrony Theory for P/T Nets. In: *Concurrency and Nets*, Voss, Genrich, Rozenberg eds., Springer Verlag (1987).

[SOUI 88]   SOUISSI, Y: *Les systemes deterministes de processus séquentiels*, MASI Report (February 1988).

[THIA 84]   THIAGARAJAN, P.S.; VOSS, K.: A Fresh Look at Free Choice Nets, *Information and Control*, vol. 61, n² 2, (May 1984).

ANNEX 1. PROOF OF THEOREMS 3.2, 4.2 AND 6.1

The proof of theorem 3.4 uses a result of [HACK 74], which requires a previous definition.

Definition 3.4 [HACK 74]

Let $N = (P, T; F)$, $p \in P$ and $t \in T$ such that $|p^{\bullet}| > 1$, $|^{\bullet}t| > 1$ and $t \in p^{\bullet}$. The arc (p, t) becomes *released* iff we modify the net in the following way (see Figure A1):

$P' = P \cup p'$

$T' = T \cup t'$

$F'= [F - (p, t)] \cup (p, t') \cup (t', p') \cup (p', t).$

A net is in *released form* when all arcs from a place to a transition satisfying the conditions above have been released. ♦

Proposition 3.4 [HACK 74]

Let N' be the released form of a net N. Then:

a)   N' is Free Choice

b)   If N' is structurally live, so is N. ♦

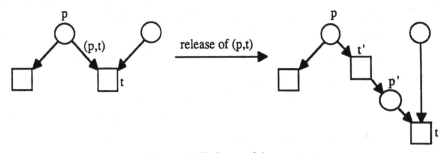

Figure A1. Release of the arc (p, t).

Theorem 3.2

Let N= (P, T; F) be a strongly connected net such that no circuit of N has a PT- nor a TP-handle. Then :

(a)   N is structurally live.

(b)   N can be covered by P-components (therefore it is conservative).

(c)   The previous properties are also true for the reverse, dual and reverse-dual of N.

(d)   N can be covered by T-components (therefore it is consistent).

Proof.

(a) Let D be a minimal deadlock of N'= (P', T'; F'), the released form of N. We prove that D is a trap.

Notice first that N contains a circuit with a certain type of handle iff N' does (follows easily from the definition of N').

Assume D is not a trap. We see that N' must contain a circuit with either a TP- or a PT-handle. Let $N_D'= (D, T_D'; F_D')$ be the I-subnet of N' generated by D. N_D' is strongly connected by proposition 2.1. As D is not a trap, there exist $p \in D$ and $t \in T' \cap p^{\bullet}$ such that $t \notin T_D'$. As N' is strongly connected, there must exist a bridge B in N' from t to N_D'. The last node of B cannot be a place, because N_D' is an I-subnet. Therefore it has to be a transition t'. We consider two cases:

i) There exists a circuit Γ of N_D' that contains p and t'. Call $\Pi=(p, t)$. Then $H=\Pi;;B$ is a PT-handle of Γ

ii) There is no such circuit. Then there exists a circuit Γ in N_D' that contains t' but not p. As N_D' is strongly connected, we can find a bridge B' in N_D' from Γ to p . If B' is a PP-bridge, then H=B';;B is a PT-handle of Γ. If B' is a TP-bridge, there exists another bridge B"in N_D' from p to Γ, which must be a PP-bridge because no transition of N_D' has two input places in N_D' (remember that N' was a Free Choice net and N_D' is the I-subnet generated by a minimal deadlock). H= B';;B" is a TP-handle of Γ (Figure A2).

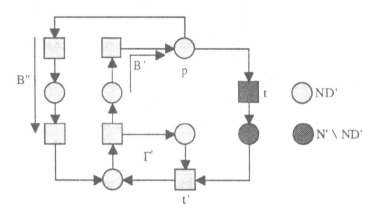

Figure A2. Illustration of the proof of theorem 3.2.

Therefore every minimal deadlock of N' is a trap and, by theorem 2.1, N' is structurally live. By proposition 3.4, N is also structurally live.

(b) Take p∈ P and let N_1= (P_1, T_1; F_1) be the maximal P–graph described in the proof of theorem 3.1. It is proved there that if no circuit of N has PT–handles and p'∈ P_1 then $^\bullet(p')\subset T_1$. It can be shown taking the reverse net that if no circuit of N has TP-handles also $(p')^\bullet \subset T_1$. Therefore N_1 is a P-component of N containing p.

(c) The reverse, dual and reverse-dual of N contain circuits with TP– or PT–handles iff N does.

(d) Follows from (b), the fact that the reverse-dual of a P-component is a T-component and (c). ◆

Theorem 4.2

Let N=(P, T; F) be a Free Choice net. N is SL&SB if:

(a)   N is strongly connected

(b)   No circuit of N has TP-handles

(c)   Every PT-handle of a circuit is bridged to it through a TP-bridge.

Proof.

$\Rightarrow$) Follows from propositions 4.1 and 4.2 and the known result that SL&SB nets are strongly connected [BEST 87].

$\Leftarrow$) We prove that, if conditions (a), (b) and (c) hold, every minimal deadlock of N is the P-support of a P-component. From theorem 4.1bis, N is then SL&SB.

Let $D \subseteq P$ be a minimal deadlock of N and N' the I-subnet generated by D. It is be shown that N' is a P-component of N. The proof is decomposed into two parts.

(i) *N' is a strongly connected P-graph.*

This is the easy part of the proof, that can be divided again in three statements:

(i1) N' is strongly connected. See proposition 2.1.

(i2) N' does not contain two input places of the same transition. Follows from the Free Choice property and the minimality of D. It is also true for Simple nets.

(i3) N' does not contain two output places of the same transition.

Assume it does. Then there exists $p_1, p_2 \in D$ and $t \in T$ such that $t \in {}^\bullet p_1 \cap {}^\bullet p_2$. It is clear that a circuit Γ of N' can be found (N' is strongly connected) that contains p_1 or p_2 but not both. Assume, without loss of generality, that Γ contains p_1. There must be a bridge B in N' from p_2 to Γ. The last node of B can not be a transition, because it contradicts (i2). But it can neither be a place, because it contradicts hypothesis (b).

N' contains all input transitions of its places because N' is a I-subnet. It remains to prove that contains also all output transitions. This is equivalent to proving that D is a trap.

(ii) *D is a trap.*

Assume it is not. By definition of trap, there exists $p \in D$ and $t \in p^\bullet$ such that $t \notin N'$ (Figure A3, left). The nodes that do not belong to N'_D are depicted shaded.). Consider the set $T'' \subseteq T'$ given by

$T'' = \{t' \in T'$ such that there exists a TT-bridge $B_1(t')=(t, ..., t')$ from t to N'$\}$ (FigureA3, right).

T'' is nonempty, because N is strongly connected, and all the bridges to I-subnets end at a transition (if they ended at a place, the input transition of this place that belongs to the bridge would belong also to the I-subnet, against the definition of bridge).

We select now carefully a circuit of N' with a PT-handle. Due to this care, we will be able to show that no TP-bridge can lead from this handle to the circuit, unless there exists another circuit with a TP-handle. This will complete the proof.

As N' is strongly connected, every transition t' of T'' is connected to p by an elementary path $\Pi(t')$ in N'. We select one of the transitions of T'', t_1, such that $\Pi(t_1)$ has maximal length. From now on we will refer to this transition, and will shorten $\Pi(t_1)$ by Π. There must also be at least a PT-bridge from Π to t_1. We choose one B_2 in N' whose first node $p' \in P$ is closest to p along Π. We have thus constructed (Figure A4) a circuit Γ with a PT-handle H.

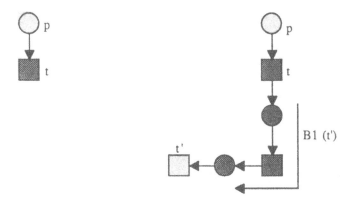

Figure A3. Illustration of the proof of theorem 4.2

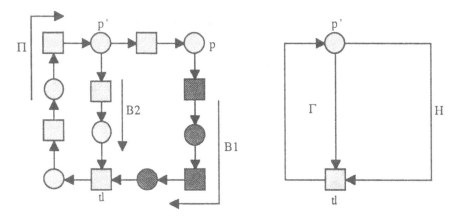

Figure A4. Illustration of the proof of teorem 4.2.

Assume now that there exists a TP-bridge from H to Γ; call it $B3=(t_0, p_0, ...,t_r, p_r)$. We consider two cases:

Case 1 . $t_0 \notin N'$. Let t_i be the first node of B3 that belongs to N' (this node exists because $p_r \in P'$, and is a transition because N' is an I-subnet). Since N' is strongly connected, there exists a bridge B4 from t_i to $B2 \cup \Pi$, whose last node must be a place p", because N' is a P-graph.

- If p"∈ Π, then N contains a circuit with a TP-handle (Figure A5).
- If p"∈ B2, then there exists an elementary path from t_i to p longer than Π, against the hypothesis (Figure A6).

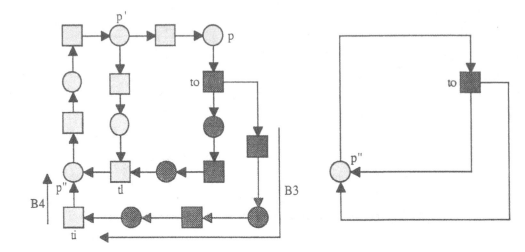

Figure A5. Illustration of the proof of theorem 4.2.

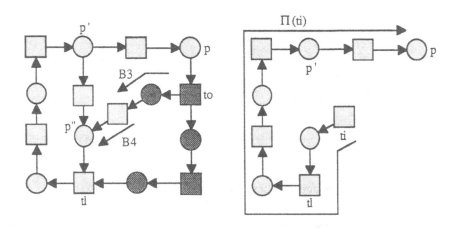

Figure A6. Illustration of the proof of theorem 4.2.

Case 2 . $t_0 \in N'$. As N' is a P-graph, $p_0 \notin N'$. Take the first node of B3, $t_i \neq t_0$ such that $t_i \in N'$ (this transition exists by the argument of Case 1). There exists a bridge B4 from t_i to B2 $\cup \Pi$, whose last node must be a place p" (again by an analogous argument to the used in the previous case).

- If p"$\in \Pi$, N contains a circuit with a TP-handle (similar to Figure A5).
- If p"$\in$ B2, as N' is strongly connected, there exists a TP-bridge B5 from t_0 to the circuit Γ, ending at a place p"'.

- If p'''∈ B₂, B₂ was not the bridge from Π to t₁ whose first place was closest to p, against the hypothesis.
- If p'''∈ Π, N contains a circuit with a TP-handle (Figure A7).

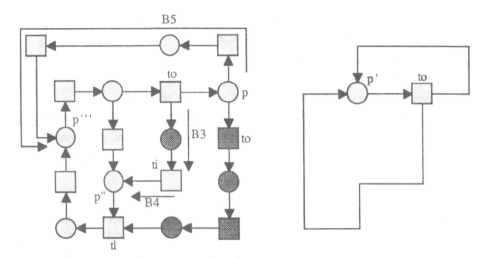

Figure A7. Illustration of the proof of theorem 4.2.

Theorem 6.1

Let N=(P, T; F) be a Strict Free Choice net. Then:

a) N contains a killing choice iff it contains a circuit with a TP-handle .

b) If N contains a circuit with a PT-handle, then it also contains a circuit with a TP-handle.

Proof.

a.⇒) Assume there exists a killing choice p. Call N' the P-component of N to which p belongs, and let t_1, t_2 be the two transitions required in definition 6.1. There exists by proposition 6.1 a circuit Γ of N that contains one and only one of transitions t_1 and t_2. We show that Γ has a TP-handle.

Suppose $t_1 \in$ Γ. As both transitions belong to the same neighbour NE, there exists an elementary path Π in NE whose first and last nodes are t_1 and t_2 respectively. Call x the last node of Π such that x∈ Γ. If x is a place, x is a choice that belongs to both N' and NE, what contradicts the fact that N is Strict Free Choice. Therefore x is a transition. This implies that the subpath B of Π with first and last nodes x and t_2, respectively, is a TT-bridge from Γ to t_2. As $t_2 \in$ N', there exists also a TP-bridge B' from t_2 to Γ. H=B;;B' is a TP-handle of Γ.

a.⇐) Suppose there exists a circuit Γ of N with a TP-handle H. As in Figure A''.b, call t and p the first and last nodes of H, respectively, and Π_H the path of Γ that has also t and p as first and last nodes. Take a P-component of a strict decomposition of N, $N'=(P', T'; F')$, such that $p \in N'$. Call t_1, t_2 the transitions of $^\bullet p$ in Π_H and H respectively. It is clear that t_1, $t_2 \in N'$.

Consider the following set of pairs of transitions of N':

Pairs=$\{(t_i, t_j)$ with $t_i, t_j \in (H \cup \Pi_H) \cap T'$, such that there exist two elementary paths $\Pi_i=(t_i, ..., p)$ and $\Pi_j=(t_j, ..., p)$ Π_i, Π_j in N', satisfying $\Pi_i \cap \Pi_j = \{p\}$ $\}$.

This set Pairs has the two following properties:

(i) Pairs $\neq \emptyset$, because $(t_1, t_2) \in$ Pairs.

(ii) If $(t_i, t_j) \in$ Pairs and $t_k \in (H \cup \Pi_H) \cap T'$, then either $(t_i, t_k) \in$ Pairs or $(t_j, t_k) \in$ Pairs or both. This property derives easily from the fact that N' is strongly connected.

We associate to each $(t_i, t_j) \in$ Pairs a natural number n_{ij} as follows: call Π_{ij} the *non-directed* path in $H \cup \Pi_H$ that connects t_i and t_j such that $p \notin \Pi_{ij}$. Then $n_{ij} :=$ length of Π_{ij}. It follows from the definition that $\forall (t_i, t_j) \in$ Pairs: $n_{ij} > 1$. Choose $(t_a, t_b) \in$ Pairs (it can be done because of (i)) such that n_{ab} is minimal. We prove that:

- t_a, t_b are synchronizations. If at least one of them were not, the previous and posterior transitions to it along the path would also belong to N' and n_{ab} would not be minimal.

- t_a, t_b belong to the same neighbour. It suffices to show that $\Pi_{ab} \cap (P' \cup T') = \{t_a, t_b\}$. Assume $\Pi_{ab} \cap (P' \cup T') \subset \{t_a, t_b\}$. Then, as N' is a P-component, there exists $t_c \in T' \cap \Pi_{ab}$. But in that case, by property (ii) above, either (t_a, t_c) or (t_b, t_c) belongs to Pairs and clearly n_{ab} is not minimal.

- there exists a circuit Γ' in N' that contains one and only one of synchronizations t_a, t_b. This is true for every node of Pairs.

So far we have not used that N is Strict Free Choice. We do it now, in order to be able to apply proposition 6.1, what finishes the proof.

b) We show that, if N contains a circuit with a PT-handle, then it contains also a killing choice. This part is easier. Consider the reverse net N of N. N contains a circuit with a TP-handle. Applying the same argument used to prove (a) $\Leftarrow$ (b), we obtain a pair of transitions (t_a, t_b) with the same properties as before. This means that N also contains this pair with same properties. We can then apply proposition 6.1 again to show that N contains a killing choice. But then, by part a), it also contains a circuit with a TP-handle. ♦

On the Analysis and Synthesis of Free Choice Systems

Javier Esparza
Institut für Informatik, Universität Hildesheim
Samelsonplatz 1
e-mail:esparza@infhil.uucp
D-3200 HILDESHEIM (FRG)

Manuel Silva
Depto. Ingeniería Eléctrica e Informática
Universidad de Zaragoza
C/María de Luna 3
e-mail:silva@etsii.unizar.es
50015 ZARAGOZA (SPAIN)

Abstract: This invited paper present in a semi-formal illustrative way several new results concerning the analysis and synthesis of free choice systems. It is a complementary work of the survey by E. Best [Best 87]. In the *analysis* part, we characterize liveness and boundedness in *linear algebraic* terms. As a consequence of the new characterizations, both properties are shown to be decidable (as a whole) in polynomial time. We also provide two different kits of sound and complete *reduction rules* (the one reverse-dual of the other).

We address then the problem of synthezising live and bounded free choice systems within the two basic design methodologies: *top-down* and *modular* (synthesis by *composition of modules*). Two complete kits of top-down synthesis rules are provided. They are essentially the reduction kits obtained before, but this time considered in the reverse direction. The completeness of the kits can be used to prove new results (or give new proofs of old results) using *structural induction* on the chain of applications of the rules that synthezise a given system. In the modular approach, exact conditions for the preservation of liveness and boundednes under compositions of systems are given. These conditions are the absence of certain design errors, called *killing choices, killing joints, synchronic mismatches* and *state mismatches*. They help to understand why a certain system is not well behaved.

Keywords: Analysis, free choice nets, linear algebra techniques, reduction, state refinement, structure of systems, modular synthesis, top-down synthesis, transformation.

CONTENTS

1 Introduction

Petri Nets (PNs) are well known abstract models of concurrent systems, with an intuitively appealing graphical representation, very appreciated in engineering circles. They provide a formal frame where the two basic problems, *analysis* and *synthesis*, can be investigated.

The analysis problem can be stated as follows: given a model (a PN model in our case), does it satisfy a certain set of properties of good behaviour? The indigenous PN techniques developed for this problem can be classified into three groups: *reachability*, *reduction* and *structural* techniques. In systems with a finite number of states (i.e. bounded systems), the reachability approach permits to answer all analysis questions. However, this technique requires an exhaustive exploration of the state space, which hinders its application to large systems. In non-bounded systems only some analysis questions can be answered (e.g. regularity problems [Fink 90]).

Structural techniques are based on the relationships between the behaviour of a system and the structure of its underlying net. More precisely, given a behavioural property, the structural approach tries to find structural properties characterizing it partially (only necessary or sufficient conditions) or totally (necessary and sufficient conditions). Structural analysis techniques use basically *graph theory* (e.g. [Best 87, TV 84]) and *linear algebra/convex geometry* arguments (e.g. [CCS 90b, CS 89a, CS 89b, Laut 87a, MR 80]).

Reduction (or abstraction) techniques [Bert 87, Silv 85] simplify the system by means of *reduction rules* which *preserve* the properties under study (the reduced systems enjoys the property if and only if the original one enjoys it as well). Applying reduction rules in an iterative way, a sequence of progressively more simple models is obtained, in which it is easier to check if the desired property holds. Sometimes the final system is trivial, and the question can be immediately answered; otherwise other analysis techniques are needed.

Synthesis is the second basic, and more difficult, problem. It can be stated as follows: given a set of properties of good behaviour, how to construct systems enjoying them? This problem is strongly related to *design methodologies*. The two basic and complementary approaches are the *top/down* (sometimes *refinement*) and the *modular* (or *compositional*). The first one is just the reverse of the reduction analysis approach. In the second case modules (subsystems) are merged (composed) into new systems.

Petri nets permit to combine in easy and powerful ways three fundamental situations: *sequence, conflict (choice)* and *concurrency*. The interplay of the last two situations can make it very difficult to find relationships between behaviour and structure. To obtain structural characterizations of behavioural properties, the only actual possibility is to restrict the class of nets in such a way that the interplay between concurrency and choice is particularly simple. The analysis and synthesis problems are trivial for systems in which synchronization is structurally forbidden such as *State Machines*. For *Marked graphs*, systems in which choices are structurally forbidden, they are not so trivial but have been both extensively studied (see [CHEP 71, ES 89b, GL 73, Mura 89]), and are very well understood.

Free Choice systems are located at an interesting place in the tradeoff between *practical modeling power* and *analyzability*. An ordinary net (i.e. arc weights equal to 1) is free-choice iff all the transitions in a conflict have only one input place. This way, choices cannot be influenced by the environment (a concept similar to the internal nondeterminism of TCSP). Partially based on works by Commoner, Hack's thesis [Hack 72] is the pioneer reference for FC nets theory. Two surveys on the results obtained till 1987 are [Best 87, BT 87]. Since then, further contributions are [BCDE 90, BD 90, Des 90, DE 90, ES 89a, ES 89b, Espa 90a, Espa 90b, ES 90a, ES 90b, ES 90c, Vogl 89]. To maintain this work at a semiformal illustrative level, the analysis works surveyed concern only two basic properties: *liveness* and *boundedness*. Analogously, only the synthesis of live and bounded free choice (LBFC) systems is considered. In [Des 90] the reduction/synthesis of live and *safe* FC systems *without frozen tokens* is done using a kit of four rules. Result concerning *home states* in LBFC systems are reported in [BCDE 90, Vogl 89], while the *reachability problem in the home space* for LBFC systems is solved in [DE 90]. The main topics selected for presentation in this paper are the three following:

(1) liveness and boundedness (as a whole) can be linearly characterized for FC systems.

(2) the class of LBFC systems can be reduced/top-down synthetized by means of kits of two rules (one non local).

(3) the class of LBFC systems can be synthetized (and also reduced) by means of modular compositions.

Given the above selection, the concepts of *handles* and *bridges* [ES 89a] are not considered here, basically because they are specially useful for proof techniques, that provide results on LBFC systems that are interpretable at higher-level [ES 90a, ES 90b].

Sections 2 and 3 are devoted to the analysis problem. Section 2 introduces our linear algebraic characterization of liveness and boundedness. It is shown how Hack's duality theorem can be derived from it. Section 3 introduces the kits of reduction rules.

The synthesis of LBFC systems is considered in sections 4 and 5. Two reverse-dual kits of top-down rules are introduced. They are, informally speaking, the reverse of those of reduction rules. The completeness of the kits permits to state a *generative definition* for LBFC systems: those that can be generated by them. Using this alternative definition new results or new proofs of known results can be given using structural induction on the chains of applications of the rules.

We present then exact conditions for the preservation of liveness and boundedness under *synchronisations* of nets (a particular kind of composition in which, essentially, transitions are merged). They are the absence of two design errors called *killing choices* and *synchronic mistmachs*. Using the duality theorem, it is shown that the absence of other two errors (*killing joints* and *state mismatches*) characterize the preservation of liveness and boundedness under *fusions* (compositions in which, essentially, places are merged).

In the sequel $N = (P, T, F)$ is a net, where P represent the set of places, T the set of transitions and F is the flow relation. A marked net or system, (N, M_0), is obtained by associating an initial marking, M_0, to the net N: usually N is said to be the underlying net of the system (N, M_0).

2   A linear algebraic approach to the analysis problem

Our linear algebraic characterization of liveness and boundedness is splitted into two parts. We characterize first the *structure* of the FC nets which can be endowed with a live and bounded marking. The second part characterizes the markings that make such a lively and boundedly markable net live and bounded.

2.1   Some definitions and results

Let us recall structural boundedness and structural liveness notions.

A net N is said to be *structurally bounded* (SB) iff for every initial marking M_0, the system $\langle N, M_0 \rangle$ is bounded. The interest of structural boundedness is that it does not depend on any initial marking, but only on the underlying net N.

A net N is *structurally live* (SL) iff there exists at least one initial marking, M_0, for which $\langle N, M_0 \rangle$ is live. Structural liveness is a necessary condition for liveness. Once again, structural liveness depens only on the net N.

Our first result, in the next section, characterizes structural liveness and structural boundedness (SL&SB). This is not in general what we promised above, since not every net that can be endowed with a live and bounded marking is SL&SB (although the converse obviously holds). But the following result, a consequence of classical results [Hack 72], shows that both notions collapse for FC nets.

Proposition 2.1 [Espa 90b] *Let N be an FC net. Then, there exists M_0 such that $\langle N, M_0 \rangle$ is live and bounded iff N is SL&SB.*

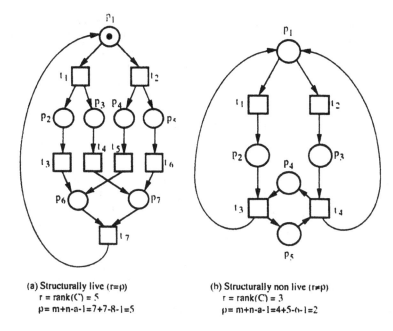

Figure 2.1. Two consistent and conservative free choice nets.

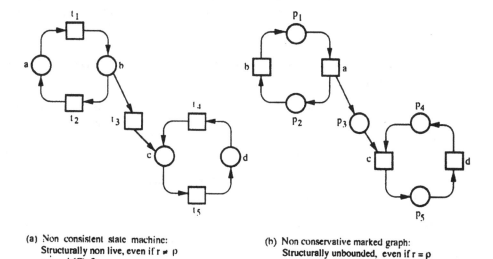

Figure 2.2. Non consistency or non-conservativeness destroy the algebraic characterization of theorem 2.3.

The characterization we provide of SL&SB is given in linear algebraic terms. It complements for FC nets the following well known result, in which SL&SB are related to two properties of the incidence matrix, called *conservativeness* and *consistency*. A net $N = (P, T, F)$ with incidence matrix C is *conservative* iff ($Y > 0$ means $Y(p) > 0$, $\forall p \in P$):

$$\exists Y > 0 : Y^T \cdot C = 0$$

N is *consistent* iff ($X > 0$ means $X(t) > 0$, $\forall t \in T$):

$$\exists X > 0 : C \cdot X = 0$$

Conservativeness and consistency can be stated in term of p- and *t-semiflows*, respectively. A rational-valued vector $Y \gneq 0$ ($X \gneq 0$) is a p-semiflow (t-semiflow) of $N = (P, T, F)$ iff $Y^T \cdot C = 0$ ($C \cdot X = 0$). The *support* of a p-semiflow Y, denoted by $\|Y\|$, is the set $\|Y\| = \{p \in P : Y(p) > 0\}$. Analogously, $\|X\| = \{t \in T : X(t) > 0\}$ is the support of the t-semiflow X. Therefore:

$$N \text{ is conservative} \quad \Leftrightarrow \quad \exists Y, \text{ a p-semiflow such that } \|Y\| = P$$
$$N \text{ is consistent} \quad \Leftrightarrow \quad \exists X, \text{ a t-semiflow such that } \|X\| = T$$

Theorem 2.2 [Sifa 78, MR 80] *Let N be an SB&SL net. Then N is conservative and consistent.*

Unfortunately, the converse of this result is not true. The net of Figure 2.1b is an example. This net is conservative and consistent, but structurally non live. The question is, which condition should be added to conservativeness and consistency in order to get a characterization of SL&SB? We do not know the answer in general, but the main result of the next section gives the answer for FC nets.

2.2 A linear algebraic characterization of structural liveness and consequences

The 'missing condition' for FC nets is, maybe surprisingly, that the rank of the incidence matrix (i.e. the maximal number of linearly independent rows and columns) has to be a very simple function of the number of places, denoted by n, the number of transitions, denoted by m, and the number of arcs leading from a place to a transition, denoted by $a = |F \cap (P \times T)|$.

Theorem 2.3 (Rank Theorem) *Let N be an FC net. N is SL&SB iff it is conservative, consistent, and $rank(C) = m - 1 - (a - n)$.*

This result is illustrated in Fig. 2.1, 2.2 and 2.3. The net of Fig. 2.1.a satisfies the conditions, and is hence SL&SB (a live and bounded marking is shown). The other nets show that all conditions are necessary.

- Fig. 2.1.b: the net is FC, conservative and consistent but does not satisfy the rank equation. It is not SL.

- Fig. 2.2.a: the net is FC, conservative and satisfies the rank equation but it is not consistent. It is not SL.

- Fig. 2.2.b: the net is FC, consistent and satisfies the rank equation, but it is not conservative. It is not SB.

- Fig. 2.3.a: the theorem is false for Extended FC nets. The net is SL&SB, but does not satisfy the rank equation. Let us point only that the theorem could be reformulated in a less elegant way to make it hold for this subclass [CCS 90b].

- Fig 2.3.b: the theorem is false for non-FC nets. The net is SL&SB, but does not satisfy the rank equation.

This characterization was conjectured by the second author, together with J. Campos and G. Chiola, while studying performance bounds for LBFC stochastic systems. We will expose here part of the original argumentation [CCS 90a] that lead to one half of the property, since we think it can provide good insight on the result. Assume $\langle N, M_0 \rangle$ is an LBFC system, and a probabilistic prescription to solve the conflicts of N is given (e.g. if a place has three output transitions t_1, t_2, t_3, firing probabilities r_1, r_2, r_3 are associated to them with the constraint $r_1 + r_2 + r_3 = 1$). Let now G be a vector of dimension $|T|$ expressing the *relative frequency of firings* of the transitions in the steady-state of the net (the reader will have to believe that this steady state exists). After a little thought, it can be guessed that this vector is *unique*, once it has been properly normalized by setting the frequency of an arbitrary transition to 1. This means that G is completely characterized by

- The *structure* of the net N, that is represented by the incidence matrix C, provided there are no self-loops (i.e. $\forall t \in T \ Pre(t)^T \cdot Post(t) = 0$).

- The *probabilities* assigned to transitions in conflict. They can be represented by a matrix R, having a row for each pair of transitions in conflict and a column per transition.

For instance, consider the net of Fig. 2.1.a. It has one single pair of transitions in conflict, namely the pair formed by t_1 and t_2, the two output transitions of p_1. Thus, R has only one row. Let the conflict be solved with probability r for t_1, and $1 - r$ for t_2. Then:

$$\frac{G(t_1)}{G(t_2)} = \frac{r}{1-r} \Leftrightarrow (1-r)G(t_1) - rG(t_2) = 0$$

Therefore $R = (1 - r, -r, 0, 0, 0, 0, 0)$.
The fact that G is unique implies that, for any assignation of probabilities, the system

$$\begin{pmatrix} C \\ R \end{pmatrix} \cdot G_n = 0, G > 0$$

has a unique solution. This means that the space of right annullers of the matrix has dimension 1, and hence the dimension of the space generated by the rows of the matrix has dimension $m - 1$. Since this happens for all the possible assignations of probabilities, the spaces generated by the rows of C and R must be *disjoints*, and hence

$$rank(C) + rank(R) = m - 1$$

Now, we can observe that the number of linearly independent rows of R is $a - n$: each place p contributes with $|p^\bullet| - 1$ independent constraints to R (e.g. if p has three output transitions t_1, t_2, t_3, only two probabilities r_1, r_2 can be set up independently, the third one being given by the constraint $r_1 + r_2 + r_3 = 1$). Adding up the constraints corresponding to all the places, this number is obtained. Hence, we have

$$rank(C) = m - 1 - (a - n)$$

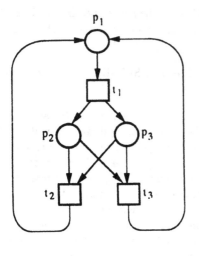 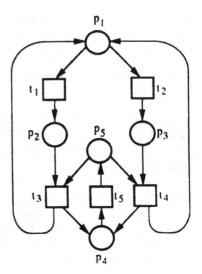

(a) Extended free choice net
r = rank(C) = 1
ρ = m+n-a-1 = 3+3-5-1= 0

(b) Asymmetric choice net
r = rank(C) = 3
ρ= m+n-a-1 = 5+5-7-1= 2

Figure 2.3. Two live and structurally bounded nets with $r \neq \rho$.

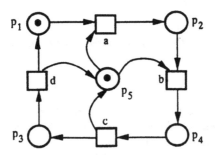

Figure 2.4. An SL&SB asymmetric choice net: It is non live even if all p-semiflows are marked.

In [Espa 90a] the algebraic characterization of structural liveness is proven for the particular case of *state machine decomposable free choice* (SMD-FC) nets. Independently of stochastic concepts, in [ES 90c] a formal proof of the theorem will be given. The necessary condition follows the above line of though, while the sufficiency is more complicated.

The first important fact about this theorem is that many of Hack's classical results can be derived from it or the proof process. In particular, the one which has an immediate proof is the so called "duality theorem". We need a previous definition: given a net $N = (P, T, F)$, its *reverse-dual* is the net $N_{rd} = (T, P, F^{-1})$ (i.e we replace places by transitions, transitions by places, and reverse the direction of the arcs). It is easy to see from the definition that if N is FC, then N_{rd} is FC as well.

We can now state the result.

Corollary 2.4 (Duality Theorem) *Let N be an FC net and N_{rd} its reverse-dual net. N is SL&SB iff N_{rd} is SL&SB.*

Proof: It follows easily from the definition of the reverse-dual net that $C_{rd} = -C^T$, where C and C_{rd} are the incidence matrices of N and N_{rd} respectively. Some consequences of this fact are:

(a) $rank(C) = rank(C_{rd})$

(b) N_{rd} is conservative iff N is consistent

(c) N_{rd} is consistent iff N is conservative

Using theorem 2.2, we have that N_{rd} is FC, conservative and consistent. Moreover

$$rank(C_{rd}) = rank(C) = n - 1 - (a - m) = m_{rd} - 1 - (a_{rd} - n_{rd}) = n_{rd} - 1 - (a_{rd} - m_{rd})$$

Hence, by theorem 2.3, N_{rd} is SL&SB. ∎

A second immediate consequence of theorem 2.3 is that SL&SB of an FC net is decidable in polynomial time.

Corollary 2.5 *Let N be an FC net. Then it can be decided in polynomial time if N is SL&SB.*

Proof: Linear programming problems have polynomial complexity [Karm 84, GT 89]. Conservativeness of a net can be decided by means of the following *linear programming problem* (LLP) (which is a little bit tricky, because the optimization function is identically zero)

$$\begin{aligned} \max \quad & Y^T \cdot 0 \\ \text{s.t.} \quad & Y^T \cdot C = 0 \\ & Y(i) \geq 1 \quad \forall i \in (1, n) \end{aligned}$$

A similar LLP can be used to decide consistency. Finally, the rank of a matrix can be calculated using standard methods of linear algebra. All these problems have polynomial complexity. Apply then theorem 2.3. ∎

2.3 A linear algebraic characterization of liveness for structurally live and structurally bounded free choice nets

Theorem 2.3 characterizes the lively and boundedly markable FC nets. Once we have one of these nets, we would like to know which are exactly the markings that make it live and bounded. By proposition 2.1, we know that the net is SL&SB, and hence bounded for any marking. It remains to characterize which markings make it live. The answer can be given in terms of the p-semiflows of the net, again a linear algebraic concept. A p-semiflow is *marked* at a marking M iff at least one of the places of its support is marked at M.

Theorem 2.6 [Espa 90b] *Let N be an SL&SB FC net. $\langle N, M_0 \rangle$ is live iff all p-semiflows of N are marked at M_0 (i.e $\forall Y \gneq 0, Y^T \cdot C = 0 : Y^T \cdot M_0 > 0$).*

The "only if" part holds in general: if a p-semiflow is unmarked at the initial marking, it remains unmarked at any reachable marking. But then the output transitions of the places of its support never fire. The "if" part can be proved from basic results in [Hack 72].

Theorem 2.6 is not true for non-FC nets. The net in Fig. 2.4 is SL&SB, and all its p-semiflows are marked at the initial marking shown. Nevertheless, the corresponding system is non-live.

A first corollary of theorem 2.6 is the well known result that the addition of tokens preserves liveness and boundedness in LBFC systems (this can be also directly derived from Commoner's Theorem, [Hack 72]), something that is not true for asymmetric choice nets (add a token to p_3 in Fig. 2.5).

Corollary 2.7 (Liveness Monotonicity) *Let $\langle N, M_0 \rangle$ be an LBFC system. Then, for every $M_0' \geq M_0$, $\langle N, M_0' \rangle$ is live and bounded as well.*

Proof: By proposition 2.1, N is SL&SB. By theorem 2.6, M_0 marks all p-semiflows of N. Then M_0' marks them as well. Applying theorem 2.6 again, $\langle N, M_0' \rangle$ is live and bounded. ∎

A second corollary states that liveness and boundedness, as a whole, are decidable in polynomial time.

Corollary 2.8 (Polynomial Complexity) *Let $\langle N, M_0 \rangle$ be an FC system. It can be decided in polynomial time if $\langle N, M_0 \rangle$ is live and bounded.*

Proof: By proposition 2.1 and theorem 2.6, $\langle N, M_0 \rangle$ is live and bounded iff N is SL&SB and all p-semiflows of N are marked at M_0. The first condition can be checked in polynomial time (corollary 2.5). The second condition can be checked solving, also in polynomial time, the following LPP:

$$
\begin{aligned}
\max \quad & Y^T \cdot 0 \\
\text{s.t.} \quad & Y^T \cdot C = 0 \\
& Y^T \cdot M_0 = 0 \\
& Y \gneq 0
\end{aligned}
$$

It is obvious that all p-semiflows are marked iff this LPP has no solutions. ∎

This result can be compared with the one obtained by Jones, Landweber and Lien in [JLL 77]: deciding if an FC system is live is an coNP-complete problem.

To finish the section, let us remark that in [ES 89b] a quite different approach for deciding liveness and boundedness of FC nets, also polynomial, was presented. The method is based on an extension of Lautenbach's ideas relating deadlock, traps and p-semiflows [Laut 87b].

3 Analysis through reduction

The idea underlying reduction techniques is the following: given some properties to be analysed, transform the system into another one such that

- The properties hold in the transformed system if and only if they hold in the initial system. When this happens the transformation is said to *preserve* the properties.

- The properties are easier to analyse in the transformed system.

The transformations are performed by repeated application of a kit of *reduction rules* (elementary transformations) preserving the considered properties. A reduction rule consists on two parts:

- The *conditions* that have to be satisfied for the rule to be applicable

- The *changes* that specify the transformation

Both of them can be divided again into conditions and changes concerning the structure of the system and conditions and changes concerning its marking.

One of the problems of reduction analysis is that there can be systems to which the rules are not applicable. If these systems have a large size, their reachability analysis can be also computationally very complex. Here is where the notion of completeness of a kit of rules plays a rôle. A kit of rules is *complete* w.r.t. a class of systems if *all* the systems of the class satisfying the properties are transformed after the iterative application of the rules into one or more particularly simple systems (called *elementary systems*). In this case, we can decide if a system enjoys the properties just checking which is the final system after the transformation, and no further analysis is needed.

The goal of this section is to introduce two complete kits of reduction rules for the class of FC systems with respect to liveness and boundedness. In the first part of the section we introduce the two rules of the first kit. They are, essentially:

- Removal of so called marking structurally implicit places

- Substitution of certain P-graphs by a place

This kit can be hence considered as *place-oriented*. In the second part we introduce, making use of the duality theorem, a *transition-oriented* kit consisting of

- Removal of certain transitions, called structural bypasses

- Substitution of certain T-graphs by a transition

3.1 A place-oriented kit of reduction rules

Let us consider first the rule of removal of places. As usual, C denotes the incidence matrix of a net N. N^{-p} denotes the net obtained from N by removing the place p, together with its tokens and its input and output arcs. The corresponding incidence matrices are denoted by C and C^{-p}. It is then clear that

$$C = \left[\begin{array}{c} C^{-p} \\ C(p) \end{array} \right]$$

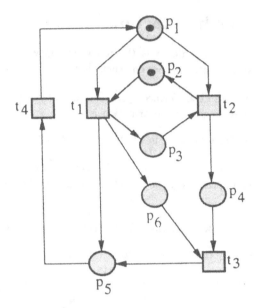

Figure 2.5. Marking liveness monotonicity does not hold for asymmetric choice nets.

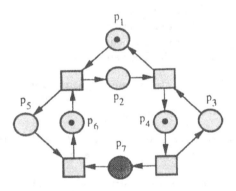

Figure 3.1. Place p_7 is 2-bounded, while the other places are safe.

where $C(p)$ is the row associated to p in C.

The places that can be removed are those whose rows in the incidence matrix are non-negative linear combinations of the rows of other places. We call them *marking structurally implicit places* (MSIPs for short) [CS 89b]. The reason of the name is given below.

Definition 3.1 *A place p is an MSIP of $N = (P, T, F)$ iff $C(p)$ is a positive linear combination of the rows of C^{-p}:*

$$\exists Y_p \gneq 0: \quad C(p) = Y_p^T \cdot C^{-p}$$

The following property can be easily derived from the definition.

Property 3.2 [Silv 85] *Let p be a MSIP. Then $\forall t \in {}^\bullet p \ |t^\bullet| > 1$ and $\forall t \in p^\bullet \ |{}^\bullet t| > 1$.*

This property provides an easy to check necessary condition for a place to be an MSIP. In particular. it is obvious that P-graphs are MSIP-free nets.

The reason of the name is that for every marking of the net N^{-p}, there is a marking of p that makes it *implicit*, meaning that the language of the net before and after adding this place does not change.

Property 3.3 [CS 89b] *Let p be an MSIP of N. Then, for every M_0^{-p}, there is M_0 (equal to M_0^{-p} in $P \setminus p$) such that the languages of $\langle N, M_0 \rangle$ and $\langle N^{-p}, M_0^{-p} \rangle$ are equal.*

This property will be used later on in some proofs.

The following theorem shows that the removal of an MSIP from an FC net preserves SL&SB. The proof is given to show an application of the rank theorem.

Theorem 3.4 *Let $N = (P, T, F)$ be an FC net and $p \in P$ an MSIP of N. Then N^{-p} is SL&SB iff N is SL&SB.*

Proof: First, it is obvious that N^{-p} is FC with $n-1$ places, m transitions and $a-1$ input arcs to transitions. We show that, under the conditions above, N is conservative, consistent and $rank(C) = n - 1 - (a - m)$ iff N^{-p} is conservative, consistent, and $rank(C^{-p}) = (n-1) - 1 - ((a-1) - m) = rank(C)$. Applying then theorem 2.3, the result follows.

Let $Y_p \gneq 0$ be the vector such that $Y_p^T \cdot C^{-p} = C(p)$.

(i) N is consistent $\Leftrightarrow N^{-p}$ is consistent

    ($\Rightarrow$): Obvious, because no transition has been removed.

    ($\Leftarrow$): Since N^{-p} is consistent, there is $X > 0$, $C^{-p} \cdot X = 0$. We show that $C \cdot X = 0$, what implies that N is consistent as well.

$$C \cdot X = \begin{bmatrix} C^{-p} \cdot X \\ C(p) \cdot X \end{bmatrix} = \begin{bmatrix} C^{-p} \cdot X \\ Y_p^T \cdot C^{-p} \cdot X \end{bmatrix} = 0^T$$

(ii) N conservative $\Leftrightarrow N^{-p}$ is conservative

($\Rightarrow$): Since N is conservative, there is $W > 0$, $W^T \cdot C = 0$. This vector W can be written

$$W = \begin{bmatrix} Y \\ k \end{bmatrix}$$

with $k > 0$. Hence

$$0 = W^T \cdot C = Y^T \cdot C^{-p} + kC(p) = (Y + kY_p)^T \cdot C^{-p}$$

Since $Y + kY_p > 0$, N^{-p} is conservative.

($\Leftarrow$): Since N^{-p} is conservative, there is $W > 0$, $W^T \cdot C^{-p} = 0$. Take $\lambda > 0$ such that $Y' = \lambda W - Y_p \geq 0$. Then:

$$0 = \lambda W^T \cdot C^{-p} = (Y' + Y_p)^T \cdot C^{-p} = Y'^T \cdot C^{-p} + C(p) = [Y'^T \mid 1] \cdot C$$

Since $Y' > 0$, N is conservative

(iii) $rank(C) = n - 1 - (a - m) \Leftrightarrow rank(C^{-p}) = (n - 1) - 1 - ((a - |p^\bullet|) - m)$

a) by property 3.2 and the FC definition, $|p^\bullet| = 1$. Hence

$$n - 1 - (a - m) = (n - 1) - 1 - ((a - 1) - m)$$

b) by the MSIP definition, $rank(C) = rank(C^{-p})$

and the result follows. ∎

It can be shown that the "if" part of this theorem holds in general. The "only if part" does not. The net of Fig. 2.5 is an example. The place p_3 is an MSIP of the net: $C(p_3) = C(p_6) + C(p_5) + C(p_1)$. Nevertheless, removing p_3 the net becomes structurally non live.

We already know that the removal of an MSIP preserves SL&SB for FC nets. We should see now which are the conditions for the removal to preserve liveness. It is not difficult to prove that, if every p-semiflow of N is marked at M_0, so is every p-semiflow of N^{-p} at the marking M_0^{-p}, consisting of the projection of M_0 on $P \setminus \{p\}$. Using then theorem 2.6, we obtain that if $\langle N, M_0 \rangle$ is live, so is $\langle N^{-p}, M_0^{-p} \rangle$. Unfortunately, the converse does not hold. It can be the case that, when removing p, we destroy unmarked p-semiflows of N, and pass from a non-live to a live system. That is why the rule requires that all p-semiflows of the source net have to be marked. The existence of an unmarked p-semiflow can be detected in polynomial time, by means of the LPP used in the proof of corollary 2.8. Fortunately, it is not necessary to check this condition every time we want to apply this rule, but *only the first one*. The reason is that, if the net contains an unmarked p-semiflow, it follows immediately that it is not live (the p-semiflow remains always unmarked, which implies that the output transitions of the places contained in its support can never fire). In this case the analysis is finished. On the other hand, if all the p-semiflows of the initial net are marked, this property is transmited to the reduced systems by the rule we introduce now, and the second one presented next.

Structural conditions : N is an FC net containing an MSIP p

Marking conditions : Every p-semiflow of N is marked

Changes : Remove p with its tokens, input and output arcs.

Theorem 3.5 [Silv 85] [ES 90a] *RIM preserves liveness and boundedness, but not the bound of the net.*

The preservation of liveness and boundedness follows, essentially, from theorems 2.6 and 3.4. Figure 3.1 shows that the bound is not preserved.

Let us now introduce the second rule of this first kit, which consists of the substitution of a P-graph (N is a *P-graph* iff $\forall t \in T, |{}^\bullet t| = |t^\bullet| = 1$) by one single place. A previous definition is needed.

Let $N' = (P', T', F')$ be a subnet of $N = (P, T, F)$ [i.e. $F' = F \cap ((P' \times T') \cup (T' \times P'))$]. A place $p' \in P'$ is a *way-in* place of N' iff ${}^\bullet p \cap (T \setminus T') \neq \emptyset$, where the dot refers to N. Analogously, p' is a *way-out* place of N iff $p^\bullet \cap (T \setminus T') \neq \emptyset$. That is, the way-in places are those that can be used to "enter" into the subnet, and the way-out places the ones through which we can "get out" of it. *Way-in* and *way-out transitions* are defined analogously. They will be used later on.

Definition 3.6 *Let N' be a subnet of N. $N' = (P', T', F')$ is reducible to a place if:*

(a) *N' is a P-graph containing at least one transition and $\forall t \in T' : |t^\bullet \cap P'| \leq 1$ and $|{}^\bullet t \cap P'| \leq 1$.*

(b) *For every $p' \in P'$, there exists at least an F'-path from a way-in place of N' to P'.*

(c) *For every $p' \in P'$ and every way-out place p'_o of N', there exists an F'-path from p' to p'_o.*

The next definition, although somewhat complex, expresses no more than the standard notion of substitution of a net by a place.

Definition 3.7 *Let $\langle N = (P, T, F), M_0 \rangle$ be a system and $N' = (P', T'; F')$ a subnet of N reducible to a place. The net $N_r = (P_r, T_r; F_r)$, with*

- $P_r = (P \setminus P') \cup \{\pi\}$

- $T_r = (T \setminus T')$

- $F_r = (F \cap ((P_r \times T_r) \cup (T_r \times P_r))) \cup F_\pi$, *where*

    - $(t, \pi) \in F_\pi$ *iff there exists $(t, p') \in F$ with $p' \in P'$*
    - $(\pi, t) \in F_\pi$ *iff there exists $(p', t) \in F$ with $p' \in P'$*

is a macroplace reduction of N, *and* π *is the* macroplace *that replaces* N'. *The system* $\langle N_r, M_r \rangle$, *where* N_r *is the reduction of* N *and* M_r *is given by:*

- $M_r(p) = M_0(p)$ *if* $p \neq \pi$

- $M_r(\pi) = \sum_{p \in P'} M(p)$

is called a macroplace reduction of $\langle N, M_0 \rangle$.

REDUCTION RULE RMP

Structural condition : N contains a subnet N' reducible to a place.

Marking condition : none.

Changes : $\langle N, M_0 \rangle$ is reduced to $\langle N_r, M_r \rangle$, macroplace reduction in which N' is substituted by a macroplace

---

Figure 3.2 illustrates the macroplace reduction rule. In order to apply RDMP it is necessary to find the subnets of a net that can be reduced to a place. In [Silv 81] an efficient (polynomial) algorithm for this purpose is given. It consists of removing first all the transitions with more than one input or one output arc, what splits the net into one or more P-graphs (Fig. 3.2b is obtained from Fig. 2.1a removing t_3, t_4 and their incident arcs). Then simple recursive procedures are applied to each connected subnet to check conditions (b) and (c) of definition 3.6. The subset of places $\{p_1, p_2, p_3\}$ cannot be reduced to a single place because liveness would not be preserved (e.g. do this reduction in the context of Fig. 2.1b).

The utility of the macroplace concept lies in the following result, which holds in general.

Theorem 3.8 [Silv 81] *RMP preserves liveness and the bound of the system (thus boundedness).*

Figure 3.3 illustrates an application of the macroplace reduction rule. Let us see how we could go on reducing the net after that. The reader can easily check that $C(MP1) = C(MP2)$, and hence any of these two places is an MSIP. Removing any of them a strongly connected state machine is obtained. The application of the macroplace reduction rule leads to a net with one place and one transition, which is trivially live and bounded. A more complex reduction process is presented in Fig. 3.4. In the first step the macroplaces "B+D+F+G" and "M+J" are created. They can be removed one after the other, since both are MSIPs in the corresponding nets. After that, the macroplace rule can be used again, leading to the macroplaces "K+A+C" and "L+H+I". This last place is an MSIP. Removing it, and applying the macroplace rule again, a system with one place and one transition is obtained. Thus the original system was live and bounded. The procedure followed in these two examples is the following Reduction Algorithm.

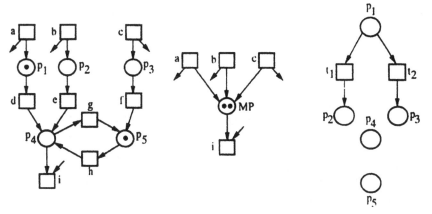

(a) Reducible subnet and its reduction

(b) $\{p_1, p_2, p_3\}$ cannot be reduced to a single place

Figure 3.2. Macroplace reduction rule.

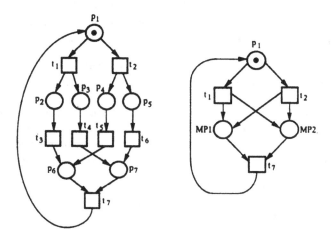

Figure 3.3. An application of macroplace reduction rule.

Reduction algorithm
begin
   input $:= < N, M_0 >$, a FC system
   $i = 0$;
   $< N_i, M_i >:=< N, M_0 >$;
   do while $(< N_i, M_i >$ is reducible)
      do while $(< N_i, M_i >$ is RMP-reducible)
         let $< N_{i+1}, M_{i+1} >$ be the result of applying RMP to $< N_i, M_i >$;
         $i := i + 1$;
      od
      do while $(< N_i, M_i >$ is RIM-reducible)
         let $< N_{i+1}, M_{i+1} >$ be the result of applying RIM to $< N_i, M_i >$;
         $i := i + 1$;
      od
   od
   output $< N_i, M_i >$
end

The importance of this algorithm is that it is *complete*. In order to state this result we need first the concept of elementary system. A system $< N = (P, T, F), M_0 >$ is *elementary* iff $P = \{p\}$, $T = \{t\}$, $F = \{(p, t), (t, p)\}$ for some elements p, t and $M_0 > 0$.

Theorem 3.9 [ES 90a] (Soundness and Completeness of the Reduction Algorithm) *Let $\langle N, M_0 \rangle$ be an FC system. The application of the reduction algorithm to $\langle N, M_0 \rangle$ yields as output an elementary system iff $\langle N, M_0 \rangle$ is live and bounded.*

If we apply the above algorithm to any system constructed by marking the net in Fig. 2.1b, we see that the system cannot be reduced. Being not elementary, it follows that it is non-live or non-bounded.

We would like to expose briefly an outline of the completeness proof, because it provides good insight about how FC systems work. The proof relies heavily on Hack's decomposition result, whose statement requires some previous notions. A *P-component* of a net $N = (P, T. F)$ is a subnet $N' = (P', T', F')$ of N with the two following properties:

- N' is a strongly connected P-graph

- $^\bullet P' = P'^\bullet = T'$, where the dot refers to N

Notice that a P-component N' is characterised by the set of its places, P'. Moreover if $Y \in (0, 1)^n$ with $Y(p) = 1$ iff $p \in P'$, Y is a p-semiflow of N (i.e. $Y^T \cdot C = 0$).

N is said to be *covered* by a set of P-components if every place belongs to at least one of the P-components of the set. This set is called a *cover*. The net of Fig. 3.4 is covered by the P-components with sets of places $\{A, B, D, F, G\}$, $\{A, C, E, K\}$, $\{H, I, E, L\}$ and $\{H, I, J, M\}$. Hack's decomposition theorem states that this is always the case for LBFC systems.

Theorem 3.10 [Hack 72] (Decomposition Theorem) *Let $\langle N, M_0 \rangle$ be an LBFC system. Then N can be covered by P-components.*

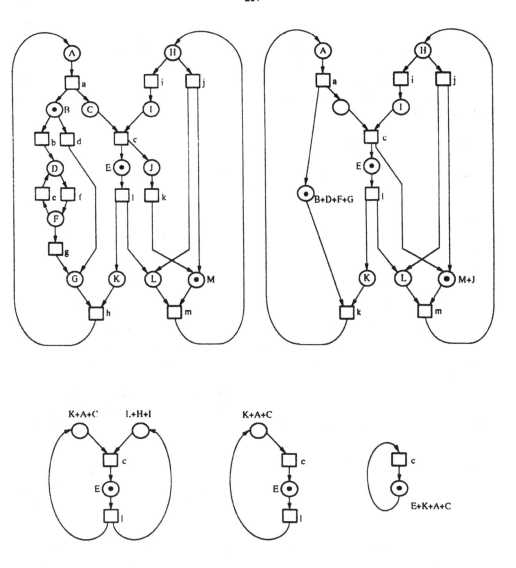

Figure 3.4. A reduction of a historical FC system (from [Hack 72]).

The completeness of the Reduction Algorithm is shown by proving the following result: it is always possible to apply the reduction rules to an LBFC system in such a way that the reduced system can be covered by a *smaller* number of P-components. Iterating this sequences of reductions, we get at the end a system covered by one single P-component, which implies that the system itself is a strongly connected P-graph. It is then possible to apply the macroplace rule to reach an elementary system.

We have to show hence how to reduce a system covered by r P-components to another one covered by $r - 1$. We need a couple of previous notions.

Definition 3.11 *Let* $\mathcal{C} = \{N_1, \ldots, N_r\}$ *be a cover of P-components of* N. *The net* $\hat{N}_1$ *covered by* $\{N_2, \ldots N_r\}$ *is called the* environment *of* N_1.

Let now N_1' *be a subnet of* N_1. N_1' *is a* private subnet *of* N_1 *iff the following three conditions hold:*

(a) N_1' *is connected*

(b) N_1' *and* $\hat{N}_1$ *are disjoint*

(c) N_1' *is maximal, in the sense that no bigger subnet of* N_1' *satisfies both (a) and (b).*

Private subnets are those parts of a P-component in which the environment does not interfere. In our example of Fig. 3.4, with the cover given above, the subnet with $\{B, D, F, G\}$ as places and $\{b, d, e, f, g\}$ as transitions is a private subnet of the P-component characterised by $\{A, B, D, F, G\}$.

Consider now a P-component such that when we remove all its private parts what remains (its environment) is strongly connected. It is not difficult to show that such a P-component always exists. In our example, the P-component generated by $\{A, B, D, F, G\}$ satisfies this condition.

We proceed in two steps. First, we show by means of the next theorem that the private subnets of such a P-component, let us call it N_1, can be reduced to a place. Then, we show that the macroplaces so obtained are MSIPs, and hence can be removed. After this, the reduced system is just the environment of N_1, which can be covered by $(r-1)$ P-components (the old cover without N_1).

Theorem 3.12 [ES 90a] [Espa 90b] *Let* N_1 *be a P-component of an LBFC system, such that its environment is strongly connected. Let* N_1' *be a private subnet of* N_1. *Then* N_1' *has exactly one way-out place.*

The only way-out place of the private subnet mentioned above is G. This theorem shows immediately that these private subnets fulfil the three conditions of definition 3.6. The third condition is immediately satisfied, because all places are connected to the only way-out place of the subnet, and hence to all of them. But the theorem has a clear interpretation as well. Private subnets of a P-component, which structurally can be considered as a sequential process, represent the part of the behaviour that the process can perform independently, without having to agree with other processes. Theorem 3.12 points out that this private behaviour is strongly constrained. Since private subnets have one single way out place, the environment, once a token has been put into the subnet, knows that eventually it will reach this place. The process can *delay* this final outcome, maybe for ever if the private subnets contains cycles and no fairness assumption is made, but cannot choose between different outcomes. Freedom of choice requires to pay a high price: *no process can take privately a decission which could have influence on the environment.* This result should not be surprising: if nobody can be forced to do anything that (s)he does not want to do, then nobody should be able to decide privately things that concern other people. From this point of view, theorem 3.12 just *formalises* this idea, giving a precise interpretation of the concepts *concern* and *privacy*.

The second part of our procedure requires to prove that the macroplaces we obtain after the reduction are MSIPs. This is done by means of the following result, which characterizes MSIPs in LBFC systems in terms of a surprisingly simple graph theoretical condition.

Theorem 3.13 [ES 90a] [Espa 90b] *Let $\langle N, M_0 \rangle$ be an SL&SB FC net and p a place of N. If N^{-p} is strongly connected, then p is an MSIP of N.*

As a last comment, the reader can check that both reduction rules can be applied by means of polynomial time algorithms. Because of the completeness of the reduction process, this provides an alternative polynomial algorithm to decide liveness and boundedness.

3.2 The reverse-dual kit

If we consider the structural parts of the place-oriented reduction rules (the structural conditions and the structural changes) we get *structural rules*. They transform nets, not systems, and *preserve the existence* of a live and bounded marking, instead of liveness and boundedness. In the case of FC nets, we know by proposition 2.1 that they preserve SL&SB as well. We can now profit from the duality theorem (corollary 2.4) to obtain what can be called structural *reverse-dual rules*. They are defined as follows:

- The strucural reverse-dual rule can be applied to N iff the structural rule can be applied to N_{rd}.

- If the structural rule transforms N into N', then the structural reverse dual rule transforms N_{rd} into N'_{rd}.

It is easy to see that if a structural rule preserves SL&SB, so does its structural reverse-dual rule (direct application of the duality theorem).

In order to get reverse-dual rules, acting on systems and preserving liveness and boundedness, we still have to care of the markings. We solve this problem using theorem 2.6.

Let us obtain the reverse-dual of the MSIP rule. If we removed places before, now we remove transitions, whose column in the incidence matrix is a positive linear combination of the columns corresponding to other transitions. We call these transitions *structural bypasses*. The reason is that their firing produces just the same effect than the firing of all the transitions present in the linear combination, each one as many times as the corresponding coefficient of the combination indicates. That is, firing this transition we *bypass* firing the other ones.

Let us now denote by N^{-t} the net obtained removing the transition t from N, together with its input and output arcs. The corresponding incidence matrices are denoted by C and C^{-t}. It is then clear that

$$C = [C^{-t} \; C(t)]$$

where $C(t)$ is the column associated to t in C.

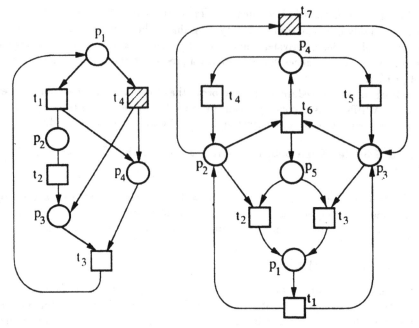

(a) The original is a LBFC net: the addition of the structural bypass $t_4 = t_1 + t_2$ preserve structural liveness

(b) The original is a live and bounded P/T net. The addition of the structural bypass $t_7 = t_1 + t_2 + t_5 + t_6$ kill the net for any initial marking.

Figure 3.5. Structural bypass: positive linear combination of transitions.

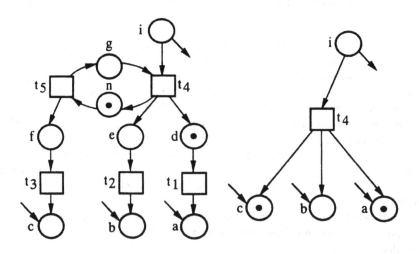

Figure 3.6. Macrotransition subnet reduction rule (ignoring the marking it is the reverse-dual schema of that in Fig. 3.2).

Definition 3.14 *A transition t is a structural bypass of the net $N = (P, T, F)$ iff $C(t)$ is a positive linear combination of the columns associated to other transitions:*

$$\exists X_t \geqslant 0: \ C(t) = C^{-t} \cdot X_t$$

The two shaded transitions of Fig. 3.5 are structural bypasses.

Property 3.15 *Let t be a structural bypass. Then $\forall p \in {}^\bullet t: |p^\bullet| > 1$ and $\forall p \in t^\bullet: |{}^\bullet p| > 1$.*

The above property (dual of property 3.2) provides an easy to check necessary condition for a transition to be a structural bypass. In particular, it points out that T-graphs have no structural bypass.

The following result is easily obtained from the duality theorem and theorem 3.4.

Theorem 3.16 *Let t be a structural bypass of an FC net N. Then N is SL&SB iff N^{-t} is SL&SB.*

This theorem is not true in general. The structurally bounded net of Figure 3.5b is non-live for any marking, but removing the shaded structural bypass it becomes structurally live.

It can be proved that if t is a structural bypass then all the p-semiflows of N are marked iff all the p-semiflows of N^{-t} are marked. This shows that we do not need to care about the markings in order to preserve liveness and boundedness.

REDUCTION RULE RBY

Structural condition : N is an FC net containing a structural bypass t

Marking condition : none

Changes : Remove t with its input and output arcs.

Theorem 3.17 *RBY preserves liveness and boundedness, but not the actual bound of the system.*

Let us now introduce the reverse-dual of the macroplace rule. The next definition contains the reverse-dual concept of subnet reducible to a place. Way-in and way-out transitions are defined analogously to way-in and way-out places.

Definition 3.18 *Let N be an FC net and $N' = (P', T'; F')$ be a subnet of N (i.e. $F' = F \cap ((P' \times T') \cup (T' \times P'))$). N' is reducible to a transition if:*

(a) N' is a T-graph and $\forall p \in P': |p^\bullet \cap T'| \leq 1$ and $|{}^\bullet p \cap T'| \leq 1$

(b) For every $t' \in T'$, there exists at least an F'-path from t' to a way-out transition of N'.

(c) $\forall t' \in T'$, $\forall$ way-in transition t'_i of N': there exists an F'-path from t'_i to t'.

Figure 3.6 shows the macrotransition reduction rule. The intuition of the reduction process is straighforward and we skip to give a formal definition of the rule (in any case, is the reverse dual of that considered in definition 3.7). The reader can easily check that now T-graphs are reduced to a single macrotransition.

Figure 3.7 is self-explicative on an alternative reduction of the net in Fig.3.3a.

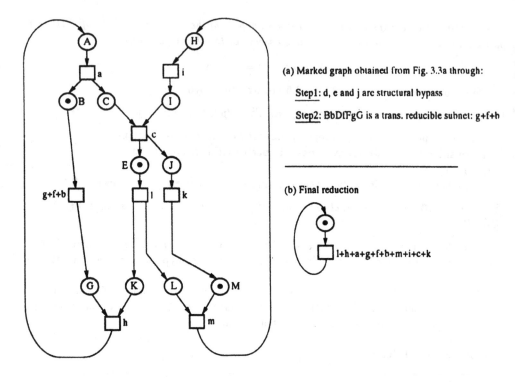

(a) Marked graph obtained from Fig. 3.3a through:

  Step1: d, e and j are structural bypass

  Step2: BbDfFgG is a trans. reducible subnet: g+f+b

(b) Final reduction

l+h+a+g+f+b+m+i+c+k

Figure 3.7. Structural bypass and macrotransition subnet reduction. of FC in Fig. 3.3a.

Structure condition : N contains a subnet N' reducible to a macrotransition.

Marking condition : There is no unmarked p semiflow in N'.

Structural changes: • Substitute N' by the macrotransition.
Marking changes: • M_o^* is the restriction of M_0 to $P \setminus P'$.
           • The final marking is obtained adding to each output place of a way-out transition the minimum number of tokens found in the different paths from the way-in transition.

The utility of the macrotransition concept lies in the following result.

Theorem 3.19 *RMT preserves liveness and boundedness, but not the actual bound of the system.*

Using the *duality theorem*, we can easily prove that this second kit of reduction rules is also *complete*. We have then provided two kits of reduction rules which characterize liveness and boundedness in FC systems. Since nothing prevents to interleave the applications of the four rules, faster (i.e. in less steps) reduction processes can be expected.

4 Top-down synthesis

Sections 2 and 3 have been devoted to analysis techniques. These techniques detect non-correct systems, but in general do not give any hint about how to proceed in order to improve the design.

This section and the next present an interesting alternative to this *trial and error* procedure based on *analysis and modification*: The use of *strict design methodologies*.

In these cases, the designer restricts him/herself to modifying and developing the model using only some very specific rules of *top-down transformation* and *composition* (modular approach), which can be safely applied because they are known to *preserve* the properties (here liveness and boundedness) desired for the system.

In the top-down design paradigm, to which this section is devoted, the synthesis procedure starts from an elementary one place-one transition system which is trivially live and bounded. This initial system is then enlarged in a stepwise way using the synthesis rules kit.

Synthesis (or design) rules are the reverse of reduction rules: instead of reducing the net system, a more detailed (enlarged) model is obtained. In section 3 a place-oriented and a transition-oriented complete reduction rules kits were presented. Their reverse will constitute *complete synthesis* rules kits: all LBFC systems can be generated stepwisely. Thus any of these synthesis kits provide an *alternative definition* of LBFC systems: instead of defining FC nets, and liveness and boundedness properties, LBFC systems are those that can be generated by means of rules of the identified synthesis kits. The important point with this idea in mind is that many net or system properties can be now proved in a relatively easy way by *inductive* reasoning: checking that the property is true for the elementary net/system and is preserved by any of the refinement rules in one of the kits.

4.1 The two synthesis kits

This section is devoted to the introduction of the two synthesis kits corresponding to the reduction kits introduced in the past section.

Place-oriented synthesis kit. This kit is composed by the reverse of the marking structurally implicit place (MSIP) and the macroplace reduction rules.

Let N_p be the net obtained adding a place to a net N. Given a marking M_{0p} of N_p, let M_0 be the marking obtained projecting M_{0p} on the places of N.

SYNTHESIS RULE SIM

Structural conditions : N is an FC net

Marking conditions : none

Structural changes: An MSIP p is added to N to yield an FC net N_p
(in particular, $|p^\bullet| = 1$)
Marking changes: • The marking of places of N remains unchanged.
• if $\exists Y \geq e_p, Y^T \cdot C_p = 0$ such that $Y^T \cdot M_{op} = 0$
then $M_{op}(p) > 0$
else $M_{op}(p) \geq 0$ fi

We can easily prove now the following result.

Property 4.1 *SIM preserves liveness and boundedness, but not the bound of the net.*

Proof: By theorem 3.4, N_p is SL&SB iff N is. Due to the nature of the marking changes, N_p contains no unmarked p-semiflow containing the new place p. This implies that N_p contains an unmarked p-semiflow iff N also contains one. Applying theorem 2.6, it follows that $\langle N_p, M_{0p} \rangle$ is live and bounded iff $\langle N, M_0 \rangle$ is live and bounded. ∎

SIM, like RIM, does not preserve the bound of the system (Fig. 3.1) and does not preserve liveness for bounded asymmetric choice systems (Fig. 2.5).

Let us introduce now the macroplace refinement rule.

SYNTHESIS RULE SMP

Structural and marking conditions : none

Structural and marking changes : Transform $\langle N, M_0 \rangle$ into $\langle \tilde{N}, \tilde{M}_0 \rangle$, such that $\langle N, M_0 \rangle$ is a macroplace reduction of $\langle \tilde{N}, \tilde{M}_0 \rangle$

Property 4.2 *SMP preserves liveness and the bound of the system (thus boundedness).*

Proof: Follows easily from theorem 3.8. ∎

Transition-oriented synthesis kit. This kit is composed by the synthesis rules corresponding to the structural bypass and the macrotransition reduction rules.

Let N_t be the net obtained by adding transition t to N.

SYNTHESIS RULE SBY

Structural condition : N is FC

Marking condition : none

Structural change: N_t is an FC net obtained adding a structural bypass t to N
(in particular, $|{}^\bullet t| = 1$)

Marking change: The old marking is preserved.

Property 4.3 *SBY preserves liveness and boundedness, but not the bound of the system. Nevertheless, if the system is live the bound is also preserved.*

Using the duality theorem and theorem 3.5, it follows that N_t is SL&SB iff N is SL&SB. The rest of the proof uses the following two facts: (1) the addition of a structural bypass preserves the p-semiflows, and (2) the behavioural bound of any place can be computed from the p-semiflows for LBFC systems [Espa 90b].

Let us now introduce the macrotransition refinement rule.

SYNTHESIS RULE SMT

Structural and marking conditions : none

Structural and marking changes : Transform $\langle N, M_0 \rangle$ into $\langle \tilde{N}, \tilde{M}_0 \rangle$, such that $\langle N, M_0 \rangle$ is a macrotransition reduction of $\langle \tilde{N}, \tilde{M}_0 \rangle$

Property 4.4 *SMT preserves liveness and boundedness, but not the actual bound of the system.*

The synthesis procedure. Any of the two refinement kits, place and transition-oriented, permit to construct all and only LBFC systems. This result, which follows easily from the completeness of their corresponding reduction kits, is formally stated next.

Theorem 4.5 $\langle N, M_0 \rangle$ *is an LBFC system iff* $\langle N, M_0 \rangle$ *is:*

a) *an elementary system, or*

b) *the result of a finite sequence of transformations from a marked elementary system using the place-oriented or the transition oriented synthesis kits.*

270

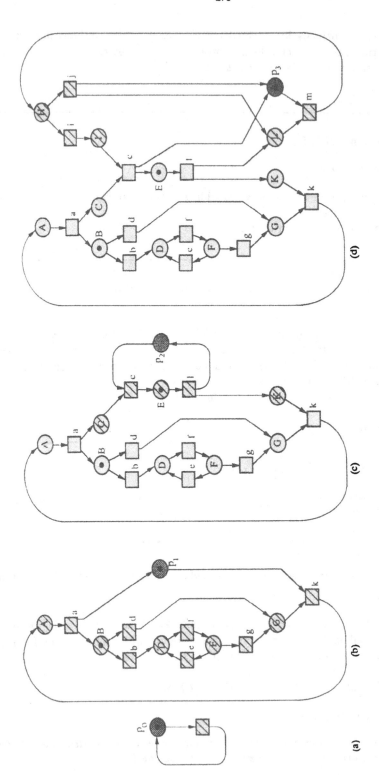

Figure 4.1. Top-down obtention of a system: The refinement of p_3 gives the Fig. 3.3a system.

Figure 4.1 shows a sequence of place-oriented synthesis. The initial place is refined into the shaded subnet. After that the MSIP p_1 is added. The refinement of p_1 leads to the shaded subnet in Fig. 4.1c. Later the MSIP p_2 is added. Its refinement leads to Fig. 4.1d, where the MSIP p_3 is added. Refinement of p_3 leads finaly to the net in Fig. 3.3a.

In the example of Fig. 4.1 places p_1, p_2 and p_3 when added are *implicit*: they do not change the behaviour of the model. In other words, these places being implicit do not constraint the firing language (i.e. the firing language is preserved) of the original net.

Let us suppose now that the elementary net (Fig. 4.1a) were marked with two tokens: $M_0(p_0) = 2$. If $M_0(p_1) = 1$ and $M_0(B) = 2$, the addition of p_1 does not kill the net (the new p-semiflow is obviously marked) but p_1 is no more an implicit place: p_1 constraints the behaviour. For example, transition k cannot be fired twice from M_0 without firing transition a.

4.2 Consequences of the completeness of the synthesis kits for the analysis of properties

Theorem 4.5 shows that LBFC systems can be defined *recursively* using any of the two refinement kits. Hence, if a property π is true for the elementary system chosen as *seed* of the synthesis procedure, and this same property is preserved for the two rules of one of the refinement kits, π is also true for all LBFC systems. We develop this idea using it to prove a couple of interesting results, whose proofs are only sketched. The first one is already known (see [BD 90]). The second can be deduced from Best/Voss/Vogler result on the existence of home states for LBFC systems [BV 84, Vogl 89] and proposition 2.1.

Proposition 4.6 (Relationship between T-components and minimal T-semiflows)
Let (N, M_0) be an LBFC system where $N = (P, T; F)$ and $X \geq 0$. X is a minimal T-semiflow iff the two following conditions holds:

(a) $\forall t \in T : X(t) \in \{0, 1\}$

(b) *There exists a T-component $N_1 = (P_1, T_1; F_1)$ of N such that the support of X (i.e. $\|X\| = \{t \in T : X(t) > 0\}$) is T_1, $\|X\| = T_1$.*

Proof idea:
($\Leftarrow$): This part holds in general.
($\Rightarrow$): We prove this part by induction.
Base: The statement is trivially true for elementary systems.
Step: It is easy to see that the property is preserved by the macroplace rule, because the macroplace is substituted by a P-graph . We show now that the MSIP refinement rule preserves the property as well. In fact, if a vector X is a T-semiflow of the net before adding an MSIP, then it is also a T-semiflow of the net after adding it, because the MSIP place is a (positive) linear combination of rows in C, and no change can be produced on its right annulers.

Assume now we have a minimal T-semiflow satisfying the conditions of the theorem. By the induction hypothesis, to this T-semiflow corresponds a T-component. Moreover we know that this vector is also a T-semiflow of the final net. In particular, for SL&SBFC nets this means that the new place has as many input transitions in the support of the T-semiflow as output transitions: the number of both is exactly 0 (when the new place has no interference with the T-semiflow) or 1 (otherwise). In the first case, the old T-component is also a T-component of the new net. In the second case, the old T-component plus the new place is a T-component of the new net. ∎

The second result requires to introduce the notion of *reversibility*. A system $\langle N, M_0 \rangle$ is reversible iff from every reachable marking M there is a firing sequence leading to M_0 (i.e. M_0 is a home state). As we have done with the notions of liveness and boundedness, we can also define *structural reversibility*. A net N is structurally reversible iff there exists an initial marking, M_0, such that $\langle N, M_0 \rangle$ is reversible.

Theorem 4.7 *Let N be an SL&SB FC net. Then N is structurally reversible.*

Proof: We generate inductively a reversible system $\langle N, M_0 \rangle$ using the place oriented kit.

Base: We start from the elementary system with one token on the place. This system is reversible.

Step: We use the two following particularizations of the two refinement rules.

i) The marking of the new MSIP places is large enough to make them implicit.

With this restriction, we ensure that the language of the net does not change. Let then (N, M_0) be the old system and (N_p, M_{0p}) the new one, where p is implicit. Consider then $M_{0p} |\sigma\rangle M_p$. Since the language has not changed, $M_0 |\sigma\rangle M$. By the induction hypothesis, there exists σ' such that $M |\sigma'\rangle M_0$. Since the language is preserved, $M_p |\sigma'\rangle M_p'$. It remains to show that $M_p' = M_{op}$. This can be done taking into account that the Parikh vector of the sequence $\sigma\sigma'$ is a T-semiflow of N. It was proved in the past result that if a vector is a T-semiflow in a net, it is also a T-semiflow after the addition of an MSIP. Hence $\overrightarrow{(\sigma\sigma')}$ is a T-semiflow of N_p, and $M_{0p} |\sigma\sigma'\rangle M_p' = M_{0p}$.

ii) The macroplace rule allows us to distribute arbitrarily the tokens of the substituted place on the new P-graph. Now we restrict this freedom, imposing that all the tokens have to be placed on the only way-out place of the new P-graph (see theorem 3.12).

Take now a reachable marking M of the system after substituting the macroplace. We sketch the procedure to find a firing sequence leading from M to M_0. The idea is the following: take the markings M_0' and M' of the system before the P-graph is substituted which correspond to M_0 and M (that is, they are like M_0 and M, with the exception that all the tokens of the P-graph are now in the macroplace). By the induction hypothesis, there is a sequence $M' |\sigma'\rangle M_0'$. Now, every appearance of a transition in σ' that puts a token on the macroplace is substituted by a sequence composed by this transition and a firing sequence of transitions of the P-graph that put this token on the way out place. This way we produde a firing sequence σ of the system after the substitution. It is not difficult to see that $M |\sigma\rangle M_0$.

Therefore giving some restrictions on the markings of the place oriented kit only reversible systems are produced. Since we have not constrained the structural parts of the rules, we can still generate all the SL&SB FC nets with this new kit (although not all the LBFC systems). We have proved then that every SL&SB FC net can be endowed with a marking that makes it reversible. ∎

LBFC systems are not reversible in general. An example is the net of Fig. 2.1a with initial marking $M_0^T = (0\ 1\ 0\ 0\ 1\ 0\ 0)$.

5 Modular synthesis

The design of large systems requires the use of *teams of designers*, each one in charge of a particular *subsystem* or *module*. The final system is built *composing* the subsystems. In this section we define two ways of composing subsystems and show how to interconnect them to preserve the properties of good behaviour that both the subsystems and the global system should enjoy.

Within our context, the above problem can be formulated in a very simple way: given several LBFC systems, characterize the compositions that preserve liveness and boundedness. We should warn the reader that we present a compositional solution of only the *structural part* of the problem. That is, we give exact conditions for the preservation of SL&SB under the compositions of nets we consider. Once we have obtained an SL&SB net, the initial markings making it live can be obtained applying theorem 2.6.

Since compositions of k nets can be splitted into $k-1$ compositions of 2 nets, we consider only this latter particular case.

5.1 Synchronizations and fusions

A very general notion of composition of two nets can be given as follows: a net $N = (P, T, F)$ is the *composition* of $N_a = (P_a, T_a, F_a)$ and $N_b = (P_b, T_b, F_b)$ iff N_a, N_b are subnets of N and $N = N_a \cup N_b = (P_a \cup P_b, T_a \cup T_b, F_a \cup F_b)$.

As an example, the net of Fig. 5.1.b is a composition of the two nets of Fig. 5.1a. An important notion for us concerning compositions is that of *interface*. The interface I between N_a and N_b in N is a subset of nodes defined as follows. A node x of N is in I iff:

- x is in both N_a, N_b

- There is at least one node of $^\bullet x \cup x^\bullet$ that is not in both N_a and N_b.

That is, we define the interface as the nodes where the two components "meet". Nodes "between" interface nodes need not be interface nodes themselves (e.g. Fig. 5.1c.2). In the example of Fig. 5.1a, the interface between the two components is formed by a place and a transition. The transition can be interpreted as a communication by *rendez-vous* between the two components, while the place corresponds to a communication by *shared states (common variables)*. Compositions in which these two types of communication mechanisms are present in the interface are difficult to interpret and lead to difficult to handle constructions. That is why we would like to consider compositions in which the interface is composed by only one type of nodes.

Definition 5.1 *Let $\{N_a, N_b\}$ be two nets. N is a synchronization of N_a and N_b iff*

$$p \in P_a \cap P_b \Rightarrow {}^\bullet p \cup p^\bullet \in T_a \cap T_b$$

(i.e. no place belongs to the interface).
   N is a fusion of N_a and N_b iff

$$t \in T_a \cap T_b \Rightarrow {}^\bullet t \cup t^\bullet \in P_a \cap P_b$$

(i.e. no transition belongs to the interface).

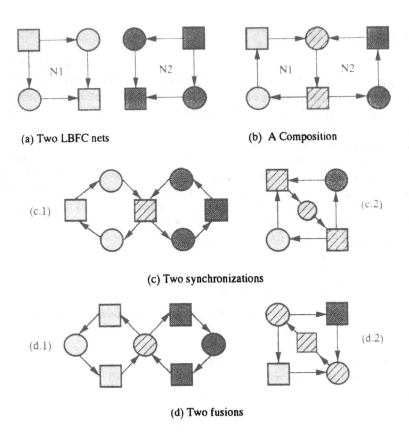

(a) Two LBFC nets

(b) A Composition

(c.1)

(c.2)

(c) Two synchronizations

(d.1)

(d.2)

(d) Two fusions

Figure 5.1. Composition, synchronization and fusion (the reverse-dual of synchronization) of free choice nets.

The nets of Fig. 5.1c are two different synchronisations of the nets of Fig. 5.1.a. The ones of Fig. 5.1d are two different fusions of the same nets.

We are interested on those synchronisations and fusions producing FC nets. We call them *FC-synchronisations (fusions)*. Obviously, the two components of an FC-synchronisation (fusion) must be FC. The net in Fig. 5.2 shows how the net in Fig. 3.3a can be obtained through FC-synchronizations.

Let us focus on the case of synchronisations. How to check that the synchronization of two SL&SB FC nets produces an SL&SB net? We could apply theorem 2.3 and check in polynomial time that the synchronisation is consistent and satisfies the rank equation (it can be shown that the synchronisation is conservative by construction). A possible question is: when the system is produced through several synchronisations, why not just check the final model? The answer is that, if we perform a check after each synchronisation, the possible design error is detected as soon as it is introduced. And this is particularly interesting in the context of FC nets, because the following *monotonicity* property can be proved.

Proposition 5.2 [ES 90b, Espa 90b] *Let N be an FC-synchronisation (FC-fusion) of $\{N_a, N_b\}$. N is SL&SB only if N_a and N_b are SL&SB.*

Hence, *if after a synchronisation of two conservative FC nets the composed net becomes non SL, it remains non SL.* Further synchronisations cannot *repair* design errors. Nevertheless, the reader can easily check (see Fig. 5.3) that this property does not holds when asymmetric choice nets are considered!

As a last remark, Fig. 5.4 shows that non-liveness of the FC-synchronized net can be originated on the initial marking obtained by the composition and not on the structure.

5.2 Interpreting FC-synchronization design errors

Theorem 2.3 can be used to detect when a bad composition was performed, but does not give information about the location and nature of the design error. We introduce in this section the results of [ES 90b] on this problem, which can be summarized as follows: the only possible design errors are two, called *synchronic mismatches* and *killing choices*.

The first structural design error: synchronic mismatches. Let us make first an informal introduction. Consider the two nets of the upper part of figure 5.5. They model the behaviour of John and Mary, two millionaires of Palm Beach. Every day John decides whether he well play tennis or not. If he does not play tennis, he goes dancing and then has a drink. If he does play tennis, then he is too tired to go dancing and just drinks. After the drink a new day comes and everything starts again.

Also Mary decides every day to play tennis or not. But, since she is in better shape than John, she always goes dancing after, and then has the drink. The question is: if John and Mary get married, and want to play tennis or not, go dancing and drink together, will the marriage eventually reach a deadlock? The marriage corresponds to the FC-synchronization at the bottom of the figure, and it is easy to see that the system will eventually deadlock. The reason is that John can execute the action "do play tennis" an arbitrarily large number of times without executing "go dancing", and Mary will be waiting to "go dancing".

To formalize the above problem, let us introduce a *synchronic relation*. Synchronic relations [Silv 87, SC 87] are tools of Synchronic Theory, which is a branch of net theory devoted to the study of dependences between the firings of transitions.

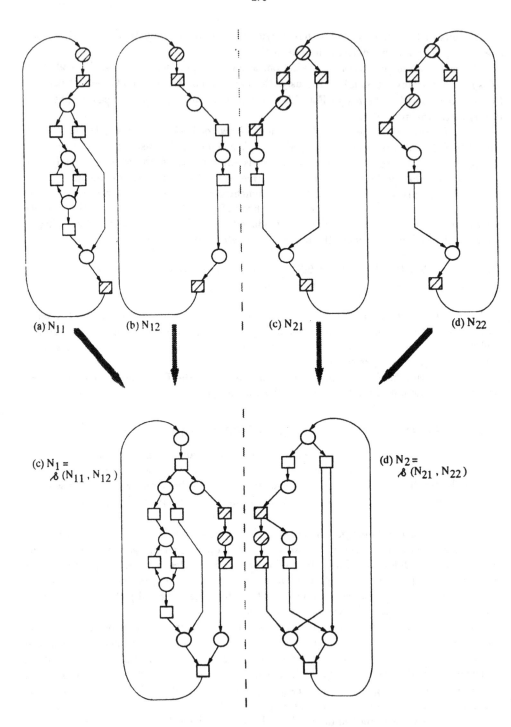

Figure 5.2. Modular composition (through synchronizations) of nets: The net in Fig. 3.3a is obtained synchronizing N1 and N2.

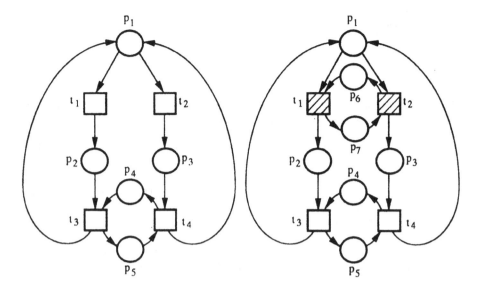

Figure 5.3. A structurally non-live FC net becomes a structurally live asymmetric choice net when the synchronization with a two place cycle is performed.

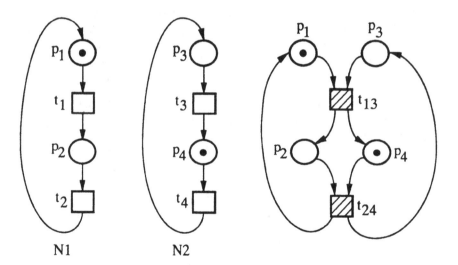

Figure 5.4. The synchronization of N_1 and N_2 leads to a structurally live net but non-live system (the cycle $p_3 - t_{13} - p_4 - t_{24}$ is unmarked!).

Definition 5.3 (Bounded Deviation, BD) *Let* $< N, M_0 >$ *be a system and* $R(N, M_0)$
its marking reachability set.

(1) $T_1, T_2 \subseteq T$ *are in* k-bounded relation *in the system iff* $\forall M \in R(N, M_0)$ *and* $\forall \sigma$ *applicable at* M *(i.e.* $M[\sigma >)$, $\vec{\sigma}(T_2) = 0 \Rightarrow \vec{\sigma}(T_1) \le k$.

(2) $T_1, T_2 \subseteq T$ *are in (behavioural)* bounded deviation relation *in* $< N, M_0 >$ *iff* $\exists k \in \mathbb{N}$ *such that* T_1, T_2 *are in* k-bounded deviation relation.

(3) $T_1, T_2 \subseteq T$ *are in* structural bounded deviation relation *in* N *iff* $\forall M_0, \exists k \in \mathbb{N}$ *such that* T_1, T_2 *are in* k-bounded deviation relation.

In the case of John and Mary, the two actions "do not play tennis" and "go dancing" are in structural BD-relation for John but not for Mary. That is, the synchronic relations of the two "partners" (subsystems) do not "match".

Definition 5.4 *Let* N *be a synchronization of* $\{N_a, N_b\}$. *The transitions* $t_i, t_j \in T_a \cap T_b$, *are a synchronic mismatch iff they are in structural BD-relation in one and only one of* N_a, N_b.

In our example, the two transitions corresponding to "do not play tennis" and "go dancing" constitute a synchronic mismatch.

Proposition 5.5 [ES 90b] *Let* N *be an FC-synchronization of* $\{N_a, N_b\}$, *where both* N_a, N_b *are SL&SB. If* N *contains a synchronic mismatch, then* N *is not structurally live.*

The second structural design error: killing choices. Let us go back to John and Mary. They have changed of hobbies, and like now to go to the cinema every day. There are two cinemas for millionaires in Palm Beach, the "Odeon" and the "Capitol". John decides each day which of the two cinemas he wants to go to, and so does Mary.

John and Mary want to get married and go to the cinema together, but both want to decide, without consulting the other, which of the two cinemas they will go to. The corresponding synchronisation is shown at the bottom of figure 5.6. Notice that the net contains no synchronic mismatches, but nevertheless leads to a deadlock for any marking. The deadlock is produced by the fact that the choices of John and Mary are *private*, but *concern the partner*. It is intuitively reasonable that these choices lead to non liveness for any marking. We call them *killing choices*.

Definition 5.6 *Let* N *be a FC-synchronisation of* $\{N_a = (P_a, T_a; F_a), N_b = (P_b, T_b; F_b)\}$. *A place* $p \in P_a$ *is a* killing choice *of* N_a *iff the following three conditions hold:*

(a) $p \notin P_b$

(b) *There exists a* T-component N_a^1 *of* N_a *containing* p *and a transition* $t_i \in T_a \cap T_b$.

(c) *There exists an elementary path* $B = (p, \ldots, t_j)$, $t_j \in T_a \cap T_b$, *such that* p *is the only node of* N_a^1 *in* B.

A killing choice of N_b *is defined analogously. It is said that* N *contains a killing choice iff it contains a killing choice of* N_a *or a killing choice of* N_b.

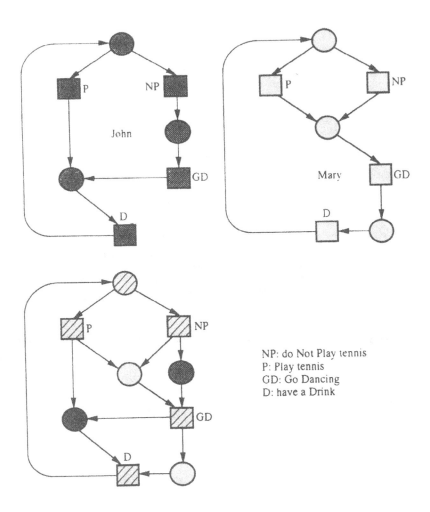

John

Mary

NP: do Not Play tennis
P: Play tennis
GD: Go Dancing
D: have a Drink

Figure 5.5. The transitions NP and GD are in synchronic mismatch.

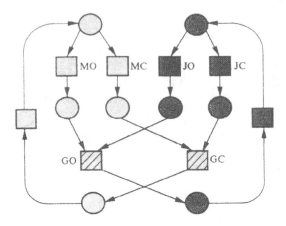

MO / JO: Mary / John decides to go to the Odeon
MC / JC: Mary / John decides to go to the Capitol
GO: John and Mary go to the Odeon
GC: John and Mary go to the Capitol

Figure 5.6. Both components of the synchronization contain a killing choice.

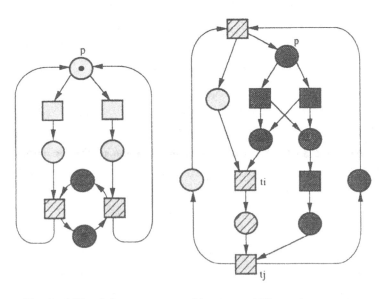

(a) p is a killing choice   (b) p is not a killing choice

Figure 5.7. Killing choices leads to deadlocks.

Notice that p is a place with more than one output transition, because it has at least one output transition in the T-component and another one out of it. In fact, N_a can decide freely at p whether the tokens are kept in the T-component or are taken out of it.

It could be thought at first sight that condition (b) of the definition is too complicated: apparently, in order to affect the behaviour of the other subnet, it would be sufficient the existence of two paths starting from the candidate to killing choice and ending at the two transitions t_i, t_j, paths with only the initial place in common. This is not enough, as the net in figure 5.7b shows. Place p seems to be a killing choice of N_b. Nevertheless, in spite of the existence of the two paths leading to t_i, t_j, the solution given by N_b to the conflict in p has no relevance for N_a. N_a only "sees" that N_b is always willing to fire both t_i and t_j, whichever was the branch selected by N_b at p. This is due to the fact that every T-component of N_b containing p and one of the transitions t_i, t_j contains also the other.

Proposition 5.7 [ES 90b] *Let N_a and N_b two SL&SB FC nets and N be an FC-synchronization of $\{N_a, N_b\}$. If N contains a killing choice, then N is structurally non live.*

This proposition is not true for asymmetric choice nets obtained by synchronization (Fig. 2.3b, with $t_i = t_3$ and $t_j = t_4$).

Completeness of the design errors. We hope that both killing choices and synchronic mismatches are intuitively seen as design errors, so it shouldn't be surprising that they lead to bad behaviours. What is not so intuitive is that every (structural) design error can be interpreted in terms of these two, or, in some sense, that these two are the only possible design errors.

Theorem 5.8 [ES 90b] *Let N_a and N_b two SL&SB FC nets and be N and FC-synchronization of $\{N_a, N_b\}$. N is structurally live iff it contains no synchronic mismatch and no killing choice.*

As a final remark, it can be pointed out that synchronic mismatches and killing choices can coexist in a bad design.

5.3   Fusions and design errors

Applying the duality theorem we can obtain similar results to those of the past section about the reverse-dual concepts of synchronization, synchronic mismatch and killing choice. Due to lack of space we will not deal with them here.

Nevertheless, it is important to point out that *FC-fusions* (the reverse-dual of FC-synchronizations) are net compositions in which the interface is formed only by places. The reader is referred to Fig. 5.8 for illustrations of the *fusion* (or place) *mismatch* error, the reverse-dual of the synchronic mismatch, and the *killing joint* error, the reverse-dual of killing choice.

Once again, particular attention must be payed to the *completeness* of fusion mismatches and killing joints in order to explain all the possible errors. The reverse-dual of theorem 5.8 states that an FC-fusion of two SL&SB FC nets is SL&SB iff it contains no place mismatches and no killing joints.

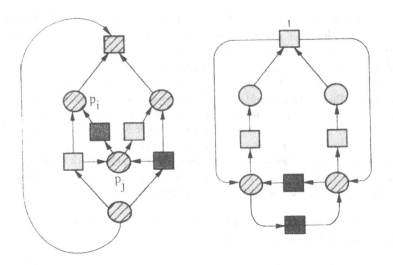

(a) p_i and p_j represent a fusion
(place) mismatch

(b) t is a killing joint

Figure 5.8. Fusion mismatch and killing joint design errors.

6 Conclusion

Arrived at this point. we should confess that our main goal has been to convince the reader of how nice, simple, powerful and computationally efficient the theory of LBFC systems can be. We have tried to state clearly concepts and results, illustrating them by means of examples and omitting the lenghty proofs. For more technical presentations the readers should consult the references. where the results are usually stated using quite different approaches. The cited works of Best. Commoner, Desel, Hack, Thiagarajan and Voss introduce many other beautiful results of the theory of Free Choice systems. In particular, it may be interesting to record two related recent results concerning home states and reachability in LBFC systems:

(1) In [BCDE 90], *home states* of LBFC systems are characterized as those for which all traps are marked.

(2) In [DE 90], the *reachability problem* is solved in polynomial time for reversible (i.e. M_0 is a home state) LBFC systems.

Free choice nets are rather limited for practical applications. For example, they cannot model systems with shared resources. On the other hand, as was pointed out in [Best 87], the research on FC systems has shown the existence of a big gap between them and asymmetric choice systems, which could appear to be the next natural class to consider. A possible solution to this conflict between the solutions offered by the theory and the requirements of practice could be the following: systems of practical interest are usually not FC, but we have observed that *they are often composed by subsystems which are FC*. These subsystems represent functional entities (i.e. the work we want to perform) which *compete* for resources or *cooperate* through message passing, modelled by means of *monitors* (a shared place implementing mutual exclusion mechanisms) and *buffers* (or mail boxes) respectively. We suggest *to extend the class of nets adding* some restricted communication mechanism like these mentioned here which, while representing a significant improvement in the expressive power, preserve some of the nice properties of FC systems. Some research is going on in this direction.

Acknowledgement

This work was partially supported by the DEMON Esprit Basic Research Action 3148 and the Spanish Plan Nacional de Investigación, Grant TIC-0358/89. The authors are indebted to J. Campos, J.M. Colom and E. Teruel, colleagues at the University of Zaragoza, for fruitful discussions and the three referees for valuable hints for improving the paper.

References

[Bert 87]   BERTHELOT, G.: Transformations and Decompositions of Nets. In [BRR 87],*LNCS 254*, pp. 359-376.

[BRR 87]   BRAUER, W.; REISIG, W.; ROZENBERG, G.; (EDS.): *Advanced Course on Petri Nets*, Lecture Notes on Computer Science 254 and 255, Springer-Verlag, Berlin.

[Best 87]   BEST. E.: Structure Theory of Petri Nets: the Free Choice Hiatus. In [BRR 87], *LNCS 254*, pp. 168-205.

[BV 84]   BEST, E.; VOSS, K.: Free Choice Systems Have Home States. *Acta Informatica 21*, pp. 89-100.

[BT 87]   BEST, E.; THIAGARAJAN, P.S.: Some Classes of Live and Save Petri Nets. *Concurrency and Nets (Voss, K.; Genrich, H.J., Rozenberg, G., eds.)*, Springer-Verlag, Berlin, pp. 71-94.

[BD 90]   BEST, E.; DESEL, J.: Partial Order Behaviour and Structure of Petri Nets. *Formal Aspects of Computing*, FACS-Vol 2, No. 2, pp. 123-138.

[BCDE 90]   BEST, E.; CHERSAKOVA, L.; DESEL, J.; ESPARZA, J.: Characterization of Home States in Free Choice Systems. *Hildesheimer Informatik-Berichte Nr. 7/90* (July).

[CCS 90a]   CAMPOS, J.; CHIOLA, G.; SILVA, M.: Properties and Performance bounds for closed free choice Synchronized Monoclass Queueing Networks. *Departamento de Ingeniería Eléctrica e Informática, Universidad de Zaragoza, Research Report 90.02*, January (27 pages).

[CCS 90b]   COLOM, J.M.; CAMPOS, J.; SILVA, M.: On liveness analysis through linear algebraic techniques. *Departamento de Ingeniería Eléctrica e Informática, Universidad de Zaragoza, Research Report GISI 90.10*, June (17 pages)

[CHEP 71]   COMMONER, F.; HOLT, A.W.; EVEN, S.; PNUELI, A.: Marked Directed Graphs. *Journal of Computer and System Sciences, Vol. 9, No. 2*, pp. 72-79.

[CS 89a]   COLOM, J.M.; SILVA, M.: Convex geometry and semiflows in P/T nets. A comparative study of algorithms for computation of minimal p-semiflows. *Proceedings of the Xth International Conference on Application and Theory of Petri nets*, June, Bonn, pp. 74-95.

[CS 89b]   COLOM, J.M.; SILVA, M.: Improving the linearly based characterization of P/T nets. *Proceedings of the Xth Int. Conf. on Application and Theory of Petri nets*, June, Bonn, pp. 52-73.

[Des 90]   DESEL, J.: Reduction and Design of Well-behaved Concurrent Systems. *Proceedings of CONCUR'90 (Baeten, J.C.M.; Klop, J.W.; eds.)*. Amsterdam, August, LNCS 458, Springer-Verlag, Berlin, pp. 166-181.

[DE 90]   DESEL, J.; ESPARZA, J.: Reachability in Reversible Free-choice Systems. *Technical University of Münich, SFB-Bericht Nr 342/11/90A*, June.

[Espa 90a] ESPARZA, J.: Synthesis rules for Petri Nets, and how they lead to new results. *Proceedings of CONCUR'90* (Baeten, J.C.M.; Klop J.W., eds.), Amsterdam, August. LNCS 458, Springer-Verlag, Berlin, pp. 182-198.

[Espa 90b] ESPARZA, J.: *Structure Theory of Free Choice nets*. Ph. D. thesis, Departamento de Ingeniería Eléctrica e Informática, Universidad de Zaragoza, June.

[EBS 89]   ESPARZA, J.; BEST, E.; SILVA, M.: Minimal deadlocks in Free Choice Nets. *Departamento de Ingeniería Eléctrica e Informática, Research Report GISI 80.07*, March (16 pages). Also: *Hildesheimer Informatik Fachberichte, 89/1*.

[ES 89a]   ESPARZA, J.; SILVA, M.: Circuits, Handles, Bridges and Nets. *Proceedings of the Xth Int. Conf. on Application and Theory of Petri nets*, June, Bonn, pp. 134-153.

[ES 89b]   ESPARZA, J.; SILVA, M.: A polynomial time algorithm to decide liveness of bounded free choice nets. *Departamento de Ingeniería Eléctrica e Informática, Universidad de Zaragoza, Research Report GISI 89.04*, May (28 pages). To appear in *Theoretical Computer Science*.

[ES 90a]   ESPARZA, J.; SILVA, M.: Top-down Synthesis of Live and Bounded Free Choice nets. *Proceedings of the XIth. International Conference on Application and Theory of Petri nets*. Paris, June, pp. - .

[ES 90b]   ESPARZA, J.; SILVA, M.: Modular Synthesis of free-choice nets. *Departamento de Ingeniería Eléctrica e Informática, Universidad de Zaragoza, Research Report GISI 90.06*, March (29 pages).

[ES 90c]   ESPARZA, J.; SILVA, M.: Free Choice nets, a Rank Theorem and its Consequences. To appear.

[Fink 90]   FINKEL, A.: A minimal coverability graph for Petri Nets. *Proceedings of the XIth Int. Conf. on Applications and Theory of Petri Nets*. Paris, June.

[GL 73]   GENRICH, H.J.; LAUTENBACH, K.: Synchronisationsgraphen. *Acta Informatica 2*, pp. 143-161.

[GT 89]   GOLDFARB, D.; TODD, M.J.: Linear Programming. In *Optimization (G.L. Nemhauser et al eds.)*, North Holland, Amsterdam, pp. 73-170.

[Hack 72]   HACK, M.H.T.: *Analysis of Production Schemata by Petri Nets*. Cambridge, Mass.: MIT, Dept. Electrical Engineering, MS Thesis (1972). Corrected June 1974

[Hill 85]   HILLEN, D.: Relationship between Deadlock-freeness and Liveness in Free Choice Nets. *Newsletter of the GI Special Interest Group in Petri Nets and Related System Models, No. 19*, pp. 28-32.

[JLL 77]   JONES, N.D.; LANDWEBER, L.H.; LIEN, Y.E.: Complexity of Some Problems in Petri Nets. *Theoretical Computer Science 4*, pp. 277-299.

[Karm 84]   KARMARKAR, N.: A new polynomial-time algorithm for linear programming. *Combinatorica, Vol. 4*, pp. 373-395.

[Laut 87a]   LAUTENBACH, K.: Linear Algebraic Techniques for Place/Transition Nets. In [BRR 87], *LNCS 254*, pp. 142-167.

[Laut 87b]   LAUTENBACH, K.: Linear Algebraic Calculation of Deadlock and Traps. *Concurrency and Nets (Voss, K.; Genrich, H.J., Rozenberg, G.; eds.)*, Springer-Verlag, Berlin, pp. 315-336.

[MR 80]   MEMMI, G.; ROUCAIROL, G.: Linear Algebra in Net Theory. *Net Theory and Applications. (Brauer, W.; ed.), LNCS 84*, Springer Verlag, Berlin, pp. 213-223.

[Mura 89]   MURATA, T.: Petri Nets: Properties, Analysis and Applications. *Proceedings of the IEEE, Vol. 77, No. 4*, April, pp. 540-580.

[Sifa 78]   SIFAKIS, J.: Structural Properties of Petri nets. *Mathematical Foundations of Computer Science 1978 (Winkowski, J.; ed.)*, Springer-Verlag, Berlin, pp. 474-483.

[Silv 81]   SILVA, M.: Sur le Concept de Macroplace et son Utilisation pour l'Analyse des Reseaux de Petri. *RAIRO-Systems Analysis and Control, Vol. 15, No. 4*, pp. 335-345.

[Silv 85]   SILVA, M.: *Las redes de Petri: en la Automática y la Informática.* Editorial AC, Madrid.

[Silv 87]   SILVA, M.: Towards a Synchrony Theory for P/T Nets. *Concurrency and Nets (Voss, K.; Genrich, H.J., Rozenberg, G.; eds.)*, Springer-Verlag, Berlin, pp. 315-336.

[SC 87]   SILVA, M.; COLOM, J.M.: On the computation of Structural Synchronic Invariants in P/T nets. *Advances in Petri Nets'87 (G. Rozenberg, ed.), LNCS 340*, Springer-Verlag, Berlin, pp. 306-417.

[TV 84]   THIAGARAJAN, P.S.; VOSS, K.: A Fresh look at free Choice Nets. *Information and Control, Vol. 61, No. 2*, May, pp. 85-113.

[Vogl 89]   VOGLER, W.: Live and Bounded Free Choice Nets have Home States. *Newsletter of the GI Special Interest Group in Petri Nets and Related System Models, No. 32*, pp. 18-21.

Petri Net Models of a Distributed Election Protocol on a Unidirectional Ring

Gérard FLORIN,

Claude KAISER,

Stéphane NATKIN

CEDRIC (Centre d'Etudes et de Recherche en Informatique du CNAM)

CONSERVATOIRE NATIONAL DES ARTS ET METIERS

292, rue Saint Martin - 75141 PARIS cedex 03 - FRANCE

Tel.: (1) 40 27 22 77

ABSTRACT This paper is devoted to the performance analysis of an election protocol for a unidirectional ring proposed by C.Kaiser. We give two models of increasing complexity in order to compute several performance criteria. The two models (called initiation model and evaluation model) are defined using coloured Petri nets. For these models several qualitative properties are proven. Then the required performance criteria are computed using an original computation method defined for non repetitive stochastic Petri net.

Keywords:distributed algorithms, election protocols, formal proof, performance evaluation, stochastic Petri nets.

CONTENTS

INTRODUCTION

An election protocol on a unidirectional ring of processors [GAR 81, LEL 77, RAY 85] is a distributed algorithm that elects a unique processor as a leader. This selected processor act, for instance, as a distributed protocol coordinator.

This problem has been stated by Lelann [LEL 77] for recovering from token failure. Chang and Roberts [CHA 79] have proposed the idea of message extinction which is the underlying principle of all the classical algorithms for unidirectional as well as for bidirectional rings. The Chang-Roberts protocol leads to a traffic in $O(n.\log n)$ elementary messages and to a response time in $O(3n)$.

This paper deals with the analysis of a distributed algorithm proposed by C.Kaiser [KAI 89]. The discussion that follows and another analytic study [JEA 88] show that this algorithm leads to a higher traffic but to a lower response time than the classical algorithms. The latter performance aspect may be of particular interest for real time applications.

The first section of the paper is devoted to an unformal presentation of the algorithm. Although our focus is indeed on analytic techniques, the methodology presented here starts from coloured Petri nets models [JEN 81]. These models are designed to prove some properties of the algorithm but mainly to compute several performance criteria using the stochastic Petri net and coloured stochastic Petri net method [FLO 85] [ZEN 85]. So in the second section we present two coloured stochastic Petri nets models of the election algorithm. These models have an increasing complexity and are designed to apply to the evaluation of specific criteria with the minimum expansion of the state space. The last section is devoted to the formal proofs and to the presentation of numerical results.

I ELECTION ON A UNIDIRECTIONAL RING

I.1 Hypothesis

We consider a set of n processors linked by a ring network. We number processors according to their relative positions on the ring (processor P_i is linked to its predecessor $P_{i-1 \bmod(n)}$ and its successor $P_{i+1 \bmod(n)}$). We assume that the processors work fully asynchronously and communicate by messages. Messages can be sent on the network in one direction only, from a processor to its successor.

We assume also that the processors and the communication subsystem work error-free during the election. The transmission delays are variable but finite.

At the beginning of an election each processor knows its name, which is unique in the ring. Without loss of generality we consider that names of processors are defined as a permutation of their numbering. A processor does not know neither the name of other processors nor the number n of processors i.e. the ring size.

I.2 Election Protocol

Initially a processor (Ni) is in the *neutral* state. This processor can decide to begin an election and to be an enabled candidate. It reaches the initiator state and sends a recognition message *recognition (Ni,Nl)*. The first field is the initiator name and remains constant during the election. Nl is initially set to Ni. During a traversal of the ring by the the recognition message, this field contains the lowest name of the "candidate" processors which have been visited by the message.

But the processor may receive a message before sending its own recognition message. The processor then knows that an election is in progress. In this case the processor will not be candidate. It reaches the *inhibited* state.

In the initiator state, when processor Ni receives a recognition message: recognition (Nj,Nl), two cases must be considered. If Nj≠Ni, the processor modifies the lowest name field and sends the recognition message: recognition(Nj,inf(Nl,Ni)). If Nj=Ni, the message generated by Ni has completed a traversal of the ring. The processor knows the name of the leader Nl. It becomes *informed* and sends an election message *election (Nl)*.

In the same initiated state, a processor can receive an election message: election (Nl). Then the processor knows the name of the leader Nl. It becomes informed and propagates the election message.

The only action performed by a processor in the inhibited state is the propagation of messages. Moreover the reception of an election message induces a transition to the informed state.

In informed state, the leader is known : redundant recognition messages or election messages must be withdrawn.

The possible state transitions are given Figure 1.

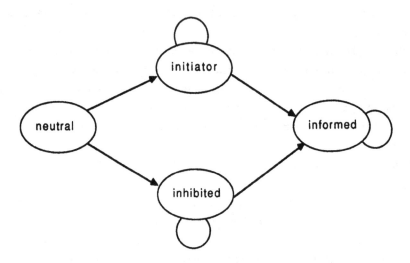

Figure 1 : State transitions diagram

I.3 Basic properties of the protocol

The uniqueness of the processor identification is sufficient to determine the leader : it is the minimum of the finite set of names (the names of processors which have sent a recognition message). Thus an enumeration of the complete set, i.e. a traversal of the whole ring, allows finding the leader.

Once initiator, a processor cannot be able to initiate a recognition. Thus the presence or absence of a processor in the set of enabled candidates is the first decision performed by this processor and its decision will never be reconsidered.

This stable property of each processor guarantees that each sequential computation performed uses the same set of decision data. Therefore, the same result is delivered to each candidate processor. This is the key of the proof of the protocol.

With this protocol, any initiator knows the leader when its recognition message has returned, i.e. after exactly one round on the ring. The election is completed, i.e. every processor knows the leader, after at most two rounds on the ring. If p initiators are present, there is a corresponding traffic of n x p elementary messages for recognition, and n elementary messages for election. So the traffic is (p + 1) x n elementary messages for an election.

II PETRI NETS MODELS

II.1 Modeling principles

II.1.1 Modeling requirements

Petri nets can be used to prove the correctness of election protocols: all the sites have to be informed of the existence of a new leader, the leader identification must be unique and the same for all sites, and the leader itself must be aware of its new role.

Stochastic Petri nets can be used for performance evaluations of distributed algorithms: they allow to model the asynchronous behaviour of the processors and to cope with variable and unbounded transmission delays.

Two performance aspects are of interest: traffic and time.

The traffic is measured by the number of elementary messages exchanged between two adjacents processors.

The time efficiency of the protocol is measured by:

-the *recovering time*, or the *restarting time*, which is the delay between the emission of the first recognition message and the moment at which a processor is the first informed of the leader name.

-the *completion time* which is the delay between the emission of the first recognition message and the reception of the last message exchanged on the ring,

-the *initiation period* which is the delay between the emission of the first recognition message and the departure from neutral state by the last processor.

II.1.2 Modeling approach for the election protocol

In this section, we recall the usual applications of Petri nets, we propose a "one execution" model corresponding to election protocols and present our methodology.

II.1.2.1 Usual applications of Petri nets

Petri nets and stochastic Petri nets modeling generally deal with systems designed to perform infinitely often some sequences of operations in a steady state behaviour. Validation methods try to prove properties of the model as : assertions on the reachable markings, liveness of the net, existence of home states etc ...

Stochastic evaluation often assumes a recurrence property of the marking process [FLO 85] and try to compute steady states mean markings or expected firing flows of transitions. Recurrent Markov stochastic Petri net performance evaluation relies on the Petri net reachability graph generation followed by linear systems resolution. For these systems the rank is equal to the number of reachable markings.

II.1.2.2 One execution models

We have taken another point of view in the modeling of election protocols. As a matter of fact an election is basically a "one shot" operation which is performed when some exceptional event occurs. A typical application is the election of a new master station in an IEEE 802.5 token ring. Such an election is done when the preceding master has failed.

So we have designed Petri nets, the behaviour of which describes one execution of the election protocol. We prove in the last section of this paper that these nets are non repetitive, i.e. Petri nets that does not have repetitive firing sequences of transitions. These nets are bounded and are not alive. The reachability relation between marking is a partial order. Non repetitive nets invariants allow to prove some election models qualitative properties (for instance the termination property).

The preceding modeling approach can also be efficiently applied to performance evaluation. Non repetitive stochastic Petri net performance criteria, can be computed during the reachability generation phase, storing a few markings and without backtracking. The theoretical basis of this approach has been settled to compute the reliability of non repairable systems [FRA 88], [BAR 88]. In the last section of the paper we briefly summerize the principles of this evaluation method.

II.1.2.3 Methodology

The validation method is based on invariants of the nets, the computation complexity of which depends essentially on the number of places and transitions. But the performance evaluation needs the generation of the reachability graph the complexity of which drastically increases with the number of reachable markings.

So we have designed two election models of increasing complexity. Each model involves only the information needed to compute a given performance criterion. This approach allows to master the complexity of Petri net models. The simplest net is designed to compute the mean number of elementary message (traffic criterion) and the mean duration of the initiation phase (initiation period criterion). It allows to compute quantitative results for larger ring than the second one. The second model can be used to compute all others time performance criteria (mean response time, mean restarting time and mean completion time). Two performance evaluation models using the same stochastic Petri net are distinguished by a boolean function (mission function) that select a set of markings such that a given phase is in progress.

II.2 The Initiation Petri net

II.2.1 Modeling principles

As it was stated in the first section, the number of messages sent during the election protocol is proportional to the number of initiators p. This number is known when the initiation phase ends. Our first and simplest Petri net is designed to model the behaviour of processors in initiation phase. It allows to compute the distribution of the initiators number and the moments of the initiation phase duration.

An election starts when a first processor decides to send a recognition message and becomes initiator. The initiation period ends when the last processor leaves the neutral states. At this time the number of initiator p is determined. As no messages have completed a turn of the ring, all messages are of the recognition kind and the number of these messages is equal to p.

So the first Petri net model does not distinguish neither the type of messages (which are all recognition messages) nor the data included in these messages which are only used to determine the end of the election and the name of the leader.

II.2.2 Petri Net description

We assume without loss of generality that the processor P_0 is the first initiator. We model an "open" ring, where no messages are received by P_0 from its predecessor P_{n-1} on the ring. As a matter of fact recognition messages received by P_{n-1} before the arrival of P_0 recognition message, are stopped in P_{n-1}. The first recognition message passing determines the state of a processor (initiator or inhibited) and the following messages only visit the site.

The set of colors used in this model are associated with n processors connected in the ring topology:

$$processors = \{ P_0, P_1, \ldots P_{n-1}\}$$

We use also the two following subsets of Processors:

$$predecessors = \{ P_0, P_1, \ldots P_{n-2}\}$$

$$successors = \{ P_1, P_2, \ldots P_{n-1}\}$$

The net has three places:

- neutral which is marked by a P_i coloured token when the ith processor is in the neutral state.
- advertized which is marked by a P_i coloured token when the ith processor is initiator or inhibited.
- ring which is marked by k P_{i-1} coloured tokens when the ith processor has k recognition messages received from its predecessor and waiting in its input message queue.

The three transitions are associated with the following events:

- neutral_to_initiator is fired when a processor decide to be a candidate. This processor becomes advertized and a message is send to its successor.
- neutral_to_inhibited is fired when a processor receives a recognition message in the neutral state. The processor becomes

advertized and the message is propagated to its successor.

- message_propagation is fired when a processor receives a recognition message in the advertized state. The message is propagated to the successor.

All these transitions are coloured on the set of processors.

The routing of messages along the ring is modelled using the function pred from the set of successors into the set of predecessors:

$$pred(P_i) = P_{i-1}$$

A message in the input queue of processor i is represented by a $pred(P_i)$ coloured token in place ring. When this message is sent to processor P_{i+1} , the token color becomes P_i.

The function id is the identity mapping.

As the election begins when processor P_0 decides to be the first initiator, initially places advertized and ring contains a P_0 coloured token, and place neutral contains a token of each color in the set successors.

According to these notations our first coloured Petri Net model is given figure 2. We present figure 3 the listing of the same coloured Petri net model in the DEOL language which is the interface language of the RDPS tool used for the validation and evaluation given in this paper [FLO 86]. The text can be easily understood from the preceding Petri net definition. Just notice that in this language the notation neutral(X) is an abbreviation for neutral(id(X)).

II.3 A complete evaluation Petri net model

The next model allows to compute all performance criteria (more precisely the moments of response time, restarting time and completion time). The election feature which is not modeled is the leader name. Hence the known extremum field of recognition messages and the leader number field of election messages is not described. The ring model is now a closed ring where P_{n-1} is the predecessor of P_0.

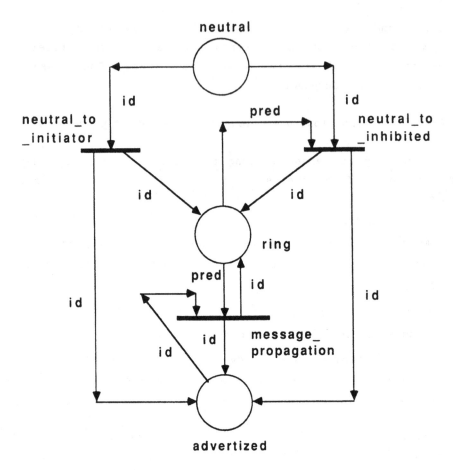

Figure 2: The initiation period Petri net model

```
/* Initiation phase for a 4 processor ring                        */
PROGRAM initiation_4 ;

/* Color sets declaration                                         */
TYPE processors   = [P0,P1,P2,P3] ;
TYPE predecessors = [P0,P1,P2] ;
TYPE successors   = [P1,P2,P3] ;
VAR X : successors ;

/* Place and transition declaration                              */
PLACE neutral, advertized, ring : processors ;
TRANS neutral_to_initiator, neutral_to_inhibited : processors ;
TRANS message_propagation : processors;

/* Function pred declaration                                      */
FUNCTION pred(successors)->predecessors ;
P1->P0; P2->P1; P3->P2;
END_FUNCTION;

/* Coloured Petri net graph declaration                          */
WHEN neutral(X) DO
              neutral_to_initiator : advertized(X) AND ring(X);
WHEN neutral(X) AND ring(pred(X)) DO
              neutral_to_inhibited: advertized(X) AND ring(X);
WHEN advertized(X) AND ring(pred(X)) DO
           message_propagation: advertized(X) AND ring(X);

/* Initial marking declaration                                    */
INITIAL
advertized.P0 :=1 ;
ring.P0       :=1 ;
neutral.P1    :=1 ;
neutral.P2    :=1 ;
neutral.P3    :=1 ;
END

/* End of initiation_4 program                                    */
END
```

Figure 3: The initiation period Petri net DEOL program

II.3.1 Colors

a) Processors (defined as in the preceding Petri Net)

processors = { P_o, P_1, ... P_{n-1}}

b) Recognition messages

rec_mes = { R_o, R_1, ... R_{n-1} }

R_i is the recognition message send by the ith processor.

c) Election messages

elc_mess = { election }

d) The following sets derived from the preceding ones are used in the Petri net model:

- messages = rec_mess U elc_mess

(where operator U denotes the union of sets)

- messages_on_ring = processors X messages

(where operator X denotes the cartesian product of sets)

An element $(P_{i-1 \ mod(n)}, M_k)$ of this set is used to define an M_k message stored in the input queue of the processor P_i.

The three following sets define a partition of messages_on_ring into :

a) election messages,

- elc_on_ring = { $(P_i, \text{election})$ }

b) recognition messages when they are first emitted,

- rec_from_me = { (P_i, R_i) }

c) recognition messages received by a processor which is not their emittor.

- rec_from_others = { $(P_i, R_k) / i \neq k$ }

II.3.2 Functions

The following functions are used in the coloured Petri net model. In order to simplify the presentation we use the same name for functions defined on subsets of a given set .

a) Function site defines the receiver of a message.

site (messages_on_ring->processors) : site$((P_i, M_k))$ = P_i

b) Function pred models the routing on the ring.

pred(messages_on_ring -> messages_on_ring)

pred$((P_i,M_k)) = (P_{i-1 \bmod(n)},M_k)$

c) Function send_elc is used when a recognition message comes back in a processor. This processor generates an election message.

send_elc (rec_from_me -> elc_on_ring)

send_elc$((P_i,R_i)) = (P_i,$election $)$

II.3.3 Places and transitions

a) Places

Places neutral, initiator, inhibited, informed contain a P_i coloured token if the ith processor is in the corresponding state. Place ring contain messages_on_ring tokens and has the same meaning than in the previous net.

b) Transitions

- Neutral_to_initiator is a rec_from_me coloured transition. If place neutral contains a P_i = site$((P_i,R_i))$ token then the state of the corresponding processor becomes initiator and a (P_i,R_i) token is added to place ring (this means that this message is sent).

- Neutral_to_inhibited is a rec_from_others coloured transition. If the ring place contains a pred$((P_i,R_k)) = (P_{i-1\bmod(n)},R_k)$ token such that i≠k this means that the ith processor has received a recognition messaged issued fom an other processor. If the ith processor is in neutral state (place neutral contains a P_i=site$((P_i,R_k))$ token) then this processor becomes inhibited and a R_k message is propagated along the ring (a (P_i,R_k) token is added to the mark of ring).

- Inhibited_propagation is a rec_from_others coloured transition. If place ring contains a pred$((P_i,R_k))$ token such that i≠k and the ith processor is in the inhibited state (inhibited contains a P_i=site (P_i,R_k) token) then the state of this processor remains unchanged and the R_k message is propagated.

- Leader_known is an elc_on_ring coloured transition. If place ring contains a pred$((P_i,$election $))$ token and the ith processor is in the inhibited state (inhibited contains a site$(P_i,$election$)$

token) then the name of the leader is known by this processor. The ith processor reaches the informed state and the election message is propagated.

- Elc_mess_arr is also an elc_on_ring coloured transition. It has quite the same meaning than leader_known, except that it is fired when the ith processor is in the initiator state. The ith processor reaches the informed state and the election message is propagated.

- End_of_turn is an elc_on_ring coloured transition. If a processor receives its recognition message in the state initiator (initiator marked by a site$((P_i,R_i))$ token and ring marked by a (P_i,R_i) token), it knows the leader name. The ith processor reaches the informed state and an election message is sent (ring marked by a $(P_i,$election$)=$ send_elc$((P_i,R_i))$ token).

Notice that in the two preceding transitions the leader can be either the ith processor itself or an other processor. The distinction between these two cases depends on the extremum field value. This is not described in this model.

- Initiator_propagation is a rec_from_others coloured transition. It is similar to the inhibited_propagation transition fired from the initiator state.

- Destroy_messages is a message_on _ring coloured transition. If a processor receives a message when it is informed (ring marked by a (P_i,M_k) token and informed marked by a site$((P_i,M_k))$ token it destroys the message and remains in the same state.

III MODEL ANALYSIS

III.1 Non repetitive stochastic Petri nets

III.1.1 Introduction

In this section we present the qualitative and quantitative properties for the preceding election protocol models.

These models are defined using coloured Petri nets but the analysis is expressed in term of the corresponding expanded Place Transition nets [JEN 81].

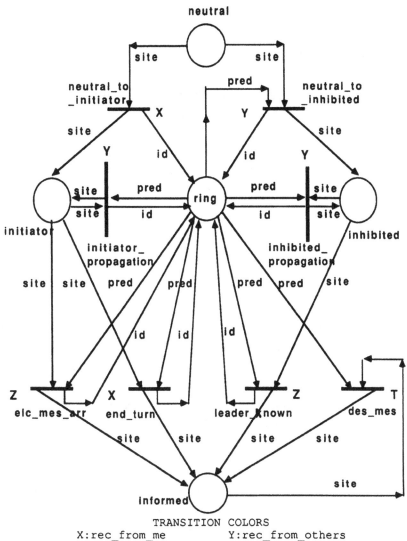

TRANSITION COLORS
X:rec_from_me   Y:rec_from_others
Z:elc_on_ring   T:messages_on_ring

FIGURE 4: THE EVALUATION PETRI NET

We denote in the expanded P-T net:

- P the set of places (with cardinality |P|)
- T the set of transitions T (with cardinality |T|)
- C the incidence matrix of the net
- M_0 the initial marking of the net.

Performance evaluations are carried out using markovian
stochastic Petri nets [Flo 85]. The infinitesimal generator
associated with a markovian SPN is denoted by A = (a_{ij}) where a_{ij} is

the firing rate of the transition which firing leads from a marking M_i to a marking M_j. Numerical computation are done using the RDPS stochastic Petri net tool [Flo 86].

III.1.2 Definition and properties of non repetitive stochastic Petri nets (SPN)

The election protocol is an example of a system that evolves in the following way. A state reached and left will never be reached again. This property can be expressed in term of Petri nets invariants.

Definition

A non repetitive markovian Petri net is a markovian SPN such that:

$$\not\exists X \in \mathbb{N}^{|T|} , \quad X \neq 0 , \quad \text{such that } C.X \geq 0$$

As a consequence of this definition ,for all initial marking, the net is bounded, not alive and has no repetitive sequences [BRA 81}.

Theorem

For any initial marking the relation M_i is directly reachable from M_j is a strict partial order relation on the set of markings.

Corollary

All strongly connected sets of the reachability graph are reduced to one marking and, consequently, minimal strongly connected sets are pending markings (absorbing states in stochastic processes terminology).

The principles of the qualitative and quantitative analysis of non repetitive SPN rely on the following result, which is a consequence of classical nets invariant theory.

Theorem

A SPN is non repetitive if and only if:

$$\exists f \in \mathbb{N}^{|P|} \quad \text{such that} \quad f^t.C < 0$$

f is called a sub p-invariant and f^t is the transposed vector of f.

Corollary

Let f be a sub p-invariant of a non repetitive SPN. The function $LV(M_i) = f^t.M_i$ defined on the set of markings M_i reachable from an initial marking M_0 is strictly decreasing with the lenght of the longest path leading from M_0 to M_i. Such a function is called in the sequel a level function.

III.1.3 Qualitative Analysis

The validation of the election model is developped as follows.

a) We find a sub p-invariant of the net. Hence the net is non repetitive and the protocol terminates. The sub invariant is chosen such that the function $LV(M_i)$ is lower bounded by some value Vmin.

b) We show that this bound is reached on all pending markings. Thus the protocol terminates always in the same manner with no more messages on the ring.

c) Finally the value Vmin is used to prove that pending markings verify an assertion on informed processors. Thus the protocol implements this assertion which one of its main specifications.

Computation of sub invariants in the RDPS tool relies on the solution of linear programs [FRA 88]. This numerical solution depends of course on the ring size. From several experiences on various ring models we have been able to derive a formal expression of sub invariants and to give a proof that does not depend on the ring size. The full demonstration is given for the evaluation net.

III.1.4 Quantitative Analysis

The main parameters to be computed on a non repetitive SPN are the moments of the sojourn time in transient states, the absorption probability distribution. In this section we just recall the principles of this computation on an absorbing continuous time Markov chain [COR 75].

The generator $A = (a_{ij})$ has only two non null submatrices:

- The matrix A1 of transitions rates leading from a transient state to an other transient state. If k_1 is the number of transient states the order of A1 is (k_1, k_1).

- The matrix A2 of transitions rates leading from a transient state to an absorbing state. If k_2 is the number of absorbing states the order of A2 is (k_1, k_2).

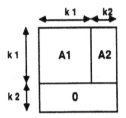

Let $T^{(o)} = (1, 0, ..., 0)$ be the (k_1) initial distribution vector (the probability of the initial marking at time 0 is equal to 1), P^* the (k_2) vector which component $P^*(i)$ is the probability to be absorbed by state M_i; $e(k_i)$ is the (k_i) column vector which components are all equal to one and $t^{(n)}$ the nth moment of the sojourn time in the set of transient states. P^* and the moments $t^{(n)}$ can be computed as follows.

Let $T^{(n)}$ be the solution of the linear system :

$T^{(n)} \cdot A1 = -n \cdot T^{(n-1)}$ with $n > 0$

then $P^* = T^{(1)} \cdot A2$ and $t^{(n)} = T^{(n)} \cdot e(k_1)$

Theorem

There is a numbering of the markings of a non repetitive SPN such that the infinitesimal generator A is triangular.

It is clear that, since in our case the matrix A has a triangular structure, the previous set of linear equations can be easily solved. Moreover if the markings are generated in a "correct" order (if a marking is generated after all its predecessors) this computation can be done during the the reachability graph generation without storing the whole matrix and without backtracking. This goal is reached using a level function.

The generation algorithm proceeds as follows.

- At a given iteration of the generation, let V be the greatest value of the level function such that all the markings with value V are generated and all their consequent transitions are fired. Let V' be the highest value such that V'<V and $\exists$ M_i such that $f^t M_i = V'$. From the monotonic property of the level function it can be easily shown that all markings with level value V' are then generated.

- All the enabled transitions in markings such that $f^t M_i = V'$ are then fired .If M_i is transient, the values $T^n(i)$ are computed and for each marking M_j directly reachable from M_i, the contributions of M_i to the jth moments equations are computed. If M_i is absorbing the absorption probability is computed. In both cases M_i is forgotten.

III.2 Qualitative analysis of the evaluation net

We denote <name_of_a_place>.<name_of_a_color> the name of a place in the expanded place transition net of a coloured net, f(<name_of_a_place>.<name_of_a_color>) is the corresponding component of the sub p-invariant f.

Theorem

The vector f defined by :

$$f(neutral.P_i) = n+3$$
$$f(initiator.P_i) = 1$$
$$f(inhibited.P_i) = 1$$
$$f(informed.Pi) = 0$$
$$f(ring.P_iR_k) = (n+k-i-1) \bmod (n) + 2$$
$$f(ring.P_ielection) = 1$$

is a sub invariant of the evaluation net

The proof relies on the following lemma which demonstration is left to the reader.

LEMMA $\forall i$, $\forall k$ $0 \leq i < n$ $0 \leq k < n$ $i \neq k$

$$-f(ring.P_{i-1 \bmod (n)}R_k) + f(ring.P_iR_k) = -1$$

We prove that $f^t \cdot C < 0$ by considering successively each transition.

a) neutral_to_initiator:

- $f(\text{neutral}.P_i) + f(\text{initiator}.P_i) + f(\text{ring}.P_iR_i) = -(n+3)+1+n+1 = -1$

b) neutral_to_inhibited:

$-f(\text{neutral}.P_i)+f(\text{inhibited}.P_i)-f(\text{ring}.P_{i-1\text{mod}(n)}R_k)+f(\text{ring}.P_iR_k)=$
$$-(n+3)+1-1 = -(n+3)$$

c) initiator_propagation:

$-f(\text{initiator}.P_i)+f(\text{initiator}.P_i)-f(\text{ring}.P_{i-1\text{mod}(n)}R_k)+f(\text{ring}.P_iR_k)=$
$$-1+1-1 = -1$$

d) inhibited_propagation:

$-f(\text{inhibited}.P_i)+f(\text{inhibited}.P_i)-f(\text{ring}.P_{i-1\text{mod}(n)}R_k)+f(\text{ring}.P_iR_k)=$
$$-1+1-1 = -1$$

e) elc_mess_arr

$-f(\text{initiator}.P_i)+f(\text{informed}.P_i)-f(\text{ring}.P_i\text{election})$
$$+f(\text{ring}.P_i\text{election})=-1+0-1+1 = -1$$

f) end_turn

$-f(\text{initiator}.P_i)+f(\text{informed}.P_i)-f(\text{ring}.P_{i-1\text{mod}(n)}R_i)+$
$$f(\text{ring}.P_i\text{election})=-1+0-2+1 = -1$$

g) leader_known

$-f(\text{inhibited}.P_i)+f(\text{informed}.P_i)-f(\text{ring}.P_{i-1\text{mod}(n)}R_i)+$
$$f(\text{ring}.P_i\text{election})=-1+0-2+1 = -1$$

h) destroy_messages

$$- f(\text{ring}.P_iM_k) - f(\text{informed}.P_i) + f(\text{informed}.P_i) < 0$$

Theorem

The reachability graph has only one pending marking which is such that all processors are informed and no messages are on the ring.

a) In the sub p-invariant f, all places (informed excepted) have a strictly positive weight. So it is clear that $LV(M_i) \geq 0$ for all markings. If $LV(M_i)=0$ there is no more messages on the ring and all processors are informed.

b) We prove that there is no pending markings such that

$LV(M_i)>0$.

- If $LV(M_i)>0$ at least one processor is not informed or a message is still on the ring.

If Mi is a pending marking no processor can be in state neutral for neutral_to_initiator would be enabled.

- Mi cannot be such that all processor are informed and some messages are still on the ring since in that case destroy_messages would be enabled.

- If we assume that at least one processor Pi is not informed (it can be either initiator or inhibited) and no message are on the ring. Its predecessor $P_{i-1mod(n)}$ cannot be informed for transitions to the informed state generate P_{i-1} election messages sent to P_i, and P_i would be informed.

So by transitivity no processor is informed. As in states inhibited and initiator no message is destroyed, this is possible only if no messages have never been on the ring. This is impossible for one message is initially on the ring.

- If we assume now that there is, in a pending state at least one message on the ring and a processor not informed. Let PiMk be such a message. Pi cannot be informed for destroy_messages would be enabled. Pi cannot be in initiator state because :

if Mk=Ri then end_turn would be firable,

if Mk=Rs s≠i initiator_propagation would be enabled

if Mk=election elc_mess_arr would be enabled.

For the same arguments Pi cannot be inhibited (any type of messages enables one transitions from this state).

Hence there is no pending marking such that $LV(M_i) > 0$.

c) As the net is non repetitive it is bounded and it has at least one pending marking. This marking must be such that $LV(M_i) = 0$. It is the unique marking such that all processors are informed and there is no message left on the ring.

III.3 Quantitative Analysis

III.3.1 Introduction

In this section we present the numerical results obtained using the non repetitive stochastic Petri net computation method.

There are two classes of results.

- First and second moment of time spent in a transient class of markings selected by a boolean function before absorption by the complementary class.
- Absorption probability distribution.

Numerical results computation needs to associate with each coloured net transition a firing rate. These rates are defined on the following basis:
- All operations duration are exponentially distributed
- The mean time to send a message on a communication line is

$1/\mu$

- The mean time spent by a processor to decide to become an initiator and to send its recognition message is $1/\lambda$ $(\lambda < \mu)$.

In all considered experiences we have taken $1/\lambda = 1$ (which can be considered as the time unit).

III.3.2 Initiation Petri net results

In the following experiences μ is constant (=2.) and the ring size (n) is taken as variable.

The initiation phase boolean function defines the set of markings such that there is at least one processor in neutral state.

The following array (figure 5) gives the mean number of initiators p, the mean initiation·period and the standard deviation of initiation period.

ring size	2	4	6	8	10
p	1,33	2,40	3,58	4,77	5,97
mean initiation period	0.333	0.767	1,011	1,169	1,297
standard deviation of initiation period	0.333	0.456	0,487	0,496	0,497
number of markings	3	37	508	8346	114495

Figure 5 :Means of the initiation net model criteria

Notice that the mean initiation period increases approximatively with the ring size logarithm. It can be shown [JEA 88] that this relation is asymptotically exact.

The software tool computes the distribution of p (i.e. the number of initiators) (figure 6). This unimodal distribution seems to be closed to a truncated gaussian functions. It tends asymptotically to a Dirac distribution [JEA 88].

DISTRIBUTION OF p

n	1	2	3	4	5	6	7	8	9	10
2	0,667	0,333								
4	0,133	0,422	0,356	0,089						
6	0,013	0,128	0,331	0,345	0,157	0,026				
8	0,001	0,019	0,116	0,274	0,321	0,199	0,062	0,008		
10	2.E-4	0,002	0,023	0,104	0,233	0,295	0,221	0,097	0,023	0,002

Figure 6 : Number of initiators distribution

A ten processor ring initiation period model leads to generate about 115000 reachable markings (and to solve two linear systems of the same order). As shown before our algorithm does not imply to keep the whole reachability graph in memory. Nevertheless in the worst computation phase it is necessary to store up to 22000 markings simultaneously.

A non repetitive stochastic petri net model of the SIFT computer system reliability has been solved using the same algorithm [FRA 88]. It leads to a one million markings graph, the computation of which takes about twenty four hours on a VAX 8250.

III.3.3 Evaluation net results

We have used the evaluation net to study the transmission delay influence on the main performance criteria. The ring size is constant (n=4). The figure 7 shows the mean values of initiation period, recovering time, completion delay and number of initiators p as function of μ.

Several comments can be made on this figure:

- Previous models of election protocols assume a synchronous behaviour of the communication ring (i.e tokens moves together from processors to processors). In a synchronous model the mean recovering time is equal to $(n-1)/\mu$ (by hypothesis the election begins when the first message is sent) and mean initiation period, mean recovering time and mean transmission time are proportional to $1/\mu$. As our model is fully asynchronous, this introduces queuing transmission delays and explains why the previous parameters are greater in our model than in synchronous ones.

- It is intuitively clear and it can be proved that p tends to 1 as $1/\mu$ tends to 0. The model shows that this convergence is very slow.

μ	2	4	8	16
mean initiation period	0,767	0,500	0,298	0,162
mean recovering time	1,527	0,833	0,447	0,235
mean completion time	2,794	1,500	0,795	0,414
P	2,40	1,94	1,57	1,325

**Figure 7 Mean times and number of initiators
as a function of μ (n=4)**

CONCLUSION

In this paper we have presented two non repetitive stochastic coloured Petri net models. These models are designed to evaluate distributed computations on unidirectional rings. The distributed computation is done by traversal on a ring and stabilization of the number of simultaneous traversals. We have considered as an example an election protocol proposed by C Kaiser. This protocol finds an extremum on a set of values.

A method which allows validation and performance of non repetitive stochastic petri nets models has been developped. This method, which was initially designed for reliability analysis, has been successfully applied to this distributed computing problem. We have been able to prove that the algorithm terminates correctly and we have obtained several numerical results. The first model allows to count the number of simultaneous traversals and to determine the date of the stabilization. The second model allows to evaluate several durations related to the traversal of the ring and in particular the computation of duration moments.

A full election protocol model can be derived from the evaluation net. The leader number determination modeling is obtained by a slight modification of color sets and of the functions definition. But these modifications increase drastically the model computation complexity. The only purposes of such a complete model is specification and validation since the evaluation net allows to compute all performance criteria needed.

Extensions of this work may be the analysis of communications or processors failure influence on the previous algorithm and the study of distributed computation on bidirectional rings [CHA 79], [KAI 89].

REFERENCES

[BAR 88] K.Barkaoui, G.Florin, C.Fraize, B.Lemaire, S.Natkin Reliability Analysis of Non Repairable Systems using Stochastic Petri Nets, proc FTCS 18, Tokyo ,july 88.

[BRA 81] G. W. Brams, Les réseaux de Petri: Théorie et pratique, Masson ed, Paris 1981.

[CHA 79] CHANG E.J., ROBERTS R. An Improved Algorithm for Decentralized Extrema - Finding in Circular Configurations of Processors. Comm.ACM vol 22,5 (May 1979) pp 281-283.

[COR 75] M.Corazza, Techniques mathématiques de la fiabilité prévisionnelle, Cepadues ed, Toulouse 1975.

[FLO 85] FLORIN G., NATKIN S. Les réseaux de Petri stochastiques.TSI vol 4,1 (1985) pp 143-160.

[FLO 86] G. Florin, S. Natkin, "RDPS: a software package for the evaluation and the validation of dependable computer systems", SAFECOMP86, Sarlat, France, 1986.

[FRA 88] FRAIZE C. Les réseaux de Petri stochastiques a graphe de marquages sans circuits: Theorie et application a l'analyse de la fiabilite et des performances des systemes informatiques Ingeneer dissertation, CNAM, Paris, October 1988.

[JEA 88] JEAN-MARIE A.,BACCELLI F. The Centaurs race, INRIA research report, august 88.

[JEN 81] JENSEN K. Coloured Petri Nets and the Invariant Method, Theoretical Computer Science 14 (1981)

[GAR 81] GARCIA MOLINA H. Elections in a Distributed Computing system. IEEE Trans on Soft.Eng. Vol 31,1 (Jan 1981) p 48-59.

[KAI 89] KAISER C. Election sur un anneau par parcours de reconnaissance ;TSI vol 8 No 3, 1989 (Also available as CEDRIC research report).

[LEL 77] LELANN G. Distributed Systems. Towards a Formal Approach. IFIP Congress 1977. North Holland (1977) pp 155-160.

[RAY 85] RAYNAL M. Algorithmes distribués et protocoles. Eyrolles (1985) 142 p.

[ZEN 85] ZENIE A. Coloured Stochastic Petri nets,Int . Workshop on Timed Petri nets, Torino,Italy, July 1985

Hierarchies in Coloured Petri Nets

Peter Huber*, Kurt Jensen*† & Robert M. Shapiro*

* Meta Software Corporation
150 Cambridge Park Drive
Cambridge, MA 02140, USA

† Aarhus University
Computer Science Department
DK-8000 Aarhus C, Denmark

ABSTRACT The paper shows how to extend Coloured Petri Nets with a hierarchy concept. The paper proposes five different hierarchy constructs, which allow the analyst to structure large CP-nets as a set of interrelated subnets (called pages). The paper discusses the properties of the proposed hierarchy constructs, and it illustrates them by means of two examples. The hierarchy constructs can be used for theoretical considerations, but their main use is to describe and analyse large real-world systems. All of the hierarchy constructs are supported by the editing and analysis facilities in the CPN Palette tool package (see [1-5]).

<u>Keywords</u> high-level nets, Coloured Petri Nets, structuring mechanisms, hierarchies, re-usable components, subnets.

CONTENTS

0. Introduction

This paper is an introduction to hierarchical Coloured Petri Nets (CP-nets). It shows how a set of subnets, called pages, can be related to each other – in such a way that they together constitute a single model. The basic idea is to allow the system modeller to describe a set of submodels which all contribute to a much larger model – in which the submodels interact with each other in a well-defined way. This idea is well known from other kinds of artificial languages, e.g. submodels in SADT and subroutines in programming languages. The purpose is to break down the complexity of the large model, by dividing it into a number of submodels.

It is important not to confuse this idea of hierarchical nets with the many approaches which relate two or more separate subnets to each other *without* combining them into a single model. In these approaches each page defines its own model – and the goal of the approach is to compare these individual models – e.g. showing that they have an equivalent behaviour or that they describe the system from different viewpoints [6,7]. In the domain of programming languages, these latter approaches are equivalent to program transformations. The models are different descriptions of the same system – and they are not used to obtain a larger and more complex description.

Although our main objective is to synthesize large models from smaller submodels, our approach also has some elements which allow the user to create a number of related models. However, each of these models are usually synthesized from several submodels. The idea is most easily explained by considering our notion of a substitution node, which is a place or a transition related to a submodel. Usually, the submodel totally replaces the substitution node and the surrounding arcs, and hence it doesn't make sense to say that a substitution transition occurs or a substitution place is marked. The substitution node is not itself part of the final model – its role is merely to describe how the related submodel is inserted in the synthesized model (in the same way as an in-line subroutine call describes where to insert the subroutine code). During the analysis of a complex system it is often convenient temporarily to be able to ignore parts of the model – or replace them with simpler components. In our methodology we achieve this by allowing the user to specify, for each substitution node, whether the related subpage should be included in the current synthesized model or not. When the submodel isn't included, the substitution node becomes an ordinary node. This means that the node can occur (if it is a transition) or become marked (if it is a place). In order for this to be useful it is of course necessary that there be some formal or informal correspondence between the behaviour described by the model in which the submodel is inserted and the model in which the substitution node is an ordinary node. Probably the most obvious relationship is to make the two models equivalent. This means that the substitution node with its surrounding arcs is behaviourally equivalent to the related submodel. Such a strict equivalence is, however, by no means the only interesting kind of relationship. Another possibility is to let a substitution transition describe the normal behaviour of an activity while the related submodel in addition describes several kinds of abnormal behaviour (e.g. time-outs and loss of messages or signals). This allows the user to have two related models: a crude one in which he can investigate the normal behaviour and a more complex one also coping with abnormal behaviour. The user can switch between the two models, e.g. first investigate the simple one and then go on with the more complex one. The two models share most of the submodels, and this means that changes in one of them automatically apply to the other.

Our hierarchy constructs do not extend the theoretical modelling power of CP-nets, and some readers might at a first glance be tempted to characterize at least some of them merely as graphical conveniences. This may be justifiable from a theoretical point of view. However, from a practical point of view, we do not think that this is a fair characterization. To cope with large systems in practice we need to develop strong structuring tools. The first very substantial step on this path was to replace ordinary Petri Nets with high-level Petri nets, such as Predicate/Transition-nets [8,9] and Coloured Petri Nets. The second step is, in our opinion, to introduce hierarchical models. In terms of programming languages, the first step can be compared to the introduction of types – allowing the programmer to work with structured data elements instead of single bits. The second step may then be compared to the development of programming languages with subroutines – allowing the programmer to work with reusable patterns. From a theoretical point of view machine languages (or even Turing machines) are equivalent to the most powerful modern programming languages. From a practical point of view, this is of course not the case. One of the most important limitations that system developers face to day, is their own inability to cope with many details at the same time. In order to develop and analyse complex systems they need structuring tools which allow them to work with a selected part of the model – without being distracted by the low-level details in the remaining parts. Hierarchical CP-nets is an attempt to provide the Petri Net modeller with such abstraction mechanisms. From a theoretical point of view it can be judged whether our framework has a sound mathematical basis. Its real success or failure can, however, only be judged by Petri Net modellers using the concepts to develop large models.

This paper assumes that the reader is familiar with non-hierarchical CP-nets – as defined in [10,11,12]. The paper gives a rather informal description of hierarchical CP-nets and concentrates on the explanation of the intuition behind the different hierarchy constructs. It is, however, not particularly difficult to give a formal definition of hierarchical CP-nets, and that will be done in a future paper.

The paper describes five different ways to relate submodels to each other. These five hierarchy constructs are not at all independent, and it is often possible to choose between them – in order to obtain a certain modelling goal (in the same way as many programming tasks can be achieved either by means of a while loop or a recursive procedure). The current formulation of the hierarchy constructs is very general – and gives the user many modelling choices. Practical experiences will probably lead to a number of more restricted hierarchy constructs – perhaps aimed at different application areas. The hierarchy constructs are in this paper formulated in terms of CP-nets. We are, however, convinced that it will be nearly trivial to reformulate them to apply to most other kinds of Petri Nets.

The remaining part of the paper is organized as follows: First we take a closer look at the idea of hierarchies in behavioural models in general. Then we present our five hierarchy constructs: substitution transitions, substitution places, invocation transitions, place fusion and transition fusion. We introduce our constructs by means of a small, original example. At the end of the paper we discuss two examples known from the Petri Net literature.

1. Hierarchies in Behavioural Models

In the area of system modelling and design the inadequacies of single level system models are well known:

- missing overview,
- too many details at one time,
- the structure of the system in question is not mirrored adequately.

Hierarchical modelling languages have been introduced to overcome these problems and have been in practical use for quite some time. Among others we have SADT and IDEF [13], Yourdon's data flow diagrams [14], and Statecharts [15]. For the majority of such hierarchical modelling languages we can list a set of nice features:

- hiding of details in a consistent way,
- separation into well defined components,
- reusable components,
- support of both top down and bottom up development strategies,
- strong graphical expressive capabilities.

However, at present − on the threshold of the development of powerful execution and simulation tools − we have to look for yet another model quality: executability. This implies that the modelling language must:

- support the notion of behaviour for its components *in a precise and consistent way*,
- make it possible to observe the execution of large, complex system models at different levels of detail.

Most of the modelling languages in the group above do not possess these executability properties. In contrast, high-level Petri Nets have in recent years been acclaimed as excellent modelling languages for expressing concurrent behaviour in a natural and sound way. Part of the reason is the mathematical (formal) basis of high-level Petri Nets, see [8,9,10,11,12].

Recently the practical use of CP-nets (and Predicate/Transition-nets) has been accelerating in such diverse areas as protocol verification, design of computer integrated flexible manufacturing systems, air traffic control problems, hardware and operating system design, and real time banking applications. However, up to recently the CP-nets and most other kinds of Petri Nets have been considered as flat models. Our rationale here is to start out from this well-proven framework for behavioural modelling and add hierarchical structure. We hope this will be an important step towards a more easy and widespread practical use of CP-nets for many different kinds of complex systems. Although the hierarchy constructs are general, their design is closely related to the CPN Palette project [1-5]. This means that the hierarchy constructs are designed in a way which makes it easy to support them by computer tools.

In the literature there is almost no work on hierarchies in Petri Nets, which take a behavioural point of view. The concept of net morphisms [16] is in its present formulation too general to be used as a basis for computer supported modelling and execution. Thus our work is more related to hierarchy concepts found in other kinds of system description languages. In both literature and practice, Petri Nets models with a consistent use of hierarchical structuring are sparse and isolated. Some ideas can be found in papers like [17,18,19,20,21,22,23]. Recently several articles showing rather complex high-level Petri Net models have been presented, e.g. [24,25]. However, these models only use multi-level structuring in an informal and rather ad-hoc way. Especially for computer supported editing, execution and formal analysis of such models a more consistent framework is necessary. In [3] we illustrate our framework by means of nine medium size examples – some known from the literature [11,24,25] and some original ones.

We have tried to look at hierarchies in an as general way as possible and impose as few restrictions on the hierarchy constructs as possible. From discussions, experiments, application of metaphors and comparison to related models, we have then developed five hierarchy constructs. Each of these gives CP-nets a more useful and more flexible expressive power. The aim of the hierarchy constructs is to guide the analyst to produce structured models by supplying a set of sound and consistent structuring concepts.

2. Hierarchies in CP-nets

Our point of departure is the ordinary non-hierarchical CP-nets as presented in [10,11,12]. A brief review of the terminology is given below:

A **place** is a node, where **tokens** from a specified **colour set** may reside. The distribution of tokens in the CP-net is called a **marking**. A place has an **initial marking**, which specifies the initial load of tokens. Places represent states and are normally drawn as ellipses. A **transition** is a node representing an action and it is normally drawn as a box. For each transition a **guard** can be specified. This is a boolean expression restricting the conditions under which the transition can occur. Places and transitions are called **nodes**. An **arc** represents an input or output relationship between a place and a transition. The actual amount and the colours of tokens moved are specified by the corresponding **arc expression**. Arc-expressions may be non-simple and may evaluate to a multi-set with 0 to n tokens.

From the arcs, the current marking, the arc expressions, and the guards one can calculate which transitions are **enabled** with respect to which **bindings** (of the **variables** in the arc expressions). If not in conflict with other transitions, an enabled transition may **occur**, whereby tokens are removed from the **input places** of the transition, and tokens are added to the **output places** of the transition, as specified by the arc expressions. The transitions can be seen as *schemes* for behaviour, in the sense that the actual binding determines the details of the behaviour. The number of tokens moved along an arc may depend upon the actual binding and it may even for some bindings be zero. A set of transitions and bindings occurring concurrently is called a **step**. A **diagram** is a set of related non-hierarchical CP-nets, called **pages**.

We define the semantics of the new hierarchy constructs by showing how each use of them can be translated into an **equivalent non-hierarchical CP-net** which has exactly the same reachable system states and enabled steps. This approach of introducing new language constructs by specifying a translation to well-known old constructs is traditional. Exactly the same thing was done, when CP-nets (and Predicate/Transition Nets) were defined by means of ordinary Petri Nets (PT-nets). It should be stressed that the only purpose of this translation is to define and present the hierarchy constructs in a precise way. The analyst works directly with the hierarchy constructs – without constructing an intermediate flat CP-net. Our extension of CP-nets implies that the existing analysis methods must be extended to cope directly with hierarchical CP-nets. For place invariants, occurrence graphs and reductions [11,26,27,28] we are convinced that this extension will present no serious conceptual problems. There are, however, a very large number of technical details which have to be worked out.

3. Substitution Transitions

We now take a closer look at the first metaphor used to develop our CP-net hierarchies: the hardware plug-in, e.g. a silicon chip. Imagine a component with a set of interface posts. We can connect such a component to a given environment by means of eyelet connectors, which are attached to the posts. Whenever a specific component of this kind is used, the only thing to be done is to specify the eyelet/post correspondence. Going back to the CP-nets, we will consider a transition as such a component and its surrounding places as the interface to the environment.

Example 1: Simple assembly line

Let us explain the idea by means of a small example. We consider a simple assembly line in a factory consisting of three machines and two intermediate buffers. The machines are identical, hence we only want to model them once. The same is the case for the buffers. The page in the left part of Figure 1 represents each machine (Mach1-Mach3) and each buffer (Buf1-Buf2) as a **substitution transition**. The details of the machines and buffers described on two other pages in the right part of Figure 1. The result is a hierarchical CP-net where five substitution transitions at page AssemblyLine#1 are related to two **subpages** Machine#2 and Buffer#3 (we denote each page by a page name, followed by "#", followed by a page number). The interfaces of Machine#2 and Buffer#3 are defined by the B-tags and the inscriptions next to them (B≈Border). The relationship between each of the substitution transitions and the corresponding subpage is defined by the inscription next to the HS tag (HS≈Hierarchy+Substitution). This inscription tells the name and the number of the subpage and it describes how each of the places surrounding the compound transition is assigned to one of the border nodes of the subpage. We have omitted most of the other net inscriptions, e.g. initial marking, since we are focussing more on the net structure than the details of colour sets, arc expressions, etc.

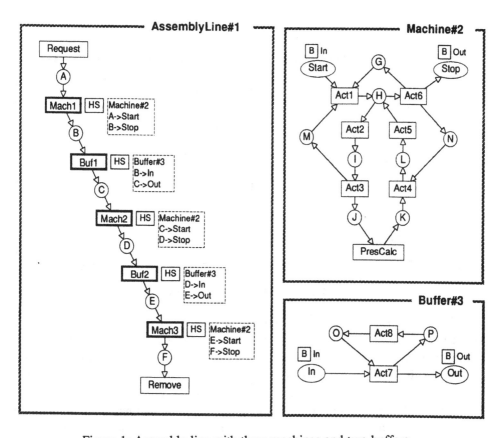

Figure 1: Assembly line with three machines and two buffers

From page AssemblyLine#1 the reader gets an overview of the assembly line. To feed the line and remove the produced items we have added two ordinary transitions: Request and Remove. The behaviour of the machines is described at Machine#2 by means of seven lower level activities (transitions). The buffers are described at Buffer#3. They are very simple and thus we might instead have inserted them at AssemblyLine#1. However, by describing them on a separate page we have abstracted them, in a way which later allows for confined experimentation with the details of the buffers without altering any other part of the diagram.

Let us pause for a moment and compare this approach with the earlier abstraction mechanisms in CP-nets. In order to represent three instances of the same machine in a compact way, we could have folded them into the CP-net of Machine#2 by introducing an additional machine-id component of the colour sets for all the places representing the machine states. We could then have done a similar thing with the buffers. The problem would however arise when we afterwards tried to relate the machines and buffers to each other. For example the fact that Mach1 is the only machine that delivers input to Buf1 would then have had to be encoded in the guard of transition Act7 in Buffer#3. To continue in that way would soon become cumbersome. Folding is well suited, when we have exactly identical objects, but less suited for asymmetrical arrangements.

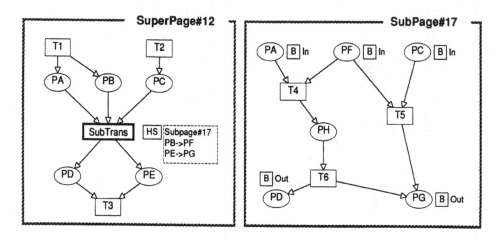

Figure 2: Substitution transition

We will now be more precise on the terminology: Each **substitution transition** designates a page. This page is said to be a **subpage**. The substitution transition represents the component seen as a black box, whereas the subpage contains the details of how this component actually performs the activity. The substitution transition is a short hand for the CP-net on the subpage. Figure 2 illustrates the idea of this node-to-page relationship for an abstract net. The substitution transition and its page are, with respect to the subpage, said to be a **supernode** and a **superpage**. For simplicity, most of the CP-net inscriptions are again omitted. The substitution transition, named SubTrans, can be recognized by the HS-tag. SubTrans has five surrounding places, which are called **socket places**: three input socket places and two output socket places. Five places on the subpage are defined to be **port places** and hence marked by B-tags. The port places represent the posts from the hardware metaphor. They are the interface to the upper level, at which the subpage is plugged in and used. The relationship between socket places and port places is called the **port assignment**. It is a function mapping sockets into ports. The port assignment is shown in the inscription next to the HS-tag of the substitution transition: The first line tells the name and number of the subpage. Each of the remaining lines describe the assignment between a socket and a port. By convention we only mention sockets which are unassigned or assigned to a port with a different name. In this case, we have omitted the lines PA->PA, PC->PC and PD->PD. We require that all socket nodes must be assigned, and that a socket node must be assigned to a port node with an identical colour set. The port assignment function is, however, allowed to be non-injective and non-surjective. The inscriptions next to the B-tags of port nodes tell whether the assigned socket node has to be an input, output or input/output node for the substitution transition. The modeller can also define a port node to be general and this means that all three kinds of socket nodes can be assigned.

It has been important for us to design concepts, which allow system components to be reusable. Once a given building block has been designed and verified it should be possible to use it at several locations. Hence, an important feature of our framework is that the same page may be used as a subpage for several substitution transitions, even on different pages. The assembly line example uses both Machine#2 and Buffer#3 as multiple plug-ins.

In the CPN Palette there are facilities for manual and automatic port assignment, optional syntax restrictions and system-aided editing. All these facilities are set up to help the user produce a consistent diagram in an easy way: It is possible to move part of a page to a subpage, whereby a supernode is created and the port assignment automatically performed. It is also possible to replace a supernode by the contents of its subpage. Finally there are facilities for connecting compound nodes to already constructed pages. For more details, see [4].

Semantics of substitution transitions

To define the semantics of a substitution transition we show how to translate it into an equivalent non-hierarchical CP-net. This is done in two steps:

a) Delete the substitution transition (together with the surrounding arcs).

b) Insert a copy of the subpage.

The left-hand side of Figure 3 illustrates steps a + b for the net from Figure 2.

c) **Merge** each socket place with the assigned port node. The result of a merge of two nodes A and B is a node C with a set of arcs which is the union of the arcs of A and B. In the case where two or more socket places are assigned to the same port, we only merge one of them with the port place and then "glue" all the socket places together by means of an instance fusion set (which we introduce later in this paper). Unassigned ports are left alone, i.e. they are not merged into another node.

The right-hand side of Figure 3 shows the result of step c for the net from Figure 2.

Each subpage is a template. From that *copies* can be made to replace the corresponding substitution transitions. We refer to such copies as (substitution) **instances** of the actual page. The initial marking of the subpage is copied together with the net structure. Each port place, however, inherits (and shares) the initial marking of the assigned socket (if any). The page instances form the **instance hierarchy** and we speak about **superinstances** and **subinstances**, in a similar way as we talk about superpages and subpages.

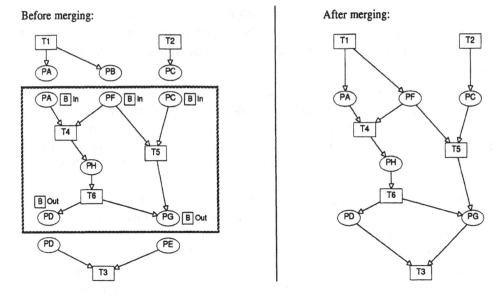

Figure 3: Semantics of substitution transitions:

The subpage replaces the substitution transition:

1. Each socket is merged into the corresponding port.

Given the semantics above, it should be clear why it makes no sense to talk about enabled or occurring substitution transitions. They are not an executable part of the model, because they are substituted by the subpage.

At this point we would like to stress, that a substitution transition should *not* be considered as a normal transition.– it has a special tag signifying this fact. The semantics is defined as a substitution by its subpage as shown above. In order to make a model more readable, it is up to the modeller to write some meaningful arc-expressions surrounding the substitution transition. Typically, the modeller would leave inscriptions empty for some of the surroundings arcs. In some nets it would make sense to exhibit a strong equivalence, but more often the modeller would choose to exhibit *some* of the possible behaviour at the upper level. The other extreme would be to have no equivalence what so ever. More work will go into defining a notion of equivalence in between these extremes. In Section 8, we explore the relationship between upper and lower level inscriptions by means of an example.

4. Substitution Places

Analogous to the substitution transitions we use the plug-in metaphor for places. We let a substitution place be a short hand for a more detailed subnet, which the analyst want to hide at the upper level of abstraction. Each substitution place has an interface which consists of transitions and it behaves in a way which resembles an abstract data type. Figure 4 shows a **substitution place** SubPlace together with its subpage Queue#4.

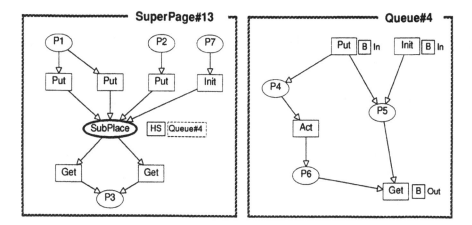

Figure 4: Substitution place

At the superpage, the substitution place outlines a simple data type: a queue with three operation handles: Init, Put, and Get. In this case Init is called once, Put three times and Get twice. These calls are represented by the six **socket transitions** surrounding Sub-Place. As for substitution transitions we allow that some port nodes are unassigned. Moreover, as illustrated above, we often assign several socket transitions to the same port. At the subpage the three operations are described in more detail and the interface to them is represented by the three **port transitions**.

Semantics of substitution places

The semantics of substitution places is similar to the semantics of substitution transitions. The roles of places and transitions are, however, reversed and in addition to this there are a number of minor differences:

a) Delete the substitution place (together with the surrounding arcs).

b) Create a copy of the subpage and **duplicate** each port transition to obtain a copy for each of the assigned socket transitions. The result of a duplication of a node A is a new node B which have exactly the same set of arcs as A. When a port has only one assigned socket node, no duplication is needed. Un-assigned ports are deleted. The left-hand side of Figure 5 illustrates steps a + b for the net in Figure 4.

c) Merge each socket transition with a copy of the port transition to which it is assigned. The guard in the resulting transition is the conjunction of the guards for the socket node and and the port node. The merge implies that a socket transition has to occur together with its corresponding port transition, as a single indivisible state change. The right-hand side of Figure 5 illustrates step c for the net in Figure 4.

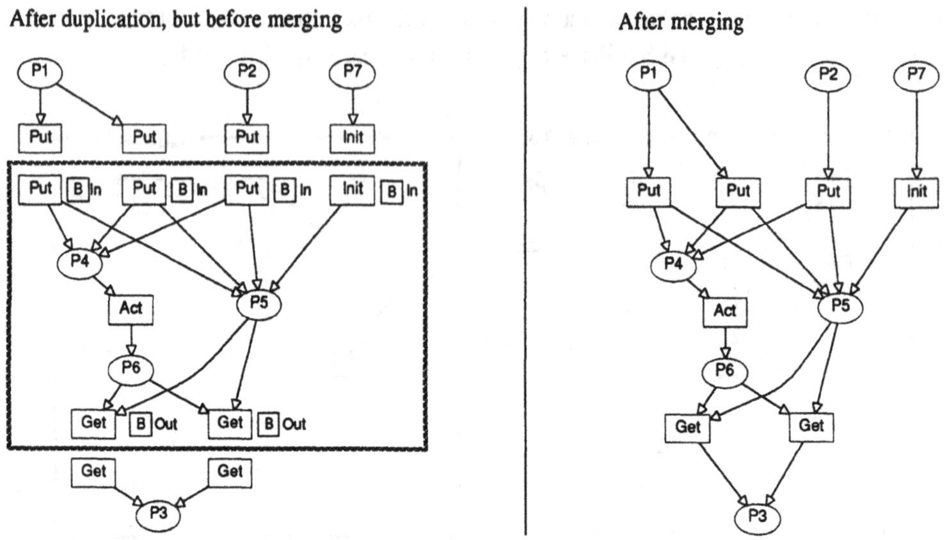
After duplication, but before merging
After merging
P1
P2
P7
Put
Put
Put
Init
B
In
B
Out
P4
P5
Act
P6
Get
Get
P3

Figure 5: Semantics of substitution places:

The subpage replaces the substitution place:

1. Each port is duplicated to match the number of attached sockets.

2. Each socket is merged into its own copy of the corresponding port.

Example 2: Small factory unit

Let us now return to the assembly line. We want to use it as a building block in a larger system. Hence, we define Request and Remove to be port transitions (by placing a B-tag next to them). We then use AssemblyLine#1 as a subpage for two substitution places Assembly1 and Assembly2, as shown in Figure 6. In addition we use Queue#4 from Figure 4 as a subpage for a front-end queue named InQueue and a back-end queue named OutQueue. This small example illustrates how it is easy to extend the scope of a model by inserting it as a submodel in a larger model.

We do not allow a substitution place SP to be neighbour to a substitution transition ST. The reason is that it then would be impossible to construct an equivalent non-hierarchical CP-net by the method defined above – because SP is socket for ST and vice versa. It is possible to extend our concepts to cover such a case. We have, however, not been able to do this in a natural and simple way, and we do not think that the restriction presents a serious problem. In the models we have been working with there has been a tendency to use either compound places or compound transitions in a given part of the diagram.

Moreover, should two substitution nodes come too close together, they can always be separated by inserting an extra place and an extra transition between them.

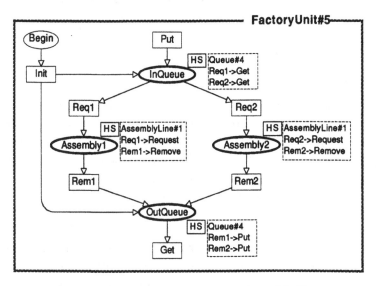

Figure 6: Factory unit with two assembly lines

Abstract data types is one of the most well-known and useful abstraction mechanisms in computer science, and it has been important for us to allow the user to apply a similar concept for CP-nets. As shown above, this can be done by means of substitution places where the port transitions represent the exported operations and the socket transitions the operation calls. There is, however, an additional set of problems which we have to solve: Suppose that the three calls of Put in Figure 4 use different expressions to describe the tokens which are given to the queue. Such a difference should not be specified at the sub-page, but at the socket transitions. Thus we allow the arc expressions of the port transitions to refer to the arc expressions of the socket transitions by means of special identifiers (details are described in [3]). However, we think this method is too primitive, and it will be refined as we get more experience with the use of our framework. One solution might be to allow the supernodes to specify instance dependent properties of their sub-pages. This would also make it possible for arbitrary places to have different initial markings in different page instances. For the moment this is only possible for port places, since they inherit their marking from the assigned socket nodes.

As for substitution transitions, substitution places should not be considered as real places, since they are substituted by a subpage. Accordingly, the substitution places carry a tag.

5. Invocation Transitions

In our search for useful constructs we have been looking for other ways to relate nodes and pages. For transitions it was rather obvious to apply the metaphor of subroutines, as known from many programming languages. A subroutine is declared with a set of formal parameters and it can be invoked (i.e. called) from different locations by supplying a set of actual parameters. Each call implies a temporary instantiation of the subroutine.

Example 3: Pressure calculation

Let us again return to the assembly line and let us assume that the machines use a complicated recursive algorithm for calculating the correct work pressure for Act4. To specify this we define in Figure 7 a subpage PresCalc#6 which is invoked by three different invocation transitions: PresCalc (at Machine#2) and PC1 and PC2 (at PresCalc#6). In contrast to substitution nodes, the invocation transitions are *not* substituted by their subpage. This means that they can occur and each of their occurrences triggers the creation of a new instance of the subpage. These subpage instances are executed concurrently with the other page instance in the model, until some specified exit condition is reached (more details below). When an invocation page instance is created or terminated, tokens are passed between the invocation transition and the subpage instance in a similar way as parameters are passed between a subroutine call and the subroutine execution (more details below).

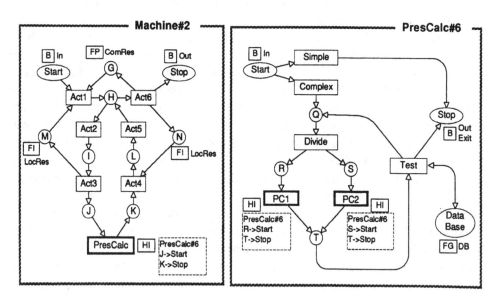

Figure 7: Recursive pressure calculation

Each invocation of PresCalc#6 receives a token from the input node of the calling invocation transition, and then classifies the task as either simple or complex. In the first case the result is immediately calculated and passed back to the invocation transition via Stop – and the execution of the subpage is destroyed, because an exit place received a token. In the second case the task is divided into two recursive subtasks (represented by PC1 and PC2), the results of the two subtasks are tested against a database, and finally a token is put either on Stop (if the test was positive) or on Q (if the test was negative) – remember, that in CP-nets am arc-expression may evaluate to the empty multi-set for certain bindings. For the moment ignore the FG/FP/FI-tags – we will return to them later.

In terms of the subroutine metaphor, the invocation subpage represents the subroutine description, while the three invocation transitions represent the subroutine calls. All the ports must be places and they represent the formal parameters. The places surrounding the invocation transitions are called **parameter places** and they represent the actual parameters. The invocation transitions are distinguishable by the HI-tags (HI≈Hierarchy+Invocation) and the inscription next to them specifies the **subpage** and the **port assignment**, relating parameter nodes to port nodes. The rule for port assignment is identical to that of substitution nodes and this means that there may be more formal than actual parameters.

The termination of a subroutine execution is usually triggered by execution of the last statement or by an explicit exit statement. In our framework it is not always possible to talk about the last node and thus we allow the analyst to define **exit nodes**. The execution is terminated the first time an exit transition occurs or an exit place receives a token.

Semantics of invocation transitions

The enabling rule for invocation transitions is identical to that of ordinary transitions, but an occurrence of the invocation transition implies a temporary *extension* of the CP-net:

a) A new instance of the invocation subpage is created. This subpage may contain substitution nodes, and when this is the case it is necessary also to create new page instances of the corresponding substitution subpages. These page instances become subinstances of the invocation page instance and they may themselves have subinstances (if they contain substitution nodes).

The arc expressions on the input arcs of the invocation transition are evaluated and the corresponding tokens are subtracted from the input parameter places and added to the assigned port places (in the invocation instance).

Multiple assignment of parameter nodes to the same port implies, as for substitution transitions, that the parameter nodes are "glued" together by means of an instance fusion set (which we introduce later in this paper).

b) The invocation instance and its subinstances are executed as a normal part of the diagram. This execution is concurrent to the rest of the diagram and it continues until an exit transition occurs or an exit place receives a token.

c) All the tokens on output port places are copied to the assigned parameter places. The invocation instance and its subinstances are removed from the CP-net, and any token information which might be left in them are lost.

Multiple assignment of parameter nodes to the same port implies, as for substitution transitions, that the parameter nodes are "glued" together by means of an instance fusion set (which we introduce later in this paper), so that tokens are copied back into that fusion set.

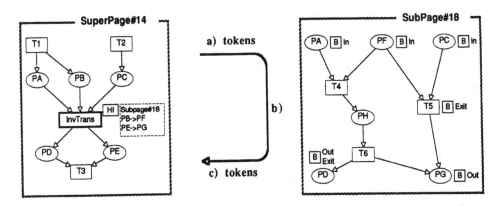

Figure 8: Semantics of invocation transitions:

When the invocation transition occurs a new instance of the subpage is created:

1. Tokens are transferred from the input places of the invocation transition to the input ports of the subpage

2. The subpage instance is executed concurrent to the other page instances until an exit is reached.

3. Tokens are transferred from the output ports of the subpage to the output places of the invocation transition.

For substitution nodes we could (although we in practice never want to do it) statically calculate the equivalent non-hierarchical CP-net. For invocation transitions this is not possible and it is necessary dynamically to extend and shrink the equivalent non-hierarchical CP-net. Without invocation each page has a constant number of instances, but with invocation the number of page instances may change (even for pages which only are substitution subpages). Moreover, each invocation transition can have any page as a subpage (as long as the ports are places). This means that the invocation hierarchy is allowed to contain circular (i.e. recursive) dependencies, while the substitution hierarchy is demanded to be acyclic (to avoid infinite substitution).

The token passing in step a) and c) is analogous to the use of in, out, and in+out parameters in subroutines. This is also sometimes known as call-by-value and call-by-result. Some programming languages, e.g. Pascal, allow subroutines to be passed as parameters to other subroutines. Analogously, we might allow token colours to represent CP-nets – but for the moment we don't allow this.

6. Fusion Sets

The main idea behind fusion is to allow the system modeller conceptually to fold a set of nodes into a single node – without graphically having to represent them as a single object. A fusion is obtained by defining a **fusion set** containing an arbitrary number of places or an arbitrary number of transitions. The nodes of a fusion set are called **fusion set members**. This idea is illustrated in Figure 9, where the leftmost CP-net has a fusion set called FusA. This fusion set contains the fusion set members A1 and A2, which are distinguishable by the FP-tags (FP≈Fusion+Page). FusA is a page fusion set and this means that it only is allowed to have fusion set members from a single page in the diagram. For the moment let us assume that this page only has one instance. Then the equivalent non-hierarchical CP-net is shown in the right part of Figure 9. It is obtained by merging A1 into A2 (or vice versa). Intuitively, this semantics means that the places A1 and A2 share the same marking.

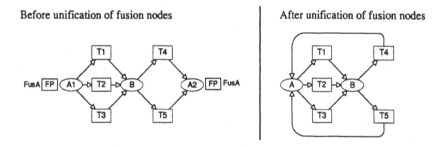

Figure 9: Semantics of fusion set

Now let us consider the case where the page of FusA has more than one page instance. We then have two possibilities. Either we can merge all instances of all fusion set members into a single conceptual node, or we can merge them into a node for each instance, i.e. only merge node instances which appear in the same page instance. The two possibilities are illustrated in Figure 10 where we have assumed that the page has two page instances. Both possibilities are useful and thus we allow the user to specify which of them he wants. The leftmost is obtained by making FusA a page fusion set while the rightmost is obtained by making it an instance fusion set (with FI-tags).

Finally we allow global fusion sets (with FG-tags). This allows fusion set members from all pages in the diagram and all instances of these nodes are merged into a single conceptual node. This means that a page fusion set is a special case of global fusion set, and seen from a theoretical point of view we could have omitted the concept of page fusion sets. However, when CP-nets are used to model large systems, it is important to be able to distinguish between global fusion sets and page fusion sets. In a computer supported environment, such as the CPN Palette, this gives the analyst an easy way to avoid unintended fusion of two fusion sets which by coincidence have the same name.

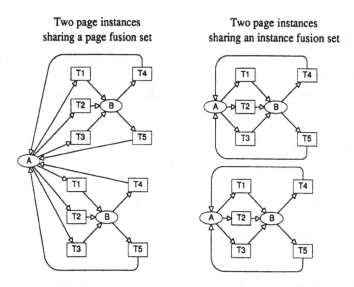

Figure 10: Page fusion set versus instance fusion set

The members of a fusion set must be comparable to each other. For places this means that they must have the same colour set and the same initial marking. It also means that they either all must be ordinary places or all be substitution places, and in the latter case they must all have the same subpage. Fusion of substitution places is useful, when we want to apply the same instance – e.g. an abstract data type – at several locations in the diagram. The cache coherence protocol modeled in [3] illustrates the use of this facility.

Above we have concentrated on fusion sets with places. However, exactly the same set of concepts applies to transition fusion. For transitions we do not demand that the guards are identical. Instead we form the conjunction of the guards. The members of a transition fusion set must either all be ordinary transitions, all be substitution transitions or all be invocation transitions. In the latter two cases they must all have the same subpage. In addition, it is not allowed to use global and page fusion for transitions, which appear on subpages of invocation transitions (or on subpages of such pages).

When applied to nodes at a single page with only one page instance, fusion is mainly a drawing convenience. However, when applied to nodes at different pages, or pages which have several instances, fusion becomes a strong description primitive of its own right, and it supplements the notions of substitution and invocation in a very fruitful way.

Example 4: Resources in the assembly line

In Figure 7 we have illustrated the use of all three kinds of fusion sets. Resources shared by all machines are modeled by a page fusion set ComRes, while resources local to one machine are modeled by an instance fusion set LocRes. Finally, the Data Base is modeled by a global fusion set DB, since another page (not shown) has the responsibility of updating the database. If we want to model the data base as an abstract datatype, the corresponding places become both substitution and fusion places.

7. Page Hierarchy

To get an overview of a given hierarchical CP-net we use a graph called the **page hierarchy.** Each node represents a page, and the shape of each such **page node** tells what kinds of supernodes the page can have. Ellipse shape indicates that all supernodes must be places, box shape that they must be transitions and rounded box shape that there is no restriction. Each arc represents a hierarchical relationship between two pages, and the graphics tells whether the arc represents a substitution relationship, an invocation relationship or a global fusion set. Page and instance fusion sets are not represented in the page hierarchy, because they involve only a single page. Figure 11 contains the page hierarchy for the small factory unit described earlier in this paper. The page hierarchy graph is generated automatically by the CPN Palette. The user can, however, change the layout and graphics in any way he might want. The page hierarchy is an integrated part of the user interface. As an example, the user deletes a page by deleting the corresponding page node in the page hierarchy.

To specify the initial state for an execution of a hierarchical CP-net, the user must define a set of starting pages, called **prime pages.** Declaring FactoryUnit#5 to be a prime page means that the execution will start with one instance of FactoryUnit#5, two instances of Queue#4, two instances of AssemblyLine#1, six instances of Machine#2 and four instances of Buffer#3. Instead we could have declared AssemblyLine#1 to be a prime page and then we would only have executed a single assembly line containing one instance of AssemblyLine#1, three instances of Machine#2 and two instances of Buffer#3. In general we allow the user to have more than one prime page and he can even let the same page be a multiple prime. Intuitively, the prime pages tell what should be included in the execution. It is, however, also possible, explicitly, to exclude certain pages. If we in the factory unit exclude Buffer#3, no instances will be created for this page, and Buf1 and Buf2 will be treated as if they were ordinary places. It is important to be able to include and exclude parts of a model – without having to change the model itself.

The CPN Palette applies an elaborated naming scheme for page instances: As an example consider "(5:Machine#2) Mach2@(2:AssemblyLine#1) Assembly2@(1:FactoryUnit#5)" which denotes the fifth instance of Machine#2, which is a subinstance of the transition Mach2 at the second instance of AssemblyLine#1, which in turn is a subinstance of the transition Assembly2 at the first instance of FactoryUnit#5. More details about naming schemes, prime pages and exclusion of pages can be found in [4-5].

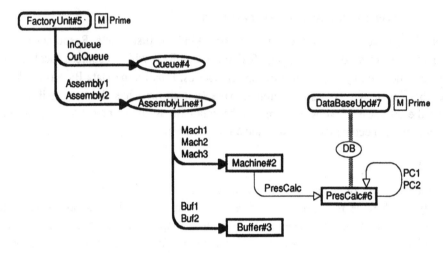

Figure 11: Page hierarchy for the factory unit

8. Example 5: Telephone System

This section presents a hierarchical version of the telephone system from [11]. It contains a single prime page Phone#51 (see Figure 13) and five substitution subpages (see Figure 13-14). In the original non-hierarchical model the place Engaged is defined to be complementary to the place Inactive (and all arcs surrounding Engaged are omitted). In the hierarchical version we update Engaged explicitly and to do this we use a global fusion set, called Engaged. The arc expression "1`x+1`y" denotes the multi-set which contains one x-token and one y-token.

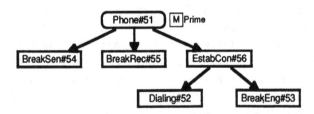

Figure 12: Page hierarchy for the telephone system

The arc expressions of the substitution transition BreakSen at Phone#51 gives a slightly less detailed description of the corresponding activity than the subpage BreakSen#54. The substitution transition doesn't show that the activity has two subactivities (which are executed after each other) and it doesn't show that Engaged is updated. However, BreakSen still gives the reader a very good idea about what the activity does. It describes the combined effect of the two subactivities on the markings of the socket places.

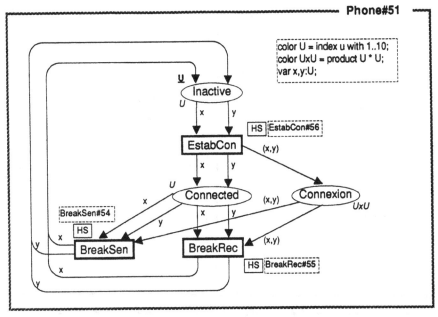

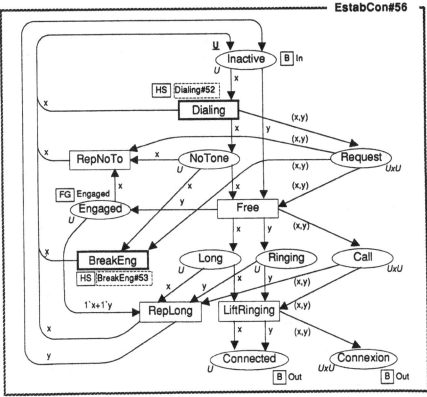

Figure 13: Telephone system, part I

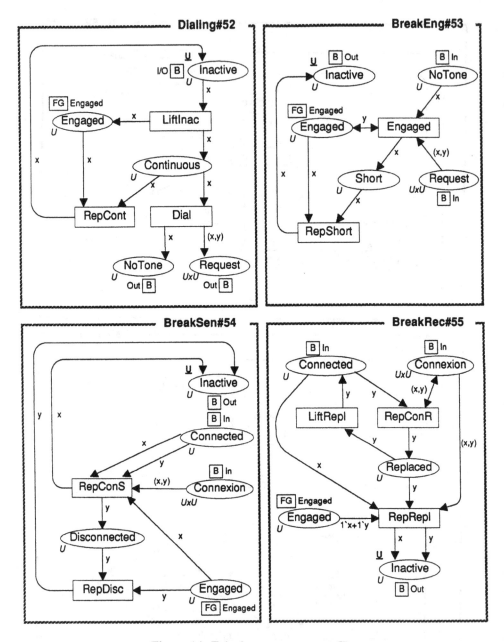

Figure 14: Telephone system, part II

The arc expressions of the substitution transition EstabCon at Phone#51 are used in another way. They describe what happens in the normal case, where a connexion is established. However, they do not say that the result of the subpage activities may be that no connexion is established (routing both the x and y token to Inactive instead of

Connected). It would not have been particularly difficult to describe this possibility in the arc expressions, but the analyst has – at Phone#51 – chosen to concentrate on the normal case.

For substitution transitions the arc expressions at the upper level never influence the execution – unless the corresponding subpage is excluded from the execution. However, for substitution places and invocation transitions this is not always true (cf. section 4 and 5).

9. Example 6: Multi-Token Ring Protocol

This section presents a hierarchical version of the net from [24], where a protocol called PLASMA is proposed. The protocol uses several tokens rings, switching and re-transmission to ensure the network service. The protocol fits between the LLC and MAC sublayers in the ISO standard for local area networks.

Our model contains a single prime page Prot#61 (see Figure 15) and seven subpages (reproduced in Figures 16-18). At execution time, we have eight page instances – one for each page in the net.

Each of the seven main components are here formally made into substitution nodes at different levels in the hierarchy. Due to their nature five of them are represented by substitution places with shared socket transitions – subpages #62–66. The last two are represented as substitution transitions, which share information (places) with the environment – subpages #67–68.

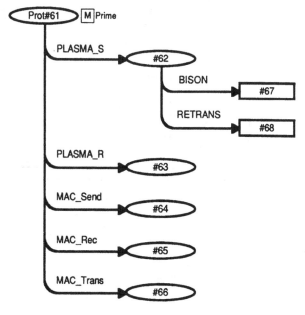

Figure 15: Page hierarchy for the multi-token ring protocol

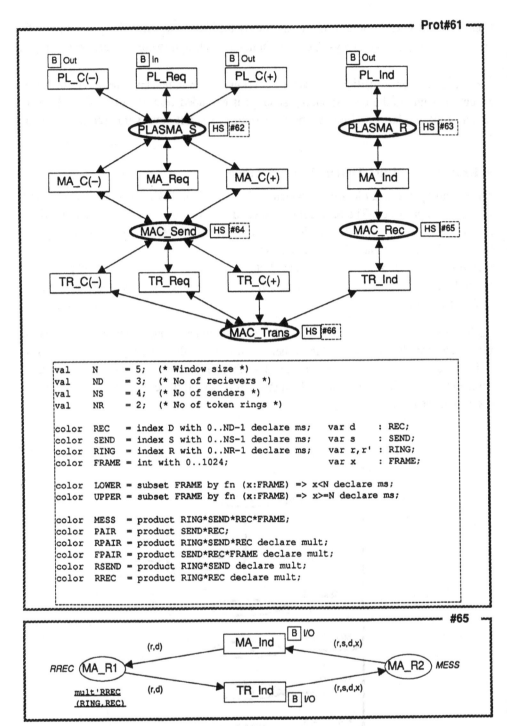

Figure 16: Multi-Token Ring Protocol, part I

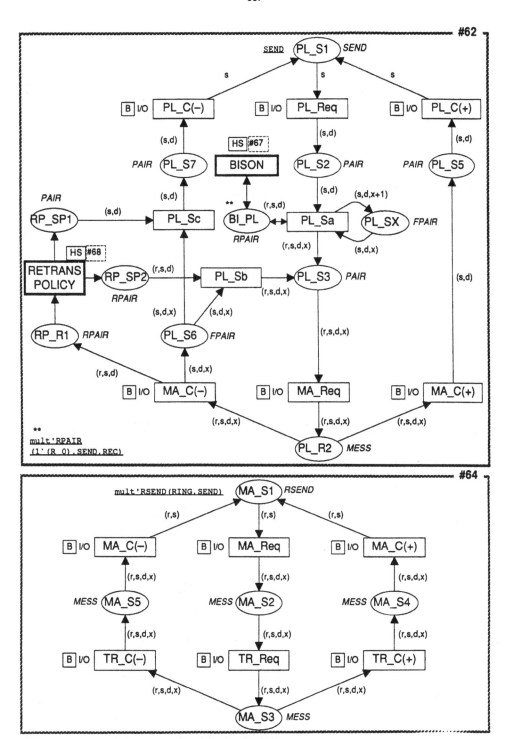

Figure 17: Multi-Token Ring Protocol, part II

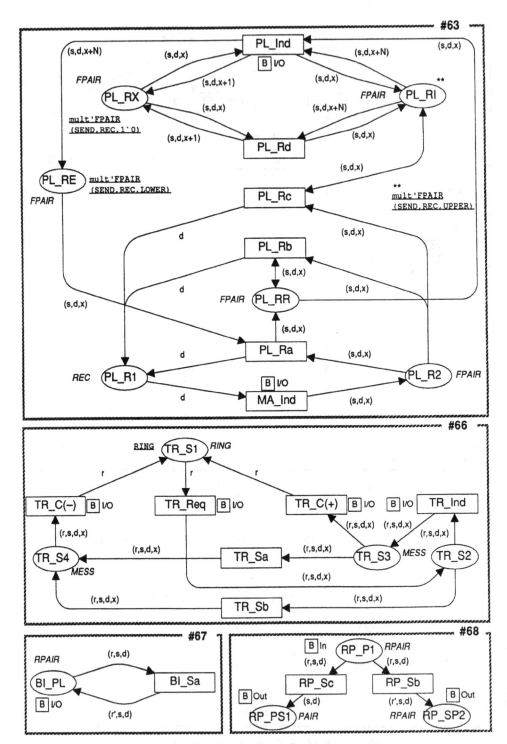

Figure 18: Multi-Token Ring Protocol, part III

We have subordinated the BISON and the Retransmission Policy process to the PLASMA_Send process, since it is the only one that uses them. Even though they are small, it is nice to have them on separate pages. This allows us to hide and experiment with the strategies for these error detection and ring switching processes separately.

We have specified port nodes for the top page Prot#61, even though it is not used as a subpage for the moment. However, this indicates, that we later might use it as a subpage for a substitution place in an even larger network system.

The definition of constants and colour-sets is given on page Prot#61 as well. Note, that we in the net only used functions, which are *predefined* in the CPN Editor. We have used the multi-set multiplication operator – mult'<Color set name> - to formulate the initial markings for product color sets in a compact form.

10. Conclusion

We have explored hierarchies in a specific behavioural modelling language: the CP-nets. This led us to the formulation of hierarchical CP-nets, which contains ordinary CP-nets as a subclass. We have introduced the notions of pages and page instances together with five elaborated concepts for hierarchical relationships:

- substitution transitions,
- substitution places,
- invocation transitions,
- fusion sets for places,
- fusion sets for transitions.

We do not claim that our five hierarchy constructs are the only sensible ones for CP-nets. As we get more experience with the modelling of large systems, the hierarchy constructs will probably be modified and perhaps augmented by new kinds. However, based on our present experience with a number of very different and rather complex examples, we believe that the current hierarchy constructs will form the base for a useful and theoretically sound extension of CP-nets.

Acknowledgements

Some of the ideas in our hierarchy concepts originates from the coarsen operation described in [19].
The participation by Kurt Jensen in the CPN Palette project is partially supported by a grant from the Danish National Science Research Council.

Reference List

[1] K. Albrect, K. Jensen & R.M. Shapiro: **CPN Palette. A Tool Package Supporting the Use of Coloured Petri Nets.** The Petri Net Newsletter, April 1989.

[2] K. Jensen: **CPN ML.** Specification paper for the CPN Palette – Part 1. Meta Software Corporation, Cambridge, Massachusetts, USA, 1989.

[3] P. Huber: **Hierarchies in Coloured Petri Nets.** Specification paper for the CPN Palette – Part 2. Meta Software Corporation, Cambridge, Massachusetts, USA, 1989.

[4] K. Jensen and S. Christensen: **CPN Editor.** Specification paper for the CPN Palette – Part 3. Meta Software Corporation, Cambridge, Massachusetts, USA, 1989.

[5] K. Jensen and S. Christensen: **CPN Simulator.** Specification paper for the CPN Palette – Part 4. Meta Software Corporation, Cambridge, Massachusetts, USA, 1989.

[6] W. Reisig: **Petri Nets in Software Engineering.** In: W. Brauer, W. Reisig and G. Rozenberg (eds.): Petri Nets: Applications and Relationships to Other Models of Concurrency,
Advances in Petri Nets 1986-Part II, Lecture Notes in Computer Science, vol. 255, Springer-Verlag 1987, 207-247.

[7] H. Oberquelle: **Human-machine Interaction and Role/Function/Action Nets.** In: W. Brauer, W. Reisig and G. Rozenberg (eds.): Petri Nets: Applications and Relationships to Other Models of Concurrency, Advances in Petri Nets 1986-Part II, Lecture Notes in Computer Science, vol. 255, Springer-Verlag 1987, 207-247.

[8] H.J. Genrich and K. Lautenbach: **System Modelling with High-level Petri Nets** Theoretical Computer Science 13. 1981, 109-136.

[9] H.J. Genrich: **Predicate/Transition Nets** In: W. Brauer, W. Reisig and G. Rozenberg (eds.): Petri Nets: Central Models and Their Properties, Advances in Petri Nets 1986-Part I, Lecture Notes in Computer Science, vol. 254, Springer-Verlag 1987, 207-247.

[10] K. Jensen: **Coloured Petri Nets. A Way to Describe and Analyse Real World Systems – Without Drowning in Unnecessary Details.** Proceedings of the 5'th International Conference on Systems Engineering, Dayton 1987, New York: IEEE, 395-401.

[11] K. Jensen: **Coloured Petri Nets.** In: W. Brauer, W. Reisig and G. Rozenberg (eds.): Petri Nets: Central Models and Their Properties, Advances in Petri Nets 1986-Part I, Lecture Notes in Computer Science, vol. 254, Springer-Verlag 1987, 248-299.

[12] K. Jensen: **Informal Introduction to Coloured Petri Nets.** Chapter 1 of a three-volume book on CP-nets. The book will be published by Springer-Verlag in the series: EATCS Monographs on Theoretical Computer Science.

[13] D.A. Marca and C.L. McGowan: **SADT.** McGraw-Hill, New York, 1988.

[14] E. Yourdon: **Managing the System Life Cycle.** Yourdon Press, 1982.

[15] D. Harel: **Statecharts: A Visual Formalism for Complex Systems.** In: Science of Computer Programming, Vol. 8, North-Holland 1987, 231-274.

[16] H.J. Genrich, K. Lautenbach and P.S. Thiagarajan: **Elements of General Net Theory.** In: G. Goos and J. Hartmanis (eds.): Net Theory and Applications, Lecture Notes in Computer Science, vol. 84, Springer-Verlag 1980, 248-299.

[17] R.M. Shapiro and P. Hardt: **The Impact of Computer Technology. A Case Study: The Dairy Industry.** GMD Internal Report, ISF-76-11, 1976.

[18] R.R Razouk and M.T. Rose: **Verifying Partial Correctness of Concurrent Software using Contour/Transition Nets.** In: Proceedings of the Hawaii International Conference on System Sciences, 1986.

[19] H.J. Genrich and R.M. Shapiro: **A Diagram Editor for Line Drawing with Inscriptions.** Proceedings of the 3'rd European Workshop on Applications and Theory of Petri Nets, Varenna, Italy, 1982, 193-212.

[20] **Network Tool Net: System Analysis and Simulation with Petri-Nets.** PSI Gesellschaft für Prozesssteuerungs- und Informationssysteme, Berlin, undated, 23 pages.

[21] H. Oberquelle: **Some Concepts for Studying Flow and Modification of Actors and Objects in High-level Nets.** Proceedings of the 3'rd European Workshop on Applications and Theory of Petri Nets, Varenna, Italy, 1982, 343-363.

[22] A. Kiehn: **A Structuring Mechanism for Petri Nets.** Institut für Informatik der Technischen Universität München, 1988, 127 pages.

[23] K.M. van Hee, L.J. Somers, and M. Voorhoeve: **Executable Specifications for Distributed Information Systems.** In: E.D. Falkenberg and P. Lindgreen (eds.): Information System Concepts: An In-depth Analysis, North Holland, 1989, 139-156

[24] B. Cousin et. al.: **Validation of a Protocol Managing a Multi-token Ring Architecture.** Proceedings of the 9'th European Workshop on Applications and Theory of Petri Nets, Vol. II, Venice 1988.

[25] C. Girault, C. Chatelain and S. Haddad: **Specification and Properties of a Cache Coherence Protocol Model.** In: G. Rozenberg (ed.): Advanced in Petri Nets 1987, Lecture Notes of Computer Science, vol. 266, Springer-Verlag, 1987, 1-20.

[26] S. Haddad.: **Generalization of Reduction Theory to Coloured Nets.** Proceedings of the 9'th European Workshop on Applications and Theory of Petri Nets, Vol. II, Venice 1988.

[27] P. Huber, A.M. Jensen, L.O. Jepsen and K. Jensen: **Reachability Trees for High-level Petri Nets.** Theoretical Computer Science 45 (1986), 261-292.

[28] K. Jensen: **How to Find Invariants for Coloured Petri Nets.** In: J. Gruska, M. Chytill (eds.): Mathematical Foundations of Computer Science 1981, Lecture Notes in Computer Science vol. 118, Springer-Verlag 1981, 327-338.

Coloured Petri Nets: A High Level Language for System Design and Analysis

Kurt Jensen
Computer Science Department, Aarhus University
Ny Munkegade, Bldg. 540
DK-8000 Aarhus C, Denmark

Phone: +45 86 12 71 88
Telefax: +45 86 13 57 25
Telex: 64767 aausci dk
E-mail: kjensen@daimi.aau.dk

Abstract

This paper describes how Coloured Petri Nets (CP-nets) have been developed – from being a promising theoretical model to being a full-fledged language for the design, specification, simulation, validation and implementation of large software systems (and other systems in which human beings and/or computers communicate by means of some more or less formal rules).

First CP-nets are introduced by means of a small example and a formal definition of their structure and behaviour is presented. Then we describe how to extend CP-nets by a set of hierarchy constructs (allowing a hierarchical CP-net to consist of many different subnets, which are related to each other in a formal way). Next we describe how to analyse CP-nets, how to support them by various computer tools, and we also describe some typical applications. Finally, a number of future extensions are discussed (of the net model and the supporting software).

The non-hierarchical CP-nets in the present paper are analogous to the CP-nets defined in [35] and the High-level Petri Nets defined in [33]. In all three papers CP-nets (and HL-nets) have two different representations: The *expression representation* uses arc expressions and guards, while the *function representation* uses linear functions between multi-sets. Moreover, there are formal translations between the two representations (in both directions). In [33] and [35] we used the expression representation to describe systems, while we used the function representation for all the different kinds of analysis. It has, however, turned out that it only is necessary to turn to functions when we deal with invariant analysis, and this means that we now use the expression representation for all purposes – except for the calculation of invariants. This change is important for the practical use of CP-nets – because it means that the function representation and the translations (which are a bit mathematically complex) no longer are parts of the basic definition of CP-nets. Instead they are parts of the invariant method (which anyway demands considerable mathematical skills).

The development of CP-nets has been supported by several grants from the Danish National Science Research Council.

Contents

To find a given page please add the page number in this table to the page number that precedes this article.

1. Informal Introduction to Non-Hierarchical CP-nets

High-level nets, such as Coloured Petri Nets (CP-nets) and Predicate/Transition Nets are now in widespread use for many different practical purposes.[1] The main reason for the large success of these kinds of net models is that they – *without loosing the possibility of formal analysis* – allow the modeller to make *much more succinct and manageable descriptions* than can be produced by means of low-level nets (such as Place/Transition Nets and Elementary Nets). In high-level nets the complexity of a model can be divided between the net structure, the net inscriptions and the declarations. This means that it is possible to handle the description of much larger and more complex systems. It also means that we can describe simple data manipulation (such as the addition of two integers) by means of arc expressions (such as x+y) – instead of having to describe this by a complex set of places, transitions and arcs. The step from low-level nets to high-level nets can be compared to the step from assembly languages to modern programming languages with an elaborated type concept: In low-level nets there is only one kind of token and this means that the state of a place is described by an integer (and in many cases even by a boolean). In high-level nets each token can carry a complex information (which e.g. may describe the entire state of a process or a data base).[2]

However, looking at the history of high-level programming languages, it is obvious that their success also to a very large degree depends upon issues that do not concern typing. In particular, the development of subroutines and modules has played a key role, because they have made it possible to divide a large description into smaller units which can be investigated more or less independently of each other. In fact, the absence of compositionality has been one of the main critiques raised against Petri net models. To meet this critique hierarchical CP-nets have been developed. In this net model it is possible to create a number of individual CP-nets, which then can be related to each other in a formal way – i.e. in a way which has a well-defined behaviour and thus allows formal analysis.

The remaining parts of this chapter contains an informal introduction to non-hierarchical CP-nets and their behaviour.

1.1 A simple example of a non-hierarchical CP-net

The non-hierarchical CP-net in Fig. 1 describes a system in which a number of processes compete for some shared resources. As in all other kinds of Petri nets there is a set of places (drawn as circles/ellipses) and a set of transitions (drawn as rectangles). The places and their tokens represent states, while the transitions represent state changes. However, each place may contain several tokens and each of these carries a data value – which may be of arbitrarily complex type (e.g. a record where the first

---

[1]   A selection of references can be found in section 6.5.
[2]   We shall in this paper not use any more space to compare high-level and low-level Petri nets. The reason is that we primarily are interested in the practical applications of Petri nets – and in this field the superiority of high-level nets is now generally accepted. A more detailed comparison of high-level and low-level nets can be found in [20] and [22].

field is a real, the second a text string, while the third is a list of integer pairs). The data value which is attached to a given token is referred to as the **token colour**.

In Fig. 1 there are two kinds of processes: three q-processes start in state A and cycle through five different states (A, B, C, D and E), while two p-processes start in state B and cycle through four different states (B, C, D and E). Each of these five processes is represented by a token – where the token colour is a pair such that the first element tells whether the token represents a p-process or a q-process while the second element is an integer telling how many full cycles that process has completed. In the initial marking, there are three (q,0)-tokens at place A and two (p,0)-tokens at place B.

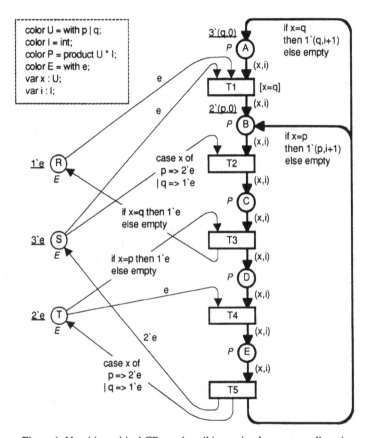

Figure 1. Non-hierarchical CP-net describing a simple resource allocation

There are three different kinds of resources: one r resource, three s resources and two t resources (each resource is represented by an e-token, on R, S or T). The arc expressions tell how many resources the different kinds of processes reserve/release. As an example, "case x of p=>2`e | q=>1`e" (at the arc from S to T2) tells that a p-process needs two s resources in order to go from state B to C, while a q-process only needs one.[3] Analogously, "if x=q then 1`e else empty" (at the arc from T3 to R) tells that each

---

[3] The operator ` takes an integer n and a colour c and it returns the multi-set that contains n appearances of c (and nothing else).

q-process releases an r resource when it goes from state C to D, while a p-process releases none.[4] It should be noticed that the processes in this system neither consume nor create tokens (during a full cycle the number of releases matches the number of reservations). Now let us take a closer view of the CP-net in Fig. 1. It consists of three different parts: the **net structure**, the **declarations** and the **net inscriptions**.

The net structure is a directed graph with two kinds of nodes, **places** and **transitions**, interconnected by **arcs** – in such a way that each arc connects two different kinds of nodes (i.e. a place and a transition).[5] In Fig. 1 the right hand part of the net (describing how processes change between different states) is drawn with thick lines. This distinguishes it from the rest of the net (describing how resources are reserved and released). It should, however, be stressed that such graphical conventions have no formal meaning. The only purpose is to make the CP-net more readable for human beings.

The declarations in the upper left corner tell us that we in this simple example have four **colour sets**, (U, I, P, and E) and two **variables** (x and i). The use of colour sets in CP-nets is analogous to the use of types in programming languages: Each place has a colour set attached to it and this means that each token residing on that place must have a colour (i.e. attached information) which is a member of the colour set. Analogously to types, the colour sets not only define the actual colours (which are members of the colours sets), they also define the operations and functions which can be applied to the colours. In this paper we shall define the colour sets using a syntax that is similar to the way in which types are defined in most programming languages. It should be noticed that a colour set definition often implicitly introduces new operators and functions (as an example the declaration of a colour set of type integer introduces the ordinary addition, subtraction, and multiplication operators). In our present example, the colour set U contains two elements (p and q) while the colour set I contains all integers.[6] The colour set P is the set of all pairs, where the first component is of type U while the second is of type I. Finally, the colour set E only contains a single element – and this means that the corresponding tokens carry no information (often we think of them as being "ordinary" or "uncoloured" tokens).

Each net inscription is attached to a place, transition or arc. In Fig. 1 places have three different kinds of inscriptions: **names**, **colour sets** and **initialization expressions**, transitions have two kinds of inscriptions: **names** and **guards**, while arcs only have one kind of inscription: **arc expressions**. All net inscriptions are positioned next to the corresponding net element – and to make it easy to distinguish between them we write names in plain text, colour sets in italics, while initialization expressions are underlined and guards are contained in square brackets.

Names have no formal meaning. They only serve as a mean of identification that makes it possible for human beings and a computer systems to refer to the individual places and transitions. Names can be omitted and one can use the same name for several nodes (although this may create confusion). As explained above each place must have a

---

4   *empty* denotes the empty multi-set.
5   Such a graph is called a bipartite directed graph.
6   To be more precise, I only contains the integers in the interval MinInt..MaxInt – where MinInt and MaxInt are determined by the implementation of the Integer data type. In general, each colour set is demanded to be finite, although it (as I) may have very many elements.

colour set and this determines the kind of tokens which may reside on that place. The initialization expression of a place must evaluate to a multi-set over the corresponding colour set. Multi-sets are analogous to sets except that they may contain multiple appearances of the same element. In the case of CP-nets, this implies that two tokens on the same place may have identical colours. By convention we omit initialization expressions which evaluate to the empty multi-set.

The guard of a transition is a boolean expression which must be fulfilled before the transition can occur. By convention we omit guards which always evaluate to true. The arc expression of an arc is an expression, and it may (as the guard) contain variables, constants, functions and operations that are defined in the declarations (explicitly or implicitly). When the variables of an arc expression are bound (i.e. replaced by colours from the corresponding colour sets) the arc expression must evaluate to a colour (or a multi-set of colours) that belong to the colour set attached to the place of the arc. When the same variable appears more than once, in the guard/arc expressions of a *single* transition, all these appearances must be bound to the same colour. In contrast to this appearances, in the guard/arc expressions of *different* transitions, are totally independent, and this means that they may be bound to different colours. As explained in the sequel, a CP-net may have several other kinds of inscriptions (e.g. used to describe hierarchical relationships and time delays).

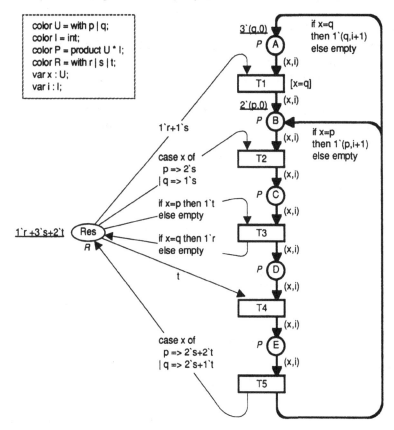

Figure 2. A slightly different CP-net describing the same resource allocation

As mentioned above a CP-net consists of three different parts: the net structure, the declarations and the net inscriptions. The complexity of a description is distributed among these three parts and this can be done in many different ways. As an example, each arc to or from a resource place could have had a very simple arc expression of the form f(x), where the function f was defined in the declaration part. As another, and perhaps more sensible example, we could have represented all resources by means of a single place RES, as shown in Fig. 2. The + operator in the arc expressions denotes addition of multi-sets. As an example, $2`s+1`t$ is the multi-set that contains two appearances of s and one appearance of t:

1.2 Dynamic behaviour of non-hierarchical CP-nets

One of the most important properties of CP-nets (and other kinds of Petri nets) is that they – in contrast to many other graphical description languages – have a well-defined semantics which in an unambiguous way defines the behaviour of the system. The ideas behind the semantics are very simple, as we shall demonstrate by means of Fig. 3 - which contains one of the transitions from Fig. 1.[7]

The transition has two variables (x and i) and before we can consider an occurrence of the transition these variables have to be bound to colours of the corresponding types (i.e. elements of the colour sets U and I). This can be done in many different ways: One possibility is to bind x to p and i to zero. Then we get: $b_1 = <x=p,i=0>$. Another possibility is to bind x to q and i to 37. Then we get: $b_2 = <x=q,i=37>$.

For each **binding** we can check whether the transition, with this binding, is **enabled** (in the current marking). This is done by evaluating the guard and all the input arc expressions: In the present case the guard is trivial (a missing guard always evaluates to true). For the binding b_1 the two arc expressions evaluate to (p,0) and $2`e$, respectively. Thus we conclude that $b_1$ is enabled – because each of the input places contains at least the tokens to which the corresponding arc expression evaluates (one (p,0)-token on B and two e-tokens on S). For the binding $b_2$ the two arc expressions evaluate to (q,37) and $1`e$. Thus we conclude that b_2 is *not* enabled (there is no (q,37)-token on B). A transition can be executed in as many ways as the variables (in its arc expressions and guard) can be bound. However, for a given state, it is usually only a few of these bindings that are enabled.

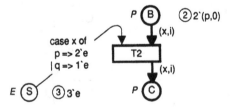

Figure 3. A transition from the resource allocation system

When a transition is enabled (for a certain binding) it may **occur** and it then removes tokens from its input places and adds tokens to its output places. The number of re-

---

7   The inscriptions at the right hand side of the places indicate the current marking. The number of tokens are indicated in the small circle while the colours are described by the multi-set next to the circle.

moved/added tokens and the colours of these tokens are determined by the value of the corresponding arc expressions (evaluated with respect to the binding in question). An occurrence of the binding b_1 removes a $(p,0)$-token from B, removes two e-tokens from S and adds a $(p,0)$-token to C.[8] The binding b_2 is not enabled and thus it cannot occur.

A distribution of tokens (on the places) is called a **marking**. The **initial marking** is the marking determined by evaluating the initialization expressions. A pair, where the first element is a transition and the second element a binding of that transition, is called an **occurrence element**. Now we can ask whether an occurrence element O is enabled in a given marking M_1 – and when this is the case we can speak about the marking M_2 which is **reached** by the occurrence of O in M_1. It should be noticed that several occurrence elements may be enabled in the same marking. In that case there are two different possibilities: Either there are enough tokens (so that each occurrence element can get its own share) or there too few tokens (so that several occurrence elements have to compete for the same input tokens). In the first case the occurrence elements are said to be **concurrently enabled**. They can occur in the same **step** and they each remove their own input tokens and produce their own output tokens. In the second case the occurrence elements are said to be in **conflict** with each other and they cannot occur in the same step.

In the initial marking of Fig. 1 we observe that the occurrence element $O_1 = (T1,<x=q,i=0>)$ is concurrently enabled with $O_2 = (T2,<x=p,i=0>)$. This means that we can have a step where both O_1 and O_2 occur. Such a step is denoted by the multi-set $1`O_1 + 1`O_2$ and when it occurs a $(q,0)$-token is moved from A to B and a $(p,0)$-token from B to C. Moreover, an e-token is removed from R and three e-tokens from S. It should be noticed that the effect of the step $1`O_1 + 1`O_2$ is the same as when the two occurrence elements occur after each other in arbitrary order. This is an example of a general property: Whenever an enabled step contains more than one occurrence element, it can (in any thinkable way) be divided into two or more steps, which then are known to be able to occur after each other (in any thinkable order) and together have the same total effect as the original step.[9]

The above informal explanation of the occurrence rule, tells us how to understand the behaviour of a CP-net – and it explains the intuition on which CP-nets build. It is, however, very difficult (probably impossible) to make an informal explanation which is complete and unambiguous, and thus it is extremely important that the intuition is complemented by a more formal definition (which we shall present in chapter 2). It is the formal definition that has formed the basis for the implementation of a CP-net simulator, and it is also the formal definition that has made it possible to develop the analysis methods by which it can be *proved* whether a given CP-net has certain properties (e.g. absence of dead-locks).

---

[8]   We often think of the $(p,0)$-token as being moved from B to C. However, in the formal definition of CP-nets, the $(p,0)$-token added to C has no closer relationship to the $(p,0)$-token removed from B than it has to the two e-tokens removed from S.

[9]   Without this property it is very difficult to construct occurrence graphs because it no longer is sufficient to consider steps that correspond to single occurrence elements. It is, however, easy to violate this property and this is in fact done by many of the ad hoc extensions which are presented in the Petri net literature (e.g. the use of inhibitor arcs and some definitions of capacity).

Consider again the resource allocation system. It can easily be proved that this system has no dead-lock.[10] Now let us, in the initial marking, add an extra s resource (i.e. an extra e-token on S). Obviously, this cannot lead to a dead-lock (dead-locks appear when we have too few resource tokens and thus an extra resource token cannot cause a dead-lock). Is this argumentation convincing? At a first glance: yes! However, the argument is *wrong*, and the extra s resource actually means that we can reach a dead-lock (by letting the two p-processes advance to state D while the q-processes remain in state A). Hopefully, this small exercise demonstrates that informal arguments about behavioural properties are dangerous – and this is our motivation for the development of more formal analysis methods. We shall return to such methods in chapter 4.

2. Formal Definition of Non-Hierarchical CP-nets

The non-hierarchical CP-nets in the present paper are analogous to the CP-nets defined in [35] – but not identical to them (for more details see the abstract).

2.1 Multi-sets and expressions

In this section we define multi-sets and introduce the notation which we use to talk about expressions:

Definition 2.1: A **multi-set** m, over a non-empty and *finite* set S, is a function $m \in [S \to N]$.[11] The non-negative integer $m(s) \in N$ is the **number of appearances** of the element s in the multi-set m.

We usually represent the multi-set m by a formal sum:

$$\sum_{s \in S} m(s) \, s.$$

By S_{MS} we denote the **set of all multi-sets** over S. The non-negative integers $\{m(s) \mid s \in S\}$ are called the **coefficients** of the multi-set m, and $m(s)$ is called the **coefficient** of s. An element $s \in S$ is said to **belong** to the multi-set m iff $m(s) \neq 0$ and we then write $s \in m$. The **empty multi-set** is the multi-set in which all coefficients are zero, and it is denoted by $\emptyset$ (or by *empty*).[12]

As an example, consider the set $S = \{a,b,c,d,e\}$ and the two multi-sets $m_1 = a+2c+e$, and $m_2 = a+2b+3c+e$ which both are members of S_{MS}. As it can be seen, we usually omit S-values which have a zero coefficient and we also omit coefficients which are equal to one.[13] For multi-sets we define the following operations:

---

10   This can e.g. be done by means of occurrence graphs or by means of place invariants.

11   N denotes the set of all non-negative integers while $[A \to B]$ denotes the set of all functions from A to B.

12   To be precise there is an empty multi-set for each element set S. We shall, however, ignore this and allow ourselves to speak about *the* empty multi-set – in a similar way as we speak about *the* empty set and *the* empty list.

13   When the CPN tools described in chapter 5 was designed, it turned out to be convenient to insert an explicit operator between the coefficients and the S-values and include coefficients which are equal to

Definition 2.2: Summation, scalar-multiplication, comparison, and **multiplicity** of multi-sets are defined in the following way, for all m, m_1, $m_2 \in S_{MS}$ and $n \in \mathbb{N}$:

(i) $m_1 + m_2 \;=\; \sum_{s \in S} (m_1(s) + m_2(s))\, s$ (summation).

(ii) $n * m \;=\; \sum_{s \in S} (n \cdot m(s))\, s$ (scalar-multiplication).

(iii) $m_1 \neq m_2 \;=\; \exists s \in S: [m_1(s) \neq m_2(s)]$ (comparison).

      $m_1 \leq m_2 \;=\; \forall s \in S: [m_1(s) \leq m_2(s)]$ (the relations $<$, $\geq$, $>$, and $=$ are defined analogously to $\leq$).

(iv) $|m| \;=\; \sum_{s \in S} m(s)$ (multiplicity).

When $m_1 \leq m_2$ we also define **subtraction**:

(v) $m_2 - m_1 \;=\; \sum_{s \in S} (m_2(s) - m_1(s))\, s$ (subtraction).

It can be shown that the multi-set operations above have a number of nice properties. As an example $(S_{MS}, +)$ is a commutative monoid.

For CP-nets, we use the terms *variables* and *expressions* in the same way as in typed lambda-calculus and functional programming languages. This means that expressions do *not* have side-effects and variables are *bound* to values (instead of being assigned to). It also means that complex expression are built, from variables and simpler subexpressions, by means of functions and operations. To give the abstract definition of CP-nets it is not necessary to fix the concrete syntax in which the modeller writes expressions, and thus we shall only assume that such a syntax exists (together with a well-defined semantics) – making it possible in an unambiguous way to talk about:

• The *type of a variable* v – denoted by Type(v).

• The *type of an expression* expr – denoted by Type(expr).

• The *set of variables in an expression* expr – denoted by Var(expr). The set of variables only includes the free variables – i.e. those which are *not* bound internally in the expression (e.g. by a local definition).

• A *binding of a set of variables* $V = \{v_1, v_2, \ldots, v_n\}$ – denoted by $\langle v_1 = c_1, v_2 = c_2, \ldots, v_n = c_n \rangle$. It is demanded that $c_i \in \mathrm{Type}(v_i)$ for each variable $v_i \in V$.[14]

• The *value obtained by evaluating an expression* expr *in a binding* b – denoted by expr$\langle$b$\rangle$. It is demanded that Var(expr) is a subset of the variables of b, and the evaluation is performed by substituting each variable $v_i \in \mathrm{Var}(expr)$ with the value $c_i \in \mathrm{Type}(v_i)$ determined by the binding.

---

one. In this case we write $m_1 = 1`a + 2`c + 1`e$ and $m_2 = 1`a + 2`b + 3`c + 1`e$. This makes it easier to perform type checking (and it makes it easier to deal with multi-sets over integers, e.g. $3`1 + 2`35 + 1`59$).

[14]   For a type A we also use A to denote the *set of elements* in A, and we use $c \in A$ to denote that the value c is an element of A.

As an example, illustrating this notation, we may have:

$Type(x) = Type(y) = S$.
$Var(2 * (x + 3y)) = \{x,y\}$.
$Type(2 * (x + 3y)) = S_{MS}$.
$(2 * (x + 3y))<x=b,y=d> = 2`b+6`d$.

2.2 Definition of non-hierarchical CP-nets

In this section we define non-hierarchical CP-nets as a many-tuple. It should, however be understood, that the only purpose of this is to give a mathematically sound and unambiguous definition of CP-nets and their semantics. Any concrete net – created by a modeller - will always be specified in terms of a CP-graph (i.e. a diagram similar to Fig. 1). In the following Bool is the boolean type (containing the elements Bool = {False,True} and having the standard logic operations). Some motivation and explanation of the individual parts of the definition is given immediately below the definition:

Definition 2.3: A **non-hierarchical** CP-net is a tuple CPN = $(\Sigma, P, T, A, N, C, G, E, IN)$ satisfying the requirements below:

(i) Σ is a finite set of types, called **colour sets**. Each colour set must be finite and non-empty.

(ii) P is a finite set of **places**.

(iii) T is a finite set of **transitions**.

(iv) A is a finite set of **arcs** such that:
   - $P \cap T = P \cap A = T \cap A = \emptyset$.

(v)   N is a **node** function. It is defined from A into $P \times T \cup T \times P$.

(vi) C is a **colour** function. It is defined from P into Σ.

(vii) G is a **guard** function. It is defined from T into expressions such that:
   - $\forall t \in T: [Type(G(t)) = Bool \land Type(Var(G(t))) \subseteq \Sigma]$.

(viii) E is an **arc expression** function. It is defined from A into expressions such that:
   - $\forall a \in A: [Type(E(a)) = C(p(a))_{MS} \land Type(Var(E(a))) \subseteq \Sigma]$
   where p(a) is the place of N(a).

(ix) IN is an **initialization** function. It is defined from P into expressions such that:
   - $\forall p \in P: [Type(IN(p)) = C(p)_{MS} \land Var(IN(p)) = \emptyset]$.

(i) The set of **colour sets** determines the types, operations and functions that can be used in the net inscriptions (i.e. arc expressions, guards, initialization expressions, colour sets, etc.). If desired, the colour sets (and the corresponding operations and functions) can be defined by means of a many-sorted sigma algebra (in the same way as known from the theory of abstract data types). We demand all colour sets to be finite - although they may have a very large cardinality (e.g. be equivalent to all the real numbers which can be represented on a given computer). This restriction means that the linear extension of a function $F \in [A \rightarrow B_{MS}]$ to a function $\hat{F} \in [A_{MS} \rightarrow B_{MS}]$ always is known to be convergent. Such functions are used in the theory of place invariants and transition invariants.

(ii) + (iii) + (iv) The **places, transitions** and **arcs** are described by three sets P, T and A which are demanded to be finite and pairwise disjoint. In contrast to classical Petri nets, we allow the net structure to be empty (i.e. $P \cup T = \emptyset$). The reason is pragmatic: It allows the user to define and syntax check a set of colour sets without having to invent a dummy net structure.

(v) The **node** function maps each arc into a pair where the first element is the source node and the second the destination node. The two nodes have to be of different kind (i.e. one must be a place while the other is a transition). In contrast to classical Petri nets, we allow a CP-net to have several arcs between the same ordered pair of nodes (and thus we define A as a separate set and not as a subset of $P \times T \cup T \times P$). The reason is pragmatic: We often have nets where each occurrence element moves exactly one token along each of the surrounding arcs, and it is then awkward to be forced to violate this convention in the cases where an occurrence element removes/adds two or more tokens to/from the same place. It is of course easy to combine such multiple arcs to a single arc by adding the corresponding arc expressions (which must be of the same multi-set type). We also allow nodes to be isolated. Again the reason is pragmatic: When we build computer tools for CP-nets we want to be able to check whether a diagram is a CP-net (i.e. fulfils the definition above). There is, however, no conceptual difference between an isolated node and a node where all the arc expressions of the surrounding arcs always evaluate to the empty multi-set (and the latter is difficult to detect in general, since arc expressions may be arbitrarily complex). It is of course easy to exclude such degenerate nets when this is convenient for theoretical purposes.

(vi) The **colour** function C maps each place p into a set of possible **token colours** C(p). Each token on p must have a colour that belongs to the type C(p).

(vii) The **guard** function G maps each transition t into an expression of type boolean, i.e. a predicate. Moreover, all variables in G(t) must have types that belong to Σ.[15]

(viii) The **arc expression** function E maps each arc a into an expression which must be of type $C(p(a))_{MS}$. This means that each evaluation of the arc expression must yield a multi-set over the colour set that is attached to the corresponding place. We shall, as a shorthand, also allow an arc expression to be of type C(p(a)). In this case the arc expression evaluates to a colour in C(p(a)) which we then consider to be a multi-set with only one element.

(ix) The **initialization** function IN maps each place p into an expression which must be of type $C(p)_{MS}$ – i.e. a multi-set over C(p). The expression is not allowed to contain any variables. Analogously to (viii), we shall, as a shorthand, also allow an initial expression to be of type C(p).

As mentioned in the abstract, the "modern version" of CP-nets (presented in this paper) uses the expression representation (defined above) – not only when a system is being described, but also when it is being analysed. It is only during invariant analysis that it may be adequate/necessary to translate the expression representation into a function representation.

---

[15] For a set of variables Vars we use Type(Vars) to denote the set {Type(v) | v ∈ Vars}.

In addition to the concepts introduced in Def. 2.3, we use $X = P \cup T$ to denote the set of all **nodes**, and we define the following functions:[16]

- $s \in [A \to X]$ maps each arc a into the **source** of a, i.e. the first component of $N(a)$.

- $d \in [A \to X]$ maps each arc a into the **destination** of a, i.e. the second component of $N(a)$.

- $p \in [A \to P]$ maps each arc a into the **place** of $N(a)$, i.e. that component of $N(a)$ which is a place.

- $t \in [A \to T]$ maps each arc a into the **transition** of $N(a)$, i.e. that component of $N(a)$ which is a transition.

- $A \in [(P \times T \cup T \times P) \to A_S]$[17] maps each ordered pair of nodes (x_1, x_2) into the set of **connecting arcs**, i.e. the arcs that have the first node as source and the second as destination:
  $A(x_1, x_2) = \{a \in A \mid N(a) = (x_1, x_2)\}$.

- $A \in [X \to A_S]$[18] maps each node x into the set of **surrounding arcs**, i.e. the arcs that have x as source or destination:
  $A(x) = \{a \in A \mid \exists x' \in X: [N(a) = (x, x') \lor N(a) = (x', x)]\}$.

- $X \in [X \to X_S]$ maps each node x into the set of **surrounding nodes**, i.e. the nodes that are connected with x by an arc:
  $X(x) = \{x' \in X \mid \exists a \in A: [N(a) = (x, x') \lor N(a) = (x', x)]\}$.

All the functions above can, in the usual way, be extended to take sets as input (then they all return sets and thus all the function names are written with a capital letter).

2.3 Dynamic behaviour of non-hierarchical CP-nets

Having defined the static structure of CP-nets we are now ready to consider their behaviour – but first we introduce the following notation where Var(t) is called the set of **variables** of t while $E(x_1, x_2)$ is called the **expression** of (x_1, x_2):

- $\forall t \in T: [Var(t) = \{v \mid v \in Var(G(t)) \lor \exists a \in A(t): v \in Var(E(a))\}]$.

- $\forall (x_1, x_2) \in (P \times T \cup T \times P): [E(x_1, x_2) = \sum_{a \in A(x_1, x_2)} E(a)]$.[19]

Next we define what we mean by a binding. Intuitively, a binding, of a transition t, is a substitution that replaces each variable of t with a colour. It is demanded that each colour is of the correct type and that the guard evaluates to true:

---

16 Each function name indicates the range of the function – as an example p maps into places, while A maps into *sets* of arcs.

17 A_S denotes the set of all subsets of A.

18 From the argument(s) it will always be clear whether we deal with the function $A \in [X \to A_S]$, the function $A \in [(P \times T \cup T \times P) \to A_S]$ or the set A.

19 The summation indicates addition of expressions (and it is well-defined because all the participating expressions have a common multi-set type). From the arguments(s) it will always be clear whether we deal with the function $E \in [A \to Exp]$ or the function $E \in [(P \times T \cup T \times P) \to Exp]$.

Definition 2.4: For a transition $t \in T$ with variables $Var(t) = \{v_1, v_2, \ldots, v_n\}$ we define the **binding type** $BT(t)$ as follows:

$$BT(t) = Type(v_1) \times Type(v_2) \times \ldots \times Type(v_n).[20]$$

Moreover, we define the set of all **bindings** $B(t)$ as follows:

$$B(t) = \{(c_1, c_2, \ldots, c_n) \in BT(t) \mid G(t) < v_1 = c_1, v_2 = c_2, \ldots, v_n = c_n > \}.[21]$$

For convenience we denote bindings in two different ways: Either in the form $< v_1 = c_1, v_2 = c_2, \ldots, v_n = c_n >$ or in the form $(c_1, c_2, \ldots, c_n)$. In both cases this denotes an element of $BT(t)$. Next we define token distributions, binding distributions, markings and steps:[22]

Definition 2.5: A **token distribution** is a function M, defined on P such that $M(p) \in C(p)_{MS}$ for all $p \in P$. The set of all token distributions (for a given CP-net CPN) is denoted by TD_{CPN}, and for all $M_1, M_2 \in TD_{CPN}$ we define the relations $\neq$ and $\leq$ in the following way:

(i) $M_1 \neq M_2 \;\Leftrightarrow\; \exists p \in P : [M_1(p) \neq M_2(p)]$.

(ii) $M_1 \leq M_2 \;\Leftrightarrow\; \forall p \in P : [M_1(p) \leq M_2(p)]$.

The relations $<, \geq, >$, and $=$ are defined analogously to $\leq$. When $c \in M(p)$ for some $c \in C(p)$, we say that the pair (p,c) is an **element** of M, and we write $(p,c) \in M$. Moreover, we say that M is **non-empty** iff it has at least one element.

A **binding distribution** is a function Y, defined on T such that $Y(t) \in B(t)_{MS}$ for all $t \in T$.[23] The set of all binding distributions (for a given CP-net CPN) is denoted by BD_{CPN}, and the relations $\neq, \leq, <, \geq, >$, and $=$ are defined analogously to the way they were defined for token distributions. When $b \in Y(t)$ for some $b \in B(t)$, we say that the pair (t,b) is an **element** of Y, and we write $(t,b) \in Y$. Moreover, we say that Y is **non-empty** iff it has at least one element.

A **marking** of a CP-net is a token distribution and a **step** is a *non-empty* binding distribution. The set of all markings (for a given CP-net CPN) is denoted by M_{CPN}, and the set of all steps is denoted by Y_{CPN}. The **initial marking** M_0 is the marking which is obtained by evaluating the initialization expressions, i.e. the marking where $M_0(p) = IN(p) <>$ for all $p \in P$.[24]

---

[20]   We assume that the set of variables $Var(t)$ is ordered – in some arbitrary way.

[21]   As defined in section 2.1, $G(t) < v_1 = c_1, v_2 = c_2, \ldots, v_n = c_n >$ denotes the evaluation of the guard expression $G(t)$ in the binding $< v_1 = c_1, v_2 = c_2, \ldots, v_n = c_n >$.

[22]   There is no difference between the set of token distributions and the set of markings, and there is very little difference between the set of binding distributions and the set of steps. In this paper we only use token/binding distributions to define markings/steps and thus it may seem unnecessary to introduce all four sets. Token/binding distributions are however, general concepts, which are useful in a number of other contexts (in which it would be misleading to talk about markings/steps).

[23]   It should be noticed that all bindings of a binding distribution, according to Definition 2.4, automatically satisfy the corresponding guard.

[24] $IN(p) <>$ denotes the evaluation of IN in the empty binding $<>$ (which is used because $IN(p)$ has an empty set of variables).

Definition 2.6: A step Y is **enabled** in a marking M iff the following property is satisfied:

$$\forall p \in P: [\sum_{(t,b)\in Y} E(p,t)<b> \le M(p)].$$

Let Y be an enabled step, with respect to a given marking M. When $(t,b)\in Y$, we say that t is **enabled** in M for the **binding** b. We also say that the pair (t,b) is enabled in M, or simply that t is **enabled** in M. When two different transitions $t_1, t_2 \in T$ satisfy $Y(t_1) \neq \emptyset \neq Y(t_2)$, we say that t_1 and t_2 are **concurrently enabled**. When a transition $t \in T$ satisfies $|Y(t)| \ge 2$, we say that t is **concurrently enabled with itself** and when it for a binding $b \in B(t)$ satisfy $Y(t) \ge 2`b$, we say that (t,b) is **concurrently enabled with itself**.

When a step is enabled it may occur and this means that tokens are removed from the input places and added to the output places of the occurring transitions. The number and colours of the tokens are determined by the arc expressions, evaluated for the occurring bindings:

Definition 2.7: When a step Y is enabled in a marking M_1 it may **occur**, changing the marking M_1 to another marking M_2, defined by:

$$\forall p \in P: [M_2(p) = (M_1(p) - \sum_{(t,b)\in Y} E(p,t)<b>) + \sum_{(t,b)\in Y} E(t,p)<b>].$$

The first sum is called the **removed** tokens while the second is called the **added tokens.** Moreover we say that M_2 is **directly reachable** from M_1 by the occurrence of the step Y, which we also denote:

$$M_1[Y> M_2.$$

Definition 2.8: A **finite occurrence sequence** is a sequence of markings and steps:

$$M_1[Y_1> M_2[Y_2> M_3 \ldots\ldots M_n[Y_n> M_{n+1}$$

such that $n \in N$, and $M_i[Y_i > M_{i+1}$ for all $i \in 1..n$.[25] The marking M_1 is called the **start marking** of the occurrence sequence, while the marking M_{n+1} is called the **end marking.** The non-negative integer n is called the **number of steps** in the occurrence sequence, or the **length** of it.

Analogously, an **infinite occurrence sequence** is a sequence of markings and steps:

$$M_1[Y_1> M_2[Y_2> M_3 \ldots\ldots$$

such that $M_i[Y_i> M_{i+1}$ for all $i \in N_+$.[26] The marking M_1 is called the **start marking** of the occurrence sequence, which is said to have **infinite length.**

---

[25] By 1..n we denote the set of all integers i that satisfy $1 \le i \le n$.

[26] N_+ denotes the set of all positive integers.

The start marking of an occurrence sequence will often, but not always, be identical to the initial marking of the CP-net. We allow the user to omit some parts of an occurrence sequence and e.g. write:

$$M_1[Y_1 Y_2...Y_n\rangle M_{n+1}.$$

Definition 2.9: A marking M" is **reachable from** a marking M' iff there exists a finite occurrence sequence having M' as start marking and M" as end marking – i.e. iff there, for some $n \in N$, exists a finite sequence of steps such that:

$$M'[Y_1 Y_2...Y_n\rangle M".$$

We then also say that M" is reachable from M' in **n steps**. The *set* of markings which are reachable from M' is denoted by $[M'\rangle$. As a shorthand, we say that a marking is **reachable** iff it is reachable from the initial marking M_0 – i.e. contained in $[M_0\rangle$.

It should be obvious that behavioural properties, such as dead-lock, liveness, home markings, boundedness and fairness, can be defined for CP-nets in a similar way as for Place/Transition Nets (PT-nets). It is well-known that each CP-net has an equivalent PT-net, and each behavioural property is defined in such a way that a given CP-net has the property iff the equivalent PT-net has. The definitions of the behavioural properties are outside the scope of this paper.

2.4 Some historical remarks about the development of CP-nets

The foundation of Petri nets was presented by Carl Adam Petri in his doctoral-thesis [48]. The first nets were called Condition/Event Nets (CE-nets). This net model allows each place to contain at most one token – because the place is considered to represent a boolean condition, which can be either true or false. In the following years a large number of persons contributed to the development of new net models, basic concepts, and analysis methods. One of the most notable results was the development of Place/Transition Nets (PT-nets). This net model allows a place to contain several tokens. The first coherent presentation of the theory and application of Petri nets was given in the course material developed for the First Advanced Course on Petri Nets [5] and later this was supplemented by the course material for the Second Advanced Course on Petri Nets [6] and [7].

For theoretical considerations CE-nets turned out to be more tractable than PT-nets and much of the theoretical work concerning the definition of basic concepts and analysis methods has been performed on CE-nets. Later, a new net model called Elementary Nets (EN-nets) has been proposed in [51] and [57]. The basic ideas of this net model are very close to CE-nets – but EN-nets avoid some of the technical problems which have turned out to be present in the original definition of CE-nets.

For practical applications, PT-nets were used. However, it often turned out that this net model was too low-level to cope with the real-world applications in a manageable way, and different researchers started to develop their own extensions of PT-nets - adding concepts such as: priority between transitions, time delays, global variables to be tested and updated by transitions, zero testing of places, etc. In this way a large number of different net models were defined. However, most of these net models were designed with a single – and often very narrow – application area in mind. This created a serious problem: Although some of the net models could be used to give adequate descriptions of certain systems, most of the net models possessed nearly no analytic power. The main reason for this was the large variety of different net models. It often turned out to be a difficult task to translate an analysis method developed for one net model to another – and in this way the efforts to develop suitable analysis methods were widely scattered.

The breakthrough with respect to this problem came when Predicate/Transition Nets (PrT-nets) were presented in [20]. PrT-nets were the first kind of high-level nets which was constructed without any particular application area in mind. PrT-nets form a nice generalization of PT-nets and CE-nets (exploiting the same kind of reasoning that leads from propositional logic to predicate logic). PrT-nets can be related to PT-nets and CE-nets in a formal way – and this makes it possible to generalize most of the basic concepts and analysis methods that have been developed for these net models – so that they also become applicable to PrT-nets. Later, an improved definition of PrT-nets has been presented in [22]. This definition draws heavily on sigma algebras (as known from the theory of abstract data types).

However, it soon turned out that PrT-nets present some technical problems when the analysis methods of place invariants and transition invariants are generalized. It is possible to calculate invariants for PrT-nets, but the interpretation of the invariants is difficult and must be done with great care to avoid erroneous results. The problem arises because of the variables which appear in the arc expressions of PrT-nets. These variables also appear in the invariants, and to interpret the invariants it is necessary to bind the variables, via a complex set of substitution rules. To overcome this problem the first version of Coloured Petri Nets (CP81-nets) was defined in [32]. The main ideas of this net model are directly inspired by PrT-nets, but the relation between an occurrence element and the token colours involved in the occurrence is now defined by functions and not by expressions as in PrT-nets. This removes the variables, and invariants can now be interpreted without problems.

However, it often turns out that the functions attached to arcs in CP81-nets are more difficult to read and understand than the expressions attached to arcs in PrT-nets. Moreover, as indicated above, there is a strong relation between PrT-nets and CP81-nets and from the very beginning it was clear that most descriptions in one of the net models could be informally translated to the other net model and vice versa. This lead to the idea of an improved net model – combining the qualities of PrT-nets and CP81-nets. This net model was defined in [33] where it was called High-level Petri Nets (HL-nets). Unfortunately, this name has given rise to a lot of confusion since the term "high-level nets" at that time started to become used as a generic name for PrT-nets, CP81-nets, HL-nets, and several other kinds of net models. To avoid this confusion it was necessary to rename HL-nets to Coloured Petri Nets (CP87-nets). CP87-nets have two different representations (and formal translations between them). The expression representation is nearly identical to PrT-nets (as presented in [20]), while the function representation is nearly identical to CP81-nets. The first coherent presentation of CP87-nets and their analysis methods was given in [35].

Today most of the practical applications of Petri nets (reported in the literature) use either PrT-nets or CP-nets – although several other kinds of high-level nets have been proposed. There is very little difference between PrT-nets and CP-nets (and many modellers do not make a clear distinction between the two kinds of net models). The main differences between the two net models are today hidden inside the methods to calculate and interpret place and transition invariants (and this is of course not surprising when you think about the original motivation behind the development of CP[81]-nets). Instead of viewing PrT-nets and CP-nets as two different modelling languages it is, in our opinion, much more adequate to view them as two slightly different dialects of the same language.

3. Hierarchical CP-nets

Hierarchical CP-nets were first presented in [31] and it should be understood that this (as far as we know) was the very first successful attempt to create a set of hierarchy concepts for a class of high-level Petri nets. This means that the proposed concepts are likely to undergo many improvements and refinements (in the same way as the first very simple concept of subroutines has undergone dramatical changes to become the procedure concept of modern programming languages). In other words: We do not claim that our current proposal will be the "final solution". However, we do think that it constitutes a good starting point for further research and practical experiences in this area. In chapter 6 we describe a number of industrial applications of hierarchical CP-nets and more information about some of these can be found in [49], [54] and [55].

In [31] individual CP-nets, called pages, are related in five different ways, known as the five **hierarchy constructs**: substitution of transitions, substitution of places, invocation of transitions, fusion of places and fusion of transitions. In the present paper we shall, however, only deal with the first and fourth of these hierarchy constructs.[27] For an explanation of the other three hierarchy constructs the reader is referred to [31].

The intention has been to make a set of hierarchy constructs, which is general enough to be used with many different development methods and with many different analysis techniques. This means that we present the hierarchy constructs *without* prescribing specific methods for their use. Such methods have to be developed and written down – but this can only be done as we get more experiences with the practical use of the hierarchy constructs. Eventually the new development methods and analysis techniques will influence the definition of the hierarchy constructs – in the same way as modern programming languages have been influenced by the progress in the areas of programming methodology and verification techniques.[28]

3.1 Substitution of transitions

The intuitive idea behind substitution transitions is to allow the user to replace a transition (and its surrounding arcs) by a more complex CP-net – which usually gives a more precise and detailed description of the activity represented by the substituted transition.

---

[27] These are the two hierarchy constructs that are supported by the current version of the CPN tools described in chapter 5 – and they are the easiest to define, understand and use.

[28] During the design of the hierarchy constructs we have, of course, been influenced by the constructs and methods used with other graphical description languages and with modern programming languages.

The idea is analogous to the hierarchy constructs found in many graphical description languages (e.g. IDEF/SADT diagrams [43] and Yourdon diagrams [64]) – and it is also, in some respects, analogous to the module concepts found in many modern programming languages: At one level we want to give a simple description of the activity (without having to consider internal details about how it is carried out). At another level we want to specify the more detailed behaviour. Moreover, we want to be able to integrate the detailed specification with the more crude description and this integration must be done in such a way that it becomes meaningful to speak about the behaviour of the *combined* system.

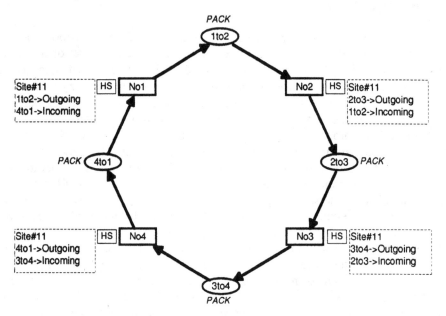

Figure 4. NetWork#10 describes a ring network with four different sites

As mentioned above, we want to relate individual CP-nets to nodes, which are members of other CP-nets, and this means that our description will contain a *set* of (non-hierarchical) CP-nets – which we shall call **pages**. Now let us consider a small example.[29] Imagine that we have a ring network with four different sites. This can be described by the page NetWork#10 in Fig. 4.[30] The four sites are represented by the four substitution transitions – NO1, NO2, NO3 and NO4 – each of which has an HS-tag adjacent (HS ≈ Hierarchy + Substitution). The inscription next to the HS-tag is called a **hierarchy inscription** and it defines the details of the actual substitution. We shall return to the hierarchy inscriptions in a moment, but let us first consider Site#11 in Fig. 5. This page describes an individual site.

---

[29] The purpose of the example is to explain the semantics of substitution transitions. The described ring network is far too simple to be realistic.

[30] To be able to refer to the individual pages we give each of them a page name (e.g. NetWork) and a page number (e.g. 10).

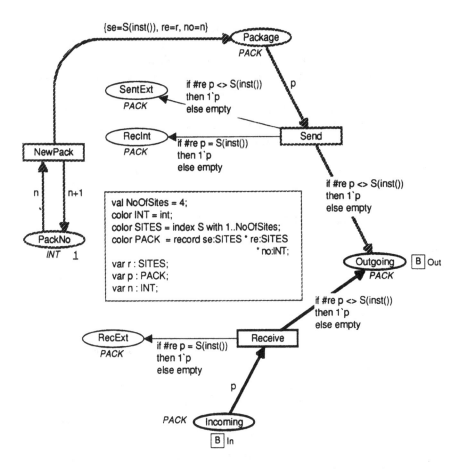

Figure 5. Site#11 describes an individual site of the ring network

Some of the declarations in the middle of Fig. 5 need a little explanation: The first line declares a constant NoOfSites. It is used in one of the other declarations – and it could also have been used e.g. in the arc expressions of NetWork#10 and Site#11, if desired. The colour set SITES contains four different elements which are denoted by S(1), S(2), S(3) and S(4).[31] The colour set PACK contains all records which have an se-field (identifying the sender), an re-field (identifying the receiver) and a no-field (containing a package number).

Site#11 has three different transitions: Each occurrence of NEWPACK creates a new package. The se-field of the new package becomes identical to S(inst()) where the pre-declared function inst() returns the identity number of the page instance on which the transition occurs[32] while the no-field is read from PACKNO. The re-field is determined

---

[31] The idea behind index colour sets is to make it easy for the user to define colour sets which are of the form {S₁, S₂,…Sₙ}.

[32] Allowing net inscriptions (such as arc expressions, guards and initialization expressions) to be dependent on the page instance is a generalization – with respect to the class of hierarchical CP-nets formally defined in section 3.4. The extension, which has turned out to be extremely useful, will be

by the variable r – which does not appear anywhere else, and this means that r can take an arbitrary value (from SITES). The created packages are handled by SEND, which inspects the re-field of the package.[33] When the re-field indicates that the receiver is different from the present site, the package is transferred to the network via OUTGOING (and a copy is put on SENTEXT). Otherwise the package is sent directly to RECINT. Finally, RECEIVE inspects all packages which are transferred from the network via INCOMING. Again the re-field is inspected, and based on this inspection the package is routed, either to OUTGOING or to RECEXT.

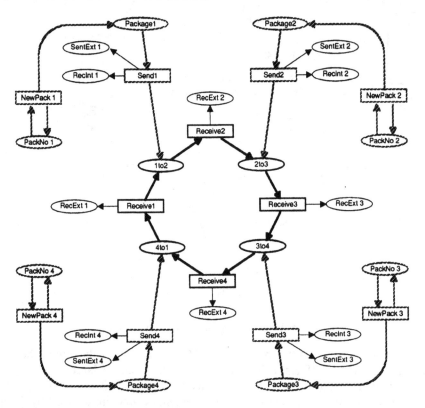

Figure 6. Non-hierarchical CP-net with the same behaviour as the hierarchical CP-net that contains the pages NetWork#10 and Site#11

Now let us return to the hierarchy inscriptions of the four substitution transitions on NetWork#10: The first line of each hierarchy inscription identifies the **subpage**, i.e. the page that is going to replace the substitution transition. In our present example, the four substitution transitions are being replaced by the same subpage Site#11. Each substitution transition gets, however, its own "private copy" of Site#11.

---

supported by one of the next versions of the CPN tool described in chapter 5. The page instance numbers are consecutive positive numbers, starting from 1 (i.e. in this case: 1, 2, 3, and 4).

[33] We use *#re p* to denote the re-field of a package p.

The remaining lines of the hierarchy inscription contain the **port assignment** which tells how the subpage (Site#11) is going to be inserted into the **superpage** which contains the substitution transition (NetWork#10). Each line of the port assignment relates a **socket node** on the superpage (i.e. one of the nodes surrounding the substitution transition) to a **port node** on the subpage (i.e. one of the nodes which have a B-tag next to it (B ≈ Border)). In our example, let us now consider the hierarchy inscription next to NO2. The first line of the port assignment tells us that the socket node 2TO3 is assigned to (i.e. "glued" together with) the port node OUTGOING. Analogously, the second line tells us that 1TO2 is assigned to INCOMING. The remaining three hierarchy inscriptions (of NO1, NO3 and NO4) are interpreted in a similar way – and this tells us that the hierarchical CP-net with the two pages NetWork#10 and Site#11 is equivalent – i.e. has the same behaviour – as the non-hierarchical CP-net in Fig. 6 (where we for clarity have omitted the net inscriptions).

When we consider the behaviour of a hierarchical CP-net each page has its own marking. We allow a single page to replace several substitution transitions, and then the page has several **page instances**, each having its own marking. In the example above, their are four instances of Site#11 – and thus four different markings.[34]

3.2 Fusion of places

The intuitive idea behind fusion of places is to allow the user to specify that a set of places are considered to be identical – i.e. they all represent a single place even though they are drawn as individual places. This means that when a token is added/removed at one of the places, an identical token has to be added/removed at all the others. The places of a fusion set may belong to a single page or to several different pages.

When all members of a fusion set belong to a single page and that page only has one instance, place fusion is nothing other than a drawing convenience that allows the user to avoid too many crossing arcs. However, things become much more interesting when the members of a fusion set belong to several different pages *or* to a page that has many different page instances. In that case fusion sets allow the user to specify a behaviour which it might be cumbersome to describe without fusion. To allow modular analysis of hierarchical CP-nets, global fusion sets should be used with care.

There are three different kinds of fusion sets: Global fusion sets are allowed to have members from many different pages, while page and instance fusion sets only have members from a single page. The difference between the last two is the following: A page fusion unifies all the instances of its places (independently of the page instance at which they appear), and this means that the fusion set only has one "resulting place" which is "shared" by all instances of the corresponding page. In contrast to this, an instance fusion set only identifies place instances that belong to the *same* page instance, and this means that the fusion set has a "resulting place" for each page instance. A global fusion set is analogous to a page fusion set, in the sense that it only has one "resulting place" (which is common for all instances of all the participating pages).

---

[34] When a CP-net is simulated by means of the CPN tools described in chapter 5, we have a window for each page. The window shows the marking of one instance at a time, and it is possible for the user to switch from one instance to another.

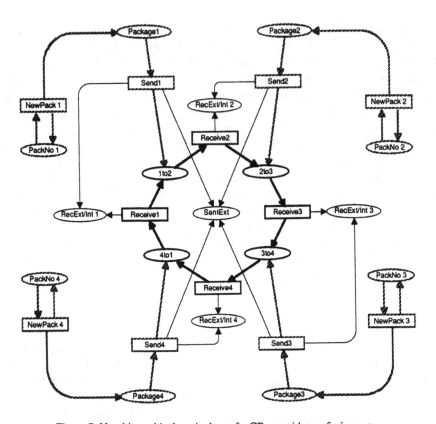

Figure 7. Non-hierarchical equivalent of a CP-net with two fusion sets

The difference between page and instance fusion sets can be illustrated by the ring network. In Fig. 7 we show how the non-hierarchical CP-net in Fig. 6 is modified when we on Site#11 define two fusion sets: An instance fusion set containing {RECEXT, RECINT} and a page fusion set containing {SENTEXT}.

Above we have illustrated the difference between page and instance fusion sets by drawing a non-hierarchical CP-net which is behaviourally equivalent to our hierarchical CP-net. It should, however, be understood that hierarchical CP-nets is a modelling language in its own right. This means that it is possible (and desirable) to model and analyse a complex system by a hierarchical CP-net – without ever constructing the equivalent non-hierarchical CP-net.

3.3 Partitions

To give a formal definition of hierarchical CP-nets we need the concept of a partition. Intuitively, a partition is a division of a set into a number of subsets, which are non-empty and pairwise disjoint:

Definition 3.1: Let a finite set Z be given. A **partition** of Z is a family of sets $X = \{X_i\}_{i \in I}$ such that:

(i) The **index set** I is a finite set.

(ii) Each **component** X_i is a non-empty subset of Z:
   - $\forall i \in I: [\emptyset \subset X_i \subseteq Z]$.

(iii) The components are pairwise disjoint:
   - $\forall (i,k) \in I: [i \neq k \implies X_i \cap X_k = \emptyset]$.

The **range** of the partition is the set:

$$X_R = \bigcup_{i \in I} X_i \subseteq Z.$$

The partition is said to be **total** iff $X_R = Z$. Otherwise it is **partial**.

It should be obvious that there is a very close relationship between partitions and equivalence relations: On the one hand, each partition determines an equivalence relation for its range (two elements are equivalent iff they belong to the same component - and each component is an equivalence class). On the other hand, each equivalence relation determines a total partition (two elements belong to the same component if they are equivalent – and each equivalence class is a component).

3.4 Formal definition of hierarchical CP-nets

This section contains the formal definition of hierarchical CP-nets. Some motivation and explanation of the individual parts of the definition is given immediately below the definition:

Definition 3.2: A **hierarchical CP-net** is a tuple HCPN = (S, SN, SA, PN, PA, FS, FT, PP) satisfying the requirements below:

(i) $S = \{S_i \mid i \in I\}$ is a finite set of **pages** such that:
   - Each page is a non-hierarchical CP-net:
     $S_i = (\Sigma_i, P_i, T_i, A_i, N_i, C_i, G_i, E_i, IN_i)$.
   - The sets of net elements are pairwise disjoint:
     $\forall (i,k) \in I: [i \neq k \implies (P_i \cup T_i \cup A_i) \cap (P_k \cup T_k \cup A_k) = \emptyset]$.

   When XX_i is a set, relation or a function, defined for all $i \in I$, we use XX to denote the union.[35] When YY is a set, relation or function, defined for HCPN, we use YY_i (and YY_{S_i}) to define the restriction to S_i.

(ii) $SN \subseteq T$ is a set of **substitution nodes**.

(iii) SA is a **page assignment** function. It is defined from SN into S such that:
   - No page is a subpage of itself:[36]
     $\{i_0 i_1 \ldots i_n \in I^* \mid n \in \mathbb{N}_+ \wedge i_0 = i_n \wedge \forall k \in 1..n: S_{i_k} \in SA(SN_{i_{k-1}})\} = \emptyset$.   *(cont.)*

---

35 The union of a set of functions is the union of the corresponding set of relations and this is known to become a function (because the set of domains are pair-wise disjoint).

36 I* denotes all finite sequences with elements from I, and we extend SA so that it can be used on a *set* of substitution nodes..

(iv) $PN \subseteq P$ is a set of **port nodes**.

(v) PA is a **port assignment** function. It is defined from SN into binary relations such that:
- Socket nodes are related to port nodes:
  $PA(x) \subseteq X(x) \times PN_{SA(x)}$.
- Related nodes have identical colour sets and equivalent initialization expressions:
  $\forall x \in SN \ \forall (x_1, x_2) \in PA(x): [C(x_1) = C(x_2) \wedge IN(x_1)<> = IN(x_2)<>]$.

(vi) $FS = \{FS_r\}_{r \in R}$ is a finite set of **fusion sets** such that:
- FS is a partition of P.
- Members of a fusion set have identical colour sets and equivalent initialization expressions:
  $\forall r \in R \ \forall x_1, x_2 \in FS_r: [C(x_1) = C(x_2) \wedge IN(x_1)<> = IN(x_2)<>]$.

(vii) FT is a **fusion type** function. It is defined from fusion sets such that:
- Each fusion set is of type: global, page or instance.
- Page and instance fusion sets belong to a single page:
  $\forall r \in R: [FT(FS_r) \neq global \Rightarrow \exists i \in I: FS_r \subseteq P_i]$.

(viii) $PP \in S_{MS}$ is a multi-set of **prime pages**.

(i) Each **page** is a non-hierarchical CP-net. We use Σ to denote the union of all the colour sets Σ_i of the individual pages (these colour sets do *not* need to be disjoint). The pages have pairwise disjoint sets of nodes and arcs, and this means that for functions and relations, defined on places, transitions and arcs, we can omit the page index without any ambiguity. As an example we can write C(p), G(t) and E(a) instead of $C_i(p)$, $G_i(t)$ and $E_i(a)$. Analogously, we use P, T and A to denote the set of all places, the set of all transitions and the set of all arcs in HCPN. The notational conventions described above allows us to move our point of focus from a given page to the entire CP-net by omitting the page index. It is, however, also possible to do the opposite and this means that we restrict a set, relation or function, defined for elements of the entire CP-net, to elements of a particular page. As an example, we use SN_i (and SN_{S_i}) to denote the subset of substitution nodes that belong to page S_i.

(ii) Each **substitution node** is a transition.[37]

(iii) The **page assignment** relates substitution transitions to pages. When a transition $t \in SN_i$ is related to a page S_k, we say that S_k is a *direct subpage* of the page S_i which is a *direct superpage* of S_k. Analogously, we say that S_k is a *direct subpage* of the node x which is a *direct supernode* of S_k. These four relations are in the usual way extended by taking the transitive closure and we then omit the word "direct" and talk about subpages, superpages and supernodes. It is demanded that no page is a subpage of itself. Otherwise, the process of substituting supernodes with their direct subpages will be infinite and it would be impossible to construct an equivalent non-hierarchical CP-net (without allowing P, T and A to be infinite).

(iv) Each **port node** is a place. It should be noticed that we allow a page to have port nodes even when it is not a subpage. Such port nodes have no semantic meaning

---

[37] As described in [31] it is also possible to allow places to be substitution nodes. The semantics of such a model is, however, slightly more complex.

(and thus they can be turned into non-ports without changing the behaviour of the CP-net).

(v) The **port assignment** relates *socket nodes* (i.e. the places surrounding a substitution transition) with port nodes (on the corresponding direct subpage). Each related pair of socket/port nodes must have identical colour sets and equivalent initialization expressions. It should be noticed that it is possible to relate several sockets to the same port and vice versa. It is also possible to have sockets and ports which are totally unrelated. Usually, most port assignments are bijective functions and in that case there is a one to one correspondence between sockets and ports.

(vi) The **fusion sets** are the components in a partition of P and this means that a place can belong to at most one fusion set. All members of a fusion set must have identical colour sets and equivalent initialization expressions. Usually, it is only a few places that belong to fusion sets and thus the partition is partial.

(vii) The **fusion type** divides the set of fusion sets into global, page and instance fusion sets. For the last two kinds of fusion sets all members must belong to the same page.

(viii) The **prime pages** is a multi-set over the set of all pages and they determine, together with the page assignment, how many instances the individual pages have. Often the multi-set contains only a single page (with coefficient one).

It should be obvious that each non-hierarchical CP-net is a hierarchical CP-net with a single page. There are no substitution, port and fusion nodes – and thus the page assignment, port assignment and fusion type functions become trivial. The single page belongs to the multi-set of prime pages, with coefficient one.

3.5 Page, place, transition and arc instances

A page may have several instances: There is a page instance for each time the page appears in the multi-set PP and, moreover there is a page instance for each way in which the page is a subpage of an element of PP.

In the following definition s and n identify the element of PP from which the page instance is constructed, while $x_1 x_2 ... x_m$ identifies the sequence of substitution nodes that leads to the page instance (in this sequence each node x_{k+1} belongs to the direct subpage of x_k). It should be noticed that the sequence may be empty:

Definition 3.3: The **page instances** of a page $S_i \in S$ is the set SI_i of all triples $(s, n, x_1 x_2 ... x_m)$ that satisfy the following requirements:

(i) $s \in PP \land n \in 1..PP(s)$.

(ii) $x_1 x_2 ... x_m$ is a sequence of substitution nodes, with $m \in N$, such that:
$$m > 0 \Rightarrow (x_1 \in SN_s \land [k \in 1..(m-1) \Rightarrow x_{k+1} \in SN_{SA(x_k)}] \land SA(x_m) = S_i).$$

When a page has several page instances each of these have their own instances of the corresponding places, transitions and arcs. It should, however, be noticed that substitution nodes and their surrounding arcs do not have instances (because they are replaced by instances of the corresponding direct subpages):

Definition 3.4: The **place instances** of a page $S_i \in S$ is the set PI_i of all pairs (p,id) that satisfy the following requirements:
(i) $p \in P_i$.
(ii) $id \in SI_i$.

The **transition instances** of a page $S_i \in S$ is the set TI_i of all pairs (t,id) that satisfy the following requirements:
(iii) $t \in T_i - SN_i$.
(iv) $id \in SI_i$.

The **arc instances** of a page $S_i \in S$ is the set AI_i of all pairs (a,id) that satisfy the following requirements:
(v) $a \in A_i - A(SN_i)$.
(vi) $id \in SI_i$.

Place instances may be related to each other, either by means of fusion sets or by means of port assignments and this leads to the following concepts:

Definition 3.5: The **place instance relation** is the smallest equivalence relation on PI[38] containing all those pairs $((p_1,(s_1,n_1,xx_1)),(p_2,(s_2,n_2,xx_2))) \in PI$ that satisfy one of the following conditions:
(i) $\exists r \in R:$ $[p_1,p_2 \in FS_r \wedge (FT(FS_r) = instance \Rightarrow (s_1,n_1,xx_1) = (s_2,n_2,xx_2))]$.
(ii) $\exists t \in SN:$ $[(p_1,p_2) \in PA(t) \wedge (s_1,n_1) = (s_2,n_2) \wedge xx_1{}^\wedge t = xx_2]$.[39]

An equivalence class of the place instance relation is called a **place instance group** and the set of all such equivalence classes is denoted by PIG.

3.6 Equivalent non-hierarchical CP-net

In sections 3.1 and 3.2 we have sketched how to define the behaviour of a hierarchical CP-net – by constructing a non-hierarchical CP-net that is behaviourally equivalent. In this section we define the non-hierarchical equivalent in a much more formal way, but before doing this we again want to stress that the construction of the non-hierarchical equivalent plays a similar role as the unfolding of a CP-net to a behaviourally equivalent PT-net: The construction is only performed in order to define and understand the semantics. When we describe a system we directly use hierarchical CP-nets – and we never construct the non-hierarchical equivalent. Analogously, we directly analyse a hierarchical CP-net – without having to construct the non-hierarchical equivalent. The existence of the non-hierarchical equivalent is, however, very important – because it tells us how to generalize the basic concepts and the analysis methods of non-hierarchical CP-nets to hierarchical CP-nets.

---

[38] Following our notational conventions we use PI to denote the set of all place instances in the entire CP-net (i.e. the union of PI_i over $i \in I$).
[39] The $^\wedge$ operator denotes concatenation of two sequences.

Definition 3.6: Let a hierarchical CP-net HCPN = (S, SN, SA, PN, PA, FS, FT, PP) be given. Then we define the **equivalent non-hierarchical** CP-net to be CPN = (Σ*, P*, T*, A*, N*, C*, G*, E*, IN*) where:

(i) Σ* = Σ.

(ii) P* = PIG.

(iii) T* = TI.

(iv) A* = AI.

(v) $\forall a$* = (a,id) $\in$ AI $\forall$(p,t) $\in$ P $\times$ T:

$\quad\quad\quad$ [N(a) = (p,t) $\Rightarrow$ N*(a*) = ([(p,id)],(t,id)) $\wedge$

$\quad\quad\quad$ N(a) = (t,p) $\Rightarrow$ N*(a*) = ((t,id),[(p,id)])].[40]

(vi) $\forall p$* = [(p,id)] $\in$ PIG: [C*(p*) = C(p)].

(vii) $\forall t$* = (t,id) $\in$ TI: [G*(t*) = G(t)].

(viii) $\forall a$* = (a,id) $\in$ AI: [E*(a*) = E(a)].

(ix) $\forall p$* = [(p,id)] $\in$ PIG: [IN*(p*) = IN(p)].

(i) The non-hierarchical CP-net has the same set of colour sets as the hierarchical CP-net.

(ii) The non-hierarchical CP-net has a place for each place instance group of the hierarchical CP-net. This means that there is place for each place instance – unless that place instance either belongs to a fusion set (in which case the place instance is merged with the other members of the fusion set) or it is an assigned socket/port node (in which case it is merged with the place instance to which it is assigned).

(iii) + (iv) The non-hierarchical CP-net has a transition for each transition instance of the hierarchical CP-net. Analogously, it has an arc for each arc instance of the hierarchical CP-net.

(v) The basic idea behind the definition of the node function is that each page instance has the same arcs as the original page. This means that a place instance and a transition instance only can have connecting arcs if they belong to the same page instance – and in that case they have connecting arcs iff the original place and transition have. It should, however, be noticed that the node function (due to place fusion and socket/port assignment) maps into place instance groups (and not into individual place instances). This is done in such a way that each place instance group gets a set of surrounding arcs that is the union of those arcs that the corresponding place instances would have got (if they had not participated in any fusion or socket/port assignment).

(vi) The colour set of a place instance group is determined by the colour set of the participating places. From Def. 3.2 (v) + (vi) it follows that all these places must have identical colour sets.

(vii) The guard of a transition instance is determined by the guard of the corresponding transition.

(viii) The arc expression of an arc instance is determined by the arc expression of the corresponding arc.

(ix) The initialization expression of a place instance group is determined by the initialization expression of one of the participating places. From Def. 3.2 (v) + (vi) it

---

40　We use [(p,id)] to denote the equivalence class to which (p,id) belongs.

follows that all these places must have initialization expressions which evaluate to the same value, and thus it does not matter which one we choose.

3.7 Dynamic behaviour of hierarchical CP-nets

Having defined the static structure of CP-nets we are now ready to consider their behaviour – but first we introduce the following notation, where $E'(p',t')$ and $E'(t',p')$ are called the **expressions** of (p',t') and (t',p'):[41]

- $\forall p'=(p,id_p)\in PI \ \forall t'=(t,id_t)\in TI:$
  $$[\ id_p = id_t \Rightarrow (E'(p',t') = E(p,t) \ \wedge \ E'(t',p') = E(t,p)) \ \wedge$$
  $$id_p \neq id_t \Rightarrow (E'(p',t') = E'(t',p') = 0) \ ].$$

Next we define token distributions, binding distributions, markings and steps:

Definition 3.7: A **token distribution** is a function M, defined on PIG such that $M(p^*)\in C(p)_{MS}$ for all $p^*=[(p,id)]\in PIG$ and a **binding distribution** is a function Y, defined on TI such that $Y(t^*)\in B(t)_{MS}$ for all $t^*=(t,id)\in TI$. We define TD_{HCPN}, BD_{HCPN}, $\neq, \leq, <, \geq, >, =$, **element** and **non-empty** in exactly the same way as for non-hierarchical CP-nets.

A **marking** is a token distribution and a **step** is a *non-empty* binding distribution. The set of all markings is denoted by M_{HCPN}, and the set of all steps is denoted by Y_{HCPN}. The **initial marking** M_0 is the marking where $M_0(p^*) = M_0(p)$[42] for all $p^* = [(p,id)]\in PIG$.

Finally we define enabling and occurrence:

Definition 3.8: A step Y is **enabled** in a marking M iff the following property is satisfied:
$$\forall p^*\in PIG: [\ \sum_{\substack{(t',b)\in Y \\ p'\in p^*}} E'(p',t')<b> \ \leq \ M(p^*)].$$
We define **enabled** transition instances and **concurrently enabled** transition instances/bindings analogously to the corresponding concepts in a non-hierarchical CP-net.

(continues)

---

41 We use p' and t' to denote a place instance and a transition instance, respectively.
42 We use M_0 for two different purposes: On the left-hand side of the equation it denotes a marking of HCPN (i.e. a function defined on PIG). On the right-hand side it denotes the union constructed from the initial markings M_{0i} of the individual pages (i.e. a function defined on P). From the argument it will always be clear which of the two functions we deal with.

When a step is enabled in a marking M_1 it may **occur**, changing the marking M_1 to another marking M_2, defined by:

$$\forall p^* \in PIG: [M_2(p) = (M_1(p) - \sum_{\substack{(t',b) \in Y \\ p' \in p^*}} E(p,'t)'<b>) + \sum_{\substack{(t',b) \in Y \\ p' \in p^*}} E(t',p')<b>].$$

The first sum is called the **removed** tokens while the second is called the **added** tokens. Moreover we say that M_2 is **directly reachable** from M_1 by the occurrence of the step Y, which we also denote:

$$M_1 [Y > M_2.$$

We define **occurrence sequences** and **reachability** analogously to the corresponding concepts for a non-hierarchical CP-net.

The following theorem shows that there is a one to one correspondence between the behaviour of a hierarchical CP-net and the corresponding non-hierarchical equivalent:

Theorem 3.9: Let HCPN be a hierarchical CP-net and CPN the non-hierarchical equivalent. Then we have the following properties:

(i) $M_{HCPN} = M_{CPN}$.

(ii) $Y_{HCPN} = Y_{CPN}$.

(iii) $\forall M_1, M_2 \in M_{HCPN} \; \forall Y \in Y_{HCPN}: [M_1 [Y >_{HCPN} M_2 \Leftrightarrow M_1 [Y >_{CPN} M_2].$

Proof: Property (i) is an immediate consequence of Def. 2.5, Def. 3.6 (ii) and Def. 3.7, while property (ii) is an immediate consequence of Def. 2.5, Def. 3.6 (iii) and Def. 3.7. Property (iii) follows from Def. 2.6, Def. 2.7, Def. 3.6 and Def. 3.8. The proof is omitted. It is straightforward but tedious – due to the large number of details which have to be considered.

4. Analysis of CP-nets

This chapter describes how CP-nets can be analysed. The most straightforward kind of analysis is simulation – which is very useful for the understanding and debugging of a system, in particular in the design phase and the early validation phases. There are, however, also more formal kinds of analysis – by which it is possible to *prove* that a given system has a set of desired properties (e.g. absence of dead-lock, the possibility to return to the initial state, and an upper bound on the number of tokens). This chapter contains a brief introduction to the main ideas behind the most important analysis methods and it contains references to papers in which the technical details of these methods can be found.

4.1 Simulation

Simulation can be supported by a computer tool or it can be totally manually (e.g. performed on a blackboard or in the head of the modeller). Simulation is similar to the debugging of a program, in the sense that it can reveal errors, but in practice never be sufficient to prove the correctness of a system. Some people argue that this makes simulation uninteresting and that the user instead should concentrate on the more formal analysis methods. We do not agree with this conclusion but consider simulation to be just as important and necessary as the more formal analysis methods.

In our opinion, all users of CP-nets (and other kinds of Petri nets) are forced to make simulations – because it is impossible to construct a CP-net without thinking about the effects of the individual transitions. Thus the proper question is not whether the modeller should make simulations or not, but whether he wants computer support for this activity. With this rephrasing the answer becomes trivial: Of course, we want computer support. This means that the simulation can be done much faster and with no errors. Moreover, it means that the modeller can use all his mental capabilities to interpret the simulation results (instead of using most of his efforts to calculate the possible occurrence sequences). Simulation is often used in the design phases and the early investigation of a system design (while the more formal analysis methods are used for the final validation of the design). In section 5.5 we give a detailed description of an existing CPN simulator.

4.2 Occurrence graphs

The basic idea behind occurrence graphs is to construct a graph which contains a node for each reachable state and an arc for each possible change of state. Obviously such a graph may, even for small CP-nets, become very large (and perhaps infinite). Thus we want to construct and inspect the graph by means of a computer – and we want to develop techniques by which we can construct a reduced occurrence graph without loosing too much information. The reduction can be done in many different ways:[43]

One possibility is to reduce by means of covering markings. This method looks for occurrence sequences leading from a system state to a larger system state (one with additional tokens) and the method guarantees that the reduced occurrence graph always becomes finite. The method has, however, some drawbacks. First of all it only gives a reduction for unbounded systems (and most practical systems are bounded). Secondly, so much information is lost by the reduction that several important properties (e.g. liveness and reachability) no longer are decidable. For more information see [18] and [40].

A second possibility is to reduce by ignoring some of the occurrence sequences which are identical, except for the order in which the elements occur. This method often gives a very significant reduction, in particular when the modelled system contains a large number of relatively independent processes. Unfortunately, it is with this method necessary to construct several different occurrence graphs (because the construction method depends upon the property which we want to investigate). For more information see [59].

A third possibility is to reduce by means of the symmetries which often are present in the systems which we model by CP-nets. To do this the modeller defines, for each colour set, an algebraic group of allowed bijections (each bijection defines a possible way in which the elements of the colour set can be interchanged with each other) – and

---

[43] For all the methods described below, it is possible to construct the reduced occurrence graph without first constructing the full occurrence graph.

this induces an equivalence relation on the set of all system states. The reduced occurrence graph only contains a node for each equivalence class and this means that it often is much smaller than the full occurrence graph. The reduced graph contains, however, exactly the same information as the full graph – and this means that the reduced graph can be used to investigate all the system properties which can be investigated by means of the full graph.[44] For more information see [30] and [35].

A fourth possibility is to construct an occurrence graph where each state is denoted by a symbolic expression (which describes a number of system states, in a similar way as the equivalence classes in method three). For more information see [9] and [42].

Finally, it is possible to construct occurrence graphs in a modular way. The model is divided into a number of submodels, an occurrence graph is constructed for each submodel, and these subgraphs are combined to form an occurrence graph for the entire model. For more information see [60].

When an occurrence graph has been constructed it can be used to prove properties about the modelled system. For bounded systems a large number of questions can be answered: Dead-locks, reachability and marking bounds[45] can be decided by a simple search through the nodes of the occurrence graph, while liveness and home markings can be decided by constructing and inspecting the strongly connected components. One problem with occurrence graph analysis is the fact that it, usually, is necessary to fix all system parameters (e.g. the number of sites in a ring protocol) before an occurrence graph can be constructed – and this means that the found properties always are specific to the chosen values of the system parameters. In practice the problem isn't that big: If we e.g. understand how a ring protocol behaves for a few sites we also know a lot about how it behaves when it has more sites.[46]

As described above, the occurrence graph method can be totally automated – and this means that the modeller can use the method, and interpret the results, without having much knowledge about the underlying mathematics. For the moment it is, however, only possible to construct occurrence graphs for relatively small systems and for selected parts of large systems. This doesn't mean that the method is uninteresting. On the contrary, the method seems to be a very effective way to debug new subsystems (because trivial errors such as the omission of an arc or a wrong arc expression often means that some of the system properties are dramatically changed). In the future, it may also be possible to use occurrence graph analysis for larger systems. This can be done by combining some of the reduction techniques described above – and by using the increased computing power of the next generations of hardware. In section 7.2 we

---

[44] The reduced occurrence graph (called an OE-graph) has more complex node and arc inscriptions than the full occurrence graph (called an O-graph). The OE-graph is a folded version of the O-graph, in the same way as a CP-net is a folding of the equivalent PT-net. The O-graph can be constructed from the OE-graph, but this is never necessary since the analysis can be done directly on the OE-graph.

[45] There are two kinds of marking bounds. Integer bounds only deal with the number of tokens while multi-set bounds also deal with the token colours. It can be proved that a place is integer bounded if and only if it is multi-set bounded. There are, however, situations in which the integer bound gives more information than the multi-set bound (and vice versa) – and thus it is useful to calculate both kinds of bounds.

[46] This is of course only true when we talk about the correctness of the protocol, and not when we speak about the performance.

describe the plans to implement a CPN tool to support the calculation and analysis of occurrence graphs.

4.3 Place and transition invariants

The basic idea behind place invariants is to find a set of equations which characterize all reachable markings, and then use these equations to prove properties of the modelled system (in a way which is analogous to the use of invariants in program verification). To illustrate the idea, let us consider the resource allocation system from Fig. 1. This system has the five place invariants shown below.[47] A place invariant is a linear sum of the markings of the individual places: Each place marking is by a weight function (attached to the place) mapped into a new multi-set. All the new multi-sets are over the same colour set and thus they can be added together – to give a **weighted sum** (determined from the given marking by the given set of weight functions).

The invariants use the three functions P, Q and PQ as weight functions. Each of them maps P-colours into multi-sets of E-colours. Intuitively, P "counts" the number of p-tokens (it maps (p,i) into $1`e$ and (q,i) into the empty multi-set). Analogously Q counts the number of q-tokens and PQ counts the number of p/q-tokens (i.e. the total number of tokens).[48] The invariants also use identity functions and zero functions as weights. The five invariants are satisfied for all reachable markings M (later we shall discuss how this can be proved). The right hand side of the invariants are found by evaluating the left hand side in the initial marking.

Intuitively PI_P and PI_Q tell what happens to the two different kinds of processes, while PI_R, PI_S and PI_T tell what happens to the three different kinds of resources. Each invariant can be seen as a way of extracting specific information – from the general information provided by the entire marking.

PI_P	$P(M(B) + M(C) + M(D) + M(E)) = 2`e$
PI_Q	$Q(M(A) + M(B) + M(C) + M(D) + M(E)) = 3`e$
PI_R	$M(R) + Q(M(B) + M(C)) = 1`e$
PI_S	$M(S) + Q(M(B)) + 2 * PQ(M(C) + M(D) + M(E)) = 3`e$
PI_T	$M(T) + P(M(D)) + (PQ + P)M(E) = 2`e$

The five invariants above can be used to prove that the resource allocation system doesn't have a dead-lock. *The proof is by contradiction:* Let us assume that we have a reachable state with no enabled transitions. From PI_P we know that there are two p-tokens distributed on the places B-E and from PI_Q that three are three q-tokens distributed on A-E. Now let us investigate in more detail where these tokens can be positioned. *First, assume that there are tokens on E:* Then T5 is enabled (and we have a contradiction with the assumption of no enabled transitions). *Secondly, assume that*

---

[47] There are many other place invariants for the system – but these are the most simple and useful.

[48] A weight function is usually specified as a function $f \in [C(p) \rightarrow A_{MS}]$ (i.e. a function from the colour set C(p) of the place into multi-sets over a colour set A). We always extend f to a function $f_{ext} \in [C(p)_{MS} \rightarrow A_{MS}]$ (for each multi-set $m \in C(p)_{MS}$ we calculate $f_{ext}(m)$ by adding the results of applying f to all the individual elements of m). Usually we do not distinguish between f and f_{ext} (and we use f to denote both functions).

there are tokens on C and/or D (and no tokens on E): From PI$_S$ it follows that there can be at most one such token and then PI$_T$ tells that there is at least one e-token on T (because $P(M(D)) \leq 1\text{`e}$ and $(PQ + P)M(E) =$ empty). Thus T3 or T4 can occur. *Thirdly, assume that there are tokens on B (and no tokens on C, D and E):* From PI$_R$ it follows that there can be at most one q-token on B and then PI$_S$ tells us that there is at least two e-tokens on S (because $Q(M(B)) \leq 1\text{`e}$ and $2 * PQ(M(C) + M(D) + M(E))$ = empty). Thus T2 can occur. *Now we have shown that it is impossible to position the two p-tokens (without violating the dead-lock assumption) – and thus we conclude that all reachable states have at least one enabled transition.* From the fact there are no dead-locks and the cyclic structure of the net, it is easy to prove other system properties e.g. that the initial marking is a home marking, that the system is live and that all reachable markings are reachable from each other.

Next let us discuss how we can find place invariants: As mentioned earlier, each CP-net has a function representation – which is a matrix where each element is a function (mapping multi-sets of bindings into multi-sets of token colours).[49] The matrix determines a homogeneous matrix equation and the place invariants are the solutions to this matrix equation (each solution is a vector of weight functions).[50] The matrix equation can be solved in different ways: One possibility is to translate the matrix of functions into a matrix of integers[51] for which the homogeneous matrix equation can be solved by standard Gauss elimination. Another, and more attractive, possibility is to work directly on the matrix of functions (this is, however, more complicated e.g. because some functions do not have an inverse). With both methods we do not explicitly find all solutions (there are usually infinitely many). Instead we find a basis from which all invariants can be constructed (as linear combinations). This leaves us with a second problem: How do we from the basis find the interesting place invariants – i.e. those from which it is easy to prove system properties? In our opinion, the best solution is to allow the user to tell the analysis program where to look for invariants – and thus calculate invariants in an interactive way. For more details about the calculation of invariants, see [12], [35], [44] and section 7.2.

Above, we have discussed how to calculate invariants by solving a homogeneous matrix equation. The problem is, however, often of a different nature – because we (instead of starting from scratch) already have a set of weight functions and just want to verify that these are invariants. This task is much easier and it can, without any problems, be done totally automatically. The potential invariants, to be checked, can be derived from the system specification and the modellers knowledge of the expected system properties. The potential invariants may be specified after the system design has been finished. It is, however, much more useful (and easier) to use CP-nets during the design and construct the invariants as an integrated part of the design (in the same way as a good programmer specifies a loop invariant at the moment he creates the loop). For this use of invariants it is important to notice that the check of invariants are constructive – in the sense that it, in the case of failure, is told where in the CP-net the

---

[49] The translation into the function representation can easily be defined by means of the lambda calculus. For more details see [35].

[50] Each solution to the matrix equation is a place invariant. The other direction is, however, only true when it is known that each occurrence element is enabled in at least one reachable marking.

[51] This is exactly the same as unfolding the CP-net to the behavioural equivalent PT-net.

problems are. Thus it is often relatively easy to see how the CP-net (or the invariant) should be modified.

Transition invariants are the duals of place invariants and the basic idea behind them is to find occurrence sequences with no effects (i.e. with the same start and end marking). Transition invariants can be calculated in a similar way as place invariants[52] - but, analogously to place invariants, it is more useful to construct them during the system design. Transition invariants are used for similar purposes as place invariants (i.e. to investigate the behavioural properties of CP-nets).

Place/transition invariants have several very attractive properties: First of all invariant analysis can be used for large systems – because it can be performed in a modular way[53] and does not involve the same kind of complexity problems as occurrence graph analysis. Secondly, invariant analysis can be done without fixing system parameters (e.g. the number of sites in a ring protocol). Thirdly, the the use of invariants during the design of a system will (as described above) usually lead to a better design. The main drawback of invariant analysis is that the skills, required to perform it, are considerably higher than for the other analysis methods. In section 7.2 we describe the plans to implement a CPN tool to support the interactive calculation and use of place/transition invariants.

4.4 Other analysis methods

CP-nets can also be analysed by means of reduction. The basic idea behind this method is to select one or more behavioural properties (e.g. liveness and dead-locks), define a set of transformation rules, prove that the rules do not change the selected set of properties, and finally apply the rules to obtain a reduced CP-net – which usually is so small that it is trivially to see whether the desired properties are fulfilled or not. Reduction methods are well-known for PT-nets and they have in [25] been generalised to CP-nets. A serious problem with reduction methods is that they often are non-constructive (because the absence of a property in the reduced net, usually, do not tell much about why the original net doesn't have the property).[54]

Most applications of CP-nets are used to design and validate the correctness of a system (e.g. whether the system executes the desired functions and whether it is dead-lock free). CP-nets can, however, also be used to investigate the performance of a system (i.e. how fast it executes). To perform this kind of analysis it is necessary to specify the time consumption in the modelled system, and this can be done in many different ways: As a delay between the enabling and occurrence of a transition, a delay between the removal of input tokens and the creation of output tokens, or as a delay between the creation of a token and the time at which that token can be used. In all three cases, the delay may be a fixed value, a value inside a given interval, or a value deter-

---

[52] Transition invariants are found by solving a homogeneous matrix equation (obtained by transposing the matrix used to find place invariants). Each transition invariant is a solution to the matrix equation. The opposite is, however, not always true (even for "nice" CP-nets).

[53] As shown in [45] invariants can be obtained by the composition of existing invariants and this means that we can construct invariants of a hierarchical CP-net – from invariants of the individual pages.

[54] An exception is the reduction method to calculate place/transition invariants, mentioned in section 7.2. In this case it is, from the reduced net, possible to determine a set of the invariants for the original net – and this means that the analysis results can be interpreted in terms of the original net.

mined by a probability distribution. Performance analysis is often made by simulation, and we shall in section 7.1 briefly describe how this can be done. For some kinds of delays, it is also possible to translate the net model into a Markovian chain – from which analytic solutions of the performance values can be calculated. For more information about performance analysis see [47].

For ordinary Petri nets at least two other kinds of analysis methods are known. One method translates the net structure into a set of logical equations, transforms the equations by a general theorem prover, and obtains results above the behaviour of the system. For more information see [10]. The other method uses structural properties[55] of a Petri net to deduce behavioural properties. For more information see [3]. Unfortunately, neither of these methods have yet been generalized to CP-nets (or other kinds of high-level Petri nets).

5. Computer Tools for CP-nets

The practical use of Petri nets is, just as all other description techniques, highly dependent upon the existence of adequate computer tools – helping the user to handle all the details of a large description. For CP-nets we need an editor (supporting construction, syntax check and modification of CP-nets) and we also need a number of analysis programs (supporting a wide range of different analysis methods). The recent development of fast and cheap raster graphics gives us the opportunity to work directly with the graphical representations of CP-nets (and occurrence graphs). This chapter describes some existing CPN tools (the CPN editor and CPN simulator from [1]). In chapter 7 we discuss other kinds of CPN tools that are needed, but have not yet been fully developed.

5.1 Why do we need computer tools for CP-nets?

The most important advantage of using computerized CPN tools is the possibility to create *better results*. As an example, the CPN editor provides the user with a precision and drawing quality, which by far exceeds the normal manual capabilities of humans beings. Analogously, computer support for complex analysis methods (e.g. occurrence graphs) makes it possible to obtain results, which could not have been achieved manually (since the calculations would have been too error-prone).

A second advantage is the possibility to create *faster results*. As an example, the CPN editor multiplies the speed by which minor modifications can be made: It is easy to change the size, form, position and text of the individual net elements without having to redraw the entire net. It is also possible to construct new parts of a net by copying and modifying existing subnets. Analogously, analysis methods may be fully or partially automated. As an example, the manual construction of an occurrence graph is an extremely slow process – while it can be done on a computer in a few minutes/hours (even when there are several hundred thousand nodes).

---

[55] Structural properties are properties which can be formulated *without* considering the behaviour (i.e. occurrence sequences). In a CP-net structural properties may involve properties of the net structure, but also properties of the net inscriptions and the declarations.

A third advantage is the possibility to make *interactive presentations* of the analysis results. The CPN simulator makes it easy to trace the different occurrence sequences in a CP-net. Between each occurrence step, the user can (on the graphical representation of the CP-net) see the transitions which are enabled, and choose between them in order to investigate different occurrence sequences. Analogously, it is possible to make an interactive investigation of a complex occurrence graph – using an elaborated search system.

A fourth advantage is the possibility of *hiding technical aspects* of the CP-net theory inside the tools. This allows the users to apply complicated analysis methods without having a detailed knowledge of the underlying mathematics. Often the analysis is performed in an interactive way: The user proposes the operations to be done. Then the computer checks the validity of the proposals, performs the necessary calculations (which often are very complex) and displays the results.

For industrial applications the possibility of producing fast results of good quality - without requiring too deep knowledge of Petri net theory – is a necessary prerequisite for the entire use of CP-nets. Furthermore it is important to be able to use CP-nets together with other specification/implementation languages (we shall return to this question in chapters 6 and 7).

The remaining sections of this chapter describe the basic design criteria behind the CPN editor and the CPN simulator. For a more complete and detailed description the user is referred to [36]. The sections can also be seen as a list of design criteria which is relevant for all high-quality Petri net editors and simulators. There are a large number of different groups which work with the development of Petri net tools. Many of the tools are, however, still research prototypes – and for the moment it is only few of them which are able to deal with large high-level nets and are sufficiently robust to be used in an industrial environment. A list of available Petri net tools can be found in [17].

5.2 CPN editor

The CPN editor allows the user to construct, modify and syntax check hierarchical CP-nets. It is also easy to construct and modify many other kinds of graphs (but they can of course not be syntax checked).[56] All figures in this paper has been produced by means of the CPN editor.

A CP-net constructed by means of the CPN editor is called a **CPN diagram** and it contains a large number of different types of graphical **objects**. Each object is either a **node**, a **connector** (between two nodes) or a **region** (i.e. a subordinate of another object). Places and transitions are nodes, arcs are connectors, while all the net inscriptions are regions. As examples, colour sets and initialization expressions are regions of the corresponding places, guards of the corresponding transitions and arc expressions of the corresponding arcs.

The division of objects into nodes, connectors and regions reflects the fact that the CPN editor works with the **graph** (and not just an unstructured set of objects, as it is the case for most general purpose drawing tools, such as MacDraw™ or MacDraft™).

---

[56] In this paper, the word graph denotes the mathematical concept of a graph (i.e. a structure which consists of a set of nodes interconnected by a set of edges).

This is important because it means that the construction and modification of the CPN diagrams become much faster (and with more accurate results): When the user constructs a connector he identifies the source and destination nodes (and perhaps some intermediate points). Then the editor automatically draws the connector in such a way that the two endpoints are positioned at the border of the two nodes. When the user changes the position or size of a node the regions and surrounding arcs are automatically redrawn by the editor. A repositioning implies that the regions keep their relative position (with respect to the node). A resizing implies that the relative positions of the regions are scaled while their sizes are either unchanged or scaled (depending upon an attribute of each region). When a node is deleted the regions and arcs are deleted too. This is illustrated by Fig. 8 where the node X is first repositioned, then resized and finally deleted. Similar rules apply for the repositioning, resizing and deletion of arcs and regions.

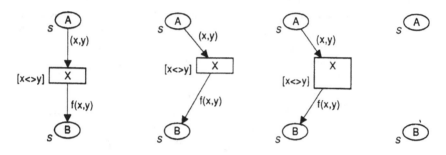

Figure 8. When a node is repositioned, resized or deleted, the regions and surrounding arcs are automatically updated.

In addition to the **CPN objects** (e.g. places, transitions, arcs and net inscriptions), which are formal parts of the model there may also be **auxiliary objects** which have no formal meaning but play a similar role as the comment facilities in programming languages. Finally, there are **system objects** which are special objects created and manipulated by the CPN editor itself. Each object has an **object type** and it should be noticed that it is the object type which determines the formal meaning of the object - independently of the object position and object form. The CPN editor distinguishes between nearly 50 different object types.

It is possible for the user to determine, in great detail, how he wants the CPN diagram to look. One of the most attracting features of CP-nets (and Petri nets in general) is the very appealing graphical representation, and it would be a pity to put narrow restrictions on how this representation can look (e.g. by making an editor in which the user cannot give two transitions different forms and/or sizes). In our opinion a good editor must allow the user to draw nearly all kinds of CP-nets which can be constructed by a pen and a typewriter. In the CPN editor each object has its own set of **attributes** which determine e.g. the position, shape, size, line thickness, line and fill patterns, line and fill colours and text type (including font, size, style, alignment and colour). There are 10-30 attributes for each object (depending upon the object type). When a new object is constructed the attributes are determined by a set of **defaults** (each object type has its own set of defaults). At any time the user can change one or more attributes for each individual objects.[57] Moreover, it is easy to change the defaults and it can be specified whether such changes apply to the current diagram or to future diagrams (or both).

In addition to the attributes the CPN editor (and in particular the CPN simulator) has a large set of **options** – which determines how the detailed functions in the editor are performed (e.g. the scroll speed, the treatment of duplicate arcs when two nodes are merged, and details about how the syntax check is performed). The difference between attributes and options is that the former relate to an individual object while the latter do not. Also options have defaults and these can be changed by the user.[58]

The CPN editor supports hierarchical CP-nets[59] and this means that each CPN diagram contains a number of pages. Each page is displayed in its own window (which in the usual way can be opened, closed, resized and repositioned). The relation between the individual pages is shown by the **page hierarchy** (which is positioned on a separate page called the **hierarchy page** and automatically maintained by the CPN editor). The page hierarchy is a graph in which each node represents a page and each connector a (direct) superpage/subpage relationship. The nodes are **page nodes** and each of them contains the corresponding page name and page number. The connectors are **page connectors** and each of them has a set of **page regions** containing the names of the involved supernodes.[60] The page objects can be moved and modified in exactly the same way as all other types of objects, and this means that the user can determine how the page hierarchy looks. The editor uses the line pattern of a page node to indicate whether the corresponding page window is active, open or closed. As an example, the ring network from Fig. 4-5 has a hierarchy page with three page nodes and one page arc, and it may look as shown in Fig. 9, where NetWork#10 is open but not active, Site#11 is closed, while the hierarchy page Hierarchy#10010 is open and active. In general, the hierarchy pages are much more complex.

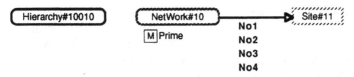

Figure 9. Hierarchy page for the ring network

The hierarchies in a CPN diagram can be constructed in many different ways – ranging from a pure top-down approach to a pure bottom-up: Part of a page can by a single editor operation be *moved to a new subpage:* The user selects the nodes to be moved and invokes the operation, then the editor checks the legality of the selection,[61] creates

---

57   This is done by specifying an explicit value, selecting another object (from which the attribute is copied) or by resetting the attribute to the current default.

58   For options a change in the default value only effects future diagrams (while a change in the option value itself, of course, effects the current diagram).

59   For the moment the CPN editor supports substitution transitions and place fusion. The other hierarchy constructs from [31] will be added later (some of them perhaps in an improved form).

60   Page nodes, page connectors and page regions are system objects.

61   All perimeter nodes (i.e. nodes with external arcs) must be transitions – in order to guarantee that the selection forms a closed subnet.

the new page, moves the subnet, creates the port nodes (by copying those nodes which were next to the selection), creates the border regions for the port nodes, constructs the necessary arcs between the the port nodes and the subnet, asks the user to create a new transition (which becomes the supernode for the new subpage), draws the arcs surrounding the new transition, creates a hierarchy inscription for it, and updates the hierarchy page. As it can be seen, a lot of rather complex checks, calculations and manipulations are involved. However, nearly all of these are automatically performed by the CPN editor. The user only selects the subnet and creates the new supernode.

There is also an editor operation to *turn an existing transition into a supernode* (by relating it to an existing page). Again most of the work is done by the editor: The user selects the transition and invokes the operation, then the editor makes the hierarchy page active and enters a mode in which the user by means of the mouse can select the desired subpage,[62] the editor creates the hierarchy inscription,[63] and updates the hierarchy page. To destroy the hierarchical relationship between a supernode and a subpage the user simply deletes the corresponding hierarchy inscription (or the corresponding page connector/region). It is also possible to *replace the supernode by the contents of the subpage:* This involves a lot of complex calculations and manipulations, but again all of them are carried out by the CPN editor. The user simply selects the supernode, invokes the operation and uses a simple dialogue box to specify how the operation shall be performed – e.g. he tells whether the page shall be deleted (in the case where no other supernodes exist).

The user works with a high-resolution raster graphical screen and a mouse.[64] The CPN diagram under construction can be seen in a number of windows (where it looks as close as possible to the final output obtained by a matrix or laser printer). The editor is menu driven and have self-explanatory dialogue boxes (as known e.g. from many Macintosh programs). The user moves and resizes the objects by direct manipulation - i.e. by means of the mouse (instead of typing coordinates and object identification numbers on the keyboard). This also applies to the pages which can be opened, closed, scrolled and scaled by means of the corresponding page node. When the user deletes a page node the corresponding page is deleted (after a confirmation). Analogously, the deletion of a page connector or a page region means that the corresponding hierarchical relationship is destroyed (and thus the corresponding supernodes become ordinary transitions).

One important difference between the CPN editor and many other drawing programs is the possibility to work with **groups** of objects. This means that the user is able to select a *set* of objects and *simultaneously* change the attributes, delete the objects, copy them, move them or reposition them (e.g. vertical to each other). The user can select groups in many different ways (e.g. by dragging the mouse over a rectangular area or by pressing a key while he points to a sequence of objects). The CPN editor

---

62 When the mouse is moved over a page node it blinks – unless it is illegal (because selection of it would make the page hierarchy cyclic). Only blinking page nodes can be selected.

63 The user can ask the editor to try to deduce the port assignment by means of a set of rules (which looks at the node names, the port types and the arcs between the transition and the sockets).

64 For the moment the CPN tools are implemented on Macintosh, SUN and HP machines – and they can easily be moved to other machines running UNIX and X-Windows. It is recommended, but not necessary, to have a large colour screen.

allows the user to perform operations on groups in exactly the same way as they can be performed on individual objects[65] – and this has the same effect as when the corresponding operation is performed on each group member one at a time. All members of a group has to belong to the same page and be of the same kind – i.e. all be nodes, all be connectors or all be regions.[66] Otherwise there are no restrictions on the way in which groups can be formed. The group facility has a very positive impact upon the speed and ease by which editing operations are performed. By selecting a group of page nodes it is possible to work on several pages at the same time.

In the design of the CPN editor it has been important for us to make it as flexible as possible. As described above, this means that it is possible to construct CPN diagrams which *look* very different. However, it also means that each diagram can be *created* in many different ways. One example of this principle is the many different ways in which the page hierarchy can be constructed. Another example is the fact that the CPN editor allows the user to construct the various objects in many different orders: Some users prefer first to construct the net structure (i.e. the places, transitions and arcs). Later they add the net inscriptions (i.e. the CPN regions) – and doing this they either finish one node at a time or one kind of CPN regions at a time, and they either type from scratch or copy from existing regions. Other users prefer to create templates - e.g. a place with a colour set region and an initialization region. Then they create the diagram by copying the appropriate templates to the desired positions and modifying the texts (if necessary).[67] Finally, most users work in a way which is a mixture of the possibilities described above. We think that this kind of flexibility – where the user controls the detailed planning of the editing process – is extremely important for a good tool. Thus the CPN editor has been designed to allow most operations to be performed in several different ways.

A CPN diagram contains many different kinds of information and this means that the individual pages very easy become cluttered. To avoid this the user is allowed to make objects invisible (without changing the semantics of the objects). As an example the user may hide all colour set regions and instead indicate the colour sets by giving the corresponding places different attributes (e.g. different line patterns/colours). In this case it is still the invisible regions that determine the formal behaviour, and it is the responsibility of the user to keep the pattern/colour coding of the places correctly updated (there are several facilities in the CPN editor which helps him in this task). Another facility, which also helps avoiding cluttered diagrams, is the concept of key and popup regions, which are used for a number of different object types (both in the editor and the simulator). The idea is very simple: Instead of having a single region (containing a lot of information) we have both a **key region** (which is a region of the object to which we want to attach the information) and a **popup region** (which is a region of the key). The key region is small (it usually only contains one or two characters) and its main purpose is to give access to the popup region which contains the ac-

---

65 There are only very few operations which do not make sense for groups.

66 In a later version of the CPN editor, we may allow a group to have members from different pages. This is easy to implement and it creates no conceptual problems. It is, however, unlikely that we will allow mixed groups. The reason is that the semantics of many operations then become a bit obscure.

67 When the user copies a node, the editor automatically copies the regions. Analogously, when a group of nodes is copied, the internal connectors (between two members of the group) are copied too.

tual information. A double click on the key region makes the popup region visible/invisible and in this way it is extremely easy to hide and show large amounts of information. For examples of key/popup regions see the hierarchy regions in Fig. 4 (with the HS-keys), the border regions in Fig. 5 (with the B-keys) and the marking regions in Fig. 3 (containing the current marking). It should be noticed that the use of key/popup regions is more general than the use of popup windows (in which information can be displayed on demand). The difference is that the popup regions are objects in the diagram itself and thus the user can leave all of them or some of them permanently visible. Actually, it is an attribute of each key region that determines whether the corresponding popup region is visible or not.[68]

It should be noticed that the generality of the CPN editor means that the user can create very confusing CPN diagrams. As examples, it may be impossible to distinguish between auxiliary objects and CPN objects (because they have been given identical attributes), transitions may be drawn as ellipses while places are boxes, and some or all of the objects may be invisible – just to mention a few possibilities. We do *not* believe it is sensible to try to construct a tool which makes it *impossible* to produce bad nets. Such a tool will, in our opinion, inevitably be far too rigid and inflexible. However, we do of course believe that the tool should make it easy for the user to make good nets.

There are many other facilities in the CPN editor: Operations to open, close, save and print diagrams.[69] An operation which allows the editor to import diagrams created by other tools (e.g. SADT diagrams created by the IDEF/CPN tool described in section 6.3). The standard Undo,[70] Cut, Copy, Paste and Clear operations known e.g. from the Macintosh concept. Operations to define fusion sets, specify port nodes and perform port assignments. Operations to create many different types of auxiliary objects (e.g. connectors, boxes, rounded boxes, ellipses, polygons, wedges and pictures[71]). Operations to turn auxiliary objects into CPN objects (and vice versa). An operation to syntax check the CPN diagram (and other operations to start/stop the ML compiler, see section 5.3). A large set of operations to change attributes and options – and their defaults. Operations which assist the user to select the correct object (when many are close to each other or on top of each other), move objects to another position (on the same page or on another page), change object size (e.g. to fit the size of the text in the object), change object shape (e.g. from ellipse to box),[72] merge a group of nodes into a

---

[68] For efficiency reasons the popup region can also be missing. In this case a double click on the key implies that the popup is generated (with the correct information) and becomes visible.

[69] It is also the intention to allow the user to save part of a diagram and later load it into another diagram. In this way it will be possible to create libraries of reusable submodels. This facility is, however, not yet implemented.

[70] For the moment, Undo only works for a limited set of operations.

[71] A picture is a bit map which is obtained from a CPN diagram (by copying part of a page) or from another program (via the clipboard). Pictures makes it easy to work with icons.

[72] All objects can take many different shapes. Nodes and regions can e.g. be boxes, rounded boxes, ellipses, polygons, wedges and pictures. Connectors can be single headed, double headed and without heads. As an example, of a creative use of this generality, it is possible to let a substitution transition be a picture which is a diminished version of the corresponding subpage.

single node, duplicate a node[73], hide and show regions and change the graphical layering of the objects. Operations to redraw the page hierarchy – when this has become too cluttered (e.g. because the user has made a number of manual changes to the automatic layout proposed by the CPN editor). Operations to select groups (e.g. by means of fusion sets, text searches and object types).[74] Operations to search for specified text strings and replace them by others (either in the entire diagram, on a single page, or in one or more selected objects). Operations to search for matching brackets, create hyper text structures,[75] and copy the contents of external text files into nodes (and vice versa). A large number of alignment operations. Some of these make it easy to position nodes and regions relative to each other (e.g. vertically below each other, with equal distances, on a circle, with the same center, etc.). Others make it easy to create arcs with right angles and vertical/horizontal segments.

The CPN editor can be used at many different skill levels. Casual and novice users only have to learn and apply a rather small subset of the total facilities. The more frequent and experienced users gradually learn how to use the editor more efficiently: All the more commonly used commands can be invoked by means of key shortcuts, and these can be changed by the users. Many commands have one or more modifier keys, allowing the user, in one operation, to do things which otherwise would require several operations. The user can create a set of templates (e.g. a set of nodes with different attributes and object types). These nodes can then be positioned on special palette pages, from where they, in one operation, can be copied to the different pages of a diagram. In this way it is easy to make company standards for the graphics of CPN diagrams.

To make it easier to use the CPN editor we have tried to make the user interface as consistent and self-explanatory as possible. To do this, we have defined a set of concepts allowing us to give a precise description of the different parts of the interface: As an example, a list box with a scroll bar can behave in many slightly different ways: It may be possible to select only a single line at a time, a contiguous set of lines, an arbitrary set of lines, or no lines at all – and when the dialogue box is opened, the list box may have the same selection as last time, have the first line selected, have no lines selected, or have a selection which depends upon the current selection in the diagram. Hopefully, this simple example demonstrates that it is important to identify the possibilities – and use them in a consistent way.

When the user creates a CPN diagram, the editor stores all the semantic information in an abstract data base – from which it easily can be retrieved by the CPN simulator (and other analysis programs). The abstract data base was designed as a relational data base but for efficiency implemented by means of a set of list structures (making the most commonly used data base operations as efficient as possible). The existence of the abstract data base makes it much easier to integrate new/existing editors and analysis programs with the CPN tools – and for this purpose there are three sets of predeclared functions: The first set makes it possible to read the information which is present in the abstract data base (e.g. get information about the colour set of place). The second set

---

[73] The new node get a set of regions and connectors which are similar to the original node. By using the command on a group of nodes, it is possible to get a subnet which is identical to an existing subnet (and has the same connectors to/from the environment).

[74] Some of the group selection facilities are not yet implemented.

[75] This facility is not yet fully implemented.

makes it possible to create auxiliary objects (which have a graphical representation but no representation in the abstract data base). Finally, the third set makes it possible to convert auxiliary objects to CPN objects (which means that the abstract data base is updated accordingly). Using these three sets of predeclared functions it is a relatively straightforward task to write programs which translates textual/graphical representations of a class of Petri nets (or another formalism with a well-defined semantics) into CPN diagrams – and vice versa.

Finally, it should be mentioned that the CPN editor is designed to work with large CPN diagrams – i.e. diagrams which typically have 50-100 pages, each with 5-25 nodes (and 10-50 connectors plus 10-200 regions).

5.3 Inscription language for CP-nets

When the user creates a CPN diagram he simultaneously creates a *drawing* and a *formal model*. The behaviour of the formal model is determined by the objects, their object types, the relationships between the objects[76], and the text strings inside the objects. Obviously these text strings need to have a well-defined syntax and semantics, and this is achieved by using a programming language called Standard ML (SML). It is by means of this language we declare colour sets, functions, operations and specify arc expressions and guards. SML has been developed by a group at Edinburgh University and it is one of the most well-known functional languages. For details about SML and functional languages, see [26], [27], [50] and [63].

By choosing an existing programming language we obtained a number of advantages. First of all we got a much better, more general and better tested language than we could have hoped to develop ourselves.[77] Secondly, we only had to port the compiler to the relevant machines and integrate it with our editor (instead of developing it from scratch).[78] Thirdly, we can use the considerable amount of documentation and tutorial material which already exists for SML (and for functional languages in general).

Why did we choose SML? First of all, we need a functional language: Arc expressions and guards are not allowed to have side effects and when a CP-net is translated into matrix form (e.g. for invariant analysis) the arc expressions and guards are, via lambda expressions, translated into functions. Secondly, we need a strongly typed language: Because CP-nets use colour sets in a way which is analogous to types in programming languages. Thirdly, we need a language with a flexible and extendible syntax: This makes it possible to allow the user to write arc expressions and guards in a form which is very close to standard mathematics (as an example, multi-set plus is de-

---

[76] There are many different kinds of relationships – e.g. the relationship between connectors and their source/destination nodes, between nodes and their regions, and between substitution transitions and their subpages.

[77] The development of a new programming language is a very slow and expensive process that requires resources comparable with the entire CPN tool project.

[78] The CPN tools use two different SML compilers. On the Macintosh we use the original compiler developed at Edinburgh University. On the Unix machines we use a more modern compiler developed by AT&T. It is also possible to run the graphics on one machine and the SML compiler on another (connected to the first by a local area network).

noted by "+").[79] SML is only one out of a number of languages which fulfil the three requirements above. SML was chosen because it was one of the best known, it had commercially available compilers, and some of us already had good experiences with the language.

We have many times been amazed by the high quality of SML, the generality of the language, and the ease by which complex programs can be written.[80] Thus we consider the choice of SML as one of the most successful design decisions in the CPN tool project. This choice has given us a very powerful and general inscription language and it has saved a lot of implementation time. As we shall see in section 5.5, the use of SML also makes it easy to make a smooth integration between the net inscriptions of a CP-net and code segments (which are sequential pieces of code attached to the individual transitions and executed each time a binding of the transition occurs).

To make it easier for the user we have made three small extensions of SML – and this yields a language called CPN ML: As the first extension, syntactical sugar has been added for the declaration of colour sets. This makes it easy to declare the most common kinds of colour sets, and it also means that a large number of predeclared functions and operations can be made accessible, just by including their names in the colour set declaration.[81] As examples, each enumeration type has a function mapping colours into ordinal numbers, each product type has a function mapping a set of multi-sets into their product multi-set, and each union type has a set of functions performing membership tests. SML allows the user to declare integers, reals, strings, enumerations, products, records, discrete unions and lists – and nest the type constructors arbitrarily inside each other. As an example we may declare the following colour sets (which should be rather self-explanatory):

```
color Name = string;
color NameList = list Name;

color Year = int;
color Month = with   Jan I Feb I Mar I Apr I May I Jun I
                     Jul I Aug I Sep I Okt I Nov I Dec;
color Day = int with 1..31;
color Date = product Year * Month * Day;

color Person = record name : Name * BirthDay : Date * Children : NameList;
```

---

[79]   The "+" operator is infixed (i.e. written between the two arguments). It is polymorphic (i.e. it works for multi-sets over all different types) and it is overloaded (i.e. it uses the same operator symbol as integer plus and real plus).

[80]   Much of the more intrinsic code of the CPN simulator is written in SML. In particular, all the code that calculates the set of enabled bindings. This code is rather complex: It defines a function which maps an arbitrary set of arc expressions (plus a guard) into a function mapping a set a multi-sets into a set of enabled bindings.

[81]   This convention saves a lot of space in the ML heap, because it turns out that most CPN diagrams only use few of the predeclared functions. A later version of the CPN editor will automatically detect the predeclared functions applied by the user (and then it will no longer be necessary to list their names).

Via the syntactic sugar, it is in CPN ML easy to declare colour sets from all the SML types mentioned above (and from subranges, substypes, and indexed types, which do not exist as standard SML types). In SML it is also possible to declare function types and abstract data types. However, such types do not have an equality operation and thus it does not immediately make sense to use them as colour sets (because you cannot talk about multi-sets without being able to talk about equality).[82]

As the second extension, we have added syntax which allows the user to declare the CPN variables – i.e. the typed variables used in arc expressions and guards. This extension is necessary because SML do not have variable declarations (in SML a value is bound to a name and this determines the current type of the name; later the name may get a new value and a new type).

As the third extension, we have added syntax which allows the user to declare three different kinds of reference variables. This is a non-functional part of SML and we only allow reference variables to be used in code segments. We distinguish between global, page and instance reference variables – in the same way as we distinguish between global, page and instance fusion sets: A global reference variable can be used by all code segments in the entire CPN diagram, while a page and instance reference variable only can be used by the code segments on a single page. A page reference variable is shared by all instances of the page, while an instance reference variable has a separate value for each page instance.

SML (and thus CPN ML) can be viewed as being a syntactical sugared version of typed lambda calculus, and this means that it is possible to declare arbitrary mathematical functions (as long as they are computable). It should be noticed that the use of SML gives an immense generality: The user can declare arbitrarily complex functions[83] and, if he wants, he can turn them into operations (i.e. use infix notation). This generality has been heavily used in the implementation of the CPN tools. Multi-sets are implemented as a polymorphic type constructor "ms" which maps an arbitrary type A into a new type, denoted by A ms and containing all multi-sets over A. Then we have declared a large number of polymorphic and sometimes overloaded operations/functions – by which multi-sets can be manipulated (e.g. operations to add and subtract multi-sets and functions to calculate the coefficients and the size of multi-sets).

The generality of the CPN ML language means that some legal CPN diagrams cannot be handled by the CPN simulator. As an illustration consider the transition in Fig. 10, where x is a CPN variable of type X, while $f \in [X \to A]$ and $g \in [X \to B]$ are two functions. To calculate the set of all enabled bindings for such a transition it is either necessary to try all possible values of X or use the inverse relations of f and g (and neither is possible, in general – because X may have two may values and the inverse relations may be unknown).

---

[82] The user can, with some extra work, use an arbitrary ML type as a colour set – as long as the standard equality operator "=" exists (and the type is non-polymorphic). In this way it is possible to declare abstract data types and turn them into colour sets. Details are outside the scope of this paper.

[83] Many CPN diagrams use recursive functions defined on list structures.

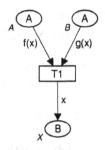

Figure 10. A syntactically legal CPN transition which cannot be handled by the CPN simulator

To avoid such problems the CPN simulator demands that each CPN variable, used around a transition, must appear either in an input arc expression without functions or operations[84] (then the possible values can be determined from the marking of the corresponding input place), be determinable from the guard, have a small colour set (in which case all possibilities can be tried),[85] or only appear on output arcs (in which case all possible values can be used). It is very seldom that these restrictions present any practical problems. Most net inscriptions, written by a typical user, fulfil the restrictions – and those which do not, can usually be rewritten by the user, without changing the semantics. As an example, consider the three transitions in Fig. 11. None of these can be directly handled by the CPN simulator. The first transition is identical to the transition in Fig. 10. The second transition has a guard which is a list of boolean expressions, and this means that each of the expressions must be fulfilled. The third transition uses the function exp(x,y) which takes two non-negative integers as arguments and returns x^y.

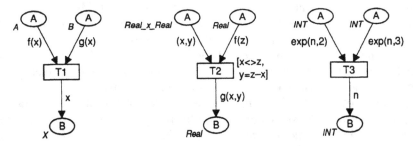

Figure 11. Three transitions which cannot be handled by the CPN simulator

Now let us assume that f has an inverse function $f1 \in [A \rightarrow X]$. Then we can, as shown in Fig. 12, rewrite the three transitions – so that their semantics is unchanged and they can be handled by the CPN simulator. In the first transition z is a variable of type A. In the second transition z can now be determined from the guard – because there is an equality in which z appears on one side (alone or in a matchable pattern) while the value of

---

84 The arc expression is allowed to contain matchable operations such as the tuple constructor (,,) in (x,y,z), the list constructor :: in head::tail, and the record constructor {,,} in {se=S(inst()), re=r, no=n}. It is also allowed to contain multi-set "+" and "`".

85 Intuitively a small colour set is a type with few values. A precise definition can be found in [36].

the other side is known (x and y are bound by one of the input arc expressions). In the third transition the function sq(x) takes a non-negative integer as argument and it returns the integer which is closest to √x.

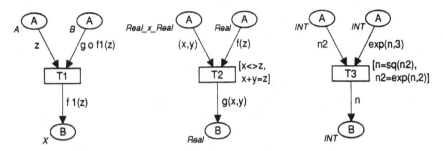

Figure 12. Three transitions that are behaviourally equivalent to those in Fig. 11 and which can be handled by the CPN simulator

It is important to understand that the general definition of CP-nets talks about expressions and colour sets – without specifying a syntax for these. It is only when we want to implement a CPN editor and a CPN simulator (and other kinds of CPN tools) that we need a concrete syntax. Thus it is for the CPN tools, and not for CP-nets in general, that CPN ML has been developed. Other implementations of CP-nets may use different inscription languages – and still they deal with CP-nets.

5.4 Syntax check

The CPN editor is syntax directed – in the sense that it recognizes the structure of CP-nets and prevents the user to make many kinds of syntax errors. This is done by means of a large number of **built-in** syntax restrictions. All the built-in restrictions deal with the net structure and the hierarchical relationships. As examples, it is impossible to make an arc between two transitions (or between two places), to give a place two colour set regions (or give a transition a colour set region), to create cycles in the substitution hierarchy, and to make an illegal port assignment (involving nodes which aren't sockets/ports or are positioned on a wrong page).

The CPN editor also operates with **compulsory** syntax restrictions. These restrictions are necessary in order to guarantee that the CPN diagram has a well-defined semantics – and thus they must be fulfilled before a simulation (and other kinds of behavioural analysis) is performed. Many of the compulsory restrictions deal with the net inscriptions and thus with CPN ML. As examples, it is checked that each colour set region contains the name of a declared colour set A (and that all surrounding arc expressions have a type which is identical to either A or A ms), that all members of a fusion set have the same colour set and equivalent initialization expressions, and that all identifiers in arc expressions and guards are declared (e.g. as CPN variables or functions). Many of the compulsory syntax restrictions could have been implemented as built-in restrictions. This would, however, have put severe limits on the way in which a user can construct an edit a CPN diagram. As examples, we could have demanded that each place always has a colour set (and this would mean that the colour set has to be specified at the moment the place is created) and we could have demanded that each arc expression always is of the correct type (and this would mean that a colour set cannot be changed without simultaneously changing all the surrounding arc expressions).

Finally, the CPN editor operates with **optional** syntax restrictions.[86] These are restrictions which the user imposes upon himself – e.g. because he knows that he usually does not use certain facilities of the editor and wants to be warned when he does (in order to check whether this was on purpose or due to an error). As examples, it can be checked whether port assignments are injective, surjective and total, whether all arcs have an explicit arc expression (otherwise they by default evaluate to the empty multi-set) and whether the place/transition names are unique (on each page).

All the type checking is done by the SML compiler and it is the error messages of this compiler which is presented to the user (together with a short heading produced by the CPN editor). The fact that these messages are easy to understand and uses CP-net terminology tells a lot about the generality and quality of SML. To illustrate this, let us imagine that we, in Fig. 1, change the arc expression between A and T1 from (x,i) to x. This will result in an error message which looks as follows:[87]

```
C.11 Arc Expression must be legal
Type clash in: x:((P)ms)
Looking for a: P ms
I have found a: U
««135»»
```

To speed up the syntax check we avoid duplicate tests: As an example, the same arc expression may appear at several arcs and it is then only checked once (provided that the places have identical colour sets). We also apply incremental tests: When the user changes part of a CPN diagram as little as possible is rechecked. Changing an arc expression or a guard means that the use of variables in the code segment must be rechecked. Changing a colour set means that the initialization expression and all surrounding arc expressions have to be rechecked.[88] Changing the global declaration node (which contains the declarations of colour sets, functions, operations, and CPN variables), unfortunately means that the entire CPN diagram has to be rechecked. To avoid using too much time for such total rechecks, the CPN editor allows the user to add a temporal declaration node which extends the declarations of the global declaration node.[89]

The CPN editor allows the user to give each page, transition and place a name (i.e. a text string) and a number (which must be non-negative).[90] It should, however, be un-

---

[86] Optional syntax checks are not implemented in the current version of the CPN editor.

[87] This is how the error message looks when the SML compiler runs on a Macintosh (on a Unix system another SML compiler is used, and thus the error messages looks a little bit different). C11 means that it is the 11th kind of compulsory restriction, while ««135»» is a hyper text pointer which allows the user to jump to the error position (i.e. to the arc with the erroneous arc expression).

[88] If the place belongs to a fusion set or is an assigned port/socket it also has to be checked whether the restrictions in Def. 3.2 (v) and (vi) still are satisfied.

[89] It is also possible, but not recommended, to use the temporal declaration node to overwrite existing declarations.

[90] In the current version it is not possible to give transitions and places a number.

derstood that these names have no semantic meaning.[91] Names are used in the feedback information from the editor to the user (e.g. in the page hierarchy and in the hierarchy inscriptions). To make this information unambiguous it is recommended to keep names unique,[92] but this is not enforced (unless the user activates an optional syntax restriction). Many users have a large number of transitions and places with an empty name (and this is no problem, as long as these nodes are not used in a way which generates system feedback).

The possibility of performing an automatic syntax check means that the user has a much better chance of getting a consistent and error-free CPN diagram. This is very useful – also in situations where the user isn't interested in making a simulation (or other kinds of machine assisted behavioural analysis).

5.5 CPN simulator

The CPN editor and CPN simulator are two different parts of the same program and they are closely integrated with each other: In the editor it is possible to prepare a simulation (e.g. change the many options which determine how the simulation is performed). In the simulator it is possible to perform simple editing operations (those which change the attributes of objects without changing the semantics of the model).[93]

The CPN simulator is able to work with large CP-nets, i.e. CP-nets with 50-500 page instances, each with 5-25 nodes. Fortunately, it turns out that a CP-net with 100 page instances, typically, simulates nearly as fast as a CP-net with only a single page instance (measured in terms of the number of occurring transitions). This surprising result is due to the fact that the CPN simulator, during the execution of a step, goes through three different phases: First it makes a random selection between enabled transitions, then it removes and adds tokens at the input/output places of the occurring transitions, and finally it calculates the new enabling. The first of these phases is fast (compared to the others), the second is independent of the model size and the third only depends upon the model size to a very limited degree. This is due to the fact that the enabling and occurrence rule of CP-nets are strictly local – and this means that it only is the transitions in the immediate neighbourhood of the occurring transitions that need to have their enabling recalculated.[94] Without a local rule the calculation of the new enabling would grow linearly with the model size and that would make it very cumbersome to deal with large systems. We have not yet tried to work with very large systems (e.g. containing 10.000 page instances) but our present experiences tell us that the upper limit is more likely to be set by the available memory than by the processor speed.

The user must be able to follow the on-going simulation – and it is obvious that no screen (or set of screens) will be able simultaneously to display all page instances of a large model. Like the editor, the CPN simulator uses a window for each page and in

---

[91] In the current version of the CPN editor the names of fusion sets play a semantic role, and thus they have to be unambiguous. This will be changed in a later version.

[92] For places and transitions it is sufficient to demand the names to be unique on each individual page.

[93] In one of the next versions of the CPN simulator we will also allow the user to make changes that modify the behaviour of the model – as long as these changes cannot make the current marking illegal.

[94] When the neighbourhood of an occurring transition is defined, fusion sets and port/socket assignments must be taken into consideration.

this window the simulator displays the marking of one of the corresponding page instances. The user can see the names of the other page instances and switch to any of these. When a transition occurs the simulator automatically opens the corresponding page window (if necessary), brings it on top of all other windows, switches to the correct page instance, and scrolls the window so that the transition becomes visible. The user can, however, tell that he doesn't want to observe all page instances. In that case the simulator still executes the transitions of the non-observed page instances but this cannot be seen by the user (unless the relevant part of corresponding page instance happens to be visible on the screen without any rearrangements). The user can set breakpoints and in this way ask the simulator to pause before, during, and/or after each simulation step. Breakpoints can be preset or added on the fly, i.e. at any point during a simulation. At each breakpoint the user can investigate the system state (and decide whether he wants to continue or cancel the remaining part of the step).

It is possible to simulate a selected part of a large CPN diagram (without having to copy this part to a separate file, which would give all the usual inconsistency problems). This is achieved by allowing the user to change the multi-set of prime pages and tell that certain page instances should be temporarily ignored. When a page instance is ignored it is no longer generated, and this means that the corresponding direct supernode becomes an ordinary transition with enabling and occurrence calculated in the usual way (i.e. by means of the surrounding arc expressions and guard). As a short hand, it is also possible to ignore a page and this means that all instances of the page are ignored.

When we simulate a CP-net it is sometimes convenient to be able to equip some of the transitions with a **code segment** – i.e. a sequential piece of code which is executed each time a binding of the transition occurs. Each code segment has a code guard, an input pattern, an output pattern and a code action. The code guard replaces the corresponding guard (in a simulation with code segments). A missing code guard means that the ordinary guard is used. The input pattern contains some of the CPN variables of the transition, and this indicates that the code action is allowed to use (but not update) these variables. Analogously, the output pattern contains some of the CPN variables (but only those which do not appear in the input arc expressions and the code guard) and this indicates that the binding of these variables is determined by the code segment. Finally, the action part is an SML expression (with the same type as the output pattern).[95] The action part may declare local variables, share reference variables with other code segments, use the CPN variables from the input pattern and manipulate input/output files. When the transition occurs the action part is evaluated and the resulting value determines the binding of the CPN variables in the output pattern. It should be noticed that the code segment is executed once for each occurring binding, and this means that it may be executed several times in the same step.[96]

---

[95] In a later version of the CPN simulator it will also be possible to use other programming languages in the code action, e.g. C++, Pascal and Prolog.

[96] The order of these executions is non-deterministic (but it is guaranteed that each execution is indivisible, in the sense that it is finished before the next is started).

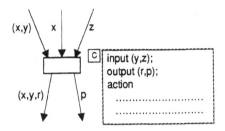

Figure 13. A simple example of a code segment

Code segments can be used for many different purposes: They can be used to gather statistical information about the simulation: It is easy to dump the value of all occurring bindings on a file (which then later can be analysed e.g. by means of a spread sheet program). It is also possible to use the graphic routines of the CPN tools (which can be invoked via predeclared SML functions) and in this way make a visual representation of the simulation results (as an example, it is easy to make a window which has an node for each site in a communication network and a connector for each pair of sites which are engaged in a communication).[97] Code segments also allow interactive user input, and they can be used to communicate with other programs (as an example, it is possible to run different parts of a very large CPN model on separate computers and let the different submodels communicate via input/output statements).

Although code segments are extremely useful for many purposes, they also have severe limitations. This is due to the fact that they allow the occurrence of transitions to have side effects and allow bindings to be determined by input files (and other kinds of user input). This means that it doesn't make sense to talk about occurrence graphs for CP-nets with code segments, and it also becomes more difficult to use the invariant method for such nets (because the relation between the CPN variables surrounding a transition may be determined by the code action, instead of the arc expressions). For this reason it is important to have a well-understood relationship between a CPN diagram executed with code segments and the same CPN diagram executed without code segments. This is one of the main reasons for the introduction of the input and output patterns.

It is possible to perform both **manual** and **automatic** simulations. In a manual simulation the simulator calculates and displays the enabling, the user chooses the occurrence elements (i.e. the transitions and bindings) to be executed and finally the simulator calculates the effect of the chosen step. During the construction of a step, the simulator assists the user in many different ways: First of all, the simulator always shows the current enabling (and updates it each time a new occurrence element is added/removed at the step). Secondly, the user can ask the simulator to find all bindings for a given enabled transition – or he can specify a partial binding and ask the simulator to finish it, if possible. In an automatic simulation the simulator chooses among the enabled occurrence elements by means of a random number generator. It is possible to specify how large each step should be: It may contain a single occurrence element or as

---

[97] We do not allow code segments to create or delete CPN objects (but the attributes can be changed).

many as possible (and between these two extremes there is a continuum of other possibilities).

It is possible to vary the amount of graphical feedback provided by the CPN simulator. In the most detailed mode the user sees the enabled transitions, the occurring transitions, the tokens which are being moved and the current markings. Each of these feedback mechanisms is, however, controlled by one or more options, and thus they can be fully or partially omitted. In this way it is possible to speed up the simulation. As an extreme a special **super-automatic** mode has been provided. In this mode there is no user interaction (for the selection of bindings) and there is no feedback during the simulation (on the CPN diagram) – and this means that the simulation runs much faster than usual, because the simulation is performed by a SML program alone (while an ordinary simulation is performed by a SML program and a C program, with a heavy intercommunication).[98] At the end of a super-automatic simulation it is possible to inspect the effect of the simulation. This can be done either by means of the usual page windows (in which the marking is updated when the super-automatic simulation finishes) or by means of files manipulated by code segments. Finally, the code segments may, as described above, use the graphic routines of the CPN tools to create a visual representation of the simulation results – and this can be inspected while a super-automatic simulation is going on.

The user can, at any time during a simulation, change between manual, automatic and super-automatic simulation (and there are many other possibilities in between these three extremes).[99] It is usual to apply the more manual simulation modes early in a project (e.g. when a design is being created and investigated) while the more automatic modes are used in the later phases (e.g. when the design is being validated). There are no restrictions on the way in which the different simulation options can be mixed and this means that each of them can be chosen totally independently of the others (as an example manual/automatic/semi-automatic simulation can be with/without code (and with/without time, see section 7.1)).

There are many other facilities in the CPN simulator: An operation that proposes a step (which can be inspected and modified by the user before it is executed). Operations to return to the initial marking of the CPN diagram and to change the current marking of an arbitrary place instance (this means that it often is possible to continue a simulation in the case where a minor modelling error is encountered). Operations to save and load system states. Operations to activate/deactivate a large number of warning and stop options (i.e. different criteria under which a manual simulation issues a warning while an automatic simulation stops).[100] An operation to determine the order in which the different occurrence elements in a step is executed. Moreover, the earlier comments about different skill levels and a consistent and self-explanatory user interface also apply to the CPN simulator.

---

[98] Super-automatic simulation is not available in the released version of the CPN simulator, but a prototype version has been used in several projects (e.g. the one described in section 6.1). One of the next versions of the CPN simulator will contain a super-automatic mode which is fully integrated with the rest of the simulator.

[99] In the current version of the CPN simulator it is, during a simulation, not possible to change to/from super-automatic mode. This will, however, be possible in one of the next versions.

[100] The load/save operations and the warning/stop options are not yet implemented.

Finally, it should be mentioned that many modellers use simulation during the construction of CPN diagrams – in a similar way as a programmer tests selected parts of the program which he is writing. It is thus very important that it is reasonably fast to shift between the editor and the simulator (and that it is possible to simulate selected parts of a large model).

6. Applications of CP-nets

This chapter describes a number of projects which have used hierarchical CP-nets and the CPN tools. All the described projects have worked with reasonably large models and this have been done in an industrial environment – where parameters such as turnaround time and use of man-hours have been important.

6.1 Communication protocol

This project was carried out in cooperation with a large telecommunications company and it involved the modelling and simulation of selected parts of an existing ISDN protocol for digital telephone exchanges.[101] The modelling started from an SDL diagram, and it was straightforward to make a manual translation of the SDL diagram to a hierarchical CP-net.[102] The translation and simulation of the basic part of the protocol was finished in 16 days by a single modeller (which had large experience with the CPN tools, but no prior knowledge of communication protocols). The model was presented to engineers at the participating company. This was done by making a manual simulation of selected occurrence sequences – and by a super-automatic simulation, where code segments were used to update a page containing a visual representation of the travelling messages and the status of the user sites.[103] According to the engineers, who all had large experience with telephone systems, the CPN diagram provided the most detailed behavioural model which they had seen for this kind of system.

Later the modelling of a hold-feature was included in the CPN diagram. This was done in a single day, and it tuned out that it could be done by adding two extra pages, and making a simple modification of the existing pages (a colour set was changed from a triple to quadruple). In SDL the inclusion of the hold-feature made it necessary to duplicate the entire model, i.e. include many new pages – and so did three other features (which were not modelled in the project, but could have been handled in a similar way). Obviously, this makes it easier to maintain the CPN diagram (because it is sufficient to make modifications to one page instead of five).

---

[101] ISDN stands for Integrated Services Digital Network. The protocol is a BRI protocol (Basic Rate Interface) and it is the network layer which has been modelled.

[102] SDL is one of the standard graphical specification languages used by telecommunications companies. For information about SDL and how it can be translated into high-level Petri nets, see [13], [41] and [53].

[103] The simulation traces a call from the originating user to the terminating user, and to do this it was necessary to include a page which models the underlying protocol layers.

Fig. 14 shows the page hierarchy for the CPN diagram.[104] The subpages of UserTop#2 describe the actions of the user part while the subpages of NetTop#19 describe the actions of the network part. Most of these pages have a supernode which is called Ui (or Ni) and this indicates that the page describes the activity which can happen when the user part is in state Ui (the network part is in state Ni). The bracket in front of the pages U_PROG#41...U_REL_CO#40 indicates that they are subpages of all the pages in Null#3...Release_#17. The five pages describe activities which are carried out in the same way in all user states. If one of these activities is to be changed it is sufficient to modify one page of the CPN diagram (while it in the SDL diagram would be necessary to modify a large number of pages). The hold-feature is modelled by U_HOLD#45 and N_HOLD#44, while ROUTING#24 models the underlying protocol layers.

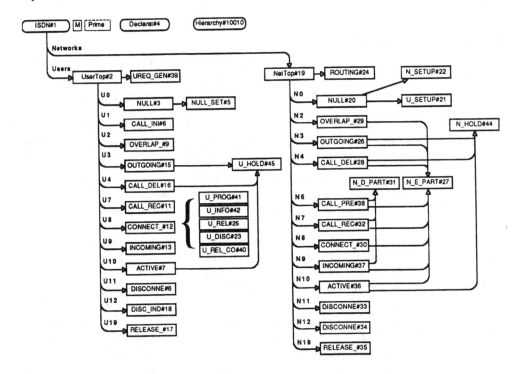

Figure 14. Page hierarchy for the ISDN protocol

A typical representative of the Ui/Ni pages is shown in Fig. 15.[105] It shows that, in the state U8, there are six different possibilities. When there is an internal user request the

---

[104] Names are truncated to the first eight characters, unless one of these is a format character (such as space, TAB, RETURN, etc). This convention keeps the feedback readable (also in diagrams with very long text strings). One of the next versions of the CPN tools will have a set of name options allowing the user to specify how names are truncated.

[105] The vertical lines and triangular figures inside the transitions are carried over from the SDL diagram, where they have a formal meaning. In the CPN diagram they have no formal meaning but they are retained, because they make the diagram more accessible for people who have experience with SDL.

first transition can occur. It creates a message to the network and the new user state becomes U11. When there is a message from the network one of the last five transitions can occur (the guards determine which one).[106] Two of the transitions create a message to the network, and the new user state becomes either U10, U12, U0, or U8. Three of the transitions are drawn with thick borders, this indicates that they are substitution transitions (having the pages U_DISC#23, U_REL#25 and U_REL_CO#40 as subpages). It should also be noticed that a global fusion set is used to glue all the U0-places together (and analogously for all the other 23 kinds of Ui/Ni-places).[107]

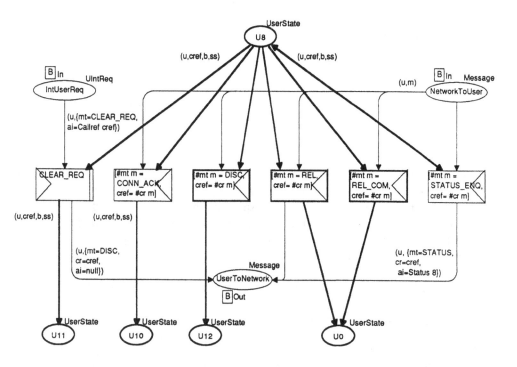

Figure 15. A typical page in the ISDN protocol (CONNECT_#12)

A typical representative of a transition is shown in Fig. 16 – together with the declarations of the appropriate colour sets. The transition is enabled when the user is in state U8 and there is a message with STATUS_ENQ as message type (on NetworkToUser). When the transition occurs the user remains in U8 and a message is created (on UserToNetwork). The new message has the same user and the same CallRef as the received message, it has STATUS as message type and Status 8 as data.

---

[106] To improve the readability the modeller has made some of the arc expressions invisible. All output arcs of NetworkToUser have identical arc expressions – and only one of these is visible.

[107] To improve the readability the modeller has made all the fusion regions invisible.

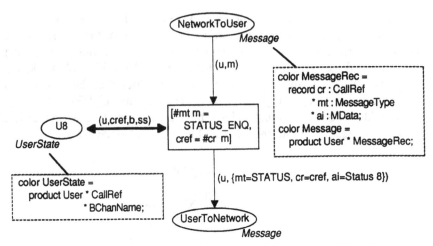

Figure 16. A typical transition in the ISDN protocol (rightmost on CONNECT_#12)

6.2 Hardware chip

This project was carried out in cooperation with a company which, among many other things, is a manufacturer of super-computers. The purpose of the project was to investigate whether the use of CP-nets is able to speed up the design and validation of VLSI chips (at the register transfer level). Below we sketch the main ideas behind the project and the most important conclusions. A much more detailed description of the project, the model, and the conclusions can be found in [54].

Let us first describe the existing design/validation strategy (without CP-nets): The chip designers specify a new chip by means of a set of block diagrams. Each diagram contains an interconnected set of blocks (activities), where each block has a specified input/output behaviour. A complex block may be specified in a separate block diagram, which is related to the block in a similar way as a substitution subpage in a CP-net is related to its supernode. When the designers have finished a new chip, the block diagrams are (by a manual process) translated into a simulation program written in a dialect of C. The simulation program is then executed on a large number of test data and the output is analysed to detect any malfunctions. The design/validation strategy described above has a number deficiencies – and we shall come back to these later (when we compare it to an alternative strategy which involves CP-nets).

Now let us describe the alternative design/validation strategy (involving CP-nets): The basic idea is to replace the manual translation (from the block diagrams into the C program) with an automatic translation into a CP-net. It is important to understand that it is *not* the intention to stop using block diagrams. The designers will still specify the designs by means of block diagrams, and they will during a simulation of the CP-net see the simulation results on the block diagrams. To support the new strategy three things are needed: The existing drawing tool for the block diagrams must be modified (to have a formal syntax and semantics). The set of block diagrams must be translated into CP-nets. Finally, it must be investigated whether the CPN simulator is powerful enough to handle complex VLSI designs.

The project only dealt with the last two issues (which were considered to be the most difficult). It was shown that the block diagrams could be translated into hierarchical CP-nets. This was done manually, but the translation process is rather straightforward and we see no problems in implementing an automatic translation. The obtained CP-net only contained 15 pages, but during a simulation there is nearly 150 page instances (due to the repeated use of substitution subpages representing adders and multipliers). The CP-net was simulated on the CPN simulator.[108]

Fig. 17 shows a subpage from which it can be seen that the VLSI chip has a pipelined design with six different stages. Each stage is modelled on a separate subpage and two of the more complex stages are shown in Fig. 18.[109] The eight transitions in the leftmost part of stage 1 are all substitution transitions (and they have the same subpage). In stage 2 the four transitions SUM1L, SUM1R, SUM2L and SUM2R represent registers. These registers establish the border to stage 3, and the transitions can only occur when they receive a clock pulse from stage 3 (via the two c-transitions in the rightmost part of stage 2). All the remaining transitions in stage 2 are substitution transitions (OR3 and OR4 denote or-gates while "+" denotes 16 bit adders).

Now let us compare the new design/validation strategy with the old: First of all, it is easier to translate the block diagrams into a CP-net than it is to translate them into a C program (the latter takes often several man-months while the construction of the CP-net only took a few man-weeks). The translation is also more transparent – in the sense that it is much easier to recognize those parts of the CP-net which models a given block than it is to find the corresponding parts in the C program (each page in the CP-net has nearly the same graphical layout as the corresponding block diagram). This means that it is relatively easy to change the CP-net to reflect any changes in the design, while this (according to the chip manufacturer) often is rather difficult for the C program. As stated above we think that it will be easy to automate the translation.

Secondly, the new strategy (when it is fully implemented) allows the designer to make simulations during the design process. This means that the knowledge and understanding which is acquired during the simulation of the model can be used to improve the design itself (in a much more direct way than in the old strategy where the validation is performed after the design has been finished).

Thirdly, the validation techniques of the old strategy concentrates on the logic correctness (tested by an inspection of the output data from the C program) and very little concern is given to those design decisions which deal with timing issues (e.g. the division into stages and the clock rate).[110] Using CP-nets it is possible to validate both the logic correctness and the timing issues – inside the same basic model.[111]

---

[108] When maximal graphical feedback was used the simulation was slow (due to the many graphical objects which had to be updated in each step). However, when a more selective feedback was used, the speed became reasonable.

[109] It is our intention to give the reader an idea about the complexity of the model (without explaining it in any detail).

[110] This is surprising, because the timing issues are crucial for the correct behaviour and the effectiveness of the chip (too fast clocking means malfunctioning while too slow means loss of speed).

[111] The timing issues were not modelled in the project – but with the time extensions of the CPN simulator (described in section 7.1) this can easily be done.

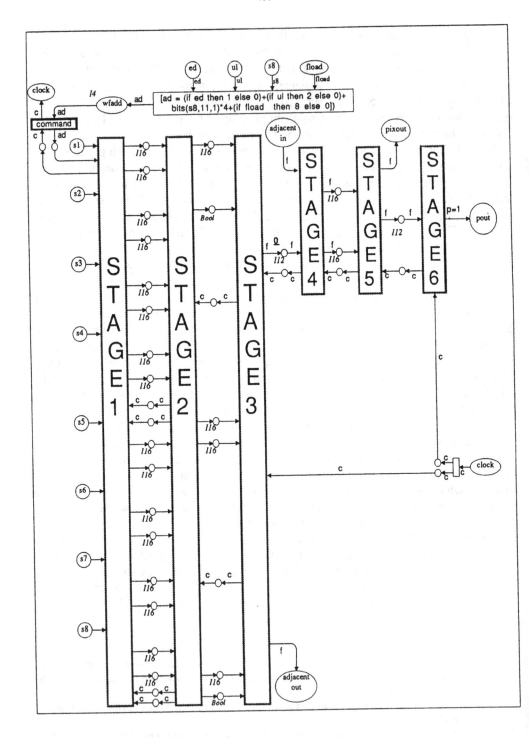

Figure 17. A page from the VLSI chip (showing the division into six pipe-lined stages)

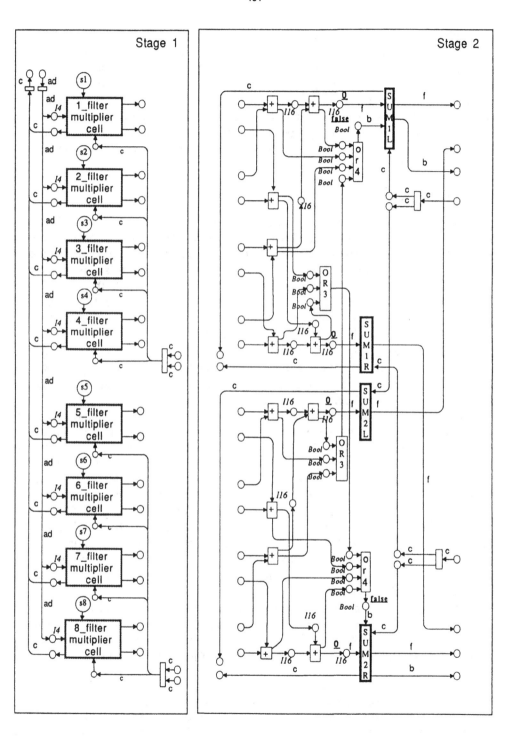

Figure 18. Two subpages of the page in Fig. 17 (modelling stage 1 and 2)

Finally, it was noticed that the execution of the C program was much faster than the CPN simulator – and that it with the latter would be impossible to make the usual amount of test runs (which typically include 10-20.000 sets of test data). It should, however, be noticed that the project was carried out immediately after the first version of the CPN simulator had been released – and that we (based on the experience with this and other large models) now have improved the speed of the CPN simulator with more than a factor 10. Moreover, super-automatic mode has been provided – and this means that we now are in a situation where it makes sense also to deal with large sets of test data.

6.3 Radar surveillance

This project was carried out in cooperation with Armstrong Aerospace Medical Research Laboratory (AAMRL) and it involved the modelling of a command post in the NORAD system.[112] The responsibility of the command post is to recommend different actions – based upon an assessment of the (rapidly changing) status of surveillance networks, defensive weapons and air traffic information. To do this the individual crew member communicates with many different types of equipment, other control posts and other members of the crew, and there is a complex set of detailed rules telling what he must do in the different types of situations. The entire system can be compared to a very complex communication protocol (although a large part of the communication is between human beings and not between computers). The proper design of command posts, including procedures, equipment and staffing, is an on-going problem – typical of the *Command and Control* area.

The purpose of the project was to get an executable model of the command post and use this model to get a better understanding of the command post – in order to improve its effectiveness and robustness. It was never the intention to use the CPN tools directly in the surveillance operations. A team of modellers working at AAMRL created a description of the command post, by means of SADT [43] (which in the United States is known as IDEF). This description was then augmented with more precise behavioural information, and the augmented model was automatically translated into a CP-net and simulated on the CPN simulator (for more details see below). The simulation gave (according to the people at AAMRL) an improved understanding of the command post, and they are now continuing the project modelling other parts of the NORAD system.[113] A much more detailed description of the project, the translation to CP-nets, and the model can be found in [55].

SADT diagrams are in many respects similar to CP-nets: Each SADT model consists of a set of pages,[114] and each of these contains a number of activities (playing a similar role as transitions in CP-nets). The activities are interconnected by arcs (these are called channels and there are three different kinds of them: representing physical flow,

---

112 NORAD is the North American Radar Defense system.

113 It is the plan to model a number of command posts – and run the submodel for each of these on a separate machine (using a separate copy of the CPN simulator). The submodels will then communicate via input/output statements in code segments (and this will be similar to the way in which the real control posts communicate with each other via electronic networks).

114 In the SADT terminology each page is called a diagram. In this paper we shall, however, use the term diagram for the *set of pages* which constitutes a model.

control flow and availability of resources). SADT has no counterpart to places, but each channel has an attached date type (playing a similar role as the colour sets in CP-nets). Each SADT page (except for the top page) is a refinement of an activity of its parent page (and this works in a way which is totally analogous to transition substitution in CP-nets).

SADT diagrams are often ambiguous. As an example, a branching output channel may mean that the corresponding information/material sometimes is sent in one direction and sometimes in another. It may, however, also mean that the information/material is split in two parts, or that it is copied (and sent in both directions). Although some ambiguity may be tolerable as long as SADT is used to describe the structure of a system,[115] it is obvious that all ambiguity must be removed before the behaviour of a SADT model can be defined (i.e. before simulations can be made) – and this means that SADT must be augmented with better facilities to describe behaviour (e.g. to tell what a branching output channel means).

There are many different ways in which this can be done. One possibility (proposed in several SADT papers) is to attach a table to each activity. Each line in the table describes a possible set of acceptable input values and it specifies the corresponding set of output values. Another, and in our opinion much more attractive possibility, is to describe the input/output relation by a set of channel expressions and a guard – in exactly the same way as the behaviour of a CP-net transition is described by means of a set of arc expressions and a guard. Thus we introduce a new SADT dialect – called IDEF/CPN. In addition to the added channel expressions and guards there is a global declaration node (containing the declarations of types, functions, operations and IDEF variables). Finally, it is possible to use place fusion sets in a similar way as in CPN diagrams.

It is easy to translate an IDEF/CPN diagram into a behavioural equivalent CPN diagram, and this means that the CPN simulator can be used to investigate the behaviour of IDEF/CPN models. For the moment there is a separate IDEF/CPN tool which allows the user to construct, syntax check and modify IDEF/CPN diagrams. This tool works in a similar way as the CPN editor (and many parts of the two user interfaces are identical or very similar). The IDEF/CPN tool can create a file containing a textual representation of the IDEF/CPN diagram, and this file can then be read into the CPN simulator (where it is interpreted as a CPN diagram). The translation from IDEF/CPN to CPN diagrams is thus totally automatic. Later it is the plan to integrate a copy of the CPN simulator into the IDEF/CPN tool itself, and this will mean that the turn-around time will be faster (because it then is possible to edit and simulate in the same tool). Such an integration will also mean that the user will see the simulation results directly on the IDEF/CPN diagram. For the moment he sees the results on the CPN diagram – but this is not a big problem because the two diagrams look nearly identical (except that the former does not have places). Fig. 19 shows an IDEF/CPN page (from the radar surveillance system) and Fig. 20 shows the corresponding CPN page (as it is obtained by the automatic translation).

---

[115] The designers of SADT argue that it is fine to allow such ambiguities – because SADT should be used to "design" the information/material flow, without having to worry about the detailed behaviour (which in their opinion is an "implementation detail").

404

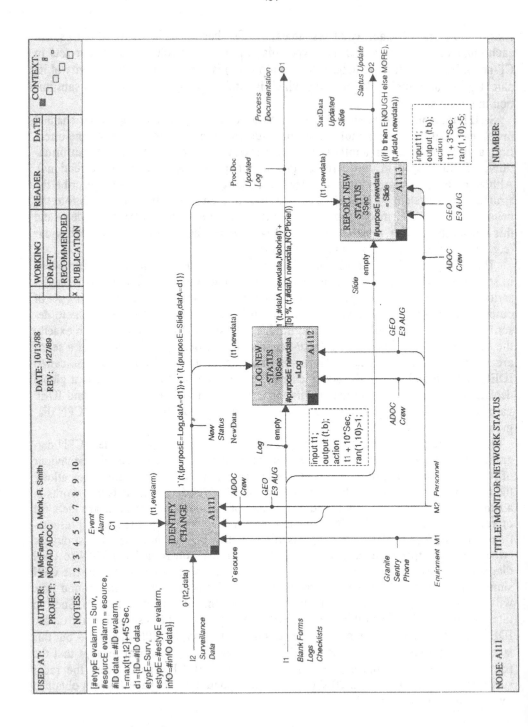

Figure 19. An IDEF/CPN page from the radar surveillance model

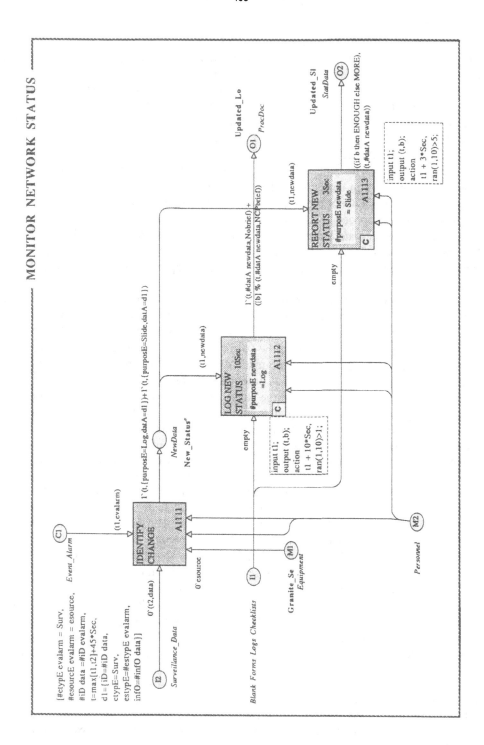

Figure 20. The CPN page obtained from the IDEF/CPN page in Fig. 19

6.4 Electronic funds transfer

This project was carried out in cooperation with two banks (Societé Générale and Marine Midland Bank of New York) and it involved the design and implementation of software to *control* the electronic transfer of money between banks. The speed of modern bank operations means that banks often make commitments which are based on money which they do not have (but expect to receive inside the next few minutes). What happens if these money are delayed – or never arrive? Two managers (at the involved banks) had an idea for a new control strategy – allowing the responsible staff to use computer support to control the electronic funds transfer.[116] The two managers concretized their idea in terms of a relatively small SADT diagram which was created by means of the IDEF/CPN tool (see section 6.3) and contained a rather informal description of the proposed algorithm. The IDEF/CPN diagram was translated to a CP-net and more accurate behavioural information was added, by a CPN modeller.[117] The translation was done in close cooperation with the two bank managers and they participated in the debugging (which also resulted in improvements of the original proposal).

During the project there were several different versions of the CPN model. The first of these was obtained more or less directly from the IDEF/CPN diagram, and it was rather crude (with simple arc expressions and very simple types). This model was primarily used to describe the data flow (while the actual data manipulations were ignored). Later the arc expressions were made more precise, a large number of complex data types were declared (and used as colour sets), complex CPN ML functions were declared (e.g. to search, sort and merge files), and finally most of the behavioural information were moved to code segments. In the final CPN model most transitions have arc expressions which consist of a single variable, and complex code segments determining the values of the output variables from the values of the input variables. It took 5 man-weeks to create the IDEF/CPN diagram, 1 man-week to get the first CPN diagram, and 16 man-weeks to develop this into the final CPN model.

In the first part of the project the graphical interface (in the editor/simulator) was of very large importance– and it was the graphical aspects of IDEF and CP-nets which made it possible for the bank managers to concretize their ideas. Later, however, it turned out that the graphical interface became less important while the output files produced by the simulation became more important – and thus the project started to use a stand-alone SML program (which was generated by the simulator in a similar way as the internal SML code needed for super-automatic simulation).

Now a simulation works with a number of input files (describing transfers which have already been made that day, and transfers which are registered but not yet executed). From these input files (which typically contains 15-50.000 records) a number of output files are produced (in 5-10 minutes) – and it is from these output files the

---

[116] Today the control of the transfer (i.e. the decisions about acceptance/rejection of the individual transactions) is made totally manual – although the transactions themselves are performed via special computer networks.

[117] The additional behavioural information could just as well have been added before the translation (i.e. by means of the IDEF/CPN tool instead of the CPN editor).

staff determine the transfer strategy to be used for the next 15-20 minutes (at which time a new set of simulation results is ready).

In this project the CPN tools (together with the IDEF/CPN tool) was used as a case tool. When the new strategy had been specified (by means of IDEF/CPN and the CPN editor) and validated (by means of the CPN simulator) the resulting SML code was automatically produced (by the CPN simulator).[118] The new control strategy, proposed by the two bank managers, seems to be working as expected – and it is for the moment being tested on historical bank data (using the SML code produced by the CPN simulator). When these tests are finished it will be determined whether the project will continue. If the project is continued the CPN model (and the IDEF/CPN model) will be extended to reflect additional aspects of funds transfer – and a graphical user interface will be added allowing the staff to interact with the model in a more natural way. The user interface will be created by letting the code segments use the graphical routines of the CPN tools. These routines are also available in the stand-alone ML environment, and thus it will still be possible to obtain the final SML code automatically from the CPN simulator (including the added graphical interface). A much more detailed description of the project, the models, and the conclusions can be found in [49].

6.5 Other application areas

CP-nets and other kinds of high-level Petri nets are used in many other application areas. For more information see e.g. [56] (flexible manufacturing systems); [28] and [52] (distributed algorithms); [58] (computer organization); [61] (data bases); [62] (office automation); [2] (computer architecture); [46] (human-machine interaction); [34] (semantics of programming languages); [15] and [29] (software development methods); [4], [8], [11], [14], [16], [19] and [24] (protocols).

From the applications reported in sections 6.1-6.4 (and some of the applications mentioned above) two interesting observations can be made: First of all, it is often adequate to use CP-net models in connection with different front-end languages (e.g. SDL, SADT and block diagrams). The reason may be that there already exist descriptions in these languages, or that the projects involve people who are familiar with some of the languages and thus prefer to use them (instead of learning a totally new formalism). It will also sometimes be sensible to make a tailored language (with a semantics based on CP-nets, but a syntax adopted to the problem area). This is for instance done by the designers of the Vista language [38], who have defined the semantics of their graphical specification language in terms of CP-nets.

Secondly, it is often the case that the graphical representation (which is very important in the early phases) later becomes less interesting. In this case the modellers may turn to super-automatic simulation and this yields a prototype implementation – or (for certain applications areas) even a final implementation. In this way the CPN tools are used as a case tool – and this will be even more attractive when it becomes possible to write code segments in different languages (such as C++, Pascal and Prolog).

---

[118] It was necessary to make a few manual operations to create the stand-alone SML code. These operations were trivial, and with the full support of super-automatic simulation they will disappear.

7. Future Plans for CP-nets

This chapter describes our plans for the further development of CP-nets. First we describe a number of extensions which is being made to the existing CPN tools (i.e. the CPN editor and the CPN simulator). Then we describe a number of new CPN tools which are being developed (e.g. to support occurrence graph analysis and invariant analysis). Finally we describe a book project which will provide the necessary introduction and documentation for CP-nets, their analysis methods, and selected examples of industrial applications.

7.1 Extensions of the CPN editor and CPN simulator

The CPN editor/simulator are being extended to handle timed CP-nets, which is an extension of ordinary CP-nets making it easy to describe systems which are time-driven. It will then be possible to use the same net model to analyse both the logic correctness and the time performance of a system. A timed CP-net has a global clock and the value of this is called the current *model time*.[119] The user can specify that certain colour sets are *with time* and this means that the corresponding tokens carry a time stamp (in addition to the ordinary colour information). Intuitively, the time stamp tells when the token is ready to be used (i.e. consumed by a transition). An occurrence element is said to be *colour enabled* if it satisfies the usual enabling criteria (defined by the arc expressions and the guard) and it is then said to have an *enabling time* which is the maximum of all the time stamps in the input tokens and the current model time. A colour enabled occurrence element is *time enabled* iff no other colour enabled occurrence elements have a smaller enabling time.[120] Only time enabled occurrence elements are allowed to occur (and this means that the transitions are executed in the order in which their tokens become ready). The occurrence rule is the same as for CP-nets without time – except that the time stamps of timed output tokens are determined by adding a delay to the current model time. The delays are specified by SML expressions and they may depend upon the colours of the input and output tokens (and via code segments also depend on reference variables and input files).[121] Each time a step has been executed the model time is advanced to match the minimal enabling time in the new system state[122] and this works very much like an event queue in a traditional simulation language. For more information about timed CP-net and the corresponding editor/simulation extensions see [37].

The CPN simulator is also being extended with a set of reporting facilities which will allow much easier visualization of the simulation results (e.g. during a super-automatic simulation). By means of code segments the user will be able to manipulate a

---

[119] The values of model time may be discrete (integers) or continuous (reals). In both cases each system state exists at a given model time – and the model time is monotonically increased throughout the simulation.

[120] A set of occurrence elements can be concurrently time enabled, but this requires that they all have the same enabling time.

[121] It is also possible to specify that different output tokens get different delays.

[122] The new model time may be identical to the old. This can e.g. happen when some (non conflicting) time enabled occurrence elements do not participate in the step or when some output tokens are created with a time stamp identical to the old model time (or without a time stamp).

large number of different charts (e.g. bar charts, function charts, pie charts and matrix charts). For each chart the code segments update an SML structure (with a predeclared type) while it is the CPN simulator which automatically updates the graphical representation of the chart (based on the value of the SML structure). The frequency by which the chart is updated is specified by the user (either in terms of the number of steps or in terms of model time). The charts are constructed by a special command in the CPN editor and they each consist of a number of auxiliary objects (which can be modified, e.g. resized, recoloured and repatterned, by the same editor operations as the other objects in the CPN diagram). For more information about the reporting facilities and their implementation see [37] and [39].

The implementation of timed CP-nets and the reporting facilities will be finished during the first half of 1991. Later we will also extend the CPN editor to allow the user to construct and modify CP-nets by means of a set of behaviour preserving transformation rules (for more information see [23]). We will also extend the CPN simulator to handle code segments written in other languages[123] and we will extend the CPN editor/simulator to handle the remaining hierarchy constructs and different extensions of CP-nets (e.g. capacities, inhibitor arcs and FIFO places). These projects have, however, lower priority than the creation of the occurrence graph and invariant tools described in section 7.2.

7.2 Additional CPN tools

A CPN tool will be created to support occurrence graph analysis. The tool will construct occurrence graphs for CP-nets (with/without equivalence classes) and it will also assist the user in the analysis of the constructed graphs. As described in section 4.2, a large number of system properties can be automatically determined from the occurrence graph (by an inspection of the individual markings and from the strongly connected components). There is, however, also a need to develop more complex search systems by which the user can perform an interactive inspection of a large occurrence graph. The CPN occurrence graph tool will be able to handle hierarchical CP-nets[124] and it will be tightly integrated into the existing CPN tools. It will e.g. be possible to ask the CPN simulator to execute an occurrence sequence which is found in the occurrence graph – or ask the occurrence graph analyser to search for markings which are identical to or larger than the current marking of the CPN simulator.

To keep the size of occurrence graphs manageable it will be necessary to create occurrence graphs for selected parts of a large model (and this will be done in exactly the same way as in the simulator – i.e. by defining prime pages and being able to ignore specified page instances). It will, moreover, be possible to simplify a model by means of *colour set restrictions*. The basic idea behind this concept is to be able to ignore parts of complex token colours – e.g. one or more components of a record type.[125] As an example, it may during the analysis of a communication protocol be adequate to ig-

---

[123] With the SML compiler running under Unix it is already today possible to use object code produced by other compilers.

[124] It is straightforward to extend the theory of occurrence graphs with equivalence classes to hierarchical CP-nets with transition substitution and place fusion (and this has already been done).

[125] This is analogous to (and inspired by) the concept of projections defined in [21].

nore the data contents of the messages. The restrictions are specified together with the colour set declarations, and this means that it is unnecessary to change the arc expressions or other net inscriptions. Colour set restrictions are also useful for simulation and it will in the future be possible to simulate a model with/without restrictions. For more information about colour set restrictions see [37].

Occurrence graphs can, for a given model, be constructed with/without time and with/without colour set restrictions. It makes, however, no sense to create occurrence graphs with code segments (at least not when these have side effects). The first version of the occurrence graph tool will be available during 1991. Later we will try to integrate our occurrence graph technique (building upon equivalence classes) with the techniques of other groups (see section 4.2).[126]

Analogously, a CPN tool will be created to support invariant analysis. The tool will calculate and check invariants for CP-nets and it will also assist the user when he applies the invariants to prove properties of the modelled system. The calculation of invariants are done in two steps: The first step is automatic and performs a reduction of the CP-net by a set of transformation rules which are proved to preserve the set of invariants.[127] The second step is interactive and it is performed directly on the CPN diagram (i.e. upon the graphical representation of the CP-net): The user proposes weight functions for a number of places. Typically he will define a small number of non-zero weight functions for places he is interested in (but also tell that certain places have zero weight). Then the invariant tool calculates those weight functions which can be uniquely determined from the weights proposed by the user. In this process the tool may also determine that some weights are inconsistent and high-light those transitions that create problems.[128] To calculate new weights and detect inconsistencies the invariant tool uses the reduced matrix obtained in the first step – but it shows the weights and the inconsistencies on the CPN diagram (i.e. in terms of the original CP-net). The user inspects the calculated weights and the high-lighted transitions – and based on this he may add new weights, modify existing weights, or change the behaviour of transitions (e.g. by modifying arc expressions and guards). The process continues, with a number of iterations, and at the end an invariant will be constructed (with some weights specified by the user and the remaining calculated by the invariant tool). The method described above may seem primitive and cumbersome – but this is *not* the case. On the contrary, it is often possible for the user to obtain useful invariants by defining a few weights.[129] It should, moreover, be remembered that the user often have a good idea about what the invariants will be (and thus e.g. knows that certain weights should be zero).

---

[126] In particular the technique described in [59] is interesting, because it seems to be orthogonal to our equivalence class technique (in the sense that the former exploits concurrency while the latter exploits symmetries).

[127] There are two different sets of reduction rules. One of them preserves place invariants while the other preserves transition invariants.

[128] To have an invariant each transition must be neutral, in the sense that the input tokens balance the output tokens (when the weights are taken into account).

[129] Each of the five place invariants PI_X from section 4.3 can be determined by specifying the weight of the single place X (and telling that some other places have weight zero).

To check a proposed invariant is even simpler: The user specifies all the weights and the invariant tool checks their consistency. When a set of invariants have been found they can be used to prove system properties, and this is also supported by the tool: As an example, the user may specify the marking of some places. Then the invariant tool calculates upper and lower bounds for other places (by means of the invariants) and in this process the tool may also determine that the specified set of place markings is inconsistent (i.e. impossible in all reachable markings).[130] The invariant tool will be able to handle hierarchical CP-nets[131] and it will, as described above, be tightly integrated into the existing CPN tools. The first version of the invariant tool is planned to be available during 1992. It is, however, obvious that this, among other things, will depend upon the priority given to the improvement of the new occurrence graph tool (and other extensions of existing CPN tools).

Finally we want to develop CPN tools to support reduction methods and the analysis of special subclasses of CP-net – e.g. as described in [9], [12] and [25]. Such tools have, however, lower priority than those described above.

7.3 CPN book

It is our plan to develop a coherent course material for those who want to study the theoretical and practical aspects of CP-nets. This material will be published as a three volume book in EATCS Monographs on Theoretical Computer Science. The book will contain the formal definition of CP-nets and the mathematical theory behind their analysis methods. It is, however, the intention to write the material in such a way that it also becomes attractive to people who are more interested in applications than the underlying mathematics. This means that a large part of the book will be written in a way which is closer to an engineering text book (or a users manual) than it is to a typical textbook in theoretical computer science.

The first volume of the book will introduce and define the net model (i.e. hierarchical CP-nets) and the basic concepts (e.g. the different behavioural properties such as dead-locks, fairness and home markings). It will in detail present a number of small examples and have brief overviews of some industrial applications. It will also contain a description of the CPN editor and the CPN simulator. Most of the material in this volume will be application oriented. The purpose of the volume is to teach the readers how to construct CPN models and how to analyse these by means of simulation.

The second volume will describe the theory behind the formal analysis methods – in particular occurrence graphs with equivalence classes, place/transition invariants and reductions. It will also describe how these analysis methods can be supported by CPN tools, and illustrate this by means of a number of examples. Part of this volume will be rather theoretical while other parts will be application oriented. The purpose of the volume is to teach the readers how to use the formal analysis methods (and this will not necessarily require a deep understanding of the underlying mathematical theory - although such knowledge of course will be a help).

---

[130] Performed in this way, the non dead-lock proof in section 4.3 becomes much easier, faster and more reliable.

[131] It is straightforward to extend the theory of invariants to hierarchical CP-nets with transition substitution and place fusion (and this has already been done).

The third volume will contain a detailed description of approximately ten different industrial applications. The purpose is to document the most important ideas and experiences from the projects – in a way which is useful for people who do not yet have personal experiences with the construction and analysis of large CPN diagrams. Another purpose is, of course, to document the feasibility of using CP-nets and the CPN tools for such projects.

For the moment approximately 400 pages have been written. Volume 1 will be available at the end of 1991 and we hope that volume 2 will be available during 1992/93. This depends, among other things, upon the speed by which the additional CPN tools are implemented.

8. Conclusions

This paper has presented the theory behind CP-nets, the supporting CPN tools and some of the practical experiences with them. In our opinion it is extremely important to develop these three research ares simultaneously. The three areas influence each other and none of them can be adequately developed without the other two. As an example we think it would have been totally impossible to develop the hierarchy concepts of CP-nets without simultaneously having a solid background in the theory of CP-nets, a good idea about a tool to support the hierarchy concepts and a thorough knowledge of the typical application areas.

TOOLS
- editing
- simulation
- analysis

THEORY
- models
- analysis methods

PRACTICAL USE
- specification
- analysis
- implementation

Acknowledgments

Many different persons have contributed to the development of CP-nets and the CPN tools. Below some of the most important contributions are listed:

- CP-nets were derived from Predicate/Transition Nets which were developed by *Hartmann Genrich & Kurt Lautenbach.*
- The first version of occurrence graphs with equivalence classes was developed together with *Peter Huber, Arne Møller Jensen & Leif Obel Jepsen.*
- Many students and colleagues – in particular at *Aarhus University* – have influenced the development of CP-nets.
- *Grzegorz Rozenberg* has been a great support and inspiration for my book project (and for many other of my Petri net activities).
- The hierarchy constructs and the basic structure of the CPN tools were developed together with *Peter Huber & Robert M. Shapiro.*
- The idea to use an extension of Standard ML for the inscriptions of CP-nets is due to *Jawahar Malhotra.*
- The idea of a super-automatic simulation mode and a stand-alone SML program is due to *Valerio Pinci & Robert M. Shapiro..*
- The user interface of the CPN tools was designed together with *Søren Christensen* and it was implemented by *Ole Bach Andersen.* Valuable critique and suggestions were provided by *Michel Beaudouin-Lafon.*
- The abstract date base of the CPN tools was designed by *Peter Huber* and it was implemented by *Vino Gupta.*
- The ML functions to calculate enabling and bindings were designed and implemented together with *Søren Christensen & Peter Huber.*
- IDEF/CPN was designed and implemented by *Robert M. Shapiro.*
- The Unix + X-Windows version of the CPN tools was implemented by *Jane Eisenstein, Ivan Hajadi & Greg Alonso.*
- The reporting facilities was implemented by *Alain Karsenty.*
- Some of the first hierarchical CPN models were made by *Vino Gupta, Peter Huber, Robert Mameli, Valerio Pinci & Robert M. Shapiro.*
- *Hartmann Genrich* has participated in many parts of the development of the CPN tools.
- *Bob Seltzer* has been a continuous supporter of the CPN tool project (and the daily chats with him have been of great importance for the mood of the project group).
- *Meta Software* has provided the financial support for the CPN tool project. So far more than 25 man years have been used. The project is also supported by the Danish National Science Research Council, the Human Engineering Division of the Armstrong Aerospace Medical Research Laboratory at Wright-Patterson Air Force Base, and the Basic Research Group of the Technical Panel C3 of the US Department of Defense Joint Directors of Laboratories at the Navel Ocean Systems Center.

Finally I thank the anonymous referees for their contributions to this paper.

References

[1] K. Albert, K. Jensen and R.M. Shapiro: **Design/CPN. A tool package supporting the use of Coloured Petri Nets.** Petri Net Newsletter 32 (April 1989), 22-36.

[2] J.L. Baer: **Modelling architectural features with Petri nets.** In: W. Brauer, W. Reisig and G. Rozenberg (eds.): Petri Nets: Applications and Relationships to Other Models of Concurrency, Advances in Petri Nets 1986 Part II, Lecture Notes in Computer Science vol. 255, Springer-Verlag 1987, 258-277.

[3] E. Best: **Structure theory of Petri nets: the free choice hiatus.** In: W. Brauer, W. Reisig and G. Rozenberg (eds.): Petri Nets: Central Models and Their Properties, Advances in Petri Nets 1986 Part I, Lecture Notes in Computer Science vol. 254, Springer-Verlag 1987, 168-205.

[4] J. Billington, G. Wheeler and M. Wilbur-Ham: **Protean: a high-level Petri net tool for the specification and verification of communication protocols.** IEEE Transactions on.

Software Engineering, Special Issue on Tools for Computer Communication Systems, SE-14(3), 1988, 301-316.

[5] W. Brauer (ed.): **Net theory and applications**. Proceedings of the Advanced Course on General Net Theory of Processes and Systems, Hamburg 1979, Lecture Notes in Computer Science vol. 84, Springer-Verlag 1980, 213-223.

[6] W. Brauer, W. Reisig and G. Rozenberg (eds.): **Petri nets: Central models and their properties**. Advances in Petri Nets 1986 Part I, Lecture Notes in Computer Science vol. 254, Springer-Verlag 1987

[7] W. Brauer, W. Reisig and G. Rozenberg (eds.): **Petri nets: Applications and relationships to other models of concurrency**. Advances in Petri Nets 1986 Part II, Lecture Notes in Computer Science vol. 255, Springer-Verlag 1987

[8] G. Chehaibar: **Validation of phase-executed protocols modelled with coloured Petri nets**. Proceedings of the 11th International Conference on Application and Theory of Petri Nets, Paris 1990, 84-103.

[9] G. Chiola, C. Dutheillet, G. Franceschinis and S. Haddad: **On well-formed coloured nets and their symbolic reachability graph**. Proceedings of the 11th International Conference on Application and Theory of Petri Nets, Paris 1990, 387-411.

[10] C. Choppy and C. Johnen: **Petrireve: proving Petri net properties with rewriting systems**. J.P. Jouannaud (ed.): Rewriting Techniques and Applications, Lecture Notes in Computer Science vol. 202, Springer-Verlag 1985, 271-286.

[11] B. Cousin et. al.: **Validation of a protocol managing a multi-token ring architecture**. Proceedings of the 9th European Workshop on Applications and Theory of Petri Nets, Vol. II, Venice 1988.

[12] J.M. Couvreur: **The general computation of flows for coloured Petri nets**. Proceedings of the 11th International Conference on Application and Theory of Petri Nets, Paris 1990, 204-223.

[13] F. De Cindio, G. Lanzarone and A. Torgano: **A Petri net model of SDL**. Proceedings of the 5th European Workshop on Applications and Theory of Petri Nets, Aarhus 1984, 272-289.

[14] M. Diaz: **Petri net based models in the specification and verification of protocols**. In: W. Brauer, W. Reisig and G. Rozenberg (eds.): Petri Nets: Applications and Relationships to Other Models of Concurrency, Advances in Petri Nets 1986 Part II, Lecture Notes in Computer Science vol. 255, Springer-Verlag 1987, 135-170.

[15] R. Di Giovanni: **Putting Petri nets into use: the Columbus programme**. Proceedings of the 11th International Conference on Application and Theory of Petri Nets, Paris 1990, 123-138.

[16] P. Estraillier and C. Girault: **Petri nets specification of virtual ring protocols**. In: A. Pagnoni and G. Rozenberg (eds.): Applications and Theory of Petri Nets, Informatik-Fachberichte vol. 66, Springer-Verlag 1983, 74-85.

[17] F. Feldbrugge: **Petri net tool overview 1989**. In: G. Rozenberg (ed.): Advances in Petri Nets 1989. Lecture Notes in Computer Science vol. 424, Springer-Verlag 1990, 151-178.

[18] A. Finkel: **A minimal coverability graph for Petri nets**. Proceedings of the 11th International Conference on Application and Theory of Petri Nets, Paris 1990, 1-21.

[19] G. Florin, C. Kaiser, S. Natkin: **Petri net models of a distributed election protocol on undirectional ring**. Proceedings of the 10th International Conference on Application and Theory of Petri Nets, Bonn 1989, 154-173.

[20] H.J. Genrich and K. Lautenbach: **System modelling with high-level Petri nets**. Theoretical Computer Science 13 (1981), 109-136.

[21] H.J. Genrich: **Projections of C/E-systems**. In: G. Rozenberg (ed.): Advances in Petri Nets 1985. Lecture Notes in Computer Science vol. 222, Springer-Verlag 1986, 224-232.

[22] H.J. Genrich: **Predicate/Transition nets**. In: W. Brauer, W. Reisig and G. Rozenberg (eds.): Petri Nets: Central Models and Their Properties, Advances in Petri Nets 1986 Part I, Lecture Notes in Computer Science vol. 254, Springer-Verlag 1987, 207-247.

[23] H.J. Genrich: **Equivalence transformations of PrT-nets**. In: G. Rozenberg (ed.): Advances in Petri Nets 1989, Lecture Notes in Computer Science, vol. 424, Springer-Verlag 1990, 179-208.

[24] C. Girault, C. Chatelain and S. Haddad: **Specification and properties of a cache coherence protocol model.** In: G. Rozenberg (ed.): Advances in Petri Nets 1987, Lecture Notes in Computer Science, vol. 266, Springer-Verlag 1987, 1-20.

[25] S. Haddad: **A reduction theory for coloured nets.** In: G. Rozenberg (ed.): Advances in Petri Nets 1989, Lecture Notes in Computer Science, vol. 424, Springer-Verlag 1990, 209-235.

[26] R. Harper: **Introduction to Standard ML.** University of Edinburgh, Department of Computer Science, The King's Buildings, Edinburgh EH9 3JZ, Technical Report ECS-LFCS-86-14, 1986.

[27] R. Harper, D. MacQueen and R. Milner: **Standard ML.** University of Edinburgh, Department of Computer Science, The King's Buildings, Edinburgh EH9 3JZ, Technical Report ECS-LFCS-86-2, 1986.

[28] G. Hartung: **Programming a closely coupled multiprocessor system with high level Petri nets.** In: G. Rozenberg (ed.): Advances in Petri Nets 1988, Lecture Notes in Computer Science vol. 340, Springer-Verlag 1988, 154-174.

[29] T. Hildebrand, H. Nieters, and N Trèves: **The suitability of net-based Graspin tools for monetics applications.** Proceedings of the 11th International Conference on Application and Theory of Petri Nets, Paris 1990,139-160.

[30] P. Huber, A.M. Jensen, L.O. Jepsen and K. Jensen: **Reachability trees for high-level Petri nets.** Theoretical Computer Science 45 (1986), 261-292.

[31] P. Huber, K. Jensen and R.M. Shapiro: **Hierarchies in coloured Petri nets.** In: G. Rozenberg (ed.): Advances in Petri Nets 1990, Lecture Notes in Computer Science, Springer-Verlag.

[32] K. Jensen: **Coloured Petri nets and the invariant method.** Theoretical Computer Science 14 (1981), 317-336.

[33] K. Jensen: **High-level Petri nets.** In: A. Pagnoni and G. Rozenberg (eds.): Applications and Theory of Petri Nets, Informatik-Fachberichte vol. 66, Springer-Verlag 1983, 166-180.

[34] K. Jensen and E.M. Schmidt: **Pascal semantics by a combination of denotational semantics and high-level Petri nets.** In: G. Rozenberg (ed.): Advances in Petri Nets 1985. Lecture Notes in Computer Science vol. 222, Springer-Verlag 1986, 297-329.

[35] K. Jensen: **Coloured Petri nets.** In: W. Brauer, W. Reisig and G. Rozenberg (eds.): Petri Nets: Central Models and Their Properties, Advances in Petri Nets 1986 Part I, Lecture Notes in Computer Science vol. 254, Springer-Verlag 1987, 248-299.

[36] K. Jensen et. al.: **Design/CPN: A tool supporting coloured Petri nets.** User's manual, vol 1-2. Meta Software Corporation, 150 Cambridge Park Drive, Cambridge MA 02140, USA, 1988.

[37] K. Jensen et. al.: **Design/CPN extensions.** Meta Software Corporation, 150 Cambridge Park Drive, Cambridge MA 02140, USA, 1990.

[38] E. de Jong and M.R. van Steen: **Vista: a specification language for parallel software design.** Proceedings of the 3rd International Workshop on Software Engineering and its Applications, Toulouse, 1990.

[39] A. Karsenty: **Interactive graphical reporting facilities for Design/CPN.** Master Thesis, University of Paris Sud, Computer Science Department, 1990.

[40] R.M. Karp and R.E. Miller: **Parallel program schemata.** Journal of Computer and System Sciences, vol. 3, 1969, 147-195.

[41] M. Lindqvist: **Translation of the specification language SDL into predicate/transition nets.** Licentiate's Thesis, Helsinki University of Technology, Digital Systems Laboratory, 1987.

[42] M. Lindqvist: **Parameterized reachability trees for predicate/transition nets.** Proceedings of the 11th International Conference on Application and Theory of Petri Nets, Paris 1990, 22-42.

[43] D.A. Marca and C.L. McGowan: **SADT.** McGraw-Hill, New York, 1988.

[44] G. Memmi and J. Vautherin: **Analysing nets by the invariant method.** In: W. Brauer, W. Reisig and G. Rozenberg (eds.): Petri Nets: Central Models and Their Properties, Advances in Petri Nets 1986 Part I, Lecture Notes in Computer Science vol. 254, Springer-Verlag 1987, 300-336.

[45] Y. Narahari: **On the invariants of coloured Petri nets.** In: G. Rozenberg (ed.): Advances in Petri Nets 1985. Lecture Notes in Computer Science vol. 222, Springer-Verlag 1986, 330-345.

[46] H. Oberquelle: **Human-machine interaction and role/function/action-nets.** In: W. Brauer, W. Reisig and G. Rozenberg (eds.): Petri Nets: Applications and Relationships to Other Models of Concurrency, Advances in Petri Nets 1986 Part II, Lecture Notes in Computer Science vol. 255, Springer-Verlag 1987, 171-190.

[47] **Petri nets and performance models.** Proceedings of the third international workshop, Kyoto Japan 1989, IEEE computer society press, order number 2001, ISBN 0-8186-20001-3.

[48] C.A. Petri: **Kommunikation mit automaten.** Schriften des IIM Nr. 2, Institut für Instrumentelle Mathematik, Bonn, 1962. *English translation:* Technical Report RADC-TR-65-377, Griffiss Air Force Bas, New York, Vol. 1, Suppl. 1, 1966.

[49] V.O. Pinci and R.M. Shapiro: **Development and implementation of a strategy for electronic funds transfer by means of hierarchical coloured Petri nets.** Proceedings of the 11th International Conference on Application and Theory of Petri Nets, Paris 1990, 161-180.

[50] C. Reade: **Elements of functional programming.** Addison Wesly, International Computer Science Series, ISBN 0-201-12915-9, 1989.

[51] G. Rozenberg: **Behaviour of elementary net systems.** In: W. Brauer, W. Reisig and G. Rozenberg (eds.): Petri Nets: Central Models and Their Properties, Advances in Petri Nets 1986 Part I, Lecture Notes in Computer Science vol. 254, Springer-Verlag 1987, 60-94.

[52] M. Rukoz and R. Sandoval.: **Specification and correctness of distributed algorithms by coloured Petri nets.** Proceedings of the 9th European Workshop on Applications and Theory of Petri Nets, Vol. II, Venice 1988.

[53] **Functional specification and description language SDL.** In: CCITT Yellow Book, Vol. VI, recommendations Z.101 - Z.104, CCITT, Geneva, 1981.

[54] R.M. Shapiro: **Validation of a VLSI chip using hierarchical coloured Petri nets.** Proceedings of the 11th International Conference on Application and Theory of Petri Nets, Paris 1990, 224-243.

[55] R.M. Shapiro, V.O. Pinci and R. Mameli: **Modelling a NORAD command post using SADT and coloured Petri nets.** Proceedings of the IDEF Users Group, Washington DC, May 1990.

[56] M. Silva and R. Valette: **Petri nets and flexible manufacturing.** In: G. Rozenberg (ed.): Advances in Petri Nets 1989, Lecture Notes in Computer Science, vol. 424, Springer-Verlag 1990, 374-417.

[57] P.S. Thiagarajan: **Elementary net systems.** In: W. Brauer, W. Reisig and G. Rozenberg (eds.): Petri Nets: Central Models and Their Properties, Advances in Petri Nets 1986 Part I, Lecture Notes in Computer Science vol. 254, Springer-Verlag 1987, 26-59.

[58] R. Valk: **Nets in computer organization.** In: W. Brauer, W. Reisig and G. Rozenberg (eds.): Petri Nets: Applications and Relationships to Other Models of Concurrency, Advances in Petri Nets 1986 Part II, Lecture Notes in Computer Science vol. 255, Springer-Verlag 1987, 218-233.

[59] A. Valmari: **Stubborn sets for reduced state space generation.** Proceedings of the 10th International Conference on Application and Theory of Petri Nets, Bonn 1989, Vol II.

[60] A. Valmari: **Compositional state space generation.** Proceedings of the 11th International Conference on Application and Theory of Petri Nets, Paris 1990, 43-62.

[61] K. Voss: **Nets in data bases.** In: W. Brauer, W. Reisig and G. Rozenberg (eds.): Petri Nets: Applications and Relationships to Other Models of Concurrency, Advances in Petri Nets 1986 Part II, Lecture Notes in Computer Science vol. 255, Springer-Verlag 1987, 97-134.

[62] K. Voss: **Nets in office automation.** In: W. Brauer, W. Reisig and G. Rozenberg (eds.): Petri Nets: Applications and Relationships to Other Models of Concurrency, Advances in Petri Nets 1986 Part II, Lecture Notes in Computer Science vol. 255, Springer-Verlag 1987, 234-257.

[63] Å. Wikström: **Functional programming using Standard ML.** Prentice Hall International Series in Computer Science, ISBN 0-13-331968-7, ISBN 0-13-331661-0 Pbk, 1987

[64] E. Yourdon: **Managing the system life cycle.** Yourdon Press, 1982.

A SIMULATION SYSTEM ARCHITECTURE FOR GRAPH MODELS*

Gary J. Nutt†
University of Colorado (USA)

ABSTRACT

The paper describes a distributed modeling system architecture, designed to support various graph models of computation, including predicate/transition nets and colored Petri nets. To demonstrate the utility of the architecture, we describe an implementation for a specific graph model (one that is related to, but distinct from, Petri nets). The architecture provides for interactive editing and interpretation facilities employing a graphic point-and-select user interface. A user can define a model, then mark it with tokens and observe the operation of the net through real time animation. The model and the marking can be rapidly altered, even as an interpretation is in progress. The system also supports simultaneous use among multiple users, including concurrent editing and interpretation. Thus the system supports cooperative model design and interpretation by a group of designers at different nodes in a network of workstations.

1. INTRODUCTION

The paper describes a distributed modeling system architecture, designed to support various formal graph models of computation. To demonstrate the utility of the architecture, we describe an implementation for a specific graph model (one that is related to, but distinct from, Petri nets -- see [9, 20, 21, 26]).

Formal graph models are an invaluable tool for analyzing the behavior of a concurrent system prior to its implementation. A sound model can be used to predict performance, represent concurrency and synchronization, and to impart fundamental knowledge about the relative merits of alternative designs for the system.

A Petri net can represent control flow, concurrency, synchronization, and nondeterminacy in systems. Petri nets represent considerable more detail than static models such as precedence graphs. Execution of the Petri net is represented by the marking sequence of the Petri net, thus there are dynamic aspects represented by the static net and an initial marking.

Petri net theory is devoted to the study of properties of Petri net variants and their behavior under various markings. Petri net application focuses on the use of the model family to represent prospective concurrent systems and to derive an understanding of the behavior of the system based on the properties of the model.

There is a spectrum of applications, ranging from model instances that can be analyzed for fundamental behavior such as safety and liveness; to timed Petri nets that predict system performance in terms of resource utilization, throughput, and turnaround time; to predicate/transition and colored Petri net models that can be used to simulate the system activity.

The *Olympus Modeling System Architecture* described in this paper can be used to build tools that support the application of Petri nets and other graph models to systems analysis and simulation. In particular, the architecture can be used to define systems that create and analyze the static version of a model as well as to exercise the dynamic execution of the model under various initial conditions.

The goal of the paper is to describe the Olympus Architecture for modeling systems, and to illustrate how the architecture can be used to support dynamic models of computation.

1.1. Background

There are a number of machine-supported, interactive modeling systems in existence, e.g., see PAWS/GPSM [3, 14], the Performance Analysis Workstation [17], PARET [19], Quinault [22], Raddle/Verdi [13], and GreatSPN [1].

Each of these systems has a specific, underlying graph model. The companion system is built to implement the syntax of the graph model and to analyze or simulate the semantics determined by the formal behavioral specification of the model.

---

* This research has been supported by NSF Grant No. CCR-8802283, NSF cooperative agreement DCR-8420944, and a grant from U S West Advanced Technologies. This paper is a substantial revision of a paper entitled "A Flexible, Distributed Simulation System" presented at the Tenth International Conference on Application and Theory of Petri Nets.

† Department of Computer Science, Campus Box 430, University of Colorado, Boulder, CO 80309-0430, (303) 492-7581, nutt@boulder.colorado.edu

These systems are implemented in bitmap graphics environments in which a designer constructs models in the language supported by that system. Typically, the user employs a graphic point-and-select editor to construct a visual model; he may then provide annotation for the model through a wide variety of annotation mechanisms, ranging from popup windows through preparing separate files in a distinct editing session. Systems such as PAWS/GPSM will also predict performance of the model using queueing network analysis techniques (a GPSM model is a queueing network).

The dynamics of model operation can be observed by supplying data to the model, then causing the model to execute in the supplied environment. Most of the systems provide an animation of the simulation execution. The modeling system may allow the user to observe the operation of the model through the changing state of the model (in the case of marked models such as Petri nets), or through the display of distributions, gauges, etc.

The operation of a model is ordinarily controlled through the use of checkpoints. That is, the model can have a flag set at some particular point in the model. When the interpretation encounters the flag, then it suspends execution and interacts with the user, allowing him to interrogate the state of the execution, change internal conditions in the model, etc.

The power of these modeling systems is in their ability to allow a user to quickly and easily build a model and then to view the dynamics of the operation of the model. The designer is able to quickly converge on "correct" models through this interactive, experimental testbed approach.

Because of the importance of these "what if" type experiments, the modeling system must be very easy to use for constructing and editing the model, it must allow the designer to easily alter the loading conditions of an individual experiment, and it must provide intuitive feedback to the designer by providing appropriate measures of the activity in a language that is familiar to the designer.

Most of today's modeling systems can be criticized on the following grounds: They often leave the user in a particular *mode* during a session, e.g., the user cannot edit if he is in the process of interpreting. It is awkward to change loading conditions while the model is in execution, since the interpretation can only be interrupted through checkpoints. Once the model is being interpreted, any editing change to the model requires that the model be halted and the editor be started (mode change) in order to accomplish the change. The modeling language is specific to the system rather than to the designer. Only a single user can interact with any particular model at any given time.

In the Olympus Architecture, we attempt to address these issues. There are no modes in a modeling session; the user is allowed to edit the model or the load characterization at any time -- including during interpretation. The interpreter can be suspended or halted at any time, then restarted or resumed later. Multiple users can be involved in an individual modeling session.

The logical interpretation and the presentation of the model and its execution are separated into model syntax and semantics. The model syntax -- the appearance of the model at a workstation screen -- is independent of the logical specification of the model -- the model's semantics.

We have built an instance of the Olympus Architecture, bound to a particular graph model. Next we provide an overview of the example system.

1.2. An Experiment

The *Olympus BPG Modeling System* (Olympus-BPG) provides machine support for a specific formal graph model, Bilogic Precedence Graphs (BPGs) [26]. It provides a model simulation environment, so that a group of designers can use interactive graphic-based tools to create, maintain, modify, and exercise an interpreted, marked network model.

Olympus-BPG is an instance of the Olympus Architecture, and is intended to address the general problems described above with architectural solutions. In addition, Olympus-BPG addresses various other modeling problems, through specific solutions as opposed to architectural solutions. For example, Olympus-BPG supports hierarchical refinement of elements of BPG models -- a solution that is specific to BPGs, but which is applicable to other models that support hierarchy.

Further, the BPG semantics are implemented in Olympus-BPG by a distinct process (optionally on a distinct machine) from the process that implements the BPG syntax. As a result, the BPG user interface contains a BPG graph editor and console, while the logical storage and interpretation of the BPG occur in a different environment interconnected via a well-defined network interface. The presentation syntax of the model is distinct from the semantics of the model's execution. The Olympus-BPG interpreter can interact with a BPG viewer/console or any of a number of types of viewer/consoles.

Instances of Olympus are designed as *distributed* modeling systems, one aspect of which we have just described. These systems support groups of users interacting with a single model, thus allowing the system to be a common, interactive design environment. The concurrency aspects mentioned above (i.e., simultaneous editing and interpretation) provides a very general modeling facility for cooperative model construction.

2. THE OLYMPUS SYSTEM ARCHITECTURE

2.1. Characteristics of Models Supported by the Architecture

The Olympus Architecture is designed to create, store, and interpret a wide class of graph models. The class is large enough so that the architecture is applicable to many systems, yet specific enough so that there is some advantage to employing a common architecture for various modeling systems.

Marked graph models supported by the Olympus architecture are of the form

$$\Gamma = ((\Xi, \Phi, M), \Delta)$$

where Ξ is a control flow graph with interpretation Φ and marking M, and Δ is a data flow graph. More specifically,

$$\Xi = (\Pi, E_C)$$

where

$$\Pi = \Pi_1 \cup \Pi_2 \cup ... \cup \Pi_K$$

$\Pi_i = \{p_{i,1}, p_{i,2}, ...\}$ is a finite set of tasks of type i (for $1 \leq i \leq K$)

$E_C \subseteq \Pi \times \Pi$ is a finite set of edges interconnecting tasks

$\Phi = \{f_i \mid 1 \leq i \leq |\Pi|\}$ is a set of interpretations for each task,

$f_i:\Pi \rightarrow$ *interpretation language* $\cup \Gamma'$

$M:\Pi \cup E_C \rightarrow \{null, \tau_i\}$ is the marking of the graph.

τ_i is a name for a token of unspecified type

$$\Delta = ((R \cup \Pi), E_D)$$

where

$R = \{r_1, r_2, ... \}$ is a finite set of data repositories

$E_D \subseteq (\Pi \times R) \cup (R \times \Pi)$ is a finite set of edges interconnecting tasks and repositories

Informally, the graph has one component to represent the flow of control among a set of task nodes, Ξ. Nodes in the graph, each representing a task, can be any of K different types, e.g., nodes with disjunctive input and output logic, or perhaps nodes with disjunctive input logic and conjunctive output logic. Every task node can have an interpretation. The interpretation is specified in an arbitrary procedural language, or it can be defined by another marked graph. The data flow graph adds nodes to represent data storage; write operations can be performed by a task if and only if there is an edge (in E_D) from the task to the repository, and read operations are represented by an edge from the repository to the task node. The marking of the control flow graph represent a distribution of tokens on task nodes and control flow edges, i.e., this model allows tokens to reside on a node or on an edge.

The graphs supported by the architecture are very general, too general for extensive analysis. However, the architecture is intended to provide a framework in which specific systems for specific graph models can be easily constructed. In particular, the architecture can be used to support Petri net models.

Murata [18] defines a Petri net as a 5-tuple, (P, T, F, W, M_0) where

$P = \{p_1, p_2, ... p_m\}$ is a finite set places

$T = \{t_1, t_2, ... t_n\}$ is a finite set of transitions

$F \subseteq (P \times T) \cup (T \times P)$ is a finite set of arcs (flow relation)

$W:F \rightarrow \{1, 2, 3, ...\}$ is a weight function

$M_0:T \rightarrow \{0, 1, 2, 3, ...\}$ is the initial marking

$P \cap T = \emptyset$ and $P \cup T \neq \emptyset$

There are at least two ways that the marked graph model could be used to represent Petri nets: By mapping places into nodes, or by mapping them into multiarcs. It is necessary to map the places to nodes if the Petri net is to represent predicate/transition nets [12] or colored Petri nets [15], since they rely on interpretations for places. Our example maps places to nodes with disjunctive (OR) input and output logic, and transitions to nodes with conjunctive (AND) logic.

Considering only the case that $W:F \rightarrow 1$, a marked graph can represent a Petri nets as follows. Let:

$$\Gamma = ((\Xi, \Phi, M), \varnothing)$$

$$\Xi = (\Pi, E_C)$$

$$\Pi = \Pi_1 \cup \Pi_2$$

where

$\Pi_1 = P = \{p_1, p_2, ...\}$ is a finite set of tasks with disjunctive input and output logic (places)

$\Pi_2 = T = \{t_1, p_2, ...\}$ is a finite set of tasks with conjunctive input and output logic (transitions)

$E_C = F$

$f_1 = f_2 = \varnothing => \Phi = \{\varnothing\}$

$M = M_0$

Type 1 nodes represent places (nodes with OR logic) and type 2 nodes represent transitions (nodes with AND logic). As stated above, the general graph model semantic of firing for type 1 nodes is degenerate, inasmuch as there is no corresponding semantic in Petri nets. To complete the semantics of transition firing (as it reflects on the activity at a place node), it is necessary to make place "firing" be passive, yielding tokens to downstream transition nodes as required by the transition's activity. (This is particularly obvious in situations involving forward conflict.)

It is possible to describe the characterization of Olympus graph models more precisely, and to make the mapping to Petri nets more specific. However, the goal of this paper is to illustrate an architecture for simulation systems that can be used to support Petri nets and other models.

The Olympus Architecture isolates the semantics of the firing rules, thus firing rules can be encoded as required without affecting the operation of other parts of the architecture. The node interpretation mechanism, hierarchy in node interpretations, data flow, token data, editing, storage, etc. are all independent of the details of the firing rules.

2.2. Characteristics of the Modeling System

The graph model provides a language for describing target systems behavior. A simulation system provides a medium for expressing models, and for studying these models by observing their reaction to different conditions. An interactive system (using bitmap workstation technology), creates an environment in which alternatives -- changes in loading conditions, changes in parameters, or changes in the model itself -- are easy to explore.

Olympus systems provide the following specific features to their users:

(1) It provides a *simple* mechanism to interactively create and edit model instances.

(2) Detailed behavior of a model can be expressed as a hierarchical model or a procedural interpretation.

(3) The presentation and the semantics of the model can be represented independently.

(4) The user can exercise a model with complete control over the interpretation, e.g., the user should be able to interrupt the interpretation at any moment (without setting breakpoints *a priori*).

(5) When an interpretation is interrupted, the user can browse and change the state of the interpretation prior to continuation.

(6) If the system is interpreting a model in scaled real time, then the user can change the time scale while the model is in operation.

(7) The interactive system allows editing and interpretation to proceed in parallel.

(8) It is possible to reuse large parts of a system instance, within the architecture, to build a comparable modeling system for related models of computation.

These are general goals, but they are useful guidelines for constructing the modeling system. We now explain how these goals are addressed in the architecture.

2.3. The Architecture

Any instance of Olympus is a collection of copies of the following modules: *Console, Model Storage, Marking Storage, Task Interpreter*, and *Repository Interpreter*. Optionally, it may also include a *Model Editor* or an arbitrary *Observer*.

Each module can be thought of as an object *class*, where any particular implementation incorporates specific instances of the different classes. For a simple Olympus configuration, there may be only one instance of each class type statically generated when Olympus is started. For example, the Sun implementation of Olympus-BPG implementation allows for multiple instances of the Console, Model Editor, Task Interpreter, and Repository Interpreter classes to operate on distinct workstations.

Console

A Console is a window onto the model which illustrates the activity of the other modules; it is used to control all parts of the system and may also act as a viewport onto the model that is being interpreted. During animation, it is the medium for displaying the dynamics of the interpretation. The Console determines the details of the model from the Model Storage and the status of the interpretation from the Marking Storage. Notice that a Console display is only interested in the marking of a small portion of the model -- a portion small enough to fit into a window; it also need not operate synchronously with the Marking Storage.

Model Storage

This module provides information about the model that defines the model or program to be interpreted. For example, the module responds to messages such as "return the identity of the task that is connected to the head of this arc," or "return the body of the procedure to be interpreted when this task is fired."

Model Editor

This module is used to define a graph model and place it in the Model Storage. The Model Editor is responsible for implementing the visual aspects of the model, thus it can be used to map various other model types into a specific model by translating the model syntax that it supports prior to storage.

Marking Storage

This module responds to a message to update the BPG marking, or to indicate the current marking of an arc (as part of an atomic transaction).

Observer

An Observer is a module that performs system-specific computational tasks. It is characterized by its absorbing information from other parts of the system without providing any particular commands or information back to the system. Thus an Observer is similar to a Console with no input operations. Observers are used to analyze a model, to display performance statistics, and other similar tasks.

Task Interpreter

The Task Interpreter evaluates a task procedure. Whenever tokens enable a task, the Task Interpreter will query the Model Storage to obtain a procedure definition, then interpret the procedure on the token. Upon completion of the interpretation, the Task Interpreter will notify the Marking Storage. The Task Interpreter will repeat the interpretation cycle on successor tasks as determined by the marking.

Repository Interpreter

A Repository Interpreter is a passive interpreting machine, i.e., it will interpret a procedure for a BPG repository when it is requested to do so, but it does not enable any subsequent activity (other than response from the request). Repository interpretation can be viewed as (remote) procedure call into a monitor. Once the Task Interpreter calls a Repository Interpreter, the Repository Interpreter cannot respond to another request until it completes the current operation.

An Olympus instance may be a statically bound set of the modules described above; it is convenient to divide the groups into the *frontend* and *backend* groups as indicated in Figure 1.

The backend -- also called the Olympus server -- is a persistent process that is started independently of any particular frontend -- also called an Olympus client. (The boxes with rounded corners in the Figure can be roughly equated to processes, although that view will be refined below.)

The client establishes a network communication socket with the Olympus server when it is initiated; all intercommunication between the client and the server take place over the socket. The server obtains commands to perform storage and interpretation control operations from the socket, and sends display instructions to the client via the same socket.

Since the client, contains the Editor, the model can be modified even as the Task Interpreter is in execution; the Console need only be able to multiplex control information to the appropriate module.

2.4. The Olympus Server

In our example instance, four of the modules are implemented in the server, making it necessary for the server to provide a demultiplexing function to call different modules as required by the client. The server dispatcher is a

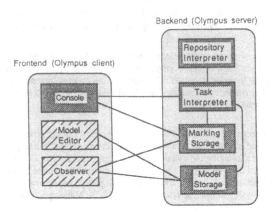

Backend (Olympus server)

Frontend (Olympus client)

Figure 1: Olympus System Architecture

cyclic program that blocks on a socket read for the socket connecting the client and the server. Whenever a message arrives from a client -- the server can support multiple clients simultaneously using the single client(s)-server socket pair -- it dispatchs the message to the appropriate module.

The set of messages recognized by the server is listed in [24]. There are three classes of messages: Editing directives to modify the Model Storage, editing directives to modify the Marking Storage, and control messages to the Task Interpreter. The dispatcher parses the incoming message, then passes the message to the appropriate module using procedure call.

The modules that implement the server need not have been implemented as a single process. For example, the procedure call interface among the modules can be replaced by a remote procedure call interface to achieve functional distribution. Notice, also, that the modularization is intended to isolate different aspects of the model; the two storage modules need not know the semantics of interpretation, and the Task Interpreter need not know any of the details of storage.

Model Storage

The Model Storage is required to remember a model definition from session-to-session, and to remember the details of a particular model while it is being interpreted. The long term storage is accomplished by saving the definition on secondary storage (using standard Unix files). The *load_model* and *save_model* messages are used to cause the Model Storage to load/save a model image into primary store from/to the file system. When a model is loaded into the Model Storage from the file system, the client does not know anything other than the name of the model. The client can send a *redraw* message to the Model Storage, which will cause it to send a full description of the model to the client.

Thus, loaded files are stored entirely in the server process's virtual memory. There are *add_<atom>* and *delete_<atom>* messages to create atoms in the model; the details of the atom definition can be added and changed using other messages, e.g., *arc_label* is used to add a label to an existing arc.

Marking Storage

The Marking Storage is relatively simple; it is only required to remember the current state of the interpretation in terms of the token distribution on a model. The *add_* and *delete_token_from arc/node* place and replace tokens on different parts of the model. The two commands to *delete_all_tokens_from arc/node* are used to reinitialize a model.

Task and Repository Interpreters

The semantics of the firing and interpretation of a model class are implemented in the Task Interpreter. The graph portion of a model defines the control and data flow of the model of operation, while interpretations may be added to individual nodes.

The Task Interpreter module reads the current marking from the Marking Storage, then determines which task nodes can be fired in their current state. Firable task nodes are scheduled for interpretation. After the interpretation has been completed, then the Task Interpreter updates the marking and again determines the set of firable tasks.

Node interpretations are procedures that can be executed on a set of local variables and global data obtained from a data repository node in the model. That is, when a task is interpreted, then some procedure is interpreted on its local data; if the graph indicates that the task has read or write access to a data repository, then the procedure may reference that data repository using a built-in repository access function corresponding to the *access-repository* procedure.

Each task interpretation also has an associated *time to execute*, which defines the real time to be used by the Task Interpreter if the marking is to be changed in scaled real time, i.e., the client is using the server as an animator. Since such times are often determined by a probability distribution function, Olympus provides a special facility for obtaining a firing time from a probability distribution function without actually executing an arbitrary procedure. The more general interpretation specification -- a procedure declaration -- may be expressed in an arbitrary, pre-compiled language invoked using Sun's RPC/XDR (Remote Procedure Call/eXternal Data Representation) protocol [30].

Whenever the Task Interpreter fires a node, it reads the procedural interpretation for the node from the Model Storage. (Actually, it reads *the name and location* of the procedure from the Model Storage.) The Task Interpreter then performs a special nonblocking RPC on the procedure, allowing it to be interpreted by a distinct process, possibly located on another host machine, see Figure 2. The RPC is nonblocking, since the intent is to allow procedures that define tasks which fire simultaneously to be interpreted simultaneously. When the procedure has been evaluated, it notifies the Task Interpreter via another nonblocking RPC call, at which time the Task Interpreter can update the marking.

After carefully evaluating the cost of using remote procedures versus statically-bound procedures [8], we chose to use RPC to separate the environment in which task interpretations are executed from the environment in which Olympus executes, and to postpone procedure binding until run time. The particular implementation supports parallel interpretation on distributed computers as a bonus. This allowed us to use the standard system facilities for compiling node interpretations, rather than implementing our own facilities. As a consequence, node interpretations can be written in C, Fortran, Lisp, Prolog, or any other language which produces a compiled object module which can be invoked using RPC. The Task Interpreter (a client program, in this case) invokes the appropriate procedure (a server program with the node interpretation) whenever the control flow dictates.

Depending upon the implementation of the firing policy, Uninterpreted models may be nondeterministic at the OR nodes, i.e., when control flows into an OR node with multiple output edges, the system may place the output token

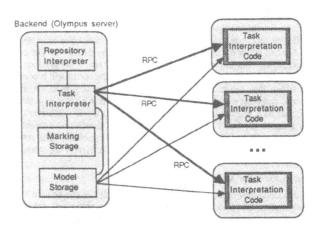

Figure 2: RPC Task Interpretation

on any of the edges. Task interpretations for OR nodes can make this decision explicit by executing an arbitrary algorithm to make the decision, then by calling a built-in procedure to tell the control flow portion of the system how to place the output token when the interpretation terminates. It is also possible to simply use stochastic functions to randomly choosing an output arc in Olympus.

As described above, the family of graph models may incorporate data flow between tasks and nodes representing data repositories. The meaning of an edge in the data flow diagram is that the task node *may* access any repository to which it is connected (using a data flow arc), although it is not required to do so. The direction of the arc implies the nature of the access, i.e., arcs from tasks to repositories imply write operations and arcs from repositories to tasks imply read operations. Each repository implements an *access procedure* corresponding to the read/write arcs incident to the repository, and thus to each *access-repository* procedure call that can exist in a task interpretation.

A repository is implemented as a set of remote procedures. Each repository has default read and write procedures that are invoked by the task interpretation (using the access function). The user must define repository interpretations in exactly the same manner as he would specify a task interpretation.

Access procedures provide a mechanism for executing arbitrary repository interpretations, but they do not explicitly handle data types. Since Olympus uses Sun's RPC for invocation of these procedures, it also employs the related external data representation (XDR) for defining the types of the information exchanged between the Task and Repository Interpreters.

The server also collects statistics on the operation of any model. Actual measures are only meaningful to the Olympus user, since some of the tasks and repositories represent resources and queues in the target system, while others are modeling overhead. Olympus provides a facility for instrumenting any arc or node in the graph, enabling data gathering on the modeling atom during interpretation. The resulting data are kept in a file for subsequent analysis. There are currently no additional facilities for analyzing the interpretation of a model.

2.5. Olympus Clients

An Olympus client is used to implement the Console, Model Editor, and various Observers. The server is an engine that stores and interprets graph models, and the client is the mechanism for implementing any function that can use the engine. For example, a client that implements a Console and Editor provides a user interface to the server engine. Because of the separation of the frontend and the backend, and because of the nature of the protocol that is used to allow the frontend and backend to communicate, the client user interface is almost completely independent of the operation of the server. In particular, the client Editor is free to use any visual representation of the graph model stored in the server that fits the need of the user.

One result of the approach is that any Editor that conforms to the client-server intercommunication protocol can be used with the server. Thus, if the server is implemented to support Petri nets, several different clients can be developed to present different visual representations of the Petri net (e.g. representations with bars or rectangles to denote transitions), and to provide different man-machine interaction paradigms. The operation of the server is oblivious to differences in these client frontends.

Because of the limited assumptions that the server makes about the operation of the client, it is possible for the client to perform different functions than the Console and Editor tasks. For example, suppose that one wished to implement a syntax-directed editor for the graph model supported by the server. The conventional approach to constructing such an editor is to either implement the parser in the server, or in the editor itself. If the parser is implemented in the server, then the interactions between the client and the server will become inefficient. If the parser is implemented in the editor, then the editor will become slow (and annoying to use, since the user will tend to be waiting for the parser to complete even though the current graph may be only an interim state.) Beguelin has used the Olympus architecture as a framework in which he implements a *critic* Observer client in addition to an editor client for his server instance [2] (see Figure 3). The critic is an asynchronous client that parses his graph model independent of the actual operation of the client that implements the editor. This results in a system with a critic that is independent of the editor, yet which parses (and otherwise analyzes) the model in the server as the editor is used to create and modify models.

2.6. General Remarks about the Architecture

While we have not described how hierarchical refinement is handled, it can be seen from the graph definitions that the server is required to allow task nodes to be defined in terms of a procedural interpretation or by a refined graph. The server implements *functional hierarchy* by allowing any interpretation to be specified as a graph. When the server is interpreting a model and it encounters such a node interpretation, then the server will use the refined node definition recursively, up to a predefined depth. We will report extensively on our research with hierarchy in a separate paper.

We have used the remote procedure call idea to interconnect the frontend and the backend, and to connect the Task Interpreter manager with the actual Task Interpretations. Sun's RPC is built on top of Berkeley UNIX *sockets* [16], which provide a network-wide means for processes to identify remote processes in terms a simple address -- a *well-known address*. Since a process's IPC port is identified by a simple address, any other process can "connect" to the

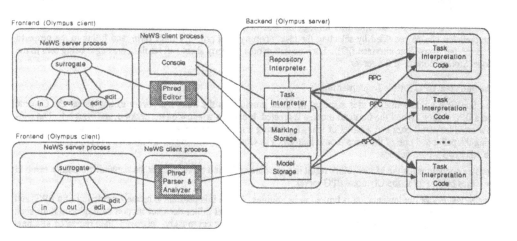

Figure 3: Beguelin's Phred System

process with the well-known socket, i.e., establish communication with the first process using the well-known address. The Olympus server has a well-known socket address which can be connected to by any number of client processes at any given time. Each client can send the server a message over the socket, causing the server to take some action, e.g., update the Model Storage, etc. *as an atomic operation.* When a client wishes to update its picture to show token movement, net changes, etc., then it sends a request for an update to the server; the server responds by placing the update on the socket. Every client is designed to react to updates from the server whether they were requested or not, thus each client has the most current information sent out by the server. As a consequence, any Olympus server supports multiple clients, the number depending only on the number of independent client processes that connect to the server.

Since the client(s) are independent of the Olympus server, editing operations can take place in parallel with the server's operation. This allows the user to edit a model while the server is in the process of animating or simulating its activity. Any change in the status of the model, as maintained by the server, results in an update being sent to the client(s). Therefore, if one client edits the model, then all clients see the change at the same time.

Olympus is a very general distributed system, enabling it to provide important interactive simulation facilities such as multiple users with simultaneous updating of screens. The separation of the work into clients and servers along with a carefully designed protocol between them allows the frontend to be asynchronous with the backend, yet allows close interaction of the console with the server.

3. THE OLYMPUS-BPG MODELING SYSTEM

The Olympus architecture has been used to support three different models extensively: BPGs, ParaDiGM [5-7], and phred [2]. In addition, we have experimented with a Petri net frontend to the BPG backend.

In this Section, we describe the instance of Olympus that has been used to support BPGs. (BPGs are a subclass of the general modeling system described above; while the details of BPGs are not especially relevant to the architectural discussion, a brief description of the model is provided in the Appendix.)

The Olympus-BPG server has been implemented in a SunOS environment (on Sun 3 and Sun 4 workstations), and on an Encore Multimax shared memory multiprocessor [25]. Various clients have been built to work with the server, including a line-oriented console, a SunView interactive editor, a Sun NeWS interactive editor, a Sun NeWS performance statistic display, a Sun NeWS interactive editor that employs Petri nets at the user interface, and a Symbolics LISP interactive editor.

Most of the editor clients are window-based interfaces that employ pointing devices to implement visual BPGs (or Petri nets). Icons are drawn on the screen, under the control of the Model Editor, then stored in the server using the messages described above. When a model is loaded into the server, then the server sends messages to the client (display portion of the client, shared by the Console and the Model Editor) so that it can present the model in its chosen method.

Node and arc properties are specified through the use of property sheets. Thus, a task can be labeled and an interpretation can be provided by selecting the task, popping up a property sheet form, and filling in the property sheet (cf. the Xerox Star interface [29]). Each operation on a property sheet will result in messages being sent to the Model Storage portion of the server.

The SunView BPG Editor Implementation

The SunView implementation uses standard facilities provided in the SunView library to implement the Console and a BPG Editor. When the frontend process is created, it opens a window on the desktop, see Figure 4. The window provides scroll bars and a pallet of icons for editing a model. Model editing operations are accomplished by using the pallet and one of the three mouse buttons. The Console operations are all invoked via popup menus from the other two mouse buttons.

Console operations for the Model Editor result in procedure calls, and operations for the remaining modules result in messages being sent to the Olympus-BPG server.

This Model Editor implementation is limited in its abilities. While it is possible to create a rendering of a BPG, and to supply interpretations and other details for each node, the Model Editor does not support editing operations such as moving an object around on the screen. Instead, the original object must be destroyed, then recreated at a new

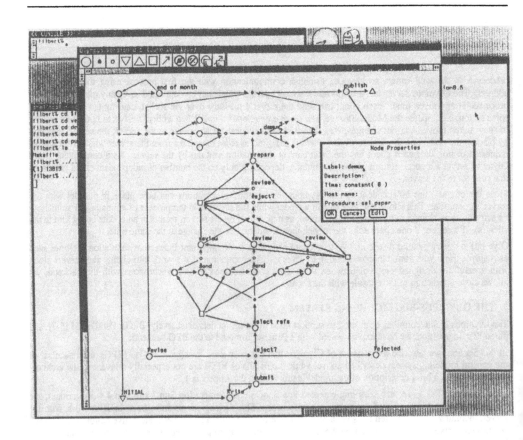

Figure 4: The SunView Client Window

screen location. However, it is possible to completely specify a model in the Model Storage.

The structure of the SunView editor was a direct outgrowth of previous work done on the Alto workstation [22]. In the Alto window environment the mouse was under program control, i.e., it was read like any other device. This structure was also natural for the very first line-oriented interface, since input events all came from the keyboard.

However, SunView (like many modern window systems) is an event-driven environment. The user defines a number of event routines, then registers them with the SunView window manager. All execution takes place under the control of the window manager; thus, execution is driven by the occurrence of events detected by the window manager, not by the user's program.

Because of the replacement of SunView by NeWS in Sun environments, the emergence of X Version 11, and because of the limitations in the design, the SunView client was not a good base from which to build other clients. Therefore, we have built subsequent frontends in the NeWS environment.

The NeWS BPG Editor Implementation

The requirements for the NeWS implementation included one that would make it easier to reuse the code than was the case for the SunView client. We had decided that we would build the next client on top of a set of libraries, at a minimum, and as an object-oriented program if that were feasible (within our other constraints).

The NeWS architecture divides any implementation into two parts: A NeWS server and a NeWS client, i.e., the Olympus client is implemented as another client and a server, see Figure 3. The NeWS client is responsible for

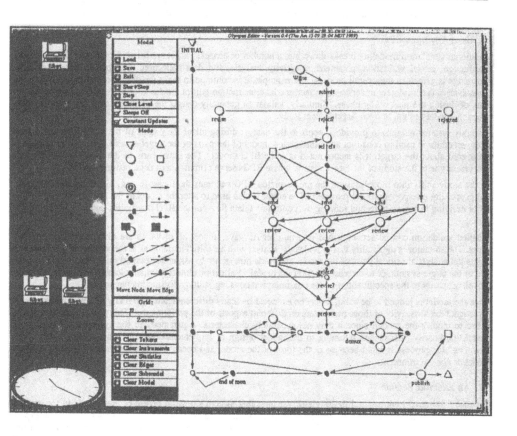

Figure 5: The NeWS Client Window

implementing the services of the Console and the Model Editor. The NeWS server is responsible for managing the display, based on a specific protocol between the client and the server.

The NeWS client Console implements the same function as the SunView Console, i.e., it accepts commands from the user (via the NeWS server), then routes them to the backend process (Olympus server dispatcher) -- see Figure 5.

The Model Editor is a new design, based on type hierarchies of visual network models. The Model Editor implements the syntax of BPGs, even though the server implements the visual aspects of BPGs, e.g., a task is drawn as a circle. The type hierarchy treats model atoms as objects; thus an object may be a node or an arc. Properties that distinguish arcs and nodes are defined in subclasses. Within the node subclass are additional refinements to distinguish between the way the editor treats a task node and a repository node (e.g, arcs between tasks and repositories are data flow arcs and arcs between tasks are control flow arcs; the appearance of the two arc types is different on the screen).

The use of object types allows the editor to be built without being dependent upon specific presentation properties of the nodes. As a result, the same editing functions can be used to construct an editor for BPGs and other models.

In Figure 3, the NeWS server is shown as a collection of *lightweight process*. Each lightweight process can be dedicated to editing tasks without incurring full Unix process context switching costs whenever work is passed among them. There is a surrogate lightweight process in the server to direct the other lightweight processes on behalf of the (Unix heavyweight) NeWs client editor. The surrogate controls a lightweight process to handle input events, another for output events, and other for specific editing tasks (such as "track the mouse").

Our experimental Petri net editor (used with the BPG server) was built by modifying the NeWS editor. The modifications did not require server changes (even though the "place firing semantics" were specialized for Petri nets). The BPG server is the same for the BPG frontend as for the Petri net frontend in this experiment.

3.1. Using Olympus-BPG

Traditional simulation modeling breaks down into a number of phases: Target system studies, model design, model construction, model validation, parameter sensitivity analysis, and data collection. The phases overlap as new knowledge is gained in the overall process. For example, it is common to begin the design of the model before the target system is completely understood; in fact, model construction guides the designer to questions that he did not think of during the pure study phase. Similarly, validation generally causes the designer to return to model construction, model design, or even target system study.

Olympus systems attempt to provide support to the analyst during all of the phases of the study. During system study, an editor is used to construct an uninterpreted model of the parts of the target system. As new knowledge is discovered about the target, it is incorporated into the BPG model. The initial parts of the model design proceed concurrently with the study of the target system, where BPGs serve primarily as a documenting device.

As the study shifts into model design, the uninterpreted BPG becomes the focus; timing, hierarchical refinements, and procedural interpretations are provided. The editor is also used to alter the model as the analyst reviews it. The act of deriving interpretations and refining the control and data flow for the BPG constitutes the model construction phase.

Detailed validation can be accomplished in a number of ways, almost all of which are outside the scope of this paper. The animator is the facility that provides the analyst with his initial intuition as to the validity of the model. It points the analyst at critical parts of the model and leads him or her to ask more detailed question about the operation of the target system, or to increase detail in the model. Validation almost inevitably leads to modification of the model, primarily to the specifications of the task interpretations, eg., tuning distribution parameters.

Once the model is judged to be valid, it may be executed on many different loads with many different parameters to investigate the sensitivity of those parameters on different aspects of the performance. This phase often leads to the desire to modify the model, since it may not accurately characterize a parameter in the system that exists in the model. Ordinarily, this means returning to the model design or implementation phase and starting again. With Olympus, that process is rapid because of the form of the model and because of the integration of the tools in the model design environment.

3.2. An Example Session

Suppose that we had constructed the single-server queueing system shown in Figure 6. Each node in the graph is created with a default (unit) time to execute. It is useful to draw the graph, mark the idle nodes, then begin experimenting with arrival and service times. These times are specified by time distributions for p_1 (the arrival distribution), p_4 (the CPU service time distribution), and p_9 (the device service time distribution). Initially, the "depart" node (p_6) will randomly choose output edges for a token, hence jobs will randomly request device I/O or be complete.

The model is refined by attaching probabilities to the two arcs (p_6, p_7) and (p_6, p_8) corresponding to the probability that a job is complete when it finishes a time quantum. A more precise interpretation can be supplied by writing a C

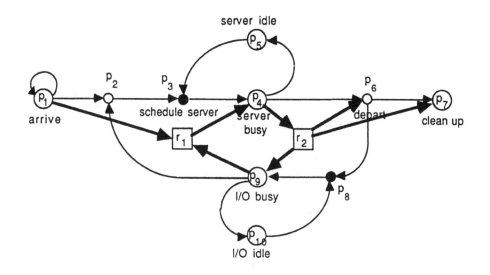

Figure 6: A BPG Queueing Model

procedure for p_6 such that a specific output arc is selected to receive a token representing a job (thus BPGs can be made deterministic by specifying the action in forward conflict situations).

The graph model suggests that there is one server and one I/O device in the system, however, we can simulate two different I/O devices by initially marking the "I/O idle" node with two tokens. This will allow two different jobs to be performing I/O -- reside on the "I/O busy" node at one time. Any of these changes to the model be implemented as the model is being interpreted.

As we continue to use the model, we may wish to distinguish between the two I/O devices, perhaps one is slow and the other is fast. A stochastic model of such operation would simply suggest that a bimodal distribution be used to specify the firing time for the "I/O busy" node. However, such a model will not prevent us from simulating two instances of the slow device being in operation at one time.

An alternative is to change the graph to the one shown in Figure 7. The graph editor has been used to copy p_8, p_9, and p_{10}, to add p_{15}, and to add new arcs connecting the subgraph. It is also necessary to either specify the stochastic conditions under which a job uses device 1 or device 2 (by annotating arcs (p_{15}, p_8) and (p_{15}, p_{13}) with probabilities) or by writing a deterministic procedure for node p_{15} to specify conditions for a job choosing one device or the other.

4. SUMMARY

We have described the Olympus Modeling System Architecture, designed on a distributed client-server architecture in which the implementations of the client and the server also employ client-server and remote procedure call models of computation.

The Olympus Architecture supports very general usage; because of the isolation of interpretation in the server, the client need not know any details of the model interpretation. The server will support multiple clients operating on a single model in the server; thus, users can cooperatively construct and analyze a model (or program) using the common server with their individual clients.

Modeling is most useful when the system that supports it is easy to use, and very flexible. The independence of the console from the server not only allows the user great freedom in applying different loads to the model, it also allows the user to dynamically change the load -- the specification of the load or the specific instance of the load -- while the model is being interpreted. More importantly, Olympus allows the user to "correct" the model during interpretation, instead of requiring that the user halt the model, change it with an editor, recompile it, reinitialize it, and wait for it to get to the loading condition in which it was halted. If alterations of the model should be performed

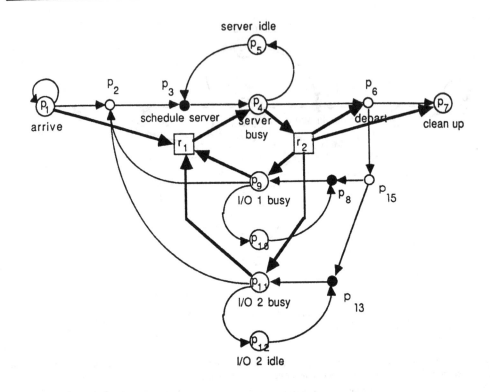

Figure 7: A Two-Device System

while the interpretation is inactive, then the interpretation can be temporarily interrupted, the model changed, and the interpretation resumed.

Our overall research program is concerned with modeling various aspects of complex systems, particularly distributed computer systems. The fundamental assumption behind our approach is that such systems are sufficiently complex that a designer can benefit considerably from interactive support systems to experiment with behavior prior to implementation.

Choosing a particular model on which to base the man/machine interface is very important to the success of the support system, and very difficult to do so that it is acceptable to a wide range of users. We each have a set of preconceived notions about modeling primitives, often based largely on aesthetics. Olympus provides fundamental operation as a simulation and animation system allowing one to use a somewhat arbitrary user/model interface.

Our overall research projects center around the application of several different formal models of computation as bases for interactive system support. In this paper we have described a simulation system while in other projects we study multi-tiered modeling systems [6, 23] and deterministic, visual programming systems [2]. The support systems for these other studies are all based on the Olympus Architecture.

Finally, we expect to use Olympus as the basis of a cooperative, distributed software development environment. The current architecture and implementation support multiple users working on a common model with atomic transactions and simultaneous update of state at the clients. We feel that this is a promising basis for general cooperative problem solving systems.

5. ACKNOWLEDGEMENTS

Several people have worked on the Olympus system including Mohammad Amin, Zuraya Aziz, Adam Beguelin, Mimi Beaudoin, Isabelle Demeure, Steve Elliott, John Hauser, Art Isbell, Nikolay Kumanov, Jeff McWhirter, and Bruce Sanders.

This research has been supported by NSF Grant No. CCR-8802283, NSF cooperative agreement DCR-8420944, and a grant from U S West Advanced Technologies.

6. REFERENCES

1. G. Balbo and G. Chiola, "Stochastic Petri Net Simulation", *1989 Winter Simulation Conference Proceedings*, Washington, D. C., December 1989, 266-276.

2. A. L. Beguelin, "Deterministic Parallel Programming in Phred", University of Colorado, Department of Computer Science, Ph. D. Dissertation, May 1990.

3. J. C. Browne, D. Neuse, J. Dutton and K. Yu, "Graphical Programming for Simulation of Computer Systems", *Proceedings of the 18th Annual Simulation Symposium*, 1985.

4. M. Broy, *Control Flow and Data Flow: Concepts of Distributed Programmings*, Springer Verlag, 1985.

5. I. M. Demeure, S. L. Smith and G. J. Nutt, "Modeling Parallel, Distributed Computations using ParaDiGM -- A Case Study: The Adaptive Global Optimization Algorithm", *Fourth SIAM Conference on Parallel Processing for Scientific Computing*, Chicago, IL, December 1989.

6. I. M. Demeure, "A Graph Model, ParaDiGM, and a Software Tool, VISA, for the Representation, Design, and Simulation of Parallel, Distributed Computations", University of Colorado, Department of Computer Science, Ph. D. Dissertation, June 1989.

7. I. M. Demeure and G. J. Nutt, "Prototyping and Simulating Parallel, Distributed Computations with VISA", submitted for publication, May 1990.

8. R. S. Elliott and G. J. Nutt, "Remarks on the Cost of Using A Remote Procedure Call Facility", University of Colorado, Department of Computer Science Technical Report No. CU-CS-426-89, February 1989.

9. C. A. Ellis and G. J. Nutt, "Office Information Systems and Computer Science", *ACM Computing Surveys* 12, 1 (March 1980), 27-60.

10. G. Estrin, "A Methodology for Design of Digital Systems -- Supported by SARA at the Age of One", *AFIPS Conference Proceedings of the National Computer Conference 47* (1978), 313-324.

11. G. Estrin, R. S. Fenchel, R. R. Razouk and M. K. Vernon, "SARA (System ARchitects Apprentice): Modeling, Analysis, and Simulation Support for Design of Concurrent Systems", *IEEE Transactions on Software Engineering SE-12*, 2 (February 1986), 293-311.

12. H. J. Genrich, "Predicate/Transition Nets", in *Petri Nets: Control Models and Their Properties, Advances in Petri Nets 1986, Part 1*, W. Brauer, W. Reisig and G. Rozenberg (editor), Lecture Notes in Computer Science, Springer Verlag, Berlin, Heidelberg, New York, 1987.

13. M. L. Graf, "Building a Visual Designer's Environment", MCC Technical Report No. STP-318-87, October, 1987.

14. *PAWS/GPSM marketing brochures*, Information Research Associates, Austin, TX, 1988.

15. K. Jensen, "Coloured Petri Nets", in *Petri Nets: Control Models and Their Properties, Advances in Petri Nets 1986, Part 1*, W. Brauer, W. Reisig and G. Rozenberg (editor), Lecture Notes in Computer Science, Springer Verlag, Berlin, Heidelberg, New York, 1986, 248-299.

16. S. J. Leffler, R. S. Fabry, W. N. Joy and P. Lapsley, "An Advanced 4.3BSD Interprocess Communication Tutorial", in *Unix Programmer's Manual Supplementary Documents 1*, Computer Systems Research Group, Computer Science Division, Department of Electrical Engineering and Computer Science, University of California, Berkeley, April 1986.

17. B. Melamed and R. J. T. Morris, "Visual Simulation: The Performance Analysis Workstation", *IEEE Computer 18*, 8 (August 1985), 87-94.

18. T. Murata, "Petri Nets: Properties, Analysis and Applications", *Proceedings of the IEEE 77*, 4 (April 1989), 541-580.

19. K. M. Nichols and J. T. Edmark, "Modeling Multicomputer Systems with PARET", *IEEE Computer 21*, 5 (May 1988), 39-48.

20. J. D. Noe and G. J. Nutt, "Macro E-Nets for Representing Parallel Systems", *IEEE Transactions on Computers C-12*, 8 (August 1973), 718-727.

21. G. J. Nutt, "The Formulation and Application of Evaluation Nets", Ph.D dissertation, Computer Science Group, University of Washington, 1972.

22. G. J. Nutt and P. A. Ricci, "Quinault: An Office Environment Simulator", *IEEE Computer 14*, 5 (May 1981), 41-57.

23. G. J. Nutt, "Visual Programming Methodology for Parallel Computations", *MCC-University Research Symposium Proceedings*, Austin, Texas, July 1987.

24. G. J. Nutt, "Olympus: An Extensible Modeling and Programming System", Technical Report No. CU-CS-412-88, Department of Computer Science - University of Colorado, Boulder, October 1988.

25. G. J. Nutt, A. Beguelin, I. Demeure, S. Elliott, J. McWhirter and B. Sanders, "Olympus User's Manual", Technical Report CU-CS-382-87, Department of Computer Science - University of Colorado, Boulder, December 1987 (revised June, 1989).

26. G. J. Nutt, "A Formal Model for Interactive Simulation Systems", Technical Report No. CU-CS-410-88, Department of Computer Science - University of Colorado, Boulder, September 1988 (Revised May 1989).

27. C. Ramchandani, "Analysis of Asynchronous Concurrent Systems by Timed Petri Nets", Ph.D. dissertation, MIT, 1974.

28. R. R. Razouk and C. V. Phelps, "Performance Analysis Using Timed Petri Nets", *Proceedings of 1984 International Conference on Parallel Processing*, August 1984, 126-129.

29. D. Smith, E. Harslem, C. Irby and R. Kimball, "The Star User Interface: An Overview", *Proceedings of the AFIPS National Computer Conference 51* (1982), 515-528.

30. "Networking on the Sun Workstation", Document Number 800-1345-10, Sun Microsystems, Inc., September 1986.

APPENDIX: THE BILOGIC PRECEDENCE GRAPH MODEL

Bilogic Precedence Graphs (BPGs) are composed from a set of *tasks*, a set of *control dependencies* among the tasks, and a specification of *data references* among tasks. A BPG can be thought of as the union of a control flow subgraph and a data flow subgraph. The control flow subgraph is made up of nodes that correspond to tasks and edges that specify precedence among the tasks. The node set for the data flow subgraph is the union of the task node set with another set of nodes representing data repositories; edges in the data flow graph indicate data references by the tasks.

BPGs are directly descended from Information Control Nets [9], which evolved from our work with data flow models and E nets [20]; and E nets are a derived directly from Petri nets [21]. The control flow subgraph is similar to the UCLA Graph Model of Behavior (GMB) [10,11] in that it specifies conjunctive ("AND") and disjunctive ("OR") input and output logic specifications for each task. Let small, open circles represent tasks with exclusive OR logic; and small, closed circles represent tasks with AND logic (see the examples on the left side of Figure A1). OR-tasks are enabled by control flow into any input arc, and upon task termination, control can flow out on any output arc. AND-tasks are not enabled until control flows to the task on every input arc, and upon termination control flows out every output arc. Large circles represent tasks with OR-input logic and AND-output logic; ordinarily, we only use single input and single output arcs on these circles since we use them to emphasize the notion of nontrivial processing. Our choice of these primitives is based on our users' preferences (from the E-net and ICN studies). Other logic combinations can be built from these primitives, e.g., AND-logic input and OR-logic output is attained by connecting the output of a multi-input, single-output AND-node with to a single-input, multiple-output OR-node.

As in other marked graphs, the control flow state is represented by tokens (data flow state is not explicitly represented in BPGs). Thus, one can think of markings and firings of the various tasks in the control flow subgraph just as in Petri nets. A BPG is activated by marking appropriate tasks with tokens, at which time the BPG firing rules (control flow logic rules) describe sequences of markings corresponding to control flow among the tasks.

A single-entry, single-exit task directly maps to a Petri net transition with one input and one output place, see Figure A1a. That is, the task fires whenever a token arrives at the input, and a token leaves the task when it has completed firing. A BPG AND-task corresponds to a set of Petri net places and a transition, see Figure A1b. The OR-task is similar to a Petri net with forward/backward conflict, see Figure A1c. Token paths can merge or separate at an OR-task. As in Petri nets, an uninterpreted OR-task in nondeterministic. (However, we will provide interpretations for BPG tasks -- see below.)

Data flow is represented by adding data repository nodes to the control flow graph, and arcs interconnecting nodes and data repositories. (Squares are used to represent data repositories in BPGs.) Data flow in a BPG does not correspond directly to data flow in a traditional data flow graph (see, for example, [4]). That is, task firing is specified by tokens in the control flow subgraph, whereas the data flow subgraph represents data references by the tasks. Thus, an arc from a task to a repository represents the case that the task *may* write information to the repository, and an arc from a repository to the task represents that the task *may* read information from the repository. An interpretation for the task specifies whether or not the task references the repositories to which it is connected for any particular task firing. The resulting model is used to represent storage references and inter-task

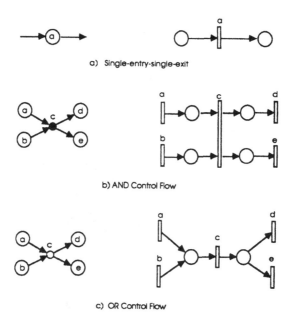

a) Single-entry-single-exit

b) AND Control Flow

c) OR Control Flow

Figure A1: BPG Primitives

communication.

Figure A2 is a Petri net model of a simple queueing system with jobs requesting CPU service and I/O service alternately. The leftmost portion of the Petri net represents the arrival of jobs and the rightmost portion represents their departure. The places labeled "server idle" and "I/O idle" must initially contain a token for the model to behave properly. (Multiple servers and multiple I/O devices could be represented by corresponding numbers of tokens on the respective idle locations.)

Figure 6 is the corresponding BPG. Task p_1 has AND output logic and OR input logic, so the edge from p_1 to itself will cause the task to be cyclic, corresponding to the job arrival portion of the Petri net. When a job is created, a record describing the job is written to repository r_1 by p_1. Task p_2 is used to merge two OR paths, and p_3 fires only when the server is idle (there is a token on the edge (p_5, p_3)) and there is a job to serve (a token is on edge (p_2, p_3)). Task p_4 models the job receiving service by reading the details of the job description from r_1 and writing the updated job status to r_2 when the time slice has been completed (p_4 terminates). When the job leaves the server, then the server becomes idle AND a decision is made as to whether or not the job is done or requires I/O (task p_6). Tasks p_8, p_9, and p_{10} model the I/O device operation, updating the job status in r_1 and r_2 during the process.

While tasks share the firing rule properties of pure Petri net transitions as described in Figure A1, they also employ the notion of non-zero transition time of E-nets, ICNs, and Timed (Performance) Petri Nets [27,28]. This is the means for introducing time into the simulation. For example, in Figure 6, the job's service time is represented by the amount of time that the token resides on task p_4.

Each task may have a procedural *interpretation*, to specify the amount of time required for firing the task. Thus, task p_4 can determine the desired amount of service time by evaluating a function such as shown in Figure A3. The evaluation of the procedure results in a simulated time being returned. (Notice that the interpretation for p_4 references repositories r_1 and r_2 using the *access-repository* procedure without specifying read/write commands. The arcs in the graph description, passed as an argument to *access-repository* determine the direction of information flow, i.e., this is the mechanism for data flow in the model.)

The interpretation is evaluated each time the task is fired. Tasks with OR (output) logic may use interpretations to specify deterministic behavior; the procedure evaluates information available to it (from repositories), then selects an output arc to receive the resulting token. We represent this choice as a second value returned from the

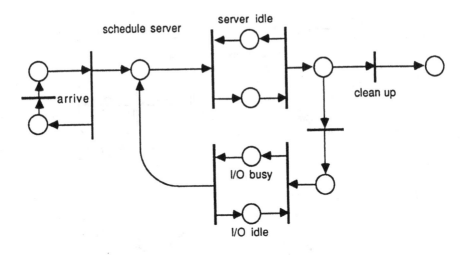

Figure A2: A Queueing System

interpretation of an OR-task, i.e.,

(time, out-arc) = f(OR-task)

BPG tasks are hierarchical. Any task may be refined by defining a new BPG which has the same input/output behavior as the parent task. Using ideas similar to those in macro E-nets [20], it is possible to define subnets that have the same logical input/output properties as an individual task in the BPG. For example, suppose that the server task were actually two subservers, only one of which could be busy at any time (this is a hypothetical example to describe hierarchical nodes in the graph). Then, the sub-BPG shown in Figure A4 would be one hierarchical refinement of p. Task $p_{4,1}$ would be a decision task that decided which of the two units were to be used for this operation. One unit would be represented by task $p_{4,2}$ and the other by $p_{4,3}$. Tasks $p_{4,4}$ and $p_{4,5}$ would be used to produce the correct token response to the outputs of the original p_4.

This is a brief, intuitive description of BPGs, particularly as they relate to Petri nets. Part of the motivation for using BPGs is that they are sufficiently simple, and similar to other commonly used models, that they are natural for representing the individual events involved in the simulation of a system. (A similar argument was used to justify the formulation of E-nets [20,21]. The other rationale for using BPGs is that they encompass the semantics of several other formal models, including other variants of Petri nets, queueing networks, and several CASE models; by implementing the modeling system so that it interprets the semantics of BPGs, it is possible to provide a user interface that employs the syntax of these other models at a particular user's design workstation.

For the interested reader, a more complete and more formal description of BPGs can be found in [26].

$p_4()$
{
    struct *job;

/* Read r_1 */
    access_repository((r_1, p_4), job)
/* Change a field in the record read from the repository */
    update(job.statistics);
/* Write r_2 */
    access_repository((p_4, r_2), job);
/* Return the amount of time required for the task to fire */
    return(job.service_time);
}

Figure A3: A Node Interpretation

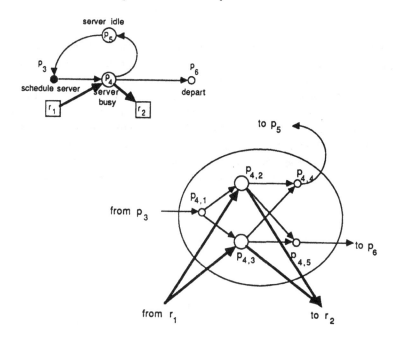

Figure A4: A Refined Task

A State Transformation Preorder
over a class of EN systems

L. Pomello and C. Simone

Dipartimento di Scienze dell'Informazione
Universita' degli Studi di Milano
via M. Da Brescia 9- 20133 Milano - Italy

ABSTRACT The paper introduces a notion of preorder between Elementary Net Systems which is based on the observability of places. This latter allows one to define the notion of Observable Local States whose transformations are the main concern of the proposed preorder, called State Transformation (ST) preorder. ST preorder compares systems with a different level of granularity in local states transformation by requiring an injective morphism between their algebraic structures of observable local states. In addition, it allows one to define in a standard way a notion of ST equivalence. This latter is related to a previous notion, EF equivalence, for which the existence of canonical representatives has been previously proved. Finally, ST preorder and equivalence over a subclass of EN systems (the S-observable systems) are discussed in the framework of system development.

Keywords behaviour of systems, equivalence, morphisms, observability of states

CONTENTS

This research has been conducted with the financial support of the Italian Ministero della Pubblica Istruzione

1. Introduction

The duality between places and transitions characterizing Petri Nets allows one to define in their regard two notions of observability: the first one based on <u>observable transitions</u>, the second one based on <u>observable places</u>.

While the first type of observability has been exploited extensively in different models of concurrent systems (e.g., [Mil80], [Hen88], [DDM87], [DDPS85], [Abr87] etc.) giving rise to a set of confrontable proposals [Pom86], the second one remains poorly exploited. Within net theory, works in various ways implicitly related to it can be: the notion of Interface Equivalence introduced by K. Voss [Vos87] based both on places and transitions observability; the notion of morphism as defined by C.A. Petri ([Pet73],[GS80]), which is very flexible but disregards dynamical properties; the notion of refinement as defined by Valette [Val79], which substitutes for a transition predefined structures of subnet; and finally, the reduction rules defined by Berthelot [Ber86], which consider both structural and dynamic aspects by preserving system behaviour, but are oriented more toward system analysis than toward system development.

The research on place observability (motivated in [DDS87] and formalized in [DDPS88]) aims at defining a notion of <u>functional equivalence</u> which is both <u>flexible</u> (allowing a wide set of system manipulations) and <u>sound</u> (allowing manipulations which preserve the state transformations of the system). Specifically, [DDPS88] introduces the notion of Exhibited Functionality (EF)-equivalence on the class of conctact-free Elementary Net (EN) systems in which some places are considered as observable (S-labelled systems). EF-equivalence requires an isomorphism between the state structures of the two systems (i.e., the algebras generated by the observable reachable markings by means of the operations of intersection and difference) and a correspondence between sequences of so called elementary observable paths (i.e. informally, the minimal portion of behaviour leading from one observable marking to another without containing intermediate observable markings). When restricted to S-observable systems (i.e., informally, S-labelled systems in which the pre and post sets of each elementary observable path are disjoint), this notion is such that each equivalence class contains a unique (up to isomorphism) EN system minimal w.r.t. the net structure in which each place is observable. This system is in canonical form, i.e., it is the canonical representative of the class and can be constructed by a reduction algorithm starting from any element of the class.

The present paper can be considered as a step forward in the study of place observability from two standpoints. First of all, the usability of place observability in system design. In fact, as will be discussed in section 4, we recognize the usefulness of having a relation which allows one to confront systems at different levels of granularity in observable state transformations. This is not the case of EF-equivalence, which prevents the designer from modifying the structure of the observable states of the system under development, and requires an 'a priori' complete knowledge about the observable parts of the system. In fact, by using such an equivalence notion, the refinements can involve the unobservable parts only. To this aim we define a preorder between systems which considers a system less or equal to another one if the second shows a behaviour (in terms of state transformations) which is an 'extension' or an 'expansion' of the behaviour of the first one. Secondly, from the technical point of view, the paper introduces a functional equivalence notion, based on the previous preorder, which fully takes into account the algebraic structure of state space. In fact, unlike EF-equivalence, it requires a correspondence between any possible local state transformation inside any two equivalent systems.

The paper is organized as follows: section 2 contains some preliminary definitions; in section 3 we define a preorder over the class of S-labelled systems, which is called State Transformation (ST) preorder, and the related notion of functional equivalence: the ST-equivalence. Then we show that EF-equivalence and ST-equivalence coincide on the class of S-observable systems, while ST-equivalence is stronger on the class of S-labelled systems. This allows one to apply to ST-equivalence the characterization in terms of canonical representatives discussed above. In section 4 we discuss how the class of S-observable systems together with ST-preorder and equivalence can be used in system design. Finally, section 5 contains some considerations on the possible developments of the present work.

2 Preliminary definitions

In the paper we assume the basic definitions of Net Theory as given in [Bra87] and we consider concurrent systems modelled by contact-free EN systems [Thi87], whose underlying nets are finite and T-restricted (i.e., for each transition t of the net pre-t and post-t are not empty). In the following when we say EN system we always mean EN system with the above properties.

Definition 1 *Notations*

Let $\Sigma = (S, T; F, M_0)$ be an EN system.

For all $w \in T^*$:

* $\forall M, M' \in [M_0\rangle \quad M[w\rangle M'$ iff

$(w = \varepsilon$ and $M = M')$ or $(\exists t_1, ..., t_k \in T: k \geq 1$ and $w = t_1 ... t_k, \exists M_1, ..., M_k \in [M_0\rangle$ such that: $M[t_1\rangle M_1 ... M_{k-1}[t_k\rangle M_k = M')$

* Perm(w) is the set of all permutations of the transitions constituting w.
* F-Perm(w) is the subset of the firable permutations, i.e.,

  F-Perm(w) = { $w' \in$ Perm(w) | $\exists M, M' \in [M_0\rangle$ such that $M[w'\rangle M'$ }.

* if $\exists M \in [M_0\rangle$ such that $M[w\rangle$, then the pre-set of w, written •w, is the minimal set $X \subseteq M$ such that $X[w\rangle$;

  the post-set of w, written w•, is the set $X' \subseteq S$ such that •w $[w\rangle X'$.

  It follows that if $w = \varepsilon$ then •w = w• = Ø.

Since we want to observe system behaviours in terms of the states they go through, we need to introduce the notions of observable places and of systems having observable places (S-labelled systems). In particular, we require that each observable place belongs to at least one observable marking, since we choose to observe the system behaviour when each component is in an observable local state.

Definition 2 *S-labelled system*

A couple $<\Sigma,0>$ (Σ for short) is an S-labelled EN system , abbreviated <u>S-labelled system</u>, iff:

i) $\Sigma = (S, T; F, M_0)$ is an EN system;

ii) $0 \subseteq S$ is such that $\forall s \in 0\ \exists M \in [M_0>: s \in M$ <u>and</u> $M \subseteq 0$. 0 is called the set of <u>observable places</u> of Σ;

iii) $M_0 \subseteq 0$;

iv) $M_{oss} = \{M \in [M_0> \mid M \subseteq 0\}$ is the set of <u>observable markings</u> of Σ.

Remark

The name "S-labelled" is used in analogy with the definition of observability of transitions, even if a real labelling is not used here. In addition, we keep this name to be consistent with our previous work [DDPS88].

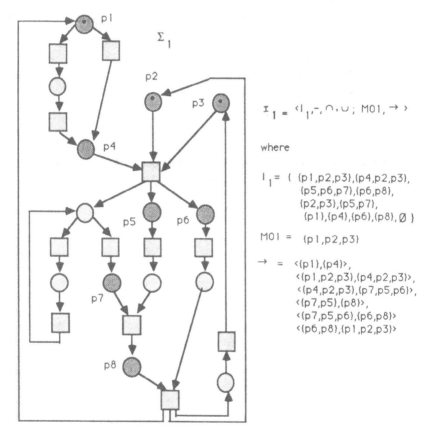

$$\Sigma_1 = <I_1, -, \cap, \cup ; \ M01, \rightarrow >$$

where

$$I_1 = \{\ \{p1,p2,p3\},\{p4,p2,p3\},$$
$$\{p5,p6,p7\},\{p6,p8\},$$
$$\{p2,p3\},\{p5,p7\},$$
$$\{p1\},\{p4\},\{p6\},\{p8\}, \emptyset \ \}$$

$$M01 = \{p1,p2,p3\}$$

$$\rightarrow\ =\ <\{p1\},\{p4\}>,$$
$$<\{p1,p2,p3\},\{p4,p2,p3\}>,$$
$$<\{p4,p2,p3\},\{p7,p5,p6\}>,$$
$$<\{p7,p5\},\{p8\}>,$$
$$<\{p7,p5,p6\},\{p6,p8\}>$$
$$<\{p6,p8\},\{p1,p2,p3\}>$$

figure 1

Example 1

<u>Example 1</u>

Σ_1, given in Figure 1, is an S-labelled system, while Σ_2, given in Figure 2, is not an S-labelled system since the place p_2 does not belong to any observable marking. (From now on observable places are represented by shaded circles).

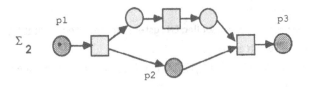

figure 2

Once defined which are the observable states, we define an occurrence sequence as minimal w.r.t. this kind of observation when it and any of its firable permutations leads from one observable marking to another without passing through intermediate observable markings.

Definition 3 *elementary observable path*

Let Σ be an S-labelled system and w∈T⁺ be a sequence of transitions $t_1...t_k$, k≥1, leading from an observable marking to an observable marking, i.e., such that ∃ M, M' ∈ M$_{oss}$: M[w>M'. Then w is an <u>elementary observable path</u> of Σ iff

∀ M[u_1>M$_1$ ... M$_{k-1}$[u_k> M' : u_1... u_k ∈ F-Perm(w) it holds: ∀ i=1,...,k −1 M$_i$ ∉M$_{oss}$.

M[(w>>M' denotes the occurrence of an elementary observable path w.

W$_Σ$ denotes the set of elementary observable paths of Σ.

Remark

Unlike [DDPS88] the empty word is not an elementary observable path. This choice simplifies the technical aspects in the presentation without influencing our results.

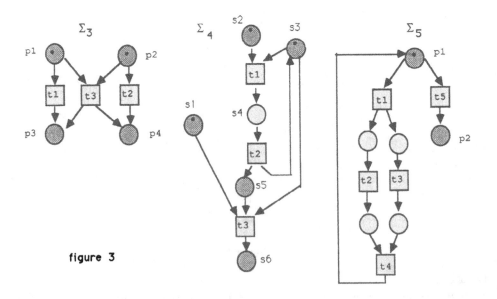

figure 3

figure 4

figure 5

Example 2

* Let us consider the system Σ_3 in figure 3: $w=t_1$, $w=t_2$ and $w=t_3$ are elementary observable paths, while $w=t_1 t_2$ is _not_ an elementary observable path since (p_1,p_2) $[t_1 \rangle$ (p_2,p_3) $[t_2 \rangle$ (p_3,p_4), and (p_2,p_3) belongs to M_{oss}.

* Let us consider the system Σ_4 in figure 4: $t_1 t_2$ and t_3 are both elementary observable paths.

* Let us consider system Σ_5 in figure 5: $w=t_5$ and $w=t_1 t_2 t_3 t_4$ are elementary observable paths, while $w=t_1 t_2 t_3 t_4 t_5$ is _not_ since, being a prolongation of an elementary observable path, it passes through an intermediate observable marking.

We characterize system behaviour in terms of state transformations within the system state space. This is done by using the notions of observable local states and of elementary observable paths.

Definition 4 OLST algebra

To each S-labelled system Σ can be associated the _observable local state transformation algebra_ (OLST algebra) $I = \langle I, -, \cap, \cup ; M_0, \rightarrow \rangle$, where

i) $\langle I,-,\cap,\cup \rangle$ is the _observable local state algebra_ (OLS algebra) of Σ where I is the minimal set of subsets of O that contains M_{oss} and is closed under the operations of difference (−) and intersection ($\cap$): $\cap$, −, $\cup$ are the intersection, difference and union as defined in set theory; while $\cap$ and − are total, $\cup$ is partial and defined as follows:

$$\forall x,y \in X, \ x \cup y \in X \ \text{iff} \ \exists z \in X : x \subseteq z \text{ and } y \subseteq z;$$

ii) M_0 is the initial marking of Σ;

iii) $\rightarrow \subseteq I \times I$ is a not transitive relation which is called _local state transformation relation_ and is defined as follows:

$$\forall x,y \in I \ \ x \rightarrow y \quad \underline{\text{iff}} \quad \exists w \in W_\Sigma : \bullet w \subseteq x \ \underline{\text{and}} \ y = (x - \bullet w) \cup w \bullet$$

M_{oss} is the set of _generators_ of I; we call I_{min} the set of the _minimal elements_ of $I - \{\emptyset\}$, where x is a minimal observable local state of I if there is no y in I such that $y \subset x$.

Remarks

− The definition of the OLS algebra was already introduced in [DDPS88] to support the definition of EF-equivalence (see definition 8). The OLS algebrs given in [DDPS88] did not contain the union operation which has been introduced here for simplifying the notation used in various proofs. The definition of OLST algebra was given also in [PS90] for EN systems without requiring contact-freeness. However, the results presented in this paper strongly depend on the assumption that the EN systems are contact-free.

− The minimal elements of $I - \{\emptyset\}$ are sets of observable places such that are _all together either marked or not marked_ in each observable marking. We exclude the empty set as an element of I_{min} since we are interested in not trivial minimal elements which will play a relevant role in the construction of the canonical reperesentative of the equivalence notion we are going to introduce (see section 3 and 4).

Example 3

Figure 1 contains the S-labelled system Σ_1 and the related OLST algebra I_1. The observable local state (p_2,p_3) is obtained from the intersection of (p_1,p_2,p_3) and (p_4,p_2,p_3), while the observable local state (p_5,p_7) is obtained from the difference between (p_5,p_6,p_7) and (p_6,p_8).

Lemma 1

Let Σ_1, Σ_2 be S-labelled systems with I_1, I_2 their OLST algebras, then:

1) $\forall x,y \in I_1 : x \rightarrow_1 y$ it holds: $x \in M_{oss1} \Rightarrow y \in M_{oss1}$.

2) If $h : \langle I_1, -, \cap, \cup \rangle \dashrightarrow \langle I_2, -, \cap, \cup \rangle$ is an isomorphism then:

$$x \in I_{1min} \Leftrightarrow h(x) \in I_{2min}$$

Proof

1) From the definition of the relation $\rightarrow$ it directly follows that if two observable local states x and y are related by $\rightarrow$ and x is an observable marking, then also y is an observable marking.

2) Let $x \in I_{1min}$ and, by contradiction, let $h(x) \notin I_{2min}$. Then $\exists y \in I_2$ such that $y \neq h(x)$ and $h(x) \cap y = y$. Since h is an isomorphism we derive $h^{-1}(h(x)) \cap h^{-1}(y) = h^{-1}(y)$, and since $x \in I_{1min}$, we derive $x = h^{-1}(y)$ and then $h(x) = y$ which contradicts the hypothesis. The truth of the viceversa is proved in a similar way.

3 The State Transformation preorder and equivalence

We now introduce a preorder, i.e., a reflexive and transitive relation, over the class of S-labelled systems. The intuition behind it is the following: a system Σ_1 precedes a system Σ_2 in the preorder if and only if 1) the OLST algebra of Σ_1 is a substructure of the OLST algebra of Σ_2; 2) to each elementary observable path producing a local state transformation in Σ_1 there is a (sequence of) elementary observable path(s) in Σ_2 producing a corresponding local state transformation.

Definition 5 ($\Sigma_1 \subseteq^{ST} \Sigma_2$)

Let Σ_1 and Σ_2 be S-labelled systems with $I_1 = \langle I_1, -, \cap, \cup, M_{01}, \rightarrow_1 \rangle$ and $I_2 = \langle I_2, -, \cap, \cup, M_{02}, \rightarrow_2 \rangle$ their OLST algebras.

Σ_1 is less or equal than Σ_2 w.r.t. State Transformation, written $\Sigma_1 \subseteq^{ST} \Sigma_2$, iff there is an injective morphism $h : \langle I_1, -, \cap, \cup \rangle \dashrightarrow \langle I_2, -, \cap, \cup \rangle$ such that :

i) $h(M_{01}) \subseteq M_{02}$;

ii) $\forall x, y \in I_1 : x \rightarrow_1 y \Rightarrow [h(x) \rightarrow_2 h(y)$ or
$\exists n \geq 1, \exists i_1, i_2, ..., i_n \in (I_2 - h(I_1)) : h(x) \rightarrow_2 i_1 \rightarrow_2 ... i_n \rightarrow_2 h(y)]$.

Lemma 2

The relation $\subseteq^{ST}$ is a preorder over the set of S-labelled systems.

Proof

It is immediate to verify that the relation $\subseteq^{ST}$ is reflexive and transitive.

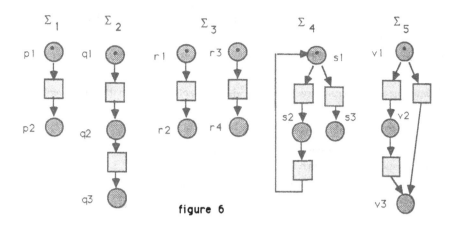

figure 6

Examples 4

Let us consider the systems Σ_i given in figure 6 with their related OLST algebras $I_i = \langle l_i, -, \cap, \cup,$ $M_{0i}, \rightarrow_i \rangle$ (i = 1,..., 5).

a) $\Sigma_1 \subseteq^{ST} \Sigma_2$: in fact, since $l_1 = \{\{p_1\},\{p_2\}\}$, $l_2 = \{\{q_1\},\{q_2\},\{q_3\}\}$, $\rightarrow_1 = \{\langle p_1,p_2 \rangle\}$, $\rightarrow_2 =$ $\{\langle q_1,q_2 \rangle, \langle q_2,q_3 \rangle\}$, there are two possible injective morphisms h, k: $\langle l_1, -, \cap, \cup \rangle \dashrightarrow \langle l_2, -, \cap, \cup \rangle$ defined respectively by: $h(p_1)=q_1$ and $h(p_2)=q_3$; $k(p_1)=q_1$ and $k(p_2)=q_2$ and such that $M_{02} =$ $h(M_{01})$ and $h(p_1) \rightarrow_2 q_2 \rightarrow_2 h(p_2)$; $M_{02} = k(M_{01})$ and $k(p_1) \rightarrow_2 k(p_2)$.

On the basis of the morphism h, $\Sigma_1 \subseteq^{ST} \Sigma_2$ means that $\underline{\Sigma_2 \text{ is an expansion of } \Sigma_1}$, i.e., Σ_2 refines the observable state transformations performed by Σ_1 in a sequence of more elementary transformations of observable states.

On the basis of the morphism k, $\Sigma_1 \subseteq^{ST} \Sigma_2$ means that $\underline{\Sigma_2 \text{ is an extension of } \Sigma_1}$, i.e., in addition to the observable state transformations performed by Σ_1, Σ_2 performs other observable state transformations.

b) $\Sigma_1 \subseteq^{ST} \Sigma_3$: in fact, since

$l_3 = \{\{r_1,r_3\},\{r_2,r_4\},\{r_2,r_3\}, \{r_1,r_4\} \{r_1\},\{r_2\},\{r_3\},\{r_4\}\}$,

$\rightarrow_3 = \{\langle \{r_1,r_3\},\{r_2,r_3\} \rangle, \langle \{r_1,r_4\},\{r_2,r_4\} \rangle, \langle \{r_1,r_3\},\{r_1,r_4\} \rangle,$

$\langle \{r_2,r_3\},\{r_2,r_4\} \rangle, \langle \{r_1\},\{r_2\} \rangle, \langle \{r_3\},\{r_4\} \rangle\}$,

there is an injective morphism h: $\langle l_1, -, \cap, \cup \rangle \dashrightarrow \langle l_3, -, \cap, \cup \rangle$ defined by: $h(p_1)=r_1$ and $h(p_2)=r_2$. Σ_3 is an extension of Σ_1 obtained by adding to this latter a concurrent component.

c) $\Sigma_1 \subseteq^{ST} \Sigma_4$: in fact, considering $l_4 = \{\{s_1\},\{s_2\},\{s_3\}\}$ and $\rightarrow_4 = \langle \{s_1\},\{s_2\} \rangle, \langle \{s_1\},\{s_3\} \rangle,$ $\langle \{s_2\},\{s_1\} \rangle$, there are two injective morphisms h, k: $\langle l_1, -, \cap, \cup \rangle \dashrightarrow \langle l_4, -, \cap, \cup \rangle$ defined respectively by: $h(p_1)=s_1$ and $h(p_2)=s_2$; $k(p_1)=s_1$ and $k(p_2)=s_3$.

In both cases Σ_4 is an extension of Σ_1.

d) $\Sigma_1 \subseteq^{ST} \Sigma_5$: in fact, considering $l_5 = \{\{v_1\},\{v_2\},\{v_3\}\}$ and $\rightarrow_5 = \langle \{v_1\},\{v_2\} \rangle, \langle \{v_1\},\{v_3\} \rangle,$ $\langle \{v_2\},\{v_3\} \rangle$, there is an injective morphism h: $\langle l_1, -, \cap, \cup \rangle \dashrightarrow \langle l_5, -, \cap, \cup \rangle$ defined by: $h(p_1)=v_1$ and $h(p_2)=v_3$.

In this case Σ_5 is both an extension and an expansion of Σ_1.

e) Let us consider the systems Σ_5 given in figure 5 and Σ_1 given in figure 6. It is easy to see that $\Sigma_1 \subseteq^{ST} \Sigma_5$ and <u>not</u> ($\Sigma_5 \subseteq^{ST} \Sigma_1$).

f) Two systems which are not in the $\subseteq^{ST}$ relation are given in Example 6.

We now introduce an algebraic structure which will play a relevant role in the subsequent proofs.

Definition 6 I'_2: *image of I_1 under h.*

Let Σ_1 and Σ_2 be S-labelled systems with I_1 and I_2 their OLST algebras such that $\Sigma_1 \subseteq^{ST} \Sigma_2$ by means of the injective morphism h.

Let $I'_2 = \langle I'_2, -, \cap, \cup, M'_{02}, \rightarrow'_2 \rangle$ be the OLST algebra in which:

a) $I'_2 = h(I_1)$;

b) $M'_{02} = h(M_{01})$;

c) $\rightarrow'_2 \subseteq I'_2 \times I'_2$ is defined as follows:
$$\forall x,y \in I'_2 \quad x \rightarrow'_2 y \quad \underline{iff} \quad h^{-1}(x) \rightarrow_1 h^{-1}(y).$$

I'_2 is called <u>image of I_1 under h.</u>

Remarks

- It is easy to see that: $\forall x,y \in I'_2 : x \rightarrow'_2 y \Rightarrow$
  $[x \rightarrow_2 y \text{ <u>or</u> } \exists i_1, i_2, ..., i_n \in (I_2 - I'_2): x \rightarrow_2 i_1 \rightarrow_2 ... i_n \rightarrow_2 y].$

- An isomorphism h: $I_1 \dashrightarrow I_2$ between two OLST algebras can be seen as an isomorphism h: $\langle I_1, -, \cap, \cup \rangle \dashrightarrow \langle I_2, -, \cap, \cup \rangle$ such that:
  i) $h(M_{01}) = M_{02}$;
  ii) $\forall x,y \in I_1 : x \rightarrow_1 y \Leftrightarrow h(x) \rightarrow_2 h(y).$

Lemma 3

Let Σ_1 and Σ_2 be S-labelled systems with I_1 and I_2 their OLST algebras and h: $I_1 \dashrightarrow I_2$ be an isomorphism, then: $x \in M_{oss1} \Leftrightarrow h(x) \in M_{oss2}$

Proof

It follows from Lemma 1 point 1) and from the previous characterization of an isomorphism.

<u>Example 5</u>

Let us consider the systems Σ_1 and Σ_6, given respectively in figure 1 and figure 7, with OLST algebras I_1 and I_6. The last one is such that $I_6 = \{\{q_1,q_2\}, \{q_4,q_2\}, \{q_5,q_6\}, \{q_1\}, \{q_2\}, \{q_4\}\}, \rightarrow_6 = \{\langle\{q_1,q_2\}, \{q_4,q_2\}\rangle, \langle\{q_1\},\{q_4\}\rangle, \langle\{q_4,q_2\}, \{q_5,q_6\}\rangle\}$.

$\Sigma_6 \subseteq^{ST} \Sigma_1$ holds by means of the injective morphism h: $\langle I_6, -, \cap, \cup \rangle \dashrightarrow \langle I_1, -, \cap, \cup \rangle$ defined by: $h(\{q_1\})=\{p_1\}$, $h(\{q_2\})=\{p_2,p_3\}$, $h(\{q_4\})=\{p_4\}$, $h(\{q_5\})=\{p_8\}$ and $h(\{q_6\})=\{p_6\}$.

The image of I_6 under h is the algebraic structure $I'_1 = \langle I'_1, -, \cap, \cup, M'_{01}, \rightarrow'_1 \rangle$ in which: $I'_1 = \{\{p_1\}, \{p_2,p_3\}, \{p_4\}, \{p_6\}, \{p_8\}, \{p_1,p_2,p_3\}, \{p_4,p_2,p_3\}, \{p_6,p_8\}\}$, $\rightarrow'_1 = \langle\{p_1,p_2,p_3\}, \{p_4,p_2,p_3\}\rangle, \langle\{p_1\},\{p_4\}\rangle, \langle\{p_4,p_2,p_3\}, \{p_8,p_6\}\rangle$.

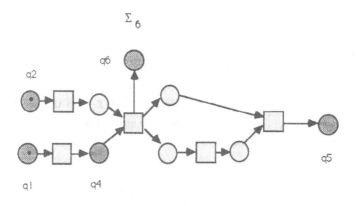

Σ_6

q2

q6

q1

q4

q5

figure 7

Lemma 4

Let Σ_1 and Σ_2 be S-labelled systems such that $\Sigma_1 \subseteq^{ST} \Sigma_2$ by means of the morphism h. Let I_1, I_2 be their OLST algebras and I'_2 be the image of I_1 under h. Then I_1 and I'_2 are isomorphic.

Proof

The proof is directly derived from the definition of $\Sigma_1 \subseteq^{ST} \Sigma_2$ and of I'_2.

Theorem 1

Let Σ_1 and Σ_2 be S-labelled systems and I_1, I_2 be their OLST algebras.

Then $\Sigma_1 \subseteq^{ST} \Sigma_2$ <u>and</u> $\Sigma_2 \subseteq^{ST} \Sigma_1 \Leftrightarrow I_1$ and I_2 are isomorphic.

Proof

a) $\exists\, h\colon I_1 \dashrightarrow I_2$ isomorphism $\Rightarrow \Sigma_1 \subseteq^{ST} \Sigma_2$ <u>and</u> $\Sigma_2 \subseteq^{ST} \Sigma_1$.

   h and h^{-1} are the two required injective morphisms. In fact, being isomorphisms between I_1 and I_2, they preserve the initial markings and the relations $\rightarrow_1$ and $\rightarrow_2$.

b) $\Sigma_1 \subseteq^{ST} \Sigma_2$ <u>and</u> $\Sigma_2 \subseteq^{ST} \Sigma_1 \Rightarrow I_1$ and I_2 are isomorphic.

b1) $\langle I_1, -, \cap, \cup \rangle$ and $\langle I_2, -, \cap, \cup \rangle$ are isomorphic.

   In fact, by definition $\Sigma_1 \subseteq^{ST} \Sigma_2 \Rightarrow \exists\, h\colon \langle I_1, -, \cap, \cup \rangle \rightarrow \langle I_2, -, \cap, \cup \rangle$ injective morphism and, by Lemma 4, I_1 is isomorphic to I'_2. Therefore it holds: $|I'_2| = |I_1| \leq |I_2|$ and $I'_2 \subseteq I_2$. Analogously, $\Sigma_2 \subseteq^{ST} \Sigma_1$ implies $|I'_1| = |I_2| \leq |I_1|$ and $I'_1 \subseteq I_1$.

   Hence $I_1 = I'_1$ and $I_2 = I'_2$ and then $\langle I_1, -, \cap, \cup \rangle$ and $\langle I_2, -, \cap, \cup \rangle$ are isomorphic.

b2) $h(M_{01}) = M_{02}$

   This is proved per absurdum by using the fact that $M_{01} = \cup_1^n x_i$ and $M_{02} = \cup_1^m y_j$ with $x_i \in I_{1min}$ and $y_j \in I_{2min}$, and that h is an isomorphism between $\langle I_1, -, \cap, \cup \rangle$ and $\langle I_2, -, \cap, \cup \rangle$; and then by applying Lemma 1-2).

b3) $\forall\, x, y \in I_1\colon x \rightarrow_1 y \Leftrightarrow h(x) \rightarrow_2 h(y)$.

   i) $\forall\, x, y \in I_1\colon x \rightarrow_1 y$ implies $h(x) \rightarrow_2 h(y)$. In fact: $\forall\, x, y \in I_1\colon x \rightarrow_1 y$ implies $h(x) \rightarrow'_2 h(y)$ since I_1 and I'_2 are isomorphic.

By definition $h(x) \to'_2 h(y)$ means: $h(x) \to_2 h(y)$ <u>or</u> $\exists u_1, u_2, ..., u_n \in (l_2 - l'_2)$:
$h(x) \to_2 u_1 \to_2 ... u_n \to_2 h(y)$; since $l_2 = l'_2$ it holds: $h(x) \to_2 h(y)$.

ii) $\forall x,y \in l_1$: $h(x) \to_2 h(y) \Rightarrow x \to_1 y$. In fact: let $G_1 = \{\langle x,y \rangle \mid x,y \in l_1 \text{ and } x \to_1 y\}$
and $G_2 = \{\langle u,v \rangle \mid u, v \in l_2 \text{ and } u \to_2 v\}$ then from b3-i) and the fact that h is an isomorphism
between $\langle l_1, -, \cap, \cup \rangle$ and $\langle l_2, -, \cap, \cup \rangle$ it follows that h is an injective morphism from G_1
into G_2; analogously, it can be proved that since $\Sigma_2 \subseteq^{ST} \Sigma_1$ then the injective morphism
$g : \langle l_2, -, \cap, \cup \rangle \dashrightarrow \langle l_1, -, \cap, \cup \rangle$ is also an injective morphism from G_2 into G_1. Then h and g
are isomorphisms between G_1 and G_2.

Definition 7 $\Sigma_1 \approx^{ST} \Sigma_2$

Let Σ_1 and Σ_2 be S-labelled systems and I_1, I_2 be their OLST algebras. Then Σ_1 and Σ_2 are
equivalent with respect to State Transformations, abbreviated <u>ST-equivalent</u> and written $\Sigma_1 \approx^{ST} \Sigma_2$,
iff $\Sigma_1 \subseteq^{ST} \Sigma_2$ <u>and</u> $\Sigma_2 \subseteq^{ST} \Sigma_1$ (or equivalently, iff I_1 and I_2 are isomorphic).

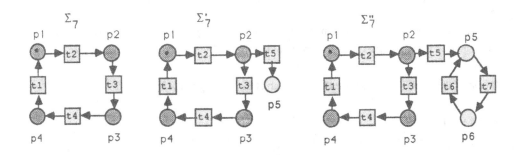

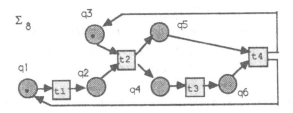

figure 8

Example 6

Let us consider the S-labelled systems Σ_7 and Σ_8 of figure 8. They are <u>not</u> ST-equivalent. In fact,
there is no isomorphism between their OLST algebras: the cardinality of the sets $l_7 = \{\{p_1\}, \{p_2\}, \{p_3\}, \{p_4\}\}$, and $l_8 = \{\{q_1, q_3\}, \{q_2, q_3\}, \{q_4, q_5\}, \{q_5, q_6\}, \{q_3\}, \{q_4\}, \{q_1\}, \{q_2\}, \{q_5\}, \{q_6\}\}$ are
different.

Moreover <u>not</u>$(\Sigma_7 \subseteq^{ST} \Sigma_8)$; in fact it is possible to show that any possible injective morphism
between l_7 and l_8 does not preserve local state transformations. For example, if we consider the
morphism h: $\langle l_7, -, \cap, \cup \rangle \dashrightarrow \langle l_8, -, \cap, \cup \rangle$ defined by $h(p_1) = q_1$, $h(p_2) = q_2$, $h(p_3) = q_4$,

$h(p_4)=q_6$, then we have $p_2 \rightarrow_7 p_3$ but $\underline{not}(h(p_2) \rightarrow_8 h(p_3))$ and also there are no intermediate states such that $h(p_2) \rightarrow_8 \ldots \rightarrow_8 h(p_3)$.

The S-labelled system Σ_1 of figure 1 is ST-equivalent to the S-labelled system Σ_8.

ST equivalence between S-labelled systems does not preserve deadlock-freeness. In fact, an S-labelled system can reach a marking in which no transition has concession (a marking in which the system is blocked) and which is unobservable.

Example 7

The S-labelled system Σ_7 and Σ'_7 from figure 8 are ST-equivalent. While Σ_7 is deadlock-free, Σ'_7 can reach an (unobservable) marking in which no transition has concession.

ST-equivalence preserves deadlock-freeness if the compared systems satisfy the requirement that any reachable marking gives concession to a finite sequence leading to an observable marking or to an infinite sequence which does not reach any observable marking. In fact the following theorem holds.

Theorem 2

Let Σ_1 and Σ_2 be S-observable systems such that $\Sigma_1 \approx^{ST} \Sigma_2$ and Σ_1 is deadlock-free. Then Σ_2 is deadlock-free if and only if Σ_2 is such that:

(*) $\quad \forall M_2 \in [M_{02}> \quad [\exists M'_2 \in [M_2>: M'_2 \in M_{oss2} \quad \underline{or}$
there exists an infinite sequence $M_2[t_1> M^1_2 [t_2> M^2_2[t_3> \ldots\ldots$
such that: $\forall j \geq 1 \quad t_j \in T_2 \quad \underline{and} \quad M^j_2 \notin M_{oss2}]$.

Proof

a) Σ_2 deadlock-free implies the condition (*): this follows from the hypothesis that $\Sigma_1 \approx^{ST} \Sigma_2$ and Σ_1 is deadlock-free.

b) The condition (*) implies Σ_2 deadlock-free: let us suppose, per absurdum, that Σ_2 reaches a marking M_2 in which no transition has concession. Two cases are possible:

1) $M_2 \in M_{oss2}$. This contradicts the fact that I_1 and I_2 are isomorphic.

2) $M_2 \notin M_{oss2}$. This contradicts the condition (*) which guarantees that M_2 cannot be a marking in which Σ_2 is blocked.

Example 8

The S-labelled system Σ_7 and Σ''_7 from figure 8 are ST-equivalent and deadlock-free. It is immediate to verify that both satisfy the condition (*) of Theorem 2; while Σ'_7 does not.

As recalled in the introduction, in [DDPS88] was given the definition of EF equivalence on S-labelled systems, which is formulated in a slightly different way w.r.t. ST-equivalence. Let us now give this definition and state the correspondence between the two equivalence notions.

Definition 8 $\Sigma_1 \approx^{EF} \Sigma_2$

Let Σ_1 and Σ_2 be two S-labelled systems, then Σ_1 and Σ_2 are equivalent with respect to Exhibited

Functionality, abbreviated **EF-equivalent** and written $\Sigma_1 \approx^{EF} \Sigma_2$, iff there is an isomorphism $h: \langle I_1, -, \cap, \cup \rangle \longrightarrow \langle I_2, -, \cap, \cup \rangle$ such that:

$\forall w_1,...,w_n \in W_{\Sigma_1}$, such that $M_{10}[(w_1 \rangle\rangle M_{11}...[(w_n \rangle\rangle M_{1n}$

$\exists v_1,...,v_n \in W_{\Sigma_2}$, such that $M_{20} = h(M_{10})[(v_1 \rangle\rangle h(M_{11})...[(v_n \rangle\rangle h(M_{1n}))$

and viceversa.

Remark

EF-equivalence could be formulated in a way similar to ST-equivalence by requiring an isomorphism between the OLST algebras in which the relation $\rightarrow$ is contained in $M_{OSS} \times M_{OSS}$. Anyway in the following theorems we will use the formulation of Definition 8.

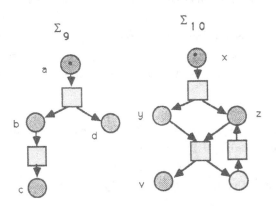

Σ_9 Σ_{10}

figure 9

ST-equivalence is stronger than EF-equivalence. In fact the following theorem holds.

Theorem 3

Let Σ_1 and Σ_2 be S-labelled systems. Then $\Sigma_1 \approx^{ST} \Sigma_2$ implies $\Sigma_1 \approx^{EF} \Sigma_2$, while $\Sigma_1 \approx^{EF} \Sigma_2$ does not imply $\Sigma_1 \approx^{ST} \Sigma_2$.

Proof

Let I_1, I_2 be the OLST algebras associated to Σ_1 and Σ_2.

i) Using Theorem 1, i.e., $\Sigma_1 \approx^{ST} \Sigma_2 \Leftrightarrow I_1$ and I_2 are isomorphic, we only have to prove that: I_1 and I_2 are isomorphic implies $\Sigma_1 \approx^{EF} \Sigma_2$. Let h be an isomorphism between I_1 and I_2, then h is an isomorphism between $\langle I_1, -, \cap, \cup \rangle$ and $\langle I_2, -, \cap, \cup \rangle$ and $h(M_{01}) = M_{02}$. In addition, to each sequence of elementary observable paths $M_{01}[(w_1 \rangle\rangle M_{11}[(w_2 \rangle\rangle ..... [(w_{n-1} \rangle\rangle M_{n1}$ can be associated the sequence $M_{01} \rightarrow_1 M_{11} \rightarrow_1 ... \rightarrow_1 M_{n1}$. Then it follows that $h(M_{01}) \rightarrow_2 h(M_{11}) \rightarrow_2 ... \rightarrow_2 h(M_{n1})$, and for the definition of the relation $\rightarrow$ (see Definition 4) there are $u_1, u_2,....u_n$ elementary observable paths in Σ_2 such that $M_{02} = h(M_{01})[(u_2 \rangle\rangle h(M_{11})[(u_2 \rangle\rangle .... [(u_{n-1} \rangle\rangle h(M_{n1})$. The the truth of the viceversa (required by EF-equivalence, see Definition 8) can be proved analogously by using the isomorphism h^{-1}.

ii) $\Sigma_1 \not\approx^{EF} \Sigma_2$ does not imply $\Sigma_1 \not\approx^{ST} \Sigma_2$ is proved by the following counter-example: the two S-labelled systems Σ_9 and Σ_{10} given in figure 9 are EF-equivalent and not ST-equivalent. In fact, in Σ_9 we have $b \rightarrow_9 c$ while in Σ_{10} $y=h(b)$ and $v=h(c)$ are not related by $\rightarrow_{10}$.

Remark

It easy to see that, even if EF-equivalence is weaker that ST-equivalence, Theorem 2 holds for EF-equivalent systems too.

In theorem 4 we will prove that ST- and EF-equivalences coincide over a subclass of S-labelled systems, called in [DDPS88] S-observable systems. The interest of this class of systems has been mentioned in the introduction and will be motivated further in §4. Intuitively, S-observable systems are S-labelled systems which cannot contain "observable side conditions" on elementary observable paths

Definition 9 *S-observable systems*

Let Σ be an S-labelled system, then Σ is <u>S-observable</u> iff $\forall w \in W_\Sigma$ it holds: $\bullet w \cap w\bullet = \emptyset$.

Remark

The previous definition implies that for each M, M'$\in$ M$_{oss}$ and for each $w \in W_\Sigma$ it holds: $M[(w\gg M'$ iff $M - M' = \bullet w$ and $M' - M = w\bullet$.
In addition, Theorem 2 concerning deadlock-freeness holds a fortiori for S-observable systems.

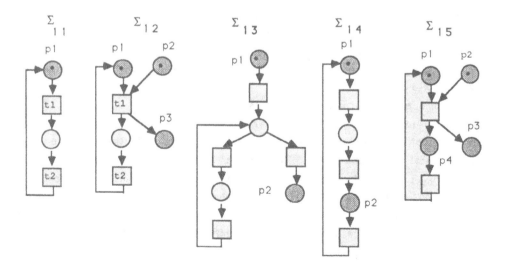

figure   10

Example 9

The S-labelled systems Σ_{11} and Σ_{12} in figure 10 are not S-observable since place p_1 belongs to both $\bullet w$ and $w\bullet$, with $w = t_1 t_2$.
On the contrary, the S-labelled systems $\Sigma_{13}, \Sigma_{14}, \Sigma_{15}$, given in figure 10, are all S-observable.

Intuitively, S-observable systems are such that places inside loops are either all unobservable (Σ_{13}) or at least two of them are observable (Σ_{14}, Σ_{15}).

Furthermore, the systems Σ_1 of figure 1 and Σ_7, Σ_8 of figure 8 are S-observable.

Lemma 5

Let Σ be an S-observable system, then for each $w \in W_\Sigma$: $\bullet w, w\bullet \in I$.

Proof

The result follows from the definition of $\bullet w$ and $w\bullet$, the definition of S-observable systems and from the construction of the set I.

Remark

Lemma 5 does not hold in the case of S-labelled systems. In fact, the S-labelled system Σ_4 of figure 4 is not S-observable since the elementary path $w = t_1 t_2$ is such that $\bullet w = \{s_2, s_3\}$ and $w\bullet = \{s_3, s_5\}$ and $\bullet w \cap w\bullet \neq \emptyset$. In addition, both $\bullet w$ and $w\bullet$ do not belong to I.

Theorem 4

Let Σ_1 and Σ_2 be S-observable systems. Then $\Sigma_1 \approx^{EF} \Sigma_2 \Leftrightarrow \Sigma_1 \approx^{ST} \Sigma_2$.

Proof

Let I_1, I_2 be the OLST algebras associated to Σ_1 and Σ_2.

i) $\Sigma_1 \approx^{ST} \Sigma_2$ implies $\Sigma_1 \approx^{EF} \Sigma_2$ follows from Theorem 3 applied to the subclass of S-observable systems.

ii) $\Sigma_1 \approx^{EF} \Sigma_2$ imples $\Sigma_1 \approx^{ST} \Sigma_2$ is obtained by means of Theorem1 and by proving that: $\Sigma_1 \approx^{EF} \Sigma_2$ implies I_1 and I_2 are isomorphic.

From the definition of EF-equivalence it follows that there is an isomorphism h between $\langle I_1, -, \cap, \cup \rangle$ and $\langle I_2, -, \cap, \cup \rangle$ and that $h(M_{01}) = M_{02}$.

What remains to be proved is that: $\forall x,y \in I_1 : x \rightarrow_1 y \Leftrightarrow h(x) \rightarrow_2 h(y)$.

a) $\forall x,y \in I_1 : x \rightarrow_1 y \Rightarrow h(x) \rightarrow_2 h(y)$.

The proof is carried on by considering two cases:

a1) $\forall x,y \in I_1 : (x \rightarrow_1 y$ and $x \cap y = \emptyset) \Rightarrow h(x) \rightarrow_2 h(y)$.

By the definition of $\rightarrow_1$ and the hypothesis $x \cap y = \emptyset$, there is $w \in W_{\Sigma_1}$ such that: $x = \bullet w$ and $y = w\bullet$. Then, since Σ_1 is S-observable there are $M, M' \in M_{oss1}$ such that: $M - M' = x$ and $M' - M = y$. By using the isomorphism h we obtain: $h(M) - h(M') = h(x)$ and $h(M') - h(M) = h(y)$ where, because of Lemma 3, $h(M'), h(M)$ belongs to M_{oss2}. Since $\Sigma_1 \approx^{EF} \Sigma_2$ there is a sequence M_{10} $[(w_1 \gg M_{11} ... M[(w \gg M'$ and a corresponding sequence $M_{20} = h(M_{10})$ $[(v_1 \gg h(M_{11}) ... h(M)[(v \gg h(M'))$ from which, and from the fact that Σ_2 is S-observable, we derive $\bullet v = h(M) - h(M'), v\bullet = h(M') - h(M)$, $\bullet v \rightarrow_2 v\bullet$, and therefore $h(x) \rightarrow_2 h(y)$.

a2) $\forall x,y \in I_1 - M_{oss1} : [x \rightarrow_1 y$ and $x \cap y \neq \emptyset] \Rightarrow h(x) \rightarrow_2 h(y)$

Since Σ_1 is S-observable it follows from the hypothesis that: $\exists w \in W_{\Sigma_1} : (\bullet w = x - y$ and $w\bullet = y - x)$. Then, $x - y \rightarrow_1 y - x$. From a1) it follows that: $h(x-y) \rightarrow_2 h(y-x)$ and since h is an isomorphism $h(x) - h(y) \rightarrow_2 h(y) - h(x)$. From the definition of $\rightarrow_2$ it follows that there is $u \in W_{\Sigma_2}$ such that: $h(y) - h(x) = h(x) - h(y) - \bullet u \cup u \bullet$, from which we can derive $h(y) = h(x) - \bullet u \cup u \bullet$ (e.g., by adding $h(y) \cap h(x)$ on both sides), which proves that $h(x) \to_2 h(y)$.

b) $\forall x,y \in I_1 : h(x) \to_2 h(y) \Rightarrow x \to_1 y$.

This is proved in two steps in a way analogous to the previous ones, by using the isomorphisms h^{-1}, the fact that h preserves the observable markings and that Σ_1 and Σ_2 are S-observable systems.

4. ST-canonical representatives and degree of concurrency

Theorem 4 says that EF and ST equivalence coincide on the class of S-observable systems. Moreover, such class guarantees that it is possible to construct a unique (up to isomorphism) canonical representative of each ST (EF)-equivalence class [DDPS88]. The canonical representatives are simple, pure EN systems without dead transitions, in which every place is observable. We now give some hints on how such representatives are constructed and how they play a role in the equivalence verification process.

Given an S-observable system and its OLST algebra, the canonical representative of the equivalence class to which it belongs is constructed by associating a place to each element belonging to I_{min} and a transition to each equivalence class of local state transformations, where two local state transformations $x \to y$ and $v \to z$ are equivalent iff $x-y = v-z$ and $y-x = z-v$, i.e.: iff they transform exactly the same local states. The flow relation connects a place p to a transition t if p corresponds to an element of I_{min} contained in the precondition of a local state transformation corresponding to t, and a transition to a place in a similar way. The initial marking is the set of places corresponding to the elements of I_{min} constituting the initial marking of the given system.

We note that the previous construction could be applied to S-labelled systems too: in this case purity of the canonical representative is no longer guaranteed since in the canonical representative a dead transition could be associated to a sequence of transitions having concession in the given system, because the disjointness of the pre-set and post-set of this sequence is not guaranteed.

Then the proof of ST-(EF) equivalence between two S-observable systems can be carried on by reducing them to their canonical representatives and then verifying if they are isomorphic. We are now developing the implementation of the reduction algorithm for the construction of the canonical representatives as the basis for an (interactive) tool for the verification of the $\subseteq^{ST}$ and $\approx^{ST}$ relations between systems.

In [PS90] we proved that the class of canonical representatives together with ST-preorder (which becomes a partial order) is a complete partial order, i.e., each increasing sequence of canonical representatives $CR_1 \subseteq^{ST} CR_2 \subseteq^{ST} \dots CR_n \subseteq^{ST} \dots$ has a limit, and the least element is the undefined system whose OLST algebra is $\emptyset = \langle \emptyset, -, \cap, \cup, \emptyset, \to \rangle$.

Let us define the degree of concurrency of an S-observable system as the maximal number of elements of I_{min} constituting a reachable observable marking (i.e., Degree of Concurrency(Σ)= Max $\{n \, / \, M = y_1 \cup ... \cup y_n$ where $M \in Moss$ and for $i=1,...,n$ $y_i \in Imin\}$). In the case of systems in canonical form, being I_{min} equal to the set of places, the degree of concurrency is the maximal number of places constituting a reachable marking.

Since two equivalent S-observable systems have isomorphic OLST algebras they necessarily show the same degree of concurrency on the observable states; otherwise, their canonical representatives cannot be isomorphic.

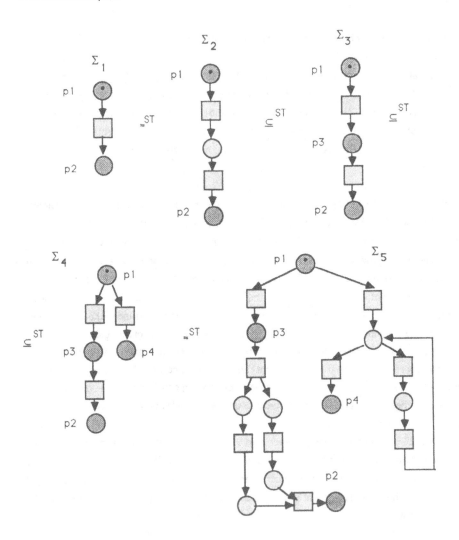

figure 11

Example 10

The S-observable systems Σ_1 and Σ_3 of figure 6 are in canonical form, they are not isomorphic and then not ST equivalent, while $\Sigma_1 \subseteq^{ST} \Sigma_3$. Σ_3 has a higher degree of concurrency on the observable states.

If we consider the S-observable systems Σ_4 and Σ_5 of figure 11, they are ST equivalent and the first one is the canonical form of the equivalence class to which they belong. They show the same degree of concurrency on the observable states, while the concurrency in Σ_5 is unobservable and then has no influence on ST equivalence.

Then we can deduce that it is meaningless to define notions of functional equivalence based on the OLST algebra by distinguishing between interleaving or partial order semantics (i.e., by using traces, posets, etc. instead of sequences). In fact, the OLST algebra associated to each system allows the distinction between systems having sequential non-deterministic behaviours and systems having concurrent behaviours (e.g., there is no system having a sequential non-deterministic behaviour which is ST-equivalent to the system Σ_3 given in figure 6).

5. ST-preorder and ST-equivalence in system design

At this point we can motivate why we are interested in a preorder instead of a simple equivalence relation between systems. From the previous section, it follows that the use of only the equivalence notion requires the system designer to have an a priori complete knowledge about the degree of concurrency needed by the final system. In fact, this notion prevents him from introducing new concurrent observable state transformations without losing the equivalence between the new and the old system (which is not true, by the way, for the equivalence notions based on observable transitions, when interleaving semantics is considered). In addition, the designer should have an 'a priori' knowledge about the system states he wants to observe, since the notion of equivalence prevents him from introducing new observable places and confronting systems with sets of observable local states which are not isomorphic. Indeed, this is what characterizes ST-preorder through the notions of 'expansion' and 'refinement' illustrated in examples 4 of section 3. By the way, we note that the designer could add unobservable places too, provided that they do not alter the set M_{OSS}, i.e. the set of the generators of the OLST algebra.

The above considerations should have shown that the class of S-observable systems, the preorder defined on them and the related equivalence notion provide the designer with a set of useful tools. The possibilities he has available can be depicted by the grid of related systems shown in figure 12. CR_i are the canonical representatives of the equivalence classes in increasing order; $\Sigma_{i,j}$ is the generic system belonging to the ith class and at the jth level of detail, m being the level the designer possibly chooses as the final step in the refinement. The designer can move inside this grid either changing the equivalence class in which he operates, i.e., the structure of observable system states (by moving along the $\subseteq^{ST}$ path) or adding more unobservable details inside the same equivalence class (by moving along the $\approx^{ST}$ paths).

$$\ldots \subseteq^{ST} CR_1 \subseteq^{ST} \ldots CR_i \subseteq^{ST} \ldots CR_n \subseteq^{ST} \ldots$$

$$\approx^{ST} \qquad \approx^{ST} \qquad \approx^{ST}$$

$$\ldots \qquad \ldots \qquad \ldots \qquad \ldots \qquad \ldots$$

$$\ldots \subseteq^{ST} \Sigma_{1,j} \subseteq^{ST} \ldots \Sigma_{i,j} \subseteq^{ST} \ldots \Sigma_{n,j} \subseteq^{ST} \ldots$$

$$\approx^{ST} \qquad \approx^{ST} \qquad \approx^{ST}$$

$$\ldots \qquad \ldots \qquad \ldots \qquad \ldots \qquad \ldots$$

$$\ldots \subseteq^{ST} \Sigma_{1,m} \subseteq^{ST} \ldots \Sigma_{i,m} \subseteq^{ST} \ldots \Sigma_{n,m} \subseteq^{ST} \ldots$$

figure 12

In particular, one path is worth noting to highlight a possible use of the grid, since it can be associated to two classic activities in the system development process, namely system specification and implementation. In fact, when the designer moves along the paths of canonical representatives he can be considered inside the specification step, in which only the essentials, i.e., the observable states, are considered and their causal relatioships are stated. Once the canonical representative satisfying all the requirements is found (i.e., the representative is the specification of the system), then the implementation step can start. In fact, ST equivalence (preserved by moving along the $\approx^{ST}$ paths) disregards any unobservable system state structure, which can depend on some implementation constraints, and only requires to maintain the observable states structure, guaranteeing in this way the fulfillment of the specification itself.

It is evident that all the other paths inside the grid correspond to system development modalities in which the specification and implementation steps are in some way interleaved. These modalities are by far the more used in practice and can find in the above mentioned grid a support to a controlled system development, as is sketched in the path shown in figure 11.

6. Conclusions

The research on ST preorder and equivalence will continue in the following directions.

First of all, we want to evaluate the possibility of relaxing, in the definition of ST-preorder and equivalence, the hypothesis that EN systems are contact-free and based on T-restricted nets.

Secondly, we want to compare ST-equivalence with other related notions in the literature. We started in [DDPS88] showing that EF (ST)-equivalence and Interface Equivalence [Vos87] are disjoint. In addition, we want to investigate the relationships between the notion of 'implementation' informally introduced in section 5 on the one hand with the analogous notion based on transition observability, namely the notion of 'organizational refinement' ([Mil80], [DDS87]); on the other hand, with the notion of 'implementation' introduced by Lamport in [Lam86].

Finally, we want to use the algebra of local states transformations to characterize the EN system they represent. Some preliminary results are presented in [PS90].

Acknowledgements
The research presented in this paper originates from previous works done in cooperation with F. De Cindio and G. De Michelis. The authors want to thank G. De Michelis for some stimulating discussions, and the four referees for their helpful remarks which led in particular to the correct formulation of Lemma 5.

7. References

LNCS stands for Lecture Notes in Computer Sciences, Springer Verlag, Berlin

[Abr87]   S. Abramsky, <u>Observation Equivalence as a Testing Equivalence</u>, Theor. Comp. Science 53, pp. 225-241, 1987

[Ber86]   G. Berthelot, <u>Checking Properties of Nets Using Transformations</u>, LNCS 222, pp. 19-40, 1986.

[Bra87]   W. Brauer, W. Reisig, G. Rozenberg (eds.), <u>Petri Nets: Central Models and Their Properties</u>, LNCS 254, 1987.

[DDM87]   P. Degano, R. De Nicola, U. Montanari, <u>Observational equivalences for concurrency models</u>, in 'Formal description of Programming Concepts III' (M.Wirsing ed.), North Holland, 1987.

[DDS87]   F. De Cindio, G. De Michelis, C. Simone, <u>GAMERU: a language for the analysis and design of human communication pragmatics</u>, in G. Rozemberg (ed) "Advances in Petri Nets 86' ", LNCS 266, 1987.

[DDPS85]   F. De Cindio, G. De Michelis, L. Pomello, C. Simone, <u>Exhibited-Behaviour Equivalence and Organizational Abstraction in Concurrent System Design</u>, Proc. 5th International Conference on Distributed Computing, IEEE, Denver,1985.

[DDPS88]   F. De Cindio, G. De Michelis, L. Pomello, C. Simone, <u>A State Transformation Equivalence for Concurent Systems: Exhibited Functionality Equivalence</u>, in F.H. Vogt (ed) "CONCURRENCY 88", LNCS 335, 1988.

[GS80]   H.J. Genrich, E. Stankiewicz-Wiechno, <u>A Dictionary of Some Basic Notations of Net Theory</u>, in W. Brauer (ed) Net Theory and Applications, LNCS 84, 1980.

[Hen88]   M. Hennessy, <u>Algebraic Theory of Processes</u>, The MIT Press, 1988.

[Lam86]   L. Lamport, <u>On Interprocess Communication. Part 1: Basic Formalism.</u> Distributed Computing, Vol. 1, pp. 77-85, 1986.

[Mil80]   R. Milner, <u>A Calculus for Communicating Systems</u>, LNCS 92, 1980.

[Pet73]   C.A. Petri, <u>Concepts in Net Theory,</u> Mathematical Foundations of Computer Science: Proc. of Symposium and Summer School, High Tatras, sept. 1973, Math. Inst. of the Slovak Acad. of Sciences, pp.137-146, 1973.

[Pom86]   L. Pomello, <u>Some Equivalence Notions for Concurrent Systems: An Overview</u>, in "Advances in Petri Nets 1985" (G.Rozenberg ed.), LNCS 222, pp. 381-400, 1986.

[PS90]   L. Pomello, C. Simone, <u>Concurrent Systems as Local State Transformation Algebras: the case of Elementary Net Systems</u>, DSI Internal Report n.77/90, Univ. of Milano, 1990.

[Thi87]   P.S. Thiagarajan, <u>Elementary Net Systems</u>, in [Bra87], pp. 26-59, 1987.

[Val79]   R. Valette, <u>Analysis of Petri Nets by Stepwise Refinements</u>, J. of Computer and System Science, vol.18-1, 1979.

[Voss87] K. Voss, <u>Interface as a Basic Concept for Systems Specification and Verification</u>, in "Concurrency and Nets" (eds) K. Voss, H.J. Genrich, G. Rozenberg, Springer Verlag, Berlin, pp.585-604, 1987.

COMPOSITION OF NETS
VIA A COMMUNICATION MEDIUM (1)

Younes SOUISSI
and
Gérard MEMMI

Bull Research and Advanced Programs
68 route de Versailles.
78430 Louveciennes. FRANCE

ABSTRACT : The general idea of this paper is to build a system in a modular way and to deduce its properties only by analysing its smaller components. Since, in general, composing subnets does not preserve properties (especially liveness) at the level of the global net, the problem is to find constraints on the subnets for establishing such results. We have discovered that in some cases it is sufficient to put structural constraints (instead of constraints on the subnets languages) only on the medium, that is the subnet generated by the elements (places and transitions) shared by the two nets to be composed. Our theoretical study includes as media of communication: places (one way communication), a rendez-vous, a sequential process, and finally a well-formed block.

KEYWORDS : Composition via shared places, separation line, composition via a sequential process, composition by rendez-vous, composition via a well-formed block, boundedness, liveness.

I INTRODUCTION

One major question that has to be tackled when aiming at introducing any verification method into industry, is the ability to manipulate and to analyse large systems. Abstraction and modularity are two ways to handle relatively efficiently systems of millions of states. Abstraction has already been studied in net theory (see the notions of equivalences [André 82], [André 83], [Pomello 88]) but to our knowledge, few results have been published on modularity although the two methods obviously overlap in the sense that it is possible, in some cases, to obtain the same subnets via a modular approach or via some abstractions. Also, the two methods aim at generating the smallest reachability graph as possible (see also

(1) This work has been done within the context of Demon project (Esprit BRA 3148).

[Berthelot 85] for transformations of nets).

Introducing modularity in order to analyse a net means finding how to decompose it into subnets such that properties of the net can be deduced from properties of the subnets. The theory that arises is fundamental in algebra. But again, very few results have been obtained on this topic, for the simple reason that subnets in general does not preserve, properties at the level of the global net, especially liveness. The problem is to find constraints on the subnets for establishing such results.

This paper aims at gathering and extending some pioneering results in |Memmi 78|, |Valette 79|, [Resig...83]. The originality here is to view a composition of nets as a composition using three subnets instead of two, where two of them are connected via the third one, the medium. We have discovered that in some cases it is sufficient to put structural constraints (instead of constraints on the subnets languages) only on the net which represents the medium.

After recalling some definitions and notations we give a first rule of composing nets via shared places while preserving liveness, then we show how to find in a given net all separation lines, the sets of shared places which allow us to decompose the net into subnets. We also give three other rules of composing nets while preserving liveness. Composition via a sequential process for which the medium is connected to the rest of the net by a set of buffers. We show that this rule generalizes the composition by rendez-vous [Memmi 78]. Finally, by using Valette's result [Valette 79] together with the preservation result when composing nets by rendez-vous, we give a result on composition of nets via a well-formed block [Valette 79]. Boundedness is preserved when using the rules of composition via a sequential process and a rendez-vous.

II BASIC NOTIONS ON NETS

Definition 2.1   net

A net is a triplet $N=<P,T,W>$ where P and T are two finite sets such that $P \cap T = \emptyset$ and $W : (PxT) \cup (TxP) \rightarrow \mathbb{N}$ ($\mathbb{N}$ is the set of natural numbers). P is the set of places, T the set of transitions and W the flow function of N.

For $x \in P \cup T$ we define $\Gamma^-(x)=\{y \in P \cup T : W(y,x)>0\}$, $\Gamma^+(x)=\{y \in P \cup T : W(x,y)>0\}$ and $\Gamma(x)=\Gamma^-(x) \cup \Gamma^+(x)$.

We generalize these definitions to sets of transitions and sets of places:

For a subset X of $P \cup T$ $\Gamma^-(X)= \cup_{x \in X} \Gamma^-(x)$, $\Gamma^+(X)= \cup_{x \in X} \Gamma^+(x)$ and $\Gamma(X)= \cup_{x \in X} \Gamma(x)$.

Let $N=<P,T,W>$ be a net. We say that N' is the subnet of N generated by (P',T'), where P' is a subset of P and T' a subset of T, if and only if $N'=<P',T',W'>$ is the net such that for any $(x,y) \in (P'xT') \cup (T'xP')$, $W'(x,y)=W(x,y)$.

Let $N=<P,T,W>$ be a net and let T' be a subset of T.

We define the projection of T over T' as $Proj : T^* \rightarrow (T')^*$ with :

$$\text{Proj}(\varepsilon, T') = \varepsilon \quad \varepsilon \text{ is the empty word of } T^*$$

for $t \in T$ $\qquad \text{Proj}(t,T') = \{ \begin{array}{l} t \quad \text{if } t \in T' \\ \varepsilon \quad \text{if } t \notin T' \end{array}$

for $\sigma \in T^*$ and $t \in T$ $\qquad \text{Proj}(\sigma t, T') = \text{Proj}(\sigma, T').\text{Proj}(t, T').$

$\text{Proj}(\sigma, T')$ is the sequence got from σ by removing all occurrences of transitions not belonging to T'.
For a subset L of T^* we note $\text{Proj}(L, T') = \{\text{Proj}(\sigma, T'), \sigma \in L\}$.

Let $N = <P,T,W>$ be a net and let M be a marking of N (M is a function of $P \to \mathbb{N}$). Using the usual definitions of an enabled sequence $\sigma \in T^*$ at M (noted M ($\sigma >$)) and occurrence of σ changing M into a marking M' (noted M ($\sigma > M'$)), we recall that $L(N,M) = \{\sigma \in T^* : M (\sigma >\}$ is the langage of (N,M) and that $[N,M> = \{M' : \exists \sigma \in T^*, M (\sigma > M'\}$ is the set of reachable markings of (N,M).

Definition 2.2 **liveness, boundednes** [BRAMS 83]
Let $(N,M) = (<P,T,W>,M)$ be a marked net. We say that a transition t of T is live if and only if : $\forall \alpha \in L(N,M), \exists \sigma \in T^*$ such that $\alpha \sigma t \in L(N;M)$. We say that (N,M) is live (or also that M is live) if and only if any transition of T is live.
We say that (N,M) is bounded if and only if : $\exists n \in \mathbb{N}$ such that $\forall M' \in [N,M> \forall p \in P \; M'(p) \leq n$.

Notations
Let $N = <P,T,W>$ be a net. For $\sigma \in T^*$ and $t \in T$ we note : $|\sigma|$ the length of σ (the number of transitions in σ), $|\sigma|_t$ the number of occurrences of the transition t in σ and $\text{im}(\sigma) = \{t \in T / |\sigma|_t > 0\}$.

Compositions of nets can be seen in several ways. The subnets constituting a global net can be associated with a partition of the set of places and transitions [Baumgarten 88]. Then the only edges are shared between subnets. More generally, the subnets constitute a covering of $P \cup T$, it is to say that subnets share common transitions [André 83] or places [Reisig 82]. We name medium of communication between two subnets N_1, N_2 the subnet generated by the shared places and transitions between N_1, N_2. The idea is then to explore how fundamental properties (as liveness) are preserved from the subnets to the global net under structural constraints on the media.

III COMPOSITION OF NETS VIA SHARED PLACES

Here, we consider the medium uniquely constitued with places. This kind of composition has already been introduced in [Reisig 82] for a particular class of nets. For this composition, a first result of liveness preservation has been given in [Souissi...88]. To our knowledge, no genral result of liveness preservation exists. This time we want to connect two given subnets (without particular constraint) via a set of shared places. We add the assumption that one of these subnets does not have any input in the set of shared places.

III.1 Definition and liveness preservation result

Definition 3.1　　　　**composition via shared places**

Let $N_1=<P_1,T_1,W_1>$, $N_2=<P_2,T_2,W_2>$ be two nets such that $P_1 \cap P_2=P_c$ and $T_1 \cap T_2=\emptyset$. We say that $N=<P,T,W>$ is resulting of the composition of nets N_1, N_2 via shared places (P_c) if and only if:

(1) $P=P_1 \cup P_2$, $T=T_1 \cup T_2$, $W=W_1 \cup W_2$

(2) $\Gamma_1^+(P_c) = \emptyset$

(3) P_c is included in $\Gamma_1^+(T_1)$.

The composition via shared places can be seen as a composition using three subnets: N'_1, N'_2 the two subnets of N generated by (P'_1,T_1) and (P'_2,T_2) respectively (where $P'_1=P_1-P_c$, $P'_2=P_2-P_c$) and N'_0 the subnet of N which have P_c as set of places and no transition (see figure 1). As we state it in the following theorem, this composition preserves liveness. Moreover, by analysing (N'_1,M'_1), (N'_2,M'_2) (M'_1,M'_2) are the restriction of M to P'_1, $P'_2)$ instead of (N_1,M_1) and (N_2,M_2) we can take advantage of the fact that, in some cases, certainly the most interesting, (N'_1,M'_1), (N'_2,M'_2) are bounded whereas (N_1,M_1), (N_2,M_2) are not. Indeed, from the structure of connections of N'_1, N'_2 to the medium (P_c) (see definition 3.1), in case of liveness (of (N,M)), P_c is a set of unbounded places.

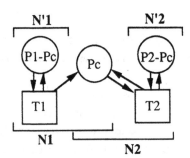

Figure 1: Composition via shared places

Theorem 3.1　　　　**liveness preservation**

Let $N=<P,T,W>$ be the net obtained by composition of nets $N_1=<P_1,T_1,W_1>$, $N_2=<P_2,T_2,W_2>$ via a set of shared places P_c. Let M be a marking of N and let M'_1, M'_2 be the restrictions of M to P'_1,P'_2 (sets defined above) respectively, then the two following properties are equivalent :

(1) (N,M) is live

(2) (N'_1,M'_1) and (N'_2,M'_2) (defined above) are live.

Proof

Let us write the two points which are the basis of our proof.

(i) The subnet N'_1 of N verifies :

$$\Gamma'_1{}^-(T'_1)= \Gamma^-(T'_1)$$

and therefore we have $L(N'_1,M'_1)= Proj(L(N,M),T_1)$.

(ii) The subnet N'_2 of N verifies :

$$\Gamma'_2(P'_2)= \Gamma(P'_2) \text{ and } (\Gamma^-(T'_2) - \Gamma'_2{}^-(T'_2)) \text{ included in } P_c$$

and therefore the following properties :

(N'_1,M'_1) live

and any place $p \in P_c$ is unbounded because of the liveness of (N'_1,M'_1)

imply that $L(N'_2,M'_2)= Proj\ (L(N,M),T_2)$.

($\Rightarrow$) By using the point (i): (N,M) live implies (N'_1,M'_1).

By the fact that (N'_1,M'_1) is live and the point (ii): (N,M) live implies (N'_2,M'_2).

($\Leftarrow$) Let $\alpha \in L(N,M)$ and $t \in T$, let us prove that there exist $\sigma \in T^*$ such that $\alpha\sigma t \in L(N,M)$.

Let $\alpha_k = Proj(\alpha,T_k)$, α_k is a sequences of $L(N'_k,M'_k)$, $k \in \{1,2\}$.

If $t \in T_1$ then let $\sigma \in T_1^*$ such that $\alpha_1 \sigma t \in L(N'_1,M'_1)$. $\alpha_1\sigma t \in L(N,M)$ since $\Gamma^-(\alpha_1\sigma t)=\Gamma_1^-(\alpha_1\sigma t)$.

If $t \in T_2$ then let $\sigma_2 \in T_2^*$ such that $\alpha_2\sigma_2 t \in L(N'_2,M'_2)$.

let $\sigma_1 \in L(N'_1,M'_1)$ such that : $\forall\, p \in P_c\ \Sigma_{t\in Im(\sigma 1)}\ W(t,p) \geq \Sigma_{t\in Im(\sigma 2)}\ W(p,t)$

then $\alpha\sigma_1\sigma_2 t \in L(N,M)$. ◆

III.2   Separation line

Now, we can try to use such a result not for analysing a net composed of two known subnets, but for analysing a given net by splitting it into two subnets communicating via shared places. The type of connections between the shared places and one of the subnets involves to consider the strongly connected components (s.c.c.) of the net viewed as a graph (see [Berge 83] for definitions and results on graph theory).

Definition 3.2   **separable net, separation line**

Let $N=<P,T,W>$ be a net. N is said to be separable if and only if there exists a partition of $P=\{P'_1,P'_2,P_c\}$ and a partition of $T=\{T_1,T_2\}$ such that N is resulting of the composition via shared places (P_c) of N_1, N_2 the two subnets of N generated by (P_1,T_1) and (P_2,T_2) respectively, where $P_1=P'_1\cup P_c$ and $P_2 =P'_2\cup P_c$.

Then, P_c is said to be a separation line of N.

Now we are able to characterize the existence of a separation line.

Poposition 3.1   **characterization of a separation line**

Let P_c be a subset of P, P_c is a separation line of N if and only if there exists a subset $\{G_1=<S_1,V_1,w_1>,..., G_k=<S_k,V_k,w_k> \}$ of the set of the strongly connected components of N such that:

(i) $\Gamma^-(\cup_{i=1}^k S_i)$ included in $\cup_{i=1}^k V_i$, $\Gamma^-(\cup_{i=1}^k V_i)$ included in $\cup_{i=1}^k S_i$

(ii) $\Gamma^+(\cup_{i=1}^k V_i) - (\cup_{i=1}^k S_i)=P_c$, $\Gamma^+(\cup_{i=1}^k S_i)$ included in $\cup_{i=1}^k V_i$.

Proof

Let P_c be a separation line and P'_1,P'_2 two subsets of P satisfying definition 3.2.

Let $c=(x_1,...x_j)$ be a path directed from x_1 of $P_2\cup T_2$ to x_j of $P'_1\cup T_1$ (T_1 and T_2 are defined by the splitting of N into N_1,N_2).

Let x_i be the first vertex of $P'_1 \cup T_1$ on this path (i.e $\{x_1,...x_{i-1}\}$ included in $P_2 \cup T_2$).

If $x_i \in P'_1$ then by definition 3.1, we have $\Gamma(x_i)$ in T_1 then $x_{i-1} \in T_1$ which leads to a contradiction.

If $x_i \in T_1$ then by (ii) of definition 3.1, we have $\Gamma^-(x_i)$ in P'_1 which also leads to a contradiction.

Then, there is no path from $P_2 \cup T_2$ to $P'_1 \cup T_1$. This means that any s.c.c. of N has its vertices either in $P'_1 \cup T_1$ or in $P_2 \cup T_2$. Moreover, no s.c.c. in $P_2 \cup T_2$ precedes any s.c.c in $P'_1 \cup T_1$. This leads to the decomposition of the proposition with $G_1,...G_k$ the s.c.c. partitionning $P'_1 \cup T_1$.

$\Gamma^-(P'_1 \cup T_1)$ included in $P'_1 \cup T_1$ implies (i) of the proposition

$\Gamma^+(P'_1)$ included in T_1 implies $\Gamma^+(\cup_{i=1}^k S_i)$ included in $\Gamma^+(\cup_{i=1}^k V_i)$

$\Gamma^+(T_1)$ included in P_1 and P_c included in $\Gamma^+(T_1)$ ((iii) of definition 3.1) implies $\Gamma^+(\cup_{i=1}^k V_i) - \cup_{i=1}^k S_i = P_c$.

Reversely, let $G_1,...G_k$ be s.c.c. of R verifying the conditions of the proposition. Let $P'_1 = \cup_{i=1}^k S_i$, $T_1 = \cup_{i=1}^k V_i$, $P'_2 = P - (P'_1 \cup P_c)$, $T_2 = T - T_1$. Then $\{P'_1, P'_2, P_c\}$ is a partition of P. Let $N_1 = \cup_{i=1}^k G_i$; let N_2 be the net generated by $(P'_2 \cup P_c, T_2)$. Point (i) of definition 3.1 holds by construction. We have, $\Gamma_1^-(T_1)$ included in P'_1 from (i) of our proposition then $\Gamma_1^+(P_c)=\emptyset$. We have $\Gamma^+(T_1) - P'_1 = P_c$ from (ii) of our proposition then P_c is included in $\Gamma^+(T_1)$. This proves that P_c is a separation line. ◆

This last proposition induces straightforwardly an algorithm to compute all separation lines for a given net N. It consists of first computing the set of all s.c.c. of N, then starting from the sources s.c.c. [Berge 83] building subsets of s.c.c. verifying (i) and (ii) of proposition 3.1; doing this, (ii) of proposition 3.1 clearly defines a separation line. Each separation line being associated with at least one subset of s.c.c. verifying our proposition, we are sure to reach all separation lines of N.

IV A STRUCTURED COMPOSITION

IV.1 Composition via a sequential process

In this subchapter we present a composition of nets which preserves liveness and boundedness. The restrictions we put on the subnets which are going to be composed are structural ones and concern only the medium. More precisely the medium to which we connect the two other subnets is a sequential process [Souissi...88].

Definition 4.1   **sequential process**

A net $N = <S \cup K, T, W>$ is a sequential process (SP) if and only if :

i) $S \cap K = \emptyset$ (S is called the set of states of the process while K is the set of its buffers)

ii) The subnet generated by (S,T) is a state machine

i.e $\forall t \in T \ |\Gamma^+(t) \cap S| = |\Gamma^-(t) \cap S| = 1$

$\forall x,y \in S \cup T : W(x,y) \leq 1$

iii) $\forall p \in S$ if $|\Gamma^+(p)| > 1$ then $\forall t, t' \in \Gamma^+(p) \ \forall x \in K: W(x,t)=W(x,t')$.

This definition of a sequential process is a generalization of Reisig's [Reisig 82]. The generalization is based on the free choice notion [Commoner 72] [Hack 72]. Indeed this extension is similar to the one which consist to extend the properties of free choice nets [Hack 72] to the extented free choice nets [Commoner 72].

Definition 4.2   **composition via a sequential process**

Let $N=<P,T,W>$ be a net. We say that N is obtained by composition of nets $N_1=<P_1,T_1,W_1>$, $N_2=<P_2,T_2,W_2>$ via a sequential process $N_0=<S\cup(K_0\cup K_1\cup K_2),T_0,W_0>$ if and only if:

(1) $P=P_1\cup P_2$, $T=T_1\cup T_2$ and for i=1,2 $x,y\in P_i\cup T_i \Rightarrow W(x,y)=W_i(x,y)$

and by defining the following sets :

$S\cup K_0=P_1\cap P_2$, $T_0=T_1\cap T_2$, $K_1=\Gamma_1(T_0) - (S\cup K_0)$, $K_2=\Gamma_2(T_0) - (S\cup K_0)$

(2) $\Gamma(S\cup K_0)=T_0$

(3) The subnet $N_0=<S\cup(K_0\cup K_1\cup K_2),T_0,W_0>$ of N generated by $(S\cup K_0\cup K_1\cup K_2,T_0)$ is a sequential process, where S is the set of states and $K_0\cup K_1\cup K_2$ the set of buffers.

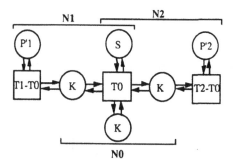

Figure 2 : Composition via a sequential process

One can note that the elements shared between N_1 and N_2 are those of $S\cup K_0\cup T_0$, when the medium is N_0 the subnet of N generated by $(S\cup K_0\cup K_1\cup K_2,T_0)$. This to express that besides the fact that N_1 and N_2 can access a common part of the system (the subnet $N'_0=<S\cup K_0,T_0,W'_0>$), each of them can access a particular set of buffers, K_1 and K_2 respectively. If we view such a net N as a model of a concurrent program , where N_1 and N_2 model two sets of tasks of this program, then K_0 can be seen as a set of global variables (since belonging in N_1 and N_2) which can be accessed only via N_0. K_1, K_2 can be seen as a set of local variables belonging to N_1,N_2 respectively. In that case, N_0 represents the synchronisation mode between N_1 and N_2.

The architecture of composition via a sequential process (see figure 2) allows us to describe via lemma 5.1 and Lemma 5.2, the link between the subnets and the global net. This link is based on inclusion languages and sub-markings equalities.

Lemma 4.1

Let $N=<P,T,W>$ be the net obtained by composition of nets $N_1=<P_1,T_1,W_1>$, $N_2=<P_2,T_2,W_2>$ via a sequential process N_0. Let M be a marking of N and M_1, M_2 the restrictions of M to P_1 and P_2. Let $\sigma\in T^*$, $\sigma_1=Proj(\sigma,T_1)$ and $\sigma_2=Proj(\sigma,T_2)$. The following property holds :

$M(\sigma > M' \Rightarrow M_1(\sigma_1 > M'_1$, $M_2(\sigma_2 > M'_2$ and $M'(p) = M'_i(p)$ for $p\in P_i$ (i=1,2) .

Proof

Let $\sigma'_2 = \text{Proj}(\sigma, T_2 \text{-} T_0)$ where $T_0 = T_1 \cap T_2$.

$\sigma_1 \in T_1{}^*$, $\sigma'_2 \in (T_2 \text{-} T_0)^*$, $P_1 \supset \Gamma_1(\sigma_1)$ and $(P_2 - (S \cup K_0)) \supset \Gamma(\sigma'_2) \Rightarrow \Gamma_1(\sigma_1) \cap \Gamma(\sigma'_2) = \emptyset$.

This last condition is sufficient to obtain that $M (\sigma > M'$ with $M(p) = M_1(p)$ for each $p \in P_1$ implies that we have $M_1 (\sigma_1 > M'_1$ and $M'(p) = M'_1(p)$ for each $p \in P_1$

In a symmetrical way we obtain $M_2 (\sigma_2 > M'_2$ and $M'(p) = M'_2(p)$ with $p \in P_2$ ♦

Lemma 4.2

Let $N = <P,T,W>$ be the net obtained by composition of nets $N_1 = <P_1,T_1,W_1>$, $N_2 = <P_2,T_2,W_2>$ via a sequential process $N_0 = <S \cup (K_0 \cup K_1 \cup K_2), T_0, W_0>$. Let M be a marking of N such that $\Sigma_{p \in S} M(p) \leq 1$. Let M_1, M_2 be the restrictions of M to P_1, P_2 respectively. Let $i,j \in \{1,2\}$ with $i \neq j$. If (N_i, M_i) or (N,M) is live then : $\sigma_j \in L(N_j, M_j) \Rightarrow \exists \sigma \in L(N,M)$ with $\sigma_j = \text{Proj}(\sigma, T_j)$.

Proof

By induction on the length n of σ_j.

(1) If $|\sigma_j| = 0$ then the result is obvious.

(2) If $|\sigma_j| = 1$,

let $\sigma_j = t$

if $t \in T_j - T_0$ then $t \in L(N,M)$ (because $\Gamma^{\cdot}(t) = \Gamma_j^{\cdot}(t)$),

if $t \in T_0$, let us study the two cases :

(a) (N_i, M_i) live

Let $\delta \in L(N_i, M_i)$ be a shorter sequence such that $\delta t \in L(N_i, M_i)$

we have $|\text{Proj}(\delta, T_0)| = 0$ (because of definition 4.1 and $\Sigma_{p \in S} M_i(p) \leq 1$)

(b) (N_i, M_i) not live

then (N,M) is live

Let $\sigma \in L(N,M)$ be a shorter sequence such that $\sigma t \in L(N,M)$

we have $|\text{Proj}(\sigma, T_0)| = 0$ (because of definition 4.1 and $\Sigma_{p \in S} M(p) \leq 1$)

Let $\delta = \text{Proj}(\sigma, T_i)$

then $\delta t \in L(N_i, M_i)$ by lemma 4.1.

From both previous cases, we deduce :

$\delta t \in L(N,M)$ with $\sigma_j = \text{Proj}(\delta t, T_j)$ since $\delta t \in L(N_i, M_i)$ and $t \in L(N_j, M_j)$ and $|\text{Proj}(\delta, T_0)| = 0$.

(3) Let's suppose that the lemma is true for any sequence $\sigma_j \in L(N_j, M_j)$ of length $k \leq n$.

Let $\sigma_j \in L(N_j, M_j)$ be a sequence with length $n+1$

Let $\sigma_j = \sigma'_j t$ with $\sigma'_j \in T^*$ and $t \in T$.

We can apply the induction hypothesis to σ'_j

then there exists $\sigma' \in L(N,M)$ with $\sigma'_j = \text{Proj}(\sigma', T_j)$

Let $\sigma'_i = \text{Proj}(\sigma', T_i)$

by lemma 4.1 we have $\sigma'_i \in L(N_i, M_i)$.

Let M', M'_j and M'_i be the markings such that $M (\sigma' > M'$, $M_j (\sigma'_j > M'_j$ and $M_i (\sigma'_i > M'_i$.

By Lemma 4.1 M'_i, M'_j are the restrictions of M' to P_i, P_j

we can apply the induction hypothesis to (N,M'), (N_i, M'_i), (N_j, M'_j) and t,

which allow us to deduce easily the final result. ♦

The following result on liveness preservation can be seen as generalizing the result which concern the decomposition of a deterministic system of sequential processes in [Souissi...88].

Theorem 4.1   liveness preservation

Let $N=<P,T,W>$ be the net obtained by composition of nets $N_1=<P_1,T_1,W_1>$, $N_2=<P_2,T_2,W_2>$ via a sequential process N_0. Let M be a marking of N such that $\Sigma_{p\in S} M(p)\leq 1$ and let M_1, M_2 be the two restrictions of M to P_1, P_2 respectively. Then we have:

     (N,M) live $\Leftrightarrow$ (N_1,M_1) and (N_2,M_2) live.

Proof

$(\Rightarrow)$ Let $\sigma_1 \in L(N_1,M_1)$ and $t \in T_1$.

By lemma 4.2 there exists $\sigma \in L(N,M)$ with $\sigma_1=Proj(\sigma,T_1)$

Let $\sigma_2=Proj(\sigma,T_2)$, by lemma 4.1 $\sigma_2 \in L(N_2,M_2)$.

Let M', M'_1 and M'_2 be the three markings such that M ($\sigma >$ M', M_1 ($\sigma_1 >$ M'$_1$ and M_2 ($\sigma_2 >$ M'$_2$.

Since (N,M) is live, there exists $\alpha \in L(N,M')$ ending with t

by application of Lemma 4.1 there exists α_1 ending with t such that M'$_1$ ($\alpha_1 >$.

The liveness of (N_2,M_2) can be proven in the same way.

$(\Leftarrow)$ Let $\sigma \in L(N,M)$ and $t \in T$.

$t \in T_1 \cup T_2$

By application of lemma 4.1 and lemma 4.2, there exists $\alpha \in T^*$ such that $\sigma\alpha \in L(N,M)$ and α containing t. $\blacklozenge$

Theorem 4.2   boundedness preservation

Let $N=<P,T,W>$ be the net obtained by composition of nets $N_1=<P_1,T_1,W_1>$, $N_2=<P_2,T_2,W_2>$ via a sequential process N_0. Let M be a marking of N such that $\Sigma_{p\in S} M(p)\leq 1$ (where S is the set of states of the sequential process via which N_1,N_2 are composed). Let M_1, M_2 be the two restrictions of M to P_1, P_2 respectively. The two following properties hold :

    (1) (N_1,M_1) and (N_2,M_2) are bounded $\Rightarrow$ (N,M) is bounded

    (2) (N,M) is live and bounded $\Rightarrow$ (N_1,M_1) and (N_2,M_2) are live and bounded.

Proof

(1) Obvious using Lemma 4.1

(2) Obvious using lemma 4.2 and theorem 4.1 $\blacklozenge$

IV.2   Composition by rendez-vous

A particular case of the previous composition is the composition by rendez-vous. Composing nets by rendez-vous means combining nets by merging transitions. In [Memmi 78], one can find a result on liveness for two combined nets using only one transition.

Let us consider the previous composition of nets in the particular case where our sequential process

$N_0=<S\cup(K_0\cup K_1\cup K_2),T_0,W_0>$ is such that :

$S=\{s\}$, $T_0=\{t_0\}$, $K_0=\emptyset$.

In this case the place s, if it is marked, becomes an implicit place [Berthelot 83] and then we can remove it from each net N, N_1 and N_2 without changing any of their properties. After this operation we say that N can be obtained by the composition by rendez-vous of N_1 and N_2.

Corollary 4.1   liveness preservation

Let $N=<P,T,W>$ be the net obtained by the composition by rendez-vous of nets $N_1=<P_1,T_1,W_1>$, $N_2=<P_2,T_2,W_2>$. Let M be a marking of N and M_1, M_2 the restrictions of M to P_1, P_2 respectively, then the two following properties are equivalent :

(1) (N,M) is live

(2) (N_1,M_1) and (N_2,M_2) are live.

Proof

Let t be the transition of T issued by merging $t_1\in T_1$ and $t_2\in T_2$. By adding to P and P_i place $s\notin T$ such that s is connected only to t (resp. t_i) in R (resp. R_i) with $W(s,t)=W(t,s)=1$ and $W(s,t_i)=W(t,s_i)=1$ we obtain the nets N', N'_i ($i\in\{1,2\}$). N can be obtained by composing N'_1 and N'_2 via a sequential process. We can then apply theorem 4.1 for establishing that (N',M') is live iff (N'_1,M'_1), (N'_2,M'_2) are live, where M,M'$_i$ are the markings such that $M(s)=M'_i(s)=1$ and $M'(p)=M(p)$, $M'_i(p)=M_i(p)$ for p$\in$ P and $p_i\in P_i$. By using the result about liveness preservation when adding an implicit place to a net [Berthelot 83], we can say that (N,M) is live iff (N',M') is live, and the same thing for (N'_i,M'_i) and (N_i,M_i) ($i\in\{1,2\}$).   ◆

Corollary 4.2   boundedness presevation

Let $N=<P,T,W>$ be the net obtained by composition by rendez-vous of nets $N_1=<P_1,T_1,W_1>$, $N_2=<P_2,T_2,W_2>$. Let M be a marking of N and let M_1, M_2 be the two restrictions of M to P_1, P_2 respectively, the two following properties hold :

(1) (N_1,M_1) and (N_2,M_2) are bounded $\Rightarrow$ (N,M) is bounded

(2) (N,M) is live and bounded $\Rightarrow$ (N_1,M_1) and (N_2,M_2) are bounded.

V   COMPOSITION OF NETS VIA A WELL-FORMED BLOCK

In his paper, R. Valette [Valette 79] aimed to depict a methodology allowing both description and analysis of a system by stepwise refinements. Here, we first recall the notions necessary to introduce our result. A first version of it can be found in [Allegre...86] [Dagron...86].

A block $B=<P,T,W>$ is a net where two transitions are distinguished, namely t_{ini} a transition called initial and t_{fin} a transition called final.

A block $B=<P,T,W>$ is a subnet of the net $\underline{B}=<P\cup\{p_0\},T,\underline{W}>$ where p_0 is called the idle place such that : $\underline{W}(p_0,t_{ini})=1$ and for any $t \neq t_{ini}$: $\underline{W}(p_0,t)=0$

$\underline{W}(t_{fin},p_0)=1$ and for any $t \neq t_{fin}$: $\underline{W}(t,p_0)=0$

Definition 5.1   **well-formed block** [Valette 79]

Let (B,M) be a marked block. (B,M) is said to be well-formed if and only if

$(\underline{B},\underline{M})$ is live

$\underline{M}$ is the only marking of $[\underline{B},\underline{M}>$ such that $\underline{M}(p_0)>0$

t_{ini} is the only transition enabled at $\underline{M}$.

$M(p_0)=1$. Where $\underline{M}$ is the marking such that M is the restriction of $\underline{M}$ to P.

Let $N=<P,T,W>$ be a net and let M be a marking of N. Let $N'=<P',T',W'>$ be a block where t_{ini} and t_{fin} are the initial and the final transitions of N'. Let M' be a marking of N'.

Let $t_i \in T$, the substitution of t_i by the block N' is a net $N''=<P'',T'',W''>$ with:

$P''= P \cup P'$ (we have $P \cap P'=\emptyset$)

$T''=(T-\{t_i\}) \cup T'$ (we have $T \cap T'=\emptyset$)

M'' is the marking of N'' such that $M''(p)= \begin{cases} M(p) & \text{if } p \in P \\ M'(p) & \text{if } p \in P' \end{cases}$

$\Gamma''^+(x) \quad = \Gamma^+(x) \qquad\qquad\quad \text{if } x \in P \cup T \text{ and } t_i \notin \Gamma^+(x)$

$\qquad\qquad =\Gamma^+(x)-\{t_i\}\cup\{t_{ini}\} \quad \text{if } x \in P \cap \Gamma^-(t_i)$

$\qquad\qquad =\Gamma'^+(x) \qquad\qquad\quad \text{if } x \in P' \cup T'-\{t_{fin}\}$

$\Gamma''^+(t_{fin}) =\Gamma^+(t_{fin})\cup\Gamma^+(t_i).$

Valette's result of preservation is the following one :

Theorem 5.1   [Valette 79]

Let (N,M) be a marked net and let t_i be a transition of N such that $t_i t_i$ does not appear in any sequence enabled at M.

Let (N',M') be a well-formed block and (N",M") the result of the substitution of t_i by N'. the three following results hold :

(a) (N",M") is bounded if and only if (N,M) is bounded

(b) (N",M") is safe if and only if (N,M) is safe

(c) (N",M") is live if and only if (N,M) is live.

Definition 5.2   **composition via a well-formed block**

Let $N=<P,T,W>$ be a net. Let $\{P_1,P_2\}$ be a covering of P such that $P_B=P_1 \cap P_2$ and $(P_B,\Gamma(P_B))$ generates a well-formed block B. Let N_i be the subnet of R generated by $(P_i,\Gamma(P_i))$, let N'_i be the result of the substitution of B by $t_i \in T$ in N_i $(i \in \{1,2\})$. Let M be a marking of N and M'_i the restriction of M to P_i-P_B $(i \in \{1,2\})$. N is said to be the result of the composition of nets N1, N2 via the well-formed block B if and only if:

(1) t_{ini} and t_{fin} are the only nodes of this block connected with the rest of the net, with $\Gamma^+(t_{ini})\cup\Gamma^-(t_{fin})$ included in P_B

(2) $t_i t_i$ does not appear in any sequence enabled at M'_i (in N_i) $(i \in \{1,2\})$.

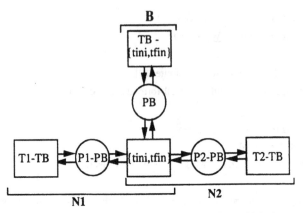

Figure 3 : Composition via a well-formed block

Theorem 5.2   **liveness preservation**

Let $N=<P,T,W>$ be the net obtained by composition of nets $N_1=<P_1,T_1,W_1>$, $N_2=<P_2,T_2,W_2>$ via a well-formed block $B=<P_B,T_B,V_B>$. Let N'_i be the result of the substitution of B by $t_i \in T$ in N_i ($i \in \{1,2\}$). Let M be a marking of N and M_i, M'_i the restrictions of M to P_i, $P_i\text{-}P_B$ respectively ($i \in \{1,2\}$). Then the three following properties are equivalent :

(a) (N,M) is live

(b) (N_1,M_1) and (N_2,M_2) are live

(c) (N'_1,M'_1) and (N'_2,M'_2) are live.

Proof

The proof is straightforward using corollary 4.1 and theorem 5.1.

Let N' be the net resulting of the substitution of the block generated by P_B by a transition t_i, M' the restriction of M to $P\text{-}P_B$. From theorem 5.1 : (N,M) is live iff (N',M') is live.

Then corollary 4.1 can be applied and therefore (R,M) is live iff (N'_1,M'_1) and (N'_2,M'_2) are live.

We apply theorem 5.1 to N'_1 and N'_2 and get the equivalence with the point (b) of our theorem.   ◆

VI   CONCLUSION

This paper presented a set of results on preservation of liveness and boundedness when composing nets.These compositions of nets have been described in two ways. First, in the construction step, we have viewed them as compositions using three subnets: two connected via the third one, the medium. Thus, we have focused on the medium and its structure. Secondly, in the analysis step, we have viewed them as compositions using two subnets which both include the medium (but in composition via shared places, where we took advantage of the elimination of the medium from both subnets). So we did not analyse three subnets but two, which is interesting, in the sense that, in general, the medium is very small with regard to the other subnets.

A comparison between our results and the works done on equivalences and abstractions have to be done within the context of lemma 4.1 and lemma 4.2. The link is based on languages inclusion and sub-markings equality.This kind of constraints has permitted to obtain results about properties preservation [André 83], [Pomello 88]. Our step is quite different in the sense that we want to derive nets structures which obey to this behavioural constraints, in the aim to optimize the verifications when composing nets. From another point of view we can say that, within the context of modularity, these first results on compositions nets and Baumgarten's ones [Baumgarten 88] are complementary, since Baumgarten focus on reusablity when we focus on construction and analysis.

We have to point out that all our schemes of composition from theorem 3.1 to theorem 5.2 allow us to create trees of components (connected via a sequential process, a rendez-vous or a well-formed block) or at most graphs without circuit (by using connections via shared places, theorem 3.1). A rule of connection creating a circuit between components and preseving liveness remains for us an unsolved problem.

The next step, for which we are working now, concerns the generalization of our rules of connecting nets to one general rule (see [Souissi 90a] and [Souissi 90b]). The idea is to derive from the less constrained hypothesis the more general structure of a medium of connection which should allows us to preserve properties by composition. This work will be done in the same time, with a more intensive exploration of the results in [André 83], [Fraisse 86], [Pomello 88], [Baumgarten 88], [Vogler 88] (see [Souissi 90a]).

We think that such modular validation methods can be easily extended to colored nets [Jensen 82] and fifo nets [Memmi...85]. Some First extensions to fifo nets can be found in [Souissi 90c].

Acknowledgements

We are sincerely grateful of the 4 anonymous referees for their useful remarks.

REFERENCES

[Allégre...86]   J.P.Allégre and N. Bobichon: "Etude de Réseaux de Petri par Décomposition." Projet de fin d'etude. E.N.S.T. Paris 1986.

[André 82]   C.André: "Use of The Behaviour Equivalence in Place-Transition Net Analysis." IFB 52, Springer (1982).

[André 83]   C.André: "The Behaviour of a Petri Net on a Subset of Transitions." RAIRO Autom. 17, pp 5-21 (1983).

[Baumgarten 88]   B.Baumgarten: "On Internal and External characterizations of PT-nets Building Block Behaviour." Advances in Petri nets, LNCS 340, pp 44-61, 1988.

[Berge 83]   C.Berge: "Graphes", Gauthiers-villars, Paris 1983.

[Berthelot 83]   G.Berthelot: "Transformations de Réseaux de Petri." T.S.I.,Vol. 4 n. 1,pp 91-101, Paris 1985.

[Berthelot 85]   G.Berthelot: "Transformations and Decompositions of Nets.", Advances in Petri Nets, LNCS 254, pp 359-376, 1986.

[BRAMS 83]   G.W.BRAMS: "Réseaux de Petri : Theorie et Pratique.", Masson, Paris, 1983.

[Commoner 72]   F.Commoner: "Deadlock in Petri Nets.", Applied Data Research Inc. Wakefiels
                 Mass. CA 7206-2311, 1972.

[Dagron...86]   N. Dagron and G. Memmi: "On the Composition of Live Subnets." FOR ME TOO
                 (BULL), Esprit project 283, Task DMC.ICPP1; march 1987.

[Fraisse 86]   P.Fraisse: "Longs Cycles dans les Graphes. Application aux Réseaux de Petri.",
                 thèse de docteur en sciences. Univeristé de Paris-sud. centre d'Orsay. 1986.

[Hack 72]   M.Hack: "Analysis of Production Schemata by Petri Nets." M.S. thesis, Dept.
                 Electrical Engineering. M.I.T. Cambridge Mass. Project MAC-TR 94, 1972.

[Jensen 82]   K. Jensen : "High Level Petri Nets". Proc. of the third European Workshop on
                 Application and Theory of Petri Nets.Varenne, Italy, June 1982.

[Memmi 78]   G. Memmi: "Fuites et Semi-flots dans les Réseaux de Petri.", thèse de
                 docteur-ingenieur. Paris VI, 1978.

[Memmi 83]   G.Memmi: "Methodes d'Analyse des Réseaux de Petri, Réseaux à Files et
                 Application aux Systèmes Temps Reels.",thèse d'état, Paris VI, 1983.

[Pomello 88]   L.Pomello: "Some Equivalence Notions for Concurrent Systems, An Overview".
                 G.Rozenberg (ed.): Advances in Petri Nets'85, LNCS 222, 1986.

[Reisig 82]   W.Reisig: "Deterministic Buffer Synchronisation of Sequential Processes.", Acta
                 Informatica 18, 1982.

[Reisig...83]   W. Reisig, G. Berthelot and G. Memmi: "A Control Structure for Sequential
                 Processes Synchronized by Buffers.", Proc. of the 4th European Work. on App. and
                 Th. of Petri nets, Toulouse, France 1983.

[Souissi...88]   Y.Souissi and N.Beldiceanu: "Deterministic Systems of Sequential Processes: Theory
                 and Tools.", Concurrency 88, LNCS 335, pp 380-400, Springer-Verlag.

[Souissi 90a]   Y. Souissi: "Préservation de Propriétés par Composition de Réseaux de Petri.
                 Extension aux Réseaux à Files et Application aux Protocoles de Communication"
                 Thèse de l'Université de Paris VI. February 1990.

[Souissi 90b]   Y. Souissi: " On Liveness Preservation by Composition of Nets via a Set of Places"
                 Proc. of the XIth Int. Conf. on Application and Theory of Petri Nets. Paris, June
                 1990.

[Souissi 90c]   Y. Souissi: " A Modular Approach for the Validation of Communication Protocols
                 Using Fifo Nets". Proc. of the Xth Int. Symposium on Protocol Specification Testing
                 and Verification. Ottawa, 13-15 June 1990.

[Suzuki...82]   I.Suzuki and T.Murata: "Stepwise Refinements of Transitions and Places.", IFB52,
                 C.Girault and W.Reisig (ed.), pp136-141, 1982.

[Valette 79]   R. Valette: "Analysis of Petri nets by Stepwise Refinements." J.C.S.S 18 pp 35-46,
                 1979.

[Vogler 88]   W.Vogler: "Failures Semantics and Deadlocking of Modular Petri Nets.MFCS 88,
                 LNCS 324.

αTrellis: A System for Writing and Browsing Petri-Net-Based Hypertext

P. David Stotts and Richard Furuta

Department of Computer Science and
Institute for Advanced Computer Studies
University of Maryland
College Park, MD 20742

ABSTRACT: We have developed a new model of hypertext in pilot studies. The traditional hypertext model resembles a directed graph, representing information fragments and the relationships that tie the fragments together. Our model, based on Petri nets, also represents the hypertext's *browsing semantics* (i.e., how the information is to be visited). The Petri net model is a generalization of traditional directed graph models. It permits development of browsing and authoring systems that can incorporate the analytical techniques that have been developed for Petri nets and also incorporate the user interface designs that have been developed for hypertext systems. The Petri net base also permits powerful specification of how the hypertext is to be browsed. New abilities include synchronization of simultaneous traversals of separate paths through a hypertext as well as of security/access control considerations into a hypertext (specifying nodes that can be proven accessible only to certain classes of browsers). In addition, different tailored versions can be generated from a single document structure in the Petri net-based model.

This report describes the Petri net-based *Trellis* model, a prototype hypertext implementation called *αTrellis*, and an early version of an authoring language for Petri net-based documents called *Alpha*.

Keywords: hypertext and hypermedia, browsing semantics, Trellis hypertext model hypertext

CONTENTS

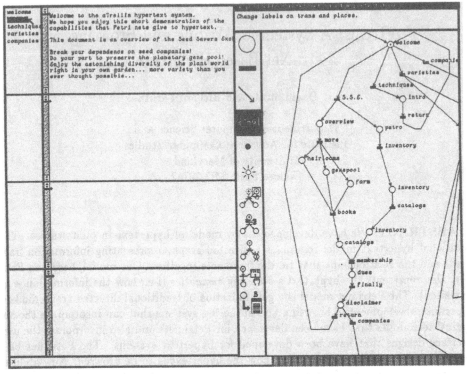

Figure 1: Initial αTrellis browsing screen.

1 Overview of hypertext

Hypertext is a structuring mechanism for information, one that is particularly well-suited for use on an interactive computer. Hypertext is not a new idea. Bush [3] is credited with the first proposal for such a system, which he called the "memex," in 1945. Brown University's HES [4] and Engelbart's NLS [10, 11] are early implementations of computer-based hypertext systems, dating from the late 1960's. Only in recent years have hypertext systems become widely available. Commercially-available systems such as Apple's Hyper-Card and Shneiderman's Hyperties [19] may be purchased for use on personal computers. Research systems such as Xerox's NoteCards [13] show the wide range of components that are useful in a hypertext and the different presentations that help make it more understandable.[1]

A hyperdocument is traditionally composed of information fragments (text, graphics, sound, video, etc.) and tangible relationships among these fragments. The traditional way to represent such a document is as a directed graph. Each information fragment is associated with a node in the graph, and the directed arcs naturally represent the relationships among nodes. A person *browsing* a hypertext traverses the graph and views (or hears) the information fragments as he visits nodes.

---

[1]We will not attempt to give a complete survey of the current state of the field. Two recent surveys are [7] and [2]. [22] presents a perspective on the history and development of the area.

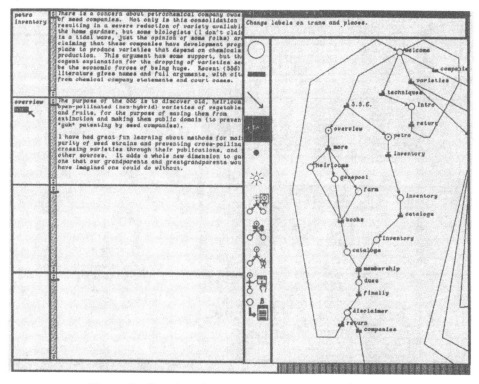

Figure 2: Creation of two concurrent browsing paths.

Some researchers, however, are beginning to realize the need for a more formal substructure for the highly implementation-defined field of hypertext; for example [9] and [12]. We are beginning to see projects that attempt to construct a more complete and descriptive mathematical basis for documents than directed graphs alone can provide. The resulting analytical frameworks will provide future solutions to the problems mentioned above that are endemic in current hypertext systems.

Our current work is based on one such mathematical framework—that provided by a Petri net. An advantage of our approach is that use of a Petri net is an incremental change to the commonly understood directed graph model, not a wholesale replacement of that model, and results developed for the directed graph model are easily adapted to our Petri net model. Unlike the directed graph model, the Petri net permits the specification of the hypertext's browsing semantics, as we will describe in more detail in the following section.

An earlier paper on this project [20] had as a goal to introduce Petri net formalism to the hypertext and electronic document processing communities. This paper has the opposite goal: to assume a working knowledge of Petri net theory and introduce the application we are making for it in the hypertext domain. In pursuit of this goal we have excluded many of the net theory definitions and expanded our discussion of hypertext and the issues related to it. Section 1.1 presents αTrellis, the hypertext browsing environment we have built based on our formalism. Following that, in Section 2 we present the

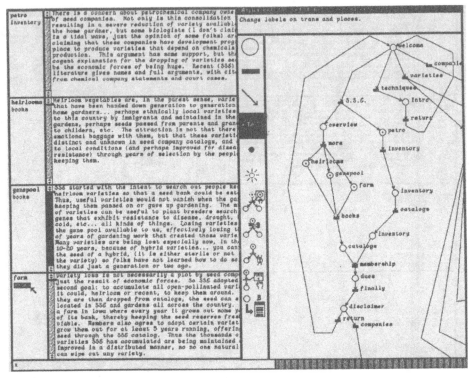

Figure 3: Synchronization of three simultaneous windows.

formal Petri net model of hypertext and some problem solutions possible with the model. Section 3 then introduces an authoring language called Alpha and discusses its utility in constructing and managing the complexity of Petri net-based hypertext documents. A discussion of useful extensions and further analysis, in section 4, completes the report.

1.1 Browsing semantics and the αTrellis system

With the increasing availability of hypertext systems has come a corresponding realization of the limitations of the current systems, particularly when dealing with large amounts of information. Two of the recognized problems in using hypertext systems [7] are *disorientation* (browsers of a hypertext can get lost within the structure, forgetting where they are and how they arrived there) and *cognitive overhead* (additional mental "effort" is required to maintain simultaneous traversals through a hypertext). We have been reexamining the underlying model on which hypertext systems are based to try and understand why these effects arise and to understand how they can be minimized. We believe that a contributing factor to the classical difficulties with disorientation and cognitive overhead has been the lack of a formal means for the author of a hypertext to express his ideas of how a document should be browsed. Our model provides this ability.

We have found that a common characteristic of existing hypertext representations is that they focus on describing the *relationships* that exist among the elements of the hypertext, and not the *browsing semantics* of the hypertext. By browsing semantics, we

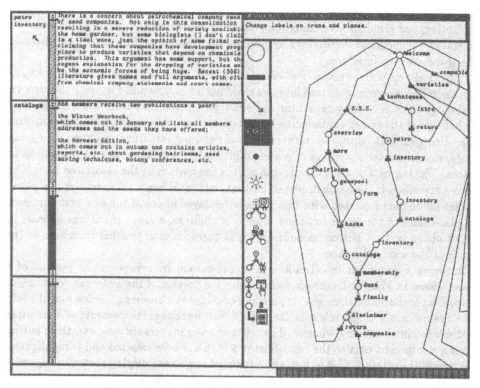

Figure 4: αTrellis display after synchronization.

mean a specification of the manner in which nodes are to be visited beyond that implied by the adjacencies defined by the arcs. Such specification of the browsing semantics of a hypertext might detail, for example, the number of nodes that may be seen at a given point in time, the number of windows that may be visible at a given point in time, and indeed the synchronization between simultaneous traversals of separate paths through the hypertext. In existing systems, specification of the browsing semantics of the hypertext has been implied by the behavior of the computer system that permits browsing of the hypertext, and is not directly incorporated into the representation of the hypertext.

To address these issues we have developed a Petri net based model of a hyperdocument. Petri nets not only naturally represent concurrent browsing paths, but as automata they also give an author some control over the experience a browser will have with his document. We have also constructed a prototype hypertext browsing and authoring environment called αTrellis based on this Petri net model. It presents a visible browsing environment in which many different elements may be viewed at a given point in time. While browsing, the user selects buttons, thereby causing the display to change to correspond to the change in the set of elements that are visible (i.e., the target elements become visible and the source element may no longer be visible). The current version of αTrellis operates on Sun-3 workstations under the Sunview window package. αTrellis is intended as an experimental platform and a proof-of-principle vehicle. As such, we have paid more attention to implementing the Petri net document representation with browsing semantics, and have not concerned ourselves for now with user interface issues like window placement, highlighting, and graphics. We are developing an expanded version called χTrellis for the workstation-independent X windows system that will incorporate a more realistic and state-of-the-art user interface.

αTrellis allows both construction and viewing of a Petri net hyperdocument. Physically, the αTrellis screen is divided into two main parts (as shown in Figures 1 through 4). On the right side is a Petri net editor and simulator, derived from Molloy's SPAN [17]. The left side of the screen contains the hypertext browser, subdivided into four text windows. Using the net editor, an author builds a Petri net structure and then, using tag strings, constructs the mappings of places to browsable text elements and transitions to buttons. The tag on a place is the name of a Unix file containing the associated text. The tag on a transition is the name displayed for that button. When a token resides in a place, the text in the file associated with that place is displayed in one of the four text windows. The place name in the upper left hand corner. In addition, a menu of buttons appears to the left of the text. A button name is displayed there for each enabled transition in the postset of the window's place.

Browsing a document in αTrellis is best understood by reviewing the portion of a session shown in Figures 1 through 4. In Figure 1 a portion of the Petri net structure of a document is shown on the right. It partially occludes the browsing windows on the left. Since the net has a single token in the place called welcome, the contents of that place are displayed in a browsing window. The token enables four transitions, and their button names are displayed next to the text. Button S.S.E has been selected and is highlighted. This causes transition S.S.E to fire, and produced the screen display shown in Figure 2. Here two parallel browsing paths have been initiated, and the reader has selected button more in window overview for further browsing. Figure 3 is the resulting display. There are now four concurrent windows, and selection of the highlighted button books will clear away three of them, as indicated by the structure of the accompanying Petri net. The resulting display is shown in Figure 4.

Note that transition (button) names do not appear in any browser window until they are enabled to fire. Note, for example, in Figure 4 that a button for transition membership does *not* appear in the window for place catalogs even though the place is marked. Further, note in Figure 3 that transition books is shown in the windows for all of its preset, that is the windows for places heirlooms, genepool, and farm.

Both the author and the reader can refer to the visual representation of the Petri net to get a graphical image of his location(s) in the document. Only an author is allowed to alter a document structure or directly place tokens in the net. Reading a hypertext is accomplished by simply executing the Petri net. Execution is controlled either (as is common in hypertext systems) by mouse selection of displayed buttons in the browser windows, or by direct firing of enabled transitions from the net editor.

2　The Petri net hypertext model

The formal model of hypertext that we propose is based primarily on a Petri net representation of a document's structure. We take advantage of the fact that Petri nets not only capture the descriptive power of directed graphs, known to be useful in hypertext systems, but provide as well a mathematically precise abstract machine for control and analysis of document "execution," or "browsing." For clarity in our discussion, we first provide a short set of definitions for the type of Petri nets we employ. Following them, we give the definitions for our hypertext model. The notation used throughout the paper is based on that in Reisig [18].

Definition 1 Petri net structure

A *Petri net structure* is a triple, $N = < S, T, F >$ in which

$S = \{s_1, \ldots, s_n\}$ is a finite set of *places* with $n \geq 0$,

$T = \{t_1, \ldots, t_m\}$ is a finite set of *transitions* with $m \geq 0$, and $S \cap T = \emptyset$,

$F \subseteq (S \times T) \cup (T \times S)$ is the *flow relation*, a mapping representing arcs between places and transitions.

The *preset* and *postset* of a node n are denoted by $\bullet n$ and $n \bullet$ respectively. In our model, we also have simplified the notation often used for Petri nets by assuming that the weight on each arc is 1, and that the token capacity of each place is ω. The standard definitions for *marking* and *net execution* otherwise apply, and the notation $M [t > M'$ is interpreted as *t fires from marking M to marking M'*.

Being a finite automaton, a Petri net has a dual mathematical nature. It can be viewed as generating (or representing) a formal language, and it can also be viewed as an abstract machine. From the formal language viewpoint, a Petri net describes a set of strings of symbols in which each symbol represents a transition in the net. From the automaton viewpoint, a Petri net is a state transition system in which the number of tokens in each place collectively constitutes the state of the abstract machine. Both views are of value to us when interpreting a Petri net in terms of a hypertext.

Definition 2 Hypertext

A *hypertext H* is a sextuple $H = < N, C, W, B, P_l, P_d >$ in which

N is a Petri net structure,

C is a set of document *contents*,

W is a set of *windows*,

B is a set of *buttons*,

P_l is a logical projection for the document,

P_d is a display projection for the document.

A hypertext consists of a Petri net representing the document's linked structure, several sets of human-consumable components (*contents*, *windows*, and *buttons*), and two collections of mappings, termed *projections*, between the Petri net, the human-consumables, and display mechanisms. A Petri net is a bipartite directed graph, and as such, is as capable of representing a linked hyperdocument as existing models using directed graphs alone.[2] An element of the set B of buttons is an action that causes the current display of a portion of a hypertext's contents to change in a specified way, as discussed later. An element of the set C of document contents can be almost anything: text, graphics, tables, bit maps, executable code, audio information, or, most importantly, another hypertext.

---

[2] Any directed graph has a simple representation as a Petri net; the bipartite nature of a Petri net is important for the execution semantics and does not restrict its structural modeling power. See Section 4.

Permitting the contents of a place to be another hypertext provides a natural hierarchy, which will be discussed at the conclusion of the paper.

Definition 3 Logical Projection

A *logical projection* of a hypertext is a triple $P_l = < C_l, W_l, B_l >$ in which

$$C_l : S \rightarrow C \cup \{\nu\}$$
$$W_l : S \rightarrow W \cup \{\nu\}$$
$$B_l : T \rightarrow B \cup \{\nu\}$$

A logical projection provides mappings from components of a Petri net to the human-consumable portions of a hypertext as mentioned above. The ν in the definition is a special item denoting a null value; it is used solely to make the functions total. The function C_l associates a *content* element with each place in the Petri net N. The function W_l associates a *logical window* with each place in N as well. The function B_l associates a *logical button* with each transition in N. Buttons can thus be thought of as names for the net transitions. A transition is designated for firing by the selection of its associated logical button.

Definition 4 Display Projection

A *display projection* of a hypertext is a pair $P_d = < W_d, B_d >$ in which

$$W_d : W \cup \{\nu\} \rightarrow Screen$$
$$B_d : B \cup \{\nu\} \rightarrow Screen$$

The intent of a display projection is to provide a link between the human-consumable components of a hypertext and the manner in which their presentation is done on a display device. The display function B_d associates a button $B_l(t)$ with a region on the screen (panel or subwindow), with a key on a keyboard, with a mouse button, or with some other device. It determines whether, for instance, buttons appear as separate menus next to text segments (as in the current αTrellis system) or as perhaps highlighted words actually in the text itself (as will be possible in the χTrellis system currently under development). Given place s, the function W_d associates the logical window $W_l(s)$ with the appropriate physical device for proper display of the contents $C_l(s)$; for example this may be a graphics window, a text scrollbar, an editor, or a sound generator. W_d could even specify that several logical windows appear overlapped on the same region of a display screen. We will not concern ourselves further with the display projection in this paper.

Definition 5 Marked Hypertext

A *marked hypertext* is a pair $H_M = < H, M >$ in which

H is a hypertext,

M is a marking for the Petri net N in H.

A marked hypertext can be thought of as representing the state of a hypertext during browsing. It is a characterization of the set of possible paths through a hypertext from a given point. A special case of marked hypertext, termed the *initial state*, is $H_{M_0} = < H, M_0 >$ where M_0 is an initial marking for the Petri net in H. Different browsing patterns can be enforced on a single hypertext simply by choosing appropriate initial states, as demonstrated in the section below on security restrictions. When a hypertext is first viewed, the node contents displayed correspond to the places that contain tokens in the initial net marking M_0; that is,

$$\{C_l(s_i) \mid M_0(s_i) > 0\}$$

is the set of elements displayed.

The execution semantics of a Petri net provides the model of browsing a marked hypertext. A token in a place s indicates that the contents of the place $C_l(s)$ are displayed for viewing (or editing, or some other interaction). When a token moves into a place, its image under C_l is mapped to the display device; likewise, when a token is removed from a place its contents are removed from the display. Tokens move through the net as transitions are fired. This is accomplished by selecting logical buttons in the display. When a transition t is enabled in the Petri net, the logical button $B_l(t)$ is visible in the window of *each* place in the preset of t. Browsing begins by starting execution of the Petri net in M_0. Browsing may terminate, depending on the structure of the hypertext, or it may cycle without end. If a state M of the Petri net is ever reached in which no transitions are enabled, then browsing ends, since no buttons are selectable at that point.

To summarize, a marked hypertext combines graphical structure with Petri net execution semantics to encapsulate all possible valid interactions that a reader may have with the document. During browsing, the current marking M of the Petri net determines which hypertext elements are viewable. The transitions enabled under M determine which buttons are visible (and hence selectable) in which windows. Selection of a button b by the reader fires the transition t where $B_l(t) = b$, thereby generating a new state M' where $M[t > M'$. The display changes appropriately to display only the windows that are visible in M'. Browsing formally terminates when no buttons are selectable.

Having a Petri net basis for hypertext allows one to apply well-known state-space analysis techniques to the solution of several interactive document problems. In the following sections we discuss several of these problems from the hypertext domain.

2.1 Display complexity

Using the reachability graph for the Petri net in a marked hypertext, we can determine some parameters of the physical presentation that cannot be determined from a directed graph alone. One such parameter is the maximum number of windows that will be required for any reading of the hypertext. Since the model associates a content $C_l(s)$ with each place s in the Petri net, and since we can assume that in most hypertexts each element of a simultaneous display will require a separate window, in any net state the number of marked places is the number of windows required to be simultaneously displayed.[3] We can then scan the reachability graph node by node and find the maximum number of marked places over all states. This information can be employed in a number of ways;

---

[3]The model, though, does not require the function W_d to be one-to-one; several elements could be mapped to the same physical window, but a clear interpretation of this is not obvious. We can imagine that two or more graphics elements might need to be overlain, perhaps for simulation of animation, with a single background and a succession of foreground images. In this situation, the number of physical windows required by a particular state can be found by counting the unique images produced by W_d for the marked places of the state.

for example, it can aid the determination of a reasonable layout for a display mechanism that, say, tiles a screen with windows.

2.2 Multiple paths and synchronization

As a computation model, Petri nets are recognized as an excellent means of representing and reasoning about parallel activities. As such, it is also a natural choice for representing concurrent multiple browsing paths in a hypertext. The advantage obtained over directed graphs alone is the author-directed synchronization of multiple traversals provided by the execution semantics of Petri nets. In traditional browsers for directed-graph-based documents, a reader often has the burden of managing multiple paths and the (perhaps) numerous windows resulting therefrom. This responsibility adds to the cognitive overhead often mentioned as a hypertext criticism. Petri nets provide an author with an elegant and succinct notation for not only the expression of parallel browsing paths but the synchronization and elimination of them as well. The browsing sequence shown in Figures 1 through 4 illustrate creation and synchronization of browsing concurrency.

2.3 Reachability and unreachability

As with directed graphs alone, the Petri net model can be used to determine if portions of a hypertext can actually be reached during browsing, or alternately, if portions can *never* be reached. This latter consideration forms the basis for a unique method of providing document security, as discussed in the following section. Given a hypertext H and an initial marking M_0, to determine if a particular element $C_l(s)$ can be viewed during browsing simply compute the reachability graph for the marked hypertext $< H, M_0 >$ (Definition 5) and scan the nodes looking for a state in which place s is marked. If no state exhibits such a marking, then the information cannot be viewed when the hypertext is browsed starting in state M_0. Similarly, we can determine if certain collections of information can be simultaneously viewed by looking for states containing sets of marked places.

Another characteristic of a hypertext that can be determined from the reachability graph is termination. If a state M exists in which no transitions are enabled, then there can be no next state M' from M, so the browsing session must terminate in M. Such terminal states appear in the reachability graph as leaves that are not duplicates of other nodes, i.e., nodes from which there are no out-arcs in the graph. If the author desires that a hypertext have no terminal states, then this property can be easily checked by scanning all nodes in the graph.

Similarly, an author may wish to verify that any terminal states in a browsing session are ones in which the screen is blank, i.e., all places are unmarked. Another state property that is reasonable to look for is that a browsing session can return to its initial state, thus making it cyclic. Any characterization one wishes to describe for a marking can be checked against the reachability graph in order to verify that a hypertext has or fails to have a particular property.

2.4 Browsing security

Unlike directed graphs alone, Petri nets can be used to enforce browsing restrictions on readers of a hypertext. In a directed graph model, if two paths share a common node, then no browser can be prevented from seeing any node past the common one by using the

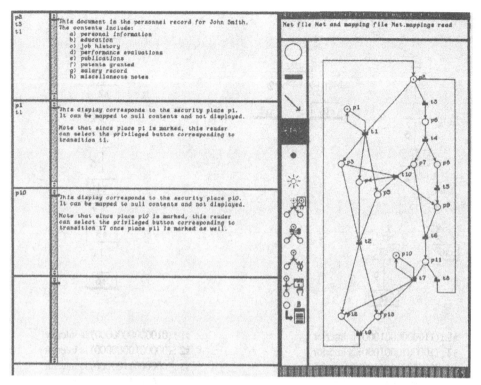

Figure 5: αTrellis display illustrating browsing security.

graph alone. An added mechanism like tagged arcs must be employed in order to provide access control. With a Petri net, however, browsing paths can share numerous common subsections and still have interspersed mutually exclusive sections as well. The restriction is again based on the idea of a marked hypertext. For a hypertext H, various classes U_i of users can be identified, depending on which portions of H the author desires to be visible to certain readers. Then each class can be given a different starting state $M_0^{U_i}$ for browsing H. Thus, each class U_i constitutes a separate marked hypertext $H_{M_i} = <H, M_0^{U_i}>$.

For example, consider a scenario in which an employment record will have two classes of reader: *privileged* (class P) and *restricted* (class R). Readers of class P can browse the entire document, but readers of class R may not see the sections containing, for example, job performance evaluations. The Petri net structure in Figure 5 illustrates this scenario. In this example, let places p_3 through p_5 have job evaluations as their images under mapping C_l; the net structure specifies that the three are to be displayed concurrently. Places p_{12} and p_{13} also contain privileged information, and their contents are to be displayed simultaneously after the evaluations have been read. The rest of the employment record (p_2, p_6 through p_9, and p_{11}) is unrestricted information. Places p_1 and p_{10} are special "security" places that serve to separate the classes of reader during browsing. On this document, readers of class P define a hypertext with initial Petri net marking $M_0^P = (1100000001000)$, whereas readers of class R define a hypertext with initial marking $M_0^R = (0100000000000)$. The initial marking shown in the figure is for class P.

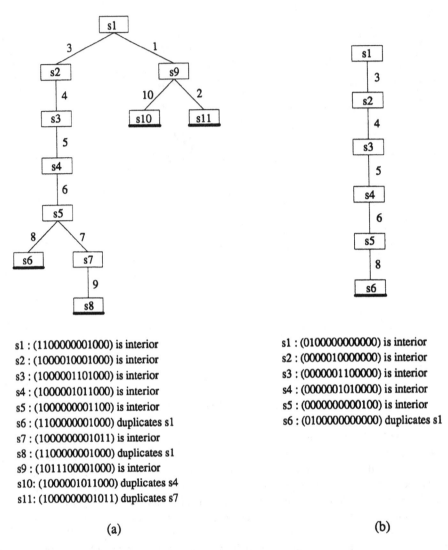

s1 : (1100000001000) is interior
s2 : (1000010001000) is interior
s3 : (1000001101000) is interior
s4 : (1000001011000) is interior
s5 : (1000000001100) is interior
s6 : (1100000001000) duplicates s1
s7 : (1000000001011) is interior
s8 : (1100000001000) duplicates s1
s9 : (1011100001000) is interior
s10: (1000001011000) duplicates s4
s11: (1000000001011) duplicates s7

(a)

s1 : (0100000000000) is interior
s2 : (0000010000000) is interior
s3 : (0000001100000) is interior
s4 : (0000001010000) is interior
s5 : (0000000000100) is interior
s6 : (0100000000000) duplicates s1

(b)

Figure 6: Reachability graph for Petri net in Figure 5

The reachability graph resulting from this marking is shown in Figure 6(a). Having a token in each of places p_1 and p_2 enables transition t_1. This in turn allows readers of class P to select a button $B_l(t_1)$ and thereby read the job performance evaluations. Readers of class R do not start with a token in the security place p_1, and a scan of the reachability graph for their initial hypertext state (shown in Figure 6(b)) shows that no token can ever be there. Since transition t_1 is never enabled for readers of class R, the evaluations can never be browsed.

Readers of class P can also choose to leave the restricted portion of the hypertext by selecting the button $B_l(t_{10})$ after reading the evaluations at places p_3 through p_5. The token in security place p_{10} allows them to re-enter the restricted section at a later point. Firing transition t_7 replaces this security token. Class R readers will never have a token in place p_{10}, so they will always be excluded from sections p_{12} and p_{13} of the hypertext (again see Figure 6(b)). Note that for both security places in this example, the net structure is such that firing the transitions they guard replaces their respective tokens.

2.5 Tailored versions of a hypertext

Tailored versions of a document are useful when the document is to contain information specific to each in a set of separate environments. Portions of the contents of the documents in a collection of such tailored versions are common to all of the versions and other portions are specific to one or to a subset of the documents. An example of a situation in which a tailored document set would be useful is to describe the invocation and use of a piece of software that runs on a number of different computers or operating systems. A similar situation is to support different user groups with different kinds of expertise (for example, a spreadsheet might be described for a user community that was expert in computer use or alternately for a group that was expert in accounting principles).

While each version could be maintained as a separate hypertext, a more attractive design is to take advantage of the commonality of structure and content in the collection of tailored versions, and to represent the collection as a single Petri net. The issue of representation and of specification of which of the alternate choices for content is appropriate is exactly the same issue discussed in the previous section on browsing security, and the same solution applies.

The reachability graph analyses needed to verify the correctness of specification for tailored versions may differ from those defined for browsing security. A property to be shown for tailored versions is that *exactly one* of a set of places is reachable (i.e., exactly one of the alternatives). A second property to be shown is that every place in a particular set is reachable (i.e., all alternatives associated with the same value for the condition that distinguishes environments from one another).

It is interesting to note that tailored versions of a hypertext may also be specified through modification to the function C_l. The mapping defined by C_l would be the same in all versions the common portions but would differ as appropriate for the alternative parts of the hypertext. This solution, however, would preclude the specification of a hypertext in which *all* alternatives were shown simultaneously—a specification that might be of use to an auditor verifying the appropriateness of the complete collection of tailorings.

3 The Alpha authoring language

αTrellis is a *browsing* environment. A complete system must also contain an *authoring* environment, and an important research topic is what the characteristics of this environment are to be. The details of how the contents of a node are to be specified can be adapted from existing interactive document preparation systems, but some of the special characteristics of the Petri net-based hypertext model deserve and require additional attention.

One issue is how to present the results from the analyses of the Petri net's structure in such a way that the author can use them. The first goal here is to identify and implement the most commonly-needed analyses. An additional goal, however, must be to

```
TITLE_PANEL {
    Space Shuttle Engine Diagram:
    The accompanying picture shows an external posterior view of the
    main engines used on the space shuttle. Many of the wires and
    supply lines have been excluded to simplify the presentation of the
    major subsystems. The diagram will remain visible as you browse the
    accompanying discussion of the individual components.
}
CLOSING_PANEL {
    Please log your session before leaving with the database editor in
    the other window. Information on other NASA projects can be found
    in the section entitled "Current Activities" in the main collection.
    Consult the article entitled "Help with Hypertext" for further
    assistance in using this system.
}
extern directional_control(), failure_detection();
extern throttle(), fuel_delivery();
engine_components ( p1 ) {--p1 specifies default initially visible elements
  cycle -> more {
    p1: 'Details are available on the follow subsystems:' ;
    set group -> options { --all choices are externally defined subnets
      p2: directional_control ( ) ;
      p3: failure_detection ( ) ;
      { p4: throttle ( ) ;
        p5: fuel_delivery ( ) ; }
} } }
extern engine_pic_1
extern in_flight_operation(), subsystem_details(), browser_log();
main shuttle_engines(g1) {--g1 specifies default initially visible elements
  set g1 -> t1 {            -- elements p1, p2, p3 are shown concurrently
    p1: engine_pic_1 ;      -- graphics in external file
    p2: TITLE_PANEL ;       -- named text definition from above
    p3: engine_components ( ) ;--invoke subnet with default initial marking
  }
  p5: in_flight_operation ( ) ;--invoke subnet with default init marking
  cycle -> again {
    p4: subsystem_details ( ) ;--subnet contents found in external file
    p8: 'Select "again" to rebrowse the details.' ;
  }
  set log -> done {
    p6: CLOSING_PANEL ;      -- named text definition from above
    p7: browser_log ( ) ;    -- external subnet, database editor
} }
```

Figure 7: A simple hypertext specification in Alpha

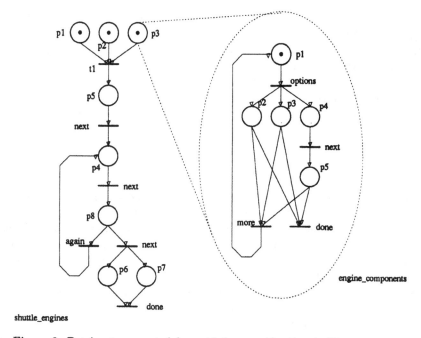

Figure 8: Petri net generated from Alphα specification in Figure 7

permit user-specified analyses of the reachability graph; a goal that requires development of user-invokable primitives for processing the tree.

Specifying a hypertext document is a form of programming. A second issue in Trellis is to determine what assistance can be provided in this programming process. It is clear that a Trellis hypertext can be *browsed* by someone with no knowledge of Petri nets or their semantics. Can similar *authoring* tools be developed? If not, to what degree can the use of Petri net templates be used to represent commonly-needed constructs, to thereby reduce the programming overhead.

An initial solution to this problem is a textual language we are designing called *Alphα*, or *Author Language for Petri-net-based Hypertext (α version)*. The author of a hypertext document will use Alphα to specify in a structured way a Petri net to represent his intentions, as well as associate text and graphics elements with the Petri net components. A textual language approach avoids some of the problems with graphical construction, namely complexity and size, while still allowing the power of a Petri net-based representation. The analogue we operate on is that Alphα does for Petri net authoring what structured programming did for assembly coding. Alphα specifications allow expression of only a subset of all Petri nets, but we are working to show that the subset is sufficient to express all useful hypertext document interactions. Again, the analogy is the same as the proof that for every possible unstructured computation, there is a structured program that will realize that computation.

The current version of Alphα allows specification of sets and sequences of hypertext elements, as well as browsing cycles. A simple Alphα program is shown in Figure 7. In this example, several different forms of hypertext entity appear. In-line text is specified with quoted strings, and will appear as the contents of a window when browsed. Similarly, larger text or graphics elements can either be defined in the program (e.g., TITLE_PANEL) or included from external files (e.g., engine_pic_1) with the "extern" directive. Subnets, that is, places with a hypertext as value instead of simply text or graphics, can be defined either explicitly (e.g., engine_components) or externally with the "extern" directive (e.g., directional_control). When a subnet is defined, the initially visible windows are specified by a list of place names in the header. When such a subnet is invoked, actual parameters may be given to override this default startup marking. The Petri net document structure generated from this Alpha program is shown in Figure 8.

4 Discussion and conclusions

The formalism we employ does not restrict current hypertext models; rather, it generalizes them. This claim is supported by the observation that any directed graph can be expressed as a Petri net by a simple transformation. The common model of the directed graph hypertext system is one in which a single element is visible at any time. The transformation to the Petri net model takes the directed graph that represents such a hypertext, makes each existing node a Petri net place, and inserts a Petri net transition on each arc. The browsing semantics under our model are then exactly as expected for the graph model. The resulting class of Petri nets is equivalent in recognition power to the class of deterministic finite automata.

In addition to translating hypertext documents from directed graph to Petri net form, we can also adopt many of the user interface techniques that have been developed for browsing directed graph hypertexts. The Petri net based model occupies the same position as does the directed graph model in a browsing tool. The results of empirical studies into visual aspects of a hypertext browsing system (see for example [19]) are relevant when applied to either model.

We also emphasize that the Petri net based hypertext model provides the author of a document with greater control over the sequences in which nodes will be browsed. Other researchers have found a similar need to permit this kind of specification (both within one document and among multiple documents [5, 6, 24, 25]). However, the Petri net model permits flexible specification of such sequencing, making it an integral part of the hypertext structure, rather than applying it in an *ad hoc* and external fashion. As such, we believe it provides a needed structuring facility to the author.

Other advantages of our Petri net based hypertext model are twofold. First, the Petri net representation is essentially graphical and consequently is only an incremental change from the common directed graph model of hypertext.[4] Second, Petri nets have been studied and analyzed for over twenty years, so an extensive theory exists that can be immediately applied to the hypertext domain. Indeed, useful extensions have been defined to Petri nets that will have direct application to hypertext as well. Three such extensions are deterministically timed Petri nets, hierarchical Petri nets, and colored Petri nets.

The incorporation of timing to the basic model makes possible hypertext documents such as timed exams and paced presentations. The inclusion can be accomplished with a

---

[4]Contrast the use of this graphically-based model with a non-graphical one such as Garg's, which is based in abstract algebra [12]. While the non-graphical models have certainly demonstrated their utility, the mental shift required to employ their results is significant.

deterministically timed Petri net [8, 21]. In such a model, an integer is associated with each place in the Petri net; it represents the number of time units (clock "ticks") that must pass before a token in the place can enable any of its output transitions to fire. In hypertext terms, the integer time on a place indicates the minimum amount of time that the contents of a place are displayed when a token arrives at the place. After the requisite number of ticks have passed, the token would participate in enabling transitions for firing, meaning either that selectable buttons would appear in display windows, or, if timing were to be strictly enforced, transitions would be fired automatically, thereby causing the displays to change.

In a hierarchical Petri net, a place can represent another Petri net. Our model already incorporates this notion of hierarchy—the contents of a place can be another hypertext rather than simply a text or graphics frame. Though a full formal semantics of hierarchical browsing has yet to be developed, we can describe the behavior informally. When a token arrives at a place that has a hypertext as its contents, a new browsing session begins layered on top of the current one. The marking of the current level is preserved, and the new level is started with its Petri net in the indicated initial marking. Browsing of the lower level document proceeds as under the definitions given here, except that any enabled transitions following the upper level place are always selectable along with the enabled transitions in the new level. Selecting an upper level button fires an upper level transition, thereby removing the upper level token and ending the lower level browsing session.

The uses for hierarchy are numerous. One obvious advantage is that each Petri net is independently analyzable. Many analysis algorithms for Petri nets are exponential in the size of the net, so a collection of smaller nets is preferable to one large net. Another advantage is that the hierarchy provides a form of abstraction. Browsing semantics can be set up so that the initial display of a lower level hypertext shows an overview of its contents. The detailed text can then be browsed for more information, or it can be skipped by moving on at the upper level.

Colored Petri nets [14] extend the classical model by associating colors with the tokens, the places, or perhaps the transitions of a net. A color is simply a method of distinguishing classes of elements that share the same structural category. The firing rule is altered to require some color property to hold in addition to having tokens in all input places for an enabled transition. For example, the rule may require all tokens being consumed by a transition to be of the same color, or to be all of the same color *and* to be the color of the transition. Color extensions increase the size of the state space that can be represented with a given net structure.

Several applications of colored Petri nets are of note in the hypertext domain. In one obvious extension, colored tokens permit multiple simultaneously-active asynchronous browsing sessions over a hypertext. It is not sufficient to permit additional sessions by simply adding (same-colored) tokens to the net as this could permit traversal of otherwise prohibited paths. Generating a new browsing session by replicating the initial marking with a previously-unused token color (or indeed by replicating the current marking in the previously-unused color) preserves the correctness of the net as tokens of differing colors do not interact. The issues surrounding the actual mapping of the separate browsing session to the display are outside of the scope of the paper, and indeed schemes such as Lifshitz and Shneiderman's [15, 16] could be adopted to provide this partitioning.

Another application for colored Petri nets is to permit definition of additional levels of granularity in security. KMS [1, page 832] has considered the case of hypertext nodes that are both readable and also modifiable by browsers (for example, to permit addition of notations and commentary). At issue is how to grant some browsers the right to modify while restricting others to reading only. One approach might be to encode the access rights in the token's color, and to generalize the logical and display projections, P_l and P_d, to associate the appropriate mappings with the specified color. Browsers receiving the appropriate color of marked hypertext would then be granted modification abilities.[5]

In summary, we have implemented αTrellis, a proof-of-principle prototype hypertext browser based on our model. We have used our experiences with this system to refine the model and to investigate the classes of problems solved by the model. Of equal importance to a complete hypertext system is the provision of an authoring environment. We have begun to design such an environment, and are paying particular attention to the ways in which the analyses permitted by the reachability graph can be made accessible to the author. As we have noted, such tools can use the reachability graph to prove that particular places can or cannot be viewed by a particular class of browser, to prove that execution of the Petri net exhibits certain temporal properties, and to give some notion of the resources that will be required to display the hypertext.

An important future project is the development of composition techniques to produce "well formed" documents, and the incorporation of these techniques into the authoring environment. One example is the heuristic mentioned earlier for constructing a hypertext with security classes. We envision an authoring language being used to structure meaningful hypertexts from meaningful Petri net fragments, much as control structures in modern programming languages alleviate the confusion of an unstructured assembly code program.[6] The authoring environment must provide tools for writing in this language, as well as the suite of analysis tools that aids the author in verifying that the hypertext will behave as expected.

The merging of hypertext and Petri nets is proving to be an advantageous combination. Much of the power of the model and corresponding implementation results from our ability to adopt already-established user interface techniques from the hypertext community and analytical techniques from the Petri net community. We believe that this formal model will allow the development of hypertexts that are not only general but also predictable in their behavior.

Acknowledgements

This material is based upon work supported by the National Science Foundation under Grant No. CCR–8810312. We wish to acknowledge the three referees for their comments.

---

[5]We note that this use of colored tokens is a special case of capability based addressing as defined in the HYDRA operating system [23]. The more general statement would be that we associate a capability with the token and that the actions carried out in the P_l and P_d mappings would be defined based on that capability.

[6]Van Dam makes a similar point in his call for identification of new flow of control kinds of hypertext constructs [22, page 894].

References

[1] Robert M. Akscyn, Donald L. McCracken, and Elise A. Yoder. KMS: A distributed hypermedia system for managing knowledge in organizations. *Communications of the ACM*, 31(7):820–835, July 1988.

[2] P. J. Brown. Hypertext: The way forward. In J. C. van Vliet, editor, *Document Manipulation and Typography*, pages 183–191. Cambridge University Press, April 1988. Proceedings of the International Conference on Electronic Publishing, Document Manipulation, and Typography, Nice (France), April 20–22, 1988.

[3] Vannevar Bush. As we may think. *The Atlantic Monthly*, 176(1):101–108, July 1945.

[4] Steven Carmody, Walter Gross, Theodor E. Nelson, David Rice, and Andries van Dam. A hypertext editing system for the /360. Technical report, Center for Computer and Information Sciences, Brown University, Providence, R.I., March 1969. Also contained in M. Faiman and J. Nievergelt, editors. *Pertinent Concepts in Computer Graphics*. University of Illinois, Urbana, Ill., March 1969, pp. 291–330.

[5] S. Christodoulakis, F. Ho, and M. Theodoridou. The multimedia object presentation manager of MINOS: A symmetric approach. In *Proceedings of ACM SIGMOD '86*, pages 295–310, May 1986. Washington, DC.

[6] S. Christodoulakis, M. Theodoridou, F. Ho, and M. Papa. Multimedia document presentation, information extraction, and document formation in MINOS: A model and a system. *ACM Transactions on Office Information Systems*, 4(4):345–383, October 1986.

[7] Jeff Conklin. Hypertext: An introduction and survey. *Computer*, 20(9):17–41, September 1987.

[8] James E. Coolahan and Nicholas Roussopoulos. A timed Petri net methodology for specifying real-time system timing requirements. In *Proceedings of the International Workshop on Timed Petri Nets*, pages 24–31, July 1985. Torino, Italy.

[9] Norman M. Delisle and Mayer D. Schwartz. Contexts—a partitioning concept for hypertext. *ACM Transactions on Office Information Systems*, 5(2):168–186, April 1987.

[10] Douglas C. Engelbart and William K. English. A research center for augmenting human intellect. *Proceedings, AFIPS Fall Joint Computer Conference*, 33:395–410, 1968.

[11] Douglas C. Engelbart, Richard W. Watson, and James C. Norton. The augmented knowledge workshop. ARC Journal Accession Number 14724, Stanford Research Center, Menlo Park, Calif., March 1973. Paper presented at the National Computer Conference, June 1973.

[12] Pankaj K. Garg. Abstraction mechanisms in hypertext. *Communications of the ACM*, 31(7):862–870, 879, July 1988.

[13] Frank G. Halasz. Reflections on NoteCards: Seven issues for the next generation of hypermedia systems. *Communications of the ACM*, 31(7):836–852, July 1988.

[14] K. Jensen. Coloured Petri nets and the invariant method. *Theoretical Computer Science*, 14:317–336, 1981.

[15] Kobi Lifshitz and Ben Shneiderman. Window control strategies for on-line text traversal, July 1987. Working paper.

[16] Gary Marchionini and Ben Shneiderman. Finding facts vs. browsing knowledge in hypertext systems. *Computer*, 21(1):70–80, January 1988.

[17] Michael K. Molloy. A CAD tool for stochastic Petri nets. In *Proceedings of the ACM-IEEE Fall Joint Computer Conference*, pages 1082–1091, November 1986.

[18] Wolfgang Reisig. *Petri Nets: An Introduction*. Springer-Verlag, 1985.

[19] Ben Shneiderman. User interface design for the Hyperties electronic encyclopedia. In *Proceedings of Hypertext '87*, pages 189–194, November 1987. Published by the Association for Computing Machinery, 1989.

[20] P. David Stotts and Richard Furuta. Adding browsing semantics to the hypertext model. In *Proceedings of ACM Conference on Document Processing Systems* (December 5–9, 1988, Santa Fe, New Mexico), pages 43–50. ACM, New York, December 1988. An earlier version of this paper is available as University of Maryland Department of Computer Science and Institute for Advanced Computer Studies Technical Report CS-TR-2046 and UMIACS-TR-88-43.

[21] P. D. Stotts, Jr. and T. W. Pratt. Hierarchical modeling of software systems with timed Petri nets. In *Proceedings of the International Workshop on Timed Petri Nets*, pages 32–39, July 1985. Torino, Italy.

[22] Andries van Dam. Hypertext '87 keynote address. *Communications of the ACM*, 31(7):887–895, July 1988.

[23] W. Wulf, E. Cohen, W. Corwin, A. Jones, R. Levin, C. Pierson, and F. Pollack. HYDRA: The kernel of a multiprocessor operating system. *Communications of the ACM*, 17(6):337–345, June 1974.

[24] Polle T. Zellweger. Directed paths through collections of multi-media documents. In *Hypertext '87*, November 1987. Position paper.

[25] Polle T. Zellweger. Active paths through multimedia documents. In J. C. van Vliet, editor, *Document Manipulation and Typography*, pages 19–34. Cambridge University Press, April 1988. Proceedings of the International Conference on Electronic Publishing, Document Manipulation, and Typography, Nice (France), April 20–22, 1988.

STUBBORN SETS FOR REDUCED STATE SPACE GENERATION

Antti Valmari

Technical Research Centre of Finland
Computer Technology Laboratory
PO Box 201, SF–90571 OULU
FINLAND
Tel. int. +358 81 509 111[1]

ABSTRACT   The "stubborn set" theory and method for generating reduced state spaces is presented. The theory takes advantage of concurrency, or more generally, of the lack of interaction between transitions, captured by the notion of stubborn sets. The basic method preserves all terminal states and the existence of nontermination. A more advanced version suited to the analysis of properties of reactive systems is developed. It is shown how the method can be used to detect violations of invariant properties. The method preserves the liveness (in Petri net sense) of transitions, and livelocks which cannot be exited. A modification of the method is given which preserves the language generated by the system. The theory is developed in an abstract variable/transition framework and adapted to elementary Petri nets, place/transition nets with infinite capacity of places, and coloured Petri nets.

Keywords   system verification, analysis of behaviour of nets

CONTENTS

---

1 The original version of this paper was written while the author was visiting Telecom Australia Research Laboratories, 770 Blackburn Road, Clayton, Victoria 3168, AUSTRALIA.

0. INTRODUCTION

Reachability analysis (or state space generation) is a widely used method for analysing concurrent systems, even though it has serious performance problems. Significant increases in the performance of state space generation would have great practical value. Unfortunately, the number of states of even moderate systems is often astronomical. As we cannot expect an astronomical number of states to be generated in a reasonable time no matter how fast an algorithm we have, it seems that the performance problems cannot be solved without reducing the number of states that are generated.

In this paper a theory is presented facilitating reduction of the number of states without modifying the answers of certain (many) analysis questions. The theory takes advantage of concurrency. Concurrency offers much potential for state space reduction, as demonstrated by the following example. The system of n non-interacting processes each executing k steps sequentially before stopping has $(k+1)^n$ states. This is exponential in the number of processes. It seems, however, intuitively clear that not all of those states are really needed. Since the processes do not interact, the end result of their execution is independent of their order of execution. Furthermore, all projections of the global state of the system to each of the processes are found if we execute the processes in any order. One might thus claim that sufficient information for the analysis of the system is achieved by simulating the processes in one arbitrarily chosen order. Simulation in one order generates only $nk+1$ states, which is linear in n and k.

The n-process example above is oversimplified, because it ignores the fact that processes do interact in practice. Two questions arise:

- How can we take advantage of situations where processes do not interact without losing the consequences of their interaction?

- What properties of the system under analysis are preserved during state space reduction?

The theory developed in this paper answers the first question through the notion of *stubborn sets*. Roughly speaking, a stubborn set is a set of transitions closed with respect to mutual interactions; all transitions interfering with the transitions in the set belong to the set. The notion is dynamic, that is, which sets are stubborn depends on the current state. In the stubborn set state space reduction method a stubborn set is computed at every state (strictly speaking, at every state with enabled transitions), and only the enabled transitions in it are used when next states are generated.

A partial answer to the second question will be given by a set of theorems, which guarantee that all terminal states (that is, states with no enabled transitions) and nontermination are preserved by the method. Furthermore, there is a version of the method which preserves livelocks (defined as unintended cyclic terminal strong components of the state space), liveness of transitions (in the Petri net sense of the word) and facilitates the detection of violations of invariant properties, expressed as fact transitions. The method can be adapted to preserve the language generated by a system, where a symbol is associated to some (but not necessarily all) transitions and transitions write their symbols when they occur.

The stubborn set method is applicable to several models of concurrency. The notion "stubborn set" captures interaction relationships between transitions. Different concurrency models express information about transition interactions in different (and sometimes non-transparent) ways, and there is often more than one way to utilise this information in the definition of stubborn sets. Therefore it is better not to tie the theory to a particular established formalism, but to develop it in a general framework, from which it can be easily adapted to other formalisms. We develop the theory in the framework of *variable/transition systems*, apply it to elementary and place/transition nets, and sketch two different applications to coloured Petri nets. As mentioned in the conclusions, the notion of variable/transition systems proved advantageous also when implementing the method.

The stubborn set theory was first introduced in [Valmari 88a], where the theory was developed directly for place/transition nets without capacity constraints. The paper also describes a linear algorithm for finding good (but not necessarily optimum) stubborn sets. The first attempt at developing the theory in a more general setting was [Valmari 88b], but the theory developed there is not well suited to Petri nets. The paper describes a quadratic algorithm for finding stubborn sets which produces optimum (in a certain sense) stubborn sets in many concurrency formalisms, including low level nets. Valmari's Ph.D. thesis [Valmari 88c] supplements the material in the papers mentioned and compares the stubborn set theory to some earlier attempts of utilising concurrency in state space reduction, including the classic static *virtual coarsening of atomic actions* (see [Pnueli 86]) and two methods by Overman [Overman 81]. [Valmari 89a] develops what is called in this paper the *weak* stubborn set theory of systems which are intended to terminate, and applies it to shared variable multi-process programs and elementary Petri nets.

The stubborn set method as developed in the above mentioned papers is suitable for analysing termination-oriented properties, that is, deadlocks, states corresponding to successful termination, and failure of termination. A certain kind of fairness problem (called *ignoring* in this paper) prevents the use of the method to analyse properties which are not directly related to termination. In this paper, after developing the basic stubborn set method, we present a solution to the ignoring problem. The solution renders possible the use of the stubborn set method to analyse liveness of transitions (in the Petri net sense of the word), livelocks, invariant properties (expressed as fact transitions) and the language generated by the system. To make the solution practical, an algorithm is described which can be embedded to reduced state space generation to ensure that ignoring is absent.

Another new result in this paper is the distinction of the *weak* and *strong* variants of the stubborn set theory. The weak theory generally leads to better state space reduction results. On the other hand, the implementation of the strong stubborn set theory is easier. For instance, the ignoring elimination algorithm given in this paper works with strong stubborn sets only.

This paper was originally published as a Petri Net Conference paper [Valmari 89b]. Changes were made to this version, most significantly the addition of Corollary 1.32 (livelock analysis) and Theorem 1.34 (language preservation). More recent development goes beyond this paper. There is now a stubborn set method which accepts a collection of linear temporal logic formulas (which are not allowed to use the "next state" operator), and preserves the truth values of them [Valmari 90]. There is also a version which preserves the "failure set semantics" [Brookes & 84] of systems.

Chapter 1 presents the theory in the variable/transition framework, and Chapter 2 demonstrates how it may be applied to Petri nets. A specific question of interest concerning Petri nets is how the stubborn set method relates to other Petri net state space reduction methods. Chapter 3 compares the stubborn set method to Jensen's equivalent marking method (see [Jensen 87]) with the aid of an example.

1. THEORY OF STUBBORN SETS

In this chapter we develop the stubborn set state space reduction method in the *variable/transition* system (*v/t-system*, for short) framework. V/T-systems resemble Petri nets, but the concepts of *token* and *place* have been replaced by the concept of *variable*. V/T-systems are defined in Section 1.1. The first key concept of the theory, namely the concept of *semi-stubborn* set of transitions is developed in Section 1.2. *Stubborn* sets are defined in Section 1.3. Section 1.4 gives the stubborn set reduced state space generation algorithm and shows that it preserves all terminal states and the existence of nontermination. Section 1.5 discusses the *ignoring* problem which arises when stubborn sets are used to analyse properties not directly related to termination, and shows how it can be avoided if the strong version of the stubborn set theory is used. In Section 1.6 we take advantage of the solution to the ignoring problem and discuss the verification of various properties not directly related to termination.

1.1 Variable/Transition Systems

1.1.1 Formal Definition of V/T-Systems

Variable/transition systems (v/t-systems) can be thought of as abstractions of shared variable multi-process programs, where the concept of the location of the control of a process has been deprived of its special significance and is replaced by an ordinary variable. People working in temporal logic use quite similar models (see e.g. [Manna & 81], [Pnueli 86]), and so do Back and Kurki-Suonio in their *joint action* research [Back & 87]. V/T-systems can also be thought of as abstractions of Petri nets, where places and tokens have been replaced by variables and their values (one should note, however, that the abstraction is valid for interleaving semantics only). The formal definition of v/t-systems is as follows.

Definition 1.1 A *variable/transition system* (*v/t-system*, for short) is a five-tuple $(V,T, type,next,ss_0)$, where

- V is a finite set of elements called *variables*
- T is a finite set of elements called *transitions*
- *type* is a function assigning a set called *type* to each variable, and
- the definition of *next* and ss_0 is deferred for a moment. $\square$

Variables may be interpreted as programming language variables, program counters, message queues, or Petri net places. The type of a variable is a set, the elements of which are called *values*. A type may be interpreted as the type of a programming language variable, as the set of locations in a process where its control may reside, as the set of message sequences that may be stored in a message queue, as the set of numbers denoting the number of tokens in a place/transition net place, as the set of multisets denoting the contents of a high level net place, or something else, depending on the intended interpretation of the variable. The interpretation of transitions will be discussed in a moment.

Without loss of generality we assume that V is ordered. We can now complete the definition of v/t-systems and define the concept of *state*.

Definition 1.1, continued

- The Cartesian product of the types of the variables is called the *set of syntactic states* and is denoted by $\mathbf{S}$. Elements of $\mathbf{S}$ are called *states*.
- *next*: $\mathbf{S} \times T \rightarrow \mathbf{S} \cup \{undefined\}$, where *undefined* is a symbol not in $\mathbf{S}$. That is, *next* is a partial function from states and transitions to states. *next* is called the *next state function*.
- $ss_0 \in \mathbf{S}$ is a distinguished state called the *initial state*. $\square$

Examples of states are the states of a concurrent program and the markings of a Petri net. The value of variable v at state s is denoted by $s(v)$. We denote the initial state by ss_0 instead of the perhaps more familiar s_0 since we want to use the latter symbol when sequences of states are discussed. The following definition gives the terms and notation associated with the occurrences of transitions.

Definition 1.2

- Transition t is *enabled* at state s, denoted by $en(s,t)$, if and only if $next(s,t) \neq undefined$. Otherwise t is *disabled*. The predicate "$next(s,t) \neq undefined$" is called the *enabling condition* of t.

- If $next(s,t) = s'$ where $s' \in S$, we say that t may *occur* at s resulting in s'. We also use the notation $s -t\rightarrow s'$. □

An occurrence of a transition changes the state of the system. Transitions can be interpreted as atomic actions in a shared variable multi-process program, or as transitions of a Petri net, etc. Some concepts related to occurrence sequences, and the reachability relation between states are defined as follows.

Definition 1.3 Let $n \geq 0$, $s, s', s_0, ..., s_n \in S$, and $t_1, ..., t_n \in T$.

- The sequence $\sigma = s_0 -t_1\rightarrow s_1 -t_2\rightarrow ... -t_n\rightarrow s_n$, where $s_{i-1} -t_i\rightarrow s_i$ for $i \in \{1,...,n\}$ is called an *occurrence sequence*. The *length* of σ is n and is denoted by $|\sigma|$. The *first state* and *last state* of σ are s_0 and s_n and are denoted by $fs(\sigma)$ and $ls(\sigma)$, respectively.

- $s \rightarrow s' \iff \exists t \in T: s -t\rightarrow s'$.

- s' is *reachable from* s, denoted by $s \rightarrow^* s'$, if and only if there is an occurrence sequence σ such that $fs(\sigma) = s$ and $ls(\sigma) = s'$. (That is, "$\rightarrow^*$" is the reflexive and transitive closure of "$\rightarrow$".) □

The initial state and the next state function of a v/t-system define a labelled directed graph in a natural way:

Definition 1.4 The labelled directed graph (W,E,T) where

- $W = \{s \in S \mid ss_0 \rightarrow^* s\}$
- $E = \{(s,t,s') \in W \times T \times W \mid s -t\rightarrow s'\}$

is called the *state space* of v/t-system $(V,T,type,next,ss_0)$. □

Assuming that two or more transitions cannot occur simultaneously, every possible finite or infinite execution of a v/t-system corresponds to a finite or infinite path in its state space. Execution models where only one transition can occur at a time are called *interleaving* models. The state space captures the interleaving semantics of v/t-systems.

We need to talk about the maximal strongly connected components (or strong components, for short) of the state space. Furthermore, we divide the strong components to terminal and nonterminal and to cyclic and acyclic ones.

Definition 1.5

- State s is a *terminal state*, if and only if no transition is enabled at s.

- $C \subseteq W$ is a *strong component*, if and only if there is $s \in C$ such that $C = \{s' \in W \mid s \rightarrow^* s' \wedge s' \rightarrow^* s\}$.

- Strong component C is *nonterminal*, if and only if $\exists s \in C: \exists s' \notin C: s \rightarrow s'$. Otherwise C is *terminal*.

- Strong component C is *cyclic*, if and only if $\exists (s,t,s') \in E: s \in C \wedge s' \in C$. Otherwise C is *acyclic*. □

An acyclic strong component contains exactly one state, but a cyclic one may contain one or more. Terminal states correspond to terminal acyclic strong components.

1.1.2 Connections of Variables and Transitions

So far we have not defined any notion of "connection" or "arc" between variables and transitions. That is, the next state function of a transition may be thought of as referring to every variable. In this section we define several notions that facilitate talking about different types of connections between variables and transitions, and help structure the next state function in a certain way.

The next definition assigns to each transition a test set, a write set, a read set and a connection set, the last one being the union of the other three. Informally, the test set is intended to represent the set of variables the transition refers to in its enabling condition. We do not, however, define it as *the* set of variables that the transition refers to in its enabling condition. Rather, we define it as a given set that must have a certain property; namely the property that if the variables in it assume equal values at two states, and the transition is enabled at one of the states, it is also enabled at the other. Clearly any set that has this property can be enlarged without violating the property. Therefore test sets can be defined in any convenient way, as long as they contain enough variables for the key property of test sets to be satisfied.

The reason for building this flexibility into the definition is that with shared variable multi-process programs it may be very difficult to compute the smallest possible legal test set. Consider a guarded programming language command with guard $(x \neq x)$. The guard is equivalent to **false**, so the reference to x in it is in a sense fake. It turns out that the empty set is a legal test set for the corresponding transition. However, it may be very difficult to distinguish between such fake references and true references. It is often easier to define that the test set is comprised of all variables appearing in the guard, plus the program counter of the process in question. This may lead to larger test sets than absolutely necessary, but promotes practicality.

Similar comments also hold for the write set and the read set. The write set of a transition is intended to contain (at least) the variables, the values of which the transition can modify when it occurs. That is, the values of variables outside the write set are not modified when the transition occurs. The read set is intended to contain (at least) the variables, the values of which are used by the transition when it determines the new values it assigns to (some) variables in its write set. To prevent the definition of the write set from interfering with the definition of the read set, the latter is made a bit complicated; it states that if a transition can occur in two states where the values of the variables in its read set agree, then for every variable the value of which is actually changed by either occurrence, the new value will be the same in both cases.

Definition 1.6 Let $(V, T, type, next, ss_0)$ be a v/t-system and let $t \in T$.

- $X \subseteq V$ has the *test set property* w.r.t. t if and only if for all states s and s':

  $$en(s,t) \wedge \forall v \in X: s'(v) = s(v) \implies en(s',t)$$

- $X \subseteq V$ has the *write set property* w.r.t. t if and only if for all states s and s':

  $$s -t \rightarrow s' \implies \forall v \notin X: s'(v) = s(v)$$

- $X \subseteq V$ has the *read set property* w.r.t. t if and only if for all states s_1, s'_1, s_2 and s'_2:

  $$s_1 -t \rightarrow s'_1 \wedge s_2 -t \rightarrow s'_2 \wedge \forall v \in X: s_1(v) = s_2(v) \implies$$
  $$\forall v \in V: s'_1(v) = s'_2(v) \vee (s'_1(v) = s_1(v) \wedge s'_2(v) = s_2(v)) \quad \square$$

From now on we assume that a unique *test set* of t satisfying the test set property is assigned to every transition t, and similarly a *write set* and a *read set*. The sets are denoted by $test(t)$, $wr(t)$ and $rd(t)$. We also define the *connection set* of t by $conn(t) = test(t) \cup wr(t) \cup rd(t)$.

The following definition allows us to look at the connections from the variables' point of view, and to talk about the connections of a set of variables or transitions.

Definition 1.7 Let v be a variable, $X \subseteq V$ or $X \subseteq T$, and $cset$ be any of $test, wr, rd$ and $conn$.

- $cset(v) = \{t \in T \mid v \in cset(t)\}$
- $cset(X) = \underset{x \in X}{\cup}\ cset(x)$ □

It is often the case that one can decide that a transition is disabled without knowing the values of all variables, or even the values of all the variables in its test set. For instance, a transition of a place/transition net is certainly disabled if it has an empty input place, independent of the markings of the other places. The stubborn set state space reduction theory takes advantage of this fact. This motivates the following definition.

Definition 1.8 Transition t is *enabled with respect to* a set of variables $U \subseteq V$ at state s, denoted by $en(s,t,U)$, if and only if

$$\exists\, s' \in \mathbf{S}:\ en(s',t) \wedge \forall\, v \in U:\ s'(v) = s(v)\ \square$$

The following properties of en are quite obvious:

$$\neg\, en(s,t,U) \Rightarrow \neg\, en(s,t)$$

$$en(s,t,U) \wedge U' \subseteq U \Rightarrow en(s,t,U')$$

$$en(s,t) \Leftrightarrow en(s,t,test(t)) \Leftrightarrow \forall\, U \subseteq V:\ en(s,t,U)$$

The stubborn set theory takes advantage of knowledge of transitions that can make a given transition enabled or disabled with respect to certain variables. In a place/transition net, for instance, assuming that there is an arc from place p to transition t but not vice versa, then only the transitions that increase the number of tokens in p can make t enabled with respect to $\{p\}$, and only the transitions that decrease the number of tokens in p can make t disabled with respect to $\{p\}$.

Definition 1.9 Let $t \in T$ and $U \subseteq V$.

- $X \subseteq wr(test(t))$ has the *write up set property* w.r.t. t and U if and only if for all states s and s' and transitions t':

$$s -t'\!\rightarrow s' \wedge \neg\, en(s,t,U) \wedge t' \notin X \Rightarrow \neg\, en(s',t,U)$$

- $X \subseteq wr(test(t))$ has the *write down set property* w.r.t. t and U if and only if for all states s and s' and transitions t':

$$s -t'\!\rightarrow s' \wedge en(s,t,U) \wedge t' \notin X \Rightarrow en(s',t,U)\ \square$$

The use of $wr(test(t))$ instead of the set of all transitions in Definition 1.9 is sound, because the transitions not in $wr(test(t))$ cannot make t enabled or disabled. From now on we assume that a unique *write up set* denoted by $wrup(t,U)$ and a unique *write down set* denoted by $wrdn(t,U)$ is attached to every $t \in T$ and $U \subseteq V$.

The final definition in this section is motivated by the fact that the enabling conditions of transitions can often be represented as conjunctions of conditions concerning small sets of variables. For instance, assuming that there are no capacity constraints, a place/transition net transition is enabled if and only if all its input places contain a sufficient number of tokens. This is the conjunction of the requirements that each individual place contains enough tokens.

Definition 1.10 Let $n \geq 1$. $\{V_1,...,V_n\}$ is a *separation* of the enabling condition of transition t, denoted by $sep(t;V_1,...,V_n)$, if and only if

- $V_1 \cup ... \cup V_n = test(t)$

- $V_i \cap V_j = \emptyset$ if $i \neq j$, and
- $\forall s \in \mathbf{S}: (en(s,t,V_1) \wedge \ldots \wedge en(s,t,V_n) \Rightarrow en(s,t))$ □

For simplicity, we will often talk of separations of transitions, when meaning separations of their enabling conditions. A separation always exists, because $sep(t;test(t))$ holds for every transition t. Because $en(s,t)$ implies $en(s,t,U)$ for every $U \subseteq V$, $sep(t;V_1,\ldots,V_n)$ implies

$$en(s,t,V_1) \wedge \ldots \wedge en(s,t,V_n) \Leftrightarrow en(s,t).$$

1.2 Semistubborn Sets of Transitions

A semistubborn set is a set of transitions satisfying a certain condition depending on the state. For the stubborn set state space reduction method to be practical, semistubborn sets should be defined statically, that is, in a way facilitating their computation using information about one state only. The following theorem plays a key role in the stubborn set theory, as it allows the permutation of occurrence sequences so that the permuted ones start with a transition belonging to a semistubborn set. It will make it possible to limit to a (certain kind of) semistubborn set when generating successors of the state. In this section we work backwards and define semistubborn sets so that the theorem can be proven.

Theorem 1.11 Let $T_s \subseteq T$ be semistubborn at state s_0, and let an occurrence sequence σ be given as below, where $t_1,\ldots,t_{n-1} \notin T_s$ and $t_n \in T_s$:

$$\sigma = s_0 - t_1 \rightarrow s_1 - t_2 \rightarrow \ldots - t_{n-1} \rightarrow s_{n-1} - t_n \rightarrow s_n$$

There is an occurrence sequence σ' as below, with the property that $s'_{n-1} = s_n$:

$$\sigma' = s_0 - t_n \rightarrow s'_0 - t_1 \rightarrow s'_1 - t_2 \rightarrow \ldots - t_{n-1} \rightarrow s'_{n-1}$$ □

Assuming that we are only interested in the states succeeding a future occurrence of a transition belonging to a semistubborn set, the theorem guarantees that we do not lose such states even if we restrict our attention to the semistubborn set when generating successors of the current state. The relation between σ and σ' can be illustrated graphically:

$$
\begin{array}{ccccccc}
s_0 & -t_1 \rightarrow & s_1 & -t_2 \rightarrow & \ldots & -t_{n-2} \rightarrow & s_{n-2} & -t_{n-1} \rightarrow & s_{n-1} \\
\downarrow t_n & & & & & & & & \downarrow t_n \\
s'_0 & -t_1 \rightarrow & s'_1 & -t_2 \rightarrow & \ldots & -t_{n-2} \rightarrow & s'_{n-2} & -t_{n-1} \rightarrow & s_n = s'_{n-1}
\end{array}
$$

We now proceed to define semistubborn sets such that Theorem 1.11 can be proven. To guarantee the existence of σ', we should establish three things:

(1) that t_n is enabled at s_0,

(2) that t_i is enabled at s'_{i-1} for $i = 1,\ldots,n-1$, and

(3) that $s'_{n-1} = s_n$ (the existence of s'_{n-1} is guaranteed by (1) and (2)).

Perhaps the most straightforward way to guarantee (1) would be to require that a semistubborn set contains only enabled transitions. It is the case, however, that to get a useful definition of semistubborn sets, we have to accept the presence of disabled transitions. Thus we should prevent a disabled transition from being the t_n of σ. This can be achieved by guaranteeing that a disabled transition cannot be enabled as a consequence of occurrences of transitions not belonging to T_s. The following condition is sufficient:

$$t \in T_s \wedge \neg en(s,t) \Rightarrow \exists U \subseteq V: \neg en(s,t,U) \wedge wrup(t,U) \subseteq T_s$$

That is, if t is disabled at s, there is a subset of variables U so that t is not enabled at s with respect to U, and all transitions that can make t enabled with respect to U belong to T_s. The condition guarantees that we have at least the following figure:

$$s_0 \xrightarrow{-t_1} s_1 \xrightarrow{-t_2} \ldots \xrightarrow{-t_{n-2}} s_{n-2} \xrightarrow{-t_{n-1}} s_{n-1}$$

$$\downarrow t_n \qquad\qquad\qquad\qquad\qquad\qquad \downarrow t_n$$

$$s'_0 \qquad\qquad\qquad\qquad\qquad\qquad s_n$$

As an intermediate step in establishing (2) and (3) we state a requirement guaranteeing that t_n is enabled at $s_1,\ldots,s_{n-2}$. It is sufficient to consider enabled transitions only since t_n is already guaranteed to be enabled at s_0. By the definition of σ, t_n is also enabled at s_{n-1}. There are two possibilities: we may either prevent an enabled transition from becoming disabled, or we may prevent it from becoming enabled again after becoming disabled. The following requirement is sufficient:

$$t \in T_s \wedge en(s,t) \implies \exists V_1,\ldots,V_m : sep(t;V_1,\ldots,V_m) \wedge$$
$$(\forall j=1,\ldots,m : wrdn(t,V_j) \subseteq T_s \vee wrup(t,V_j) \subseteq T_s)$$

That is, a separation of the enabling condition of t is given, and for each set V_j of the separation, either no transition outside T_s can make t disabled with respect to V_j, or no transition outside T_s can make t enabled with respect to V_j. Let $i \in \{0,\ldots,n-1\}$. In the former case $en(s_i,t_n,V_j)$ holds, because t_n is enabled at s_0. In the latter case, because $en(s_{n-1},t_n,V_j)$ is true, we conclude $en(s_i,t_n,V_j)$. Thus at s_i, t_n is enabled with respect to every set in its separation, which implies by the definition of separation that t_n is enabled. The figure now looks like this:

$$s_0 \xrightarrow{-t_1} s_1 \xrightarrow{-t_2} \ldots \xrightarrow{-t_{n-2}} s_{n-2} \xrightarrow{-t_{n-1}} s_{n-1}$$

$$\downarrow t_n \qquad \downarrow t_n \qquad \ldots \qquad \downarrow t_n \qquad \downarrow t_n$$

$$s'_0 \qquad s'_1 \qquad \ldots \qquad s'_{n-2} \qquad s_n$$

The final step is to require that the enabled transitions in a semistubborn set *accord left* the transitions not in the set in the sense of the following definition.

Definition 1.12 Transition t *accords left* transition t', denoted by $t \angle t'$, if and only if for every state s, s', s_1 and s'_1:

$$s \xrightarrow{-t} s' \wedge s \xrightarrow{-t'} s_1 \xrightarrow{-t} s'_1 \implies s' \xrightarrow{-t'} s'_1 \quad \square$$

This definition can be illustrated graphically:

$$
\begin{array}{ccc}
s \xrightarrow{-t'} s_1 & & s \xrightarrow{-t'} s_1 \\
\downarrow t \quad \downarrow t & \Rightarrow & \downarrow t \quad \downarrow t \\
s' \quad s'_1 & & s' \xrightarrow{-t'} s'_1
\end{array}
$$

The requirement $t \in T_s \wedge en(s,t) \implies \forall t' \notin T_s : t \angle t'$ completes the figure:

$$s_0 \xrightarrow{-t_1} s_1 \xrightarrow{-t_2} \ldots \xrightarrow{-t_{n-2}} s_{n-2} \xrightarrow{-t_{n-1}} s_{n-1}$$

$$\downarrow t_n \qquad \downarrow t_n \qquad \ldots \qquad \downarrow t_n \qquad \downarrow t_n$$

$$s'_0 \xrightarrow{-t_1} s'_1 \xrightarrow{-t_2} \ldots \xrightarrow{-t_{n-2}} s'_{n-2} \xrightarrow{-t_{n-1}} s_n$$

Putting the parts together, we have the following definition of semistubborn sets:

Definition 1.13 A set of transitions $T_s \subseteq T$ is *semistubborn* in *weak* sense at state s, if and only if for every $t \in T_s$

(1) $\neg\, en(s,t) \;\Rightarrow\; \exists\, U \subseteq V : \neg\, en(s,t,U) \wedge wrup(t,U) \subseteq T_s$

(2) $en(s,t) \;\Rightarrow\; \forall\, t' \notin T_s : t \angle t' \wedge \exists\, V_1,\ldots,V_m : sep(t;V_1,\ldots,V_m) \;\wedge$
$(\forall\, j=1,\ldots,m : wrdn(t,V_j) \subseteq T_s \vee wrup(t,V_j) \subseteq T_s)$ $\square$

In the derivation above, when ensuring that t_n is enabled at s_1 to s_{n-2}, we allowed an enabled transition belonging to a semistubborn set being disabled by the transitions not in the set, provided that it cannot be enabled again by them. When developing decision procedures for liveness etc. in Section 1.5 we will discuss an algorithm which has a stricter requirement, namely that an enabled transition belonging to a semistubborn set cannot be disabled by the transitions not in the set. Unfortunately, strengthening the requirement removes some possibilities of optimizing semistubborn sets, and is thereby likely to lead to larger semistubborn sets and less state space reduction. Therefore we have chosen to develop two versions of the stubborn set theory, weak (leading to better state space reduction results) and strong (easier to implement, decision procedures for more properties), leaving the tradeoff between them to the implementer of the stubborn set method. When we do not specify which theory is used, the discussion is valid for both.

In conclusion, the difference between the weak and the strong theory is that in the latter enabled transitions belonging to a semistubborn set cannot be disabled by transitions outside the set. We will show in a moment that in the strong theory the relation "$\angle$" can be replaced by a simpler, more symmetric relation "$\leftrightarrow$" which is defined as follows:

Definition 1.14 Transition t *accords with* transition t', denoted by $t \leftrightarrow t'$, if and only if for every state s, s' and s_1 there is a state s'_1 such that

$$s -t\rightarrow s' \wedge s -t'\rightarrow s_1 \;\Rightarrow\; s' -t'\rightarrow s'_1 \wedge s_1 -t\rightarrow s'_1 \quad \square$$

The definition is symmetric with respect to t and t'. A graphical illustration of the definition is:

$$
\begin{array}{ccc}
s -t'\rightarrow s_1 & & s -t'\rightarrow s_1 \\
| & & | \quad\quad | \\
t & \Rightarrow & t \quad\quad t \\
\downarrow & & \downarrow \quad\quad \downarrow \\
s' & & s' -t'\rightarrow s'_1
\end{array}
$$

According with is equivalent to the conjunction of according left and the requirement that t' cannot disable t. Therefore, in the strong theory it can replace according left in part (2) of the definition of semistubborn sets. The requirement that enabled transitions in a semistubborn set cannot be disabled by transitions not in the set is then automatically satisfied. The resulting strong definition of semistubborn sets is:

Definition 1.15 A set of transitions $T_s \subseteq T$ is *semistubborn* in *strong* sense at state s, if and only if for every $t \in T_s$

(1) $\neg\, en(s,t) \;\Rightarrow\; \exists\, U \subseteq V : \neg\, en(s,t,U) \wedge wrup(t,U) \subseteq T_s$

(2) $en(s,t) \;\Rightarrow\; \forall\, t' \notin T_s : t \leftrightarrow t'$ $\square$

Although Definitions 1.13 and 1.15 are not equivalent, Theorem 1.11 is valid independent of which one is used.

Semistubborn sets remain semistubborn when transitions outside them occur, thus justifying the name *stubborn*:

Theorem 1.16 If T_s is semistubborn at state s and $s -t'\rightarrow s'$, where $t' \notin T_s$, then T_s is semistubborn at s'. $\square$

Proof Let $t \in T_s$. If t is disabled at s, (1) of Definition 1.13 or 1.15 is valid and remains valid for t when t' occurs. If t is enabled at s and remains enabled when t' occurs, then (2) remains valid for t in both theories, as the right hand side of (2) is independent of the state. In the strong theory t cannot be disabled by the occurrence of t'. In the weak theory (Definition 1.13), if t is disabled by the occurrence of t', then by (2) at s' there is V_j such that $\neg en(s',t,V_j)$ and $wrup(t,V_j) \subseteq T_s$. Therefore (1) holds for t at s'. $\square$

In both theories, at every state, there are at least two semistubborn sets of transitions, namely the empty set, and the set of all transitions T.

1.3 Stubborn Sets of Transitions

Theorem 1.11 allows the permutation of execution sequences in a certain way, provided that a transition belonging to a semistubborn set is going to occur in the future. However, there is no guarantee of such an occurrence. Quite the contrary: the empty set is always semistubborn. In this section the definition of semistubborn sets is augmented by a requirement which guarantees that there is an enabled transition in the set at least until a transition belonging to the set occurs.

Definition 1.17 A set of transitions $T_s \subseteq T$ is *stubborn* in *weak* sense at state s, if and only if T_s is semistubborn in weak sense at s, and there is a transition $t \in T_s$ such that

$$en(s,t) \wedge wrdn(t,test(t)) \subseteq T_s$$

Transitions with the above property are called *key transitions*. $\square$

In the strong theory the definition of stubborn sets is simpler, because transitions outside a strong semistubborn set cannot disable transitions in the set.

Definition 1.18 A set of transitions $T_s \subseteq T$ is *stubborn* in *strong* sense at state s, if and only if T_s is semistubborn in strong sense at s, and T_s contains an enabled transition. Enabled transitions in T_s are called *key transitions*. $\square$

According to the definitions, in both theories, a stubborn set contains at least one key transition, and key transitions are enabled, remain enabled and retain the key transition property at least until a transition belonging to the stubborn set occurs. Adding Theorem 1.16 to this gives the following result:

Theorem 1.19 If T_s is stubborn at state s and $s -t'\rightarrow s'$, where $t' \notin T_s$, then T_s is stubborn at s'. $\square$

At every state at least T is semistubborn, and the key transition property is trivially satisfied for every enabled transition if $T_s = T$. Therefore:

Theorem 1.20 There are no stubborn sets if there are no enabled transitions. At least T is stubborn if there is an enabled transition. $\square$

1.4 Reduced State Space Generation

In ordinary state space generation, for every encountered state all the transitions which are enabled in it are found and used to generate the immediate successors of the state. The act of doing this is sometimes called *expanding* the state. Expanding a state without enabled transitions amounts to doing nothing, so we limit the consideration to states with enabled transitions.

Algorithm 1.21 *Reduced state space generation* is the following modification of state space generation. When expanding a state with enabled transitions, instead of using all enabled transitions for generating immediate successor states, a stubborn set is found and only the enabled transitions in it are used. $\square$

Because the set of all transitions, T, is stubborn if and only if there is an enabled transition, ordinary state space generation is a special case of reduced state space generation. However, always using T as the stubborn set leads to no reduction in the size of the state space. The intention is to use stubborn sets which contain less enabled transitions than T. This is often possible, as there are often many stubborn sets in a state.

Perhaps surprisingly, always choosing the stubborn set with as few enabled transitions as possible does not necessarily lead to maximal state space reduction results, as shown in [Valmari 88c]. It is not entirely clear what is the best way of choosing stubborn sets. Furthermore, we will encounter decision procedures which state some constraints to stubborn set selection. Fortunately, as long as the constraints are obeyed, the stubborn set selection does not affect the correctness of the analysis results. It affects only the amount of state space reduction achievable. This leaves the implementer of reduced state space generation room to choose the (constrained) stubborn sets in whatever convenient way, making a tradeoff between better reduction results and the ease of implementation. [Valmari 88a,b] contain a linear algorithm which produces "good" strong stubborn sets. In this paper we do not go further into the details of stubborn set selection, but in the (temporary?) absence of better sources refer to [Valmari 88a,b,c].

The notation used in the context of the *reduced state spaces* resulting from reduced state space generation is given below.

Definition 1.22 Let a rule be given specifying a unique stubborn set T_s for each $s \in \mathbf{S}$.

- t is *stubborn-enabled* at s, denoted by $\underline{en}(s,t)$, if and only if $en(s,t)$ and $t \in T_s$.
- $s -t\underline{\rightarrow} s'$ if and only if $s -t\rightarrow s'$ and $t \in T_s$.
- $s \underline{\rightarrow} s' \Leftrightarrow \exists t \in T_s: s -t\rightarrow s'$.
- $s -\text{key}\rightarrow s' \Leftrightarrow \exists t \in T_s: s -t\rightarrow s'$ and t is a key transition of T_s.
- "$\underline{\rightarrow}*$" is the reflexive and transitive closure of "$\underline{\rightarrow}$". "$-\text{key}\rightarrow*$" is the reflexive and transitive closure of "$-\text{key}\rightarrow$".
- The *reduced state space* is the labelled directed graph $(\underline{W},\underline{E},T)$, where

$$\underline{W} = \{s \in \mathbf{S} \mid ss_0 \underline{\rightarrow}* s\}$$
$$\underline{E} = \{(s,t,s') \in \underline{W} \times T \times \underline{W} \mid s -t\underline{\rightarrow} s' \}$$

- The *key space* is the labelled directed graph $(\underline{W},E_K,T)$, where

$$E_K = \{(s,t,s') \in \underline{W} \times T \times \underline{W} \mid s -t\underline{\rightarrow} s' \wedge t \text{ is a key transition of } T_s \} \quad \square$$

The key space is a subset of the reduced state space which, in turn, is a subset of the ordinary state space in the sense that $\underline{W} \subseteq W$ and $E_K \subseteq \underline{E} \subseteq E$. In the strong theory all enabled transitions belonging to a stubborn set are its key transitions, and the key space is thus the same as the reduced state space.

The correctness of systems which are intended to terminate is often defined as consisting of two components: the system must terminate, and it must produce the right results upon termination. If the results produced by the system are considered as part of its state, then the latter requirement reduces to the requirement that the state of the system upon termination must satisfy certain properties. For instance, if we are analysing a protocol and request for one message transmission only, we expect the protocol to terminate, and we expect to see the transmitted message being available at the receiver side upon termination.

The following two theorems show that the stubborn set method preserves all terminal states, and the possibility of nontermination. Furthermore, for every occurrence sequence leading to termination, the stubborn set method preserves a sequence which is a permutation of the former. In this sense the stubborn set method preserves everything essential regarding the verification of systems which are intended to terminate. The theorems are valid in both the strong and the weak theory, and they are independent of how stubborn sets are found.

Theorem 1.23

(1) If $s \in W$ and s is a terminal state, then $s \in \underline{W}$ and s is a terminal state of $\underline{W}$. Furthermore, if σ is an occurrence sequence from ss_0 to s, then the reduced state space contains a permutation of σ leading from ss_0 to s.

(2) If s is a terminal state of $\underline{W}$, then $s \in W$ and s is a terminal state (of W). $\square$

Proof (1) Let σ be an occurrence sequence from ss_0 to s. For $i = 0$ to $|\sigma|$ we construct s_i, $\underline{\sigma}_i$ and σ_i such that $fs(\underline{\sigma}_i) = ss_0$, $ls(\underline{\sigma}_i) = s_i = fs(\sigma_i)$, $ls(\sigma_i) = s$, $\underline{\sigma}_i$ belongs to the reduced state space, $|\underline{\sigma}_i| = i$ and $|\sigma_i| = |\sigma| - i$. Choose $s_0 = ss_0$, $\sigma_0 = \sigma$ and $\underline{\sigma}_0$ is the empty occurrence sequence starting at s_0. Now let $i > 0$. Because $|\sigma_{i-1}| > 0$, s_{i-1} has an enabled transition. Let T_{i-1} be the stubborn set used at s_{i-1}. By Theorem 1.20 T_{i-1} is not stubborn in s. By Theorem 1.19 σ_{i-1} contains at least one occurrence of a transition in T_{i-1}. Let t_i be the transition corresponding to the first such occurrence. By Theorem 1.11 there are s_i and σ_i such that $s_{i-1} - t_i \rightarrow s_i$, $fs(\sigma_i) = s_i$, $ls(\sigma_i) = s$, and $|\sigma_i| = |\sigma_{i-1}| - 1$. Because $t_i \in T_{i-1}$, $s_i \in \underline{W}$. $\underline{\sigma}_i$ is $\underline{\sigma}_{i-1}$ with the occurrence of t_i added to its end. $\underline{\sigma}_{|\sigma|}$ is a permutation of σ belonging to the reduced state space and leading from ss_0 to s. That s is a terminal state of $\underline{W}$ follows from $\underline{E} \subseteq E$.

(2) $s \in W$ because $\underline{W} \subseteq W$. s is terminal in W because otherwise Algorithm 1.21 would have chosen a stubborn set T_s at s and T_s contains an enabled transition by Definitions 1.17 and 1.18. $\square$

Theorem 1.24 There is an infinite occurrence sequence in the reduced state space if and only if there is an infinite occurrence sequence in the ordinary state space. $\square$

Proof The "only if" part is obvious, as $\underline{W} \subseteq W$ and $\underline{E} \subseteq E$. To prove the "if" part we construct for arbitrary n an occurrence sequence of length n belonging to the reduced state space using an argument resembling the one used in the proof of the previous theorem. Because T is finite, König's Lemma (see e.g. [Reisig 85] p. 141) gives then an infinite occurrence sequence in the reduced state space.

If there is an infinite occurrence sequence, then there is an infinite occurrence sequence starting at ss_0. Let σ be a prefix of such a sequence such that $|\sigma| = n$. Let s_i, $\underline{\sigma}_i$, σ_i and T_i be defined as in the proof of the previous theorem, with the exception that now $|\sigma_i| \geq |\sigma| - i$ and s is not defined. The difference to the proof of the previous theorem arises from the fact that there is now no guarantee that a transition belonging to T_{i-1} occurs in σ_{i-1}. In such a case, let t_i be a key transition of T_{i-1}. By the definition of key transitions, t_i is enabled at the end state of σ_{i-1}. Let σ'_{i-1} be σ_{i-1} with the occurrence of t_i added to its end. If a transition belonging to T_{i-1} does occur in σ_{i-1}, let $\sigma'_{i-1} = \sigma_{i-1}$. Theorem 1.11 can now be applied to σ'_{i-1}, and the proof continues as before. $\square$

1.5 The "Ignoring" Problem

In the previous section we showed that the stubborn set method preserves sufficient information for the verification of systems which are intended to terminate. However, it is often the case that the system under analysis is not intended to terminate. Such a system is sometimes called a *reactive system*. Theorems 1.23 and 1.24 are of course valid for reactive systems, too, guaranteeing among other things that all deadlocks (that is, unintended terminal states) are preserved by the stubborn set method. On the other hand, there are important properties which are not preserved by the stubborn set method as presented so far.

In the proof of Theorem 1.24 we constructed from a given occurrence sequence an occurrence sequence belonging to the reduced state space. Each construction step consumed either one or zero transition occurrences from the original sequence in the sense of moving it from σ_{i-1} to $\underline{\sigma}_i$. The no consumption case arose when a key transition was added towards the end of σ_{i-1}, because then the key transition was the only one belonging to both T_{i-1} and σ'_{i-1}, and was consequently the one moved to $\underline{\sigma}_i$. Assuming that key transitions are added only a finite number of times, the reduced state space contains a permutation of some finite extension of the original occurrence sequence. There is, however, no guarantee that key transitions may be added in a way that leads to an end. If the adding of key transitions never ends, the first unconsumed transition of the original sequence is *ignored* in the sense of the following definition.

Definition 1.25 Transition t is *ignored in state* s, if and only if $en(s,t)$ and $\forall\ s' \in \mathbf{S}$: (s –key→* $s' \Rightarrow \neg\ \underline{en}(s',t)$). t is *ignored*, if it is ignored in some $s \in \underline{W}$. $\square$

Ignoring may limit seriously the coverage of the stubborn set method. For instance, if the system under analysis contains one process running in a loop and not interacting with the rest of the system, the stubborn set method may traverse once around the loop and then stop, leaving most of the behaviour of the system uninvestigated. This is cunning behaviour if one is interested in terminal states only, because the existence of such a loop guarantees that there are no terminal states. On the other hand, it is very undesirable behaviour when analysing reactive systems. In the remainder of this section we develop algorithms for detecting and eliminating ignoring. In Section 1.6 we show that many important system properties can be decided using the reduced state space when ignoring has been eliminated.

Assume t is ignored at s and t_k is a key transition at s. By Definitions 1.17 and 1.18 t_k remains enabled when t occurs. Then by the definitions of according left and according with t remains enabled when t_k occurs. As a consequence, t is ignored in the resulting state, too. Repeating the argument reveals that t is enabled and ignored in every state reachable from s in the key space. If the key space is finite, which is the case at least if the ordinary state space is finite, then it must contain a terminal strong component C such that t is enabled but not stubborn-enabled at its every state. Let $s \in C$. Because t is enabled at s there is a stubborn set at s. Thus s has a child in the key space and C is cyclic. On the other hand, if the key space contains a terminal strong component such that t is enabled at one of its states but not stubborn-enabled at any of its states, then t is obviously ignored in s. This gives the following theorem, and a corresponding algorithm for detecting ignoring.

Theorem 1.26 Assume the state space of the system is finite. Transition t is ignored if and only if the key space contains a terminal strong component C such that $\exists\ s \in C$: $en(s,t)\ \wedge\ \forall\ s \in C$: $\neg\ \underline{en}(s,t)$. If C exists, it is cyclic, and t is enabled in its every state. $\square$

Algorithm 1.27 Assume the state space of the system is finite. Find the terminal strong components of the key space. For each of them, choose an arbitrary state and compute the set of transitions enabled in it. Subtract from this the set of all transitions which are stubborn-enabled in the component; this set is easily obtainable as it is the set of the transitions labelling the edges of the strong component. The union of the results of the subtractions for each terminal strong component is the set of ignored transitions. $\square$

Strong components can be found in time linear in the number of states and edges in the key space using Tarjan's algorithm, described in [Aho & 74 Chapter 5]. Recognizing the terminal strong components is not difficult, because Tarjan's algorithm finds the strong components in depth first order. Tarjan's algorithm produces the set of states of each strong component, making it easy to compute the set of transitions labelling the output edges of the states. Therefore ignoring can be detected very cheaply, in linear time in the size of the reduced state space.

Detecting ignoring gives information about the coverage of the analysis and makes it possible to repeat the analysis with a modified stubborn set find algorithm, thereby forcing different branches of the state space to be investigated. However, this falls short from what we wish to achieve. In the strong theory of stubborn sets the key space is the same as the reduced state space. Together with some nice properties of Tarjan's algorithm, this fact enables cheap detection and remedy of ignoring at analysis time, leading to a reduced state space where ignoring does not occur.

Algorithm 1.28 Assume the state space of the system is finite, and the strong stubborn set definition is used. Generate the reduced state space in depth-first order and apply Tarjan's algorithm along with the generation. Attach an initially empty set of transitions T_x to each state generated. Tarjan's algorithm's stack of found nodes not belonging to a completed strong component will get extra short cut links as described below; therefore we rename it *T-list*. These links are used only for ignoring detection, and affect Tarjan's algorithm in no way.

Whenever a terminal strong component C is found, compute T_u, the set of transitions used in it as shown soon. Let s_c denote the current state, and T_e the set of enabled transitions in s_c. There are ignored transitions in the current branch of the reduced state space if and only if $T_e - T_u \neq \emptyset$. Mark the component ready as required by Tarjan's algorithm and backtrack from it only if there are no ignored transitions. If there are ignored transitions, add T_u to the T_x of s_c, and create a short cut link from the current top of the T-list to s_c (note that the states belonging to C are the states above and including s_c in the T-list). Then choose a new stubborn set such that at least one of its key transitions is ignored, that is, in $T_e - T_u$, and continue depth-first analysis.

The set of used transitions is computed by traversing the T-list from top to and including s_c, using short cut links where available. During the traversal, for states not adjacent to a short cut link, add their sets of stubborn-enabled transitions to T_u. For states adjacent to the tail but not to the head of a short cut link add nothing to T_u, and for states adjacent to the head of a short cut link add their T_x to T_u. (Note that the T_x sets and the short cut links are used at most once, and before the corresponding states are popped from the T-list by Tarjan's algorithm.) ☐

The new edges introduced to the reduced state space by this algorithm do not confuse Tarjan's algorithm, as they are introduced just before Tarjan's algorithm would become aware of their non-existence. The short cut links and the T_x sets are used for speeding up the computation of the set of ignored transitions, taking advantage of the previously computed T_u sets. Because of them, each state's set of stubborn-enabled transitions is computed at most once. Short cut links are used at most once. The remaining operations related to ignoring detection are done once for every ignoring recovery, and every ignoring recovery introduces at least one new edge to the reduced state space. Thus the cost of this algorithm is at most proportional to the size of the (final) reduced state space multiplied by the number of transitions in the v/t-system.

1.6 Stubborn Sets and Reactive Systems

Let us return to the argument in the proof of Theorem 1.24. Assuming that ignoring does not occur, it is always possible to select key transitions in such a way that as i grows, σ_i eventually contains an occurrence of a transition belonging to T_i. Continuing the procedure, the transition occurrences belonging to the original occurrence sequence are eventually all consumed, justifying the following theorem:

Theorem 1.29 Assume ignoring does not occur. Let σ be a finite occurrence sequence starting at s, where $s \in \underline{W}$. There are $s' \in \underline{W}$, a finite extension of σ called σ' leading from s to s', and a permutation of σ' called $\underline{\sigma}$ leading from s to s' and belonging to the reduced state space. Each transition occurrence in $\underline{\sigma}$ either has a corresponding transition occurrence in σ, or is the occurrence of a key transition. ☐

This theorem has corollaries which are important regarding the analysis and verification of reactive systems.

Corollary 1.30 If ignoring does not occur, a transition occurs in the reduced state space if and only if it occurs in the ordinary state space. ☐

This corollary allows the use of the well known Petri net fact technique (see e.g. [Reisig 85] p. 56) for verifying invariant properties with the stubborn set method, provided that ignoring is eliminated. A *fact* is a transition t whose enabling condition $E(s) = en(s,t)$ is expected to be never satisfied. That is, $\neg E$ is intended to be an invariant property. The generation of the current branch of the state space may be quitted when an enabled fact is found. The quitting causes the state violating the fact appear as a terminal state in the reduced state space, thus confusing the ignoring elimination algorithm (Algorithm 1.28). Because of this, if invariant properties are violated, it is guaranteed only that at least one violation is found. Furthermore, other analyses (terminal state detection etc.) are guaranteed to produce correct results only if there are no violations of invariant properties. As a consequence, some errors of the system under analysis are not necessarily reported, if there is a violated invariant. This is often sufficient, because the violation of the invariant is reported, and the remaining errors will be found after the error causing the violation of the invariant is fixed.

There is also a way to restore the ignoring elimination algorithm. This is done by not taking fact violation terminal states into account when checking in the algorithm whether a strong component is terminal. Key transitions leading from a state s to a fact violation terminal state cannot any more be considered key transitions in s. If the weak definition of stubborn sets is used, this may lead to the need of finding and using a new stubborn set in s to ensure that at every state with transitions which are enabled but not stubborn-enabled, there is a key transition leading to a proper successor state.

Transition t is *live* in the Petri net sense of the word, if and only if for every $s \in W$ there is an occurrence sequence starting at s and containing an occurrence of t. We can say that t is *live in the reduced state space* if and only if for every $s \in \underline{W}$ there is an occurrence sequence starting at s, belonging to the reduced state space and containing an occurrence of t.

Corollary 1.31 If ignoring does not occur, a transition is live (in the Petri net sense of the word) if and only if it is live in the reduced state space. That is, if ignoring does not occur, stubborn set state space reduction preserves liveness. $\Box$

Proof Assume t is live. Let $s \in \underline{W}$. Take an occurrence sequence σ starting at s and ending with the occurrence of t. By Theorem 1.29 the reduced state space contains a permutation of an extension of σ starting at s. Therefore it contains an occurrence sequence starting at s and containing the occurrence of t. t is thus live in the reduced state space. Assume now that t is not live. There is then a state s such that t is disabled in every state reachable from s. Take an occurrence sequence σ from ss_0 to s. By Theorem 1.29 there is a state $s' \in \underline{W}$ such that s' is reachable from s. t is disabled in every state reachable from s', thus it cannot occur in any occurrence sequence starting at s' in the reduced state space. As a consequence, t is not live in the reduced state space. $\Box$

A *livelock* can be thought of as a mode of operation where the system is doing something but what it is doing is unproductive. We can distinguish between two kinds of livelocks: those which can be exited, and those which cannot. The latter correspond to cyclic terminal strong components C of the state space of the system such that the set of transitions occurring at the states of C is not what is expected. The following corollary shows that such livelocks are preserved by the reduced state space generation method if ignoring does not occur.

Corollary 1.32 Assume the state space of the system is finite and ignoring does not occur.

(1) Let $C \subseteq W$ be a terminal strong component. There is a terminal strong component $\underline{C}$ in the reduced state space such that $\underline{C} \subseteq C$ and for every transition t, if and only if $\exists\ s, s' \in C$: $s -t \rightarrow s'$, then $\exists\ \underline{s}, \underline{s}' \in \underline{C}: \underline{s} -t \Rightarrow \underline{s}'$.

(2) Let $\underline{C} \subseteq \underline{W}$ be a terminal strong component of the reduced state space. There is a terminal strong component C such that $\underline{C} \subseteq C$ and for every transition t, if and only if $\exists\ \underline{s}, \underline{s}' \in \underline{C}$: $\underline{s} -t \Rightarrow \underline{s}'$, then $\exists\ s, s' \in C: s -t \rightarrow s'$. $\Box$

Proof (1) Let $s \in C$ and σ be an execution sequence from ss_0 to s. Every state reachable from s belongs to C. Consider the s' the existence of which is implied by Theorem 1.29. $s' \in C$ and $s' \in \underline{W}$. Let $\underline{C}$ be a terminal strong component of the reduced state space such that $\exists \underline{s} \in \underline{C}: s' \Rightarrow^* \underline{s}$. We see that $\underline{C} \subseteq C$. Now, let $\underline{s}$ be any element of $\underline{C}$ and let $s_1, s'_1 \in C$ and $t \in T$ such that $s_1 -t \rightarrow s'_1$. Because C is a strong component, $\underline{s} \rightarrow^* s_1 -t \rightarrow s'_1$. By Theorem 1.29 there are $\underline{s}_1, \underline{s}'_1 \in \underline{W}$ such that $\underline{s}_1 -t \Rightarrow \underline{s}'_1$. $\underline{s}_1, \underline{s}'_1 \in \underline{C}$, because $\underline{s} \in \underline{C}$ and $\underline{C}$ is a terminal strong component of the reduced state space. Now let $\underline{s}_1, \underline{s}'_1 \in \underline{C}$ such that $\underline{s}_1 -t \Rightarrow \underline{s}'_1$. $\underline{s}_1, \underline{s}'_1 \in C$ and $\underline{s}_1 -t \rightarrow \underline{s}'_1$ because $\underline{C} \subseteq C$ and $\underline{E} \subseteq E$.

(2) Choose $\underline{s} \in \underline{C}$. Let C be a terminal strong component of the ordinary state space such that $\exists s \in C: \underline{s} \rightarrow^* s$. As above, Theorem 1.29 implies that there is $\underline{s}' \in \underline{W} \cap C$ such that $\underline{s} \Rightarrow^* \underline{s}'$ and $s \rightarrow^* s'$. Thus $\underline{s}' \in \underline{C}$, and because $\underline{C}$ is a strong component in the reduced state space, we get $\underline{s}' \Rightarrow^* \underline{s}$. Therefore $\underline{s}$, s and $\underline{s}'$ belong to the same strong component of the ordinary state space, that is, to C. We conclude $\underline{C} \subseteq C$. The claim "for every transition t, if and only if $\exists \underline{s}, \underline{s}' \in \underline{C}: \underline{s} -t \Rightarrow \underline{s}'$, then $\exists s, s' \in C: s -t \rightarrow s'$" is proven as above. $\square$

It is known that the stubborn set method as presented so far does not preserve livelocks which can be exited. The stubborn set method can be modified to cover the analysis of such livelocks, too, but it is beyond the scope of this paper.

The last result in this chapter is about preserving the language generated by a system. We assume that some, but not necessarily all transitions of the system have been given a symbol from some alphabet. Then the language generated by the system is the set of strings generated by the occurrence sequences of the system.

Definition 1.33 Let Σ be a set of symbols. Let $(V,T,type,next,ss_0)$ be a v/t-system and α be a function from T to Σ^* such that $\forall t \in T: |\alpha(t)| \leq 1$. Let $\sigma = s_0 -t_1 \rightarrow \ldots -t_n \rightarrow s_n$.

- $t \in T$ is *visible*, if and only if $|\alpha(t)| = 1$. Otherwise t is *invisible*. The set of visible transitions is denoted by T_V.

- The *word* generated by σ is the string $\alpha(t_1)\alpha(t_2)\ldots\alpha(t_n)$.

- The *language* generated by $(V,T,type,next,ss_0)$ with Σ and α is the set of words generated by all finite occurrence sequences of $(V,T,type,next,ss_0)$ starting at ss_0. $\square$

Assuming that the selection of stubborn sets is constrained in a certain way and ignoring does not occur, the stubborn set method preserves the language generated by the system.

Theorem 1.34 Assume that ignoring does not occur, and the stubborn sets used by Algorithm 1.21 satisfy the following for every stubborn set T_s used at state s with an enabled transition:

$$(\exists t \in T_s \cap T_V: en(s,t)) \Rightarrow T_V \subseteq T_s.$$

If there is an occurrence sequence σ starting at ss_0 generating the word x, then there is an occurrence sequence $\underline{\sigma}$ in the reduced state space starting at ss_0 and generating x, and vice versa. $\square$

Proof The "vice versa"-part is obvious. Regarding the other part, consider the $\underline{\sigma}$ of Theorem 1.29. We prove that in the construction of $\underline{\sigma}$ the order of occurrences of visible transitions does not change, implying that $\underline{\sigma}$ has a prefix generating x. Consider again the argument in the proof of Theorem 1.24. Each construction step moves a transition occurrence from σ'_{i-1} to $\underline{\sigma}_i$. If the transition is invisible, moving it does not change the order of occurrences of visible transitions. Assume now the moved transition t is visible. It is obviously enabled at $s_{i-1} = ls(\underline{\sigma}_{i-1})$ and belongs to T_{i-1}, where T_{i-1} is the stubborn set used at s_{i-1}. By the assumption of the theorem we get $T_V \subseteq T_{i-1}$. The moved transition is the first of those in σ'_{i-1} which belong to T_{i-1}, thus it is the first of those in σ'_{i-1} which belong to T_V. As a result, moving it does not change the order of occurrences of visible transitions. $\square$

In conclusion, if the strong definition of stubborn sets is used, Algorithm 1.28 can be used to eliminate ignoring. When ignoring is eliminated, the stubborn set method preserves liveness in the Petri net sense of the word, and can be used to check invariant properties. Furthermore, it preserves livelocks defined as unintended terminal cyclic strong components. Assuming an extra constraint on the selection of stubborn sets the method preserves the language generated by the system.

2. STUBBORN SETS OF PETRI NETS

In this chapter the theory of Chapter 1 is applied to three different classes of Petri nets by adapting the definitions of stubborn sets (Definitions 1.17 and 1.18). The classes are elementary nets (see [Rozenberg & 86] or [Thiagarajan 87] for definition), place/transition nets with finite capacity of places ([Reisig 85] or [Reisig 87]), and coloured Petri nets ([Jensen 87]).

Since we have used the symbols s, s', s_1,... to denote states, we denote Petri net places by symbols starting with p, to avoid confusion. We continue to use the predicate *en* for denoting that a transition is enabled. Otherwise in this chapter we use familiar Petri net notation where convenient, such as $\bullet t$ and $t\bullet$ for the sets of the input and output places of transition t, respectively. In particular, markings (the Petri net equivalent of states) are denoted by the usual M, even when they are used mixed with variable/transition system notation. That is, we write, for instance, $next(M,t) = M'$.

2.1 Stubborn Sets of Elementary Nets

An elementary Petri net system as defined in [Rozenberg & 86] or [Thiagarajan 87] can be thought of as a variable/transition system where places correspond to variables, transitions correspond to transitions, markings correspond to states and the initial marking corresponds to the initial state. The type of each variable is $\{0,1\}$, representing the corresponding place being empty or marked, respectively. The topology of the net defines the next state function in an obvious way:

$next(M,t) = undefined$, if and only if $\exists\, p \in \bullet t: M(p) = 0 \vee \exists\, p \in t\bullet: M(p) = 1$

otherwise $next(M,t) = M'$, where
$$\forall\, p \in \bullet t: M'(p) = 0 \;\wedge\; \forall\, p \in t\bullet: M'(p) = 1 \;\wedge\; \forall\, p \notin \bullet t \cup t\bullet: M'(p) = M(p)$$

Because of the form of the enabling condition of an elementary net transition, it has a separation (see Definition 1.10) consisting of single places:

$sep(t; \{p_1\},...,\{p_n\})$, if $test(t) = \{p_1,...,p_n\}$

The most natural choices for the test, write and read sets of transition t satisfying Definition 1.6 and the corresponding connection set are

if $\bullet t \cap t\bullet = \varnothing$: $test(t) = wr(t) = conn(t) = \bullet t \cup t\bullet \;\wedge\; rd(t) = \varnothing$

if $\bullet t \cap t\bullet \neq \varnothing$: $test(t) = wr(t) = rd(t) = conn(t) = \varnothing$

To keep our formulas simpler, from now on we assume that for all transitions t, $\bullet t \cap t\bullet = \varnothing$. (That is, we ban *side places*.) This is not an essential restriction, since transitions not satisfying this are never enabled.

Transition t is enabled with respect to a subset of places P' in the sense of Definition 1.8 if and only if

$$\forall\, p \in P' \cap \bullet t: M(p) = 1 \wedge \forall\, p \in P' \cap t\bullet: M(p) = 0$$

A possible choice for write up and write down sets of transition t (see Definition 1.9) is

$wrup(t,P') = \bullet(P' \cap \bullet t) \cup (P' \cap t\bullet)\bullet$

$wrdn(t,P') = (P' \cap \bullet t)\bullet \cup \bullet(P' \cap t\bullet)$

Every elementary net transition accords left (Definition 1.12) every other elementary net transition, as can be verified by algebraic manipulation based on the definitions. We can write weak definitions of semistubborn and stubborn sets of elementary net transitions (see Definitions 1.13 and 1.17):

Definition 2.1 Subset of transitions T_s of an elementary Petri net is *semistubborn* in the *weak* sense at marking M, if and only if for every $t \in T_s$

$$\neg\, en(M,t) \;\Rightarrow\; \exists\, p \in {}^\bullet t\colon M(p) = 0 \wedge {}^\bullet p \subseteq T_s \;\vee\; \exists\, p \in t{}^{\bullet}\colon M(p) = 1 \wedge p^\bullet \subseteq T_s$$

$$en(M,t) \;\Rightarrow\; \forall\, p \in {}^\bullet t \cup t{}^{\bullet}\colon {}^\bullet p \subseteq T_s \vee p^\bullet \subseteq T_s$$

T_s is *stubborn* in the *weak* sense at M, if and only if it is semistubborn in the weak sense at M, and

$$\exists\, t \in T_s\colon en(M,t) \wedge ({}^\bullet t)^\bullet \cup {}^\bullet(t^\bullet) \subseteq T_s \quad \Box$$

Strong definitions of semistubborn and stubborn sets (see Definitions 1.15 and 1.18) have the following form:

Definition 2.2 Subset of transitions T_s of an elementary Petri net is *semistubborn* in the *strong* sense at marking M, if and only if for every $t \in T_s$

$$\neg\, en(M,t) \;\Rightarrow\; \exists\, p \in {}^\bullet t\colon M(p) = 0 \wedge {}^\bullet p \subseteq T_s \;\vee\; \exists\, p \in t{}^{\bullet}\colon M(p) = 1 \wedge p^\bullet \subseteq T_s$$

$$en(M,t) \;\Rightarrow\; ({}^\bullet t)^\bullet \cup {}^\bullet(t^\bullet) \subseteq T_s$$

T_s is *stubborn* in the *strong* sense at M, if and only if it is semistubborn in the strong sense at M, and

$$\exists\, t \in T_s\colon en(M,t) \quad \Box$$

2.2 Stubborn Sets of Place/Transition Nets

The interpretation of place/transition nets (as defined in [Reisig 85] or [Reisig 87], for instance) as variable/transition systems follows the same guidelines as the interpretation of elementary nets. Since places may now contain more than one token, the type of the variable corresponding to place p is $\{0,\ldots,K(p)\}$ where $K(p)$ is the capacity of p, or $\{0,\ldots\}$ if the capacity of p is infinite. The next state function is defined by the transition rule of place/transition nets as follows. Let $W(x,y)$ be the weight of the arc from place or transition x to transition or place y, or 0, if there is no arc.

$$en(M,t) \;\Leftrightarrow\; \forall\, p \in P\colon W(p,t) \leq M(p) \leq K(p) - W(t,p)$$

$$en(M,t) \;\Rightarrow\; next(M,t) = M', \quad \text{where } \forall\, p \in P\colon M'(p) = M(p) - W(p,t) + W(t,p)$$

As with elementary nets, $sep(t; \{p_1\},\ldots,\{p_n\})$ holds for every transition t if $test(t) = \{p_1, \ldots, p_n\}$.

Let us denote the set of places with finite capacity by P_K. Test, read, write and connection sets may be defined as below:

$$test(t) = {}^\bullet t \cup (t^\bullet \cap P_K)$$

$$wr(t) = rd(t) = \{p \in P \mid W(p,t) \neq W(t,p)\}$$

$$conn(t) = {}^\bullet t \cup t^\bullet$$

Enabling with respect to a set of places can be defined as the restriction of the enabling condition to the set of places in question.

The definitions of smallest possible write down and write up sets of general place/transition nets are quite complicated, and thus so are also the definitions of (semi)stubborn sets. For simplicity, in the remainder of this section we assume that the capacity of each place is infinite. If stubborn sets of place/transition nets with capacity constraints are needed, one can use the general ideas of this paper to derive the necessary definitions.

With the assumption of the absence of capacity limitations, write up and write down sets with respect to individual places may be defined as follows:

$$wrup(t,\{p\}) = \{t' \in T \mid W(t',p) > W(p,t') < W(p,t)\}$$

$$wrdn(t,\{p\}) = \{t' \in T \mid W(p,t') > W(t',p) < W(p,t)\}$$

Theorem 2.3 Let t and t' be transitions of a place/transition net where the capacity of each place is infinite. $t \angle t'$, if and only if

$$\forall p \in P: W(t,p) \geq \min(W(p,t), W(p,t'), W(t',p)) \quad \square$$

Proof "if" part: Assume that $M -t\to M'$ and $M -t'\to M_1 -t\to M'_1$; we have to prove that $M' -t'\to M'_1$. By the assumption, for all $p \in P$, (1) $M(p) \geq W(p,t)$, (2) $M(p) \geq W(p,t')$, and (3) $M(p)-W(p,t')+W(t',p) \geq W(p,t)$. Also $M'(p) = M(p)-W(p,t)+W(t,p)$. If $W(t,p) \geq W(p,t)$, then $M'(p) \geq M(p) \geq W(p,t')$ by (2). If $W(t,p) \geq W(p,t')$, then $M'(p) \geq W(t,p) \geq W(p,t')$ by (1). If $W(t,p) \geq W(t',p)$, then $M'(p) \geq M(p)-W(p,t)+W(t',p) \geq W(p,t')$ by (3). Thus t' is enabled at M'. $M' -t'\to M'_1$, since the net result of the occurrence of two place/transition net transitions in sequence is independent of their order of occurrence.

"only if" part: Assume that there is a place p so that $W(t,p) < \min(W(p,t), W(p,t'), W(t',p))$. Consider marking M where $M(p) = W(p,t)+W(p,t')-W(t,p)-1$, and the marking of the remaining places p' is $M(p') = \max(W(p',t), W(p',t'), W(p',t')-W(t',p')+W(p',t))$. $M(p)$ is well defined, because $W(t,p) < W(p,t)$ implies $M(p) \geq W(p,t') \geq 0$. There are M', M_1 and M'_1 so that $M -t\to M'$ and $M -t'\to M_1 -t\to M'_1$, as can be verified by algebraic manipulation based on the assumption about $W(t,p)$. However, t' is not enabled at M' because of p. $\square$

Using the above definitions and Theorem 2.3, we get the following definitions:

Definition 2.4 Subset of transitions T_s of a place/transition net with infinite capacity of places is *semistubborn* in the *weak* sense at marking M, if and only if for every $t \in T_s$,

$$\neg en(M,t) \Rightarrow \exists p \in P: M(p) < W(p,t) \wedge \forall t' \notin T_s: W(p,t') \geq \min(W(t',p), W(p,t))$$

$$en(M,t) \Rightarrow \forall p \in P: (\forall t' \notin T_s: \min(W(t,p), W(t',p)) \geq \min(W(p,t), W(p,t')) \vee$$
$$\forall t' \notin T_s: \min(W(t,p), W(p,t')) \geq \min(W(p,t), W(t',p)))$$

T_s is *stubborn* in the *weak* sense at M, if and only if it is semistubborn in the weak sense at M, and

$$\exists t \in T_s: en(M,t) \wedge \forall t' \notin T_s: \forall p \in P: W(t',p) \geq \min(W(p,t'), W(p,t)) \quad \square$$

Definition 2.5 Subset of transitions T_s of a place/transition net with infinite capacity of places is *semistubborn* in the *strong* sense at marking M, if and only if for every $t \in T_s$,

$$\neg en(M,t) \Rightarrow \exists p \in P: M(p) < W(p,t) \wedge \forall t' \notin T_s: W(p,t') \geq \min(W(t',p), W(p,t))$$

$$en(M,t) \Rightarrow \forall p \in P: \forall t' \notin T_s: \min(W(t,p), W(t',p)) \geq \min(W(p,t), W(p,t'))$$

T_s is *stubborn* in the *strong* sense at M, if and only if it is semistubborn in the strong sense at M, and

$$\exists t \in T_s: en(M,t) \quad \square$$

It is interesting to compare Definition 2.4 to Definitions 2.1 and 2.3 of [Valmari 88a], as both define semistubborn and stubborn sets of place/transition net transitions, and both assume that there are no capacity constraints. The definitions in [Valmari 88a] were derived directly for place/transition nets, using heuristics to develop different strategies for establishing conditions guaranteeing Theorem 1.11, and using algebraic manipulations to find the corresponding definition. The definitions in [Valmari 88a] are not intuitive, and, as a matter of fact, not equivalent to Definition 2.4. This is because stubborn set theory aims at finding a sufficient and statically computable condition for guaranteeing Theorem 1.11, and different approaches may lead to slightly different results.

2.3 Stubborn Sets of Coloured Petri Nets

Coloured Petri nets are a high level net class defined in [Jensen 87]. Tokens of a coloured Petri net may have an identity ("colour"). Transitions may have different occurrence modes (they, too, are called "colours"), and the tokens the transition consumes from its input places and produces for its output places may be defined by arbitrary functions from occurrence colours to multisets of token colours.

There are basically two approaches to interpreting coloured Petri nets as variable/transition systems, one concentrating to the places of the coloured net as such, the other to the places of the corresponding unfolded net. In the first approach each place is thought of as a single variable the type of which is defined so that it covers all the multisets of tokens that may be stored in the place. Each occurrence colour of each transition is thought of as a unique transition. Test, write, write down etc. sets and stubborn sets are defined putting the available information of the relationships between transitions and places to as good use as conveniently possible. For instance, an easy but crude way of defining the test, read, write and connection sets of transitions is to define $test(t) = wr(t) = rd(t) = conn(t) = \bullet t \cup t \bullet$ for each transition t. The observation that for a particular transition t and place p the functions defining the tokens consumed from and produced for p by t are equal, can be taken advantage of by removing p from $wr(t)$, because then t only tests the presence of some tokens in p without modifying the contents of p. An easy definition of write up and write down sets would be $wrup(t,P') = wrdn(t,P') = wr(test(t) \cap P')$ for each transition t and set of places P'. With these definitions, the weak and strong definition of semistubborn sets agree and lead to the following simple definition (originally [Valmari 88b]):

A set of transitions $T_s \subseteq T$ is *semistubborn* at marking M, if and only if for every $t \in T_s$

$$\neg\, en(M,t) \;\Rightarrow\; \exists\, P' \subseteq test(t): \neg\, en(M,t,P') \wedge wr(P') \subseteq T_s$$

$$en(M,t) \;\Rightarrow\; conn(wr(t)) \cup wr(conn(t)) \subseteq T_s$$

The definition of stubborn sets adds the requirement of the presence of an enabled transition in the set to this. This definition is quite simple, but it leads to unnecessarily large stubborn sets and thus does not give the best possible state space reduction results. Better reduction results are achieved if the information of the relationships between places and transitions is utilised more carefully.

In the other interpretation approach each place is thought of as consisting of several variables, each corresponding to one possible token colour. That is, the coloured Petri net is interpreted as being only a concise description of the corresponding unfolded place/transition net. Then the definitions of stubborn sets of place/transition nets are used. This approach does not imply that the unfolding should be actually done; rather, it states merely that the algorithm finding stubborn sets should interpret the coloured Petri net as if it were a condensed description of the corresponding unfolded place/transition net. The advantage of this approach over the first interpretation is that better reduction results may be achieved, but the disadvantage is that algorithms searching stubborn sets become more complicated and consume more time. At the time of writing it is an open research problem as to whether using this interpretation allows stubborn sets of coloured Petri net transitions to be computed with effort proportional to the size of the coloured Petri net rather than proportional to the size of the corresponding unfolded place/transition net.

In conclusion, the best interpretation of coloured Petri nets as v/t-systems depends on the available information on what there may be in arc functions and transition guards. The ideas of this section should be applicable to most other high level net classes, too, including Genrich's predicate/transition nets [Genrich 87] and Numerical Petri Nets [Wheeler 85].

3. STUBBORN SETS AND EQUIVALENT MARKINGS

In this chapter we compare with the aid of an example, the stubborn set state space reduction method with Jensen's equivalent marking method as defined in [Jensen 87]. The example is a data base system originally presented by Genrich and Lautenbach. We use the version in [Jensen 87] p. 269. It consists of $n \geq 2$ data base managers, which modify the data base and send and receive messages to each other to ensure that they have the same idea about the contents of the data base. The model concentrates on the message exchange. In particular, the modification operations are not modelled.

Initially all managers are in inactive state. Then one of them, any one, modifies his data base. This is modelled by transition "update and send messages" which reserves the data base for that manager and sends a message to every other manager. Then all the other managers concurrently perform a two step sequence, where the first step corresponds to the reception of the message, and the second step corresponds to the sending of an acknowledgement. When all acknowledgements are available, the manager who started the game reads them, releases the data base so that the other managers can modify it if they wish, and returns to the inactive state.

The state space of the data base system has a symmetrical structure which makes it easy to compute its size when no reduction method, the stubborn set method, the equivalent marking method or both are used. The ordinary state space (no reduction method used) is as in the figure below, where usm_i is the occurrence of transition "update and send messages" with occurrence colour i, ra_i is the occurrence of transition "receive acknowledgements" with occurrence colour i, $rm_{i,j}$ is the occurrence of transition "receive message" with occurrence colour "j receives from i", $sa_{i,j}$ is the occurrence of transition "send acknowledgement" with occurrence colour "j sends to i", $cube_i$ is a subspace resembling an $n-1$ dimensional hypercube (see the example below), and in_i and out_i are the input and output states of $cube_i$. $cube_1$ for $n=3$ is shown in the following page.

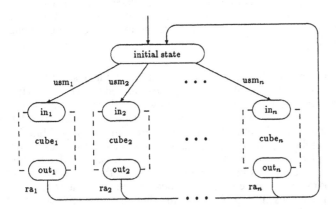

An $n-1$ dimensional hypercube with edges of length 2 has 3^{n-1} vertices and $2(n-1)3^{n-2}$ edges. Therefore the state space of the example contains $n3^{n-1}+1$ vertices and $2n(n-1)3^{n-2}+2n$ edges.

When the stubborn set state space reduction method is used and stubborn sets are computed as if from the unfolded place/transition net corresponding to the coloured Petri net representing the data base system (see Section 2.3), the stubborn set method takes advantage of the fact that the receive message — send acknowledgement sequences of different managers are concurrent with each other. Therefore it simulates only one path through each $cube_i$. This

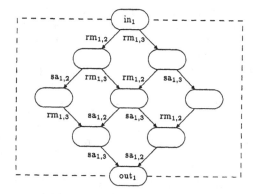

is true independent of whether the weak or strong definition of stubborn sets is used. It is, however, required that the stubborn sets used are not larger than necessary. Under these assumptions, the numbers of vertices and edges are $2n^2-n+1$ and $2n^2$.

In this example, the equivalent marking method takes advantage of the fact that the system is symmetric with respect to the data base managers. That is, it is not necessary to know the identity of the manager that is at a given state; it is sufficient to know only the number of managers at each state. Therefore only one of **cube**$_i$ is generated. Furthermore, within each **cube**$_i$ only the states (j,k,l) are generated, where j is the number of managers which have not yet received the message, k is the number of managers which have received the message but have not acknowledged it, l is the number of managers which have acknowledged their message, and $j+k+l = n-1$. There are thus $(1/2)n^2+(1/2)n+1$ vertices. A bit more complicated analysis reveals that the number of edges is n^2-n+2.

Finally, when both reduction methods are used at the same time, only one of **cube**$_i$ and only one path through it are generated. Therefore the number of vertices and edges are both $2n$. These results are summarized in the following table, where we have included only the most significant term of each formula:

	vertices	edges
no reduction	$n3^{n-1}$	$2n^23^{n-2}$
stubborn sets	$2n^2$	$2n^2$
equivalent markings	$\frac{1}{2}n^2$	n^2
both	$2n$	$2n$

In this example, the size of the state space is exponential in n if neither reduction method is used, quadratic in n if either reduction method is used, and linear in n if both are used at the same time. From this, one should not conclude that the stubborn set method and the equivalent marking method are roughly equally strong, but that they are incomparable, that they take advantage of different aspects of the system under analysis. The equivalent marking method works well when there is a suitable symmetry available; the stubborn set method works well when there is concurrency. In this example there are both, thus it is advantageous to use both reduction methods.

4. CONCLUSION

In this paper we have developed a general state space reduction theory and applied it to both low level and high level Petri nets. From the implementer's point of view the theory is very flexible. Several sets in the theory can be enlarged at will without invalidating the theorems in this paper, including write down and write up sets. Therefore the implementer may choose how carefully the relationships between transitions are captured by the definition of stubborn sets. More detailed definitions give better state space reduction results, but if the ease of implementation is preferred, the use of crude definitions is perfectly legal.

There are two versions of the theory: strong and weak. With both versions, the reduced state space contains every terminal state of the system under analysis, and facilitates the detection of nontermination. This information is sufficient to verify the total correctness of systems which are intended to terminate. If nontermination occurs, a certain kind of fairness problem called *ignoring* can take place and limit the coverage of the analysis of reactive systems. Ignoring can be cheaply detected from the reduced state space. If the strong theory is used, ignoring can be eliminated altogether without undue cost using the algorithm given in the paper. If ignoring does not occur or is eliminated, reduced state space generation can be used to decide the liveness of transitions (in the Petri net sense of the word), to detect livelocks (defined as unintended terminal cyclic strong components of the state space) and to check invariant properties. Furthermore, with a small modification the stubborn set method can be forced to preserve the language generated by attaching a symbol to some (but not to all) transitions. The preserving of linear temporal logic formulas is discussed in [Valmari 90], and also the failure set semantics [Brookes & 84] of systems can be preserved.

We compared the stubborn set method to Jensen's equivalent marking method through an example. The conclusion was that both methods are capable of giving good reduction results (the size of the state space reduced from exponential to quadratic in system size with either method in the example), but they are incomparable in the sense that they take advantage of different aspects of the system under analysis. In the example the use of both methods at the same time led to even better results (linear).

As reported before [Valmari 88a], there is a test implementation which uses the strong form of the definitions and makes a very crude analysis of the relationship between transitions. A more serious attempt of applying the stubborn set method is currently being conducted by Telecom Australia. It is developing a protocol engineering tool called Toras [Wheeler & 90]. Among other features, it can generate ordinary and reduced state spaces using the strong stubborn set method. It contains an ignoring elimination algorithm resembling Algorithm 1.28. Furthermore, it contains the language preserving and the failure set semantics preserving stubborn set methods.

The state space generator tool of Toras has been divided to two modules, one embodying knowledge about state space generation and the various stubborn set methods, the other corresponding to the semantics of the concurrency model which is used to represent the systems under analysis. The idea is that the tool can be adapted to various concurrency formalisms by changing the latter module. The modules communicate with each other at the level of variable/transition systems. The above mentioned state space generation algorithms have been implemented, and at the time of writing there is a concurrency model module for place/transition systems without capacity constraints. Another for a certain version of Numerical Petri Nets [Wheeler 85] is partially implemented. In the initial speed tests a P/T-system version of the 100 philosopher system ($\approx 10^{47}$ states) was analysed in 20 minutes CPU on a Sun 3/60, with the result of generating 29 702 states using the basic strong stubborn set method [Wheeler & 90].

ACKNOWLEDGEMENTS

As many of the ideas of this paper have been developed during my Ph.D. thesis work, I would like to thank here my supervisor, referees and opponents of the thesis, namely Professor Kurki-Suonio of Tampere University of Technology and Drs Eike Best, Pekka Orponen and Joachim Parrow. Later the comments by Geoff Wheeler of Telecom Australia have been very valuable. The quality of this paper has improved also by the comments by the unknown referees of the Tenth Petri Net Conference, and after it by the two referees of this volume. I wrote the Petri Net Conference version of this paper [Valmari 89b] while I was visiting

Telecom Australia Research Laboratories supported by Telecom Australia. That the visit was possible and I had the chance to do this work is largely due to Jonathan Billington. The Technical Research Centre of Finland (VTT) and the Technology Development Centre of Finland (Tekes) have supported this work through its all stages, including the period in Australia.

REFERENCES

[Aho & 74] Aho, A. V., Hopcroft, J. E. & Ullman, J. D.: *The Design and Analysis of Computer Algorithms*. Addison-Wesley 1974. 470 p.

[Back & 87] Back, R. J. R. & Kurki-Suonio, R.: *Distributed Cooperation with Action Systems*. ACM Transactions on Programming Languages and Systems, Vol 10, No. 4 1988, pp. 513–554.

[Brauer & 87] Brauer, W., Reisig, W. & Rozenberg, G. (ed.): *Petri Nets: Central Models and Their Properties. Advances in Petri Nets 1986, Part I, Proceedings of an Advanced Course, Bad Honnef, September 1986*. Lecture Notes in Computer Science 254, Springer 1987. 480 p.

[Brookes & 84] Brookes, S. D., Hoare, C. A. R. & Roscoe, A. W.: *A Theory of Communicating Sequential Processes*. Journal of the ACM 31 (3) 1984, pp. 560–599.

[Genrich 87] Genrich, H.: *Predicate/Transition Nets*. In: [Brauer & 87], pp. 207–247.

[Jensen 87] Jensen, K.: *Coloured Petri Nets*. In: [Brauer & 87], pp. 248–299.

[Manna & 81] Manna, Z. & Pnueli, A.: *The Temporal Framework for Concurrent Programs*. In: Boyer, R. S. & Moore, J. S. (ed.): The Correctness Problem in Computer Science. Academic Press 1981, pp. 215–274.

[Overman 81] Overman, W. T.: *Verification of Concurrent Systems: Function and Timing*. Ph.D. Dissertation, University of California Los Angeles 1981. 174 p.

[Pnueli 86] Pnueli, A.: *Applications of Temporal Logic to the Specification and Verification of Reactive Systems: A Survey of Current Trends*. In: Current Trends in Concurrency, Lecture Notes in Computer Science 224, Springer 1986 pp. 510–584.

[Reisig 85] Reisig, W.: *Petri Nets, an Introduction*. Springer 1985. 161 p.

[Reisig 87] Reisig, W.: *Place/Transition Systems*. In: [Brauer & 87] pp. 117–141.

[Rozenberg & 86] Rozenberg, G. & Thiagarajan, P. S.: *Petri Nets: Basic Notions, Structure, Behaviour*. In: Current Trends in Concurrency, Lecture Notes in Computer Science 224, Springer 1986 pp. 585–668.

[Thiagarajan 87] Thiagarajan, P. S.: *Elementary Net Systems*. In: [Brauer & 87] pp. 26–59.

[Valmari 88a] Valmari, A.: *Error Detection By Reduced Reachability Graph Generation*. Proceedings of the Ninth European Workshop on Application and Theory of Petri Nets, Venice, Italy 1988 pp. 95–112.

[Valmari 88b] Valmari, A.: *Heuristics for Lazy State Generation Speeds up Analysis of Concurrent Systems*. Proceedings of the Finnish Artificial Intelligence Symposium STeP-88, Helsinki 1988. Volume 2 pp. 640–650.

[Valmari 88c] Valmari, A.: *State Space Generation: Efficiency and Practicality*. Ph.D. Thesis, Tampere University of Technology Publications 55, Tampere 1988. 169 p.

[Valmari 89a] Valmari, A.: *Eliminating Redundant Interleavings during Concurrent Program Verification*. Proceedings of Parallel Architectures and Languages Europe '89 Vol. 2, Lecture Notes in Computer Science 366, Springer 1989 pp. 89–103.

[Valmari 89b] Valmari, A.: *Stubborn Sets for Reduced State Space Generation*. Proceedings of the Tenth International Conference on Application and Theory of Petri Nets, Bonn, West Germany 1989 Vol. 2 pp. 1–22.

[Valmari 90] Valmari, A.: *A Stubborn Attack on State Explosion*, 15 p. In: Kurshan, R. & Clarke, E. M. (ed.): Proceedings of the Workshop on Computer-Aided Verification, DIMACS Technical Report 90-31, June 1990, Volume I.

[Wheeler 85] Wheeler, G. R.: *Numerical Petri Nets — A Definition*. Telecom Australia Research Laboratories Report 7780, 1985, 42 p.

[Wheeler & 90] Wheeler, G. R., Valmari, A. & Billington, J.: *Baby Toras Eats Philosophers but Thinks about Solitaire*. Proceedings of the Fifth Australian Software Engineering Conference, Sydney, NSW, Australia, 1990 pp. 283–288.